WHAT THEY'LL NEVER TELL YOU ABOUT THE

MUSIC BUSINESS

THIRD EDITION

THE COMPLETE GUIDE FOR MUSICIANS, SONGWRITERS, PRODUCERS, MANAGERS, INDUSTRY EXECUTIVES, ATTORNEYS, INVESTORS, AND ACCOUNTANTS

PETER M. THALL

WATSON–GUPTILL PUBLICATIONS

Berkeley

CONTENTS

PREFACE

We are the music makers
And we are the dreamers of dreams,
Wandering by lone sea-breakers,
And sitting by desolate streams,
World-losers and world-forsakers,
On whom the pale moon gleams:
Yet we are the movers and shakers
Of the world forever, it seems
—ARTHUR O'SHAUGHNESSY

There are enough agents, accountants, attorneys, managers, and music publishers, not to mention friends and family, who are more than willing—for love or money—to advise young artists (musicians, singers, and songwriters) in the pursuit of their careers.

Most of this advice is well-intentioned—and it may even be timely and helpful. However, it may also be irrelevant to a particular individual's circumstances. The reasons for this are manifold.

Not the least of the problems in offering advice to young artists is the fact that they customarily have limited knowledge of the music industry. Unlike participants in other industries, the major players in the music business often enter the arena with neither a clear understanding of its workings and history nor the means to obtain the information that would convey such knowledge to them. The people who make up the heart and soul of the music industry do not usually know a break-even point from a producer point, a royalty from a prince, or a mechanical license from a synchronization license—in short, they don't know their business. In the course of writing this book, I have discussed various chapters with senior executives in different departments of major music business companies. At the end of the discussion, all of them told me, in so many words, "You know, I learned a thing or two today." This is not to criticize them. As an attorney who has practiced in the music industry for more than forty years, I learned long ago that managers and executives in the music industry, unlike their highly trained peers who choose to work in the financial or real estate worlds, rarely have the requisite background to function in the industry at an optimal level. Yet these managers and executives are ultimately responsible for making the decisions that will make or break their companies.

The music industry executive's strength is enhanced only when the company he or she joins has an established and tested management training program. Although the institutions that form the music publishing and recording industry today are very well set up for precisely this kind of training, it is unlikely that these companies will also give the fledgling executive the information that I am seeking to impart in this book. For the personal manager and business manager in whose hands the artist and the record and publishing companies place their trust, this book is intended to provide not just informational data, but also a perspective that will help them to become more aware of the parts of the business which no one will teach them, but which they must nonetheless understand if they are to perform their functions effectively.

Ironically, when it comes to artists, it is widely accepted that really creative people do not know their business. After all, aren't they living in the realm of the idea—the eigenwelt—the world that is interesting precisely because it is not the mitwelt—the shared world, the concrete, tangible world that can be objectively evaluated? The late Northrup Frye, one of the 20th century's preeminent literary critics, and a noted commentator on Canadian society and culture, gave an acclaimed series of lectures at the University of Toronto several decades ago. In these lectures, published as *The Educated Imagination*, Frye spoke of the uniqueness of creative people—how creative people see things that "aren't there." What more appropriate an image for artists? What more dangerous a situation for the creative forces of the music business? And how can the creator—a living, breathing human being from whom the art emanates—function effectively in the shared world? Those who live in the imagination cannot be expected to have either the patience or the time to attain the knowledge and experience to rule their own destiny. We are all familiar with the saying "the lawyer who represents himself has a fool for a client." How much more troublesome is the vision of artists who drift through life without an understanding of their business—the customs, traditions, contractual norms, and laws of the very industry that would not even exist but for them and their artistic contributions?

Remarkably, we are talking not just about fledgling musicians, singers, and songwriters. Many of those who have topped the charts for a generation are no more sophisticated than the novice when it comes to the business intricacies that, when all is said and done, will determine their financial outcomes. Equally remarkable is the fact that their representatives—the executives at their record labels and publishing companies; personal and business managers charged with fiduciary responsibilities toward their clients; attorneys in whose trust they place their careers; investors and others from the financial arena who follow the industry from Wall Street to the Times building—are often just as unsophisticated and unaware.

Ultimately, all of the creative people who form the heart of the music industry must depend on a network of advisors in whom they need to place their trust. Nothing could possibly constitute more of a gift to artists than a competent, hard-working, intelligent, aware, trustworthy representative. And, although artists' advisors are all too often ill-informed, there are many—managers, attorneys, accountants, and agents—who have dedicated their lives to further the artistic careers of their clients. Attorneys and accountants customarily work for agreed-upon fees. Managers and agents work for a percentage of the artists' income; in essence, they work for nothing until the day comes—if it ever does come—when the economic potential of the people they represent is realized. At their best, these people can make a difference profound enough to encourage artists and help them bring to fruition and to the world's attention the results of their creations. For many—and I include myself here—that is enough compensation for the tribulations experienced in the course of practicing our professions.

I have sought, in this book, to expose the most treacherous pitfalls faced by both creators and their representatives and have pointed out some of the most egregious examples of the ways in which artists can be affected by customs and practices to which the industry universally adheres. It is not my intent either to alarm the artist or to depict the industry or its principals as monsters of selfishness. On the contrary, as the music industry has become more sophisticated, it has come to terms with certain realities—financial and artistic—and the result has been the establishment of more thoughtful and fairer practices than existed during the heyday of Tin Pan Alley almost one hundred years ago. Nevertheless, I feel that the more one exposes the conundrums that face artists, the more likely it is that they will be solved.

The evolution of the music industry as an institution is no less a process than the evolution of any other business or political entity. In the present environment of technological advance, the artistic community must adjust to the sea changes occurring both in the creation and the delivery of music, and so there is more than ever a need to examine the underpinnings of our industry so that we can better fine-tune our business relationships and take advantage of the promises of the future.

In 2015, a dispute raged between those who think that the down years for musicians are over and the "creative apocalypse" that was forecast for musicians never happened, and those who think this is a misplaced, and ignorant, view of reality. The appropriately named The Future of Music Coalition is, of course, on the opposite side of the pundits who have judged the plight of musicians to have ended in the glory of new sources of exploitation, distribution, and income. The devil, as they say, is in the details—more appropriately the data. As can be expected, data is read differently by different people—especially those with their own agendas. But suffice it to say that the digital evolution, as I refer to it in chapter 4, page 57, has presented myriad problems for musicians, and interpreting their reality on the basis of impersonal data that lacks the human test seems quite useless. (For example, a *New York Times* feature disclosed that since 1999, "music directors and composers" have increased enormously—from 53,000 to 60,000, a 15% increase. But the data included, for the first time, music teachers, employed and hardly starving in their van performing midnight gigs at the local club. This addition skewed the results which, without including them, indicated that the number of "music directors and composers" dropped during this period from 53,000 to 47,000, a *decline* of 11%.)

Still, for those 47,000 and for all who choose to enter this extraordinary way of life for love or profit, this book will provide a foundation that will assist them in comprehending and managing *their* business throughout their careers in whichever part of the industry they choose to serve.

What They'll Never Tell You is divided into twenty-five chapters that identify and explore many of the most important issues that impact the musician, singer, and songwriter, and therefore the producer, the personal and business managers, the accountant and the attorney, and every level of music company executive. Some deal with fairly intricate issues; some are rather more accessible. None, to my knowledge, are addressed sufficiently in the principal books on the subject of educating the reader on the ins and outs of the music business. In this book, I have tried to find a common ground between the theoretical and the practical; my analysis of the issues faced by the professionals in the music business, as well as by the business entities themselves, is informed by years of experience, litigation, and both psychological and financial reinforcement. I have written this book on the theory that more knowledge is better than less, and the greater the awareness on the part of both the representatives of talent and those who exploit it, the more likely it is that an optimal collaboration between artists and companies can be achieved. I hope the information will be received as another layer of wisdom over that which already exists in significant amounts among the top professionals in the field.

Record companies, producers, and music publishers need not be concerned that all of their secrets are now out, nor should attorneys and accountants fear that their jobs will be rendered obsolete by this book. Record company personnel may feel that I have given away too many secrets, and my peers in the legal and accounting professions may feel that I have given away for free what they charge fees for. To them I respond, like a retailer who believes the best customers are educated consumers, that educated artists, producers, personal and business managers, agents, A&R (artists and repertoire) people, attorneys, and accountants will be better served, and will better serve each other, than those who have chosen, or who have been forced, to live in ignorance or, worse, in a daydream.

It is not enough to know the things you think you need to know about the music industry. Those who live within it—whether at the artistic or the business end of the spectrum or somewhere in between—must know more. They must know what they never knew or did (and do) not even think they want to know. They must know the difference between surface and substance, between truth and lie, between reality and myth. Only then can they prosper within their industry while taking genuine pleasure in their contributions to the culture that sustains them and the rest of our world.

ACKNOWLEDGMENTS

Thanks must go to all of my own mentors over the years: in particular Bernard Korman, the former general counsel of ASCAP, who taught me that it is okay to reexamine and rewrite what I have created; the legendary Harold Orenstein, the first true music business attorney, who taught me order and legal ethics; and the many people who assisted me in researching and editing this book, particularly Bob Nirkind, former acquisitions editor at Watson-Guptill; my current editors, Jenny Wapner and Clara Sankey, at Ten Speed Press, as well as Sylvia Warren, whose knowledge of the music industry was enormously beneficial to me and to the readers of this book.

I would also like to thank my former associates Scott Francis, former president of Warner-Chappell Music Publishing, and Michael Simon, the innovative and imaginative president/CEO of the Harry Fox Agency, Inc.; Stewart Hescheles; Loren Chodosh and Sandor Frankel, who give attorneys back their good name; Terri Baker, the true artist's attorney; Cheech; David Kincaid, of The Brandos, who "did it himself"; the great Anna Moffo, who sang *La Traviata* 956 times and encouraged me even more often; and Ira Sallen, formerly executive vice-president of human resources of BMG Rights Management and currently their valued consultant.

Thanks are also due the following people from whose insights I have benefited enormously—both in writing this book and in life: Maestro Gilbert Levine; Chris O'Malley; James Phelan; Deirdre O'Hara for my morning whisper line; Dr. Steven Paul; Bob Epstein, my colleague who taught me many things that I didn't know; Alex Murphy; Paul Adler; Errol Wander, CPA; Nat Farnham; Judy Corcoran; Kathleen Marsh, CEO of musicnotes.com; Martin Josman; Gilbert Hetherwick, former president of Sony BMG Masterworks; Carol Matorin, another superb and wise attorney and former vice-president, general counsel, Marc Jacobs; Joseph Dash, former head of Columbia Masterworks; the incomparable pianist and music historian Steven Blier; Jackie Kim; Natasha Azava, the new generation of music attorney, Renata Zeigeur, our valued assistant; and Carol Gigante, my secretary and assistant for twenty-five years without whom nothing would have gotten done. On a personal level, I wish to thank Theresa Wing Hines and her two amazing sons, Graham and Ian, for inspiring me to put the finishing touches on this epic work during the heat of a Connecticut summer and fall, 2015. I also owe heartfelt thanks to my daughters, Emily and Sophie, and my stepson Vincent, both for their support and for their frequent admonishment on reading a portion of the manuscript: "Are you sure you want to say that?"

1 · INTRODUCTION

It is a sobering thought that when Mozart was my age
he had been dead for two years.
—TOM LEHRER

Everyone has an idea; everyone has talent; everyone thinks that they can write or play or sing a song better than much of what they hear on the radio. There are one hundred songs on the charts. Why can't theirs be one of them? Perhaps it can. But I am fairly certain it won't.

There is an apocryphal story about David Merrick, the legendary Broadway producer. An agent said to him that his artist was talented and deserved a chance at appearing in one of Merrick's shows. Merrick went over to the window (his office, like mine, was on Broadway), opened it (you could in those days), and yelled at the top of his lungs: "TALENT!!!!" He then turned to the agent and said, "If I want talent, I can get it by the thousands. They're all out there just waiting for me to open the door. Finding talent is not my problem."

In fact, although unique talent is rare, all of us have talent to one degree or another. But what we do with our talent is the ultimate issue—and the key to opportunity. I say opportunity, not success, because all one can hope for in the music business is opportunity. Success depends on many factors: the ability and inclination to roll up one's sleeves and work at the craft of creation so as to actually improve and fine-tune one's skills; the ability to earn money and to provide oneself with food and shelter during the process, which can and will take many years; understanding one's limitations; and identifying an attainable goal and keeping it in mind over the years, amid innumerable distractions. It also depends on one factor over which even the most talented individual has no control: luck—ever-changing radio formats; the attention—or inattention—of an artist's representatives at important moments; timing (for example, the release of a key single on the same day the label is shut down and its artists moved to a sister label).

I have long been sure that most of the talented people who pursue their craft diligently and over a long period of time—those who "stay in the ring"—do realize their potential. The truth of this has been proved time after time. What I am less sure about is what advice to give to the young artists who have talent but who may not have the personal or financial resources to pursue a career in the arts. One thing is for sure: These artists will not lack for advice. There is no limit to the number of people, including top professionals in the music business, who think they know it all. Sometimes advice givers are being practical; sometimes they are simply jaded; sometimes they are dead wrong—and some are greedy and will say anything to get up-front money. So, how can the artist seriously pursuing a career in the music industry maximize the chances of getting good advice? As I emphasize throughout the book, the best approach is to assemble a team consisting of an attorney, a personal manager, a booking agent (personal managers, who are not licensed by the states, are not allowed to seek or obtain employment for their clients), and an accountant.

SELECTING THE RIGHT ATTORNEY

There is plenty of justification for seeking out a good attorney from the outset, not least because attorneys have become an important source of business to the record and music publishing companies. Record companies know that if they maintain a cordial relationship with us, they may eventually be at the top of our shopping lists when an artist of significance comes into the picture. Attorneys are also safe—in the sense that the presentation of an artist to a record or publishing company by an attorney diminishes the possibility that the artist will create problems for the company in the future. The triage—the checking out—of the artist, and of his or her bona fides, will have already been done by someone whose telephone number will be the same in the near future when a problem might arise. In addition, attorneys are licensed by state authorities and have state as well as national ethical rules that guide and bind them.

People in the entertainment industry in the United States have learned something that many in other industries—and countries—have not: the selection of an attorney should be made earlier, not later, so he or she can help you in structuring your deals and relationships in ways that can avoid problems. But, although choosing the right legal representation is one of the most important decisions that creative people make, there is no simple formula for making the right selection. Attorneys come with offices, secretaries, and occasionally ties and jackets. They come in every possible stripe and from every possible background, and it is difficult to evaluate them objectively. Attorneys with all of the trimmings appear to be more stable—more dependable—than those without. But appearances can be deceptive, and there is no substitute for extensive experience in the music industry.

It is not difficult to begin your search. Numerous websites and bar association assistance lines, as well as books and magazines, identify attorneys whose practice areas include the music business. Most attorneys, or their assistants and secretaries, are helpful and clear with callers and are happy to guide potential clients to the appropriate firm or institution for assistance. In addition, most attorneys will provide brief consultation time, at no charge, to potential clients.

Once you are in the process of narrowing down your short list of potential attorneys, however, things become more complicated. You will need to personally interview each attorney, and at some point all of the following questions must be answered to your satisfaction:

- Has the attorney had experience with your kind of music?
- Which record companies does the firm have the best relationships with?
- Which record companies have most recently signed the firm's other clients?
- What is the firm's policy with respect to introducing new clients to other clients—like producers, managers, songwriters, production companies, etc.?
- How does the firm resolve the issue of conflict of interest in the event that it sets up relationships with other clients in your area?
- How does the firm charge for services, and what are the rates (1) of the partners and (2) of lower-level associates and paralegals?
- When rates are about to change, does the firm advise the client?
- Does the firm request a retainer (an advance against fees), and how is it calculated (for example, does it reflect hourly rates times an estimated number of hours that will be invested before the retainer will have to be "refilled")?

- What are the firm's, and the artist's, short-term and long-term goals?
- If the agreed-upon goals are not fulfilled, or are not fulfilled in a timely fashion, is the unused balance of the retainer returned?
- How are nitty-gritty details handled? (For example, when the firm "shops" a demo, does it copy the artist on the correspondence? If contacts are made via email or telephone, is it the firm's policy to provide updates on each contact, or periodically on a quantity of contacts?)

Although it may appear so, I am actually not suggesting that as a potential client you interrogate potential legal representation with a machine-gun barrage of questions. Needless to say, no one wants to be subjected to this kind of questioning. And you are still the "seller," not the "buyer," so you will have to be somewhat more circumspect in your approach. Nevertheless, these are all questions that need to be explored and eventually answered.

PERSONAL REPRESENTATION

Chapters 5 and 6 cover many of the issues to be considered in selecting both personal and business managers. Though personal managers are not subject to the same rigorous licensing procedures that attorneys must pass through, a good personal manager is more likely to be a ticket to a deal than virtually any other type of professional in the entertainment business. But, as you read on, remember that your attorney of choice can be changed easily and often. In contrast, artist–personal manager relationships are usually sealed by long-term written agreements.

Other than retainer agreements establishing what services are being provided, and which are not, and the fee structure between the client and the attorney, written agreements indicating the expectations of clients are practically nonexistent. Even when an attorney agrees to work for contingent percentage income, the percentage is traditionally considerably lower than that sought by managers, and often covers a specific transaction rather than a career. In contrast, most personal managers feel it is foolish to invest their time and facilities, not to say money, in assisting an artist in career development without some contractual commitment which covers the scope and length of the artist's entire career.

Finding a Personal Manager

Barry Bergman, the founder and president emeritus of the Music Managers Forum— United States, (MMF was formerly IMF International) was once quoted as follows:

> Occasionally, someone will ask me if I'm in charge of our country's financial assets. I often look at them and in a very serious tone respond by saying "yes." After all, what greater assets do we have in our nation other than our artists, writers, producers, and musicians? We must never forget that without the musical creators there would be no artist managers, no record retailers, no record manufacturers, no record distributors, no industry . . . no kidding.

Now that is the kind of manager you want! Unfortunately, finding a good personal manager is not as easy as finding a good attorney. Law firms can—and do—"manage" hundreds of clients. But personal managers traditionally manage three or fewer clients who pay the bills; those managers with any reasonable amount of experience have very little time to explore the possibilities of exploiting the potential career of a start-up client. Most often, artists take a chance on managers just as managers take a chance on artists. The most useful advice I can offer is that you not entangle yourself too quickly or for too long a period, and that anything you sign, or agree to, be reviewed first by an attorney familiar with the entertainment industry.

You can start your search on the Internet, with the Music Managers Forum (MMF) at www.mmf-us.org. They can provide you with a head start on finding out about management opportunities and possibilities in many American cities and several foreign countries.

DEAL MAKERS: WHY YOU NEED THEM

There is something to be said for the fact that both attorneys and managers customarily socialize with executives and A&R (artists and repertoire) people at record companies (as well as with the business affairs staff with whom they may eventually be negotiating the record deal). The value of the "lunch deal," which is characteristic of virtually all businesses, is particularly consequential in the entertainment business, where ideas, not products, are the coin of the realm. A badly presented film script may never be taken seriously by the film company. A demo tape, CD, MP3 file, or link to YouTube or SoundCloud, which is presented to the record company by anybody other than someone credible, may never even get a listen. But when the material is presented by a credible and powerful representative in a way that the representative knows will be well received and reviewed, an artist or a songwriter with promise has a chance. Perception may not be everything, but don't underestimate it. In a world of images, artful and effective presentation is compelling.

Don't Worry, Be Wary

In a classic lunch deal, an agent approached one of his clients, a film actor whose last film (for which he was paid minimum scale) was a big success, to recommend an offer. A film company executive had told the agent (at lunch) that he was interested in optioning the actor for three more films—at $100,000 each. This sounded fabulous. However, the actor's attorney determined that the "three picture" deal was really a "no picture" deal. The film company did not have to make the films if it did not come up with acceptable scripts, budgets, costars, etc. In the meantime, the actor would be tied up. The actor declined the deal, and lo and behold, a few months later, with his tail between his legs, the agent called to tell the actor that the film company wanted to do a sequel to the actor's first film (which you will recall was a big success) and it needed the actor in order to produce the sequel. The fee that was ultimately negotiated? One million dollars and a percentage of the profits.

Now, of course, this benefited the agent as well as the actor. Why then, would the agent have recommended the "three [no] picture" deal? There are plenty of reasons, not the least of which is that a deal in hand—even a no-picture deal—is sometimes perceived to be worth more than no deal at all. One of the reasons agents are so valuable (and so valued) is their relationships with the buyers of talent. Of course, having such relationships is a perquisite of being a successful agent, but it can also be an affliction for the actor or artist to endure. This is all the more reason to have an attorney who is independent of the agent and who can operate as a check and balance for the client.

Similarly, in the music business, who will provide this kind of protection if the artist has only an attorney, but no personal manager? Managers are not so quick to jump on an artist's bandwagon when the band's wagon consists only of a motley crew (pardon the pun) of guitarists and drummers without a recording of any sort, or even a touring van. So the novice artist may have only one person guiding him or her. And that person is often an attorney. The healthiest situation is for a sufficient number of professionals to be engaged to guide an artist so that they each serve to keep an eye on the others. Checks and balances. Each advisor provides this service and the artist is the better for it.

However you look at it, when you put all of your eggs in one basket—any one basket—the eggs may come out scrambled. Behind all successful artists is a team that works more or less in synchronization to assist them in identifying and in reaching their goals. You have heard the Academy Award winners, the Emmy Award winners, and the GRAMMY Award winners thank these people, but now perhaps you can better understand why these faceless individuals garner so many thank-yous at awards ceremonies. Building a working team is a daunting challenge, second only to the act of creation itself in importance, but one that must be met.

DEAL BLOCKERS: HOW TO GET PAST THEM

There is no sure way to get a deal in any business. This section is not directed at artists who are creating a sensation in their home region and are attracting broad interest from various industry personnel around the country. Most artists who call upon the assistance of attorneys and managers to "shop" them—that is, to bring them, in an effective manner, to the attention of a record or music publishing company—have no such advantage. If you are a novice in the music business, three things work against you in your pursuit of a deal: insufficient time to develop your material, insufficient representative material, and insufficient attention by your representative.

Making Time

As I indicated earlier, it is also necessary for you to stay in the ring as long as possible to work on your art. Unreasonable and artificial time limits will work against you. Naturally, you have to eat; yet any day or night job will interfere with the time that needs to be spent on your efforts to manifest your talent in concrete form—songs, tapes, or CDs—or performances. Therefore, the squeeze is on. You must find a way to block out hours each day, seven days per week. You have to sacrifice everything that might distract you from your goal. In addition, you must have a sense of your direction.

Everyone wastes time. The secret is to know how to manage it—setting priorities, putting first things first, and following other rules of life you first heard (learned?) from, of all people, your parents. Perhaps it is enough simply to have this issue identified, because once the words "time flies" are posted on the mirror, the avoidance of waste becomes possible. However, although none of us experiences time in precisely the same way, most of us have jobs, salaries, projects to complete, etc. We do not have to self-start. We have a place to go at 9:00 a.m., lunches and dinners to eat (and meet at), meetings and conferences to attend. Not so with artists, who must learn to be proficient at managing time—whether "down" time or "up" time. They must understand, experience, and manage time in ways that the rest of us would never comprehend. Artists' comprehension of time is directly related to their ability to achieve their goals.

Building Your Material

Never think that whatever stock of creative materials you have on hand at any given moment will be sufficient to interest a company. You must continue to write, to perform—in a word, to develop your craft. Nothing disappoints an A&R person more than to hear a band months after its initial presentation and realize that there are no new songs, or that the arrangements have not evolved.

The more you perform, the more you improve your art. Why? For one thing, the mere process of playing in front of an audience constitutes a self-criticism that cannot be accomplished any other way. Self-congratulatory artists who decide that their creation is sacrosanct—locked in concrete—will not appeal to a record company or, in the long run, to the public.

Monitoring Your Representative

Once a representative has agreed to work with you, it should not take long to structure an approach to record and music publishing companies, to follow through on the approach, and to draw conclusions from the effort. Remember, though, the shopping function is both a privilege and a burden. Time passes; holidays intervene; people who work with a volume of beginning artists have to figure out how to organize approaches to the record and music publishing companies and then to coordinate them with the companies' responses, if any. When a representative is truly snowed under by other work, especially for "paying" clients, no amount of frustrated calls, emails, faxes, chocolates, or cajoling on behalf of an artist will be effective in getting the representative's attention. The truth is that you must set your own time limits and, if necessary, switch representatives regularly. You are, after all, number one on your own priority list and you must act accordingly.

STAYING THE COURSE OR CALLING IT QUITS

And now to the ultimate decision. When to give up! For every one hundred records on the charts, there are tens of thousands of demos filling our trash dumps or MP3 files freezing our computers waiting for the delete button. And they belong there. Why? Because they are not good enough. Now, there is no universal standard for determining what is good enough or what ought to be a hit. But, by definition, if your record does not take off, it isn't good enough. This is, of course, a psychological truth, not a real truth. Your recording may be perfect, but if it is not a hit, it is not good enough. Good enough means successful. If it is not successful, it is not good enough. This does not mean that the "essence" of the recording is not fabulous. It only means that the recording, taken together with the efforts and talent of the record company, the manager, the attorney, the publicity firm, the radio promotion people, etc., has no potency.

I was standing in the back of a theater a few years ago with the writer of the book and lyrics of the musical comedy *Annie*. The writer had an enormous reputation as a comedy writer for television, magazines, etc. If anyone knew what constituted a joke, he did. We were watching a preview of the musical a few days before the official Broadway opening. The actor on stage spoke a particular line that was supposed to be funny, and no one laughed. In fact, they had never laughed at this line. Having represented the "orphans" for more than a year, I had seen the show in its developing stages at the Goodspeed Opera House in East Haddam, Connecticut, and then at the Kennedy Center in Washington DC. This would have been my twentieth time hearing the same line that received no laughs. The book writer mumbled something which I could not make out. I asked him, "What did you say?" He said, "I guess it's not a joke." I said, "I guess not." The writer was not worried. He had a suitcase of lines that were jokes, so he never looked back from his Tony Award and he continued his illustrious career.

At any rate, the writer left the line in, and certainly it did not keep the play from becoming a big success, with a five-year run followed by a film, multiple revivals, and even another film. This does not change the fact that the line read like a joke and sounded like one. But it wasn't. You might think back to this story when you are hanging on tightly to a song or a recording that you "know" is a hit but is going nowhere. Maybe it's not a hit.

Like our writer, you may have a trunkful of songs. You may even have had a brief run on the charts with a song or two. But sooner or later, you have to confront reality and decide whether what you have accomplished is good enough.

A final point. A hit is a hit only after it has become a hit and after the artists and producers have been paid and have deposited the checks, and the checks have cleared the bank. This confluence of events may not occur until years after the climb up the Everest that is the *Billboard* 100. Or, as we will see, it may be a longer wait than that. Get as excited as you like when it appears that your song is a hit, but don't believe it until all of the above have occurred.

You have to determine for yourself when enough is enough, when it is time to quit the ring. The art may be there, but the execution may have failed. The art may be there, but the money may have run out. The art may be there, but the patience may have expired. My best advice to artists who are contemplating quitting is to seek counsel from friends and, in particular, friends intimately involved in their profession—band mates, agency and record company personnel, even club owners who originally supported them. Record and publishing companies are populated by artists who quit pursuing their own careers. They have found a way to express their artistic ideas in a different arena. And no one need stop creating just because he or she determined that a full-time career as a creator is not in the offing. The world of music is filled with stories of composers and performers who blossomed late in life. Perhaps a heavy metal career for a forty-year-old is not in the cards, but there are certainly other possibilities.

2 · INVESTORS
The High Costs of Low Finance

A bank is a place that will lend you money if you can prove you don't need it.
—ATTRIBUTED TO BOB HOPE

It is extremely difficult for struggling artists to be heard by the powers that be. Just as a song needs to be played on the radio (or available on YouTube or Facebook) in order to sell records, artists need to be seen, heard, auditioned, or played on a CD player, an MP3 player, or via YouTube or other streaming video and audio sites in order to sell themselves. This costs money, and there are individuals and companies willing to lend artists money or facilities in order to assist them in positioning themselves so they can be effectively auditioned by the ultimate buyers of talent: the record companies.

THE COSTS OF BEING HEARD

Fledgling artists need to be seen as well as heard. Record companies need to know that the sound and emotion they hear on a demo can be reproduced with sufficient virtuosity live (1) to electrify an audience when on tour and (2) to convince the public that the artistry on the record has not been faked (remember Milli Vanilli?). It is neither cheap nor easy to gather together musicians for a showcase at a live club or in a rehearsal hall. An already organized band has it hard enough; it is even more difficult and expensive for a solo singer to replicate what can be manufactured on a CD with sophisticated recording techniques.

Prior to the technological revolution spurred on by MySpace, iTunes, and subsequently Spotify, Pandora, YouTube, Tidal, and SoundCloud and other delivery systems, showcasing one's music was achieved only via a live performance or a demo, and these traditional forms remain the predominant way an artist can spread the word. Computers and the digital evolution have not done away with those who have to input information, as green-peaked accountants did for the past several hundred years, and the Internet has not done away with the need to create an effective product constituting the musical performance.

In the past, a homemade piano and vocal tape could serve as a "hard copy" of an artist's music. Times have changed. Over the last decade, it has become a necessity for artists to demo their songs for the record labels in such a highly sophisticated way that a normal person would be hard-pressed to distinguish the result from a full-priced Electric Lady master with all the trimmings. Musicians are able to make such demos because incredible innovations in recording equipment now allow them to build extremely effective home recording studios. This equipment, plus CD burners, MP3 file transfers via the Internet, YouTube, and other means of exploitation, is helping artists to find new and better ways to present themselves and to make access to their music more manageable. But the costs remain. These extend well beyond the cost of demos. They include all of the costs of beginning a career: from performing live, with the attendant costs of equipment, transportation, and mailings, to the cost of attending music conventions that cater to young artists, to the cost of legal and financial services, including the cost of creating the business entities that are necessary in order to function without unwanted liability to third parties, and, finally, to the cost of living—food and shelter for one's very survival. And these costs are greater than ever before.

OF INVESTORS AND INVESTMENT AGREEMENTS

Enter the investor. There are as many variations of investors as there are forms of investor agreements. I am not talking about moneylenders who lend funds either in a lump sum or as needed up to a maximum amount—all in return for a promise to pay back the loan within a specific period of time, often in specific balanced installments, and always with an interest factor. Banks will usually lend money only to someone who has established good credit and has assets that can be designated as security to the bank in the event of default. A mortgage on a piece of real estate is the most common example of this model.

Artists are not usually in a position to borrow from banks, not the least of the reasons being they cannot fulfill either of the requirements noted above. This does not mean that finding someone willing to invest in an artist's career or demo recording is an impossible goal. Many people—often those with no music industry background—are willing to assist an artist in achieving the wherewithal to be seen and heard by a record company. Family members, friends, and strangers often combine to finance an artist's needs. Like anyone seeking financial aid, artists must go through the process of developing a business plan. However, one of the most important parts of plans developed by entrepreneurs hoping to start up a small business, the forecast of earnings, is impossible to incorporate into an artist's plan. The highly speculative nature of all music industry endeavors reduces the artist's plan to a fairly simple agreement, one that states

- the amount of the investment;
- the purpose for which it will be used;
- some kind of time frame in which the investment will be applied to the mutual goals of the artist and the investor—or returned;
- terms affecting the manner in which the investment will be repaid (or not repaid).

The most common forms of artist-investor agreements are partnerships, including the joint venture, where the partners are active participants in the venture covered by the agreement, and the various forms of incorporated businesses, including the S corporation, the C corporation, and the LLC (limited liability company). (In this chapter, and in chapters 6 and 16, I discuss these and other types of structures available to artists seeking investment capital.)

FINDING THE MONEY

It has not gone unnoticed by many fledgling artists, or their fairly sophisticated friends and relatives, that there is a widely held perception—much of it justified—that successes in the music business can make lots of money. Therefore, those with money are susceptible to being convinced to throw some of it into a pot to help an artist, or, more frequently, a record production company, a publishing company, a label, or even a management company, break into the business. Artists or their representatives trying to raise money for demos and tours (or careers) through one of the corporate forms—by selling financial interests to nonparticipating investors in their future profits—need to be aware that raising money this way is no different from selling securities. If they seek to raise money from passive investors (that is, those who are not active participants in the project being financed), they must comply with securities laws.

Raising money is a difficult—and sometimes risky—enterprise. This goes not only for you, but also for your representative—no matter how well intentioned he or she may be. Just as you must exercise care in determining how best to raise money and on what terms you can pay it back, you must make yourself aware of how those who believe in you are seeking to raise the money as well; and if they intend to raise these funds from passive investors, then either they, or their lawyers, need to have a solid knowledge of securities law, as I will discuss in more detail below. Never forget, though, that most investors want the highest return, the highest liquidity (ability to turn their investment into cash easily and quickly), and safety. An honest advisor will tell them that is a rare combination indeed, but a dreamer won't.

Blue-Sky Laws

In 1911, Kansas passed the first set of comprehensive laws in the United States designed to prevent the sale of interests in fraudulent schemes or schemes whose likelihood of success was highly speculative. It was said that the only thing that backed the securities sold in various fly-by-night enterprises being hawked to gullible Kansans was "so much blue sky," and the Kansas laws were referred to as blue-sky laws. One judge referred to "vision" when describing the character of a particularly questionable venture. He wasn't talking about creative vision; he was talking about fantasy, and "fantasy" ventures are what the state regulatory agencies in the United States under the umbrella of the federal Securities and Exchange Commission (SEC) seek to prevent by requiring those selling securities to comply with a complex set of filing regulations.

Suppose, for example, you, or someone who believes in your talent decides to raise money from others in return for a promise to pay a percentage of profits at such time as the investment returns a profit. Say the original investor has contracted with you to provide $100,000, and subsequently decides to raise the entire amount or a portion of it from others. (In securities law lingo, he is said to be "offering" a piece of what he gets from you in return for a piece of the money he has promised to you.) That investor is, in effect, selling securities, and hence must comply with the securities laws of the states in which the various potential investors live—and possibly the securities laws of the United States as well. Note that whoever is making the offering must file—according to the specific state's rules and regulations—in each state in which the investment is being solicited, even if the potential investor eventually declines the offer. And although many state registration requirements are relatively straightforward, there are nevertheless fees that must be paid to the agencies. And don't forget the legal fees.

The good news is that when relatively insignificant amounts of investment capital are sought by the person offering the "securities," both the federal securities act and the blue-sky laws of each state offer a multitude of exemptions, thereby relieving the investor of most, but not all, of the costly and time-consuming filing and documentation procedures that would ordinarily be required for a larger investment. The bad news is that state regulations vary, and only someone thoroughly acquainted with securities law is in a position to sort them out. If an offering is made only in one state (that is, the offer would only be made to investors located in the same state as the person seeking the investment), the offering is not occurring "in interstate commerce" and therefore federal law does not apply. However, if an offering is made to potential investors located in more than one state, the offering becomes subject to both federal and state securities laws. There are generally two types of offerings: public and private. Due to the cost of registration and preparation for a public offering, most small entertainment projects obtain financing through a private offering, which is exempt from the most burdensome requirements. Both the US Federal Securities Act of 1933 and all of the various states' laws provide for private offerings.

If a person seeking investment makes an offering involving interstate commerce, the most commonly used federal law is the private placement exemption offered under Regulation D of the 1933 act. However, although the offering is exempt, there are nevertheless specific rules, requirements, and filings that must be followed. By filing a simple form—Form D—with the SEC, a small company (Friends of and Investors in Superartist?) can sell up to $1 million of security interests (that is, equity in the artist or in a production company) in a twelve-month period.[1] A word of warning: Don't forget that, in addition to compliance with federal regulations, the person seeking investment capital must also comply with each state's security laws. (Rules change frequently, so be careful!)

There is also an exemption within Regulation D that permits offerings without regard to dollar amount provided that there are no more than, or the offering party believes that there are no more than, thirty-five purchasers of securities from the offering party. Rule 501 makes it clear, however, that one does not have to count among the thirty-five those people who are considered under the law to be accredited investors. "Accredited investors" are those that are either experts in the securities field or well off financially. A definition of such investors supplied by the SEC in Rule 501 can be found at 17C.F.R. Section 230.501.

Typically, Regulation D forbids advertising or general solicitation of investors. It also stipulates that an offering document, such as a private placement memorandum, must be prepared and given to each prospective investor before he or she actually makes the investment. This document sets out the details of the investment and its potential risks.

Penalties for Failure to File

When anyone seeking to obtain passive investment to finance a demo, an album, or a career fails to file the proper documents with the applicable securities agencies, any one of the following may occur:

- having to pay fines
- having to pay punitive damages
- facing future restrictions on seeking investment for other projects— up to and including being barred for life from doing so
- having to file retroactively at considerable cost
- having to return the investment money with interest
- having to cite the violation in future private placement memoranda that he or she, either alone or in association with others, wants to use to solicit investments

It is likely that if the investor is a family member or a close friend, the securities agencies will never receive a complaint; if they do, they will usually drop the issue entirely. There are provisions in the securities laws in which the disclosure requirements are treated differently when investors are a small number of "friends and family." However, securities law compliance is more likely to become an issue when a disgruntled investor—not necessarily, but usually, a stranger—feels slighted (and when, of course, the investment has gone south). Did you forget to invite your investor to the CD listening party? Did you fail to return his telephone calls? Have you incorrectly credited or failed to credit him on the CD jacket or wherever else credit was expected or promised? Even when you have failed to follow the laws designed to protect investors, if everyone makes a profit, you are not likely to have a problem. But angry investors who have also lost money will be looking for reasons to file a complaint (the SEC provides preprinted forms for easy complaining), and they may well find them. And, once a complaint is filed by an investor who claims to have been misled by you, the securities agencies will have no choice but to investigate. Further, certain illegal actions are more visible than others, and may be noticed even when none of your investors has complained. For example, if you advertise for investors, which, as noted above, you cannot do except as part of a formal public offering, federal or state securities departments may, in the course of their routine watch policies, see the advertisements, at which point they may well decide to knock on your door and pursue you. Talk about a career bummer!

INTERNET-SPECIFIC OFFERINGS

It used to be difficult enough to identify the particular states in which a blue-sky registration had to be filed. Some were easy: the state in which you lived, the state in which your potential investor lived. Some were less easy. With the advent of the Internet, offering semianonymity and a very broad reach, things became even more complicated—and opportunities for fraudulent investment schemes multiplied. But in this country, no technological advancement can gain a footing for long before a law or rule is adopted which will regulate it.

Organized in 1919, the North American Securities Administrators Association (NASAA) is the oldest international organization devoted to investor protection. It lists on its website, www.nasaa.org, an enormous number of organizations that protect the (potentially) defrauded investor. NASAA has recognized that the Internet has become an alternative distribution channel for people who may defraud others. Reaching people via email is more efficient than the old-fashioned telemarketing method, and as this new method spread around the world, both the NASAA and the SEC had to address the issue, both to protect legitimate offerings and to identify illegitimate ones. In addition, over half the states in the United States have established Internet surveillance programs that watch for fraud. Take heed. The Internet is probably so much a part of your daily life that it would seem natural to use its long reach to interest potential supporters. But utilize a chat room, or encourage a well-heeled "fan" to donate money, and you may be headed for trouble. If you mess up once, you may be looking at jail time. If your "fairy godmother" investor decides to solicit investment funds from others and she messes up, you can be held responsible also.

THE SAFE HARBOR DISCLAIMER

Legislation and/or policies designed to protect people from certain risks and uncertainties that they might otherwise be subject to are called *safe harbors*. NASAA has created a safe harbor disclaimer whereby you (or your investor) can indicate either on your home page or via other methods those states to which you are directing your offer of investments, and you (or your investor) can then follow the blue-sky rules and regulations of those states, a move that substantially insulates you from the charge that you (or your investor) have been making offerings in states in which you have failed to register or chosen not to register.

Following NASAA's guidelines does not protect people seeking investments from others from charges of fraud if they violate any rules or regulations of the state or federal securities laws, but complying with these guidelines—which is evidence that you are really trying to do the right thing—can at least shift to state authorities the burden of proving violations of the law. Over half of the states have adopted this safe harbor disclaimer exemption. Hopefully, the rest will follow suit.

GETTING THE RIGHT ADVICE

As you have seen, this process is very dangerous. It's cliché time. The securities departments of the various states and the federal government were not "born yesterday." "There is nothing new under the sun." "It's all been done before." "The securities police can "see you coming." I am not suggesting that raising money by selling interests in a company is a bad idea. In fact, it can be a very good idea. If Microsoft can do it, why not you? If an off-Broadway show can raise a million dollars in an environment where the odds of losing it all are similar to the odds in the record business, why not your career, your record company, or your newly discovered artist?

There are plenty of lawyers who specialize in securities law. The problem is that most music industry attorneys do not. Some music lawyers are members of law firms that have securities divisions, but the majority of the boutique firms offer legal services predominantly in the area of facilitating music business transactions. So before you start raising money left and right, it's a good idea to first consult with a securities lawyer. Just as the laws are there to protect the "little old ladies" who might otherwise be taken advantage of, they are structured to assist you in doing it right. It will be money and time well spent. And besides, perhaps the securities lawyer knows a couple of people who have money, instead of CDs, to burn.

PAYING IT BACK

In return for a budgeted amount that will serve their needs for a given period, artists will agree to pay back their investors in one of the following ways, or variations of one or more of these ways. Polyphonic, a new medium for financing fledgling artists, is a special newcomer in this arena and I discuss it in some detail later in this chapter.

First Monies Plus a Percentage

The artist can agree to pay investors out of the very first cash he or she receives from a contractual relationship with a record company or a music publishing company (known as "first monies"), and, subsequently, by paying an identical amount out of, for example, 50% of the next monies received. Say an investor has invested $1,000. Under this payback method, the investor would receive the first $1,000 of money not otherwise committed for recording, and half of the next $2,000 of similarly designated money—not a bad return on a risky investment.

Straight Percentage

The artist can agree to pay the investors a percentage of receipts derived from all or some of a variety of music industry sources—everything from record royalties and advances to live performance fees and music publishing income. The nature of such receipts needs to be very carefully defined, and if you go this route, you need an accountant who is intimately acquainted with the idiosyncrasies of the music business to ensure that the parties are clear as to what investors are to receive and from which monies. Similarly, there should be a cap, or limit, on the amount of money investors can receive. For example, the agreement might specify that on a $1,000 investment, the investors will receive 25% of all advances and royalties received from the record company or publishing company up to a total payment of $2,000.

Royalty Points

An artist who has a well-negotiated record deal will generally receive (exclusive of what the producer's royalty is) from 9 to 12 points. If an artist has a 10-point deal (net of producer), if the investor is promised 1 point, this entitlement will constitute 10% of that total. That must be added to the 15% or 20% of the total earnings that a manager receives, the 5% the business manager will likely claim, and legal fees, which, even if not specifically tied to a percentage of income (a practice becoming more and more popular), can be considerable. The cost of legal services can amount to anywhere from 3% to 10% of artists' gross incomes—at least at the beginning of an artist's career, when legal services are much in demand and gross income is likely to be low.

Thus, ultimately, the artist may have to pay out as much as 45% of his or her gross income. In such cases, since any well-run "business" is likely to require as much as 50% of gross income, or more, to cover operation expenses, the artist will be left with very little or nothing—and possibly even owe money. Even assuming the lower cost figures (that is, 15% for a personal manager, 5% for the business manager, and 3% for the attorney), the artist would end up with less than 20% of gross (15 plus 5 plus 3 plus the investor's 10, plus the 50% for operational expenses, equals 83%).

Therefore, when artists still choose to pay investors a "point" or two, it is logical to establish some kind of cap on the amount of money to which investors are ultimately entitled. In this way, payments to the investors will not completely consume what is left of the artist's income after professional fees and other costs are paid. Another possibility is to limit the sources of financial return. For example, if the investor's entitlement is limited to record royalties, at least other sources are exempt from the potentially devastating effect on the artist's resources that I have described above.

OVERCALLS AND CONVERSIONS

In cases in which the initial investment proves inadequate, artists may want to seek additional money from investors. This "last" money is often the most expensive a borrower can receive. For this reason, it is extremely wise to provide in advance, in a written document, for an overcall right—that is, a right for artists to claim from the investors an additional sum of money without changing the basic parameters of the understanding.

Artists may also negotiate the right to convert the investment into a loan, with interest (the conversion right), and have the option to pay back the investment within a particular period of time at an agreed-upon rate of interest. This option is of obvious value to the artist, and may sometimes be more appealing to investors than one would initially think. This right may mature under any of the following circumstances:

- upon the artist signing an exclusive recording or music publishing agreement within a certain period of time;
- upon the artist paying back a percentage (for example, one-half) of the investment within a specified period of time, in which case the balance owed would be subject to the conversion;

- upon the artist reconstituting him- or herself with another artist or artists—for example, by changing band mates and re-forming as another band;
- upon the occurrence of negative circumstances, such as the failure of the artist's first album or the failure to enter into an exclusive recording or music publishing agreement within a certain period of time. (In such cases, all or part of the investment can be converted into a loan.)

COMMISSIONS

Borrowers may have more than investors to worry about. They may also have personal managers whose contracts permit them to commission all gross receipts. Not only may the investment itself be commissionable; when artists' earnings are being directed toward paying back investors, the record sales that generate this income may be subject to commission as well.

Only one commission is considered fair. But which one? Presumably the second—that applied to actual earnings—because investment capital is hard to come by and to reduce it by 15% to 20% at the very moment it is paid out to the artist may not be the best use to which the capital can be put. On the other hand, the personal managers may be the ones who have obtained the financing. What is that worth? Or personal managers, understandably, may not want to work for free, and part of any money that comes into the coffers of the artists may logically be money that is legitimately commissionable by them.

No one approach will fit all circumstances. But the dangers described in the previous examples warrant careful consideration and discussion by all parties involved in an investment of this nature; then, once the agreement is reached and signed, no one should have reason to be angry later.

CROWDFUNDING

In chapter 16, I discuss in detail the benefits and the risks of using crowdfunding sites such as Kickstarter. While I am aware of no artist who has been pilloried by the securities laws (federal or state) for using crowdfunding to raise capital, I should nevertheless make some mention of the nature of these types of transactions in the context of the laws designed to protect "investors."

Crowdfunding is not actually a recent concept.

For years there has existed a financial mechanism, used traditionally for financing the cost of college, which is referred to as a *human capital contract*. This product provides funds to an individual through an "equity-like" arrangement where the funding party receives, usually for a limited period of time, a portion of the individual's future income. I am not describing some kind of backroom loan-sharking scheme here. Human capital contracts have been advocated by a number of Nobel Prize–winning economists and were originally proposed by Adam Smith in *The Wealth of Nations* as a way to make human capital a tradeable asset. Most often, this arrangement is characterized by the funding party receiving different percentages of the results of the venture being funded, depending on how much the artist earns. What is attractive about this kind of funding is that the artist is neither "borrowing" nor "going into debt" but rather is utilizing a structure that provides him with what he needs, while not risking his future financial stability. Before an artist decides to take this path, I urge him to check with an attorney to ensure that what he is doing does not run afoul of the securities laws in his state, or otherwise.

There are innumerable entities that provide funding via human capital contracts, but www.upstart.com might be a good place to visit to begin to understand what they do. Upstart was established by a number of former Google employees. They have established a fairly well-respected algorithm that forecasts future income for those whose projects they fund. How they can do this in the music business is beyond me, but it is worth the time to research them and to listen to their pitch. Those seeking to raise money via crowdfunding can accept investments up to $1 million from companies and from $2,000 to $100,000 from individuals, depending on earning and net worth.

SHOULD HE WHO PAYS THE PIPER CALL THE TUNE?

Over the last decade, the music industry has begun to attract traditionally conservative Wall Street types as investors. While on the face of it, this sounds like a good thing, it can cause problems for the group or company that obtained the investment. For example, one independent company, a clever, creative group of music industry neophytes in San Francisco, was shut down by its Silicon Valley financiers after only a few months of operation. The label had signed a number of acts, but the terms of the artist deals (required by the investors) were so brutal that many of the artists represented by reasonably competent counsel were invariably lost to another, more competitive (and more experienced) label. The labels that acquired those acts had flexible, long-term thinkers who understood the concept of compromise in their negotiations. The investors in the company, who were not music industry professionals, decided that they had no time to be flexible. They wanted it all, and they felt that they knew better. The result: They ended up with nothing. All that was left was another defunct label to add to the scrap heap of the music business and one more anecdote with human consequences. Today they are probably bad-mouthing the music industry as a lousy business and a foolish place to invest one's money. They're wrong, but probably have no clue as to why.

It can seem amusing to observe the pratfalls and arrogance of people who are the "masters of the universe" on Wall Street but who are total idiots when it comes to the valuation and exploitation of intellectual property, and there are innumerable examples of investor-caused failures in the music business beyond the one cited above.

What is happening in the music industry is mirrored by what happened to the dot-com music businesses in the 1990s. The financial "experts" and their technology specialists established many music industry–oriented businesses, yet they neither understood the concepts of the industry, nor its history, nor the mistakes that were made before them from which they might have learned a thing or two. Perhaps most significantly, they did not know the people in the industry and did not gain their confidence. One particularly egregious example involved a record company that began its exploitation of music rights by appropriating digital files of sound recordings, but not the accompanying right to "reproduce" or "perform" these files. This was not a good idea.

A BACKER WHO KNOWS WHAT HE'S DOING

Brian Message, manager of Canada's Radiohead, and Adam Driscoll of the British media company MAMA Group, have teamed up with Terry McBride of Nettwerk, a Canadian company that manages, produces, and publishers artists, (www.nettwerk.com) to set up a company that may mark the future of many young artists who want to avoid the processes described above in this chapter. They call it Polyphonic.

This is how it works at its most basic level. First Polyphonic invests in a band and helps them to create a kind of minilabel whose only artist is the band which is the subject of the investment. They provide many of the tools that a record company would traditionally provide (whether promotion, marketing or A&R advice), but only when needed, so that the "label" will not be burdened with large overhead costs. You could say that Polyphonic is assisting the artist in "doing it yourself," but the artist who opts for this kind of assistance will never face the myriad situations that cause most fledgling artists to fail at their first or second attempts on their own without a professional support team. The belts and suspenders available from an institution like Nettwerk will not let that happen. In a way, Polyphonic is the ideal answer to the frustrations of depending on the majors (or even the independent record labels). Their assistance allows young bands to go beyond their own resources to establish their bona fides with the public. Polyphonic is extremely well-funded and intends to invest as much as $300,000 in each new band which they take under their wing. Frankly, they are doing what the major labels used to do, but with much more savvy in the new world of social networking and burgeoning digital services. Another company that is seeking to establish the same kind of service to bands is "Self Serve," which is an offshoot of William Morris Endeavor Agency. It will be interesting to observe whether, or which of, the two (or perhaps more manifestations in the future) will succeed in their efforts: a conglomerate of incredibly connected and experienced music business professionals or a powerful multipurpose agency whose music business credentials are limited mostly to live booking.

• • •

It would be a mistake to suggest that the music industry is not a gold mine for intelligent investors who seek advice from those who understand the industry best. It is, and has been, and will be.

Those who are reading this book with the intention of becoming investors in the music business must realize that this industry has a long, complicated history, and that there are reasons some companies have survived and others have not: The stars of Wall Street who think the music business is not "brain surgery" are wrong. It is. The lessons to be learned are many and take years; there is no easy entrance into this industry. The contribution of music industry professionals is as invaluable as the investment itself.

But lest we forget, whether investors are seeking to invest their money solely for profit, for artistic participation and expression, or merely for the opportunity to be patrons of the arts in a time-honored tradition, their contribution is enormously valued and can mean the difference between an artist's gaining the attention of the world and struggling during yet another unsatisfying—and unfulfilled—period.

---

1. There was a time when the federal government divided potential investors into two groups: sophisticated investors and the rest. There were no limitations on the number of "sophisticated investors" one could solicit. As to "the rest," there were limitations. As it turned out, the sophisticated-investor exemption was interpreted by different federal courts in different states in different ways. The result was that a person seeking investment from an array of investors would never know whether, down the road, he or she might be found to have violated the federal securities laws or not. This uncertainty resulted in an awkward and costly situation in which people raising money would set up different companies in different states to avoid running afoul of the federal laws in any state, and, ultimately, led to the creation of Regulation D. The sophisticated-investor exemption still exists, but it is rarely used. Regulation D has effectively replaced it in practice.

3 · ADVANCES
Why They Seem a Lot Like Loans
(and Vice Versa)

Ah, take the cash, and let the Credit go
Nor heed the rumble of a distant Drum
—EDWARD FITZGERALD, *THE RUBÁIYÁT OF OMAR KHAYYÁM*

The New York music business's nickname, Tin Pan Alley, hails from the early part of the 20th century, when music publishers were concentrated on Twenty-Eighth Street in Manhattan. As the story goes, the name was coined by a reporter who said that the paper-roll pianos being played in publishers' demo rooms sounded like the pianists were pounding on tin pans. In fact, he said, the whole of Twenty-Eighth Street was beginning to sound like a tin pan alley.

In the early days of the music business—from the late 19th century to the 1950s—a music publisher would take everything from a songwriter, perhaps even put the publisher's president's name down as a writer, and give the actual songwriter a bone (maybe a pink Cadillac, maybe something a bit shadier). Things have not changed so much. Only now instead of bones, they give writers advances. Remnants of Tin Pan Alley remain, even as the music industry itself has matured in a multitude of ways. The paper that muted the piano has been replaced with the paper constituting the contracts that too often compromise artists' ability to glean financial security from their creative efforts.

What is an advance? In a word, it is cash. In the music business, it is cash given by a record company, production company, or music publishing company to an artist—cash that the company is entitled to have returned, however. And there's the rub.

If you look up "advance" in the dictionary, you will find it has an unusually large number of synonyms—among them "debt," stampede," and "loan." In the music business, the word takes on an almost metaphysical dimension. Eyes light up, those who commission earnings get all excited, and everyone tries to convince everyone else that they are getting something for nothing. Although the advancing party does not receive any perceived value from the receiving party at the time the advance is given (except promises), the receiving party is now about to enjoy a bottle of champagne, a new car, and the opportunity to treat many friends (probably newfound) to a night or week on the town.

What are the real characteristics of advances? Their implications? The advantages? Whatever you can do with the money—live, eat, pay rent, pay the phone bill, buy some equipment, rent a rehearsal room, outfit your band with instruments and clothes, pay your lawyer, your accountant, and your manager something "on account," provide your fans with updated website information or postcards about upcoming dates. And don't forget union dues, without which you might not be able to afford medical insurance. There are lots of reasons for artists to take advances. Without them, most artists would be unable to function, and the record companies would be the eventual losers.

The disadvantages? The entire burden of paying back cash advances is the artist's alone. And, even if they are ultimately repaid, the publisher or record company will have acquired, via these advances, long-term equity in copyrights in both musical compositions and recordings, as well as the right to control and share financially in these potentially vast income-producing assets "in perpetuity" (read "forever"). This is because all monies going in the direction of the artist, or songwriter, are advances. Music publishers do not "purchase" your copyrights, or the right to control them, when they enter into a typical copublishing agreement. Rather, they advance, to the artist or songwriter, money that must be returned—if only out of the artist's or songwriter's share of earnings. And yet they wind up owning the writer's or artist's assets.

Shocking as it may seem, artists in the music business begin their careers more in debt than doctors who have borrowed their way through eight years of college and medical school. At least doctors own a medical degree. Artists do not even own their masters; on the contrary, as we will see, they have to pay for the records they make, for recording costs are advances, too. Songwriters have to return the money they receive for selling their copyrights and the worldwide administration rights, but they do not get their copyrights back. They receive equipment loans, but often have to return the equipment. They look to the record company to provide services including, obviously, the promotion of their records, yet they are charged for the tens of thousands of dollars that it costs the record company to hire independent promotion people—people who used to work for the record companies, but who are now operating under their own umbrellas so that record companies (at least three of which at one time were operating under federal license to run enormously lucrative broadcast networks) would not be tainted with the same brush that the less reputable promotion people have been scarred with. (For more about independent promotion, see chapter 4, page 35, and chapter 9, pages 154–156.)

As people in general have become more aware of lifetime investment needs and opportunities, a growing segment of the music industry's lawyers and accountants are no longer inclined to encourage artists to accept substantial advances. While it is true in most instances that advances are not repayable in cash, and are thus nonreturnable, they are always recoverable from royalties (that is, they are "recoupable"). That's why they are called advances. And, as we shall see, sometimes they are subject to interest charges that can inflate what seemed to be a manageable sum into a totally unmanageable debt.

A SAD STORY AND A HAPPY STORY ABOUT ADVANCES

One day, not too many years ago, a hungry manager and a greedy lawyer decided that one of their artists needed a quick infusion of money. Whether this was because they were insecure about the artist's continuing ability to feed the family of professionals around him by writing and recording hit records or because the artist had dug a financial hole for himself is not known. But the artist was not averse to a fat deposit into his bank account. What the manager and lawyer did, however, was to have a permanent effect on the artist and his family. These "caring professionals," with the songwriter's approval of course, sought and received several million dollars from the music publishing company to whom the writer had licensed his copyrights. The documentation concerning the payment referred to it as a "loan." Of course, interest was chargeable to the songwriter at the prevailing rate for personal loans, and the loan was secured by the artist's copyrights. The loan (together with its accumulated interest) was payable through the earnings of the songs, just as an advance would have been. However, it was not payable in the direct way that a loan ordinarily would have been. In other words, the loan did not have to be paid back—ever—out of the borrower's (the writer's) pocket. It just generated interest, and the accumulating interest, plus the unpaid balance of the loan, would simply be applied to the future earnings of the songs—songs that had been written over many years in the past as well as songs yet to be written.

Because both the lawyer and the manager needed money also (and, in their own view, deserved it because of their successful efforts in getting the money from which they were going to be paid the money they deserved), they obtained a combined commission rate that exceeded 30% of royalties. That left 70% for the songwriter. (This sounds like a comedy routine, but it's not funny.)

Along came the IRS. They said, "Wait a minute, this looks like an advance to us: The writer never has to pay it back except out of earned royalties, and his representatives commissioned it just as if it were income. This is no loan!" The writer's representatives cried foul. Loans are not income. Only advances are income. The IRS agreed, but found the payment to be an advance, not a loan, and therefore it was viewed as taxable income. The federal, state, and local taxes, interest, and penalties totaled—guess what—70% of the money "lent" to the artist in the first place.

Unfortunately, the artist had retained very little of the 70% he netted after his representatives took their commissions. (He was not to enjoy a fabulous lifestyle after all.) So the money owed the various government agencies began to accumulate interest and by the time the IRS asserted its claim, the money owed had doubled.

The artist not only had nothing left, but he owed the IRS an interest-accumulating amount equivalent to what he had received in the first place. Meanwhile, he owed the publishing company millions of dollars—to be recouped out of his songwriter earnings. Cash advances do not usually bear an interest rate. This "loan" did, and the debt accumulated interest charges rapidly. Remember that the publishing company could not request direct repayment, nor could the artist pay back the loan directly even were he able to raise the capital, so the publisher could forever hold on to the income generated by the musical compositions attributable to the writer.

And now for a happy story. A publishing company liked a band and its songwriters and signed them to a typical copublishing relationship. They would receive royalties—as writers—representing 50% of almost every dollar earned by their songs and an additional 25% of the same dollar by virtue of the fact that they were copublishers and co-owners of the copyrights to their music. The idea of paying writers one-half of the publisher's share of royalties in addition to their writers' share so that they ended up with 75% of every dollar was one that developed as artists began to be solely responsible for recording their own songs—a responsibility that in olden days had been the music publisher's. This particular artist's advance was modest, too. Four years later, the band still had not been signed, but each member worked at a day job and the writers had been able to develop and demo their songs (thirty songs during this period). The band also showcased regularly and developed a fan base; in essence, they were helped financially and creatively over a four-year period to sharpen their skills and improve their craft of writing and recording.

By the time a major record company recognized their appeal and signed the band to a spectacular agreement, their *red position* (the total of all unrecouped advances) under their music publishing contract was minuscule. This happy situation could not have occurred had the music publisher been simply parsimonious. It was the result of a carefully orchestrated process by the band's proactive music publisher through which the advances they received were carefully thought through before they were paid out and they were applied to expenses only as necessary. In no other way could the music publisher have afforded to stick with the act for that long. Consequently, almost as quickly as this band's records started selling, the company recouped its advances and the band started to receive additional money—money they earned, not money they had to pay back! The band was now in a position where they could actually revisit the publishing agreement from a position of strength and renegotiate some of the provisions that had given them pause at the beginning of their relationship. (There are always provisions that give one pause.)

The cautiousness with which both the band and their publishing company addressed the issue of advances and the band's responsibility toward feeding and housing themselves also had the effect of restraining the band from having to go to its record company to seek additional advances in return for which they would have had to give up even more rights and options.

A happy story.

IS ONE PERSON'S MONEY ANOTHER PERSON'S MOTIVATION?

Many of my colleagues and clients feel that if they hit up the record company or music publishing company for a lot of money by way of advances, the companies will fight harder for the artists under contract, if only to protect their own positions. On the contrary. My experience is that companies facing huge losses as a result of a contract with an artist who is not making it are more likely to write off the expense as a bad debt than to throw good money after bad. Nowhere is this more true than when a regime changes and the expenditure was authorized by the former administration!

Many lawyers and managers will seek to express their machismo and their worth by waving big bucks in front of their clients—bucks received as advances. But by the time everyone gets paid their fees, and the IRS and state tax authorities take their pounds of flesh, there often is not enough left to do a whole lot of good—certainly not enough to effect real change in the artist's life or career. And believe me, if the artist's records do not return the investment fast, the record or music publishing companies move quickly on to their next dream act without losing a beat. The only one who loses is the artist, who is history, even though the lawyers and managers are already moving toward big deals for the next generation of clients.

Obviously, I am not suggesting that artists should be underrepresented or represented less than aggressively in every way. But look at what happened to Alex Rodriguez after he signed a $252 million deal with the Texas Rangers: The public's focus turned from his art, and his skills, to his money. It was distracting, to say the least.

Commit another error or strike out too often and the money becomes the elephant in the living room that cannot be gotten rid of; the baseball player's performance on the field, previously the sole reason for the player's existence, is replaced with something totally extraneous to his function—whether or not the money that has been paid has been well spent and is being earned. This may be a mere distraction for sports stars, but in the music field it can be devastating, especially when the line between art and commercial viability is so indistinct, determined not necessarily by the artist's talent, but by that intangible called "perception" or "image"—that is, how a potential (or former) audience sees the artist.

4 · ROYALTIES
Some Unvarnished Truths

*When a little girl asked Lew Grade, founder of ATV Music,
now Sony/ATV, what two and two equals, he answered:
"It depends on whether you're buying or selling."*

Except for a few glaring examples (for example, the creators of *Superman* were paid off with a flat sum of money and the only pleasure they received from the success of the motion pictures based on their story was the buttered popcorn they purchased at the theater), most creators of intellectual property and their eventual distributors, such as record companies, acknowledge that they cannot fix a value on the created property. The result? A stratagem whereby creators receive a share of the success of the exploitation of their property. In the record business, this share is called a *royalty*. A royalty is essentially a sum of money that represents a percentage of sales. But as we shall see, the distinction between royalty and nobility has come a long way since the days of King Arthur.

The part of a recording agreement with the greatest consequence for artists is the section dealing with royalties. In contrast to salaried employees, who create a product or provide a service and receive a regular paycheck in return, artists, who produce what is known as *intellectual property*, are compensated on a totally different model—the royalty rate. But once compensation for services is calculated on the basis of a royalty, the floodgates open for every possible royalty-reduction device that can be dreamed up by the business affairs lawyers at the record labels. It is no wonder that the section in recording agreements dealing with royalties can be well over thirty pages.

Before getting into the details of the numerous charges against artists' royalties that are written into record agreements, I want to emphasize again that the cost of recording and marketing these days is astronomical, even as record sales and revenues have nosedived. Even with modern recording methods that can result in a top-quality result from essentially home studios, the costs of marketing and promoting a record remain high, and are even increasing, given the innumerable means now available to record companies on- and off-line to reach consumers. The royalty concept remains irreplaceable because record distribution, which remains the primary service provided by a record label in establishing an artist in the marketplace, still demands the royalty model in order to create manageable participation in income among all involved parties. Once royalties are implicated, charges against royalties have a rationale. Therefore, the following discussion remains as pertinent as ever.

However you may feel about the propriety of record companies charging so much against artists' accounts, you cannot deny that the investment by record companies in signing new artists is phenomenal. When A&R people observe artists at club dates, they know that if they sign the acts, their companies will have to invest upward of half a million dollars *per act* to break them. No small risk. No small risk for the A&R people either! How many acts can they sign without success before their record companies look cross-eyed at them?

It is no wonder that A&R people are extremely cautious before committing their company to a potential financial disaster. This old joke about A&R people is funny for a reason:

Question: How many A&R people does it take to screw in a lightbulb? *Answer:* I don't know. What do you think?

One or two misfortunes and the A&R person will be dusting off the old bass and looking for a gig. I use the word "misfortunes" rather than mistakes because the commercial acceptability of art being what it is—intangible, uncertain, and highly speculative—many brilliant and even potentially era-defining artists fail to break the commercial barrier for a long time, if ever.

By describing the various charges against artists' accounts with record companies, as with other descriptions and disclosures made in this book, I am not expressing an opinion about the correctness of the procedures; it is the job of artists and their representatives to seek a balance in the negotiations or renegotiations of their record agreements. However, the information needs to be in hand so that artists and their representatives can negotiate from an informed position. Remember, your adversaries are not going to transform themselves into teachers. Neither the lawyer in the negotiations nor the auditor who ultimately examines the royalty statements can look to the record or publishing company to walk them through the minefields and obstacle courses that have been set up specifically to divert and confuse. Therefore, as I repeatedly advise in this book, it is essential to call in an expert who has the experience, the relationships, and the drive (the need to win?) to ask the right questions and to elicit complete answers.

While this may sound obvious, young professionals who do not have these qualifications enter the music industry every year. What they may have is a new, nonjaded way of looking at a situation; they may have a hunger that older professionals may have lost years before, but they are nevertheless inexperienced. It should not be insulting to them to seek a second opinion or to offer to bring in a consultant to ensure that the myriad of obstacles that are placed before all negotiators in the music business (no, the companies don't discriminate) will be identified and addressed. It is never too early to call in an expert.

HOW THE ROYALTY PIE IS SLICED AND WHO GETS THE PIECES

The parameters that I have chosen for the following scenario are but one of many combinations that can describe a royalty structure. (For example, I have assumed that the producer of the record in my illustration is an independent producer and not either the artist or a producer employed on the staff of the record company.) Suppose the suggested retail selling price of a CD is $16.98, and the record company agrees by contract to pay you a royalty of 12% of the suggested retail selling price of the CD (12% or even 13% rates are the current going royalty rates for new artists). Not bad, you think: about $2.04 per copy. If you sell a mere 25,000 copies ($50,940), you're on the way to financial glory. (And that doesn't even take into account the publishing royalties, the merchandising, the touring.) Right? Wrong! (As you will soon see, this royalty is more than likely to be closer to $0.80 than $2.04—partially because the independent producer's royalty must be cut out of the 12% or 13%, leaving the artist with only 9% or 10% of the total.) In fact, you won't see $50,940 for a long, long time, if ever.

In the following sections, I will introduce you to the myriad items, in addition to advances, routinely deducted before an artist starts getting any royalties. Prices other than the suggested retail list price—for example, the published wholesale price or the ever-more-popular published price to dealers (PPD)—can be used as the royalty base (see the table on page 25 for a comparison of retail and PPD calculations for an $16.98 CD), but the examples in this chapter apply to the suggested retail selling price.

None of the following is meant to suggest that all record companies are rolling in money while their artists are starving. Since the first edition of this book was published in 2001, nothing could be further from the truth. Nevertheless, the universal music industry practice that artists pay recording costs out of their own royalties is unique to the music business. This does not happen in the book publishing business, where writers receive a royalty from the first book sold and production costs are not recoupable from the writer's royalties. The only monies recouped by the book publisher are the advances paid to the authors as cash or as a contribution toward publicity expenses and other promotional costs. The book royalty rate will invariably be lower than, say, 12 percent of retail, but it is exempt from the reductions prevalent in the music industry. Classical music record royalty rates are also traditionally lower because classical music labels do not usually recoup recording costs from the artist's royalties.

RECORDING COSTS

Recording costs are recoupable against the artist's royalties as if they were paid out in cash to the artist. These costs include everything imaginable, including studio costs, engineering costs, musicians' and singers' costs (including union payments), and the cost of tapes. They also include *mastering* (putting the recording into a form from which copies can be made), an item once absorbed by the record company as a manufacturing cost, not a recording cost, and one which can exceed $10,000 for an album. (With vinyl LPs, the mastering process involved making an acetate disc from which a metal "mother" master was created. Duplicate masters were made from the mother master, and these were used to press the records. Mastering is now a totally digital process—it consists essentially of balancing and equalizing the recording so that the copies made from the resulting master achieve the highest possible quality of sound on playback systems—yet the record companies routinely list it as a recording cost.)

Recording costs can be staggering. In 1969, the total charges applied against Simon and Garfunkel's royalty account for recording costs for the album *Bridge over Troubled Water* amounted to just over $30,000. Today the recording costs for a similar album would easily exceed $350,000, and probably approach $1,000,000.

Let's go back and see how this factor affects what the artist will actually receive in royalties on the sales of our hypothetical $16.98 CD. Since the price received by the record company from the retailer is about $10.70, we'll use $10.70 as 100 percent of the record company's receipts for each CD. (All of these costs vary from record to record and from artist to artist. But the example used here is well within the norm.) Out of the $10.70, the record company must pay the costs of manufacturing physical sound carriers (about $1.00); promotional expenses incurred by the company's own staff, as opposed to hiring an independent promoter (about $1.00); the cost of distribution (also about $1.00); union pension and welfare fees (about $0.09); and the cost of mechanical royalties to the publishers of the songs contained on the record (about $0.68). Anything left over is retained by the record company to share with the artist—but only *after* various charges, including recording costs, are recouped. Using our hypothetical deductions, this retained amount will be about $7. These are the record company's gross, or retained, earnings.

Now suppose that the recording costs listed above total $100,000. Theoretically, the record company will recoup its investment once 14,268 records have been sold ($100,000 divided by $7). However, the record company has other costs, including general overhead, tour support, independent promotion costs incurred as a result of the company's hiring promotion companies unaffiliated with themselves, marketing, and videos. Often the total amount of these other costs can be just as much as the actual recording costs; in our example, another $100,000. Taking into account these other costs, you might think the record company would *really* break even after selling 28,572 units (in contract language, a *unit* is one copy of a record), and the royalties would start flowing to you, the artist. Think again.

UNITED STATES CD ALBUM ROYALTY CALCULATION: RETAIL LIST PRICE VS. PPD

RETAIL LIST PRICE ROYALTY CALCULATION

Suggested Retail List Price	$16.98
Less	
Container Deduction	(25%) ($4.25)
Subtotal	$12.73
Standard Discounts (15%)	($1.91)
Subtotal	$10.82
Program Discounts (5%)	($0.54)
Royalty Base Price	$10.28
Artist Royalty Rate	15%
Artist Royalty	$1.54

PPD ROYALTY CALCULATION

PPD*	$10.70
Less	
Program Discounts (5%)	($0.54)
Royalty Base Price	$10.16
Artist Royalty Rate	15.1%†
Artist Royalty	$1.53
Source: Warner Bros. Records	

*For an $16.98 retail price, the PPD (WEA's base price) of $10.70 includes a 15% standard discount. (WEA, Warner/Electric/Atlantic, is the distribution arm of the Warner Music Group.)

† Note from author: So we don't really have an artist royalty rate of 15% but rather 15.1%? But what's 0.1% among friends and partners? Or up the deal by 0.1% for a true equivalency. Every little bit helps. On a million records, that's $9,000. On 10 million records—well, you get the idea.

That isn't the way it works. Why? Because recording costs are not recouped by the record company out of its retained earnings. Yes, the entire $7 mentioned above is retained by the record company, but on the books of the record company, only the amount that is owed to you, the artist's royalty, is applied against the costs of the recording project. Let's say your royalty is $0.80 per record. (Bear with me. You will soon see that a royalty of 12% on a

$16.98 CD is not $2.04, as one would presume, but about $0.80.) Given that, 125,000 records need to be sold before the $100,000 recording costs are recouped. At that point, the record company will have received $875,000 (125,000 times $7).

Unfortunately for you, your producer, who is not paid his or her share until the record company recoups all royalties owed you that are applied to recording costs, is next in line to be paid. The producer is paid on what is known as a *record one* basis (from the first record sold). At about $0.25 per record (that is, three-twelfths of your 12% royalty—or one-third of your 9% net royalty), the producer's payment on the first 125,000 units amounts to $31,250, which comes out of the record company's $875,000 gross. You have still received nothing. And, despite the fact that your royalties are calculated prospectively and not back to record one, it may be some time before you see any cash.

To review: At first, you thought that upon the sale of 25,000 units, at $2.04 per copy, you would have been paid almost $51,000. But since you have to pay *out of your own royalties* the $100,000 cost of recording, the sale of 25,000 copies will actually net you zero. In fact, it will take a total of 125,000 records (that is, 100,000 additional copies) sold to bring your account out of the red. On these 125,000 records, you will receive *no* royalty; whereas your record company will deposit into its bank account $875,000. The producer will have received $31,250—$0.25 times 125,000 units, which will be paid by the record company out of the $875,000 it will have received from its distributors. And we have not even begun to take into account other recoupable costs that the record company can (and will) charge against your royalties.

PAYMENT ON LESS THAN 100% OF RECORDS SOLD

In the old days, vinyl records (in particular 78 rpm records, which were retired as the format of choice in the late 1950s) would often break, whereupon consumers would return them to dealers and the dealers would discard them. Therefore, the record companies would promise to pay artists' royalties based on only 90% of sales on the (arbitrary) assumption that 10% of all records sold to dealers would be worthless and they would have to give dealers a credit for these shipments. This was done whether or not any of the records actually broke. Once LPs were introduced in the 1950s, there was absolutely no justification to reduce artists' royalties by 10%. Supposedly, this practice ended in the 1960s.

It's back.

Many record companies today pay royalties on less than 100% of sales. (A&M Records (now part of the Universal Music Group), the home of Carole King, Supertramp, The Police, and Peter Frampton, never paid royalties on more than 90% of records sold. The now defunct label, Jive Records (now part of Sony BMG Music), home of Britney Spears, 'NSYNC, R Kelly, Justin Timberlake, and the Backstreet Boys, also had a nostalgic tendency to play the 90% game. The record companies take what they can. Indeed, 85% is now the standard basis on which royalties are calculated. The rationale? There is none.

"NEW" TECHNOLOGY?

When CDs first came into the picture, many record companies wanted financial relief for what they termed the "incredible" cost of research and development. The relief they gave themselves was to pay royalties on anywhere from 85% to 90% of records sold to as few as 66.67%. Of course, most of the record companies had invested nothing in R&D, let alone incredible amounts. But, having been surprised by the advent of a new technology for which no special consideration had been made in their recording agreements, the record companies decided to include in their record agreements a catchall royalty reduction provision covering *any* new technology. This provision serves to reduce the royalty rate from 25% to 50% of the otherwise applicable royalty rate on formats such as digital compact cassettes or minidiscs, and now also *digital phonorecord deliveries* (DPDs) delivered to consumers via the Internet's digital download capability. These technologies are already with us. How will the companies deal with as yet unknown future inventions? Already we are seeing recording contracts that provide that, when new technologies are being used, the artist's royalty will be reduced to 50% or less of the otherwise applicable royalty rate, although 25% reductions are more common.

When audiotape was first introduced in the 1960s—and for years thereafter—record companies regularly reduced eight-track and cassette royalties by 50%. As most tapes were manufactured by licensees of the record companies, not the record companies themselves, the reduction was perhaps justified at the time, but the companies continued the practice long after they began to manufacture tapes themselves. Similarly, until CD plants became widespread, the reduction in royalties had some rational basis. But, once they did, the rationale disappeared—even as the practice continues to this day.

A common practice among more reputable, or thoughtful, record companies when negotiating royalty rates for new technologies has been to include clauses providing that while there will be a general reduction in the royalty rate during the early years of exploiting these technologies, once the majority of similarly situated artists on a particular label revert to a more reasonable royalty rate, or once the proportion of sales of the new technologies increases to an undeniably large figure, such as 50% of the total market, the reduction will be lifted and the royalty rate will return to what most of us consider to be a "full" rate. While what used to be called the "CD concession" and now is referred to as the "new technology concession" has disappeared from some companies' recording agreements, many companies still resist paying a full rate for the CD format, even though it has been twenty-five years since the format was first introduced and it is now the principal format for all records sold in the world. We can expect similar resistance to removing "concessions" for other technologies, including DPDs, for a long time to come.

There are numerous implications of the total absence of a standard with respect to how and to what extent DPDs, and electronic rights, are dealt with in recording agreements in general and in clauses pertaining to royalties in particular. Several of them are dealt with later in this chapter; see "The Myth of Royalty Escalations" (page 37) and "The Effects of Digital Downloading on Pricing and Royalties" (page 43).

"SPECIAL" CATEGORIES

Singles

Record companies traditionally pay artists a lower royalty rate on singles than on album sales even though the royalty *rate*, were it to remain the same, would be applied against a significantly reduced base. The retail cost of singles is, of course, considerably less than that of albums, thereby ensuring a lower royalty payment even if the rate remained the same. Yet artists' royalty *rates* are reduced as well. For example, if a royalty of 9% were paid on an album with a royalty base of $11, after all the deductions, the royalty would be $0.99. If the same royalty rate were applied to a single with an effective royalty base of $3, the royalty should be $0.27. Sounds proportionate. But record companies do not pay $0.27. They reduce the royalty rate by as much as half. In our example, based on the same $3 royalty base, the actual royalty that record companies would pay on the sale of a single would be $0.135. Simple. You ask why? They answer, "Why not?" And, as if this result were not bad enough, singles royalty rates most often do not escalate based on sales achievement levels, as do album rates.

Reduced-Price Records

The typical reduction in the royalty rate on midprice and budget records is 50%. A successful negotiation can increase this to a two-thirds rate for budget records and a three-quarters rate for midprice records. Often, and for no apparently good reason, the royalty rate on other types of records—such as those sold through military exchange channels, soundtracks, picture discs, etc.—is also reduced. Every reduction in rate represents another few pennies lost to the artist and producer and gained by the record company. Believe me, they add up.

Foreign Sales

Royalty rates are also traditionally reduced for foreign sales. This is true whether or not a record company owns or controls (through subsidiaries or divisions) its own companies outside of the United States. However, in the latter case, there is room for negotiation. In such a scenario, the record companies actually do have some justification for their position. They claim that they should not be penalized for having their own divisions, since these divisions or subsidiaries have the same operating costs as those of unaffiliated companies. The United States–based companies claim that it is to the artist's advantage to keep their recording careers "in the family"—that is, in one company whose interests in an artist's career are global and thus broader than those of individual companies whose interests in an artist's career are necessarily more "provincial." They argue that the benefit that accrues to the artist more than justifies the foreign divisions being compensated in the same way a company that is a stranger to the artist's record label would be compensated.

Record Clubs

Record clubs used to account for as much as 30% of a record label's sales. Over the years, they have diminished in importance to the point that in most cases they have ceased operations. Online music services, downloads, including, of course, illegal downloads, had made a dent in this market—a dent that became a chasm. Despite this, the record-club deduction is still very much alive in recording artist contracts. Why? Let's first see how they work.

In order to induce consumers to join, record clubs typically gave away a specified number of records, while others were sold at full price. Thus members were, in effect, getting a discount on their selections, but the label had no royalty obligations on the free records. After the Sony BMG merger, there was only one record club left: BMG Music Service, which went out of business in 2009. In essence, through their record clubs, Sony BMG sold records, even at the traditional record club discount, at considerably higher prices than they would have had to sell to a dealer who would then mark up the record for retail sale. In order to avoid an avalanche of giveaways of an artist's hit records, as a loss leader for the club for the purpose of selling other artists' records, the typical deal for an artist and producer was that the company was permitted to give away royalty-free only as many of the artist's records as they sold (that is, for every two records distributed, on only one will royalties be paid). It is frustrating to observe that foreign companies either do not comprehend the concept of paying on records given away for free, or will simply refuse to agree to a provision pursuant to which at least one of every two records distributed must bear a royalty. This is particularly galling when the foreign company (for example, Universal France) will be distributing the records in the United States via its US parent, and the US parent would inevitably have agreed to such a concept. It is also upsetting when the response from the foreign company is "Sorry, we don't do that in [name of country]." As the saying goes, "Duh. I know that; we're talking about applying the 1/1 concept to the United States record clubs where your affiliated company *does* do that!"

For the records that they *do* sell, and that bear royalties, the record companies typically pay 50% of the otherwise applicable royalty rate. Wow! So if they don't get you one way, they get you another.

Many artists felt that they were subsidizing the company's record club operations and would much prefer to take their chances on selling their records in traditional marketplaces at regular prices, thereby generating a full royalty for themselves. "Free" records, in reality, have been sold to induce the record club customers to buy other artists' records! Because of this, many independent record labels had always refused to allow their records to be sold via either Columbia House or the BMG Music Service. Individual artists rarely have such leverage.

In 2003, a class action suit (*Babette Ory et al. v. Columbia House Music Club, BMGDirect*) was brought against Sony BMG, charging that the record clubs' practice of paying only three-fourths of the statutory mechanical license rate was illegal and, further, that compensation was due the music publishers for years of having been underpaid or inaccurately accounted to by the record clubs. (For an explanation of the statutory rate, see below, page 31.) A tentative settlement reached in 2005 was challenged by the Harry Fox Agency, Inc., among other parties. The challengers contended that the settlement, in practice, would have made it relatively easy for Sony BMG to continue to pay less than the full rate—indeed, there was nothing in the settlement to prevent the service from paying *less* than the three-fourths rate—with the burden being on the copyright holder to object to the use. As of this writing, the court has agreed to delay implementation of the settlement so that all concerned parties will have time for additional discussion. However, the Harry Fox Agency has entered into its own agreement with the major record labels the basis of which is essentially the three-fourths rate, with an accompanying—and valuable—audit right.

Do You Want to Be a Member of This Club?

Over the past decade, since the decline of the CD as a medium to carry sound, many of the renowned record clubs (which became, of necessity, audio/video suppliers as well) were sold to a variety of private equity companies or private owners, most of whom ended up in bankruptcy; yet, in 2015, 110,000 members remained at Columbia House. Deals that used to offer ten CDs for the price of one, or even for $0.01, in return for a promise to purchase another ten are now merely offering one CD or DVD for one (plus shipping). Nevertheless, quite a few consumers apparently still like to receive that package in the mail containing new sounds, new dreams, and new experiences. Given other choices (downloading and streaming in particular), the current record club deals are not much of a bargain for consumers, but as I said, some people like their music delivered this way. Still, income from record clubs is hardly enough to make a dent in the income of artists, record labels, or publishing companies. Compare Amazon Prime's $99/year paid service (with a thirty-day free trial) that gives Amazon members a smorgasbord of benefits that no other services come close to providing. To suggest that record clubs are antiques is an understatement.

TWO DIABOLICAL DEDUCTION DEVICES

Do you think that the previous examples of royalty reduction methods are egregious? Perhaps. But diabolical? *That* adjective must surely be reserved for the following two particularly odious devices by which record companies reduce your royalties: packaging deductions and reduced mechanical royalties on controlled compositions.

Packaging Deductions

Record companies decided long ago that while they did not object to paying a royalty per record sold, they did not see why they should have to pay a royalty on the packaging. This makes some sense. When a 78 sold for $1 and four 78s in a box sold for $5, the extra dollar was obviously attributable to the cost of the package. Or was it? Perhaps the bundling of the four records constituting a concert performance or an opera simply made the entire package more valuable in the eyes of the record company and the customer. Nevertheless, it was this logic that resulted in the birth of the first packaging deduction. Clearly, the majority of the cost of a record is for the intellectual property (that is, the songs and the masters—the music) of which it is composed. But some of the cost is contained in the disc (or tape) itself and in the packaging surrounding it, and record companies have succeeded in persuading artists and their representatives that they should not pay a royalty on those components.

The packaging deduction is customarily worded in terms of a percentage of the record's *royalty base price*. A 25% packaging deduction means that for a record retailing at $16.98, $4.25 is deducted before the artist's royalty rate is applied. (The 10% packaging deduction is a thing of the past; the current going deduction for CDs, and other new technologies, is 25%.)

Let's return to our earlier example to see exactly how I got the $0.80 per-unit royalty. Suggested retail ($16.98 CD) × 90% (10% breakage deduction) × 75% (25% new technology deduction) × 75% (25% packaging deduction) × 9% royalty rate (12% less 3% for producer's royalty) = $0.77 net artist's royalty per sale

$16.98 × 90% = $15.28

$15.28 × 75% = $11.46

$11.46 × 75% = $8.60

$8.60 × 9% = $0.77 (rounded up to $0.80, the figure cited on page 25, the net artist's royalty per sale)

And, as we have seen, the net royalty will be further reduced for singles, record club sales, midpriced and budget records, and other ancillary sales.

Now there are always variations on the theme. As we have seen, the 10% breakage deduction is inching up to 15%, whereas the CD concession and new technology rate may be reduced from 25% to 20%, or even to 12.5%. If 20%, the resultant royalty will be $0.82, rather than $0.77. Furthermore, the royalty rate for a sought-after artist may be 15% to 18% rather than 12%. At the same time, many producers charge 4% (and even 5%) rather than 3%, and their royalties often escalate, based on sales achievements, by 1%. Then again, with most record companies you may be able to rid yourself of the breakage reduction. If you cannot, then the only way to ratchet up your net (that is, final) royalty is to increase the gross royalty rate from 12% (in this example) to 13% or 14%. It is all rather fungible. The bottom line is that one way or the other, when your gross royalty rate is 12% of retail, your ultimate (net) royalty will be somewhere around $0.80 on a $16.98 CD.

Further, you will not see any royalties at all until the company has sold enough records to recoup all recoupable expenses, and, as we have seen, the number of records that constitute "enough" is invariably much higher than you might imagine.

How Is a DPD Packaged?

Yes, there is an ultimate excess to point out to you. The record companies have decided to apply the standard packaging deduction of 25% to DPDs—which, in case you haven't noticed, do not even have a package! What better evidence do we need that the deduction game is just a screen for the record companies' attempts to fix a per-unit royalty to every sale—one that fits into their overall scheme, a scheme which presupposes very few hits and very many failures. I think we would all be happier if they were just a little bit more direct; it would save us the inconvenience and the cost of having to negotiate all of these intermediate provisions whose sole purpose is to get the royalty down to X dollars (cents?) anyway. See page 26 to learn how record companies have concocted a "new technology concession" deduction to replace the insidious packaging deduction (which amounts to the same "diabolical" deduction there used to be).

REDUCING MECHANICAL ROYALTIES

Every song included on a CD, other than songs in the public domain,[1] is subject to a *mechanical license fee*: a payment to the holder of the copyright, usually a music publisher, for the right to use the song. The amount of the fee depends on the length of the song and the current rate as established by the US copyright law, the *statutory rate*. Most artist–record company agreements include a provision stating that the record company will pay the mechanical license fees up to but not exceeding three-fourths of the *minimum* statutory rate without regard to length. This discounted rate is known in the business simply as a *rate*. (The "minimum" bit is important: songs over five minutes long command a higher license fee than songs less than five minutes in length.) In addition, record companies usually include a provision stipulating that no matter how many compositions are on a CD, they will pay only ten times three-fourths of the minimum rate. The amount in excess of three-fourths of the minimum rate is charged against the artist's royalties. This is true whether the composition in question is a *controlled composition*—a composition written by the artist or the artist's producer—or is not a controlled composition.

Let's say that you record eleven songs. Two are "outside" songs owned by other music publishers; the others are your own compositions. One of the outside songs is six minutes long. First of all, you or your producer will have the unpleasant task of requesting that both outside publishers grant a rate to your record company for the compositions being used, including the six-minute song, which would normally command a higher fee than the other one. Also, since the record company has agreed to pay the fees for only ten songs, the effect is that you have to license the nine songs you have written for a total royalty of eight times the three-fourths rate, not nine.

To the extent the owners of the two outside songs refuse to license their songs at three-fourths of the minimum rate, your mechanical royalties with respect to your nine songs will be further reduced. To the extent they demand payment at the so-called "long rate" for the six-minute song, your royalties will be even further cut. If your own publisher does not care about the way your record agreement is written and insists on being paid the full rates established by the Copyright Act, the excess the record company has to pay over three-fourths of ten times the minimum rate will be charged against your record royalties and any other monies the company may have to pay you contractually. (And if you cowrote any of these songs with another writer—often the producer, but just as often a totally unaffiliated writer—you would have to get *that* other writer's permission to license the song at this reduced rate as well.) So, while you are trying to do your thing, your manager or lawyer is spending valuable time, and eventually your money, trying to clear these rights, just to *save* you from an unconscionable result. And it can be enormously expensive.

Finally, the applicable minimum statutory rate provided for in the contract is customarily the one in effect at the time the record was supposed to have been delivered, not the one in effect when the record is released, or even recorded. Let me show you how sinister this tidbit in recording agreements can be. In a recent case, an artist died before he could complete the recording of his new album and deliver it to his record company. Consequently, he could not, of course, deliver the record "when due." When his recording was finally ready for posthumous release, the record company reminded the lawyers for his estate that the mechanical rate at which all of the compositions on the album (including those of the now-raging publisher of the artist's song) would be licensed was the rate that had been in effect years earlier, when the rate was considerably lower than on the date the CD was actually released. So it goes.

SPECIAL ISSUES REGARDING CONTROLLED COMPOSITIONS

But for the controlled-compositions clause, record companies claim, they could not make budget records (as stated previously, usually priced at about one-half of the suggested retail price of so-called top-line releases) available to the public; the same applies to developing new music platforms whose sales volume does not justify the expenditure of what would be acceptable for a top-line release. There has been considerable talk in recent years about replacing the statutory mechanical rate with a rate which would be calculated by a percentage of retail. This would be welcomed by record companies; they would always know what their mechanical royalty costs would be, freeing them to determine the content of releases without regard to "nonartistic" issues such as length or number of songs. On the other hand, music publishers do not like this concept. For a start, they do not know what the percentage would be, and they probably would want a guaranteed minimum rate in any event, putting us back where we started! They also feel that, while a percentage controlled-compositions rate would spread the cost risk, they should not have to bear it all. They also wonder whether, if the record is successful, they will ever get back what they discounted. Not likely.

In addition to this current controversy, the impact of the mechanical royalty cap has devastated elements of the music industry. As noted earlier, the cap affects all of the songs on the album, not just those that the artist controls. It is in the EDM (electronic dance music), hip-hop, and reggae areas that the disaster is most visible. An artist who writes (not even cowrites) every song on the album can end up receiving *nothing* if the cost of the samples he incorporates into the tracks causes the total mechanical royalty costs to exceed the cap. For the sample owners are copyright owners, too, and their demands for mechanical royalties are usually made after the fact of the recording and they have all the leverage. The owners of the samples (often the producers of the tracks) do not have to honor the cap and often will charge a full statutory rate for their miniscule contribution to the song. Guess why we never hear medleys anymore? That's right: the mechanical royalty cap. The record company's business affairs lawyers will say that it is up to the artists to control what goes on their records. (Clive Davis would respectfully disagree, but then, he is in the creative tower, not in the royalty department.) That is like telling Beethoven to forgo the choral part of his *Ninth Symphony*. Easier said than done.

As this book is being published, Congress and the Copyright Office are looking into the mechanical royalty clause in the Copyright Act and will likely rethink it in a way that will soften the blow of contractual modifications of the clause, such as is evidenced by the mechanical cap. In the meantime, I guess it is up to the artist to control what goes on the record.

THE BEAT GOES ON: OTHER IMPORTANT DEDUCTIONS

Just when you think you've heard enough, there's more. There are a vast number of additional charges that must be paid out of your royalties before you see a dollar. It is notable that none of these is applied against either your producer or your cowriters or their music publishers. While they enjoy the success of the effort of all involved in making the record, only you are expected to pay back these costs.

Promotional Videos

Prior to the early 1980s, there were no promotional videos to speak of. Video promotion and outlets for video broadcast—such as MTV and VH-1—were minimal. After 1983, however, things changed dramatically, and costs for promotional videos incurred by record companies increased geometrically. Video clips lasting fewer than four minutes can cost anywhere from hundreds of dollars to hundreds of thousands of dollars: $150,000 per video is not unusual. By the 21st century, the definition of the once-straightforward entity—"promotional video"—had expanded to include full-length DVDs, which cost upward of $400,000, as well as varieties of video "clips" for use on everything from video ringtones to MP3 players such as Apple's iPod. An artist should be concerned with several important issues affecting videos: Who pays for the costs of making them? How many videos, and of what configurations, should be made? How are royalties on the eventual commercial exploitation of videos shared?

It didn't take the record companies long to figure out how to cover these costs. An answer came from on high (or at least from the chief financial officer's floor). Charge the artist! Currently, most record agreements stipulate that one-half of promotional video expenditures be borne by the record company and one-half be paid out of the artist's *audio-only* record royalties. The half borne by the record company is maintained on the record company's books, and is eventually repaid to the record company out of 100% of the artist's share of video royalties, if any, derived from the exploitation of the video itself. These royalties are calculated at essentially the same *rate* as are the artist's record royalties; however, the price on which the royalty rate is applied differs from company to company. Escalations such as those that apply to audio-only record royalties are rarely applied to audiovisual royalties. But many record companies are so fearful of a market with which they have little experience (and even less interest) that they try to protect themselves by establishing, in contract provisions referring to audiovisual royalties, an arbitrary suggested retail selling price and then fiddling with it. Here's an example from a major Sony BMG affiliate's form agreement:

> With respect to United States sales through normal retail channels at a base price which is less than a top-line price, Company shall accrue to the artist's account a royalty of 10% of the

applicable royalty base multiplied by a fraction, the numerator of which is the suggested retail list price that equates to the applicable base price and the denominator of which is $19.95. [Note the weasel words "accrue to the artist's account" rather than "pay to the artist"!]

One further observation: Record companies are so skittish about video production that they try to maintain a very tight rein on costs. After all, a fabulous video by a major pop star could cost in excess of a small movie—$1 million or more. (U2's recent video, designed for IMAX theaters, cost more than $5 million. Scary!) So, the companies trump the artist one more time by providing that even if they are the ones who have mismanaged or incorrectly estimated the budget, once the budget hits a certain number (for example, $200,000), *all* of the excess over the original budget is recoupable from the artist's audio-only record royalties.

For years, it was common to make two or three videos to promote an album, but as outlets for video presentation have diminished, record companies in general have become more expensive to operate, record sales have tanked, and record returns from dealers have become more problematic due to the advent of MP3/Internet distribution, most companies will commit to no more than one video per album, if that. They would rather commit to spending an equivalent amount on other kinds of promotion, at their option, if they feel that paying for video production is of negligible value.

A new wrinkle affecting promotional videos appeared in 2015. Artists—and their record labels—began to claim a share of income derived from these videos which, on their creation, had solely a promotional purpose. They were offered to MTV and later to YouTube for free until the rights owners realized that "free" is no longer appropriate or necessary.

Tour Support

Artists who seek to reach their audience have to tour. Touring increases artist awareness among the broadcast industry and eventual consumers and fans, with the ultimate benefit of increased sales of records and increased interest in that artist and, down the road, a successful subsequent tour. But touring is enormously expensive. The cost of travel, food, and lodging alone can bankrupt any baby band. Individual artists have it much tougher, since they may not be able to function at all without hiring backup musicians. These backup musicians, or sidemen, may themselves make their living only by providing their services to other artists' recording sessions and they may be unwilling to travel without being paid an amount of money equivalent to that which they might have made had they remained in their own cities. The benefit of a band sharing various costs (for example, a van to transport the musicians and the equipment) is not available to an artist using sidemen.

The record company does not directly share in the earnings from tours (neither from concert fees nor, usually, from merchandising sales), except in the sense that celebrity and success help all involved. However, once artists are signed, the record company usually foots the bill for its artists' tours at the beginnings of their careers. As with most of the items listed in this section, the costs incurred are ultimately borne largely, if not solely, by the artists. While record companies risk the loss, 100% of the tour support is recouped out of the artist's royalties.

Equipment Loans

Quite simply, artists need equipment (for example, instruments, amps, speakers, tuners, computers, etc.) with which to perform. They also need equipment with which to write and demo their songs. The record company once again is the source of aid to needy artists and lends them the money they need to rent the equipment. The total cost, of course, is an advance charged against their royalties, even though the record company may ultimately be the principal beneficiary of the expenditure. In lieu of asking for equipment advances on a per-recording basis, artists should seriously consider purchasing some of the equipment they need for preproduction or even production of their recordings (for example, for a Pro-Tools kit, which is extremely expensive to rent). Many artists tell me that ownership is power. I believe it. Once you own a piece of equipment, you don't have to hit up the record company every time you want to rent a bass rig or an ADAT machine.

Independent Promotion

And now, the *coup de grâce*.

What hasn't been said about independent promotion? It has been the subject of books, exposés, television reports, and documentaries, not to mention a multitude of conversations and debates within the record industry and on Capitol Hill. An entire chapter of this book (chapter 9) has been dedicated to marketing and promotion, including independent promotion. For purposes of this chapter, though, suffice it to say that record companies now require artists to pay for what the companies used to provide via their own personnel as an ordinary part of their overhead. They do this by stipulating that part or all of promotional expenses, including the costs of promotional TV campaigns (see below), are recoupable out of royalties. And, as with other recoupable costs, they are considered advances and must be repaid before the artist's royalty payments begin to kick in.

Television and Radio Campaigns

Paragraph 7.07(b) of the Universal Records standard recording artist agreement (and, regrettably, most other record companies' contracts as well) provides that if the record company spends money on a TV campaign, the otherwise applicable royalty due the artist will be reduced (by as much as 50%) during the semiannual period when the campaign initially took place through, to, and including, the semiannual period when the campaign was concluded. (Sometimes they will agree to limit the reduction to the four-month period following the commencement of the campaign. However, since royalty departments do their accounting on a semiannual basis, the actual reduction usually ends up being taken over a six-month period—*if* they even remember to reinstate the basic rate.) Upon the expiration of the latter period, the royalty due the artist is reinstated—but prospectively only. This means that not only is the artist ultimately paying much of the cost of independent promotion, as we have seen, but is also subject to having his or her royalty rate reduced for the duration of a television or radio campaign.

In order for these provisions to take effect, there is no requirement that the record company spend a substantial amount of money on the campaign. A modest expenditure is sufficient to set the royalty reduction clause in motion—and what a furious reduction in earnings can result!

Things are different in Europe because a far greater percentage of record sales are generated there by TV advertising than are generated in the United States. But then it seems fair that the reduction in royalty should apply only to those territories in which the TV campaign is actually employed—not all foreign territories.

Now if it is appropriate or effective for expenditures to be incurred in furtherance of a common cause (that is, the sale of records), fine. But there is no rational defense I can think of for arbitrarily reducing the royalty rate for whatever number of records are sold during a period of TV advertising. And note that there is usually no cap on the number of records that can be affected by the royalty reduction. As we have seen, it does not take a lot of record sales to return to the record company a lot of money. At a minimum, the applicability of the reduction should be limited to a definite number of records sold during the TV campaign period. The practice has other implications as well. For example, if a bonus or royalty escalation is dependent on achieving a certain level of unit sales, the calculation of these sales is usually based on US sales through normal retail channels. Sales resulting from TV promotions are often exempted from the calculations.

PREPAYMENT OF ROYALTIES

In some cases, a record (or music publishing) company will voluntarily prepay royalties. A prepayment of royalties constitutes an advance, allowing a company to recoup the advance from royalties that were otherwise earned and would become payable but for the passage of time between the end of a royalty period and the date on which the royalties are due to be paid.

Let's take a common example. A company is required to pay you advances of $10,000 on the first of January of each year—and does. Meanwhile, as of December 31 of the prior year, royalties in some amount are payable, previous advances and chargeable costs having been recouped. But wait. They are not actually payable until the accounting statement is required to be prepared and sent out—usually three months later. Do you receive the royalties along with the statement submitted on March 31? Or does the company "recoup" the recently paid January advance out of the royalties that had already been earned, but were simply not yet due? In other words, are you actually being paid your advances out of your own earned royalties? In this example, if the earned royalties as of December 31 were $10,000, you could receive either $10,000 (the advance) on January 1 and no royalties come March 31, or $20,000 ($10,000 for the advance and $10,000 for the earned royalties). There's a big difference.

Now consider the following two situations: (1) you (the artist) need money in January and ask the record company to "lend" it to you; (2) the record company decides that since earned royalties are likely to become due come March 31, it is now time to spend some of that money in a hurry so that it can be deemed an advance, recoupable out of the very royalties that are coming due. In either case, the money being spent—advanced—is yours. Let's say that you have earned $50,000 in royalties as of the close of an accounting period (let's stick to December 31). You usually do not know how much, if anything, you will receive at the time the accounting is submitted three months later, at the end of March. But the record company does. What a good time to finance another video, or album, or tour, or spend some money on the release of a new single and the independent promotion services that naturally accompany the release. By March 31, that newly charged debt vacuums up money that would otherwise have been payable to you. At this point, you may justifiably wonder how it came to pass that you have just financed your own video, album, or tour— ahead of time! As if it isn't bad enough that you have to pay for these expenditures out of future royalties: now you are paying them out of past royalties.

In cases like the above, the contract language (or lack of it) either permits the chain of events or it does not, and your representatives and the record company's representatives can either address the issue or not. Therefore, a provision should be negotiated by your attorney to be added to the agreement providing that royalties earned as of the *end* of an accounting period cannot be recouped out of advances paid *subsequent* to the date on which such royalties were actually earned, even though not yet payable because the accounting is not yet officially due. We refer to this particular gambit as *forward recoupment*. And once the agreement is signed, it is too late to deal with any such problems.

THE MYTH OF ROYALTY ESCALATIONS

The term *royalty escalation* (or royalty acceleration) refers to the situation in which an artist's or producer's royalty rates rise incrementally from year to year, or from album to album, or from sales level to sales level, or sometimes a combination of these. For example, a royalty rate of 12% may rise to 12.5% on units of records in excess of 500,000 copies and to 13% on units of records in excess of 1 million copies. Customarily, the increase is limited to album sales in the United States through customary retail channels (excluding budget records, midpriced records, record club sales, records sold in conjunction with TV campaigns, etc.), and so right away, the presumed escalation does not apply to anything close to the total number of albums sold. It is also rarely applied retroactively.

In addition, the conditions giving rise to royalty escalations are customarily required to be met from album to album. In other words, if your first album achieves sales of 5 million copies, don't expect your next album to start at 13%. It won't. The whole story begins again. In fairness, there is some justification for this in that the second album may require no less a financial commitment from the record company than the first—and perhaps more. But if the prior album sells enormous quantities, the rationale is no longer valid. And, since record companies cross-collateralize album costs and royalties back and forth among albums, it is disingenuous to argue that each album "stands on its own" when it comes to escalations. (*Cross-collateralization* refers to the record company practice of recouping expenses payable according to one agreement with an artist or producers from monies received as a result of any other agreement with that same artist or producer. It also refers to the universal practice of charging costs incurred with respect to one specific product—for example, an album—against earnings generated by another.)

In the digital age, the concept of royalty escalation has taken on a new twist. What if there are no "units" in the traditional sense of the word? What if the sale occurs in cyberspace? For the purpose of determining the applicability of royalty escalations, "cybersales" do not count. Obviously, as time goes on, the trend toward instant downloading of music or sharing of music tracks will become more and more commonplace and the income generated from such exploitations will increase accordingly, and the record companies will have to adjust the definition of what is and is not a sale through normal channels. Theoretically, sales subscription services will be dealt with the same way as long as the number of actual downloads can be identified and tracked.

FREE GOODS

Practically all products are discounted from time to time, except for those that are truly in demand. (You will never see an Elsa Peretti gold pendant at Tiffany & Co. on sale; nor do NARS nor Estée Lauder allow their cosmetics and fragrance lines to be sold in stores that customarily discount products.) Yet in the record business, all records are discounted to retailers *all the time*. Everyone gets a break from the published wholesale price. This allows some price variations at record stores. But one way in which record companies discount—the distribution of free goods, or freebies, to avoid paying the royalty costs that accompany the *sale* of records—is unique.

Let's see how the free goods policy works.

First, free goods are not free, nor, in the case of digital downloads, are they even "goods" in the traditional sense of the word. Free goods are a fiction created by record companies in order to reduce their obligation to pay artist royalties, music publishing royalties, and union royalties. Furthermore, they don't count in calculating record sales for royalty escalation purposes.

Suppose a record company wants to discount a shipment to a retailer for any one of the following reasons:

- as a reward for a long and profitable relationship, giving the dealer a little advantage over other dealers

- so the dealer can sell the record company's record at a price that is more attractive to customers than other records

- as encouragement to purchase a sufficient number of records so that when the record receives radio play, there will be lots of inventory available to respond to consumer demand

As we have said, discounted records are still susceptible to the record company's having to pay royalties. So, instead of selling 1,000 records at 15% off the wholesale price, the record company "gives away" 150 records. It ships 1,150 records, but charges only for 1,000 records. In this way, it has eliminated the mechanical, artist, and union royalties on the 150 "free" records.

All music publishers, and in particular, the powerful and vocal Harry Fox Agency, abhor this practice and resist it. However, they often have no choice but to acquiesce because free-goods no-royalty provisions are written into most artist–record company agreements. For the same reason, unions (most often, the American Federation of Musicians and the American Federation of Television and Radio Artists) acquiesce in this practice as publishers do with the three-fourths mechanical royalties clauses. Were the union or the music publisher to successfully object, the record companies would simply take the excess cost out of the artist's royalty, and their right to do so is usually provided for in the recording contract.

By the way, in the case of free goods, members of the "family" of artists on a record label are treated *less* favorably than the record label treats strangers. Record companies will typically pay royalties on free goods to outside songwriters, and often producers with negotiating leverage, whereas it is rare for record companies to pay royalties on free goods to their own artists or to the music publishers that control their artists' songs.

Let us revisit our earlier example of how many records must be sold before an artist recoups a $100,000 recording cost. You will remember that at an $0.80 royalty rate, 125,000 records need to be sold to reach this level. Except for what I am about to describe, the producer will at the moment of recoupment be due a check for $31,250 ($0.25 per record) and the artist will be due zero. Now we see that even if 125,000 records are sold, only 85% of them really count. The remaining 15% were given away for free and do not bear any artist (or producer) royalty at all. Thus 147,059 records will have to be sold to net 125,000 royalty-bearing records, at which point royalties will begin to accrue to the artist.

In addition, all record companies establish what they call "special programs" for a limited time period (such as the period of initial release, or the release of a subsequent album in order to stimulate interest in the catalogue). These are referred to as "special frees," and they have to be considered as well. Typically, they amount to yet another 5% of records shipped to dealers. Thus, we are not talking about a 15% free-goods policy, but a 20% free-goods policy during what may well be the most significant sales period or periods in the album's history. And the effect of this on the artist? Figure it out: In order to get to 125,000 royalty-bearing records, 156,250 have to be shipped and sold. Someone is doing quite well here. Certainly not the artist. And probably not the producer, as the producer customarily abides by the same royalty provisions as those that apply to the artist (with the exception, of course, of the artist's contribution to such costs as the cost of recording).

LOST OR MISPLACED ROYALTIES

Each year, millions of dollars of royalty monies that might be paid to artists are not collected because the US music industry has failed to keep abreast of developments in international copyright legislation and to take advantage of opportunities that have opened up as a result of technological developments. An important example of the former is a neighboring rights law passed in Germany that recognizes the rights of producers whose work has made a significant contribution to the success of specific recordings. With regard to the latter, two important sources of potential income are (1) royalties that are collected in a growing number of countries for home taping and rental uses and (2) royalties generated by the use of audio recordings on the World Wide Web and via satellite and cable services.

For a discussion of the various sources of income that that are outside of the mainstream and out of many industry professionals' consciousnesses, see chapter 17 pages 261–266.

CHIPPING AWAY AT POST-TERM ROYALTIES: SYNCHRONIZATION LICENSES

Even after an artist's recording career is essentially over, not only will the artist's records continue to sell, but his or her recorded tracks may very well find themselves in a movie or a commercial. The use of recorded music to accompany visual images—for a theatrical-release film, a DVD-only release, a for-TV film, a commercial, or a video game—requires two synchronization licenses. One *synchronization*, or synch, *license* is granted by the music publisher. A separate license—referred to as a *master license* or a master synch license—is required to use a particular recorded performance of the music. Unlike mechanical license rates, which are set by law, synch licenses are granted on a case-by-case basis and are broadly negotiable. Although lucrative film licenses mostly occur in conjunction with films produced in the United States, uses in commercials and TV films represent a robust—and growing—worldwide business.

Traditionally, publishers remitted to their songwriters 50% of synch license receipts. Latter-day songwriters, especially those who were responsible for recording their own songs, entered into copublishing deals under which they would receive, essentially, 75% of receipts. A songwriter who owns his or her own copyrights, of course, will retain 100% of receipts. The financial splits between artists and their record companies are quite different. While record companies traditionally have shared with their artists receipts from synchronization licenses equally, in recent years, as profitability in the record industry has declined due to the diminution in record sales, certain record companies have reduced the artist's share of master synch fees to as little as 20% of receipts. In some cases, they have sought to pay a royalty as if the synchronization were a record. They ignore the fact that a synch fee is derived from a passive license—most often emanating from the label's business affairs lawyers; a record sale requires far more effort on the part of the record company. This is how that scenario works: Say an artist's royalty rate is 12% and the record company licenses a track for an IBM commercial for $1 million. In this situation, the artist will receive only 12% of the money while the record company will retain as much as 88%.

The manner in which synchronization fees are handled is important. Not only are the amounts involved usually pretty significant, but income derived from synch licenses is often received well after the heyday of the artist—when his account is "in the black." The best argument for a more generous split between record labels and artists is that the record company often has no role in obtaining, or even negotiating, the synch license, which might well have originated with the music publisher or simply "flew in the window." Therefore, whatever deal was in place at the time the artist initially recorded his or her master recordings, the artist's representative should keep in mind that at some point—probably a point well into the future—the traditional 50/50 split might no longer be appropriate. This might occur, for example, once the term of the exclusive recording agreement has expired, provided that the artist's account is in the "black," the percentages could change prospectively. If you wait too long to deal with this problem, or if you do not address it at all, your only leverage down the road is the tracks.

ACCOUNTINGS, AUDITS, AND THE STATUTE OF LIMITATIONS

More problems arise for artists from flawed accounting provisions in recording artist contracts than from just about any other provisions. When artists are dependent on a record company to determine the sales of a recording and the amount of royalties due them, many factors come into play and there are innumerable concerns that arise, all of which need attention.

For example, many companies provide accounting documentation (that is, royalty statements) only when there are royalties "shown to be due." If the record company shows the incorrect amount of royalties due, then according to this language, they did not err by paying you only what the accounting "shows" to be due. If they show no royalties to be due, they may not even bother sending a statement indicating the number of records sold during the accounting period. Furthermore, as we have seen, it may be a very long time (or never) before any royalties are actually due (shown or otherwise), so this practice may result in the artists never receiving any statement containing pertinent sales history data: information on total sales; where and to whom records were sold, and at what price and with what tax consequences; whether and to what extent reserves against the eventuality of returns were maintained (see below); whether there actually *were* any returns; and the number of records sold by foreign licensees or affiliates of the principal contracting record company. Yet without this information, the sales history of a record is hazy at best and impossible to determine at worst.

There are as many variations of accounting statements are there are companies. Only highly experienced accountants can sift through the plethora of information that a record company will thrust on them during an audit in order to determine the veracity of the statements. The royalty programs used by different record company computers also differ dramatically (and intentionally). This fact will impede any reasonable attempt at verifying not only artist royalties, but also mechanical royalties due publishers and mechanical rights societies. (See chapter 12 for a more detailed discussion of royalty audits.)

Truth in Royalty Statements

As stated earlier, all recording agreements provide that the company has the right to withhold royalties on a specified percentage of records sold, in anticipation of returns. (All records are distributed on a 100% guaranteed return basis, resulting in the bizarre possibility that every record ever shipped to a dealer might eventually be returned for credit one day.) These provisions have potentially far-reaching implications.

Let's say that, contractually, the record company is allowed to withhold royalty payments "in reserve" on 15% of all records shipped. At the same time, 15% of the shipped records constitute "free goods." Now, if 100 records are returned, shouldn't only 85 of them be charged against the artist's *account*, since the artist would never have received royalties on the remaining 15—the free goods—anyway? Shouldn't returns be applied against the artist's account in the same proportion as they are shipped—that is, with 15% of them free? Now that we have answered these questions, we ask, "How many of the 100 records should be subject to the 15% *reserve* right?" All of them? Eighty-five of them? If the answer is 85, then royalties reflecting 12.25 records will be held in reserve. If the answer is 100, then royalties reflecting 15 records will be held in reserve, which is 22% *more*. If the amount of money we are talking about is $100,000, the 22% difference is $22,000, not a small sum.

Note one exception to the rationale for maintaining reserves: DPDs (digital phonorecord downloads) cannot be returned; thus, there is no logic to retain reserves against these sales as if in anticipation of eventual returns. If your contract does not state this explicitly, the record company would have every right to add DPDs to their reserve cache according to the language they create covering the right to withhold royalties on reserved records.

Now, suppose that during a particular accounting period, 1 million records recorded by a particular artist have been manufactured and 750,000 have been shipped to dealers. Presumably, 250,000 records would remain in the record company's inventory at its manufacturing facility or at its branches. What might the artist's accounting statement look like? First of all, the actual manufacturing data will probably not appear because, contractually, the record companies do not have to provide that information. Will the number 750,000 appear? No. Because this number, as we have seen, does not really reflect the number of royalty-bearing records which have been distributed (shipped)—which is 541,875. *That* number is calculated as follows: first the 15% free-goods deduction is taken (85% of 750,000 is 637,500); then the reserve clause is applied, resulting in 541,875 units (15% of 637,500 is 95,625). So, even though 750,000 units have been shipped, the record company's statement to the artist will not exceed 541,875 units as it is still too early for actual returns to occur.

But what if the accounting statement shows royalties calculated on only 250,000 units? Is there any way to know whether this reflects a true accounting of the number of records sold during the accounting period? The answer is no. Why? Because the record companies will invariably deny the artist and his or her auditor access to manufacturing data, inventory numbers will never be provided, free goods will not be separately accounted for, and an accountant would need a crystal ball to identify how many units have been held in reserve. Sorry. Some—but not all—record companies have begun to open up some of their manufacturing records, but I have yet to learn of any true transparency in this area.

Finally, suppose that you or your accountant suspect that, due to shady or haphazard or undisclosed accounting procedures, you have not received the royalties that are due to you. What recourse do you have? Your only legal recourse is to demand that the company open its books to an audit. But artists do not get the same benefit as all other citizens when it comes to such pursuits. Remember in the film *The Sting* when the Newman/Redford operation ran out of money and could not cover Robert Shaw's bet? They shut him out. They waited until the horse race had begun and then closed the betting window. Record companies do the same thing. Just as artists begin to get a feel for the flow of royalties in relation to the success they are having, their right to audit is closed down. Audit limitations of one or two years are common—hardly enough time to get the "feel" of a series of accounting statements (especially if foreign sales are significant). Without that "feel," it is difficult to determine even if the cost of an audit is justified. Too often, the time passes, and the opportunity is lost long before a real sense of the accounting history can be experienced. (See chapter 12, the section on statutes of limitation, page 204.)

The increasingly effective alliance of artists—the Recording Artists' Coalition (RAC) (www.grammy.org/recording.academy/advocacy/rac)—has begun to look into the fundamentally unfair nature of royalty statements issued by most every record company. They have also been active in seeking the repeal of laws which tie artists to long-term record contracts and laws which surreptitiously affect artists' rights to recapture their masters under provisions of the existing Copyright Act. The RAC has enlisted the aid of the Democratic Party to introduce legislation dubbed the "Artists' Bill of Rights" that addresses injustices suffered by artists. Issues of importance to RAC include what they claim are unfair accounting practices on the part of record companies. In 2009 RAC became an arm of NARAS (National Academy of Recording Arts and Sciences), the organization responsible for the GRAMMYs, reinforcing their commitment to the rights of artists.

HOW RESPONSIBLE SHOULD RECORD COMPANIES BE?

Courts have held that a contract clause requiring payment of royalties does not create a fiduciary relationship. If it did, the burden of paying would go much more to the heart of the agreement and a breach of financial undertakings would more easily permit termination. In a fiduciary relationship, the fiduciary owes to its beneficiary obligations far more stringent than that required of ordinary contracting parties. Consequently, the customary low level of responsibility and accountability on the part of record companies means, in practice, that the burden of proof (such as proving that accountings are inaccurate) remains the artist's; the record company does *not* have the burden of proving the accuracy of its accounting statements. One might think that the fact that the payer has exclusive control over the financial receipts would help the artist to transfer this burden—but one would be wrong. Even if a fiduciary relationship were to apply, a breach of fiduciary duty is a tort (a "wrong"), and not a contract breach. The statute of limitations for redress for torts is customarily three years rather than six years, which is the standard term for contractual claims. Thus, even if a fiduciary responsibility can be established, the chances are that by the time the right to assert a claim has been discovered, the three years will have passed. But this doesn't really matter much anyway because the record contract invariably provides for a shortening of the traditional six-year *contract* statute of limitations to two or three years. Another common device that record companies use to increase their cash flow is to delay payments to artists. Book publishers rarely delay payment. Why? Because all of their costs are up front. Record companies, however, rely on the float—the use of money that they have, on paper, already dispensed. They will use *you*, the artist, as a bank. For example, Sony's bank is in North Carolina! When you receive a royalty check, or even a tour support advance from the New York "home" office, your bank has to wait for the North Carolina bank to clear the funds. What is a few extra days to you? Not so much, other than what can be a considerable inconvenience. But consider how the sheer volume of a record company's banking exchanges can affect their profitability. How clever of them. And the device appears nowhere in the record contract.

THE EFFECTS OF DIGITAL DOWNLOADING ON PRICING AND ROYALTIES

As technology continues to outpace the law, new methods of exploiting records are being discovered on a regular basis. The most important of these is the DPD, distributed via the Internet—in essence, the electronic transfer of sound (with or without video images), digitally, without an intervening sound carrier such as a CD or cassette. Methods of exploiting DPDs are also undergoing evolutionary processes such as the advent of subscription services offering digital downloads of limited, and even unlimited, quantity and duration, tethered downloads (those whose "life" expires after a certain number of days), and the like. Streaming services are becoming more and more popular as the youthful record "buyers" grow up "renting" music and not buying it.

The original grant of rights provisions (rights granted to the record company by the artist) in a record contract entered into before the era of DPDs no doubt included electronic rights such as are utilized in downloading digital copies of music. The industry has acknowledged this. But it is going to take a wizard to figure out the extent to which the royalty provisions apply to such new technological advancements as digital downloads; limited, or tethered, downloads; streaming; podcasting (permanent); and webcasting (not permanent). Areas of particular concern include identifying the territory of the sale, determining release commitments, determining the royalty rate, long-term availability, price, and licensing these rights to third parties.

Territory of Sale

In chapter 17 I discuss some of the issues involved in determining exactly *where* digital downloads may be said to take place. What country is identified as the country of sale will have on impact on royalty calculations. For example, suppose the download occurs in a country where the record company is entitled to pay a reduced royalty. Does the reduced royalty rate apply, or is the applicable royalty rate the one in effect in the territory in which the server is located—or where the original content provider is located?

Determining territoriality also impacts the recording agreement's provisions relating to release commitments. What if the Internet server is located within the United States and the actual physical record is never released outside of the United States? If artists have the right to recapture their records in territories in which the record company fails to honor its release commitment, should they, then, have the right to claim reversion of their rights for those portions of the world in which the record was not released in tangible form? And if they do, can the artists then offer the record for sale via the Internet, which will have the effect of global availability, thereby interfering with the exclusive rights of the record company?

Determining the Royalty Rate Base for Digital Downloads

What should the royalty rate for DPDs be based on? List price? Receipts? List price with a discount? Now that the volume of digital downloads has reached a kind of critical mass, record companies are hard-pressed to explain why those costs traditionally accompanying the manufacture and distribution of a record should have any place at all in the way entitlements of the record company and the artist are calculated. (For purposes of this portion of this chapter, I am treating the interests of producers and artists as being in synch with each other, since producers' entitlements are usually tied to those of the artist.) For example, when all the record company has to do is provide A&R and marketing services and present a digitized version of the music and lyric track to a server, the following costs should be out the window: the cost of artwork development and production, jewel boxes, CD manufacturing facilities, per-unit manufacturing costs, packaging the product, packing the product for shipment, and other shipping costs.

On the other hand, some costs will be specific to the sale of DPDs. The costs associated with credit card enablers, perhaps some "agent" or "dealer" fees to third-party website providers, conversion costs incurred in the course of digitizing music files, the cost of maintaining servers, and the cost of lost sales due to piracy or, conversely, the cost of preventing digital files from being pirated are all new. And, of course, record companies will remind us that the high costs of production, marketing, promotion, advertising, tour support, videos, and the like do not disappear once an artist's music is offered for transmission over the Internet. (They do have a point, of course, but what does this have to do with packaging deductions?)

However one looks at it, coming up with new royalty formulas on the basis of download-related sales is not a simple matter. Note that digital downloads are not the only media affected by this dilemma; mastertones, ringtones, even digital streams have similarly created confusion among the labels themselves as to how to interpret their own contracts in calculating royalties due their artists.

Here are four ways to calculate an artist royalty:

1. The company pays a percentage of net receipts at the same rate as the artist's royalty rate. Under this system, net receipts on a $0.99 DPD sold in the iTunes store would work out as follows: Apple takes a cut of $0.23, leaving $0.76. After deducting $0.01 for the union payment and $0.091 for copyright mechanicals (required by law), $0.659 is left. Assuming a royalty rate of 15%, the artist receives $0.10 on each sale—essentially the same amount as the owner of the musical composition.

2. The record company applies the royalty rate to the retail selling price of the DPD. For example, 15% of $0.99 equals $0.1485. This will probably be further reduced by a 25% packaging and a 25% new technologies deduction—depending on how they choose to interpret the contract. Thus it can be as low as 15% of $0.5569, which is $0.0835 (8 cents) if they play it that way. (The record companies have graduated from actual charges to virtual charges. Who says they aren't growing "with the times"?)

3. The DPD is viewed as the product of a license (which it *is*), and the artist receives 50% of the record company's net receipts of $0.659 (that is, $0.3295), the net after Apple's cut, the union share, and the musical composition mechanical fee. Of course, this is the method preferred by artists and their representatives, and were the record industry a bit healthier, it is probably the way things would have gone but for the disaster caused by peer-to-peer sharing. The major labels are so desperate now that they

are looking to find an edge every way they can. (If the music publishers/songwriters are successful in increasing their share from $0.091, then, of course, the net to the record labels will change.)

In 2011 and 2012, litigation on this subject by a class of recording artists asserted the argument cited in Number 3 above. These cases are now being settled rather than have the parties go to trial. So we will never know for sure whether DPDs were actually authorized as sales of licenses. One of these settlements involved the groundbreaking FBT Productions LLC v. Universal Group case brought by a production company which originally signed Eminem as a recording artist. In this case, following a jury verdict in favor of the record label, Universal, the Third Federal Circuit Court of Appeals sided with FBT in finding that a DPD sale by iTunes was indeed a result of a license, as provided in Eminem's agreement with Universal (FBT received an override, a percentage of sales, on certain records released by Universal after FBT was no longer officially Eminem's production company.) In March 2012, Sony Music Entertainment settled a class action brought by disgruntled former Sony and Arista recording artists and their producers which essentially resolved their dispute for past royalties by characterizing past DPD sales as derived from a license, but treating future DPD sales as if they were retail sales, for which a royalty would be paid. These, and other record company settlements becoming public in the last few years have resembled the 15% of $0.99 ($0.1485 or $0.15) model (without deductions). This is not much different a formula than the customary application of the royalty rate to the suggested retail selling price of records. The difference with digital downloads, of course, is that there is no cost applicable to the sale: no inventory, no shipping, no packaging.

4. However, never underestimate the imaginative workings of the record company's mind. There is yet a fourth formula for calculating DPD percent (to 18%), and it is applied to the record company's *receipts* ($0.659) from DPD sales through digital music services such as iTunes rather than to the online company's *gross receipts* ($0.99).

So which result do you think is fair?

15% of $0.99 with standard deductions or 15% of $0.5569: $0.08 [as if a sale]

15% of the record label's net receipts ($0.659) after publisher and union: $0.10 [as if a sale]

15% of the sale price ($0.99) without deductions: $0.15 [as if a sale]

18% of the record label's net receipts ($0.659) [recent settlements]: $0.12 [as if a sale]

50% of the record label's net receipts ($0.659) [standard licensing split]: $0.33 [as if a license]

The claims and the settlements affect only existing contracts that were entered into prior to the digital age, which both the labels and the artists fought to interpret their way. New contracts, of course, are drafted to protect the record companies from similar claims. Why did the artists involved settle for so little? My read is that their lawyers were in so deep in litigation costs, and since the artists were so poorly funded, the plaintiffs tended to grasp at almost any offer rather than continue a full-fledged war against the majors. Since Sony, Warner, and Capitol (now part of Universal) have settled, it is likely that the above solution (number 4) or something close to it will prevail. Next: the independents.

Hardly a victory for the aging, and financially challenged, artists on what will surely become the bulk of their aggregate "record" sales over time.

DPDs and Music Publishing—Implications for Mechanical and Performance Rights

Digital phonorecord deliveries also involve music publishing issues. For example, does the controlled composition rate apply to them? No, it doesn't. In 1995, the federal government passed the Digital Performance Right in Sound Recordings, a law protecting digital, but not analog (terrestrial radio, for example) performance rights. The law also permitted record companies to pass on to the online download service company (for example, iTunes) the same license, so that the third party did not have to acquire its own license. While the rate is statutory, the collector of these mechanicals is the record company, not the Harry Fox Agency or the independent music publisher. Once the record company has collected these monies, it keeps them until it must account to the publisher for ordinary brick-and-mortar sales. In the meantime, record companies are considering all sorts of ways to increase their slice of the pie. For example, can they apply the controlled-composition cap on singles? Can they recoup other costs against mechanical royalties due the artist-writer or the artist-writer's publishing company? The latest language *du jour* is that the record company will pay the "lowest applicable rate established by the applicable US or Canadian law." Put the fox (the carnivore, not Harry Fox) in charge of the henhouse and anomalies are sure to follow. Finally, who is keeping track of the accuracy of DPD-originated royalty accounting? The music publisher? The writer's accountant? The artist's account? Are they comparing notes? The natural differential in accounting periods and at least a six-month lag in reporting sound recording earnings as opposed to music publishing earnings ensures that there is no simple way to match DPD sales with mechanical royalties earned from them.

Royalty Payments Versus Licensing Fees

The question here is, Is a digital download a sale at all? The mere concept of royalty—and many of the now-antediluvian deductions on which royalty bases are formed—may be unworkable in the context of electronic rights. What is a digital download, if not a license? In licensing situations, the traditional record contract already recognizes that receipts derived from licenses should be shared. The split is usually 50/50.

How can record companies reconcile the nature of a digital delivery of *any* kind with the application of a royalty rate based on the retail or wholesale price of hard goods—sound carriers—such as CDs? Whether a download, webcast, podcast, or stream, there is very little direct cost in getting the music into consumers' hands (or at least into their computers and MP3 players—and soon into their televisions—whether or not on a permanent basis). Most intellectual property experts feel that, at most, consumers are obtaining a license when it comes to DPD deliveries. If a 50/50 license revenue share can be rationalized in some areas, why not all? But try to convince record companies of this. As far as they are concerned, they have sold a record and this sale is no different from the sale of a CD at a record store. Both go through third parties before reaching the consumer. And they will remind us that their costs of making *any* artist successful remain constant. They claim, then, that they cannot afford to share income from DPDs equally with artists when that source of money may soon approach that from customary channels. Even as consumers are thinking more in terms of "renting" music rather than building a record collection, record companies are imposing, via artists' contracts, the opposite view. And there is nothing you can do about it unless you have leverage. Once you do have the leverage, you may be able to renegotiate the provision affecting downloads prospectively but rarely, if ever, will you be able to fix the past. Record companies know this and always end up on the side they want to.

Electronic Rights and "the Catalogue"

Another consequence of the digitizing of music is that the recorded performance will always be available. It will never be deleted from the catalogue. Anyone who wants a copy of a particular piece of music can access it via the Internet and download it. This fact will wreak havoc with those artist agreements that provide for reversion of rights in the event that record companies fail to keep the artist's records in inventory or in release in whatever format is provided for. Of course the record companies, even today, repackage records from other eras into midprice and then budget formats—ever aware of the fact that somehow, somewhere, there is someone who might want to buy the record. But this possibility of permanent availability might generate whole new versions of downward pricing (and downward royalties). New York's former attorney general, Eliot Spitzer, and other attorney generals, are investigating whether the standard $0.99 DPD price is the result of an industry's fixing prices—probably legally. It is only a matter of time before we see considerable upward and downward variations in these prices. Indeed, in 2006 Beyoncé's "Check on It" was offered for download by different cell phone providers for $0.99, $1.99, and $2.99. Walmart offered it for $0.88, and Rhapsody offered it to subscribers for $0.79. And don't forget the Russian menace www.Allofmp3.com, which offered it for $0.10! No wonder that the UK phonograph industry has targeted this rogue player for destruction. In recent years, the industry seems to have settled on a $1.29 price for new and current hits.

The Bottom Line on Pricing

Ordinarily, when negotiators either compromise on a point or decide it is not worth arguing, they understand the implications of what they are doing. In the case of negotiating the impact of DPDs, however, no one can even imagine the consequences of failing to get it right, and no one even knows what getting it right means.

In the end, artists will probably pay the price for the current lack of precision in artist–record company negotiations and for the lack of clarity in achieving an understanding as to where a digital download occurs, what release commitments mean in the digital age, what royalty rate should be applied, whether a DPD is a sale or a license and how this choice impacts royalty rates and release commitments, and whether a record that is available via the Internet can ever go "out of print." And if the artists do not pay, the consumers most definitely will.

Record companies have two rationales for keeping their royalty calculations complicated: the first, which you may not hear directly (but I have), is to confound the artist and the artist's representatives; the second is that the worldwide computer systems of the companies are set up in such a way that these systems recognize only the established (what we might refer to as the "bizarre") interrelations among the various deductions. Anything simple would be a foreign language to them.

Clearly, it is very important that all accounting provisions be carefully and thoroughly considered. Their language will determine whether the artist ever receives even what the royalty provision, on its face, appears to say should be due. Attorneys and managers negotiating these agreements can fight only so hard to stop the avalanche of record companies' initiatives to cut artists' royalties down to where they want them. There is going to be a point when the party without the leverage is going to have to simply give up the fight.

• • •

In 2003, BMG gave a nod to transparency, simplicity, and fairness in recording agreement structure and language. Unfortunately, they immediately took it back. Truth be told, even the so-called transparency that they claimed to have achieved was obtained at the cost of honesty. The bottom line amount of royalties payable to artists and producers had not varied in the slightest. Anatole France said if 50 million people believe a foolish thing, it's still a foolish thing. Of course, the Sony BMG merger ended that experiment! The convoluted methodology of calculating royalty payments that shocked us for decades is still being used—and its use is even more widespread than it was in the past. They are still "foolish things."

I had thought that transparency was the wave of the future, but no, it was not to be. As the recording industry shrinks, the companies' search for the ever-imaginative edge over the artist continues apace. Universal Music Publishing was one of the first to claim transparency. As with Kobalt, you can now observe your royalty earnings online as they are recorded. But all this does is provide an early view of what you will be receiving at regular intervals of six months in the ordinary course of issuing accountings. It does not provide any in-depth breakdown of how these royalties have been calculated.

Other provisions that have found their way into recording agreements have actually evidenced a certain contempt at any attempt at transparency. *Billboard* magazine has cited several dozen examples including (a) undertakings that permit a label to use a duet's performance in video games without compensation; (b) careless use of the word "licensees" that would allow not only authorized licensees to utilize master recordings, but anyone, even a commercial product company; (c) permitting advertising on video clips on Vevo, Yahoo, YouTube, or on the artist's website without compensation; (d) the wholesale use of links on an artist's website to sites that the artist might find objectionable or in whose revenues the artist will not share; (e) charging "service fees" to music services such as iTunes for providing delivery of data to these services; (f) placing software on CDs that monetize the CDs for the label, but not for the artist; (g) haphazard use of outtakes, including those that are not actually finished recordings; (h) using artist's likeness in virtual characterizations on video games; (i) carelessly marshalling data that invades the artist's privacy after the term of the contract has ended; (j) passing along to soundtrack companies controlled compositions rates that were never intended to be applied to any records except the artist's own; and many more examples.

In general, exploitation of sound, songs, tablature, and lyrics has become so inventive these days that it is incumbent on the artist and his representatives to be extra careful to limit the right of record labels to utilize music as a means to an end that is something other than what is agreeable to the artist or that is not financially meaningful to the artist.

Consider also the impact of the 360 deal (see page 50) on all of these points—restrictions secured by the artist on the record deal portion may not apply to the publishing or touring portion unless specifically dealt with in the various interlocking agreements.

Like Hertz or Avis Rent-a-Car, surprise: the record companies are actually not in the business whose product is included in their names (for example, "car" or "record"); they are in the financial business—their concern, for their shareholders, and for their own pocketbooks is the spread between the cost of money and what they receive via rentals or sales. As record companies become more and more "media companies" or "entertainment companies" or "we don't know what we are companies," what is a truth in other businesses will more and more apply to them. No wonder that we are seeing more and more financial institutions and financiers entering the music business. Following are some examples of how 360 deals changed the face of contractual relationships between record labels and artists. The examples are gleaned from both domestic and international Sony, Universal, and Warner Music Group contracts, the three remaining majors.

- There are often virtual container charges on DPDs.
- Video costs over $125,000/$150,000 are now 100% recoupable.
- "Personal enhancement" costs (trainer/clothers/appearance) are now part of the record deal and they are, of course, recoupable.
- Websites are owned and maintained by the record company, but the artist has to pay the maintenance costs.
- The trend is to take streams of money and to apply a factor that takes into account virtual charges—for example, free goods (when there are none). Somehow or another, the "penny rate" always ends up the same.
- The maximum term can be as much as sixty-three months for a two-album deal (with an add-on of eighteen months after the end of the term just for the heck of it).
- Excuses by the multinationals regarding these excesses are actually quite amusing. For example, "Sorry, this is an international guideline." "We cannot keep advertising off of your website because it would be too difficult to handle." "You cannot, of course, share in the income." "Sorry, we do not understand forward recoupment." And the omnipresent, "This is not how we do it in this country." "Tax credits? I do not understand your request."
- Rerecording restrictions are extending to seven and even ten years versus the traditional five years after recording or two years after the end of the term, whichever is later.
- Often record companies take the royalty rate (let's say 15% of the PPD—essentially wholesale) and apply that number to all sorts of income that the record companies used to split 50/50 with the artist (for example, synchronization fees). They similarly apply the 15% to ringtone receipts from third parties, something that is inconsistent with the manner in which record companies used to divide third party licensed income. The 15% number has a certain cachet for them. They hope it has the same for you.
- The scope of record contracts now includes voice greetings that do not even utilize music. Sales via USNRC (United States Normal Retail Channels sales) which, if they reach a certain level, kick off royalty increases or improved advances or other terms, do not include DPDs, or if they do, they only include digital albums with no credit for singles. Ordinarily, the sale of ten to twelve singles would constitute an album for this purpose, but this variation would have to be separately negotiated.

It is satisfying to report, however, that Warner Bros. Records (and its affiliated label, Atlantic Recording Corporation) have made valiant efforts to simplify their contract drafts, even if the terms remain fairly much the same. The table on page 25 shows a quantitative comparison of the old versus the new method of royalty calculations. The means are different, but the ends are almost identical. On the plus side, at least the time it takes to negotiate contracts, and the attendant legal costs and management time, are considerably reduced.

Unfortunately, the 360 deal is a catastrophe for those who desire fairness and transparency in artist/record company relationships.

360 "DEALS"

Round and Round it Goes
Where it Stops Nobody Knows
—FROM *THE ORIGINAL AMATEUR HOUR* ON RADIO 1948–70

Rationale

Why the quotation marks in the title of this chapter? Because the word *deals* suggests a meeting of the minds; 360 deals are just another phrase for the impenetrable fortress that the record labels have created to protect their total hold over "their" artists. Briefly, as many of you know, 360 deals represent the effort of record labels to protect their hegemony over artists in the current era when "records" as such represent a smaller portion of the entertainment dollar than ever before. Record labels have recast themselves as "music entertainment companies." They're not entirely wrong to do so. From time immemorial, their investments in record production, marketing, promotion, sales, and general exploitation of this gold mine of an invention have generated so much money for them that they have ignored the ancillary income generated by their own investment and hard work on the record side of the artist's career: touring, merchandise sales, publishing income, tour and nontour sponsorships and endorsements, secondary ticketing (a new profitable source of income), tour VIP/travel packages, fan clubs, and the like. Once peer-to-peer sharing (stealing of music) had reached critical mass, they necessarily had to look outside of their own special milieu for other sources of income to justify the massive expenditures that they incurred each time they gambled on the possibilities of a musician/singer (who burnished their assets by calling them recordings artists) making it big. They claimed, and still claim, that this new economic model would actually build a better relationship with their artist—they even refer to that new structure as a partnership.[2]

Record labels not only bypassed the traditional sources of income for the artists they developed, but they also have only recently become conscious of "new" distribution networks, many of which were introduced by the Internet. Social networks, apps, *American Idol* and the dozens of spin-offs—none were created by the record labels. Like the image of the Big Apple that is New York City, record labels have belatedly come to recognize that the worldwide music industry is something that offers many "bites" and that they have traditionally been enjoying only one of them. It was now necessary, appropriate, and timely for them to have a larger meal. The story as to how they did this is both amusing and tragic—and not just for their artists.

At first, the monster talent/booking agencies that book and promote concerts decided to accumulate rights that ordinarily went to record labels—like the right to record their own artists. Madonna, Jay Z, and others entered into agreements with Live Nation which, in its turn, engaged selling institutions such as Momentum Worldwide to convince the public to buy what their packaged entertainment. "One-stop shopping," they called it. (Interestingly, the contract for these early beneficiaries of 360 deals was not structured in terms of a traditional record agreement, with additions. It was structured as a joint venture, a mechanism quite commonly used in genuine partnership situations. All of the parties were involved in identifying the financing to be provided as well as how it was to be spent. But as we will see later, even these agreements do not really establish traditional partnerships.) Simultaneously, record companies decided to expand the scope of rights which *they* would acquire from recording artists into a broad involvement with their entire careers. Immediate return of their investment was paramount and capturing new sources of income became their obsession. The cost? Depending on who you talk to: innovation, creativity, and mission. By 2016, Madonna's 360 deal had run its course and the appeal of such extraordinarily expensive packages had diminished; touring itself was really all that counted.

Impact of 360 Deals

Can an artist today develop organically like Billy Joel or Bruce Springstein did? Or must artists become famous first and then try to respond to the challenge of being as good as promised? For those few who were uniquely talented, there remains too little oxygen in the system in which to breathe new life into their creations as they themselves develop and grow. Beethoven didn't write his Ninth Symphony until 1824, three years before he died at 56. Verdi didn't achieve his ultimate greatness until he surprised everyone with *Falstaff* as he approached his 80th birthday. How many great potential achievements have been killed before they could bloom because the airwaves, publicity machines, etc. were filled with what *they*—not the public—determined we should be listening to? Or because the companies were so obsessed with the bottom line that they had no patience to wait long enough for the master to appear from the apprentice.

In his blog, Bob Lefsetz, who many consider to be the conscience of the music business, has often pointed out the lack of memory as to what used to be. Lyor Cohen, head of Warner Music Group, famously identified what he called 360 deals that went back into the earliest days of the modern era of music (1950s–60s). Sure, some of the writer/artists of those days would take a Cadillac over a royalty any day, but the monstrous accumulation of rights sought today by the record labels is no match for the more benign nature of the grasping common in those days.

In a recent proposal from one of the four majors, even though the artist was already signed to a seventy-plus-page recording artist agreement that cost him a fortune to negotiate, the record label advised his representatives that they would not release his second record until he would agree to convert the existing agreement into a 360 "deal." What did they want? You wouldn't believe. Not just a "piece of the action" of other sources of income which, in theory, actually had some justification given the huge investment they were making in the *recording* career of the artist and the risk that they were accordingly taking, but such a large percentage of his ancillary income as to render virtually impossible the artist's ability to engage other representatives (who actually knew what they were doing) in the other source areas of income (publishing, management, sponsorship, merchandise). Furthermore, they actually wanted not just to share in the merchandising and sponsorship income, but to *acquire* all of the artist's rights in this area.

Let me give you an example. This particular record label (via its highest business affairs executive—someone who enjoyed more than a decade of important experience at the top—someone who spent hours every day with the CEO of the label and was enormously trusted for his/her advice in all areas of the business) sought to receive for the record company, in addition to its entitlements under the record deal, 15% of the artist's live performances. Now let's consider the following: The artist plays Madison Square Garden. He receives a fee of $100,000, out of which he has to pay expenses of his staff, musicians, equipment rentals, sound system, and the cost of getting to and from the venue, his tour accountant, and, of course, his overall manager, business manager, and attorney. Let's say that a well-run business will incur costs of 50% of gross income and that this particular artist's business is very well run. His net after paying all of these expenses will be $50,000. Not bad for one night's performance. What did the record company want to receive from him? $150,000. That's right. Three times what he was netting. How is that possible? Well, they wanted 15% of his live performances, remember? But they thought that this should be 15% of the gross of the Madison Square Garden event itself. Let's say that was $1,000,000. The promoter guaranteed the artist $100,000 of this and had to pay the following out of the remainder: the rental cost of the venue; security; the cost of printing tickets; ushers; advertising; maybe even free tickets to colleagues. The record company confused the "gross" of the promoter with the "gross" of the artist. Yet they insisted that they wanted $150,000 out of this scenario. They had no clue. I sent them my book, but I don't think they read it. They held up the release of the album for more than two years and by then the momentum that the artist had achieved, worldwide, had ceased. Some attorneys in my field have not experienced such ignorance, and some record labels have themselves grown organically out of artist or producer production companies where knowledge of other areas of the music business came more naturally—by personal experience. But the story I have related is true and has been replicated too often to ignore out of hand.

A more outrageous, and yet more common, result occurs when a tour actually loses money. Let's say that the artist is invited to open for a major star. He gets paid $10,000 (a lot, believe it or not). Out of this he has to pay his manager, business manager, agent, and lawyer. These fees and commissions regularly will amount to at least 35% of the $10,000. Now, even if the record label acknowledges that it is the artist's fee, and not the show's gross that is commissionable, they want $1,500, too. As noted above, that brings the total up to 50%. Out of the remainder, the artist has to pay his band members, tour manager, tour accountant, in-ear monitors, wardrobe, equipment, guitar tuner, transportation, hotel, food, and other expenses. Am I being redundant by saying that there *is* no more money to share with anyone? Furthermore, in a scenario such as this, certainly the personal manager, and probably the other representatives, will defer all or a portion of their commissions or fees. This is an unwritten policy, but usually followed. Will the record company understand the necessity of this so that they will defer their commission as well? Their experience in touring is so deficient that they probably do not even understand what I am saying. In summation, a record label's grab for *anything* has to come out of the 15% remaining after the other professionals are paid, leaving who knows what for the artist. Of the artist's costs are 50%, nothing will remain. If they are more, well, you figure it out. This scenario, which is all too common in 360 deals, makes no sense. In legal terms, it is unconscionable.

Of course, when the label is more heavily involved in developing the artist's career, they may well fund the deficit of a tour. Although this funding will be recoupable, it is not returnable, so there is certainly risk on the record company's part. The anomaly in this scenario is that if the label has a 360 deal with the artist, they can "recoup" their tour support investment from the very sources of revenue that in the past have kept an artist alive—merchandise sales, publishing, sponsorship. They usually want to control all of this income so they are free to dip into it whenever they want to achieve their "numbers" for their own year-end bonuses. So now how the record company deals with its agreed share of income (much of which it will collect directly before the sharing occurs) depends on whether the artist is touring at the beginning or at the end of the company's fiscal year. Some partnership!

Everything that I have just referred to belies the fact that the artist is also contributing something: his or her own services and the creative resources behind them. In another ludicrous scenario which I have observed at a major record label, an artist with a six-piece band was paid $500 per date as an opening act for a big European star. This introduction into the European market could have proved invaluable, and the artist and his representatives grabbed it immediately. There were nineteen dates, generating $9,500 for the artist and his band (which he reduced to three from six—reluctantly because with half the musicians he would not be able to replicate the sound on his record very accurately). The cost for this tour was estimated to be $90,000. Therefore, the artist would require $80,500 from his record label for tour support and would end up with nothing for his considerable efforts and labor. It was at this point that his record company threw a bomb into the relationship and, out of nowhere, insisted on converting his traditional recording agreement into a 360 deal. Their actions belied the fact that they themselves would have reaped substantial benefits from the tour in terms of breaking the act overseas. (And they wanted 15% of the "show gross" besides.) The decision had to be made within twenty-four hours. It wasn't. The tour fell apart. The label ignored the fact that a successful overseas tour could establish the artist for all time as Europeans particularly are very loyal to the artists who go there to perform; either they didn't realize the ancillary benefits of helping one of their acts tour overseas, or they did and sabotaged themselves for some "greater" cause.

Even if they wanted 15% of the *artist's* gross, what about the manager's 15%? They would say that the manager is not investing $1,000,000 in the artist's recording career (which is true) and shouldn't complain. Were they capable of providing actually management (labor) services, let along management (career guidance) services to the artist? Of course not. Then they wanted 15% of the sponsorship income. Did they even know the telephone numbers of the potential sponsors (Budweiser beer, CitiBank)? Of course not. Then they wanted 15% of the artist's music publishing income. Did they have any concept of what music publishing was? Of course not. Besides, if the artist had already signed with a music publisher in order to finance his efforts to obtain a record deal in the first place, that publisher would not be willing to give up either any of its 25% of the composition's earnings, let alone the ability to recoup its advances from the remaining 75%.

And what if they "got it" and agreed to a percentage of the artist's *actual* income: remember that the artist is already paying 15% (or more) to a manager, 5% to a business manager, 10% to an agent, and legal fees that can approximate another 5% when all is said and done (and in California, the lawyers customarily charge 5% just to acknowledge the reality that all of the time-charge calculations will eventually equal that anyway, so why bother?). Adding to this is deadly for a performing artist.

Some creative managers and lawyers have considered taking 30% of the artist's net income and offering it to the entire pool of representatives (including the manager, business manager, attorney, agent, and record label) for them to work out among themselves what they respectively should be paid. The artist is free to go about his business, which is creating, recording, and touring. The representatives will have to earn their piece of the action, and there will have to be negotiated compromises as to how much of the 30% they can reasonably claim. Here is a sample split:

Management: 9%, except for touring: 7%

Agent: 8%, except for nontouring: 5%

Record Company: 6%

Business Manager: 4%, except for nontouring: 5%

Attorney: 5%

All will share in publishing net in the same percentages.

Interestingly, even if a 360 deal could have been negotiated in a manner consistent with the reality of the music business, the record labels have one card they would refuse to play—a card that eternally would throw out of balance any specter of a partnership. For however you might construct a relationship whereby the artist and the record company were essentially partners in the business of making money from the artist's talent and the record company's noble efforts, the company would nevertheless insist on (1) paying a royalty rather than a share of profits,[3] and (2) recouping, out of the artist's share, the cost of recording (including tour support and at least one-half of video expenses and independent promotional services) —thereby eliminating any chance of creating parity between them.

To the date of publication of this edition, the jury is still out on the 360 concept—both for the artist and for the label. It only appeared in any concrete form around 2007 and remains relatively untested and novel. While the concept has some rationale, the attempts at execution are dismal at their best and career destroying at their worst.

Entangling Alliances: The Ethics of Avoiding a Family Feud   *Entangling alliances got the world into World War I. How do they work in the record business?*

So what to do with the reality of record companies' obvious contributions to artists' careers and the difficulties of finding a way to carve out for the companies a piece of their ancillary income ? It may be time to consider reconstituting the respective relationships among artists' representatives. Should the record companies establish a management arm? What about the conflicts of interest? One artist client of mine was signed to a major label and the label said it would not release the record until she had replaced her manager with one who they believed in. Once she entered into a new relationship with a world-famous manager, the label asked for 15% of the artist's income which, at least in substantial part, and as a matter of practicality, would have had to come out of the manager's share. When asked how they could do this, they repeated their mantra: "We are the ones who invested a million dollars in the artist. What did the manager invest?"

The problem with this scenario is that management is, by definition, at odds with the label of their artists. Indeed, their principal function is adversarial to the record companies—all with the hoped-for result of making the company perform better. More often than not, the label wants the manager to beat up on their own staff to make sure the job is done—in industry parlance, to "work the building." Thus, a management team controlled by the record label is not likely to be effective. As for other sources of income which the record labels seek to share (merchandise, touring, sponsorship, publishing), as I have noted earlier, record labels are historically completely ignorant of these areas and can be of no help whatsoever. So is it not folly for them to insist on achieving hegemony over these very areas?

It is important to note that many 360 deals are structured so that the record company (excuse me, the music entertainment company) actually controls all of the revenue streams of the artist's creative life. All money goes to the company for division according to their agreement with the artist.

The conflicts of interest and the undesirability of putting all of the control of the artist's financial life in the hands of the one entity whose long-term management of money, rights, and new technologies has proven to be so inept are readily apparent.

A benefit to the artist from out of left field is the fact that a record company which has become part of the artist's venture via a 360 relationship may have assumed a liability far beyond that which it ordinarily would bear. Artists who have tried to rescind contracts for failure to pay royalties have usually run up against courts that rule that the record companies may owe them money, but they do not have that extra degree of responsibility toward the artists as would occur were they to be considered "fiduciaries." Trustees of other people's money are certainly bound to these special duties. But record companies, in a traditional relationship, are not. An artist who proves that his record company kept monies otherwise due him can only collect money damages if he prevails at trial. But an artist who can prove that his record company had a fiduciary relationship with him via a 360 "partnership" may have many other tools at his disposal to remedy such a situation than in a traditional artist/record company relationship. Control of the artist's revenue streams would certainly establish this requirement that the record company exercise an especially high degree of care when handling the artist's money. It may also be the case that the fiduciary duties will inure to a company such as a record company even if it does not actually control the revenue streams, because if it is going to share in those pieces of the artist's income, its actions insofar as the income it *does* control (the record income), may create a fiduciary responsibility that had previously not existed.

Solutions

Will we see the appearance of conglomerates that provide *all* services to all artists, or some variation? I don't know the answer. What I do know is that the current situation is fraught with problems, and it will take a strong personality (management, the artist, the attorney) to resist a 360 deal *per se*. The result may not be to the artist's ultimate liking either as the artist may well be without a label at all if he or she is too rigid.

One solution introduced by some is to establish a "180 deal." What is that? Well, it's certainly not one that covers all aspects of an artist's career. Maybe it excludes publishing income participation; sponsorship income participation; merchandise income participation. Maybe a portion of some or all of the above. This is not a bad idea, but it requires creativity on the part of both the record labels and the artist's representatives. During a panel discussion by the International Association of Entertainment Lawyers (IAEL) at the annual MIDEM conference a couple of years ago, when this phenomenon was just becoming part of the conscience of the entertainment bar, it was suggested that there were actually many variants of the 360 that could be explored:

The 90 deal: Just records

The 120 deal: Records plus limited tour and retail merchandise

The 180 deal: Records plus full tour and retail merchandise

The 240 deal: Records plus full tour, retail and tour merchandise, website sales

The 360 deal: Records plus full tour, retail and tour merchandise, website sales, endorsements, acting, reality TV shows, video games, digital merchandise, cookbooks, and many others. (I had one client who was a vegetarian and Sony Music wanted to control whether he would write a cookbook, and where and how he could promote it—for example, an audio book version or promoting it live on the *TODAY* show would require their permission.)

The ultimate solution is for the parties to figure out how to achieve what they need to fully function in their various capacities and to construct a relationship that accomplishes this goal in the most effective way for all parties. As always, compromise is the name of the game. But nowadays, it requires some genuine creativity in establishing realms of influence and asserting expectations from all parties. Record labels bear a certain arrogance that comes from the fact, which we cannot deny, that they are investing the largest sums of cash (if not labor) in the artist's eventual career. If they are able to respect the investments of the other professionals, perhaps we can reach some level of parity which will eventually inure to everyone's advantage.

Alternative Solutions for Various Scenarios One thing that many lawyers and managers do not consider when they eventually make a 360 deal that they believe serves their immediate needs is this: What happens if there is no long-term success? How long does the record company "commission" the revenues of the very artist whose promised success does not equal the dreams of the participants? I have always been one to bet on success, but one of our principal jobs is to protect against failure. The post-term participation by the record company in merchandising, touring, etc. can paralyze an artist for years after the relationship with the label has actually come crashing down (no matter who was at fault).

An example of the opposite situation, betting on success, would be to make sure that after the first album under the 360 structure, the artist can cancel further 360 aspects on subsequent records where the first record has been successful. Or perhaps the artist can cut it in half or establish some progressive percentages so that the "hit" isn't as great on subsequent albums. Otherwise, the record label will be sharing substantially in the artist's career long after the value of their contribution (tour support, for example) has been neutralized by the artist's having caught on with the public. While this result may be controversial, the fact is that by insisting on a 360 deal—particularly after the artist has already entered into a traditional recording agreement—the label is saying, essentially, "We cannot do the basic job for which we signed the artist in the first place." So, fine. Modify the relationship to assist the label to do its job on the first 360 album, but have the option to pull back if that modification results in a successful financial return to the label for its initial risk investment.

Another option for artists trying to scrape together some semblance of balance between the parties is to limit the impact of the 360 deal to specific territories where the artist needs the extra support of the label: for example, the US and Canada only, or Europe only, or wherever. Where the artist's career is well under way in one or the other territories, there is no desperation on the part of the record labels such as they are expressing in today's economy, and there is no need to accommodate this desperation by giving away more of the store than is necessary.

Yet another option is to give the record label shares, or stock options, in the artist's corporate family. This idea is catching on with "music entertainment" companies, but generates additional legal fees as these deals can become very complicated and implicate tax and international tax issues, securities laws, trademark and corporate matters above the expertise of your average music attorney. A more full-service law firm can provide these services, but oh the costs! On the other hand, the artist can be given shares in the record company. After all, the record company has all of these experts at its disposal and the artist will not need to engage them. Remember, this is all about achieving some balance when both parties are seeking to share in the success and to cover their losses in the event of failure.

The difficulty of achieving a workable 360 deal is exacerbated by the simple fact that the label is calling all of the shots because the label is spending all of the money. Therefore, in the standard 360 deal, the balance that the parties seek actually is never achieved. Nothing would resolve the eternal conflict between artist and record company more than a 50/50 relationship. No one doubts the contribution of a hit record to the enhancement of an artist's other income. But when a record label continues to recoup solely from the artist, at the artist's net royalty rate (see early sections of chapter 4), the recording costs, promotional costs, tour support, and video costs, when the record company calculates digital royalties as if they were actual retail sales (via a distributor or one-stop distributor),[4] demands percentages of the "show gross," or structures payments to the artist on a royalty rather than a profit-split basis, this balance is unattainable. In conclusion, in order for a record label to earn the right to a 360 deal, as Bob Lefsetz has reported in his blog, it has to be a 360 company. Live Nation has tried to accomplish this and in the course of things has convinced some extremely important artists to establish something much closer to a partnership than has been the case in the past. Madonna, Jay Z, Shakira, U2, and Nickelback all have put many eggs into the 360 basket (and have been advanced millions to do so). Unfortunately, this kind of deal is obviously not available to 99+% of artists who have not yet established an important brand. The fact that those who have accomplished essentially what they have sought from these ties have already "made it" demonstrates the futility of comparing those deals with what the record labels are demanding today. But even with the stars' deals, certain events can cause them to regret what they have done . . . long after they have paid their taxes on their enormous advances and spent the rest: for example, cross-collateralization where one record/tour cycle is successful and another one is not. If the failure comes early, and the success later, the artist will not see any additional money for years while the investor will at least be able to recoup its losses out of revenues. An ironic result was also suggested at the IAEL discussion noted earlier. The Copyright Royalty Board has established a late fee to be charged to record labels which are late in their mechanical royalty payments to music publishers. If the label and the artist rise and fall together, then if the label is late in paying mechanical royalties (which often happens because the writers are not agreed on the splits as to their respective contributions and the record label has no idea who to pay or in what percentages), the *artist* will be paying part of the late fee out of his or her own share.[5]

When all is said and done, the artist will have to make a fateful decision: do I accept a 360 (or variation) offer from a fully-staffed record company (whether or not a major), or do I try to do it myself (see chapter 16 and the pitfalls applicable to that option)? Rather than view the record company's conditions as being demanding, or grasping, the artist must consider the alternatives, and try to find a way to live with as efficient version of the 360 deal as possible—and as short a one, if possible. In the end, it's all about negotiation with an adversary who has most, if not all, of the leverage. He has to look at the situation as an investment, but, as Bob Lefsetz wrote, Do I want to invest in GM or in Toyota? Since he wrote this, GM has had a complete turnaround, and Toyota had a tsunami to deal with. Where would you place your bet?

THE DIGITAL EVOLUTION

No discussion of the modern record industry (such as it is) is complete without acknowledging the earthquake that is the digital evolution. I intentionally did not use the word "revolution" which seems to be what most observers commenting on the subject think of when they explore the seismic changes in the means of both producing and delivering music which have occurred since the 1980s. Someone once said that the only real revolution that we have seen in the last hundred years was the development of rock and roll in the first place. I tend to agree. No, digitization of music is not revolutionary; it is characterized more by progress than by disruption—more by evolution than by interruption (as much as these changes have jarred an industry that was doing just fine without it). If digitization is looked upon as an advance, then, why did its introduction to the mix cause such regression in the very industry it was supposed to help grow?

The answer lies in the inability of the "suits" who ran the industry over the past thirty-five years to understand and embrace the new technology. As I observe in chapter 5, Personal Management, skills to operate one kind of challenge rarely evolve into the kinds of skills necessary to operate another or others. Congresspeople often take the rap that they are more concerned (and better at it) about getting elected than they are at governing. The inability of executives to change with the times, to apply their management skills (such as they are) to new situations has led to the state that we are in today: failure to adopt new strategies and staffing, failure to accommodate the minimum desires and to comprehend the nature of their own consumers, and failure to respond to the passion of their former and potential to consume what they consider to be their culture, not those of the institutions. In chapter 25, Solving Piracy in the 21st Century, I point out that suing 20,000 kids, grandmothers, and parents for copyright infringement, which was the process *de jour* just a few years ago, was so counterproductive that what had been a very favorable, if benign, view of the music business by the public at large (as well as by Congress) turned into front-page derision. What kids said they were taking because it was free was called stealing by the industry leaders with disastrous public relations results.

Let's explore the ways digitalization has impacted all of us.

The Truth as seen by a Sony Consultant:

Sony consultant Dave Goldberg, a consultant at SurveyMonkey, wrote a memo to his client, Sony Music Entertainment, in 2014, which Wikileaks decided to disclose to shake up the music industry from its summer malaise. He indicated in his memo his view of the future of music and music commerce and made some pretty universal and revolutionary recommendations and forecasts about the recorded music industry (and in some respects the music publishing industry as well). Here are some of his conclusions:

1. Music is becoming a purely digital product.
2. A digital-only recorded music company will be much more profitable, delivering higher margins if lower gross revenues.
3. Record companies should look only to subscription and advertising for their revenues.
4. Since a record company's existing catalogue provides 50% of its revenue and 200% of its profits from recorded music, those are the areas deserving most attention.
5. Even streaming revenues are primarily generated by a record company's existing catalogue.
6. If Sony is netting $250 million in EBITDA, then the portion that is attributable to its existing catalogue is probably $500 million and, conversely, new releases, which cost 98% of its overhead, are losing $250 million.
7. Therefore, cutting back new releases dramatically is the formula for a record company to be profitable, or at worst, to break even or to experience small losses.
8. New releases should be in the rock or country genres; these areas are catalogue builders and are relatively less expensive to produce compared with hip-hop, etc.

9. Act like a music publisher: invest very little money, but don't try to hold artists for long contract periods.

10. The new release business would be handled like an independent label: low headcount, simple deals.

11. No new releases or signings would take place without acquiring publishing rights as well.

12. Internationally, record companies should eliminate local repertoire—sell it off to a local company that is more invested in it.

13. Focus on English language recordings except maybe for sales to Japan (currently the world's second largest music market) and China (which is next?)

14. Help digital service providers grow; Pandora should be accessed solely by subscription; Spotify should enter the radio space.

15. Get rid of the performing rights organizations and their "tax."

16. Net result: record companies will realize 40% profit margins as opposed to the current ones that range from 11% to 18% in a good year.

Impact on Commerce

As we all know, digital downloads and digital streaming are rapidly replacing traditional physical sales. In 2014 and 2015, sales of CD units still exceeded digital download transmissions. Yet by 2016, digital downloads were dropping precipitously at a rate of more than 10% a year—to 2006–2007 levels—even as streaming (over 200 *billion* total on-demand streams were logged in 2015) is fast becoming the go-to means by which the public gets its music.

One metric that provides a bit of a forecast for the future is the percentage of a country's population that has even the *means* of accessing digital deliveries of any sort. In some countries, like the United States and the United Kingdom, a large percentage of their populations have access to the Internet and know how to use it; yet a low percentage of these consumers use the Internet to obtain their music needs and desires. Fewer than 60% of the citizens of the European Union have ever accessed the Internet, let alone used it to access music. This will no doubt change over the not-so-distant future—all to the benefit of the music industry—provided it can capture and monetize the activity efficiently.

Most Favored Nations

The European Union's Commission on Competition has been a thorn in the side of the music industry as it tries to reconstitute itself after the precipitous fall of the last fifteen years. It has thrust itself into innumerable attempts by multinational companies who seek to combine music assets via merger or sale. And it has acted without mercy. For example, the Commission forced BMG Music Publishing to sell off Zomba Music and other publishing assets for Europe to a third party when it prohibited Universal from acquiring the world-wide rights to this illustrious catalogue. And EMI's renowned Parlaphone label was sliced off from Universal's purchase of the recorded assets of EMI when that company was sold.

This Commission has now reached out to those companies in the music industry (that is, almost all of them) that utilize most favored nations (MFN) clauses in their contracts. The most favored nations concept is derived from an age-old understanding reached in innumerable international multicountry transactions among sovereign governments. It has been co-opted by commerce. In essence, most favored nations clauses (also referred to as most favored customers clauses or most favored licensee or licensor clauses) is a contract provision in which a seller (or licensor) agrees to give the buyer (or licensee) the best terms it makes available to any other buyer (or licensee). In the digital service provider world, it works the other way: the buyer (or licensee—think Spotify) agrees to give the seller (or licensor—think Sony Music) the best terms it makes available to any other seller (or licensor—think Warner Records). Even if the initial contracts between parties satisfy the MFN clause, the buyer/licensee is not permitted to modify these contracts in a way that would result in the MFN clause being violated. The result is that if one party (a seller/licensor) exercises its power/size/leverage over another (a buyer/licensee) and increases the deal in its favor, even in a willing buyer, willing seller, open and free market, all of the other deals that the buyer/licensee has entered into must be automatically modified accordingly.

Yes, all of these deals are confidential—but by audits and other means, the information gets out. Of course, one company's deal is not always comparable to another company's deal beyond basic provisions such as term and royalty provisions—transferring equity to the licensing party is often part of a buyer/licensee's offer as are other "nonmaterial" provisions such as the relative amounts of advances paid or penalties for nonrecoupment at the end of a term. Creating these exceptions to the MFN is a lawyer's dream—and a draftsman's nightmare. Whether it negates the anticompetitive nature of MFN clauses is another question to be answered on a case by case basis. Still, rarely does a music industry contract exist without the inclusion of a most favored nations clause.

The view of the Commission is that if one party wants to lower its price to the consumer, and it is restricted from doing so by a MFN clause, the restriction on the party becomes anticompetitive. Merely one price reduction or increase sets off across-the-board reductions, or increases, automatically. While this practice has existed from time immemorial, the Commmission's attention has been drawn to digital music services to determine if the agreements they make with content owners are noncompetitive due to the inclusion of MFN provisions.

Streaming

Streaming—the present and the future: The future is huge; everyone knows that this is the be all and end all of music distribution. How it is achieved, through what media, how to identify the few services that will rise to the top (getting in first or early may have sealed the fates of many of the latecomers)—the jury is still out. But Spotify, Amazon, now Apple, possibly Tidal and Rdeo—these form what, in modern parlance, is often referred to as "the new music ecosystem." Some researchers have reported that well over 200 billion songs were streamed in 2015—legally! Once the major players have locked in a base level of subscribers, it will be a done deal. Those of us who even know what a cherished record collection is will be a fading few—antiques among the audience sought by the record companies. Not that most people care, except some of the older generation probably, but it is virtually impossible to "own" a stream delivered by these streaming services. So even owning a record collection is becoming less and less *possible* while being even much less likely.

Some holdouts among artists and small record labels think that they will be able to "direct stream" their recordings and keep all of the money generated from the public. Good luck with that. This has not worked very well among digital sheet music providers or download providers. We cannot underestimate the sophistication that has gone into the development of technology that achieves the smooth services represented by Spotify and a very few others. To "do it yourself" is harder than it looks.

YouTube and SoundCloud: What Exactly Are They and Whom Do They Serve?

One aspect of the digital world that is often ignored when searching for reasons why income to creators is less than reasonable people think it should be deals with the position that YouTube and SoundCloud take. These companies are a kind of blend between active exploiters of music and passive providers of broadband connection. Both companies claim to act like Internet service providers (ISPs) such as AOL, Yahoo, or Internet Explorer. They hide behind this self-designation when unauthorized content gets uploaded to their sites. They take no responsibility for obtaining permission from artists and songwriters. According to YouTube and SoundCloud, they need not go to the kind of expense incurred by Spotify, Apple and others because they are merely ISPs—passive intermediaries.

Of course, they are not.

The indisputable result is that YouTube and SoundCloud pay artists unfairly—in part because of their business model whereby, many believe, constitutes a "gaming" of the copyright law. They take advantage of copyright exemptions that were never intended to apply to them. The Digital Millenium Copyright Act (DMCA) was passed to protect ISPs, not the kind of wholesale distributors of music characterized by YouTube and SoundCloud. It provides this protection via the concept of the safe harbor. If someone posts illegal content using their service, the rights owner can demand of the ISP that the content be "taken down" and then, in most cases, the ISP will usually comply after giving the offending company which posted the content an opportunity to object.

At considerable expense, Spotify actively makes licensed music available on their site. YouTube and SoundCloud claim to be passive participants; they don't put content onto their sites; users themselves upload content and YouTube and SoundCloud serve, in their minds, as ISPs, Internet service providers no different than Yahoo, AOL, or Microsoft (via Internet Explorer), etc.

Free is a difficult model to compete with, and the Spotifys of the world are learning that the insatiable practice of peer-to-peer sharing and other forms of piracy (whose impact remains even though the mere existence of inexpensive streaming options has resulted in some softening of its impact on rights owners) still continues—but like the wolf in different clothing. An otherwise legitimate company can cause tremendous damage to the income of rights owners by invoking the safe harbor exemption when it should not.

What they do is interpose a step *prior* to taking down an offending video clip which is the subject of the takedown notice. They offer to copyright owners the option of either removing the disputed music (often well after the fact) or allowing advertising to be placed on the video clips, the income from which they will share with the copyright owners. The leverage that they have by considering themselves ISPs—by invoking the safe harbor provisions of the DMCA—allows them to "settle" claims by actually generating new money from the content for themselves, although they share it with the copyright owners. The choices that the rights holders have are limited to (1) letting the clip stay up because they cannot possibly monitor every uploaded work that happens hundreds of thousands of times a day with respect to a major copyright owner; or (2) seeking to identify what is theirs and make a deal so that they end up authorizing the advertising and forego their claims. As a result of exercising this leverage over the rights holders, both YouTube and SoundCloud now have pretty much all of the blanket licenses that they need from the major record and music publishing companies.

So, are they ISPs or infringers? Apparently neither—just clever negotiators who use the DMCA to give them the leverage they need to pay rights holders less than a free market would have forced them to. The losers? The record companies and the publishers—and, of course, the creators as well because the pot that they share in is far smaller than it could have been.

PS: PRS for Music, the British mechanical and performing rights society, sued SoundCloud in 2015 after five years of failed negotiations with that company to get them to withdraw their argument that they do not need a PRS for Music license for its streaming service in the UK and Europe.

Digital Service Income Shares

Let's talk about what the actual revenues shared between rights holders and digital service providers such as Spotify and Pandora are. Of course, very few people actually know what these interests are—and they are not talking.

Usually, receipts by a record company as a result of the exploitation of their recordings are split somehow with their artists—not usually 50/50—often quite arbitrary amounts—more like 3 to 1 in favor of the record companies (remember the various ways in which DPD royalties can be calculated discussed earlier in this chapter).

When the record labels and music publishers licensed the streaming services, in many cases, they insisted on being given equity in the services themselves. This, together with huge advances and, sometimes, catalogue "service" fees, made one question in whose interest were the rights owners working. Clearly not their artists and songwriters. (No wonder Bette Midler, and many others made very public complaints about how little they receive from the extensive number of streams that they have received.) The great David Byrne, always a force for artists' rights, says that the not-tied-to-standard provisions such as term and royalty rates result in a "black box" consisting of monies collected by the rights holders, but not shared with their artists and songwriters. This is not the black box that I identify in the audit and publishing chapters (chapters 12 and 13) which refers to foreign collection societies' secret funds reserved for their own local members. No, this black box refers to the depository of money earned, but not remitted to artists and songwrwiters, even though generated solely from their art and their appeal to the users of these services. Writers and publishers are as close to partners as is possible under the sophisticated relationship that they have with each other. Labels and artists? Not so close. But the result is the same. Amusing as it was disturbing, the secret memo from Sony's top digital consultant that went viral (and described at length earlier in this chapter) asserted that labels are justified to perform this way; that they need advances to allow them to take risks by signing and developing new acts; that their overhead demands considerable revenues to keep the machine going for their acts; that big-selling artists have always subsidized new or failed artists. Taken to its logical conclusion, his argument is that the core of an artistic enterprise must be manipulated in however many ways can be dreamed up to ensure that the corporation and its stockholders are unaffected by the rises and falls of the marketplace. The result? Artists and songwriters are actually subsidizing their record companies and music publishing companies. Who knew?

Of course, how the revenues derived from streaming is split depends on there being money to split in the first place. These are still early days of ad-supported and subscription-based delivery systems. Streaming services are figuring out how to collect revenues and how to share them—all the while being chased by rights owners to make sure that the parties reach some kind of reasonable and balanced accommodation. This is an evolving area, of course, and most pundits predict that sooner or later the availability of free music—at least the kind offered by iTunes—will be controlled and properly monetized, and things will even out to everyone's advantage.

Pulling Digital Rights as a Means of Circumventing the PROs Consent Decree Limitations. Another aspect of the digital evolution deals with the pressures being put on the American performing rights societies. As there was no royalty rate established in the streaming "space," both the American Society of Composers, Authors, and Publishers (ASCAP) and Broadcast Music, Inc. (BMI) had to go to their respective rate courts (overseen by federal judges appointed to oversee the consent decrees—issued by the US Justice Department—under which the PROs were allowed to function, being, after all, monopolies) to seek one. Their music publishing company members and affiliates were apoplectic at the decisions made by the rate court judges. Spurred on by Sony/ATV, in 2013, the large music publishers attempted to withdraw only their digital performance license rights from the PROs and to license them directly. In this way, they could negotiate individually with the digital streaming services and obtain more money in a market characterized by a willing buyer *and,* for the first time, a willing seller—not one ruled by the hand of a single judge. While they eventually failed in their quest, and have since pulled back from their stance, these and other music publishing companies are now focusing their efforts on the pursuit of modifying the consent decrees rather than merely striking at windmills.

Does Sound Matter?

One would think that, with all of the technology emanating out of the imaginations and skills of computer scientists worldwide, the quality of the sound in the digital age might have improved from the 78 rpm, but apparently consumers don't demand it and suppliers accordingly don't really bother to deliver it.

Neil Young is betting that the powers that be are wrong and "if you make it, they will buy it." So in a combination of altruistic and commercial initiative, he has developed Pono. Who better to lead the fight to replicate the highest level of studio production than this icon of the recording world who has actually experienced firsthand the incredible advancements of recording capabilities from the 1960s to the present?

Neil Young's goal is to bring high-quality-sounding music to the marketplace—"not just some 21st century fake shallow Xerox facsimile, with all of the essence taken away and replaced by a thin exterior with no passionate core." He states that he has no intention of reaching the masses of consumers who he believes are not that interested in perfection, but he feels that he can give a choice to those who are. If Young is correct, the loss of quality between a first-class master and an MP3 is almost 95%. He claims that the size of the respective files confirm this.

Gilbert Hetherwick, former head of Columbia's Masterworks and EMI's US Classical Label awards HDTracks the current high-water level of quality sound. He calls it the ULTIMATE in sound quality . . . and "provides your files [with sound capabilities] FAR exceeding the quality of your now 'primitive' CDs!"

Hashtags as a Source of Income in the Digital World

These are known to most young people—less so to their parents. Hashtags are keywords used to reach like-minded people out there in the cyberspace. Twitter is the mechanism by which hashtags are disseminated. So someone sends a message not exceeding 140 characters to the ether, which may or may not have impact on those who receive the tweets. Incredibly fast communications of likes, dislikes, recommendations, etc. regarding all things imaginable, including music, are facilitated by the use of hashtags. Hashtags seem to be here to stay. Even though their value is questionable, admittedly they disseminate information about music widely and often. I can't say that this result isn't useful in a world of overstimulation where artists and songwriters seek to be easily and broadly identified and followed.

---

1. The *public domain*, of course, is just what it says. Once the period of copyright protection expires, the public ends up owning the work and can do anything it wants with it. It can perform it, mechanically reproduce it, print it, display it, edit, arrange, adapt or translate it, use it as the basis of a dramatic work or film, download it, etc., all without permission and without the obligation to pay anyone for using the work. Its domain—its home—is the public.

---

2. For millennia, partnerships have been characterized by one characteristic above all others: the parties share in the profits; but they also share in the losses. It is not customary for one partner to share in the profits, but to have the right to recoup from the other partner's share large portions of their investment (that is, recording costs after which the record companies still claim ownership of the master recordings for ninety-five years).

---

3. The notion that promising to pay a royalty to an artist presumes that the record label will follow traditional, and substantial, release protocols such as promotion, marketing and sales, as well as other commitments customarily provided by a record label—particularly a large one. Otherwise, it would have no retort when requested to share profits.

---

4. Music publishers/songwriters still don't comprehend why they should only get $0.091 (the statutory mechanical royalty), while the record label/artist/producer retain about $0.659 (and Apple retains $0.23 off the top). After all, there are two products being sold: the song and the sound recording, according to them. Why shouldn't the song owner enjoy half the net proceeds? As noted earlier in this chapter, that would work out to $0.3295 for both the record label and the music publisher to share with their respective artists and songwriters. In the current scheme of things, the publisher/songwriter receive 25% of what is logically theirs. The artist? Less.

---

5. Now that's one for the books! In Canada the mechanical rights society (CMRRA) has worked out a deal whereby they are paid the disputed mechanicals into a suspense fund and at least the money is in the hands of the music publishers' agents rather than the record labels which are all too anxious to withhold money due on the sale of records. Similarly, Apple's deal with record labels provides that they pay to the labels the mechanical royalties, for later distribution by the labels to the music publishers/writers. In Canada, and I believe in the rest of the world, this does not happen; the music publishers and their agents collect the mechanicals directly from the eventual user, in this case iTunes.

5 · PERSONAL MANAGEMENT
The Whys, Wherefores, and Watch Outs

The man that hath not music in himself
Nor is not moved with concord of sweet sounds
Is fit for treasons, stratagems, and spoils
The motions of his spirit are dull as night
And his affections dark as Erebus.
Let no such man be trusted.
—**WILLIAM SHAKESPEARE,** *THE MERCHANT OF VENICE*

Okay, I am being a bit dramatic with the quotation. And actually, I disagree with the Bard—at least insofar as personal managers are concerned. It matters not how musical your personal manager might be. What matters is how dedicated, how energetic, and how imaginative he or she might be. Add ethics and a way with numbers and you're a long way toward having it all—professionalism, enthusiasm, and results.

What values should you apply to your choice of manager and to your rationale for entering into a formal agreement in the first place? Artists are principally concerned with, and principally adept at, only their own art; yet the business aspects of conveying and transmitting this art to the public must also be dealt with if they are interested in protecting their creations, earning a living, and communicating their art to others. What is the thought process that artists should conduct before entering into an agreement with a personal manager? Pertinent questions might include these: Why should you even consider obtaining a manager? What would and would not be included among a personal manager's duties? How should your manager be compensated? What should you expect and what should you reasonably *not* expect of this person?

First of all, let's concern ourselves with the schooling for managers. Sorry, there is none. Well, then, what about the licensing for managers? After all, accountants have to be licensed, as do lawyers, even dogs. What agency licenses managers? Sorry again; there is none.

Let's focus on something more concrete, then: the various kinds of managers waiting to assist artists in developing their careers. As you have no doubt guessed, there are as many types of managers as there are one-hit wonders. There are educated managers and uneducated managers; experienced managers and grads who ran the live music programs in college; managers who know songs and managers who know sounds; managers who are attentive to the business of their artists and managers who are as lost in the world of business as their clients profess to be (and often are); managers who are creative geniuses and managers who are public relations disasters; managers who have never left Landsdown Street in Boston, Beale Street in Memphis, or Sixth Street in Austin, and managers who understand, or at least are aware, of the world as a marketplace; managers who are happy to have the record company do its thing and managers who are hands-on and make sure the jobs expected of the record company's personnel are done efficiently and on time;

in-box managers who are reactive types and handle only what comes to their attention and managers who are proactive and initiate activities without having to be tapped on the shoulder. There are probably no managers who have either all of the negative or all of the positive attributes listed above, although most managers exhibit at least some of both.

WHAT A PERSONAL MANAGER SHOULD (AND SHOULD NOT) BE EXPECTED TO DO

Your manager is the primary contact person for all of your business affairs, and should be able to act in your place and on your behalf. In essence, your personal manager should operate as your chief of staff in reducing to their essentials all aspects of your legal, financial, and artistic career. Your manager should

- in consultation with a licensed booking agent, arrange your live performance bookings, including the size and nature of venues and the manner in which the live performance will be presented;
- work with your record company on everything from approvals of album artwork to coordinating the choice of producer, location of recording, establishment of recording budget, rental of equipment and lodging, travel, promotional appearances, press and publicity, and exploitation of your records;
- assist your attorney in negotiating record, publishing, and merchandise agreements;
- approve allocations of monies expended on your behalf for advertising;
- provide informed advice and counsel on all decisions regarding your ultimate choices of producer, agent, accountant, booking agent, video director, and, possibly, attorney as well.

Your manager should also work with you to establish the image that you wish to project and the manner best suited to project—and to protect—that image, and help you set goals and establish strategies to achieve them.

A personal manager's role is not to be underestimated, but it is not always what you think it is either. Unfortunately, management contracts do not usually cite the specific areas in which a manager provides services. For example, they do not usually include language about ensuring that your rent is paid on time, your rehearsal hall electricity bill is paid on time, or that, when you arrive in London to record your album, you are accompanied by a work permit authorizing you to do so. Without it, you'll be on the next plane home—at your own expense. Inattention to these kinds of details can wreak havoc with your career, let alone with your management relationship, and if you do not articulate your expectations, preferably in writing, you are likely to be disappointed.

Before going into details on the personal manager's role in an artist's life, a few words are in order about what a manager is *not* supposed to do. Accept the fact that it is not your personal manager's job to assume your life responsibilities, or even all of your career responsibilities. Too many artists try to delegate to others all of their responsibilities and in the end regret it. Ultimately, we are all 100% responsible for all of the decisions affecting our lives and careers. But most of us do not have "managers" or others who tell us or, worse, allow us to believe, that they will look after us. It is all too easy for the young artist to defer to someone who wants to take charge, especially if that "someone" is experienced, mature, and successful at selling him- or herself and his or her abilities in a world that most have only read about. Yet artists who look to a manager to live their lives for them and managers who claim to be able to do so are both delusional. You and your manager must also separate out your own respective interests. It is the rare manager who has the objectivity to do this.

When a manager and artist first meet, they are often on their best behavior, and their wish that their respective interests should dovetail can get in the way of objective thought processes. If they hit it off, and the prospective manager is adept at self-promotion, the artist may be so relieved, and so anxious to get the interviewing process over with, that both artist and manager rush ahead to the next step. Their "love affair" has begun. But the curse of many love-at-first-sight relationships comes along with it. I often think about how marvelously some young attorneys present themselves in interviews, only to disappoint after being asked to write their first contract. Similarly, managers, even those with the most magical appeal, may disappoint when they have to make their first practical decision. (Of course, sales talent is not such a bad attribute for an artist's personal manager to have.)

MANAGING THE FIVE STAGES OF AN ARTIST'S CAREER

There are five distinct stages in the career of a very successful artist:

1. The beginnings: Your career is just starting to develop.
2. The marketing stage: You are the opening act (that is, your on-stage time is before 9 p.m.).
3. Your career is established.
4. You are a star.
5. Your career is for all intents and purposes over, but your legacy comprises a catalogue of albums and, possibly, musical compositions—some, all, or none of which you may own or control.

Of course, not all artists reach stages 3 and 4, but stage 5 is applicable to everyone who has had even the slightest degree of success.

The roles of the personal manager differ in each of these time frames; the qualifications the artist looks for in a manager differ as well. Ideally, an artist would be able to hire five different managers, one for each stage. However, the financial consequences of attempting to replace a manager as the artist's career shifts from level to level would likely be devastating, and so the trick is to find a manager who will grow in a manner consistent with the artist's changing needs.

The Beginnings

During the first level of development, your personal manager needs to draw attention to you and build your team—and your chances of success. This is the period of rough demos; amateur-night performances at local clubs; battles of the bands sponsored by local radio; being featured in workshops sponsored by the American Society of Composers, Authors, and Publishers (ASCAP), Broadcast Music, Inc. (BMI), the Society of European Stage Authors and Composers, Inc. (SESAC), or the Songwriters Hall of Fame; postcard mailings; preliminary introductions to music business professionals such as A&R people; part-time jobs; and, above all, listening and learning—listening to everyone around you, learning the history and the lexicon of the music industry, reading the available books on the business of music, and attending educational forums sponsored by ASCAP, BMI, and SESAC, as well as the Association of Independent Music Publishers (AIMP), whose principal offices are in New York and Los Angeles.

From a musical point of view, this is the time you are sharpening your image, developing your craft, discarding almost as much as you write, replacing musicians, and replacing the replacements. It is also the time for concretizing your physical image so that you look the part of what you are trying to communicate. (For some, this is easy. I represented a band that merely wore jeans and T-shirts, which they would remove at some point during the show and throw into the audience. Other bands with fashion supervisors could never match the raw, natural energy and rebellious image that this band had.) This is the time you try to impress on others that you are something new and something special. Long hair, short hair, shaved heads—whatever floats your boat. But a statement must be made or you will be forgotten and melt into the fungible band category and disappear. "Nothing jumped out at me," the professionals will say.

Marketing

This second level of development begins just before you are "discovered" and ends after you have signed a record deal and delivered several albums that have sold in sufficient quantities for the record company to justify expending more money on your career—and not just on a particular single or two. During this stage you are the opening act for a more significant or known performing artist. By this time, your professional team is more or less solid, and you and they have to consolidate—and reconcile—your musical and professional (read "financial") goals. Do you begin to appear in public with other artists of the same level of success? Do you start writing songs with them? Guesting on their shows? Do you volunteer your time and services for charitable purposes and do you begin to identify those charities whose interests you feel you can advance by your involvement? Do you reconsider whether your band is ready for the big time or whether you need to replace or add one more musician?

This is the time when your record could be moving up the charts (with a "bullet" in *Billboard*) but is just as likely to fall off the charts (with an "anchor," in music biz vernacular) more rapidly than it climbed them. This is the time when the spin on who you are, what you represent, and where you are going (really far) is most appropriately promoted. Many decisions made during this period are of a one-time marketing nature, but at the same time you will be facing issues requiring decisions that you will have to live with for the rest of your career. For example, should you expand or contract your music publishing relationships? Should you expand your reach beyond the United States into other territories of the world, even as the demand for your services is gradually building in your home country? Do you need to revisit your contractual relationship with your manager and try to determine, with your manager, whether his or her expertise, vision, contacts, staff, etc., can support the next phase in your career without help or whether it is time for your manager to consider partnering with another—perhaps other-coast—management firm? Is it worthwhile to move to a booking agency that can partner you with their other acts in a combination that will be synergistic both from a musical and demographic level? Is it appropriate or timely to engage a full-time publicity and public relations firm? A proper consideration of these issues requires time, money, and thought—not just thought on your part and your personal manager's part, but on the part of your lawyer and business manager as well.

The Established Career

During the third level of development, your manager must juggle the various duties that are generated by the very nature of your status in the music industry. This is the time during which you are sought after around the world, and you have to make careful decisions about whether your musical style and material need to be modified or whether doing so might end up destroying a formula that works (from a business point of view). Naturally, your musical style and your songs will tend to evolve anyway, but many artists have messed up their careers at this point by making decisions that, on their face, sounded right but that resulted in their losing the very audiences that supported them in the first place. Ian Hunter left Mott the Hoople just when the band was breaking in a huge way worldwide. Neither he nor the band ever recovered. On the other hand, Phil Collins left Genesis and Rod Stewart left Faces to even greater stardom. The Beatles shifted gears, added cellos, then recorded *Sergeant Pepper*, creating a musical breakthrough whose effects are still being felt almost fifty years later.

Stardom

It is during the fourth level of development that a manager's true capability is tested. During this period, the manager's role must be to keep the artist on top by, among other things, sifting through the offers coming in for that artist's services and by being the catalyst for other opportunities that may be more fitting and appropriate to that artist's place in the world. The legendary Colonel Parker did not hesitate to maneuver Elvis Presley's career into television and film, even as his recording and performing career was at its peak. When should an artist or group perform and when not? U-2, Green Day, and the Rolling Stones have gone years between tours, but one gets the impression that their finger is not far from the pulse of their audience. At the same time, through spreading their legendary status, they welcome new and younger audiences to their shows and as purchasers of their records. Managers can help you to understand the dynamics of your audience. Some use tried-and-true marketing techniques such as focus groups and private polls.

Dealing with the Legacy

By the fifth stage, the artist's development is complete. However, there remains a residue of assets, image, and art that require of the personal manager a completely different set of responsibilities, talent, experience, and imagination. It is during this stage that the artist's catalogue of albums and musical compositions need to be attended to and exploited in order to keep them vital. This stage also requires an understanding by your manager and other professionals charged with looking after your catalogue as to what level of exploitation you want—or will permit. Some artists' catalogues are available on every compilation album imaginable—and a considerable amount of money is generated from these exploitations. Some artists' catalogues are available nowhere except as originally released and more than twenty years later are still selling for $18.98 (for example, the Rolling Stones).

The "old" artists cannot be too thrilled either. Some artists' recordings are repackaged in deluxe editions, "truck-stop" editions, etc. Some are not. How the artist wants his or her catalogue dealt with after the active career is concluded can depend on the financial security of the artist or, if a group, that of the various members of the group. Uneven needs among members of the group can result in conflict. Post-breakup decision-making should be considered in any agreements among band members.

Touring is another area in which a manager can have tremendous impact. Tim Collins believed in Aerosmith after their demise in the 1980s, and they returned bigger and better than ever—as a result, according to music business insiders, in large part to the vision and relentless effort of their manager. (Historical footnote: They subsequently fired Collins.) Bringing back Deep Purple after more than twenty years was a very successful move, but one requiring delicate management guidance as well. Pairing Mark Knopfler with Emmylou Harris in 2006 was inspired—and profitable. Most notably, in 2005, INXS auditioned a new lead singer on a TV reality show to replace the late and departed Michael Hutchens, thereby jump-starting a new career. And now: Holograms. (see chapter 10, page 179).

A final note: Your old, dusty, and yellowed contracts had better be available or you will not be able to establish ownership or royalty entitlements for such things as "previously unreleased outtakes" or "original demos." Make sure your manager or attorney provides you with a copy of everything you sign. Don't depend on them—in fact, don't depend on anyone but yourself—to keep your contractual heritage alive.

It is very difficult to maintain communication and democracy among band members during their prime; it is nearly impossible afterward. The musicians go their merry way; some prosper, others do not; some marry, others divorce; some die and their estates are ruled by their exes, their executors, or their children's guardians. Their contracts are over, their high-powered personal managers and lawyers and business managers are long gone (remember a percentage of no earnings equals zero), and their catalogues—their legacies—are slowly but surely degrading. Yet an artist's or band's catalogue is most definitely an asset, one that needs coordinating—in a word, managing.

KMMA: KEEP MY MUSIC AVAILABLE—AT ALL COSTS

One immediate concern for managers of legacy artists is the passivity of record companies who neglect the artists' recordings when they are no longer in the foreground of consumers' consciousness. These companies are usually willing to reissue their out-of-print–out-of-release recordings; they just do not care, do not respond to entreaties, or do not know what is in their catalogues in the first place. In the downsizing of record companies, those employees with corporate memory are the first to go. Perhaps income from these exploitations is not included in the calculation of their bonuses, or they simply do not have the time to deal with inquiries because they are vastly overworked and understaffed and they simply cannot be responsive.

Whatever the reasons, the recordings remain, for all intents and purposes lost to the world (and their income potential lost as well). Many artists whose recordings have met this fate have recently joined what I call the KMMA crowd—those who want to "keep my music available" at all costs. These forces join with (1) those who want copyright to end, thereby expanding the public domain (see chapter 24); and (2) those who want copyright to continue, as long as the exclusive rights of the copyright owners are bent just enough to permit them to apply for a license to allow the release of their own recordings! The Internet, of course, is assisting those forces by making virtually every record in existence available to consumers.

There is a lot of support for a pending congressional bill that would assist potential users of works which have been "orphaned" (again, see chapter 24) and the owners of which cannot be located for purposes of clearance. Such a significant modification to the exclusive rights of copyright owners would create a lot of problems for the record companies' own legacy programs, which are traditionally several years in the planning stages. Perhaps the 24/7 all-downloads-all-the time technology introduced into the mix in recent years will resolve this problem in the cyberspace environment, if not so successfully in the bricks-and-mortar world.

I was recently reminded of the nightmare sometimes experienced by creative artists who sample long-forgotten works. The artists themselves are often ecstatic that they have been remembered, but their record companies put the kibosh on the use by overcharging or threatening copyright infringement were the artist to proceed with the sample. One artist's solution? Do it without telling the record company that owns the sample. It probably has no clue as to what it owns anyway, let alone what it sounds like. Not a healthy situation when this is the most practical solution.

Regrettably, you cannot usually rely on your (former) record company or music publisher to exploit your catalogues of songs and master recordings—especially if you don't own or control them. The only way you can rejuvenate your catalogue is by being proactive, and designating capable people—whether your attorney or some combination of your attorney and the multitude of music supervisors and clearance houses that can be appointed—to take charge. In addition, there should always be a savvy accountant involved. But I have rarely known of an artist appointing anyone to take responsibility for managing a catalogue of music. Most artists think that their catalogues will be nurtured automatically. More magical thinking.

The legacies of the great composers and artists of old—the Gershwins, Irving Berlin, even Leonard Bernstein—are all handled by "executors" who are charged with maximizing the estate and protecting the artists' images. The lawyer for Cole Porter's estate was instrumental in developing the Kevin Kline film *De Lovely*, which single-handedly regenerated that great author's song legacy. Some music business professionals are uniquely positioned to coordinate the exploitation of both song and record catalogues—even if the artist owns neither the song copyrights nor the masters. If you can find someone to do this, even someone who is new to your life, you will be well served, as catalogue exploitation is a business in itself—whether accomplished by taking a song and getting it revived, by rerecording it or coupling recordings of it on compilation records, or by taking a master and finding a place for it in a film or commercial. The Buddy Holly catalogue was lying fallow until Linda Ronstadt recorded two of his songs. This was followed by the film *The Buddy Holly Story* and the musical *Buddy*, which remains a staple of the stock and amateur circuit and has had a ten-year run in London. And don't forget *Mamma Mia!*, the "tribute" to ABBA. Or *Smokey Joe's Cafe*, which gave new life to the songs of Leiber and Stoller. Or *Moving Out*, the musical featuring Billy Joel's songs, or *Jersey Boys*, the Broadway show based on the story of the Four Seasons. Ray Charles's last album, *Genius Loves Company*, was a singularly successful partnership between Concord Records and Starbucks. That album, together with the Oscar-winning film *Ray*, released around the same time, introduced Ray Charles to a new generation.

Although there is no single person who can "wake up" a catalogue, your attorney, or someone operating under the attorney's guidance, can play a kind of "central command" role. This person, working with an accountant, can also monitor the master recording licenses that will inevitably be authorized by the record company (which, through multiple sales and mergers, is most likely a successor to the artist's original company). The income from these licenses should tie in exactly with the mechanical licenses issued by the music publishing company (which, like the record company, is most likely a successor to the artist's original publishing company). Where they do not tie in, someone has either cheated or made a mistake—and the result is usually not to the artist's advantage. This comparative analysis is best handled by a person who has the time and ability to scrutinize royalty statements as they come in (or track them when they do not come in).

There is no reason why an artist or writer cannot seek permission to "work" a catalogue that he or she does not actually own or control; believe me, the record company and publishing company are likely to be thrilled, especially since in many cases they have long ago forgotten that they even own these works. Any number of deals can be worked out with them so that any income that is received can be shared with the artist and writer on the one hand and their "agent" for exploitation on the other, all the while providing unexpected new income for the record and publishing companies.

But someone has to initiate it.

As always, the best way to achieve a particular goal, in this case the optimal exploitation of one's catalogues, is to assemble a competent team of persons expert in the music field and charge them with coming up with a strategic plan for accomplishing the goal. After all, there is money to be made.

All managers bring with them their own backgrounds, prejudices, and paradigms of what they envision their role to be in the overall context of the artist's life. And, as I have said previously, the different functions for which a manager is responsible beyond the abstract known as career planning—marketing, budgeting, scheduling, promoting, communicating, investing, and training—are all important and each requires a different degree of attention at one time or another. Yet practically, there will simply not be enough money going to the bottom line for either you or your manager to achieve perfection in all of these areas on any efficient or regular basis. This is not to say, however, that the issues should not be brought up frequently by you (or by your manager) and addressed in an ad hoc way whenever possible. A failure in any one of these areas can poison the entire financial and artistic program that has been designed so painstakingly by you and your team. This is all the more reason to be careful in choosing a manager and keeping that individual's role under some contractual control. Of course, for some it will be difficult, if not impossible, to find a person who is willing to work for nothing now and a promise to be paid a percentage of some unknown sum in the future. The negotiating power—that is, the power to say no—is in the hands of the manager. Nevertheless, a few points of guidance should be useful for any artist, especially a beginning artist, in order to achieve some degree of control over how the relationship acts itself out.

You have two principal goals. The first is to find the most *effective* people to represent you to the world. The second is to establish a system of checks among all the members of your team, which is the best safeguard against failure. Any system of checks must be tailor-made for the particular participants, but here is a brief list of some of the ways one can establish such a system.

- A copy of every document signed on your behalf, whether by you or by your manager, under a power of attorney, should be delivered to you and to your attorney; if it is necessary for your accountant to have a copy, the attorney should be charged with that responsibility.

- Establish regular get-togethers among all the key professionals on your team. Set up the meetings in the same way that organizations hold board meetings: Have each person review each area that person is responsible for. Introduce new business in an orderly fashion and delegate responsibilities and deadlines for accomplishing these. Have someone take notes and provide a summary of the meeting to all of the participants within a week following the meeting.

- If the workload is getting out of hand or requires the addition of other participants, appoint someone to identify them, calculate costs, and set up a procedure and a timetable for completing the task.

- As the workload grows, consider hiring a facilitator who understands how to flesh out a larger business; but in any event start expanding the organizational chart by setting up committees and subcommittees that can meet without the entire "governing board" and establish a timetable for them to meet, identify, and pursue their goals, and report back to the "board."

- Set up individual meetings with specific team members as appropriate. It is not necessary or desirable that all team members be at all meetings. For confidentiality reasons, for example, you don't want your tour manager to know everything about your concerns about the financial viability of a planned tour because the information may seep down to hired staff who may make a run for it if they feel their jobs are not secure. It is perfectly appropriate for some people to be invited into a meeting and then excused after the need for their presence has ended. You should also establish regular meetings with your financial advisors, starting with your business manager; have your lawyer present at these meetings because it may turn out that you need to engage an outside financial advisor in addition to your accountant to serve your needs. (For obvious reasons, your accountant might not be the first to recommend this.)

- Send your manager to business school. I'm not kidding. U2's 2001 "Elevation" tour grossed $143 million from 113 shows in the United States and Europe. This is *real* money and a real business. How many businesses grossing that kind of money are run by people with zero business training? Prince Rupert Loewenstein, long-time manager of the Rolling Stones, was an investment banker. Many business schools have two-week, six-week, two-month, and longer programs specifically designed for managers of small companies, and the lessons learned can be invaluable not only as your company grows but also to *ensure* that your company grows.

- Try to protect yourself from all possibilities, whenever they present themselves, for conflicts of interest between you and any of your professional representatives so that you are all in the same boat and what's good for one is good for all and vice versa. As noted below, conflicts can arise when your manager, record company, producer, and music publisher, or any combination of these, is the same party. One of the successful ways to ensure open and honest performance by these entities, whether or not they are aligned, is by inviting their creative and administrative heads into some of your meetings to present their views of where you are and where you (and they) are going, and at the same time, to make themselves available to scrutiny and questioning from your professional team.

- Finally, remember that trust is earned over a period of time; be prepared to loosen strangleholds over your manager as the manager's worth to you is proved. Better still, don't *ever* have strangleholds over your manager—just reasonable constraints.

CHOOSING YOUR MANAGER

How do you choose a personal manager? Slowly. Carefully. Openly. As you meet more people in the music industry—record company personnel, music publishers, agents, lawyers, other artists and musicians, recording studio personnel, and others—you begin to develop a sense of proportion and perspective. You learn about historical situations concerning other artists and you learn the parameters of trust. You learn to audition those who are auditioning you, to interview those who are interviewing you. Your instincts are useful, but obtaining concrete evidence of other people's experience, willingness to help, and level of understanding of you and your music, plus cross-checking this information with others whom you have learned to trust, is the best way to choose an effective manager.

At the outset, you need to consider in what areas you require the services of a manager. If you are a musical artist who aspires to become an actor, you should find a professional experienced in both fields—or, alternatively, two professionals, each of whom is expert in one of the fields. The contracts, contacts, relationships, and methodologies of these two fields are enormously different, yet the standard management contract typically blends them (as well as other fields) together. If you are interested in a theatrical career, once again you must consider the specific experience of the person whom you would have as your personal manager. Often the expertise of a given music business professional does not cross over into the areas of musical theater or drama. You certainly do not want to be in the position of having to find a manager for your manager. Rex Smith, the actor, was REX, the hard-rock band before his Broadway debut in *The Pirates of Penzance*. Kevin Bacon has a band! Kevin Spacey toured briefly when he directed and starred in *Beyond the Sea*, the Bobby Darin biopic. And don't forget the Blues Brothers.

Once you have pinpointed the kind of experience you need your manager to have, you need to consider other crucial areas:

Does the manager work for other artists, and, if so, how many and in what genre? While you will agree to be exclusively represented by your personal manager, your manager will be free to provide similar services to other artists. (There is at least one positive aspect to the fact that your manager is working for other artists: the fact that he or she will be dealing with an array of other industry people. The broader your manager's access to these people, the greater that person's ability to utilize this network on your behalf.)

Of course, this brings us to a frequently disturbing fact: that a manager who is working for more than one artist may have a time-availability problem. Ironically, the one-act manager of today, partly because of his or her success with you, may be a multiple-act manager (with a record label) tomorrow. This is an issue not just of time availability, but also of genre of music. If you are a heavy-metal artist, for example, and all your manager's other artists are cut from the same cloth, a legion of conflicts of interest can arise. (You have just learned another lesson about clout: You want someone with it, but you also want to be the only star on the clout-master's roster. If you are the only star on the roster, where is the clout? Hint: It is you.)

THE QUESTION OF CLOUT

There seems to be a syndrome characteristic of recording artists and songwriters that encourages them to blame others when things are not the way they want them to be.

Why has your five-album publishing deal not been renegotiated even though you have only recorded one album? It has been five years, after all, since you received your first (still unrecouped) advance! Why did your record company refuse to finance a second video? Release a second single? Invest more money in independent promotion? Finance your tour to Europe?

Call it greed. Call it desperation. Whatever the problem or dissatisfaction is, it could have been avoided if your manager, or accountant, or lawyer had CLOUT. Then you would not have had to deal with these issues because the person with clout would have just gone in and simply fixed the problems or made them disappear.

Sometimes the idea that there is such a thing as clout is sold by some professionals—who, of course, claim to have it—to uninformed artists. It eases the artists' insecurity and relieves them of having to take responsibility for their own careers. But mostly, I hear the term *clout* bandied about by artists, not managers. The truth is that there is such a thing as clout, but that having a manager with clout is not always the road to success. In fact, persons with clout can even have a negative effect on an artist's career by disrupting relationships that have been carefully built over years. On the other hand, many personal managers can make a difference. Their clout works. My concern, however, is not that you should ignore power, status, prestige, contacts, or proven results from top personal managers. Obviously, sometimes, the right call to the right people can make a difference. My concern is that there is an overreliance of artists on others due to the fear that only through managers—or lawyers or accountants—with clout will the difference in a career be achieved. I don't believe it will, and if you follow the guidelines in this and other chapters, you won't either. What is forgotten in the mix is that the only real clout is the artist's, through his or her songs and recordings.

You must therefore be careful to question both the time availability of the manager and his or her career intentions with respect to other artists or other functions. You need to make sure that the managerial services reasonably expected to be provided to you will not be materially hampered by your manager's other commitments. An important exception to the above has seen a great deal of growth in recent years and deserves mention: the conglomerate management company. Several successful management companies such as Front Line and Red Light have not only grown enormously in ways that used to be enough to cause artists to jump ship for lack of attention, but they have solved this inherent problem within a large, often faceless company, by acquiring small, successful, independent management boutiques. These managment boutiques have been given autonomy to continue to act as they have in the past, but they now have the clout and the experience and roster of the largest such companies in the world. Record labels are renowned for doing this (and more often than not absorbing the smaller companies, dismantling their staffs, and effectively annihilating their identities and all that made them effective in the first place (see Virgin, Chrysalis, A & M). Other management companies that followed this model, some more successfully than others, are Vector Management, the Sanctuary Group, and The Firm. The latter is a lesson in what can happen when power overtakes purpose. Mass resignations of The Firm's most important agents left the company a shadow of its former self, and the two people who founded The Firm and ran it in its heyday in the 1990s are long gone. Sanctuary is defunct. And Vector has joined Front Line. So it goes.

And what if your manager puts all of his or her efforts into your career—full-time? One of the concerns many managers have expressed to me is that if they do so, and are fired without cause, they will be worse off than they would be in a canoe without a paddle. They won't even have the canoe. The manager who has formally contracted to manage an artist should be able to have some confidence that the professional relationship with that artist is stable. This will, in turn, allow him or her to commit more and more time to the artist as the artist's career expands. Traditional contracts that provide a term of representation and a reasonable income participation are eminently enforceable, and an artist who tries to replace a manager in changing circumstances such as those noted above will be immediately reminded of this fact. That's why they call them contracts. So have discussions about your concerns with respect to your manager's availability early and often. Once you sign the contract, the issue is closed.

Is the prospective manager related in any way to your publishing company or your recording company? If so, the conflict of interest potential is fairly serious. You should be very careful to delineate the responsibilities of your manager, your record company, and your music publisher so that each separate entity (management, recording, and publishing) can function on its own, independent of anyone's interest except yours.

Does the manager understand and share your vision—short, medium, and long range? This may be the most important criterion of all. Your manager must also bring something to the table to facilitate and implement achieving that vision—be it experience, creativity, a functioning office and staff, money, just being hungry enough, or some combination of the above.

How assertive (or aggressive) a marketer is the manager? A good manager must have the ability to energetically and effectively market you to the public and to the music industry. He or she must take a proactive role, particularly vis-à-vis the record company, and must be tenacious. A Scorpio (stubborn—never gives up) would do just fine. A tiger is an apt animal comparison. Your manager must be able to find, facilitate, and create opportunities for you.

Are the manager's people skills good? An effective manager has to be able to deal with all kinds of people.

How developed are the manager's organizational skills? We have already discussed the value of organizational structure. While it is not necessary to rise to the level of Robert's Rules of Order, tight organization can be very useful not only in tactical and strategic planning, but also in identifying patterns of problems, achieving easier and more effective communications, and avoiding problems before they occur. If neither your manager nor any other team member has the requisite organizational talent to achieve these ends, you and your manager will have to hire someone who does.

What kind of reputation does the prospective manager have? He or she should have a reputation for dedication, loyalty, and brutal honesty (and you must be able to deal with that). You do not need any more yes-men than will naturally gravitate around you. Keep them around if you want to, but don't pick one for your manager.

Is your manager willing to take calculated risks? A corollary to this is, Can you accept failure if the risky move doesn't pan out? In the event of failure, you must avoid responding by punishment or rejection. In such an event, your manager should be open and honest enough to discuss with you the thinking behind the risk taking and how to avoid failure in the future, if possible—pushing the envelope while being realistic as to the balance between risk and reward. Short of a material breach of the management agreement, there is very little that you can do to "punish" the manager anyway. Nevertheless, I have seen too many artists turn a deaf ear to the manager and disappear into the ether rather than confront the problem directly and move on from there. The "punishment" too often will end up at the artist's door if he or she has not used the negative experience to build for the future.

What abilities does the person have specific to music? Your manager should have a musical sensibility, meaning that he or she can guide you in building your musical team, and in achieving an effective musical entity and presenting it. This may involve auditioning and selecting sidemen for recording dates, and even adding or subtracting from your band if necessary. In addition, your manager must be able to understand the sound system that is or should be installed at your gigs, how to deal with its cost to minimize rental requirements, and how to identify those people who can help realize your sound needs and potential.

How well connected is your manager at that level of the music industry in which you find yourself? Does your manager have the awareness and ability to make additional contacts in order to achieve the level of familiar and effective relationships that you will need at the next level?

How well-heeled is your manager, and how willing to spend money on the right things? Particularly early in your career, your manager should be able to invest money in your career to assist you in wardrobe planning and purchase, outfitting your band's instrument and sound equipment needs, moving you around from gig to gig, and helping to defray your living costs, if possible. (I knew a manager once whose philosophy was not to spend one dime on his struggling artists. One of those artists was so frustrated that he wore a sandwich board and walked around with a monkey and a cup looking for donations. The fact that he did this most of the time in front of his manager's home office was not appreciated and the two ultimately parted ways. The manager never did change his style.)

The manager must have enough cash to maintain an office, communications (cell phone, telephone, fax, email), and minimal staff. Your manager should also have sufficient funds to travel where required on your business.

PAYING YOUR MANAGER

There are two basic ways a personal manager in the music industry can be paid: (1) on the basis of one of numerous permutations and combinations of a percentage (commission) of the artist's gross or net income and (2) by a flat fee.

Percentage of Gross Income

Most personal managers seek to be paid a 15% or 20% commission based on the artist's gross income, but 25% is not unheard of. For reasons I will never understand, rarely do managers receive commissions somewhere in between—for example, 18.5%, 16%, 14% decreasing to 11.5% after a stated amount of commissionable income has been received, etc.

Why a promised percentage? For some very good reasons. It is quite difficult for personal managers to provide management services without being paid—but that is exactly what often happens with beginning artists. As an artist's career develops, but earnings remain virtually nonexistent, managers must invest more and more of their time, money, and staff (overhead). It is easier if the artist's career starts and either succeeds or fails quickly. It is far more difficult, and complicated, when the career builds over time (for example, Billy Joel, Garth Brooks, Shawn Colvin, Moby, Death Cab for Cutie—even Lorde who was signed to Universal Music Australia when she was a young teen). For with this scenario, few managers have the wherewithal to dig in their heels for an extended—what may seem endless—period of time. The issue is a financial one, not an emotional one, and it often doesn't matter whether or not the manager believes in the artist. Belief cannot pay the rent, or the staff, or the costs associated with managing a working band. In addition, the accumulated investment, over time, can be enormous. A management business, like any other business, cannot survive without income. Not only are most managers in this situation unable to tap into unlimited resources in order to sustain their offices, they cannot staff themselves with capable assistants who, themselves, have careers to consider.

Even successful management companies will not allow a "nonprofit center" to exist for long. Without adequate recompense, good assistants will leave or—worse—be stolen by other management companies with more action—and more money to offer. The only way to compensate the manager-investor is with a percentage of income because if the artist is successful, there really is the promise of a pot of gold (or at least a paid-off mortgage) at the end of the rainbow. No pot, no manager. That's the way it is. And I, for one, cannot blame them. I know very few lawyers who will make that kind of investment in an artist's career. Sure, some will wait a while to be paid and some will shave down their fees to accommodate a fledgling artist. But it is a rare lawyer or law firm that can sustain the kinds of losses that occur when a baby band or a band in the second stage of development embarks on a recording and touring career. A lawyer's overhead is usually considerably higher than a manager's overhead; a manager is of a different mindset than a lawyer and is willing to do the things that managers do well and lawyers either do not know how to do or do not want to do (for example, play emergency doctor 24/7). And lawyers are not inclined to invest substantially all of their time chasing a career of one or two clients for percentages that are traditionally out of whack with those that lawyers, even those working for a percentage, charge in this country. Sure, a personal injury lawyer will take on a case for one-third of the recovery of a case even if the case may take five years to resolve, but John Travolta and *Civil Action* aside, such a lawyer must take on hundreds of such cases in order to sustain a law practice. Lawyers who charge a percentage for their services customarily charge between

5% and 10% of their clients' income, but they also are quite careful to accept clients who actually have income and not just the promise of income. They also operate out of offices with associates and assistants. It is the rare manager who does not leave the office, or the city, for that matter, for hours and days—and even weeks—on end. This routine will simply not work for a lawyer who desires to establish a stable law practice. So cut a little slack for managers who insist on a percentage of your future income.

How does one determine what is a fair percentage of income to pay a manager? Is it a percentage of gross income, net income, or something in between? And should there be a cap, or limit, on the amount of money that will ultimately be paid in the event the artist is really successful? We are entering the smoky and mirrored house of the Manager's Piece of the Action!

On the face of it, an 85/15 split between artist and manager sounds quite—for want of a better word—manageable. Unfortunately for the artist, the manager's 15% is almost invariably taken out of the artist's *gross* income. For example, if your live gig brings in $1,000, the manager receives $150.00. Let's say that the costs for the particular gig (hall, transportation, equipment rental, invitation cards, flyers, postage) are $500 and there are four people in the band. Your agent gets 10%, or $100. After the manager is paid $150, there is $250 for you to split four ways ($62.50 each). Now suppose that the date is so badly planned (managed?) that the costs rise to $750. Unless you have another understanding with your manager, he or she will receive $150 and you will receive—0!

Of course, this scenario deals with what I described earlier in this chapter as the first distinctive time period of an artist's career—the development level. At that level, most managers either postpone payment of their commission until you are a bit more flush, or forgo it entirely. But what happens when things are rolling (the end of the first and the beginning of the second level) and the single gig is expanded to forty dates, generating performance fees of $25,000 each? The gross is $1 million. Your manager will receive $150,000 (15% of gross). If the costs are $500,000 (costs of operation of one-half of the gross is usual), you will receive one-fourth of $250,000 (still assuming that your four-person band splits the money evenly) or $62,500, and your agent will receive $100,000 (10% of gross). (It has become fairly standard recently (much to the dismay of individual agents) that agencies will give cut rates—a percentage or two—to certain successful artists, so the long-sacrosanct 10% is no longer the rule.).

So how does the 85/15 ratio that the management agreement allegedly established *really* turn out for the artist? You may have to get out your calculators to see that, in the above example, of the $400,000 paid to the manager and artist combination—the net profits—your manager receives 37.5% and your band receives 62.5% ($250,000). Looking at it another way, the relationship between you and your personal manager in terms of the gross income is 25% for you and your band mates ($250,000) and 15% for your manager ($150,000). Remember the 85/15 ratio? It's long gone. (It never really existed!) Now it's 25/15—quite a difference. As the costs increase, whether or not this is due to inefficient management or the inefficient work of other professionals, such as accountants and lawyers, or simply because the market did not perform better, the ratio decreases even more. The $150,000, after all, stays. If a snowstorm cuts into the number of performances, the costs of the touring ensemble (staff, trucks, truck drivers, lodging, travel, food, etc.) remain the same. This affects your net income more than it affects your manager's percentage of the gross. If the costs rise to $750,000? Well, you know the answer. The manager receives $150,000, the agent receives $100,000, and you receive—0!

Is this exact scenario likely? Probably not. Has it happened? Yes. Has something in between 85/15 and 0/15 happened? Often. More to the point: Is it ever 85/15? No.

Let's look into how the artist/manager split is handled when you and your manager's representatives are using their heads.

Net Versus Gross

One way to avoid the kind of disparity noted above is to deal with net touring income rather than gross touring income. In this way, your manager has an inherent interest in keeping the costs under control because the manager's percentage will be worth more and more only insofar as your net is more and more. Legend has it that Patti Page (from the 1950s—"Doggie in the Window," "Mockin' Bird Hill," "Old Cape Cod," "Tennessee Waltz") had a unique arrangement with her manager, Jack Rael, with whom she agreed to split every profit dollar down the middle. What was good for her was good for him and vice versa. If a tour made no money, neither of them did either. (I understand that they parted ways in the late 1990s after more than forty-five years—time for a change, I guess.)

You and your potential manager and your respective legal representatives will no doubt spar intensely over whether this approach is as fair as the percentage of gross structure mentioned earlier. You will both try to determine whether it is fairer to *both* parties or only to *one* party to calculate management commissions on the net rather than on the gross. Remember, managers and their staffs invest a considerable amount of their resources and living time to set up an effective tour—even an unprofitable one. And it is not always your manager's fault that the tour does not work. Is it just *possible* that you are a lousy performer? Or a brilliant performer in progress? Why should you appear full-blown like Athena from the head of Zeus? The rest of us had to develop on some kind of time line. You will most certainly have to as well. A percentage of net at this stage is usually a nonstarter for managers. On the other hand, you are investing a considerable amount of your own resources and living time to write, prepare, rehearse, and perform tours—time that puts into jeopardy family relationships and puts a strain on both yourself and your financial resources. Why should you *not* enjoy the benefits of a net calculation?

In reality, very few managers will agree to a split based on net. Why? Probably because the cash flow to keep a management office running must be maintained on some functional level or the whole house of cards may come tumbling down. Eventually, it is in your interest to have a financially viable management, and if that means that a hunk of the gross must go toward financing it, there are many in my profession who will give that arrangement their blessing.

This does not mean, however, that there exist no alternative ways to bring the ratio into some semblance of balance in the event that the financial facts are similar to those in my examples. Here are three.

The Floor

Some artists and managers create an agreement that stipulates that no matter what the profitability of a tour (or lack thereof), the artist, or the manager, or both, are guaranteed a minimum income by tour's end. In this situation, to the extent there are any profits at the end of a tour, the artist receives a minimum amount before the manager, or the manager receives a minimum amount before the artist, or both are guaranteed a minimum amount.

After all, as noted earlier, if your manager does not receive a share of the income during the actual course of the tour, he or she may not be able to finance the operation, pay staff, etc.—in short, do what the job description calls for. Big-time management companies do not have the same cash-flow pressures as fledgling management companies do, but big-time management companies are often too busy, too above it all, or simply not available to bother with a fledgling act. Similarly, if the artist receives nothing, there is no incentive to continue to tour, thus impacting not only the artist, but his or her manager as well.

When a floor is established, you can provide for a reconciliation to be made semiannually or annually by your business manager so that the actual contractual ratio (for example, 85/15 of gross income) is reestablished down the road.

The Ceiling

Whereas most people work for a fixed income (often with a contingent or even guaranteed bonus), personal managers work on the basis of financial hopes and dreams. As mentioned at the start of this chapter, they are not paid for their services other than by a share of the artist's earned income. They often work for nothing until there is something to share.

But what happens when your manager's income from your career is as good as guaranteed? You, who are creating the income by your writing, recording, and performing, often feel that a cap—a ceiling—should be placed on the income of those who originally provided their services in return for a commission—a percentage of the profits. This is true of booking agents and accountants as well as managers. It is occasionally true of attorneys as well when the attorney is compensated by being paid a percentage of your income.

While, at the beginning of an artist's career, "commission" professionals are risking time, money, and their own careers providing services to artists on contingency basis, there often comes a time when the risk is essentially gone and the compensation is truly out of proportion to the current services they are providing. Who is to say if the cap is fair, or when, if at all, it should be imposed? (For that matter, who is to say when the artist's income is out of proportion to the value of the manager's services? After all, $1 million for two hours of singing, like $40,000 per at-bat for a baseball player, is practically beyond rationalizing. Even when your manager's commission is not guaranteed, there are times when artists and managers should revisit the concept of an unlimited commission and resolve to cap the manager's income at some point below which no one could reasonably argue that this individual was being underpaid.

Some artists feel that a manager's job is simply that: to manage. The manager is not expected to "create," and his or her creative and artistic advice is not sought—or deemed to be necessary. For artists who think this way, a cap may be most appropriate. However, in situations in which artists obviously require (and receive) an enormous amount of creative guidance, it is not as reasonable or as compelling to talk in terms of a cap.

Of course, I am assuming that the parties are both able to realistically assess their respective contributions—something that is, regrettably, not often the case.

The Hybrid

Let's say your manager's commission rate is 15%. A tour grosses $100,000 and the expenses, including agent, are $70,000. Your manager would ordinarily receive $15,000 and you would receive $15,000. But if the expenses are, say, $90,000, your manager's commission would totally absorb the $10,000 profit and there would be nothing left for you. What's more, you would owe him $5,000! Some music professionals might say that poor management may have led to this problem in the first place, so why pay the manager the full commission (in this example $10,000 and another $5,000 due later)? In anticipation of this situation, the agreement between artist and manager might provide that no matter what the net is, the artist (that is, the individual or the entire band) will never receive less than the manager. In our example, they would split the $10,000 profit into two equal parts.

As noted above ("The Floor"), you can provide for a reconciliation to be made semiannually or annually by your business manager whereby the actual contractual ratio will be reestablished.

The Compromise

Pay the manager 7.5% of Gross plus 7.5% of Net, with both percentages governed by the hybrid rule just discussed.

The Flat Fee

This method of calculation is used mostly when you are an established act and it is possible to quantify objectively the value you seek to achieve from your manager. Much of what management responsibilities entail is quantifiable. Anyone can perform the requisite duties if they are well staffed and halfway organized and funded. Of course, much of what management brings to the table cannot be quantified, and this is where the conflict arises when the flat-fee approach is under consideration. Superstars are not usually any more willing to part with large sums of money than fledgling ones. If they are, their business managers and attorneys will often step in and protect them from the excesses of their own desires (or insecurities). But sometimes they are better off paying flat fees because, as we have seen, percentages have a sinister way of throwing off budget projections. Simple gross percentage commissions can be larger, or smaller, in relation to your net receipts, depending on things often out of your control. With flat fees, the artist has a much better handle on the bottom line.

Of course, even here, hybrids flower abundantly. No successful manager wants to do his or her magic for a fixed amount of money. Thus, thresholds are often established whereby flat fees are payable for a predictable result and a job well done and percentages or bonuses are payable according to targeted levels of success. (Note that "targeted" does not mean "guaranteed.") On some level, all stages of development have certain predictable plateaus of success, but this compensation method is most effective at the superstar level. With luck, the flat-fee scenario will be a subject of interest for you some day.

THE TERM OF THE AGREEMENT

In management agreements, the word *term* can mean many things, depending on the context. For example, the *basic term* is for the period of exclusivity—typically up to five years. However, managers will usually continue to commission, for many years to come, those products—such as records recorded or songs written—during the term of exclusivity. (These commissions are often reduced over a number of years following the end of the exclusive period of the management term.) More troublesome is the provision that after the exclusive period of the term has expired, the manager can commission deals entered into, or substantially negotiated, during the term. If, during the term of a management agreement, an artist enters into what can extend into a ten-year recording artist agreement, and the management agreement ends during this period, under the customary "form" contract, the manager may be entitled to a full commission on every derivative of every master recorded pursuant to the long-term recording deal. What about the impact of such a provision on an artist who signs a long-term booking agency agreement to book the artist's tours? Is the manager entitled to commission on all of the tour dates booked pursuant to such a contract long after the exclusive management agreement has expired? What a disaster that would be. Yet many agreements are susceptible of such a reading, which is all the more reason to question the contractual language and make sure it means not what it says, but what you want it to say.

EXTENDING OR TERMINATING AN ARTIST-MANAGER RELATIONSHIP

The decision as to whether or not to extend an artist-manager contract past the initial term of the agreement (which may be specified in terms of years, number of album cycles—that is, the period ending a number of months after the release of an album and its attendant tour—or both) often depends on financial criteria, for example, whether the artist grossed $X during a specified time period. But what do we mean by "grossed"? Let's say that your manager, through cleverness, persuasiveness, reputation, experience, or simply stubborn ability, has convinced third parties (record companies, investors, music publishers, and others) to advance money to you to help keep your career alive in an ever more difficult market? Let's say further that these third parties have been persuaded to invest $1 million in your career—such as by advancing recording costs, paying for equipment and costumes, tour support, independent promotion, and general cash advances to keep the band going. Hasn't this manager done a great job? None of this money is ordinarily commissionable, except for the cash advances. Should you discount the valuable service of a manager, who, through the sheer force of personality, has obtained significant investment so that you can stay in the ring?

Suffice it to say that the amount of gross commissionable earnings alone does not tell the whole story of a manager's successful contribution to the artist's career. Yet some management agreements require that in order to count for purposes of a conditional opportunity to terminate the relationship, the amount of money obtained during the specified period must be commissionable income—that is, only actual earnings—not tour support, for example. Just actual earnings. This amount would necessarily be less than the number established were it to include all of the noncommissionable items, such as the loan mentioned earlier.

Stipulating that such monies are commissionable or noncommissionable in part is the responsibility of the artist's attorney. (The *manager's* attorney should have only one role—to negotiate the management agreement with the artist. Ethical considerations come into play when the manager's attorney acts on behalf of the artist, simply because the manager is comfortable with him or her, or knows he will be protected by him or her, or doesn't trust the artist's attorney.)

Another factor to consider is that an artist's perspective at the time of signing with a manager is likely to be different from his or her perspective five years later, when the precondition comes into play. For example, suppose the precondition to extend the term of a manager-artist agreement from a two-album cycle to a four-album cycle (or from three years to five years) is the receipt by the artist of gross commissionable income of $250,000 during the first period of the term (or the expenditure by a record company of $1 million of combined commissionable and noncommissionable income to promote the artist's career).

Those numbers may look awfully large on day one of the relationship and awfully small at the end of the time when the condition permitting or prohibiting termination matures. Yet for a new artist who has never grossed a nickel to receive $250,000 in three years (or to have a record company spend $1 million on promoting his or her record and career during the same period) sounds to me like a pretty successful achievement. Human nature being what it is, artists do not always concur with this point of view.

Finally, you should be aware of the ramifications of terminating an artist-manager agreement *without cause*. These can extend well beyond the contractual provisions that specify actual sums of money. For example, managers may claim that their relationship is so unique that a replacement manager could cause irreparable damage to the strategic plan the manager and artist devised during happier times. So the manager may seek to enjoin, or stop, the artist from pursuing career decisions within the area of the manager's exclusivity. If your manager is also your producer, and you decide to contest such a claim, you are asking for a complicated legal battle, and your career could very well be placed on hold for a significant period of time. This happened to Bruce Springsteen. His manager-producer succeeded in enjoining him from recording for more than a year, claiming that anyone else who acted as producer would necessarily produce a product inferior to what he would have produced. Remember, he was asserting in his role as manager that only he, in his role as producer, should produce Springsteen's records. As exclusive manager, his advice was not being heeded. In this case, the inherent conflict of interest was not decisive, and The Boss finally had to pay off the "manager-producer" in order to resume his career. There are innumerable examples of people filling the combined roles—I would even say it occurs in the majority of cases in certain genres of music. Deals in which artists sign production deals with their manager's production (read: recording) company are back in vogue. The consequences are quite serious if the manager can find a court, as Springsteen's manager did, that is sympathetic. The consequences can also be devastating if the artist does not have the resources to bring legal action to right the wrong. The disastrous effects of enjoining a career for a year or more speak for themselves. Springsteen survived the interruption of his career, at some cost; others would surely not have. See also the sad case of Ke$ha v. Dr. Luke, her producer, and his production company/label.

Termination

What happens when the criteria established for extension—or termination—of the term of the agreement are not met—or when you and your manager simply no longer get along? Even if your career has developed to an outstandingly successful level, you may not necessarily be able to relate personally with your manager over a tedious and frequently tense period of time, a time during which interests and needs change and goals often diverge. Even the two Sirs (Elton John and John Reid) have broken up their long-term relationship. Contractual issues relating to the termination of the relationship between artist and manager are extremely important, because the relationship may be, for all intents and purposes, in effect for the entire period during which the artist has a viable career potential. And, even when the formal relationship is no longer in effect, a personal manager's financial entitlements will often last long after artist and manager have parted company—on a friendly basis or otherwise.

A word about written contracts. In most states, a contractual agreement of the length and consequence of an exclusive management agreement must be in writing to be enforced. Without a piece of paper that documents the intention of the parties, the parties will not be able to prove to anyone's satisfaction—not even each other's—what precisely constituted their "meeting of the minds." The details, and even the material elements, of their deal will be totally uncertain. As a result, both parties may suffer the consequences if they have to litigate their respective claims, and time and money—sometimes huge amounts of both—will be spent that should have been invested more constructively.

Switching Managers

Disaster can befall artists when they switch management in the middle of a management contract term. Not only might they owe commissions to the former representative for contractual commitments made during the term of the now-terminated agreement, they most likely will owe commissions to the former manager *and* the new one for *future* contractual commitments. How can they pay them both? One common solution applicable to live performances—absent offsets that might arise by virtue of the former manager's misconduct—is to pay the former manager a full commission on dates played prior to the termination and one-half commission on dates played after the termination. (After all, the new manager will be charged with "managing" the new dates, and this amounts to a considerable amount of work, resources, and time.)

The same concept may also be applied to agents, who are often replaced when a new manager steps in. But the circumstances with agents are slightly different. Often an agent can actually fulfill his or her duties with respect to dates booked before the agent was replaced, even if they are to be played later. This is because an agent's job is fairly mechanical and is not characterized by the kind of personal, intimate, and confidential relationship that an artist usually has with a manager. I have seen even broader reduction of their commission percentages based on whether the dates were (1) actually contracted for in writing with deposits received, (2) merely confirmed in writing, or (3) simply discussed as part of a tour that was being planned. In the latter two circumstances, the dates would naturally have to be more fully negotiated by the new agent, thus entitling him or her to a larger percentage of the commission than if he or she were simply completing the services with respect to an otherwise substantially finished deal.

Of course, the former manager's claims, unlike the claims of the agent, will extend beyond live dates. For example, the issue of commissioning formerly released albums and those that have been newly recorded but not yet released becomes yet another hot issue to resolve—and one that most agreements do not anticipate or provide for. (One approach is to phase out a manager's commission rate on formerly released CDs or reduce it dramatically on unreleased product if for *any* reason the manager is not actually "working" the record once it is released.)

Negotiated Settlements

Obviously, the best course for all parties involved in an artist-manager dispute involving termination of an agreement is to try to settle the dispute quickly. Litigations are costly and time-consuming. And, whatever one may say about the justice system's effectiveness in assisting litigating parties to reach a considered and correct conclusion, you never know how a litigation will end up. My clients have won cases they should not have won, and they have lost cases they should not have lost. Even when they have won, they have lost time, opportunities, and lots of money. I am not suggesting that litigation is *always* an inappropriate route through which one can seek a remedy. Sometimes it is the only one.

But negotiated settlements, or even mediations according to the producers of JAMS, are the preferred route for most people—no matter what side of the table they are on. Even disputes arising absent a breach of contract have breach-of-contract characteristics. If an artist just doesn't like the manager anymore or wants one with more clout, and if he or she is willing to take the risk, the artist will seek to terminate the agreement and list an array of things that, taken together, he or she might be able to blend into a definition of a breach of one provision or another of the agreement. When one party wants out of a contractual relationship, a dispute exists by definition, and the parties are thrust into either a litigation or settlement mode. Arbitration is often required by the terms of management agreements, but this option is often merely "litigation lite." The pitfalls of litigation remain, and arbitrations are still quite costly.

If the presumed breach is immaterial or unprovable, the consequences to the artist are much more serious. The artist may be forced into a settlement that impacts on his or her ability to pay a new manager, the outgoing manager may stonewall the artist, blocking his or her ability to sign with a new manager who is unwilling to be sued for intentional interference with a contractual arrangement, and the potential new manager may see how the artist has dealt with the old one and say, "This one's not for me." The following guidelines for achieving an equitable negotiated settlement by paying the manager an agreed-upon recompense assume that no provable breach of contract (see box, page 87) is involved.

Methods of Payment

The two most common ways to pay a manager in the event of termination are through a one-time payment of an agreed-upon sum of money, in which case the manager will be out of the artist's life forever, or on a percentage basis. There are a number of ways to pay a manager on a percentage basis.

You can pay according to a *sliding scale*, whereby you pay a full commission on product (songs and recordings) recorded and released prior to termination; a lesser commission on product recorded, but not released, prior to termination; and an even lesser commission on product recorded and released following termination up to the end of the term of the original recording agreement.

Even these already reduced commissions can be further reduced, ultimately to zero, over a number of years following termination. The length of time these commissions apply will vary, depending on the negotiators' respective strengths. A new artist will have to bear a longer phaseout of commissions, if indeed any phaseout at all is achievable; an established artist will have a shorter period during which to pay commissions on deals entered into during the term of the agreement or records recorded or songs written (and/or recorded) during the term. In the former situation, six years is not unusual, with rates being reduced gradually every two years; in the latter, two to three years seems to be the standard. (In my experience, managers will never agree that their right to commissions should end *absolutely* upon the expiration of the term of their agreement with the artist, however long it may last.) But everything is subject to the impact of other provisions in the agreement. For example, if a manager agrees to be employed for only one or two album cycles, he or she probably has enough confidence to believe that if he (or she) wants the agreement to extend beyond those cycles, the artist will be pleased to do so. But in return for agreeing not to require a longer term, the manager may demand, and receive, a provision that pays him or her a full commission forever on records recorded or songs written during the term.

You may also choose to pay with sliding-scale commissions, as described in the above paragraph, but they can be calculated differently from those provided in your agreement with your manager. For example, your manager may have agreed to "stand behind" your recording costs up to a certain amount, but not more; you can modify the base on which the commission is being applied by doing away with the cap (see page 81).

BREACH OF CONTRACT IN ARTIST-MANAGER AGREEMENTS

There are number of ways in which a contract between an artist and manager can be breached. Managers are in breach of contract if they

- steal the artist's funds;
- mix funds among the manager's and the artist's bank accounts and, perhaps, with those of other artists as well, making them hard to trace;
- make themselves totally unavailable during key moments in the artist's career development;
- participate in activities that clearly constitute conflicts of interest;
- are so totally inept as to render impossible the ability to perform the functions outlined in the standard management agreement.

An artist is in breach of contract if he or she

- refuses to take the manager's reasonable guidance in such a pervasive manner as to be "unmanageable";
- violates the exclusivity clause by utilizing others to provide the services for which the manager is exclusively selected to perform;
- fails to pay the manager commissions or expenses when due and to account to the manager in accordance with the accounting provisions (in cases in which the artist controls the receipt and disbursement of his or her earnings);
- violates the "morals" clauses of the contract (see chapter 7, page 116);
- chooses to leave the band (when the agreement is between an agent and a group) and pursue a career outside of the parameters of the manager's right to expand the management role from the band to the individuals within the band, including the artist.

Redefining "Commissionable"

You can pay your manager according to a revised version of what constitutes "commission-able contracts" as defined in your management agreement. For example, your agreement may provide that your manager is entitled to commission all record contracts entered into during the term of the manager-artist agreement *plus* all modifications, extensions, and *renewals* of such contracts.

The word *renewals* is extremely dangerous and will drag along your former manager's entitlements well into what are actually new deals that you and future managers may make. For example, let's say you had a record agreement that expired after the delivery of six albums. Your original manager would have been entitled, by contract, to commission all six of them. Now that you have terminated your agreement with the manager (after, say, two albums), and have been able, through negotiation, to substantially reduce the original manager's commission on the four remaining albums to be delivered after termination, what happens if you subsequently renegotiate and extend the original record agreement? Let's say there are four more album delivery requirements added by the amendment, for a total of eight that remain. The original manager may be entitled to a commission on the additional albums. Even if you terminate the original record agreement, or it expires on its own terms after you have recorded the originally required six albums, if you subsequently renew it, the renewal may be commissionable as well. When negotiating termination settlements, it is important for you and your attorney to catch and change those things that you may not have had the leverage to change during the initial negotiation of the agreement.

Variations on Standard Settlements

When contemplating what an artist can achieve in a negotiated settlement with a manager, there are other things that an artist's attorney can pursue beyond just seeking a reduction or termination of commissions. In situations in which the artist's manager is also his or her production company, the artist can seek to acquire control over the master recordings produced during the period of the agreement, agreeing to pay over to the production company a larger share of income derived from the exploitation of these master recordings. The value of doing this is immense, because you then have the opportunity to keep your catalogue in one place; to use the masters in negotiating a more favorable deal with a subsequent record company; and to utilize, or to authorize your new record company to utilize, the early master recordings for, say, greatest-hits recordings.

Even if you are not able to acquire control over your master recordings, you may be able to eliminate or shorten the period during which you would traditionally be prohibited from rerecording songs contained on those master recordings. As noted earlier, this rerecording restriction is universal in production and recording agreements, but if you are able to reduce or eliminate it, you will be freer to plan your future—in particular, even if a greatest-hits album is not a viable option, you will now be able to record a "live" album containing the songs embodied on your earlier master recordings—or rerecord a song for a film or TV commercial and keep all of the money generated from it.

● ● ●

In negotiating a settlement with a terminated manager, you can agree to pay the manager in a way that permits you to continue your career or in a way that jeopardizes your career. Don't be precipitous and seek to rid yourself of old problems just to strap yourself with new ones. Fortunately, your manager's interests and yours, perhaps for the first time, coincide, at least in the sense that what is good for you (an ability to pay a new manager without bankrupting yourself) is good for the former manager as well (a percentage of something is better than a percentage of nothing). Any commission you still owe your former manager will be meaningless unless you have a career that generates income, so the best thing your now-terminated manager can do is to facilitate the transition to a new manager.

6 • MANAGING YOUR BUSINESS AND YOUR FINANCIAL FUTURE
When "Show Me the Money" Isn't Enough

Charles Robertson is an accountant.
If they come any greyer than that they're squirrels
—NANCY BANKS-SMITH

Money is better than poverty, if only for financial reasons.
—WOODY ALLEN

How nice it would be to sit back and have one completely trusted person take care of everything but writing the songs or playing the music—maybe not grapes and champagne by the poolside, but a slew of far less appealing challenges and obligations that come up at various stages of an artist's career (like deciding what form of business organization is best, paying taxes, paying bills, auditing royalty statements, etc.). Finding a personal manager who has everything you are looking for is difficult enough. Finding one person who can handle all aspects of an artist's business is not only practically impossible, but, as we shall see, possibly not even desirable. Financial planning is incredibly important, perhaps the most important time spent by artists, songwriters, and record producers other than their creative time. There is nothing wrong with accumulating well-earned wealth and I do not know any professionals who are reticent to claim the rewards of their artistic efforts, yet poor advice can easily rob them of their just rewards.

This chapter will describe the choices, risks, consequences, and rewards derived from the multiple ways in which you—the creative one—may partner with others as you begin to develop a business and find the means to manage it. Whom do you look to for the kinds of services that you cannot expect from your personal manager or lawyer? Answer: A financial advisor. A financial advisor can have any one of a number of different titles: accountant, business manager, retirement counselor, or others. But before you start planning your retirement, you are first going to need a person—or more than one person—to assist you in taking charge of the myriad business and financial responsibilities you will face throughout your career. The accountant's role is more limited than that of a business manager. The designation "business manager" incorporates many functions, including those of tax preparer, personal assistant, bill payer, accountant, and auditor. Business managers are not engaged to perform these functions as distinct jobs, with separate fees negotiated for each one as would be the case with an accountant. Their very reason for being is to assume responsibility for *all* of these functions all of the time. Most artists tend toward selecting a business manager as their financial advisor of choice. Here I explore the reasons why and the things you should look out for in choosing your business manager.

WHAT A BUSINESS MANAGER DOES

Tax preparers, as their name suggests, prepare tax returns. They do not help you manage your finances or keep records for you. Personal accountants are, of course, able to prepare tax returns, but they can also provide assistance on day-to-day financial matters, help you maintain the records you need to best deal with federal and state tax authorities, and, depending on their training (see box, "Certified Public Accountants") perform audits. The business manager's role is something else entirely. Business managers can often provide the same services as a personal accountant, but they are also charged with responsibilities that touch every aspect of your business and life—for example, setting up the best form of business organization for you, obtaining and negotiating mortgages for your homes, protecting your profits through various savings techniques, paying your personal and business bills, monitoring and securing your insurance needs, and even working through the multitude of problems resulting from a divorce.

FINDING THE RIGHT PERSON

It is essential that your business manager be one who can and will agree to coordinate with the other professionals in your life: in particular, your personal manager and attorney.

Because non-CPA business managers are not licensed, artists must go beyond the title of "business manager" and explore the backgrounds of the people they interview. Certainly, one need not be a CPA in order to be a competent business manager, and many business managers who are not licensed have licensed CPAs working for them. They can also outsource work that requires a kind of expertise they might not have themselves, for example, audits.

CERTIFIED PUBLIC ACCOUNTANTS

Under most state laws, one can hang out a shingle as a tax preparer or accountant without any particular education, degree, or certification. This is not true of certified public accountants (CPAs), who are highly trained professionals. No one lucks into being a CPA. They have to have a background of business law, financial courses, tax courses, auditing courses, and government theory courses, followed by several years of apprenticeship under other CPAs. Sounds like an old movie? It is. Everything but the green eye shade.

The American Institute of Certified Public Accountants (AICPA) has recently authorized licensed professionals to receive fees and commissions from the sale of various financial products, including insurance, which means that a CPA who is also a AICPA member can now legally receive a percentage of the investments that he or she suggests that a client make. This is not necessarily a bad thing, but it is something that has in some cases caused clients to wonder whose side the CPA is on. (See page 100, "Investing: Is Anyone in Charge Here?")

Audits

An *audit* is an examination of a person's or company's books and records. When a royalty statement is received by an artist's business manager or accountant (or lawyer, particularly if the lawyer administers the artist's copyrights), it is customary for the recipient, or a accountant hired by the business manager, to perform what is known as a *desk audit*. Desk audits are distinct from formal audits, or certified audits that can only be performed by CPAs. Anyone who is responsible for collecting the artist's (or writer's) money should take the responsibility for knowing what the artist has done—songs written, albums recorded, synchronization licenses authorized, etc.—so that when a statement comes in, a quick glance can determine whether the statement is relatively accurate. Formal audits can come later, if necessary, but in many cases an error uncovered by a desk audit can be corrected immediately, often avoiding future duplications of the error. In addition, if resolved early, the irregularity will not be subject to the settlement (read: compromise) process years later, which is how most formal audits conclude.

Keeping Track

In most instances, your business manager will be working for other clients, and his or her staff, not the person you so carefully investigated and ultimately engaged, will handle the day-to-day activities of your "account." It is crucial to have firsthand knowledge of these staff members, who can range from capable to disastrously incompetent. Unfortunately, you have no choice but to depend on other people to do for you what you would do for yourself if you had the time or the training. Therefore, it is essential that you, or your lawyer or manager, review your financial status regularly—preferably together—to keep a close eye on things.

Many business managers provide to artists on a monthly basis a computer printout of monies received and deposited into their accounts, and monies spent; also identified are the source of the receipts and the destination of the outgoing monies. Absent is any regular tax planning or budgeting, and the client has no real awareness of the bottom line insofar as assets and liabilities are concerned or any true sense of the total financial picture.

Other business managers *do* provide more—specifically: budgeting, profit-and-loss statements, and a monthly analysis of investment positions. What a business manager does may be, in part, a function of the ability of the average client to pay fees, since all time spent, and all documentation, costs money; but an artist who is generating fairly substantial sums of money is not only entitled to this level of service, but probably needs it.

Some business managers (I would like to say all, but this is just not the case in the real world) meet with their clients and clients' spouses regularly—at least twice each year and sometimes four times each year. These meetings should be inviolable. Only an emergency should keep them from taking place. For a touring artist, they can be held on the road. The artist's lawyer, and sometimes the manager, should be at these meetings.

Not all clients really *want* to know the truth about their financial health. They prefer to be "in denial," despite the fact that avoiding financial reality can put them into the very position they were fearing: total collapse of security and a loss of everything they have built up over the years. So in whose hands is the responsibility for the psychological cure going to be placed? The business manager's. In the best-case scenario, information will be freely exchanged among the artist and other business professionals, and this will benefit the client by allowing reality to sink in. Decisions based on reality will obviously be more sound than those based on ignorance or—worse—fantasy.

Speaking of reality, here is an example in which an artist can be jolted into the truth. A good business manager will always give you the bad news as well as the good. When the IRS or state department of taxation examines a taxpayer's books and records, if a deficiency is found, not only does it have to be paid; the final audit report is supposed to be signed by the taxpayer. If your business manager is not straightforward with you, he or she might sign the document on your behalf. The business manager will already have your power of attorney in order to sign checks, open bank accounts, and handle other financial arrangements. In such a case, you wouldn't suspect anything was wrong unless you were diligently observing the ins and outs of your bank account. It is not only you, the artist, who benefits from openness and honesty. From the business manager's point of view, there is value in the sign-off, as it gets him off the hook because it is a formal declaration that the client has examined and understood the result of the audit. Your understanding with your business manager or accountant should specifically reserve this right to yourself—and in writing.

AUDITING THE AUDITOR

If you believe your business manager (or accountant) is guilty of shady practices, or of not following generally accepted accounting procedures, you are perfectly within your rights to institute an audit of that person's books. Sometimes such audits will turn up illegal practices. (One famous artist's accountant who ultimately went off to jail actually paid his own taxes with his clients' money, audited his own books—with predictable results—and even charged the artist with the costs of the audit!)

When you secure the services of an independent CPA to audit your business manager's books and records, the report that is issued will likely affirm that the business manager is (1) not stealing, (2) not doing things that are ridiculous (for example, putting all of your assets into a checking account earning 2% interest), (3) complying with federal and state tax laws, and (4) maintaining orderly and complete files in anticipation of a future IRS audit. Sometimes it is comforting to know that all is in fact well. That will have positive resonance for both of you.

WHAT KIND OF BUSINESS IS BEING MANAGED?

If you are a sole proprietorship and rent a van to go to a gig or if you are a corporation and rent a van to go to a gig, which rental car expense is more likely to be deductible as a business expense? Trick question. The answer is both are equally deductible. Many people going into business for themselves—and artists are no exception—are motivated to incorporate simply because they believe that unless you have a corporation, you cannot deduct certain business expenses. This is a myth. If you spend money for business purposes, it is deductible. Period. You do not need a corporation to do this. Despite this, many accountants will suggest that deductions taken by corporations are more likely to survive an auditor's sharp eye, or that the IRS regards a corporation as somehow more "legitimate" than a sole proprietorship (a so-called *dba*, which stands for "doing business as") or a partnership.

Performing rights societies do not require a music publishing affiliate or member to be a corporation.

SHOULD YOU "DO BUSINESS AS" OR FORM A PARTNERSHIP?

A dba is a totally legitimate form of business. But while it cloaks you as a business (banks love them), it does not provide the shelter from liability that a corporation does. Investors do not find the dba an appealing business structure either. From an estate planning point of view, a dba can also complicate your life because there is no differentiation between you and your business. Let me put it another way. The risks and financial liabilities that characterize your dba are absorbed into your own personal identity—and this can have an extremely negative impact on tax planning for yourself and for your family.

If there are other people who make contributions to your business and share in the profits (and losses), you might want to form a partnership, where each partner has an interest in the earnings and a responsibility for the losses consistent with such person's partnership interest. If three partners are all equal, they share these equally. Any variation is possible. But partnerships are not usually favored among individual creative people and investors, because the artistic contributions are customarily provided by only one partner and there is no rationale for a partnership structure.

One reason often given for forming a corporation is that with sole proprietorships and certain kinds of partnerships, the individual (or, in the case of general partners, the partners) is personally liable for the debts of the business. In contrast, the risk of loss for one who has incorporated is generally limited to the value of the corporation, hence the term *limited liability*. Another is that incorporating gives you—and your manager—more control over your finances. To some extent that is true. If your business is a corporation, you are paid a salary, and within a few days, withholding tax is sent to the government. Unincorporated businesses are required to file—and pay—estimated taxes four times a year (April 15, June 15, September 15, and January 15), which takes far more planning and more careful money management.

Note two things about these dates. First, the April 15 date coincides with the date on which the personal tax return for the prior calendar year must be filed. A double whammy. Second, there are no estimated taxes due during the summer or the Christmas holidays—times when most people incur out-of-the-ordinary expenses for vacations, gifts, etc.—yet overspending during these periods may result in difficulty meeting the September and January payments, respectively. If you are incorporated, you do not have to plan for those dates; otherwise, you and your business manager must burn them into your mental calendars.

Despite the above advantages, I am not a big fan of establishing a corporation unless it is absolutely appropriate—and timely. First, although I hate to say it, many lawyers and business managers set up corporations for profit-making reasons. The out-of-pocket cost to establish a corporation is in the $500 to $600 range, and the fee for doing the paperwork is about the same. So the total cost is something in excess of $1,000. Set up one hundred a year and you're talking $50,000 in fees. Easy money.

In addition, the costs associated with incorporating are not limited to the initial setup costs and fees. There is an annual franchise fee for the privilege of having a corporation, and now you must file two sets of tax returns: your personal tax return and the corporation's returns.

And then there is the little discussed, and little understood, provision of the Internal Revenue Code establishing the personal holding tax. This is a tax that the US government has established to penalize people who set up corporations and take out 100% of the earnings, after expenses, as salary, which is no different from what that person would have done had the business been a sole proprietorship. An artist who creates his or her own income (that is, as a producer, artist, or songwriter) runs the risk annually that his or her corporation may be designated a personal holding company. (In fact, the tax preparer is *obligated* to check off a box on the corporation tax return specifying that such a company is in fact a personal holding company.) What is wrong with being designated a personal holding company? For starters, the personal holding company tax is significant. I have been told by a highly regarded tax attorney that it can actually amount to as much as 100% *or more* of the gross income of the corporation once all the applicable taxes have been taken out and interest and penalties assessed.

However, while the IRS may not "like" personal holding companies, audits are not automatic, and I understand that there is a high rate of success in winning these audits. It is one of those provisions in the law that judges do not value as much as the enforcers do.

A final argument against going to the trouble of forming a corporation is that under the Copyright Act, infringers cannot hide behind a corporate "veil." Not only would the corporation be liable in the event of a determination of copyright infringement, but also the officers and writers/artists would remain liable notwithstanding the existence of a corporation.

Forming a Corporation

There are several types of corporations that you can establish: a traditional C corporation; an S corporation, and an LLC (limited liability corporation). Which one you establish may depend on whether you are a songwriter, producer, or recording artist—or some combination of both—and whether you are an individual or a group.

An *S corporation* is a corporation that has been "branded" special by the stockholder(s) because its purpose is really to protect against liability and would probably not exist but for that benefit; the IRS has determined that this kind of corporation should not subject the shareholder(s) to the same kinds of rigid standards that normal C corporations are subjected to and should allow the shareholder(s) to deal with their corporation as if it were, essentially, a sole proprietorship.

The S corporation, which is not subject to a personal holding tax, is not for everyone. For example, a foreign citizen (one without an alien resident green card) cannot be a shareholder in an S corporation. There are ways to convert a C corporation into an S corporation, but there are also risks. Because of the importance of the personal holding company status of a C corporation, the IRS may not want to lose its edge, which it may do when a C corporation is converted into the S structure. Therefore, in such a situation, there is a risk that the corporation, with its new shiny S designation, can be taxed on what the IRS deems to be "excess passive income" (for example, royalty income derived from song or record earnings). An S corporation that was once a C corporation can have its S status revoked if 25% of its income is passive for three years. Once you take out a salary in excess of $400,000 or $500,000, you are beginning to push the envelope and you may draw the attention of an IRS auditor.

S corporations still have to file corporate tax returns (1120S). Whereas, for the most part, they do not pay federal corporate taxes, there may be no way to avoid state or city corporate taxes. For example, New York City does not recognize S corporations. The state and city tax can exceed 8% and you cannot reduce profits to zero (thereby absolving your corporation any obligation to pay corporate taxes) simply by paying out high salaries. In New York City, there is an alternative tax that is charged without regard to whether or not your corporation even *had* a profit.

Pros and Cons: C Corporation, S Corporation, and LLC Let's explore first how C corporations and S corporations handle profits in the situation in which a company grosses $100,000 and has $20,000 in expenses.

If your company is a traditional C corporation, there will be $80,000 left. If $50,000 is paid out to you or to your band members, federal corporate taxes will be payable on approximately $30,000. There are two sets of tax returns to be prepared and filed: the corporation's and yours and those of your band members. If the corporation purchases capital equipment, only a certain percentage of the cost of that equipment can be expensed in the year it is purchased; taxes must be paid on the remainder. So, for example, if the corporation purchases a Pro-Tools rig for $25,000, it may be allowed to deduct 10%, or $2,500, as expenses in the year it is purchased, leaving 90%, or $22,500, spent but not deductible. (This is called *depreciation of a capital asset*.) There will be federal and state corporate taxes payable that year not only on the $30,000 referred to above, but also on the $22,500 as if it were income—which of course, as a practical matter, it is not. There may not be money left in the coffers of the corporation to pay the taxes on the $52,500. Indeed, if the $30,000 is also paid out as salary to you or to you and your band members, there won't. This reality must be taken into account each time the corporation purchases something of lasting value, such as a guitar or a van, or even if it makes capital improvements to a rehearsal hall.

If your company is an S corporation, the $80,000 will constitute income and will be divided among your band mates. Each band member will be taxed whether or not the member takes the money. This means that if some of the money is left in the corporation for contingencies or future expenses, the shareholders will nevertheless be taxed as if they had taken the money themselves. Each shareholder files his or her own tax return. There is no corporate tax return to be prepared or filed. Each of the band members can deal with his or her share of the $80,000 in whatever creative tax-planning manner they see fit—for example, paying some money into an IRA or 401(k)—and the aggregate tax paid may be well under the tax that the C corporation would have to pay. The capital equipment purchases, unfortunately, are dealt with in the same way as with the C corporation, but this time each individual shareholder has to bear his or her share of the portion that the government does not allow to be deducted as an expense (in my earlier example, 90% of $25,000, or $22,500).

Another area in which taxes will be payable on earnings never actually received is in the area of health insurance. At the end of the year, band members are faced with the fact that what their corporations paid to the insurance company for health insurance is taxed to them personally *as income*.

Those band members with extra money are able to bear the burdens of paying taxes on the nondepreciable portion of a capital asset, or on health insurance costs never actually passing through their bank accounts. Those with little money are not. Those who earn extra money through songwriting income will be better off than those who do not; those who are married presumably will be less well off than those who are not if their incomes have to be shared among their family members. In fact, the economic disparity among band members may be even more glaring after a year of S corporation activity than it would have been after a year of C corporation activity.

I am beginning to sound like Tevya in *Fiddler on the Roof*, who was fond of saying "On the one hand . . . on the other hand . . . on the other hand . . . etc." But here it is: The C corporation may in fact be more advantageous to you in this situation than the S corporation. For example, you can move money around more easily within a C corporation, and you can establish a *fiscal* tax year, which does not have to run from January 1 to December 31. You can have your corporate tax year begin in September and end at the end of August. Thus, if the corporation expects to receive a lot of money in December, instead of having to pay taxes on this by April 15 at the latest, the taxes can be delayed until, let's say, October 15, or even later, by virtue of your having manipulated the tax year. The S corporation has to maintain a traditional calendar year tax period. In addition, if you are thinking of having investors in your business, they would be far more comfortable with a C corporation or an LLC than with an S corporation structure, which is more suitable when there are a tiny number of shareholders. Even though you are permitted up to seventy-five shareholders in an S corporation, one to five is the norm among entertainers.

A partnership does not pay salaries to partners. Their share of profits is paid out as a profit participation, and a K-1, rather than a W-2, is issued by the partnership. An S corporation, being essentially a partnership, may elect not to pay salaries, but it is usually good business practice to pay out something in the form of salaries so that the self-employment tax (Social Security and Medicare combined) is paid first by the corporation and, subsequently, by the employee/shareholder as well. The IRS likes this. Under current rules, the first $90,000 of one's salary is subject to the social security tax of 6.2% and the Medicare tax of 1.45%. If your S corporation pays you a salary of $90,000, the government will be pleased because you will have caused the Social Security contribution to be made both by your corporation and by yourself, rather than just by yourself, which would be the case if your entire "salary" had been distributed to you as a share of profits. The Social Security system will have been enhanced accordingly by your "employment." A problem arises, however, with regard to the Medicare portion of the self-employment tax. This portion does not have a cap of $90,000 or, for that matter, any cap. Therefore, if you limit the portion of your profit distribution to $90,000, you will be depriving the government of the employer's portion of the Medicare tax on any excess. Many accountants will therefore recommend that you take out a salary in excess of $90,000—a good-faith attempt to take care of your federal responsibilities, even though you are probably not required to do so.

The *limited liability corporation (LLC)* provides for profit-sharing arrangements that used to be available only in limited partnerships, but it also provides the limited liability that used to be available only in C and S corporations. It is a hybrid and one that has proved extremely popular for small businesses and newly formed companies such as are the norm in the entertainment business. The LLC form is uniquely beneficial to artists who want to raise money from investors either for general career purposes or to pay for recording a master or demo.

In the past, the only protection afforded investors in a partnership was for the limited partners; the general partners (who operated the company) were personally responsible for the debts of the partnership. The limited partners were merely passive investors. Under the LLC, the general partner's equivalent, usually called the *managing member*, has the same unlimited personal liability protection afforded to those investors who are the equivalent of the limited partners in a traditional partnership.

If you want to put together a film, it is relatively easy to form an LLC that has an investor member and a managing member. To do this in a C or S corporation, you would have to have a shareholders' agreement, an annual board of directors meeting, an annual election of the officers, etc. In an LLC, you can have meetings and elections as often or as infrequently as you like.

It is relatively easy to switch from a partnership structure, which until recently was the preferred structure for bands, to an LLC. By doing this, you will have traded a general partnership with no liability protection for an LLC with absolute liability protection. In some states you do not even need to prepare and sign an operating agreement establishing how the company is to be operated. (Of course, having one is appropriate if there is more than one shareholder.)

There has been some resistance in the bigger money markets to public offerings by LLCs. Financiers who are comfortable with the old system tend to resist new structures. The LLC is less of a structure and more of a conduit. Its house is not built of brick and mortar. It does not yell out solidity, thrift, durability. It is worth noting that although technically, no corporate book, no seal, and no stock certificates are required, corporate stationery companies are not going bankrupt; they still create a virtual "corporate kit"—replete with a sample operating agreement and a seal. Although not necessary, it works for organizational purposes and makes people feel comfortable. Now, I am told, even certificates of member-ship interest (shades of stock certificates) are provided in the "LLC kit," and the managing member will often call him- or herself "president" rather than explain why there isn't any. These are all vestigial remains of the old days.

Despite the resistance to the LLC structure in some quarters, the LLC is beginning to replace the traditional C or S corporation as the vehicle used for furnishing services of artists, producers, and other creative talent.

Enter the IRS

Corporations are often established to provide the services of a creative person to a user of talent. This practice permits flexibility within the tax laws without drawing unwanted attention from the IRS. However, these "loan-out" or "furnishing" companies raise certain issues that might not be present were the client to have simply provided his or her services personally. Remember my warnings about inadvertently creating a personal holding company.

Having a corporation furnish the services of an artist, or having it own and administer one's copyrights, involves establishing, somewhat arbitrarily, a salary for the artist whose artistic creations or compensation rights are integrated into the corporation. Suppose a corporation is set up to furnish a record producer's services and to collect the producer's advances and royalties, and after a year or so, the advances and royalties amount to $400,000. The costs of operating the corporation are minimal—perhaps some equipment, legal and accountancy fees, and maybe some incidental expenses such as unreimbursed travel and accommodation costs incurred while seeking new business. Let's say these total $50,000. The balance remaining in the corporation's coffers at the end of the year will be $350,000.

Now, the business manager decides to pay out to the producer the entire $350,000 as a salary, and the producer pays taxes on this as an individual. But the IRS comes in and says, "You know, that's an awful lot of money for you to earn as a salary; we think your two months in the studio should be worth about $150,000 and that's a wonderful annual salary for an executive of this tiny corporation." Where is your employment contract, they might ask? How can you possibly justify a $350,000 salary for such a wimpy contribution of time and effort—on a Caribbean Island no less (like the legendary Nassau studio of

Island Records, Compass Sound). Put simply, the IRS does not like an individual owner of a corporation taking 100% of the money out of it for "salary."

So the corporation agrees with the IRS that the producer's salary should be $150,000. What happens to the remaining $200,000? Why, it is put back into the corporation . . . , except for one problem. You can't put back what you have taken out. The corporation winds up with a profit that year of $200,000, which is subject to a tax of more than 50%. And, once you take out of a corporation that which is not yours, it constitutes a dividend; this is further taxed so that in the end you have your $150,000 (salary), which is subject to ordinary income tax, and $200,000, which is absolutely decimated. A dangerous game.

Beyond this, there is the reality that by the time the IRS gets around to informing you that it has disallowed a portion of your salary, you will have incurred incredible amounts of interest and penalties. And that's just the federal tax. Now the state steps in and charges even more taxes, interest, and penalties, and for entertainers who work in many states, there can be multiple state taxes due as a result of an unfavorable ruling by the IRS. There may be city taxes as well (as is the case in New York City).

Worse still, your behavior may trigger a general audit, not only for the year in question but for years down the road. The IRS can go back only three years (unless fraud or substantial underreporting is involved, in which case it can go back much longer), but it can continue to knock on your door forever. It is not unusual for the IRS to audit taxpayers for as many as five consecutive years once they get started. Your cost for accounting services to assist you in dealing with all of these government agencies can be enormous.

What were your options in the first place? You could have avoided a corporation, but once the corporation is formed, and once used to funnel your income from personal services, the potential of steep taxation exists.

Given all of the potential problems associated with incorporating—no matter what kind of corporate structure you choose—it remains beyond my comprehension why so many people in the music industry want to create a new taxable entity when there is no compelling reason to do so. I don't mean to suggest that there are *never* times and reasons to form one. For example, it may be good business and sound legal management to form a corporation for touring purposes, to limit liability if someone is hurt at a show. But suffice it to say that walking away from your business manager's office on the first day carrying a corporate "set" of books and seals (not the animal kind) might not turn out to be exactly the thrill you thought it would be. And I suggest that musicians, songwriters, and producers should be highly suspicious of any business manager whose *specialty* is creating corporations.

As I have said, conducting a business through a corporate structure does not legitimize it, and doing so can *add* to your problems rather than solve them. It creates new burdens, and at the same time may not relieve you of old ones. It creates new work and costs that were not there before. It can not only be costly, but, potentially, *devastatingly* expensive.

I think I have made my point.

MONEY MEANS OPTIONS: RESISTING THE "KEEP 'EM POOR" PHILOSOPHY

When others are handling your money, anything is possible, and everything under the sun has happened to someone you know or have read about. Therefore, I feel it is necessary to describe a particular horrifying scenario. As you read on, keep in mind that if you choose your advisors wisely, and pay attention to what they are doing, this won't happen to you.

There is an old music business adage: keep 'em poor. Why? Because then they have to work. And if they work, they earn gross income. And if they earn gross income, the manager and business manager (and more and more frequently, the lawyer) will commission it. A client who is content, satisfied, and financially comfortable is not as likely to go back to the drudgery of "the road." The last thing commissioning professionals want is for their clients to retire.

Commissions are only applied against what artists earn, not what their investments generate, and therein lies a potential for abuse. Even if the client is in debt, the "gross" commissioning professional cannot lose—and therein lies another potential for abuse.

A client wants a new car. He has one by noon the same day. A client wants a new house. He has his mortgage in twenty-four hours. The business manager has done magic for him. But weren't we all taught there is no such thing as magic? There isn't. There is a cost for this convenience. A client may receive her mortgage approval in twenty-four hours, but may not be able to handle the carrying charges.

Some clients believe that if they have *some* money, they can do most anything; if they have a *lot* of money, they can do everything. This is categorically untrue. Although a fledgling artist may qualify for a car or house loan on paper, once the mortgage has been approved, the artist may end up with unmanageable cash-flow problems. The more you have, the more you can squander. If you had to be careful *before* you achieved your first successful financial goal, you will have to be even more careful afterward.

There is one caveat to this "budget alert." Sometimes artists are so bull-headed that a business manager can do only so much to protect them. Some artists simply do not want to live on a budget, or even think about retirement. (After all, they have just *begun* to live!) Ultimately, their business managers have to say, "Enough with the wise financial advice. Let them be happy." If clients are determined to consciously reject making the right decisions, what can a business manager do? Take away their credit cards? Give them a limited-amount debit card? Take away their toys? I don't think so. My advice to these well-meaning souls is, "Just make sure you have made it abundantly clear to the clients—and often—what the consequences of their actions are likely to be. Hopefully, they will come to terms with reality sooner rather than later."

At the same time, too many people telling an artist that he or she does not know anything about anything results in a certain deafness (and, I would say, an understandable deafness). Sometimes the best that a conscientious business manager can do is keep the artist, the artist's family, if possible, and the artist's other representatives advised of the status of the artist's business. This should be enough to ward off disasters while accepting that it is the client, after all, who has the *right* to be wrong.

MANAGING YOUR MONEY

Everyone has trends. Expense trends and income trends. Among the most important functions of a business manager is to identify these trends and to guide the client's expenditures and investment opportunities accordingly. Predicting trends on the basis of data gathered over a reasonably long period is relatively easy. This is especially true with respect to artists whose biggest income-producing years are behind them but who are continuing to receive significant income from catalogue sales. It is less easy—but nonetheless important—to predict trends for artists who are in the beginning—more erratic—stages of their careers.

INVESTING: IS ANYONE IN CHARGE HERE?

Let's say that you have invested your career-long savings in an IRA. How is it invested? Who is paying attention? Is it invested in a money market fund at 4.5%? Is it deposited into one, undiversified, mutual fund with the business manager's favorite broker in charge of it?

Are your investments, though sound or even shrewd, consistent with your own value system and principles? Is a portion of your portfolio invested in Philip Morris? Is this something you, who have proselytized about the dangers of smoking or alcohol, want disclosed in a tabloid or industry rag? Maybe Delta Airlines? Enron, anyone? There is no surefire investment strategy that works for everyone. But there are guidelines that you and your representatives can follow and options to consider no matter what stage of your career you are in.

The danger young artists face is to be so tunnel-visioned that they focus only on their music or their fans or their live performances, while all the people around them—their lawyers and business and personal managers—are so buried in the day-to-day effort to make all of these things work in tandem that no one is paying attention to either the economic or the tax consequences of what they are doing—or not doing.

Although the following information on investments is applicable to everyone from every walk of life, I have included it in this book because many artists, record producers, and even managers, especially those who are beginning their careers, make unwise investment decisions (or no investment decisions at all) or have unwise investment decisions made for them.

Types of Investments

Let's say you have a $10,000 surplus in your bank account. Do you want to invest it? To keep it under the mattress? And if you choose to invest it, what do you want to get out of it? The safety of knowing that the entire $10,000 will still be there when you need it? Growth? Super-growth? And what are the down-the-road tax consequences of decisions you make today? How does the rate of inflation affect your investments and your goals? These are things that you need to determine, with the informed help of your advisors.

Fixed-Interest Vehicles   Certificates of deposit (CDs) are time deposits issued by a bank at a fixed interest rate for a period of time—three months, one year, five years—whatever is offered. When considering investing in CDs, you need to consider what can be serious tax consequences. If you buy a one-year CD with your $10,000 at a 5% interest rate (I will use 5% to simplify the math although since the recession of 2007, interest on CDs has barely exceeded 2%—and that for a ten-year CD!), your return will be $500. At the end of the year, you will also get a Form 1099, a copy of which has been filed with the IRS, stating what you have earned in interest. (The same thing happens if you hold mutual funds in a taxable, versus a retirement, account.) If you are in a 50% tax bracket (federal, state, and city combined), you will owe the various governments $250, and your bottom-line return on your investment is not 5%, but 2.5%. (One rule of thumb about investment growth is called the rule of 70: Divide 70 by the current interest rate, and the result is the number of years it will take you to double your money. In my example, taking into account taxes paid, it would take twenty-eight years. A long time.) That $250 you paid in taxes could have been used for further investment or purchase of growth assets—or it could have been applied toward your winter vacation. But it is lost forever once the tax is incurred. Then again, the CD is safe and federally insured. A growth fund is not. As with all investments, performance is a balance between risk and reward: with a CD, there is little risk, little reward. And note that if you retain the CD, or its term extends, for more than one year, you will not be able to pull the $250 out of it in order to pay your income taxes. The income from a CD is the same as ordinary income. You have to make $500 to keep $250. But in the case of CDs, you will have to find the $250 somewhere else. And, since you are in a high tax bracket, you will have to have earned $500 more dollars in order to keep $250 long enough to send it to the IRS to pay the taxes due on the gain in the CD. This situation is not dissimilar to the ones earlier noted where you have to pay taxes of undepreciated capital assets, or the value of the health insurance paid on your behalf. It is all counted as income even if you never "receive" it.

Say you earn $240,000 in interest from a CD and have to pay $120,000 in taxes. This $120,000 is gone forever. Consider the following scenario. If the $240,000 were invested in a stable stock fund and allowed to grow at 10% a year (on average, about what the stock market has historically done), it would be worth $264,000 at the end of one year, $290,400 at the end of two years, $319,440 at the end of three years, $351,384 after four years, and $386,522 after five years. In order for the $120,000 remaining after taxes to build up to essentially the same level ($240,000), you would need to achieve growth of more than 25% for each of those five years—a growth rate that has never happened. Then again, the stock fund is not insured. Risk and reward again.

Individual Retirement Accounts The returns you get on the money you have invested in an individual retirement account (IRA) or 401(k) retirement account are not taxed until you pull the money out of them. The annual contribution limits for IRAs depend, in part, on the age of the contributor. In 2006–2007, the maximum allowable amount an individual can deposit into his or her IRA is $4,000 if the person is under fifty years old, and $5,000 if the person is fifty or older. In 2008, the amounts are $5,000 and $6,000, respectively. The deposits need not be made all at once as long as the total for the year does not exceed the allowable amount. You cannot deposit in one year the maximum amount *plus* the amount you were deficient in a previous year, in which you deposited less than the maximum.

Individual retirement accounts are tax-deferred, not tax-free, vehicles. If you take money out of your retirement fund before you are fifty-nine years old, you are taxed according to whatever tax bracket you are in, plus 10%. After age fifty-nine, you are taxed only according to your income bracket. But consider this. Not only are IRAs *not* tax free, they are not even safe havens. You *must* start taking money out of your IRA by April 1st in the year following the calendar year in which you turn seventy. The *amount* you must withdraw is determined by an actuarial schedule that takes into account how long the government thinks you have left to live. The trick is to live precisely as long as the government expects you to. If you disappoint them and die later, while you may not have any money left to pull out, they will not have the chance to penalize you for failing to take it all out before you die. Because when you die, if you still have money in your retirement fund, it will be taxed in the same way as income is taxed, according to what is known as "income in respect of decedent." There are possible estate taxes as well that may be assessed. The rules are complex, and unless you are an accounting whiz as well as an artist, you should make sure your business manager or account is keeping a watchful eye on your IRA.

Stocks and Bonds A *stock* is an ownership interest—a share—in a company. Stock is issued by the company to raise money that the company does not have to guarantee to pay back at any particular price. By owning stock in a company, you actually have a claim on the company's assets. These are sometimes paid out in regular dividends. Some companies do not pay dividends and your only gain comes when the stock value increases (appreciates) and you sell it. You lose when the stock value decreases (depreciates) and you sell it. Stock prices go up when the company's profits go up or there is a generally accepted expectation that they will. And vice versa. You can own stock directly in a company or through a *mutual fund*, which itself holds an array of stocks from different companies, and/or various types of bonds.

A *bond* is what you receive after you have lent money to a corporation, a municipality, or the US government in return for a promise to pay you back the loan at a certain date in the future. In the interim, the party issuing the bond and receiving your money agrees to pay you a fixed rate of interest at regular intervals, usually semiannually. Most often, you never see your bonds; they are maintained by your broker or are accumulated in mutual bond funds. As market forces change, the value of bonds changes.

The ins and outs of stock and bond purchasing and trading are complex, and rather than become an expert in yet another field outside of your own, you may want to select a broker (yet another licensed professional) to perform this function for you. One more to add to the team. But how do you know if the securities recommended by a particular broker are really the best ones for you, your income, your cash flow, and your tax situation? You don't, but your business manager can help guide you. The market is a casino. Be careful.

Let's say you buy a fund that specializes in the blue chips—stocks issued by the traditionally most stable corporations. All of these generate dividends that themselves may reflect a decent percentage, such as 3% to 4% of the value of the stocks. But you don't see the dividends. They are reinvested in the fund and contribute to its appearance of growth. Then you get a 1099. This represents the dividends that you earned during the prior year, another form of taxable income you have not actually received. If your fund has gone up, you will say, "Hey, I'm paying taxes because my fund went up. So what?" And your broker is making fees on the maintenance of the fund and your portfolio? Same thing. What do you care? Your fund went up. You ignore these two costs because everything that is presented to you shows that you are *making* money. If you don't have the cash to pay the taxes, you can sell some of your shares in the mutual fund (at a profit, remember). No problem!

Then come years like 2000, or 2008–2009, or even the summer of 2015 when China's apparent invincibility dissolved, throwing a wrench into an eight-year bull market, when the value of mutual stock funds went down! Yet, even as investors were looking at the sad state of their portfolios at the end of the year, they received 1099s showing what the IRS calls "gain." Taxable gain. These were the dividends they never saw. They had to find the money to pay the tax on the gain even though their money was still tied up in the mutual funds and they didn't have the cash to pay the tax out of their other resources. Naturally, they were reluctant to sell their shares at their low point. It was not a happy situation.

When you look at a mutual fund prospectus, it will show you a chart. Had you invested $10,000 in 1972, it would have grown to $X by now. All the mutual funds have nice charts. Lots of dot matrixes. They show that during the oil embargo, in 1964, the value would have been $Y; when Reagan was president, it would have been $Z. But they never show you that each year you would have gotten a 1099, so the *real* growth would have been only one-half of what shows on the chart. Figure it out.

Let's go back to the $500 generated by a $10,000 CD, which was discussed earlier in the chapter. If you did not have to pay the tax, you would have had the $500 back in your pocket as well as all of the options that you no longer have because the $500 that was generated to multiple federal taxes as well as state and, often, city taxes as well. The loss is not just the tax you had to pay; it represents a lost opportunity as well: the opportunity to use the $500 more effectively.

People rarely factor in the potential for loss. Dreamers *never* do. Many wealthy investors allocated their assets so poorly in the late 1990s that when the NASDAQ dropped, they lost everything. Why should artists be expected to act any more wisely?

This brings us back to sound advice and counsel from your—the artist's—business managers. They will tell you that markets do not rise in a straight line—nor do they usually fall in a straight line. A 10% average over five years may have been achieved by one year of 15% growth, one at minus 3%, one at 0%, two at 6%, and one at 26%. Markets don't move in consistent ways. They do not perform at 10%, 10%, 10%, 10%, and 10%. They never will.

People will tell you that, except for income-producing real estate, there is no return like the stock market over time. This was essentially true prior to 2000. But, as we have seen, *average* return and *actual* return are not the same. Furthermore, losses count more than gains and if you lose money and have a bad experience, you may be scared off the market forever and that is a loss that you cannot calculate. For example, if you lost money simply because the economy went south for a while, or you had a personal need for emergency money and you could not get it out of the market without taking a horrible loss, you might tire very quickly of the market as a resource for your financial well-being.

You may be thinking, "Well, I am very computer savvy and I am becoming fairly expert at dealing with E*TRADE. Why can't I do it myself?" Outside of the fact that you should be doing what you do best—writing, performing, managing, producing, whatever—why do you think that you can possibly do as well as a professional? Handicapping stocks is a complex process. Sure, when the market is going up at the rate of 30% a year, which it did in the late 1990s, you don't have to be a genius to grow your portfolio. But I suggest that spending money to get *good* advice on your investments is well worth it. Even if your broker commissions purchases and sales, it is money well spent. You should still shop around for the lowest commission rates. Online services have made strides in this area and should be seriously considered as an option. And if the uncertainty among average investors is not enough to make you wary, consider legendary financial historian and investment advisor Peter Bernstein's famous warning: "We don't know what's going to happen with anything, ever."

MAKING IT AND SAVING IT

Beware of Greeks bearing gifts. Remember the Trojan horse? How about those millionaire lottery winners? Once you start making money that you do not need for your living expenses, there are going to be a million people wanting to latch onto you.

Just as in all businesses, there are good guys and bad guys. Hundreds of thousands of people have passed the securities exam. Even Martha Stewart. But what is their motivation? Are they interested in you as a person, a husband, a father, a breadwinner—a rock star? Or are they dancing to your music as they charge you big-time fees? You have to use all of your talents of perception to consider the motivation of your representatives. There are those who will tell you that stockbrokers merely sell the flavor of the day—that if they were really that good, they would be traders—or analysts. This is obviously an oversimplification. But whenever you put your money into the hands of someone who can control its activity, you are taking a risk. Not necessarily an unreasonable one, but a risk nonetheless. And you had better be sure about the person you hope will steer you around or through that risk.

Consider the fees and expenses of maintaining your portfolio. Brokers' primary motivation is not necessarily to make money for people; it is to generate activity in accounts. I am not saying that they "churn" the accounts, but they themselves do not make any money unless they are buying and selling, that is, unless your assets move in your account. They get a percentage of every purchase and every sale. At their worst, they meet in the morning and say this is what we're going to sell today. They often do not do adequate research, and you are as anonymous as the rest of their clients. One thing is certain: in essence, they are salespeople. Often they are under pressure from their superiors to sell products that offer higher commission payouts. A friend of mine who works in the investment field says that brokers are in the moving business, not the storage business.

Remember, growth funds such as mutual stock or mutual bond funds are not federally insured by the Federal Deposit Insurance Corporation, the Federal Reserve Board, or any other government agency. And it would serve you well to also acknowledge that stocks and bonds gain, and lose, value for both direct and indirect, good and bad reasons. A company may announce horrible numbers, such as earnings, or there might be a flare-up in the Middle East affecting oil prices and, accordingly, the entire economy of the United States. Most troubling is when stock analysts devalue a company's shares (for example, Apple in 2012 when the so-called "new" iPad was offered for sale) because of extraneous stress tests applied. In Apple's case, 1,250 people had lined up at its Fifth Avenue flagship store in 2011 to buy the iPad 2. Only 750 people showed up in 2012 following the launch of the follow-up. The analysts disregarded the fact that presales were abundant with the new iPad, though not even available for the iPad 2, and that since 2011, two other huge Apple stores had opened within blocks of the flagship store—one right in the middle of Grand Central Station, the arrival and departure point of many of the former customers of the Fifth Avenue store.

Owning foreign securities is even more risky.

Am I suggesting that you revert to the mattress method of savings? No, of course not. But I would be remiss if I did not point out the dangers that should, at the minimum, be investigated and addressed before you risk your hard-earned capital.

Real Estate

I do not mean to ignore what for many has been the wisest investment of all: real estate. But therein lie many surprises. Experts in the valuation of properties often miss, but they are often corporations using bank money. Individuals who take these risks should follow two simple conservative rules: first, buy something that has value to YOU—that is, as a home or even a vacation or weekend home, and second, buy something that has inherent value: something along a beach front; an 18th-century house that will always be unique to some future purchaser; a property in a neighborhood where property is so rare that it is bound to make a comeback (sooner or later, even if much later); a house that with a little paint, a SubZero refrigerator, and some minor repairs can be returned to its former level of quality (for example, a stone barn) on five to ten acres of land. As low as interest rates have been since the recession of 2007, the interest rates on mortgages in 2012 have hovered around 3% to 5% depending on (1) the size of the loan, (2) the term of the loan, and (3) whether the rate is fixed for ten, twenty, or thirty years, or whether it is susceptible of arbitrary or agreed increase after a set amount of time.

Savings Accounts

And then there are savings accounts. Guaranteed up to $100,000 each by the federal government, the interest rates after 2007 have been minuscule—not even keeping up with the low rate of inflation, thus resulting in a net loss of purchasing power as the years go on if nothing were to change. In 2012, the best money market (super savings accounts) rates were LESS than 1%. Normal savings account rates were even less than that.

Deferred Payments Versus Cash on the Barrelhead

Successful young artists who suddenly come into more money than they have ever had in their lives are at risk of blowing most or all of it on cars, companions, or even a home recording studio that may be a luxury in view of their particular circumstances. So a business manager asks, "How can my client not take so much now and get used to having less money so later on there will be some left—especially if things do not work out as hoped careerwise?"

One answer is to defer payments. Like anything else, there are pros and cons to deferring payments. No taxes are payable on deferred payments. Then again, you have lost the opportunity to build the deferred money into a larger sum because you do not control it. So an alternative route would be to take the money when offered, provided that you are disciplined enough not to spend all of it. A good business manager will encourage you to have some kind of savings plan from day one. Combine this with the overwhelming odds that you are likely to fail *despite* how talented you may be, and you can begin to see why it would be smart to follow Grandmother's advice to put away some money for a rainy day.

One of the psychologically enticing aspects of having lots of money in your pocket when you are young is that it makes you feel as if you are on top of the world. You are likely to spend it all on things that are not enduring—that is, *not* on real estate or sound investments. Or you may think that your advisors are warning you to save because they do not believe in you. This is simply not true. They are telling you this because they care about you and know the reality of the situation. They are looking at things with a less romanticized vision than you are—which is not only sensible, but it is also what you want in a financial advisor. A business manager who says, "Let's put away some money" is saying it because he or she has seen people less (and more) talented than you and less (and more) lucky than you *not* succeed. Your manager wants to make sure that you are covered no matter what happens.

Insurance

In all likelihood, insurance protection is something that your business manager will be responsible for. As noted earlier, the business manager's aura of protection goes beyond your work—into your life.

In the past, business managers worked closely with one or more insurance agents to identify and secure the best insurance for their clients at the lowest cost: homeowners' (covering risk of theft, loss due to fire, etc.); automobile; an umbrella policy giving you an added layer of protection; and life insurance. They were not meant to profit from the choice or amount of insurance obtained, but sometimes they did, and no one—certainly not the client—was the wiser. Recently, the American Institute of CPAs changed the rules that had prohibited CPAs who are AICPA-certified from being agents for insurance companies. Now it is permitted, and the client is suddenly faced with a potential conflict of interest. If the business manager benefits from the policies he or she secures for the client, how does the client know that the advice being given is valid?

The good news is that whereas in the past clients would never know for certain that they had all of the requisite insurance to protect their assets and their heirs, now, most certainly, they will. And for the first time, insurance fees are split with your financial advisors, and this practice, and its cost, are right up there in plain sight—on the balance sheets proffered by your business manager. He or she is being paid. So what. Everyone else who provides a service is getting paid.

Life Insurance   Although there are many books and Internet articles that cover the subject of life insurance, I am giving it special attention here, in the chapter on managing your business, because the entertainment industry in general and the music industry in particular is a high-risk arena: there is a high risk of failure, of early burnout, and, sadly, of early death or disability. Musicians are always under pressure to write more music, record more hits; they have to tour and tour and tour. Drug abuse has been an occupational hazard for over a century. As a result, some artists become uninsurable at a relatively young age.

The lesson here is that any artist, songwriter, record producer, or manager who secures life insurance early has successfully "buried" a sum of money, that is, put the money away into a protected place, where it will be available no matter what happens down the road. That person will not have to pay taxes on the cash value of the policy as it grows. And in many states, the value of a life insurance policy is protected from creditors in bankruptcy proceedings. Life insurance, then, can be regarded as one kind of investment vehicle, and should be carefully considered by the artist and the artist's representatives so that an informed decision can be made.

There are essentially two kinds of life insurance: term and whole life. *Term insurance* is what it sounds like: insurance against an early demise that expires at some specific point in the future. If you die within that time, fine. If you die after that time, you're not only dead, but your estate or beneficiary does not receive the insurance. The appealing thing about term insurance is that it appears to be cheap. But once the term ends, it is over and there is no residual value remaining. *Whole life insurance*, on the other hand, appears to be expensive, but it actually works as an investment vehicle in that its cash value grows over a period of years. You can cash in your whole life insurance policy at any time, or borrow against it. Once fully paid, the policy remains in effect until you die, at which point the insurance company will pay your beneficiary the face value of the policy. What does all this have to do with you?

Consider the following scenario. A young artist wants some of the advance monies from his or her record contract to be used to purchase life insurance. The recording relationship lasts for three or four years, then the artist is dropped from the label. If the artist has purchased whole life insurance, the payments will be very expensive; if for term, they will not be. Thus we see some justification in favor of term insurance, at least at the beginning of an artist's career. Artists who subsequently make it big can convert the term policies into whole life and build equity; if they fail, the policy will end or they can keep it going for far less money than a whole life policy would have cost.

Alternatively, let us imagine that the record company can buy a whole-life cash-value life insurance policy. The company fronts enough money in the first year or two of the recording agreement for the policy to be fully funded, and does not require any further premiums for it to remain in force; the cash value can be borrowed against. The artist can now continue making payments, or, if the relationship with the record company continues, the record company can. Theoretically, this policy can be paid off quickly and it will last for the artist's lifetime. Now *that's* planning.

Note that up-front payments of a life insurance policy's premiums may have unfavorable tax consequences. However, there are ways to avoid an acute tax problem for you. Your business manager will know how.

Let's say a recording artist has succeeded over the years and makes a bundle of money year after year after year on his or her catalogue of records and/or songs. The artist's business manager wants to invest prudently. But maybe having an IRA is *not* prudent. Is an IRA creating wealth for the artist or is it just sitting there, not doing anything except grow at a snail's pace? Maybe this particular artist does not need an IRA at all. Recall that at age seventy and a half, the artist must start withdrawing the money, or be taxed on it anyway.

Suppose, instead of putting money in an IRA, the artist purchases a $5 million life insurance policy. By the time he or she reaches seventy years, this policy can be worth $10 million dollars! At that point, the artist can live high on the hog because the policy, at his or her death, will be worth so much. Without such a policy, the artist must be careful not to spend too much, so that enough will be left for his or her heirs. Putting it simply, the policy makes the artist richer.

There is another advantage to choosing this option. If the artist's advisors gamble wrong and royalties stop, the policy still has value and the artist can borrow against it or cash it in. (There are ways to withdraw money out of a life insurance policy without paying tax on the withdrawals.)

7 • WHEN YOUR JOB IS MORE THAN A GIG
Employment Agreements and Disagreements

Blessed is he who expects nothing, for he shall never be disappointed.
—JONATHAN SWIFT

For most of us, inherited wealth is not the way we will end up providing for ourselves, our families, and our progeny. This will come only through our own hard work and income. Therefore, if one is fortunate enough to be offered an important, well-paying position at a company in one's field of choice, there is no legal document in one's work life more important than the employment agreement. Being offered an employment contract and signing one (or more) are seminal events in an executive's life. Many provisions in employment agreements are standard, no matter what industry the company is in, and to provide a context for employment contract provisions that are of special concern to the music industry professional, I will first review many of the customary provisions in standard employment agreements. As some of these can mean financial success or failure for the employee signing the contract, it is crucial for the employee—and his or her advisors—to pay careful attention to all of them, including so-called "boilerplate" provisions.

TERM OF EMPLOYMENT

Assuming an employee is confident of his or her abilities, it is obvious that if that employee can keep the term shorter, rather than longer, his or her options will be increased many times over. In employment agreements, the word *options* is usually used to describe the right of the employer to determine whether to extend the term of the agreement. Surprisingly, even some of those whom one might consider the more savvy first-time contracting executives do not initially understand this. The right of the employer to control the length of the term of the agreement is a very powerful tool used by employers to wield power over their employees.

Of course, some executives, for security or other reasons, may prefer that the term be longer rather than shorter. Given the mercurial nature of some industries—including the music industry—even if an executive is confident in his or her ability, three to five years of guaranteed salary and bonuses do not look so bad. An additional reason some employees prefer to contract for a longer term is that a longer term will affect the magnitude of the payout in the event of early termination.

DUTIES

While the title of the person who is being hired is usually set forth in the agreement, it is not always clear what that person's responsibilities are, what the reporting lines are, and, ironically, what kind of flexibility the employee has in actually fulfilling his or her responsibilities—or even going beyond them in exceeding the expectations of the employer. It is important for the employee, and the person he or she is to report to, to talk through these issues and to find a way to clarify any ambiguities and to incorporate their understandings and expectations into the written document.

Here is an excerpt from a typical—and typically ambiguous—employment contract:

> Employee shall have all the authority and responsibility customarily associated with such position in a company of the size and nature of the Employer.

> During the term, Executive shall devote substantially all of his business time and his efforts, business judgment, skill and knowledge exclusively to the advancement of the business and interests of the Company and to the discharge of his duties and responsibilities hereunder.

Clear? Clear as mud. And the consequences—in terms of the provisions in the termination section of the contract, which doesn't come up until pages and pages later in the document—can be serious, as one of the bases for termination for cause is the "repeated failure or refusal to materially perform one's duties and responsibilities as set forth in this agreement." There are two things you or your representative need to consider here: securing what are called "notice and cure" provisions, which require the company to tell you of a problem and then give you the opportunity to explain or fix it, and/or articulating with precision what the employee's actual duties are supposed to be. If you do neither, you will have to live with the ambiguity of the "duties" provision and you will be relegated to a negotiation, upon termination, consisting of arguing "on the one hand, on the other hand" with the company's legal department.

REPORTING LINES

One area of concern at the time of the initial negotiation is to ensure that the employee has the right to report to a particular position in the company, for example, the president or the CEO. Prospective employees are not usually allowed to attach the name of a particular person to that position. (So-called "key man" clauses, which provide for this, are anathema to most corporations.) They can, however, try to ensure that no other person will come between them and their functions vis-à-vis the president (or CEO, or vice president of operations, or whomever). Being specific about the position to which the employee is to report protects against the employee's being marginalized or layered by virtue of the placement of another position between the employee and the person to whom he or she was expected to report. The employee may even have aspirations for the higher job—or perhaps was even promised that such advancement was in the cards—but if the employee no longer reports to the person he or she was supposed to report to, the chances of moving up are naturally reduced at best and eliminated at worst.

If the contract specifically addresses this issue and the company doesn't live up to the provisions, a variety of remedies are possible. Some of these will come out of existing applicable law; others may actually be inserted into the contract; for example, the employee will have the option to terminate the agreement—possibly with a penalty assessed against the company. Damages might include the immediate vesting of stock options, a flat-fee payout, the continuation of health-related benefits or compensation so the employee can obtain such benefits elsewhere, a reduction of the ordinary mitigation responsibilities of the employee, and relief from certain post-term responsibilities or restrictions. Another possibility is that a rerelocation provision that was supposed to have expired after a year of employment can be revived.

CONFIDENTIALITY AND COMPETITION

When an employee's skills, experience, and relationships are specialized within any particular industry, the most egregious limitation that can be placed on that person is a prohibition against competing, at a future date, with the company with whom he or she is entering into an agreement.

Anticompetition provisions take several forms and are designed to protect against different outcomes. One such provision seeks to protect against the disclosure, or use for the benefit of others, of any information regarding the activities of his or her employer that is of a secret or confidential nature. This information can take the form of financial information, contracts, contacts, contract proposals and negotiations, plan development, administrative procedures, and dealings with a party with whom the employer has entered into contracts. Obviously, in every field, and in particular in an industry whose "architecture" is essentially closed—such as the music industry—even so-called "private" information is hard to protect. Gossip runs rampant; publications (such as *Hits* magazine) and Internet sites (such as The Velvet Rope) are successful in large part because of their very active rumor mill. Anyone in the music industry, and his or her attorney, must be clear with each other as to the parameters within which they are expected—and willing—to keep a closed mouth. A music industry employee's very strengths may be as a person who knows "everything and everybody," and zipping such a person's mouth may be impossible or counterproductive.

Other anticompetition promises can ruin an employee's chance to make a decent living, or even to stay "in the game" of his or her particular profession, after the term of the employment agreement has expired or is terminated. One is the promise not to work in the employer's business for a specific period of time (it might be two years but could be as long as five, seven, or even ten years) within a limited geographical area (let's say within a radius of fifty miles from the location of that business). This promise is usually sought from someone who is an employee of a business being purchased by another entity; the purchasing company wants to keep the employee on staff for a period of time to help in the transition. Record company executives whose independent record labels are purchased by a major often are required to make this kind of promise. Naturally, to be barred from one's profession for an extended period is something not to take lightly, although the money paid to the promising party is likely to be sufficient for him or her to agree.

The same advantages are not usually offered to professionals who are not entrepreneurs. A second approach to anticompetition promises involve restrictions not on whether, but on how, or the extent to which, the terminated employee can pursue his or her profession. Take, for example, a personal manager, or a producer's manager, whose team has been "adopted" by a company that wishes to take advantage of the employee's experience, contacts, and roster. Restrictions are often placed on the employees such that they cannot solicit the artists (or producers) signed to the umbrella company during the term of the employment for a period of years (usually two or three) once their deal ends with the umbrella company. This can be devastating to people who have spent the past three to five years, say, nurturing the business. In essence, they are left with no one to manage. I alert such managers and their attorneys to be careful to at least provide that any noncompetition provision of this nature be waived if the employer terminates the agreement without cause. Of course, employers are reticent to lift restrictions at least until the date on which the term would naturally have ended if they going to have to pay out the employee's salary to the end of the term anyway. This scenario would occur after, say, they shut down the management division for whatever reason. It is very difficult to deal with a firing without cause. Although the employer usually has to pay out the remainder of its obligations, there is always some damage done to the employee, if only to his or her reputation. Building in a penalty in such situations (such as a waiver of a noncompetition provision) is often a good move.

Another aspect of anticompetition provisions applicable upon departure deals with restrictions on the part of the employee from soliciting other employees or contracting parties and bringing them to the employee's new company (whether a third-party company or the employee's own entrepreneurial venture). There exist many state, federal, and even constitutional provisions that can reduce the impact of such provisions, but a litigation may ensue that can be very expensive in terms of time, money, and the stress it brings to the litigant. At a minimum, you should try to exclude from such prohibition your personal assistant or secretary, or any person whose services are more or less indispensable and not easily replicated. Sometimes the employer may be vengeful enough to refuse to allow you to take an assistant with you, then terminate the assistant's employment shortly thereafter, thereby inconveniencing all concerned *but* the employer.

Finally, an employee may comfortably (or not) agree to refrain from soliciting former colleagues but should not be precluded from hiring them should the colleagues themselves seek such employment on their own volition. I have always been reticent to "steal" a lawyer (or secretary, or paralegal assistant for that matter) from another firm with whom I do business, but once the person announces that he or she is leaving and is going to knock on yet another competitor's door or on mine, I feel no such reluctance. This is a fine point, but it can free up the employee a bit and creates more room for discussion before a real legal claim for violation is brought. It is easy to prove that a former employee violated a "Thou shalt not hire" clause, but it is much harder if the clause is limited to "Thou shalt not solicit." The problem, of course, lies in the proof.

While it may seem premature to deal with down-the-road failure of the employer-employee relationship while negotiating the terms of an employment agreement, there is no better time to protect against possible adverse consequences of termination than when things are rolling along just fine. In instances such as those I have just referred to, the employer may actually still be paying out the employee's salary for the remainder of the contract term (no matter that the employer has shut down the division, fired all staff and assistants, removed the employee from the premises, stopped paying benefits, and stopped reimbursing the employee for expenses incurred on behalf of the employer's business). The employer may feel that, because it is still paying out the employee's salary, it is entitled to any and all anticompetition restrictions. Yet the employee is, in a sense, paralyzed—unable to build his or her profession or pursue new business opportunities. The employee's career is, in a real sense, on hold. The careers of his or her clients are also on hold, and they very well might have no other choice during this period of limbo but to move on and hire other managers to serve their professional needs. Termination without cause followed by full payout of one's salary—even in a lump sum payment—may sound reasonable on paper, but it can be a recipe for tremendous frustration and financial horror if it is not coupled with simultaneous waiver of the other rights that the employer would normally have enjoyed had the employment contract been honored in its entirety. It would not even be outside of the range of fairness to build in a penalty if the promise of the employment term is unfulfilled due to the failure of the company's executives to keep the company afloat. High-level executives (including in-house attorneys) who take a chance with a start-up company often give up solid employment to take the new job and are left in a vulnerable position professionally if the start-up goes belly up.

STOCK OPTIONS

The coming (and going) of the age of the dot-coms has universalized the subject of stock options beyond the bounds of the traditional corporate boardroom. In order to put a value on a stock option offer or even to know what to ask for, a great deal of information is necessary and it is useful to have a business manager familiar with such issues assist your attorney in counseling you as a prospective employee.

Of course, some companies (for example, Bertelsmann AG; Peermusic) are not publicly held companies, and stock options are simply not available to their employees. But there are many ways to "equalize" an offer from a public company with that from a privately held one. The principal way is to seek to ensure that the executive's compensation is commensurate with that of other people at that level in the industry. Participation in compensation programs can take many shapes, and stock options are not necessarily the most advantageous to the employee. This is especially advantageous in cases of termination with—or without—cause.

Following are a few recommendations to those who may be receiving stock options pursuant to an employment contract:

- You may secure acceleration of vesting in the event of a termination other than for cause or in the event of death, disability, or departure for "good reason."

- You may secure accelerated vesting based upon the financial performance of the company (that is, a profit metric or some aggregated stock price appreciation) or the employee's [your] performance or on other specific criteria.

- You should be sure to determine whether the options are qualified under the tax code (that is, they are capable of producing taxable value for you, the employee, at the capital gains rate) or nonqualified (that is, the proceeds will be taxed at ordinary income tax rates).

- Find out the exercise or strike price—the price you have to pay for each share of stock when you exercise the option. This price is usually the market price of the stock on the day you received the option. The difference between the strike price and the current market price on the day you exercise (buy) your stock is taxable in the year the event takes place. This tax will be a problem if the stock you buy is illiquid (does not trade on a public stock exchange). Remember, it's just as if you were holding real estate; you are holding stock, not cash. You may have to sell it to get enough cash to pay the tax, and in closely held, nonpublic companies, it is often difficult, if not impossible, to sell your shares until the company goes public or is bought out.

- Check the vesting schedule to make sure that you are receiving the best possible vesting-rate status vis-à-vis similarly situated personnel.

- Read your stock option plan and make sure your postdeparture option exercise rights are acceptable. Do unvested options lapse? Under what circumstances will you be able to exercise vested options after your departure and for how long postdeparture will this right last? Do you have to exercise the options—that is, buy the stock—on or before your departure or do you have some time after you leave? Suppose, for example, you are forced to exercise the options within, say, thirty days of leaving or lose them. Remember, you will have no job and maybe no cash. If there are taxes due (see the fourth bulleted item above), and you don't have the cash to pay the taxes, you will not be able to afford to exercise the options. Does the plan allow for "cashless" exercises, namely, the right to exercise an option and simultaneously sell the underlying security, thereby enabling you to cover the exercise price out of the sale proceeds? Or must you write a check and fork it over to the company?

Remember, stock options are merely another form of compensation—one that does not require immediate outlay of cash by the employer or the employee. You may prefer to forgo the risk of stock options becoming ultimately valueless by substituting a provision that will provide you with future bonuses to be paid in cold cash.

PERKS

Some perks are based on profitability; some are not. In some areas, parking space counts big time; in others, not at all. In some cities, the lease of a car (especially diesels during gas shortages) matters more to the employee than perhaps any other term of the employment agreement! Other perks include the reimbursement or assumption of attorneys' fees if the employee sues on the contract (and wins); reimbursement for attorneys' fees expended simply to negotiate the employment agreement in the first place; graduate schooling (for example, special weeks' or months' programs at universities for management training; MBA programs; other programs for executives offered by various business schools [sometimes with a cap of $X per year); the cost of a home office (for example, the cost of an up-to-date laptop, cell phone, DSL line); special medical plans, even gardening services and opera tickets (I refer you to Jack Welch's deal as CEO of General Electric).

There are often formulas established for bonuses based on earnings; the assumption of country or university club dues (which are otherwise not deductible by the employee); daily car service; and preferred classes of air travel and hotel accommodation. Sometimes the perks can be as simple (and as useful) as a budget to hire a staff assistant who will make the life of the executive easier and more productive. School fees for children's education is a popular perquisite, one that is nothing less than a necessity in certain cities. While the schools in Geneva or Paris or London are ostensibly better, on average, than those in American cities, the employee who is based outside of the United States may wish his or her child to obtain an "American" education nevertheless, and the cost for this is substantial, as is the cost of SAT or ACT preparation, which is practically essential for an American child brought up in a foreign country. This can amount to many thousands of dollars in the child's junior or senior year in high school.

Financial Planning Assistance

One of the more impressive perks I have seen recognizes that employees, like their bosses, have financial goals. One large company agreed to provide financial counseling through a partnership with a financial management company. The first year of counseling was 100% company paid. Each year thereafter, the company agreed to pay 50%. Alternatively, the company offered a reimbursement of $5,000 annually to be used by the employee with the financial planner of his or her choice.

Paid Time Off

As employment becomes more gender-neutral and society has embraced the fact that males as well as females might wish to spend some quality time with newborns, or even older children, some companies have established plans allowing for up to thirty days of paid time off on an annual basis in addition to the regular company-paid holidays. Some companies have tired of allowing "personal" days as these are simply taken willy-nilly as additional vacation days and do not necessarily serve the company well. How resentful an employee feels after he has taken off his allotment of personal days to run errands, or attend a parent's funeral, and then suffers a debilitating illness in November or December and the employer says, "Too bad. You've taken your share—no pay for you this week."

TERMINATION

Termination as used here means the ending of the contract other than by its natural expiration. There is a misconception held by most employees that if they sign a contract, they are assured of being employed throughout its term. Most, if not all, states in the United States are *at-will* states, which means that there is no guarantee that the employment will continue. Indeed, both parties to an employment agreement can terminate at will. Just as the employer can terminate the employee at any time, so also the employee is free to resign at any time. Both can act for any reason. (The only way at-will status does not apply is when the contract actually contains the words, "This is an express contract of employment" and is signed by an officer of the company. Companies are loath to do this.) The issue is not whether the employment *can* be terminated, but what are the consequences of the termination.

Two main categories of termination are termination *without* cause and termination *with* cause, and their consequences differ. If the termination is with cause, there may be no more payment of the contractual salary, or other compensation, such as perks, as of the date of termination, and the employer may even claim damages from the employee. (For example, the employer may require that the employee return money previously paid by the company.) Prospective employees should check the language of for-cause termination clauses carefully. Some companies, for example, are including inappropriate electronic communications (for example, offensive postings to message boards and chat rooms) as causes for termination.

Termination without cause is more difficult to define. It occurs when, for example, the employer decides that the employee's job definition is not correct or not being filled as well by employee A as it might be by employee B, or simply because the budget for the division has been reduced, leaving the employer with no alternative but to cut staff. In this situation, the contractual provision usually requires payout for the entire term of the agreement, *with mitigation*. This means that the employee must seek, in good faith, another job equivalent to the one that he or she had with the employer. During the job search, the employee's contractual salary will be paid out, for the term of the original agreement, until such time as the employee finds another job. (It is possible to negotiate provisions that state that in the case of termination without cause or termination for good reason [see below], the employer must make available out-placement services to assist the employee to find an equivalent job.)

It should be noted that in the event of termination without cause, even when the employer is paying out compensation as required by the agreement for the remainder of its term, the employer is not usually required to continue offering other benefits (for example, car allowance, health insurance, etc.). Under COBRA rules, an employee is entitled to retain medical insurance for eighteen months after leaving the job. In most cases, the employee has to pay for this continuation, although the employer will often agree to pay the COBRA amount for the duration of the unexpired term if the employee does not secure other employment. But the employer will surely not pay this absent a specific provision in the employment agreement requiring it to do so. (Note that this sum might soon constitute taxable income to the employee whether or not he or she is still employed while receiving medical benefits. The current administration and the Congress are looking for ways to increase revenues while appearing not to raise taxes.)

The negotiating strategy of an employee who might one day expect to be terminated *without cause* (for example, if the employer is a relatively new, or highly leveraged company, whose future existence is not assured) is to provide in the original contract the right to be paid out the entire balance of his or her salary *regardless of mitigation*. This is difficult to get. Yet, if the employer believes that insolvency of the business or such a severe scaling back of the business that the employee's entire division must be terminated is unlikely to occur, the employer may agree to such terms. For example, new companies flush with capital may be so optimistic about their future prospects that they will consider payment-without-mitigation terms. It is worth a try in any event.

In cases where the employer wants to limit the payout term, it is possible to agree that "with cause" results in no payment and "without cause" results in a payment equal to the lesser of base compensation for three to six months or base compensation for the then remaining natural term of the agreement.

Change of Control

In some cases, the employee may wish to end the contractual relationship if a change of control in the company occurs. This can be negotiated in the contract to constitute a termination without cause, but the consequences may be different from the consequences of other kinds of termination without cause. The new company will be responsible for the consequences of such a provision, not the contracting employer, so it is sometimes fairly easy to obtain a provision that in the event of a change in control, the employee will have the right, for example, to terminate the agreement and be paid out the balance of the contract in a lump sum without mitigation. Those doing the due diligence of the company being acquired always take care to determine if clauses like this one exist in executives' employment agreements, as the loss of high-level staff due to the exercise of such "out" clauses can be problematic for the acquiring company.

One complex issue connected with changes in control is the following. According to Section 280G of the Internal Revenue Code of 1986, an employee who receives more than 2.99 times his or her base compensation as a parachute payment in the event of termination without cause triggered by a change of control is susceptible of having to pay an additional excise tax, imposed by Section 4999 of the code, of 20% on the entire payout *in addition to all other compensation-related taxes*. (The base compensation is averaged, based on whichever is shorter, over the preceding five years or the duration of employment with that particular employer.) Big-gun employees will ask for (and occasionally obtain) a provision that authorizes the company to "gross up" a payout to compensate the employees for the cost of the excise tax in the event the payout is likely to constitute an excess parachute payment. One way or another, they will get what they want.

Termination by the Employee for Good Reason

There is a developing concept that employees have the right to terminate their own employment when there is good reason to do so. As noted in the "duties" section, above, both specificity and ambiguity regarding duties may be double-edged swords. If these provisions are ambiguous, it will be difficult for the employer to point to a specific requirement and allege failure giving rise (barring cure) to the right to terminate with cause. At the same time, it will be harder for the employee to claim termination for good reason. A decent middle ground for the employee is to have the general duties described in ambiguous terms and, then, in the good-reason section, enumerate very specific good reasons, such as

- any reduction in the executive's minimum annual compensation, target percentage of executive's annual bonus, or any other material employee benefit or perquisite enjoyed by the executive other than as part of an overall reduction in such benefits or perquisites applying to the company's senior executives generally;

- any failure to continue the executive as [insert title];

- any material diminution in executive's duties or the assignment to executive of duties that are materially inconsistent with executive's then current duties;

- any other material breach by the company of any of the provisions described in the agreement;

- the *occurrence* of a change in control (provided that the executive remains employed with the company for six months thereafter);

- the failure to obtain the assumption of the executive's employment agreement by any successor to all or substantially all of the business or assets of the company.

Morals Clauses

Most talent contracts include provisions that protect the employer from having to keep an employee whose moral character is embarrassing to the employer. Ordinarily, these provisions speak in terms of being convicted of a felony or some similar criminal act. Some companies, however, have experienced considerable embarrassment by virtue of employees' behavior that, although not rising to the level of criminal activity, is nevertheless abhorrent to whatever the company stands for or whatever it claims to stand for.

Thus arises the general "morals clause," which one should be particularly cautious to negotiate carefully. Most people will sign an agreement that permits termination with cause if the employee commits a felony. However, the language of many contracts is so general as to give the employer a right to terminate with cause a contract that otherwise would be solid and free from attack. For example, one of the television networks provides that behavior *inimical* to the employer may permit the termination of the contract for cause. During negotiation, the network in question offered, and the employee finally accepted, the following definition of "inimical" when pressed:

> Those actions that are harmful to their reputation and/or business interests as determined by the employer.

So much for the negotiation "victory" of establishing a definition.

A cause for termination that frequently finds its way into boilerplate morals clauses is the word *insubordination*. What on earth does *that* mean?

When faced with such provisions, the only thing that one can request is an additional provision establishing a right on the part of the employee to have an opportunity to correct any deficiencies based on the severity of the claimed offense. Never was an "opportunity to cure" more desired, or more warranted.

Clearly, from the employee's perspective, to have to accept a morals clause is a horrendous burden. But provision or no provision, someone who publicly embarrasses his or her employer and, by his or her conduct, jeopardizes the business relationships and business reputation of the employer, will be fired. Should the employer pay lots of money to make the miscreant leave if the contract does not provide for a breach of morals to entitle the company to fire the employee with cause?

One way to deal with this eventuality may be to provide a substantial reduction of the without-cause payout amount in the event of the violation of the morals clause. A hybrid termination—for example, "with cause when the cause is a breach of the morals clause short of a criminal act"—could trigger a situation in which *some* money can be paid, although less than that paid out without cause.

Us Weekly magazine provided us with a useful list of behavior that constitutes sufficient moral turpitude to condemn the contract (and the fee) to the trash heap. In order of disgust, it begins not with murder, but child molestation. Close behind, though, come murder, rape, blasphemy, affairs (especially with someone of the same sex), public airings of marital strife, excessive drug or alcohol use, and AIDS. "Homosexuality is not a good idea, but homophobia is not a big deal," predicted Marc Perman, a well-respected talent agent, almost twenty years ago. Lawyers have to come up with language to cover these idiosyncratic distinctions. Good luck. Companies nowadays don't seem too stressed about living, flamboyant personalities—in fact, with some products, the edgier the better. Our heroic Jack Bauer, Keifer Sutherland, spends a few nights in jail for behavioral excesses resulting from too much alcohol, but this hasn't impeded him from obtaining greater and more lucrative roles in television and film.

WORKING IN A FOREIGN LAND

When a person relocates to a foreign country, air fares, estate agents, temporary facilities for himself and his family, homes, hotels, etc. can add up. The value of these costs—upward of $30,000—will be taxable. In England, the rate approaches 40%. Accordingly, in addition to making sure that you have sufficient medical insurance and car allowance, you must take into account the taxability of these perquisites, and others. Even "end of service" gratuities—what we call severance pay—have to be accounted for as they may be taxed in the country in which they are received.

More important than at a United States–based entity where customs and traditions are fairly well understood by an American employee, it is essential that before you accept a job overseas you know precisely (a) to whom you report and are accountable, and (b) what your responsibilities are (and are not). Less specifically, but all too importantly, you had better know what your employer's expectations are. Too often these are unstated, but nevertheless very real.

RELOCATION AND RE-RELOCATION

Remarkably, relocation provisions are often ignored by employees leaving one venue and traveling to another. In initial negotiations, the company's thoughts as well as those of the employee, the employee's family, and regrettably, often the employee's attorney's as well, are, quite naturally, focused only on the future placement of the employee. No one thinks of the end; they are all focused on the beginning.

A favorable provision will provide that, whether the contract is terminated for cause or without cause, the employer must return the employee and the employee's family and belongings to the place of origin. Sometimes the provision returns the employee only to the place of origin if the contract ends in the first year; thereafter, the employee must pay. Sometimes the provision stipulates that, provided the contract runs out its entire term, the employer must return the employee to wherever he or she wants to go in the world.

Relocation and re-relocation expenses should specifically cover a trip or trips to the new location for the employee and perhaps his or her spouse so that they can establish schooling arrangements for their children and select a home prior to the official commencement of employment.

In addition to moving and relocation expenses, there are many costs involved that the relocating employee may have to assume if the employer is not asked to assume them. For example, if the employee has committed to rent a summer house or has paid a deposit on private school fees prior to the time he or she is asked to relocate, the company should be expected to reimburse the employee for such costs. These costs may be incurred at either end of an employment, and therefore reimbursement provisions should apply both to relocations and re-relocations. Similarly, there will likely be storage fees that must be assumed, costs of selling one's home (realtor's commission, attorneys' fees, document preparation, recording fees, inspection fees), whether for relocation or re-relocation. There are additional expenses, such as property taxes, interest on one's mortgage, improvements to make one's home (at the new or old site) ready for sale, and concessions that are made to sell the home (at the new or old site) to a new buyer.

VISAS

Special issues arise if an employee whom a company wishes to hire is resident in the United States via a special visa (rather than, say, a green card). Sometimes these visas are obtained by employees' own service corporations and they need to maintain the status they have acquired while they pursue their application for a green card. If a new employer requires that the employee terminate his or her application and reapply with the new employer as the sponsor for the visa, even if the employer is prepared to pay for the costs of the switch, do not forget that once the employment ends (on the contract's own terms, or with or without cause), the employee will be in serious jeopardy of having to return to his or her own country *unless the company assumes the responsibility of reinstating the employee's original visa status once the employment is ended.*

DISABILITY AND DEATH

The problem with the term *disability* is that it requires an objective standard, and a contract that ignores establishing such an objective standard is susceptible of interpretation that can be devastating to an employee who suffers an injury that *the employee* believes to be a disabling injury but that the company does not. Most companies will agree that if a competent medical authority certifies disability, they will respect the diagnosis. The contract should provide for this.

Disabilities can be either short-term or long-term, and it is a good idea to have these terms defined contractually so their different consequences can be evaluated by the employee and negotiated if they are not to his or her advantage.

Death, of course, requires no objective standard, but some consideration should be given to the need for life insurance, and the cost of such insurance. The prospective employee should discuss with his or her financial planner how much life insurance he or she would require at different points during the term (especially during extension terms, where the needs might be less (as, for example, when children have grown up), but the costs considerably more. Some planners suggest that the life insurance payout be approximately two to three times the employee's base salary, with additional insurance added during the term by one times salary for each new child born during the term. This can be a lifesaver for the surviving spouse and children.

PROVISIONS THAT SURVIVE TERMINATION

Provisions that survive the end of the agreement should be carefully considered because they may have an impact on future employment. For example, there may be promises made regarding company policies (for example, secrecy; see the section on confidentiality, page 110) that the employee will have to adhere to even long after the contract expires. For the most part, termination will have a deleterious effect on unvested stock options. Unvested options customarily expire on termination except for senior executives with some leverage. Companies are loath to extend or alter the terms of options—and it is not due to malice that they behave like this. There are considerable negative accounting consequences for a company that varies the terms of options for employees, especially if the modifications are unevenly applied.

If termination occurs without cause, or in the ordinary course of the expiration of the term of the agreement, it is possible to negotiate an immediate vesting.

Employees who share in profits or have the right to receive royalties may find that their own right to audit the company expires upon termination even though they have not yet received accountings reflecting monies earned during the term. And in some cases, monies are earned and payable after the term, even though the audit clause that would have been the basis of verifying the accountings may have been negated by the effect of termination. Similarly, profit shares and royalties may be payable only through the end of the contract term, and the language providing for this result may be so obscure as to be easily missed by someone reviewing the contract. (See below, under "A&R Incentive Plans.")

VACATIONS

Sometimes, or for some people, it is awkward to highlight vacation issues when negotiating an employment agreement. Work, compensation for work, and productivity are considered to be the real focus of the contract, and nonwork and holiday issues are not. Nevertheless, everyone (including the person you are negotiating with) considers this to be a legitimate area to discuss and the specific needs of each employee should be addressed. If one is uncomfortable allocating a block of valuable negotiating time to nonwork issues, the negotiating position can easily be presented in writing (and in detail, with recommended contract language) by the employee's attorney.

One area of concern is vacation accumulated by employees who don't take their vacation time—either because they are the most dedicated or the most neurotic employees the company has. Many companies have rules that require that vacation time must be taken during the year in which the vacation time accrues. The more structured the corporation, the more likely it is that it will have rules that affect everyone's options—no matter how highly placed the employee.

There are many and varied solutions to the problem. One that is becoming popular is the right to be permitted to take time off equivalent to two years' vacation allowances. In other words, the vacation time accumulated over two years can be joined into one long holiday. This practically amounts to a sabbatical and is understandably very appealing to prospective employees. Another solution is simply to allow the employee to take the vacation time in cash. However, while this relieves the corporation from having to replace the employee for the period of the vacation, or to do without his or her services for that period, the result may be an exhausted employee, which could threaten productivity, so many companies have a policy against that option.

One final vacation hint: Depending on how the unused vacation time can be rolled over from year to year, some senior executives use the vacation provision as an uncategorized slush fund that will be paid out on termination without (or even with) cause. Senior executives may not use the four or five weeks allotted to them, and such an employee who accumulates unused weeks (for example, two weeks a year for four years), will have additional severance on termination commensurate with the unused vacation weeks. Companies do not like this, but if the rollover practice of the company permits it, why not try for it?

RELEASE AND SETTLEMENT

In today's volatile employment market, more and more employees are switching companies, and want the right to do so written into their contracts. Employers, on the other hand, have anticipated that they themselves might very well wish to terminate these contracts early. Many companies have been faced with issues (for example, sex and age discrimination) that not only generate unanticipated costs to the company, but whose resolution may add to the cost of termination beyond the contractual requirements. As a result, many companies have begun to insert into their employment agreements provisions that are somewhat different from their traditional termination provisions (especially those affecting termination without cause or for good reason). More and more companies are requiring that a release agreement "in company's standard form" be executed and delivered at the point when the employee leaves the company. These documents include a release from any and all claims, including discrimination claims, that the employee may have relating to his or her employment and its termination. Failure to sign such a standard release agreement upon termination can result in the forfeiture by the employee of everything from the employee's right to receive salary through to the end of the term of the contract, to benefits attached to employment such as medical benefits, and even prenegotiated severance-pay provisions, and this is true even when the standard form release is not referenced in the original agreement.

EMPLOYMENT ISSUES SPECIFIC TO THE MUSIC INDUSTRY

Most industries do not face the same kinds of issues that arise when a music business executive is in the negotiating stage of an employment agreement. First and foremost is the issue of how to calculate compensation payable to those who sign artists or writers to the companies that employ them. (The issue of incentive is generally applicable to all industries, but provisions dealing with incentives for A&R executives are specific to the music industry.) Second, music industry companies have historically not been as "corporate"—as structured and as rule driven—as other, more traditional companies. (With consolidation in the record industry, this is beginning to change.) Third, there is often an urgency in placing an executive in a position quickly lest the chance to present him or her at a high-profile industry event passes while the lawyers and human resources personnel are haggling over details. Also, many executive employees in the music industry are not your usual three-piece-suit types; their raisons d'être are creative, and they themselves are likely to chafe at the stratified regulations that bind employees in companies in other industries. Indeed, more and more often, former high-profile celebrities from the creative world are being hired by record and music publishing companies, giving rise to the same kind of problems that a television network has in dealing with its talent: other commitments. Finally, the nature of their work requires that certain unique provisions be included—for example, those pertaining to fan mail—that are not an issue in other types of companies.

A&R Incentive Plans

There are a variety of ways—or incentive plans—to calculate compensation payable to those who sign artists or writers to the companies that employ them. Most companies have their own incentive plans, and most of these have specific provisions affecting the termination of benefits. Suffice it to say that the best result one can obtain in an A&R incentive plan is that the financial interest that the employee may acquire in a given artist's recordings or songs continues *after* the termination of employment. This result is rarely obtained. But as with many other positions taken by employers, there are many variations on the theme, and an employer who wants to accommodate the employee may be receptive to one or more of these.

Before addressing the amount of compensation traditionally offered to A&R executives, I first want to point out that it is important to be specific in identifying the particular artists and sound carriers (for example, records, DVDs, etc.) as to which said compensation is payable. For example, if an A&R executive is the first to notice an artist; goes to a number of that artist's showcases; participates over a period of time in discussions of material, instrumentation, selection of a manager, strategies to interest the senior record company executives, etc.; and ultimately is responsible for persuading the senior executives to sign the artist, that exec is likely to be considered qualified for the A&R incentive plan.

But what if an obscure artist already has a record released in Europe (think: *Macarena, Chant*)? Even if the A&R person "discovers" the record, identifies the artist, takes the steps necessary for the US record company affiliate to sign the artist or merely to release the record, and works the record and the artist in the United States as if he or she had gone through all of the other processes described above, that person still may not qualify for the A&R incentive plan unless the language of the plan is flexible enough to include this particular circumstance. The same concern is present when an A&R executive is successful in persuading an artist who has been previously discovered by another label to come aboard the executive's own company. Many plans exempt from coverage any artist who appeared on another label, or any artist whose records have sold, say, 250,000 or more copies on another label. (One might call this provision a *disincentive*.)

Unfortunately, many of these plans are written in stone; that is, they are not negotiable. The person negotiating for the record company will usually say that the A&R person has to trust that his or her superiors will "do the right thing" in situations other than the standard ones. So much for creative lawyering. I do not know whether this attitude is a function of orders from on high or merely of laziness on the part of the company's staff assigned to draft modifications in language, but it is prevalent, certainly among the majors.

The A&R exec trying to establish whether he or she is entitled to an incentive royalty on a particular artist or record is usually left only with the language of the company's standard incentive plan to resolve any questions, and I heartily recommend that every A&R person, before signing the employment agreement, read it *very* carefully, keeping in mind any "fluke" situations from his or her own past—or even the historical past. For example, ABBA was the direct outgrowth of the two Bs (Björn and Benny), whose single "Ring, Ring the Telephone" was going nowhere on a now-defunct label, Playboy Records. If the inducement plan for the A&R person at Atlantic who convinced the label to sign an agreement under which ABBA would spend their entire careers included language requiring that he or she had to have "discovered" the artist, the A&R person would not have been entitled to any participation in the group's success. Another remarkable turn of events (positive for the new label and horribly negative for the old) occurred when Elton John's first single was going nowhere on Bell Records, the predecessor of Arista Records. A few entreaties and a few more dollars and one of the largest-selling artists of the 20th century switched to UNI (MCA, now Universal), and the rest is history. As in the ABBA example, under similar language John's A&R person at UNI would not qualify for compensation. Now isn't that ridiculous?

Sometimes the preamble of the incentive plan itself gives some hint as to how a conflict about identifying artists or records that qualify for a royalty can be resolved. Following is an excerpt from one major label's A&R incentive plan.

> This plan is designed to meet the following objectives all of which are intended to support eligible A&R positions:
>
> 1. To reward eligible A&R employees for their contributions in maximizing roster development, recording and sales of BMG Classics' product.
>
> 2. To assist in attracting and retaining qualified A&R employees.

While this language may be in conflict with the exact language of the royalty provision, which most likely speaks in terms of acts "first signed or discovered" by the A&R person, a court could easily fit a *Macarena*, a *Chant*, an ABBA, or an Elton John into the definition if sufficient ambiguity were present to allow it to do so.

VARIATIONS OF ROYALTY CALCULATIONS

The royalty payable to the A&R person (often referred to as an "override") is customarily established at one rate for the United States and one-half of that for the rest of the world. A 1% to 1.5% royalty rate is fairly standard. This is usually calculated on the same basis as is that of the applicable artist signed by or served by the A&R person, and customarily amounts to from $0.09 to $0.12 cents. Here are some other variations:

- Sometimes the royalty is attributable only to recordings sold in the United States or in a territory somewhat less than the entire world.
- Sometimes the royalty will be capped at a certain amount of money (for example, an amount equivalent to the A&R person's salary).
- Sometimes the royalty is payable from record one after recoupment of the recording costs at the artist's net (that is, lower) rate.

- Sometimes the royalty is payable from record one after recoupment of the recording costs at the combined artist and producer rate (a faster rate of recoupment).

- Sometimes the royalty is payable prospectively from the point that the company has recouped the recording costs at the artist's net royalty rate.

- Sometimes the royalty is payable prospectively from the point that the company has recouped the recording costs at the combined artist and producer's rate.

- Sometimes the royalty is payable in the manner described in the four bulleted items immediately preceding this one, but instead of recouping only the recording costs, *all* (or many) costs attributable to a particular album (including video, marketing, promotion, touring, and other costs) are recouped at one rate or another as noted above.

- Sometimes the royalty is payable after a portion of the A&R person's salary is recouped—that is, as if a portion of the A&R person's salary is an "advance."

- Most often, the royalty is payable only until the expiration of the term of the A&R person's employment agreement or, alternatively, the royalty is payable (sometimes in a diminishing amount) over a period of years (one, two, or three) after expiration of the term of the A&R person's employment.

- Sometimes, though rarely, the royalty is payable after the expiration of the term (at least for a while) of the A&R person's employment agreement, if the employment expires on its own terms or is terminated without cause. Sometimes, also rarely, the royalty is payable after the expiration of the term (at least for a while) of the A&R person's employment agreement, if the A&R person terminates the agreement for good reason. The clauses pertaining to collection of royalties after termination can be extremely important, and the A&R person, and his or her representative, must review all such provisions carefully.

- Sometimes the royalty is payable with respect to all of the recordings made by the artist whom the A&R person signed or serviced.

- Sometimes the royalty is payable with respect to all of the recordings made by the artist whom the A&R person signed or serviced, with the exception of recordings made pursuant to a renegotiation.

- Sometimes the royalty is payable with respect to all of the recordings made by the artist whom the A&R person signed or serviced, with the exception of recordings made pursuant to an extension agreement.

- Sometimes the royalty is no longer payable if the A&R person dies or is disabled during the term. Sometimes it is.

- Sometimes the A&R person's contract requires that special credit provisions be provided on records (that is, "A&R'd" by that person) and the royalty is payable only on records containing this credit.

- Most often, the royalty is payable only on USNRC albums (United States net sales through normal retail channels—that is, not for sales outside of the United States). Thus the royalty is not paid on singles, midpriced records, budget records, records sold through record clubs, records sold via armed forces PXs, premium sales, educational and institutional means, licensed uses, governmental distribution and mail order; and tracks derived from full-length CDs sold as part of compilations. (Note that sometimes a reduced royalty will be paid for records sold in some, but not all, of these categories.) Such a provision could bar the A&R person from receiving a share of DPD sales, today's fastest-growing format, and conceivably the preferred format for most "record" sales in the future.

- Sometimes the royalty is paid not only on USNRC, but on sales outside of the United States as well, excluding ancillary sales. Sometimes the royalty is paid not only on USNRC, but on all sales outside of the United States as well, including ancillary sales.

- Sometimes the royalty is paid at the same rates as the artist's royalties are calculated; sometimes it is paid at an arbitrary "half rate."

- Sometimes, the royalty is paid only while the artist is in the "black." This has the effect of the A&R person's royalties being retained by the record company once the artist, not the A&R person, has commenced recording of a subsequent record or has been charged with video, tour support, more independent promotion costs, or even taken an advance, and has placed his royalty account "in the red" all over again.

- Sometimes royalties payable with respect to one artist whose recording costs are recouped are withheld by the record company because another artist or artists as to whose records the A&R person is entitled to receive royalties is in an unrecouped status. In other words, the accounts are cross-collateralized. This is, of course, a disaster in most situations for the A&R person.

- Sometimes (and this variation is an especially hard one to take) the A&R person is a producer of the artist's recordings as well and the contract reduces the producer's royalty by the amount that the A&R person would have received pursuant to the A&R royalty provisions.

The above list is a partial one only. The possible variations are endless. Clearly, any A&R person considering employment must read and understand the consequences of the standard provisions and, hopefully, be able to negotiate changes peculiar to the employee's own situation, needs, and as always, leverage. What will always make a diffence is the answers to these questions: how much does the label want you and what (particularly which artists) are you bringing with you?

If the foregoing is not enough to depress the A&R person, there is another truth to deal with in this area: the royalty payable to the A&R person is almost always subject to most, if not all, of the same reductions and limitations as the artist's royalty is subject to—for example, allowance for reserves; packaging deductions; a reduction for digital mediums such as DVD, CD, DAT; reductions for midprice and budget sales; reductions for military sales; reductions for Internet downloads; and reductions commensurate with how the artist's royalties are reduced (for example, if the artist is paid on 85% or 90% of records sold, the A&R person's royalties will be reduced accordingly). One trick used by some companies is to apply these reductions to the employee's already reduced royalty.

For example, let's say that the A&R person's royalty rate is reduced by one-half for overseas sales, and the artist's tracks are also reduced by, say, 25% in the United Kingdom, 40% in France, and 50% in South America (all of which are quite likely, especially for a new artist, whose records are, after all, what the A&R person is "commissioning"). It is not beyond the realm of possibility that the record company might then cut *those* percentages in half. This is not something that could ever have been intended by the A&R person or his or her attorney, I assure you.

Finally, it is not unusual for a record company to refuse to allow the A&R person (who is an employee of the company, after all) to audit the books and records of the record company with respect to his or her A&R royalty. The argument given for this is that the auditor would discover information whose confidentiality is of such consequence that the management of the record company's business would be compromised were the information to be disclosed to the A&R person. Similarly, record companies often resist attorneys' efforts to obtain for their A&R clients the right to an upward royalty adjustment if the *artist's* audit claim results in a settlement with positive implications for the A&R person. For example, if the artist, producer, and A&R person are all accounted to for 400,000 records sold in Australia and it turns out that the record company mysteriously, and erroneously, forgot to account for an additional 200,000 records, while the artist's royalty account will be adjusted upward, and most likely the producer's will as well, the A&R person's account will not be, and there is no way for the A&R person to even know that such an adjustment has taken place.

Even when the A&R person is permitted to examine the record company's books while he or she is employed, upon termination of employment, the right to audit may also be terminated, making it difficult if not impossible to verify the amounts owed—that is, amounts earned and payable during the term of employment. After all, it is far more likely that an employee will refrain from auditing during the term of his employment, as audits are often experienced by the party being audited as being aggressive and adversarial. The same reticence is not present *after* the term has expired. Sometimes profit shares and royalties may be payable only through the end of the contract term, and the language providing for this result may be so obscure as to be easily missed by someone reviewing the contract. However, as noted in the list above, payment responsibilities insofar as A&R royalties and the like are concerned may be extended if the contract has been terminated by the employer without cause or by the employee for good reason.

EMPLOYMENT AGREEMENTS WITH CELEBRITIES AND OTHERS OTHERWISE ENGAGED

When negotiating A&R agreements for a person who is also a talent in his or her own right, the attorney representing that person needs to consider carefully what is singular about the person, and whatever exceptions are appropriate to that person should be sought during the employment contract negotiation. It is surprising how many requests for exceptions are likely to be granted—even when the eventual employee's leverage is not so great. Currently there is a trend, which began, albeit slowly, a few decades ago, toward hiring celebrities for A&R positions. For example, Mitch Miller, head of A&R at Columbia in the 1950s and 1960s, also had his enormously popular television show. And, although Clive Davis has not been seen waving a baton at a chorus lately, few record executives can boast his extraordinary visibility—least of all on the final broadcasts of *American Idol*. Today L. A. Reid (Island, Def Jam), Rick Rubin (Def American, American Recordings, Columbia), Damon Dash and his colleagues (Roc-A-Fella Records) and, of course, Jay Z (Roc Nation) and other well-known music industry personages are heading up some of the industries' most visible record labels, or providing consulting services, and are also appearing on television and at high-profile parties.

Such employees, and others like them, while exclusive for a category of services—for example, A&R person—may wish to pursue other interests, from endorsements to broadcast commercials, to clothing lines, to maintaining their own websites and offering merchandise, to recording or writing for others outside of the exclusive relationship. An employee who is also a songwriter may want to pursue a separate career as a theatrical show writer, or to continue writing for motion picture or television soundtracks.

An employee who has had a prior career as a producer's manager or an artist's manager may want to continue to pursue these interests during the term of his or her employment or at least during a phaseout period during the term of employment. That person may wish to continue to receive financial compensation arising from a prior manager's agreement with an artist or producer. If so, he or she will have to provide for this in the employment contract to avoid a conflict of interest and a breach resulting from nondisclosure.

A record company A&R person with a public persona may wish to appear on *American Idol* or similar programs; to appear as a guest on talk programs and even prime-time situation comedies or specials; even to be, say, the "music minute" reporter on The *TODAY* show. A&R execs who are also performers may wish to continue to appear in front of live audiences.

All of these issues should be considered when drafting provisions affecting exclusivity, competition, confidentiality, and ownership-of-ideas provisions and should be considered in the course of the negotiation.

MAIL

In certain talent contracts (for example, video jockeys on cable channels or on Internet radio), the issue of fan mail arises. This is a real concern to people who receive it and to the companies whose employees receive it. Certainly, it should be collected and forwarded to the employee. But should it be read? The employer will often claim the right to open it, read it, and even answer it; sometimes the employer will agree to keep it private when it is marked "private" or "personal" and deliver it to the employee directly.

There are copyright issues to be considered as well. Who owns the letters? Who—the employer or the employee—can benefit from ideas expressed or suggestions offered in the letters? Obviously, fan mail can be very useful to both the employer and employee. The manner in which it is collected, read, categorized, registered in databases, etc., is of real concern to both, and the way in which this is handled can and should be specifically provided for in the employment agreement.

There are cyberspace issues here, as well. What about email? Most cases dealing with this issue have held that the employers own the email of all employees. Not only do they have the right to access the employees' email files (including their address lists), but they can snoop on employees' exchanges. What about emails from fans to the employer's website? To the employee's website? To the employee's website that is managed (and owned?) by the employer? The law in such cases is rapidly evolving, but it will apply only to those situations where the employer and employee *have not themselves dealt with the issue in their written contracts.*

THE OWNERSHIP OF IDEAS

It is not unusual for employers to attempt to treat all intellectual property created by an employee during the term of the employment as the property of the company. As such, the company will seek not only to own the results of the employee's creative thinking—that person's intellectual property—but also to bind the employee to nondisclosure of such intellectual property.

As noted in the opening sections of this chapter, uniquely in the music industry many of the very people whose professional services are sought to foster creative development in others are themselves creators. It is anathema to them to be asked to sign an agreement that assigns to the employer all the results of their creative services—including, by definition, their "ideas" and the expression of such ideas (such as songs, artistic approaches to production, arrangements, etc.). While the provision against disclosure or use of information may be said to have a generally rational purpose, it may be abusive and overreaching under certain circumstances and for certain people.

Contract language in the realm of works for hire will often specify that the employee must warrant that all ideas, creations, literary, musical, and artistic materials and intellectual properties created or developed by the employee *during the course of employment* will be owned by the company. And, often, these provisions are buried in general boilerplate warranty paragraphs. Obviously, those who are hired for creative purposes must be very cautious about agreeing to such provisions when they do not provide for additional compensation. An A&R person who contributes ideas as part of his or her job does not usually intend to relinquish ownership in songs written outside of the parameters of the job description—particularly for no compensation. While ideas, as such, are not susceptible of copyright protection, the *expression* of ideas is, and this fact should be considered carefully in each case before signing an employment agreement that contains language that is improvidently or heedlessly conceived. As with other provisions in these "standard" inducement plans, business affairs lawyers are reticent to make *any* changes in language, so your attorney's battle on your behalf to avoid a potentially catastrophic result, where your company owns your creations without having compensated you for them, will not be an easy one.

• • •

Most people at some point in their lives work for others. Most people have never had an opportunity to work for themselves. While *Forbes* magazine lists the one hundred companies that are the "best" to work for, chances are you will not be working for one of them. Insecurity is the norm and it is your reality. Many long-term music executives who have been found "redundant" in recent years as the industry has shrunk and the cost of benefits and salaries has risen have told me, with some bitterness, that the moment one feels secure, one is vulnerable. Regrettably, the quote at the beginning of this chapter is not far from the truth.

8 · RECORD PRODUCERS
Are They as Sharp as Their Points?

The first cut is the deepest Baby I know
—YUSUF ISLAM (CAT STEVENS)

In the world of recording, the media have told us more than we want to hear about artists and record companies. But one role player who has traditionally succeeded in keeping a fairly low profile is the record producer. (This is not necessarily so in urban music, where often one identifies the recording more with the producer than with the artist.) I am, of course, talking about individual producers rather than record companies that "produce" recordings.

Who was the first producer? It is hard to say, but Walter Legge, formerly the chief creative person at EMI in London, claimed to be the first. (Norman Lebrecht, in his tell-all book *Who Killed Classical Music?* refers to him as the most disagreeable personage ever to intrude upon musical performance.) It was Legge's aim to "make records that would set the standards by which public performances and the artists of the future would be judged." He tried to make records not only match live performances, but to exceed them in quality. He certainly succeeded. A huge percentage of EMI's "Recordings of the Century" bear his imprint as producer. Legge even created an orchestra, the Philharmonia of London, for recording purposes only, although today the Philharmonia is one of the world's most respected performing orchestras as well.

The old adage about the chicken and the egg has some resonance in this area. Who is responsible for an artist's success, the artist or the producer? This is a question that will, most probably, never be answered to everyone's satisfaction. The producer shapes the recording, but depending on the nature of the artist and the artist's particular talent, the producer's role will differ dramatically from artist to artist. The nature of their deals, however, will not.

HOW 25% CAN EQUAL 100%

In chapter 4, I more or less glossed over the producer's cut of the artist's royalties. Let's look more closely at the financial impact of the producer's deal on the artist's ultimate take-home pay. Let's say that an artist's royalty rate from the record company is 12% of the suggested retail selling price of records. Not unusual. A customary producer's royalty would be approximately one-fourth of that rate, or 3%, leaving the artist with 9%. Another way to put it is that the producer receives 25% of the total royalties, but 33.33% of what the artist receives. So it would seem that for every $9 credited to the artist's account (and notice the "credited"; the artist may never see this money), the producer gets $3.

Not so. Here's why.

First, and most significant, after recoupment of recording costs, the producer customarily gets paid from record one—the first record sold. The artist does not.

Let's say the recording costs are $100,000 and the 12% royalty works out to about $1.07 per record. (In this example, I am assuming that a royalty "point" is worth about $0.09. It can be higher.) The record company will usually recoup these recording costs (that is, pay themselves back) at the so-called "net artist rate," that is, 9% (12% less the producer's rate of 3%). (I am assuming, for the sake of this example, that the producer is solely responsible for producing the entire CD; it is entirely possible that the producer's share is not calculated on 100% of the tracks on the CD, as pointed out below under "Pro Rata Royalty Share.") At $0.09 a point, a 9% royalty rate works out to be about $0.80. At $0.80 per unit, it will require a sale of 125,000 records before the recording costs are recouped. A new clinker for the producer: Since about 2005, record companies insist on recouping not just the recording costs before going back to record one to calculate the producer's royalties. Now they want to wait until the recording costs *plus* the producer's advance is recouped before doing do. At $0.80 per unit, an additional 62,500 units (for a total of 187,500 units) must be sold to recoup, say, a $50,000 producer's advance. At that point, the producer is entitled to be paid his or her 3% royalty from record one. At $0.27 per record (three times $0.09), the producer is entitled to a check for $625 over his $50,000 advance. The artist? He's entitled to nothing at this point.

Is the producer receiving 25% of the total royalty paid out by the record company? No. He is receiving 100%! Meanwhile, the record company has received about $7 per record sold through its distribution system. Thus, 187,500 in sales represents more than $1,312,500 in cash receipts to the company.

Let's examine what happens when the record has achieved sales of 250,000 units. The producer's royalties have now reached $67,500. The artist royalties are now in the positive column also. Once the 125,000th sale has occurred (the record has now recouped the recording costs), the artist will be due royalties of $0.80 per record on all units sold after that. The differential between 250,000 and 125,000 is 125,000. Therefore, the artist will have earned a grand total of $100,000 ($0.80 times 125,000). This is beginning to look better for the artist. Yet at the same time that the artist will begin to receive his first royalty dollar, the producer will receive an additional $16,875 to add to his $50,625.

The total royalties payable by the record company (which, lest we forget, has received by now $1.75 million from its distributors) have amounted only to $167,500. The producer's $67,500 share amounts to 40% of the total royalties paid (hardly the 25% the artist originally had in mind), and the artist's $100,000 share will be 60% of the total royalties paid. In fact, the producer's share of total royalties will never be as low as 25%. I am not saying this is unlikely; I am saying it is impossible. Watch.

More bad news: The artist will not receive the $100,000 that he or she has earned according to the above scenario. It will take many more sales before the artist receives the first royalty check. Why? Because not only does the artist pay out of royalties the cost of producing his or her own recordings; the artist also has to pay for tour support advances, equipment advances, independent promotion expenses (more about this later), and video production expenses (or at least one-half of them). Nowadays, record companies have even added certain marketing, artwork, and other costs to the list of recoupable monies. So it can require 500,000 album units or more before the record company has recouped all of these advances and expenses. At that point, the producer will have received $135,000 in royalties ($0.27 [3 x $0.09] x 500,000 = $135,000) and the artist will still have received . . . zero.

The disparity between artist and producer royalties can be even greater—and, at the same time, camouflaged, when the producer receives a "penny rate" rather than a royalty rate (which is cast in terms of a percentage of receipts, or suggested retail, or wholesale price). On its face, the penny rate appears insignificant. But it's not. For example, let's say that the producer receives $0.50 an album rising to $0.5625 at 500,000 units and to $0.6275 at one million units. Calculated at $0.09 per royalty point, this works out to be about a 5.5% of retail royalty rate, going to 6.2% and ultimately to 7% at 1 million units. At $0.10 or $0.11, the equivalent royalty percentage would be even higher . . . . possibly so high as to be unconscionable.

In essence, record companies, unlike all other businesses that create and exploit intellectual property (movies, television, book publishing), get to make huge profits on products, the worldwide copyright to which they will own for upward of ninety-five years, without having actually paid for them. Granted, they risk losing the investment, but when a record succeeds, the only thing they have lost is the use, for a year and a half or so, of that money. Yes, they have expended a fair sum on overhead, but having observed the salaries of record company executives over the years and their generous perks, I am not too worried that they will feel taken advantage of.

CROSS-COLLATERALIZATION:
IT DOES NOT APPLY TO THE PRODUCER

Because the cross-collateralization provisions contained in most artist–record company agreements do not apply to producers, the disparity between the relative earnings of the producer and the artist on a particular record does not stop with the calculations listed above. When the artist records a subsequent album, its costs will inevitably be charged against the prior album's royalties as well, but the producer will not have to face this additional headache. Once that 125,000th sale has occurred, the producer is home free for all time and will get his or her share of every record sold, every DPD, every ringtone, every use on a compilation, synchronization in a film, soap opera, TV special, or commercial—even as the artist is wallowing in "debt" due to the right of the record company to recoup costs associated not just with that particular record but unrecouped costs related to both prior and subsequent records as well.

Whether this practice will continue or be modified in the future is something that will require some serious thinking on the part of artists' advisors who specialize in this field and who understand all of the ramifications of the producer receiving "a couple of points." It is endlessly surprising to me how many artists and their representatives do not understand the true significance of cross-collateralization provisions, or those affecting royalty calculations for producers. Perhaps when they do, the creative partnership may become a financial one as well. Meanwhile, since the industry still protects producer royalties from the application of any recording costs but those that he or she is involved in, the producer's attorney should take steps to ensure that on a particular recording project (for example, an album), only those costs attributable to the portion of the album that that particular producer is working on will be subject to recoupment. If the producer has to wait for the artist's royalties to accumulate until the entire album's recording costs are recouped at the artist's royalty rate, and the producer has either produced (or mixed) less than 100% of the whole album, or the record company has engaged other producers or mixers to fine-tune the work of the producer, the producer will have a long time to wait before receiving royalties "from record one"—if in fact they are ever received.

It should now be abundantly clear that being promised three points, calculated as producers' royalties are calculated, is a lot more attractive than being offered nine points calculated as artists' royalties are. To put it another way, the work/reward ratio is a lot more favorable for the producer, whose creative input and labor end once the recording process is completed, than for the artist, who must "work" the record for many months afterward, pursuing promotion, marketing, and touring efforts to bring the record to the attention of potential buyers.

PRODUCERS' ROYALTY PROVISIONS: THE BASICS

Despite the basic disparity between the producer's share and the artist's share of royalties—which works in favor of the producer—there are a number of contractual snares and pitfalls that producers should be aware of. From the outset, the producer's representatives must obtain a copy of the artist's royalty provisions, without which they will have no basis on which to determine what the producer is supposed to receive. This is because once the number of royalty points is agreed upon, the producer needs to keep track of reductions for foreign sales, the definition of "net" sales, packaging deductions, etc.

Although producers customarily live with the provisions in the artist's agreement, they needn't do so if they have some leverage. Here's the grandest bargain I've seen for producers with leverage: a base royalty of 5% of retail, with escalations; no free goods permitted; no packaging deduction; no TV deduction; full royalty worldwide (no territorial reductions); pro rata share (based on original artist's rate without escalations, thereby keeping the percentage at its highest potential) of 50% of net digital receipts (as if a license); no format reduction; fee not recoupable as if it were an engineering fee; and an absolute payment from record one without delay as a result of the record label recouping recording and/or other costs. Ancillary uses such as promotional giveaways are a considerable source of licensing income, and even if the record company's agreement with the artist denies the artist a share of that income, if the producer has any leverage, why be hoisted by the same petard? The artist's negotiating position might have been weak, the artist or the artist's representatives careless or not assertive, or perhaps the artist's representatives simply decided that it was not financially sound for the artist to pay the legal costs of fighting for *absolutely everything* in an eighty-page agreement. The producer need not suffer the same consequences.

It should be a given that the terms of the contract with the producer be clear to all concerned—artist, producer, producer's lawyer and manager, etc.—and that all agree on what the deal is. But you would be surprised how often this is not case. For example, did they agree to a royalty of 3% of retail, going to 3.5% at 500,000 units and to 4% at 1,000,000 units? Did they agree on the correct number of tracks? Did they agree on whether the producer would do the mix? Did they agree on whether the record company can reduce the royalty if the company brings in another person to do the mix? The remix? Does the producer realize that all recording costs in excess of the agreed-upon budget may be directly charged to him or her? Will the producer's royalty be paid after recoupment of recording costs attributable to his or her production only, or will it be paid after recoupment of the total recording costs on the album? Will the producer receive royalties directly from the record company, and has the record company formally agreed to this? Or has the record company simply acknowledged receipt of a letter of direction requesting that it honor the request of the producer—which has become the customary way record companies have chosen to deal with this issue. This latter point becomes relevant when a record company refuses to honor the letter of direction. Most often, this occurs when an artist renegotiates his deal with his record label and receives a high advance, only to see record sales dive. The record companies have been known to tell the artist, "Pay your producer out of your high renegotiation advance." Unfortunately, the artist has often spent it. Too bad. The artist owes it, however, and suddenly the producer, for the first time in his or her memory, perhaps, is at risk. It used to be that record companies would provide the producer's services as part of their A&R function; now they disclaim any responsibility whatsoever.

The following sections cover some of the important contractual issues the producer and the producer's representatives must be aware of.

The Producer's Share of Renegotiated Royalties

An artist's royalty provisions may—no, *will*—be modified upward once the record agreement is renegotiated. If the improvements are retroactive, it is important that the producer-artist agreement allow that improvements in the producer's royalty be made along with improvements in the artist's royalty—especially because the renegotiation will presumably have occurred, at least in part, because of the success of the record that the producer produced! Increased royalties may also be the order of the day upon a record's achieving certain sales levels. For example, if a record is a success, and the artist's royalty increases, from, say, 12% to 13% at 1 million units, does the producer's percentage dip from his 25% ratio to three-thirteenths, or 23%? While this is 23% of the total, it is only 30% of what the artist receives, a 10% decline from 33.33%! It might surprise you that this is exactly what happens unless specific provision to the contrary is made in the producer's agreement. Some reward for success! This would be a good place to vary the tenor of this chapter, in which I have been highlighting the advantages that a producer has over the artist. When the producer is indeed an experienced, successful producer, and the artist is not, my resistance to the inequality of the financial relationship between the producer and the artist fades. In this instance, there is no reason why such a producer cannot seek a better deal than the artist has, particularly when the artist is new and his or her recording contract reflects only the most minimal royalty and other terms. For, as we have seen, a "better deal" does not mean just the differential in the respective royalty rates, but the means by which it is calculated. There is no need for a famous producer to accept some of the "new artist" terms in a record deal such as a half-rate for sales in Europe, or a controlled compositions special rate for his or her songs.

New Technology

In the area of digital or new technology, it is not unusual to see provisions establishing that a producer's share of the royalties on such uses be calculated according to a specific percentage of the total. The figure 16.67% is one that is often used, and it is obvious that the result will be an overall reduction from the 33.33% of the artist's share cited above.

This 16.67% (or any other number used) is totally arbitrary, and can have dramatic impact on what the producer gets from ancillary sales of records, which, in the Internet age, may actually constitute a greater percentage of total sales than those through normal retail channels. Recent producer agreements have been quite innovative in ways to reduce the producer's share of income derived from digital downloads. I have seen as much as a 30% reduction in the producer's royalty share. Sometimes I think that the record companies, or the artists' attorneys, insert these provisions just for the hell of it. There certainly is no justification for them, and as the gross share of income derived by virtue of digital downloads has increased geometrically in recent years, producers' attorneys should be on the lookout for such provisions. Too often, by the time the producer's attorney gets to the bottom of the royalty provisions, his or her eyesight, let alone consciousness, is blurred and these kinds of provisions slip through the cracks.

Delays

Sometimes the negotiations on a project go on so long that it is appropriate to ask that a start-up advance (customarily 50% of the total producer's advance against royalties) be paid to the producer even though the paperwork is not complete. One reason negotiations may be dragged out is uncertainty on the part of the artist—or record company—as to the number of tracks for which the producer may be asked to perform producer services or that he or she may be asked to mix. The producer should not be penalized for this uncertainty. Recently, the parties have begun to favor a short deal memo to get things started.

Pro Rata Royalty Share

Customarily, the producer will receive a pro rata share of the total royalty, depending on how many tracks are produced in relation to the total number of tracks on the album. Note, however, that whatever percentage is decided upon can be the subject of heated renegotiation later. For example, suppose the one track that the producer produces is the track that "makes" the record. I recall a situation when a movie soundtrack was released and the only track of any significance was the title track to the film, which was a big hit in and of itself. The record company sold millions of albums, and the artist and producer's brilliant track was dealt with as if it were merely one of a dozen of tracks on the album. There is no rule that says the track cannot bear a royalty as if it were five or six tracks on the album. At least this way, the track will earn money for the artist and the producer commensurate with its real value. (The soundtrack to *Foul Play*, starring Goldie Hawn and Chevy Chase, contained "Ready to Take a Chance Again," which was the only important song in the film—or on the album. Barry Manilow sought—and received—royalties as if the recording represented 50% rather than 10% of the album's content.)

If the number of tracks to be produced is indefinite at the time of negotiation, the producer's agreement (or deal memo) can take into account the uncertainty by including a series of contingency provisions, reducing the total royalty base on which the producer's royalty is calculated by, say, 5% for each reduction in the producer's contribution by one track. For example, if ten or more songs produced by the producer appear on the album, the royalty will be calculated and paid on the basis of 100% of the base royalty (for example, 3%, going to 3.5% at 500,000 units and to 4% at 1 million units). For a nine-song contribution, the royalty would be calculated and paid on 95% of the base royalty; for an eight-song contribution, the royalty would be calculated and paid at 90% of the base royalty; etc. This is only an example. There are innumerable permutations, and the relative strength of the producer and the artist must always be taken into account when concocting the formula to be used. The point is, producers should not be penalized and have their royalties reduced by the mere addition of "filler" tracks on the record which do not bear any qualitative comparison to the tracks that they have produced.

A-Side Protection

A producer who has not produced all the tracks on an album does not want the track or tracks he or she *has* produced to lead the sale of a single or a CD single (which might contain more than two songs) and receive merely a pro rata share of royalties based on the total number of tracks on the particular recording. Customarily, when a producer produces the great majority of tracks on an album, or when he or she is a "star" producer and is brought in to produce only one or two key tracks, that producer is afforded what is known as *A-side protection*. This means that if the producer's track is on the A side (that is, the featured track on a record), he or she will receive a full royalty without regard to whether other tracks that the producer is responsible for are incorporated onto the B side (or, in the case of CD singles, the B or C sides). Producers may even insist on language in their contracts providing that their track(s) not be included on the B side, in the hopes that the track(s) will be contained on the A side one day. If a producer *does* insist on A-side protection, the record company will ordinarily counter with a demand that if another producer seeks A-side protection for his or her track, and if the first producer's track is on the B side, the first producer will receive nothing for that B side. It is important for the producer's representative to understand what is actually going on in the studio—how many tracks are being recorded, whether the artist or record company intends to bring in another producer to record additional tracks, etc.—so that he or she will be in a position to negotiate this provision effectively given the particular nature of the recordings that the client is making in relation to the album as a whole. This entire area is of steadily diminishing significance in the digital era—with the exception of the occasional CD single.

Credit Provisions

There need to be provisions setting forth the credits to be accorded the producer—size and location on the CD, back cover, liner notes, etc. One thing that is often carelessly handled is the nature of the credit when the producer is providing his or her services through a service corporation. If the producer's services are being furnished by the producer's corporation, it would be inconsistent for the CD to carry a simple credit, "Produced by [Producer's Name]." If the words "For [Name of Service Corporation]" were not included, the IRS could infer that the producer's claimed tax position, that of being employed by a corporation, was not true. There can be nasty tax consequences as a result of this apparently innocent lapse. Therefore, the contract provisions relating to credit must take this into consideration. Of course, some producers, like artists, do not want to appear too "corporate" and are willing to take the risk.

Producers may also want to avoid the situation in which their names are connected to a particularly goofy corporate name in credit lines and in advertisements. Presumably, they want their work to be taken seriously. This is not as easily achieved when the credit reads, say, "Produced by [Producer's Name] for "Take the Money and Run, Inc." Producers should make sure that provisions are included stating they will receive credit in every medium they might wish or expect and in a reasonable size and typeface. Nothing is more disconcerting than for a producer to open *Billboard* and see that no producer credit is given in the full-page advertisement celebrating the record's release—or platinum achievement. And don't neglect consumer ads. *Rolling Stone* (not considered a trade magazine), *People*, *Vanity Fair*—all are consumer publications that can reach the artist's potential audience, and there is no reason to leave out the producer's name from those ads, which will most certainly be read by industry professionals. Yes, they do read things other than the trades.

Producers might also want to consider requesting that their credits not appear with respect to mixes or remixes by third parties, or that their names as producers be retained but not as mixers. Only a provision to this effect will assure them of the right to remove their name in such circumstances.

Audits

As stated previously, the producer's royalties are dependent on the artist royalty provisions. Therefore, the producer's representatives *must* have an unredacted copy of those provisions in order to be able to determine what the producer is supposed to receive.

Other audit-related issues are the following: Are there provisions covering whether the producer is bound by the accountings to the artist and/or the audit provisions of the artist's agreement? Does the producer have the independent right to audit the record company? Can the producer piggyback on the artist's royalty audit and ensure that his or her entitlements are covered, and claimed, as well as those of the artist in any eventual claim that is asserted following the conclusion of a royalty examination?

Rerecording Restrictions

Customarily, producers are expected to warrant to the artist and the artist's record company that they will not, for a period of from two to five years after the completion of their production services, produce or coproduce a master recording for any other artist or record company that embodies any musical composition they have just produced. When the producer also writes the songs being produced, this can be an unreasonable restraint on future exploitation of the producer's own compositions. This can be even more restrictive if the producer is also an artist and might like to record his or her own versions of these compositions.

Song Authorship

It has become the norm for the contract with the producer to provide that the producer must warrant that he or she has not made and will not make any contribution to the authorship of any compositions recorded and that he or she will not claim any right, title, or interest therein. If the producer has made an authorship contribution and the contract is still in the draft stage, the language can be changed. But what happens when a producer has already signed a contract containing this provision and then makes a significant authorship contribution? In such a case, I usually advise my producer clients not the leave the studio until a piece of paper confirming the coauthorship, and the exact splits, is initialed by all contributing authors.

Sampled Material

Most producer contracts specify that delivery of the masters is deemed not to have occurred unless and until all written licenses and permissions from the owner(s) of sampled material have been obtained and delivered to the artist and record company. More often than not, except in the hip-hop and reggae genres, it is the artist who decides whether samples are necessary and who selects them, but it is the producer who is contractually responsible for obtaining the permissions, upon terms and conditions acceptable to the artist and the record company, and it is the producer who is responsible for any fee or other payment due in connection with the use of any sampled material that is not approved by the artist and the record company. That's quite a responsibility. Do all producers know that such provisions exist? Have their lawyers or managers ever told them about this particularly tricky delivery requirement? Sometimes a producer will become aware of this provision only when the back-end advance, having been used by the record company to pay for the cost of samples, does not arrive on schedule (or at all) or has been reduced. Of course, the previous example covers the situation in which the artist is signed directly to the record company and the producer is separately, and independently, engaged. When the record company signs the producer who provides the services of the artist, or when the producer is the artist, the question of sanctions on producers, which I am suggesting be avoided in sampling situations, becomes moot.

Indemnities

Producers, who by definition are supposed to be the responsible ones in charge of multi-hundred-thousand-dollar budgets, are often asked to protect the record company from eventual claims arising out of a large number of potential problem areas. Producers and their representatives must be particularly careful about what the contract requires them to indemnify. For example, if the producer has nothing to do with selecting samples, he or she should not indemnify the artist or record company against losses resulting from claims by the owners of the songs, or recordings, sampled. Furthermore, the producer is in no position to warrant the originality of musical compositions written by the artist and should not be responsible for any costs related to the fact or claim that these songs have been plagiarized by the artist. Finally, as with all indemnities, no one can guarantee that a claim will not be brought by a third party seeking compensation for damages. Even unproven claims are very costly to defend, and the only thing that the indemnity should apply to is losses resulting from these claims—presumably confirming the veracity of the claims—not the cost of a successful defense of a claim.

Claims settled without the consent of the producer should not be subject to the indemnity provision unless the producer has consented to the settlement.

Union Requirements

The standard contract requires that the producer adhere to all union agreements having jurisdiction over the recording, and producers and their representatives should be aware of what this entails.

Among the most tedious responsibilities are the filing of union session reports within a set number of days (usually fourteen) following the applicable recording session. These session reports are, in themselves, rather complicated in that the producer must accurately report the number of sessions; overtime, if any; and, in the case of the American Federation of Musicians (AF of M), indicate who is the leader of the musicians. (Every union session must have a leader, who receives double scale.) Many producers have assistants who are familiar with the rules and regulations of the two principal unions—AF of M and American Federation of Television and Radio Artists (AFTRA)—involved in the making of recordings. Union regulations for theatrical productions are especially complex and costly, and some theatrical show producers are paid substantially for the services of their assistants in addition to their own fees. But any way you look at it, the record producer is charged with these responsibilities and the ramifications for failing to honor them can be serious.

Post-Term License Income

Post-term licensing of master recordings can be extremely lucrative. Film, TV, and commercial uses of masters generate enormous sums of money for the record company. This money is customarily split with the artist on a 50/50 basis, although it can be shared more favorably. The artist's share must be split between the producer and the artist, and this division is normally made by the record company before distributing the artist's share. But unless producers see or hear, or hear about, the particular TV show, film, or commercial, they are unlikely to find out about these uses, and must rely on the record companies to pay them their shares. By the way, here is another example of how producers can profit from others' efforts long after they have completed their work and gone home. The huge staffs of the majors' synch divisions, as well as those of publishing companies, are always working overtime to generate these monies. Songwriters and artists are also often quite involved. The producers? Well, they just collect their percentages.

Producer-Engineers

When a producer provides services as an engineer as well as a producer, if the fees attributable to his or her engineering services are included in the customary advance paid against producer royalties, it is appropriate to divide the advance into (1) the engineering fee, which is not recoupable against royalties, and (2) an amount, the fee, which is recoupable against producer royalties.

The faster the advance is recouped (that is, the lower the amount of what is designated as the advance), the more quickly the producer will receive royalties that, as you will recall, go back to record one. These early royalties can accumulate in substantial amounts, and if they are never released to the producer because the advance is never recouped by the record company, there can be significant financial consequences. The lesson here is to designate as much of the signing amount as possible as an engineering cost, and as little as possible as a producer advance.

Location of Recording

Producers are often more comfortable in their own environment than in a different city. They know about the studios in their geographical area, and they are aware of the availability and level of quality of technicians, equipment, and parts, etc. If the consensus among the record company's A&R person and the artist and the artist's representatives dictates that the recording be made, in whole or in part, outside of the producer's preferred location, two factors come into play. First, there will be additional costs for transporting and housing people and equipment (for example, the Pro-Tools engineer the producer prefers to work with), all of which will add to the production budget and delay the release of the producer's royalties after the advance has been recouped. If possible, language should be added stipulating that the producer is not responsible for such additional costs. Second, the producer's own comforts must be considered—for example, travel, accommodations, rental car, per diems, perhaps a trip "home" if the process takes more than a month or two. All will have to be dealt with, and the producer's own manager or attorney—whoever is negotiating the agreement—should be familiar with the producer's minimum requirements in this area.

Complimentary Copies

The producer's representatives must make sure the contract contains a provision requiring the record company to deliver to the producer, at its expense, at least twenty-five copies of the CD as soon as it is released. You would be surprised how many times a record company will try to weasel out of giving producers the copies of the CD that are rightfully theirs and which they need for a variety of reasons, not the least of which is auditioning for new projects—often with the same record company.

THE PRODUCER AS AUTHOR OF THE SOUND RECORDING

All record companies require that producers acknowledge that their duties are performed as employees for hire and that the products of their efforts are works for hire. As discussed in chapter 23, there is a possibility that the copyright law does *not* permit such a concept—that their creations are merely *assigned* to the record company, in which case the producers may actually terminate the assignments thirty-five years after they performed the services. Section 203 of the 1976 law (which took effect in 1978) provides that authors can recapture whatever it is that they assigned, and the first test of this for records produced in 1978 was 2013.

This issue will be of particular relevance to record producers who have contributed more than traditional production services, that is, producers who have actually *created* the product no less than if they were the artists themselves. Such producers have become the norm in certain genres of music. To my mind, these producers have every right to be called "authors," and it will be interesting to see if they can garner the support for a share in the recapture wars that are certain to erupt shortly.

Record companies are now insisting that certificates of employment be signed before the actual producer agreements are concluded. This insistence on producers admitting in writing that the record they are about to produce is a work for hire—*even before they receive their start-up advance*—is becoming universal in the United States. Many lawyers are up in arms about their clients signing a document that says that the record company owns the results of the producer's services even before the deal is fully negotiated, let alone reduced to a signed writing. Some lawyers withhold their objection if they have at least a brief deal memo signed between the artist and the producer. Those with no leverage will allow the certificate of employment to be signed even if the actual deal is far from concluded—just so that the producer can go into the studio and begin working. After all, they feel, sooner or later, they will be paid for their services since a record company would be hard-pressed to say that they own something when they have not actually paid for it. In any event, here is one more document that benefits the record company. It may well turn out to be illegitimate, but it will still require expensive lawyer's services to review.

PRODUCERS AND NEIGHBORING RIGHTS

As uses of recordings in new media multiply due to the spread of the Internet among all peoples of the world, assuming that unauthorized sharing and piracy can be controlled, income for all participants will increase as well. Some institutions and mechanisms exist now, and others are in the process of being established, which can generate additional income for individual producers that they do not enjoy as of the date this book is being written. While the passage of truly meaningful neighboring rights legislation has been blocked for generations in the United States, there are some cracks in the wall of resistance—notably the

Digital Performance Right in Sound Recordings Act (DPRSRA) of 1995, which mandated licensing fees for certain digital transmissions by subscription services. (The term *neighboring rights* refers to rights that are *not* covered by US copyright law but that are related to rights conferred by copyright law and that *are* recognized by many other countries. Neighboring rights are discussed in more detail in chapter 17.)

For the first time, artists (together with their record companies and their producers) are being paid for the performance of their music. Frank Sinatra and others whose recorded performances generated fortunes for the broadcasting industry over the years, and who fought for neighboring rights legislation for decades, must be singing for joy in the other realm.

Over the last few decades, record producers have gotten into the act, claiming that radio performances of their music should generate a "residual" for them as well as for the music publishers and writers. Contemporary record producers see themselves not just as functionaries, but as intellectual property creators and contributors no less important to the ultimate product than the song itself. Of course, recording artists feel the same way, so there is quite a large population of people hungry for a larger piece of the pie. As the pie itself continues to grow, perhaps producers will receive their fair share.

Record producers note that film companies refer to the script as the "currency" of the motion picture and music publishers refer to the song as the "currency" of the recording. They contend that, by analogy, their contribution as producers is the "currency" of genres like rap, hip-hop, and dance music. And frankly, they are not wrong.

There are two issues here. The first is whether individual producers are "authors" in the sense of various world copyright conventions. For example, the Rome Convention, to which the United States is not a signatory, stipulates that when a work is broadcast, a fee must be paid to the producers, to the performers, or to both, of the broadcast work, or phonogram. The phrase "broadcasters of phonograms," has been the subject of intense litigation in Europe because individual producers are claiming that the word *producer* refers both to individual producers and corporate (record company) producers. The consensus of those who have considered this issue is that it was probably the intention of the drafters of this convention and others that the "producers" for whom the conventions have sought to provide protection are indeed the record companies and not individual producers, who are trying to slip themselves into the coverage afforded by the treaties.

The second issue is a practical one. Even if the individual producers prevail in their claim—or succeed in promoting legislation supporting their claim—is there enough support in the industry to force broadcasters to pay yet another fee for the operation of their businesses? It does not appear that there is. Currently, only some European organizations collect neighboring rights income for artists and record companies. It is probably not through the record company that the artist will be paid neighboring rights income, and therefore the traditional producer agreement and the letter of direction to the record company will not cover the issue of neighboring rights income. One of the things that the producer can do in the meantime, however, is to piggyback on the rights of artists, where they exist, and share in the same ratio as they share in other income sources via the producer agreement (for example, foreign, club, budget, and other forms of ancillary income). This will require that the producer agreement with the artist specifically identify sources of income that may not be collected directly by the record company, with the resultant pay-through of a share to the individual producer. These new sources that are collected directly by the artist will have to be accounted for and paid separately by the artist, who is not traditionally equipped to account on a regular basis to others. Thus, the producer agreement might include a letter of direction—"To Whom It May Concern"—such that in cases in which artist income for neighboring rights is paid directly from broadcasters to artists (or to artists' agents), the paying party is directed to also pay the producer his or her contractual percentage directly.

Where record companies receive neighboring rights income, they customarily share it not just with their artists, but with their producers as well, in the proportions that are established by their respective contractual arrangements. Otherwise, in order to make their argument for a share of this income, producers will have to overcome the economic resistance of a large number of interests as well as the perception that their creative contribution to a master recording is something less than authorship. In chapter 17, I discuss in more detail the concept of neighboring rights and the availability of new sources of income for producers, artists, and writers.

9 · GETTING YOUR RECORD HEARD
A Practical Guide to Marketing and Promotion

Half the money I spend on advertising is wasted;
the trouble is I don't know which half.
—LORD LEVERHULME, IN DAVID OGILVY'S
CONFESSIONS OF AN ADVERTISING MAN

The record is written and recorded. It is manifested (finally) in a master recording from which "derivatives" will be made and shipped (or digitally transmitted) to the consumer. There are now left only two functional dominions—or realms—that affect the recording artist's eventual success or failure: the contract terms and the record company's promotional tools. The contract describes the mutual promises made between the record company and the artist; it defines and delineates the structure of their relationship and it refines how their respective rights and financial entitlements are to be governed and how they are to be achieved. The promotional tools of the record company are the hundred or so actions it can take to maximize the chances that potential buyers will hear the record and that the artist(s) will achieve the highest profile possible. Of these mechanisms, which include advertising of all kinds, videos, and public appearances, the most important is radio promotion, that is, obtaining airplay time. And whereas in the past promotional campaigns were handled and paid for by the record companies, increasingly the trend has been toward independent promotion, where, although people inside the company *manage* the promotional campaigns, people outside the company are charged with the real task and costs are borne in part or in whole by the artist.

Advertising and publicity, of course, continue to have their place in the overall marketing of a record. But print advertising is not particularly effective in the music business, and radio and television advertising is prohibitively expensive. Other forms of publicity—such as interviews in trade magazines, appearances on television talk shows, or articles inserted into consumer magazines—all require a "story." Beginning artists rarely have one that can be effectively publicized. Merchandising a new artist will not be very extensive—perhaps limited to delivery of posters and in-store displays to record stores, with no guarantee they will be used. Thus in most cases, radio promotion is the only viable route with which to bring an artist and the artist's recording to the attention of eventual buyers.

MARKETING TOOLS

A well-intentioned record label executive might say, Here are one hundred things we can do to market you and your record:

1. Arrange for in-store appearances.
2. Get you mentioned in *Hits* magazine.
3. Take ads in trade publications.

4. Get you mentioned in *Billboard.*

5. Send postcards to advise everyone of the impending release.

6. Put stickers on the record and on telephone booths in towns where you have elicited interest.

7. "Snipe" the city (put posters up on abandoned buildings).

8. Bring you to conventions to perform.

9. Utilize Broadcast Data Systems (BDS) and SoundScan.

10. Hire an independent publicist.

11. Do a video. We'll post it on YouTube or SoundCloud.

12. Do another video. We'll post it on YouTube or SoundCloud.

13. Get on a television show.

14. Get a track of yours on a soundtrack to a cool movie or TV show.

15. Send you to Europe and other foreign countries.

16. Send you on tour in the United States.

17. Hire independent radio promotion people in addition to those on our permanent staff.

18. Take out ads in towns where you have fans to strengthen your core support.

19. Send you on a radio promotion tour in the United States.

20. Send you on a radio promotion tour in Europe and other foreign countries.

21. Arrange for radio interviews by satellite to foreign countries.

22. Arrange for an "event" with a flying pig balloon à la Pink Floyd.

23. Host a number of "listening" parties to introduce your album.

24. Hire ethnic-specific marketing people to reach your biggest fan base.

25. Feature your record as the "Record of the Week" on our website.

26. Co-op advertise your album (for example, by paying for one-half of Tower Records' print ads in the Sunday paper).

27. Prioritize your album by delivering it to key radio stations 120 days before the official release date so that upon release, you will have 40 parallel one-station ads (see "Airplay and Payola," page 152).

28. Place your music on the Internet and digitally download "teases" to interest consumer in purchasing the record or listening to it via downloads or streams.

29. Place a track in a TV commercial.

30. Offer free downloads on consumer products.

31. Offer free downloads or inexpensive album downloads for short periods of time via Amazon.

32. Feature your band at a music convention/festival such as SXSW, Bonnaroo, Lollapalooza, or Ozzfest.

33. Place a track on a video game.

34. Create a video moment whose goal is to "go viral" on YouTube or VEVO. Gotye ("Someone I Used to Know")—380,000,000 viewers—and Carly Rae Jepson ("Call Me Maybe") 420,000,000 viewers—did it, why not you?

35. Obtain feature articles in mainstream publications highlighting your being the cutting-edge artist of the moment. Especially useful in magazines with annual music features.

36. Similar mentions on "What We're Listening To" features.

37. Provide opportunities for in-store performances at bookstores/cafes

38. Obtain an interview at a music conference such as Music Matters, SXSW, MIDEM. This certainly helped Jason Mraz whose success in Asia-Pac territories had not yet translated in the United States.

39. Obtain an add-on to a Sirius-XM channel such as "Coffee House." Remember, they actually identify the artist. Jason Mraz was heavily featured on this channel in 2011.

40. Obtain caller ring-back tones in new markets —this has helped enormously where it has been otherwise difficult to expand an artist's commercial success into new territories.

41. Compete on broadcast television shows such as *American Idol, The Voice*, even *America's Got Talent*.

42. Have someone manage your Twitter account to increase the number and improve the demographics of your followers.

43. Try to obtain features on NPR or local public radio stations. In New York City, WNYC plays a portion of a song by a break, cutting edge, artist every morning and then advises its listeners as to when and where they can be seen live THAT NIGHT.

44. Release your CD (album or single) by surprise, virally, to garner press attention (see Drake, Kendrick Lamar's efforts in 2016).

45. You get the idea.

THE GOAL-ORIENTED CAMPAIGN

These "hundred tools" are on the table at all times, and the senior record executive who oversees marketing, publicity, and promotion departments, and is charged with breaking the act or the album, will choose among them, and others. Yet the decisions will not always be tied to an agreed-upon goal shared by the artist and the record company.

Instead of saying, "Here's our goal; let's apply the tools," record company executives often say, "Look, here are our tools. Let's apply as many as we can afford and see what sticks." While everyone (including the artist and the artist's manager and lawyer) is applauding the record executive for convincing the record company to apply any given tool (like a cutting-edge video), they often lose sight of the goal—if indeed any goal has ever been articulated, let alone agreed upon. And before the coda fades to black on the $100,000 video, an entire career may be lost. Indiscriminate application of marketing tools makes the record company no less the victim than the artist. Ironically, it is often the artist who has the creative ideas that actually push the record company in the *wrong* direction. A record company president once told me that his company's marketing should be to the eventual consumers, not to the artists or their managers.

This is top-down management, not bottom-up management, where goals are identified and money and labor are spent efficiently and effectively. To mount an effective goal-oriented marketing campaign in the music industry requires a fundamental familiarity with the practical side of the business. Yet the lawyers and business affairs executives of record companies, whose job it is to negotiate the many-faceted, intricate legal and financial relationships between the parties, are often light-years away from understanding how a record is sold—how the company can help an artist to succeed.

It is very easy to work the next Kanye West record. It is nearly impossible to work the new "new band" record. How do you get the label to work the new band product after the first week, when it has sold only 200 units nationwide? And how in fact does the label arrive at the 200-unit number? Will it rely on SoundScan, which is merely a statistical sampling? Will it totally ignore sales at mom-and-pop stores or speciality underground stores, which is where any new band's core fan base will begin to show interest? Will it recognize Internet activity as a barometer of things to come? If a record does not show a lot of sales activity in the first two weeks, not infrequently the label will give up on the record. Yet it is on these first two weeks' activity that much, if not everything, that the artist has dreamed about for a lifetime, depends. One wrong format decision, one bad decision as to where the money is spent, and the artist is history.

Identifying the goal, keeping your eye on it amid all adversity and turmoil, prioritizing functions, avoiding distractions, managing time, capitalizing on opportunities—all of these are characteristics of the highly successful entrepreneur. And all of these are characteristics of the highly successful artist. Yet just as every artist is different from every other artist, the goals of every artist are different from the goals of every other artist, and the means toward those goals will differ, even among artists who share similar aspirations. For example, some bands do not really want to be a band; they just want to make five records every ten years for five decades. Others realize that their fan base is everything and that time spent in front of two hundred people at a time will go much further toward achieving their goals than doing an in-store appearance or radio convention visit three thousand miles away. Some do not aspire to have trade magazine ads and stories, but rather prefer to utilize "bounce-back cards" to establish a database of like-minded fans. The business side of things is anathema to those kinds of artists. Their goal is to be like Hootie and Phish—that is, to reach their fan base because it is to them that they have something to say, not to the readers of *Time* magazine or people who watch PBS programming. These bands' methodologies have the intended design of making the record company irrelevant insofar as building a sales base is concerned. Michael Bolton actually held parties after his gigs, inviting fans to a hotel suite where beverages were served (nonalcoholic, I'm told). The purpose was not just to have a good time, but to use this unique opportunity to identify his true fans and to be able to contact them later—for example, on the release of an album, or when Bolton would be coming to their town or area again, maybe even a few years down the road. Then again, the methodology of a singles band may be completely different. A track on a movie soundtrack or placement on *American Idol* is golden to this kind of act.

All artists are special. They have different attributes, different natures, and different missions. Some of these differences are addressed in one way or another in the contract. Most are not. The *contractual domain* provides structure and rules to the artist's professional life. The *practical domain* is primarily concerned with the goal of success.

THE RECORD CONTRACT

The goal of "success" is never mentioned in the record contract itself, nor do artists' professional representatives always think through contract negotiations with success in mind. Too often, the negotiations center on what to do in the event of failure—not success. Most recording contracts clearly state that no provisions be made regarding eventual sale of sufficient records to meet specific goals. Yet other than the ostensible artistic purpose of creating music, is it not the perceived goal of every artist to become a hit artist? Why, then, is the contract never couched in these terms?

Suppose record executives and the artist's representatives *can* agree on what makes a particular artist unique and then agree on which tools should be utilized to promote that artist. Do any of the parties concerned know what the contract says on the subject? How often do the hundreds and thousands of music industry people involved in an artist's career make marketing decisions on the basis of the contract? I would suggest hardly ever.

Maybe they don't *want* to know what the contract says. Does the manager disclose to the record company just before a decision about tour support funding is due that a (least important) member of a band has just quit the band? After all, the contract will require that a notice be sent within a set number of days after the occurrence, but you can be sure it will not be sent even if the manager or attorney is aware of the contractual requirement.

Do the delivery requirements under the contract jibe with the likely release date six months later? Has any record *ever* been delivered on time? Has any marketing director ever said, "Don't deliver the record now; we can't do anything with it until the second quarter of next year." On the contrary, no record company business affairs lawyer ever misses the opportunity to notify an artist (certified mail, return receipt requested, with copies all over the place) that he is one hundred days late in delivering the record and therefore the contractual consequences will take effect. (For example, the mechanical royalty rate in effect when the artist "should" have delivered will apply, not the mechanical royalty rate in effect when the artist "did" deliver the record.) Ironically, when the record is actually delivered, the timing is often perfect for the record label to release the record. In other words, the delay may have worked to the record company's advantage. Yet the contract penalizes the artist for late delivery.

Is all of the money that is being charged to the artist being applied to the correct account? How does the actual way in which the marketing budget is structured affect the profit-and-loss statement of the record company with resultant decisions as to whether to pick up an option or to not throw good money after bad? What does the contract say about that? What mechanism does the contract provide to resolve the multitude of issues of this nature that arise during the course of an artist's career?

If the artist's team (manager, lawyer, business manager) believes that the contract does not contain adequate provisions for promoting the record, does the team build another 30% over-budget contingency into the recording fund to ensure that it can access this money when it is needed for promotion—not for recording? If not disclosed, is this ethical? Is it dangerous? Is it tantamount to stealing? Do the potential disadvantages of this kind of practice—for example, setting a tone and establishing a reputation that might hurt the artist and the artist's team—outweigh the potential advantages?

The label will direct its own overworked publicity department to apply its necessarily generic styles to the artist's album (although rarely to the artist's "career"), and if the publicity department cannot generate much press, the artist is usually blamed. It is nearly impossible to restructure a label's departments, least of all the publicity department, to custom-fit a particular group. It is a rare contract that will commit a record company to covering the costs of an independent publicist to market an artist's record in every important market.

Much of what is in the contract is never enforced. Here's just one among many possible examples. The last paragraph of section 11.03 of Sony Music's form agreement requires that an auditor hired by an artist to examine Sony's books may not be at the same time engaged in "any other examination." Paragraph 11.03.1 goes on to say:

> The preceding provisions of this paragraph will not apply if Sony elects to waive the provisions which require that your representative shall not be engaged in any Other Examination.

Originally, these clauses were presumably inserted to frustrate the auditor who commences an audit for one client, sees an error affecting other artists, calls the other artists, and says, "Hire me for a third of what I can dig up for you, and I will audit your account at the same time as I am proceeding with the audit I have just begun." At the request of my clients' auditors, fearing the potential consequences (especially to themselves) of this provision, I have repeatedly invested hours and hours of time negotiating modifications to such clauses. The fact is that the likelihood of their ever being enforced is nil, and so, practically speaking, my efforts are a waste of time and money.

For a seventy-page (or more) document that costs between $15,000 and $20,000 (or more) in legal fees to negotiate, that is a sad commentary on the practicality and efficacy of the services that the label forces the artist to obtain and pay for.

Tour Support

Having a provision in the contract committing the record company to provide deficit tour support guarantees that a band will have the chance to perform live. It means that the record company will absorb losses associated with an artist's tour; in essence, it is a subsidy. Customarily, record companies are very hands-on with respect to planning the tour, selecting the cities visited and the clubs played, budgeting, etc. If the budget is, say, $50,000 for a twelve-city tour, yet projected gross income is only $20,000, the record company promises to bear the burden of the $30,000 balance. The provisions that establish this in a typical contract are no different from one artist agreement to another, and most stipulate that such support will be provided for a tour schedule that is approved by the record company and the artist (so-called "mutual approval"; see below). Although such a provision may be totally satisfactory for many artists, for some it may not be. For example, the artist and the artist's manager may disagree with the record company as to what tour schedule will best achieve the aims of that particular artist and will differentiate the artist from other artists. The record company's "approval" of a tour plan is not only irrelevant in this situation, it is a waste of money—money that might more effectively be spent elsewhere, or saved until an *appropriate* tour opportunity comes along.

Here's an example that concerns a new band that was given the opportunity to be the opening act for a well-known group. Now, it is axiomatic that any good new band will be bringing to the stage a style and an interpretation that is unknown to the public, and the more talented and innovative the new group, the more likely it is that the band's style will take some getting used to. In fact, the better the new band, the more likely it is to be dismissed by an audience with an established taste. This is why radio, with its repeat-play capabilities, is still so important in introducing new art to the public. In this case, the new group knew that the audience would be likely to hoot them off the stage, but the record company and the agent thought that partnering with the famous band and playing in front of large audiences would be a great coup. The record company agreed (joyfully, I might add) to lend its contractually agreed-upon financial tour support to *that* tour and to *that* tour only. As it turned out, not only was the audience impatient to hear its favorite act, it was totally turned off by the nature of the new band's music. You can imagine the frustration of the artist and manager when a few months later the perfect tour opportunity materialized at a festival with a number of like-minded bands whose much larger audience was complementary to our—now depressed—new band. Why depressed? Because there was no money left with which to introduce the band to the very people who would have liked them and would have bought their records. To add insult to injury, the wasted tour support money was logged as an additional advance against the artist's account.

Recording Costs

What may seem to be incidental marketing costs can wreak havoc with both your marketing budget and your ever-growing royalty deficit. For example, is a radio edit a recording cost? If the royalty department codes a radio edit as a recording cost, the artist may have a surprise in store when the royalty statement arrives months later. Some singles have twelve different radio versions. At $5,000 per edit, that's $60,000. At $0.80 per CD (see chapter 4, page 25, for an analysis of the artist's "rate"), an additional 75,000 albums have to be sold to pay for these costs. It will cost $10,000 or more to do an audit before the issue is even addressed and, perhaps (or perhaps not), resolved—usually through some compromise. And meanwhile, 75,000 albums that bear no royalty for you will have generated more than $525,000 in additional revenues for the record company, even as the artist's royalty account remains in the red.

Mutual Approval

"Mutual" is an often-used contract word. Lawyers think they have attained something when an approval right (for example, tour support) is made "mutual" between the record company and the artist. In reality, even when a contract says that approval of certain matters shall be subject to mutual approval by the record company and the artist, the record company always has the last word. Further, many contracts provide that the artist shall not withhold approval "unreasonably," whatever that means.

Mixers

Not the college kind. The studio kind. Often labels will force a mixer—or a producer—of their choice on an artist. The costs of hiring a fabulous mixer (and there are a few) for two weeks—which is what it might take to remix an already finished album—can equal the costs of hiring a producer for three months! And if you are an East Coast group and the mixer of the moment lives in Hawaii or Malibu, you have to add the cost of a trip to the other coast for the band (or two of its members) and perhaps the manager. Then there are the hotel rooms and per diems. And let us not forget that the mixer will only work in such and such a studio, which charges $1,800 a day for fifteen days. Total cost: $60,000? $70,000? $80,000? Why not? After all, it will help sell records to have Mr. X's name on the back of the disc. Or will it? Some feel that Mr. X's name will mean something only to *Billboard* addicts or other industry types. No doubt some fifteen- to eighteen-year-olds have heard of Mr. X—or can distinguish between X's mix and others' mixes—but most have not. Others will tell you that the mixer is the difference. The labels will call it marketing, but your royalty account will not reflect any difference between this and other recoupable recording costs.

Maybe Mr. X *is* the only person in the world who can polish the record to the point at which it will be the hit it would otherwise never have been. I do not know whether this is usually, sometimes, or never the case. The artist and the artist's manager usually go along with the decision largely because they, too, can't be sure whether it will actually make the difference between a bubbling-under rating success and a major hit, and they themselves are susceptible to the "star" treatment. Who would not want Chris Lord-Alge or Mike Shipley to mix their record? But since so many factors enter into whether a record is a success, I am convinced that the added cost and time are of somewhat less value than the involved parties think they are. Whatever the reality, for the insecure artist and manager, not to mention the record company executives themselves—whose jobs are, in a way, on the line if the $500,000 or $1 million invested in our proverbial baby band is not earned back—what better way to cover oneself than to hire the supposedly tried . . . and true. After all, this cost, too, will ultimately be charged back to the artist.

Videos

Gotta have a video? Every band wants a video. Why? Is the money allocated to the band sufficient to produce the video and also do the other things that may be better ways to reach the artist's goal—for example, to pay for two months on the road? Which is the more efficient way to spend the limited money? It used to be that the only issue was how to convince MTV or VH-1 to *play* the video. Nowadays a video can be distributed via innumerable means including, of course, YouTube. And a video can be produced inexpensively by someone with a Canon HD Mark II and some talent. Kiesza's "Hideaway" was an inexpensive, one-take, video clip that went viral and helped to mount her career with an almost immediate #1 record in the United Kingdom. But the question remains whether one should be produced at more typical costs of from $50,000 to $100,000. The manager and record label of a client of mine insisted on producing such a video (although it cost $250,000), and it ended up being a really expensive home movie. Unfortunately, his royalties, such as they are, continue to be used to recoup these costs years later. Maybe the money could have been better spent? At the beginning of the 2000s, many record deals acquiesced in providing for a commitment of money to the promotion of the artist's record that might or might not take the form of video expenditures. However, some of these deals provided that if a record company were to take the position that a video does not make sense in the context of the marketplace, it would be obliged to invest the same amount of money in other, mutually agreed-upon, promotions. *Forcing* a label to spend money on videos can be counterproductive.

• • •

When all of the money is spent (or misspent) and the record company and the artist have the tour they do not need, the mixer they do not need, and the video they cannot use, the band members may have to return to their day jobs to survive, thereby relinquishing their one golden opportunity to work the record that took two years to make and twenty years to prepare for. The manager, the business manager, and the lawyer will also be off doing other things, since they cannot survive forever on the fumes of hope. They have overhead to pay and families to support. Their commitments can be stretched only so thin. So the implications of marketing and promotion decisions are very far-reaching indeed. The stronger the artist and the artist's representatives are, and the clearer they are as to the goals of the artist and how to reach those goals, the more likely it is they will be able to apply the artist's values to the task at hand in an efficient manner and at the same time keep costs in line.

DO RECORD COMPANIES KNOW WHAT THEY ARE DOING?

With all due respect to music industry professionals, with the exception of some A&R executives, not many of them have a clue as to how the record business really works—that is, how to make a hit record or a hit artist. Young (and some old) business affairs executives whose job it is to arrange the relationships among all the constituents of the record label often do not understand one iota of how their business works, nor, as often as not, do the artist's attorneys and managers. They have never made a record, delivered a record, experienced the recording of a record in a studio, or applied the principles in the contract to exploit the record. They do not understand whether a radio edit is a recording cost or a marketing expense.

I am not singling out young business affairs executives for any reason except to point out that while those in this department can—most impressively—dictate a fifty-page contract off the tops of their heads, it is the rare document that serves to assist either the record company *or* the artist (and manager) in choosing among the tools traditionally sought to "break" the artist or the record once the record has been delivered.

But there is an exception. Among the most important young record company executives is the A&R man or woman who championed the act in the first place and was instrumental in getting the artist signed. While the A&R person's job is officially concluded when the act is signed and the record is completed, no one can prove more of an asset to the common goal of breaking the artist and the new record than this particular professional. The A&R person is the conductor of the orchestra. The A&R person has to spot signs of weakness; cajole departments to focus on the artist; siphon off money slated for a different line item or different record; lead the participants—including the manager, lawyer, and business manager—toward understanding the common goal; watch out for people and political situations at the record company that may get in the way of reaching the common goal; and persuade the record company to believe in the band as much as the A&R person does. The A&R person coordinates the record company's worldwide efforts to bring the record—and the artist—home successfully. Conversely, the absence of an effective A&R person can have a devastating effect. The artist's representatives must be sensitive to the strengths and weaknesses of the A&R person and be ready to compensate for these weaknesses and to exploit these strengths. Failing that, the effort to make the artist and the artist's record a high priority at the record company—always an uphill battle—will be nearly impossible.

VICTIM OR VICTOR?

Most artists get one chance to make it. The days of multiple opportunities to click with the public are over. The Billy Joels, Bruce Springsteens, and Garth Brookses might have made it anyway, given their enormous talents and energies, but the fact is that they *were* given several albums' opportunity to reach their goals. The situation an artist does not want to be in is the one the overwhelming number get into, the one where they say, "Okay, we messed up. We made a lot of mistakes on that first album. Next time let's make sure we don't make the same mistakes." They won't likely get the chance. We have seen some of the mistakes. Here are a two more:

If the artist and/or the artist's team do not concur with the label's marketing people, and can't find a way to diplomatically redirect the label's focus to what they believe is the correct direction, the artist can be (1) written off as difficult, (2) avoided like the plague when subsequent marketing opportunities arise or (3) called an ass (or worse). Rarely will the artist be listened to with respect in the future.

Here is a possible scenario, one that will resonate with many artists and their managers. An artist (seeking to achieve a personal goal of reaching fans through live performing and building a fan base over however many months or years it might take) is needed by the record company in Seattle. The only problem is that the artist is in South Carolina ready to perform before his fiftieth club crowd of two hundred people. (That's ten thousand potential record buyers.) So she cancels the gig, loses $2,000, and flies to Seattle to make an in-store appearance and to stop by a radio station that has never heard of her and is doing a favor to the record company promotion person. But there is no direct flight from South Carolina to Seattle, so she has to fly to Atlanta and then to Denver and then to San Francisco and only then to Seattle. She arrives at 3 a.m. because heightened security measures have delayed departures from San Francisco and the weather in Seattle is stacking up the planes that wish to land there. She misses the radio appearance, but that's okay because the record company has another in-store scheduled for Portland, Oregon, at midnight the next night, tying in this artist's record with the crowded release event of the latest DVD of a hugely successful motion picture, one that is sure to draw hundreds of people who will, as a sort of captive audience, learn about the artist for the first time (although they could care less).

Do you see how an artist can become the victim of a goal-less label? Ironically, the record company itself is no less a victim of its own indiscriminate, injudicious application of the tools that are supposed to enhance an artist's acceptability, not to destroy it.

Sound exhausting? It is. Sleep deprivation is a leading cause of craziness among recording artists. They are forced into taking stimulants in unhealthy amounts—whether coffee, cigarettes, drugs, or all three. Welcome to the ozone that surrounds too many of our young artists. Before they know it, they're on the proverbial merry-go-round on their way to rock-and-roll hell. Their inexperienced young managers, lawyers, and business managers often have no idea how to stop the spiral, and the rest is history.

I am not suggesting that a misguided promotional trip to Seattle (or even a wisely chosen trip to Seattle) will send the artist into drug addiction. But the insanity that surrounds the period that record industry professionals call the "album cycle" is real and is fundamentally dangerous to careers and to lives. There is a saying in the record business that today's buzz is tomorrow's hangover. Nothing could be more true.

TELEVISION CAMPAIGNS

Mostly in Europe, but also in Japan and in other countries, record companies have discovered the value of television advertising for their products. Of course television advertising campaigns are very expensive, and record companies have decided that, rather than charge artists for all or a part of the cost of this form of promotion, they should reduce artists' royalties to, say, 50% of the otherwise applicable royalty during the period in which the campaign is running, or for a period of months afterward. Now it is the artist who finds that this can be very expensive.

Here are a few ways that artists can get some relief from this recent intrusion into the royalty calculation:

- Limit the effect of the provision to "substantial" television campaigns.
- Acquire the right to exercise veto rights over either the campaigns themselves or the extent and coverage of the campaigns.
- Limit the application of this provision to the locations where television campaigns have proved to be effective.
- Limit this provision so that it applies only to records sold in the specific territories reached by the television campaign and to no others.
- Try to get some handle on the projected financial impact of the promotion. As your career expands from using bounce-back cards to having your records featured in television advertisements, your manager will have to accumulate knowledge pretty quickly about the efficacy of such campaigns. The information is available, but much of it is overseas. The telephones and email servers to foreign affiliates are all operative and should be used in order for your manager to make decisions on the basis of what, for example, television advertising has done for other artists, where, at what cost—even in what seasons.

RADIO PROMOTION

What good is a good record if no one ever hears it? These days, it is easy to produce a wonderful recording in the confines of one's own home studio. But what to do once you have completed it? How do you get potential buyers to actually listen to it? The best way is for your record to be played on the radio. Really. I know, it sounds somewhat obvious on one level and ridiculous on another. But can you conceive of another means? Snipe (sticker) every city and small town and college in the world? Play every city and small town and college in the world? I don't think so. Just as television was the catalyst behind the success of Andrea Bocelli, Josh Groban, and The Three Tenors (and even The Irish Tenors), so radio is the only catalyst we know behind the success of most recording artists. Sure, the Internet is beginning to have an impact and Ani DiFranco has figured out how to sell records out of the back of her van, but for most of us, the only way we will hear about a new act is through radio performance—and possibly summer festivals. Say what you will about the power of YouTube clips gone viral, that is a very low percentage way to hope to grab peoples' attention to your record. It is in this atmosphere where the opportunities—and the headaches from radio promotion lie. Much of the remainder of this chapter is devoted to radio play and the means to obtain it. Before you read those portions, you will have to first come to terms with the fact that radio is not the be all and end all for an artist's success as it used to be. The reason is that radio has become so genre specific and yet so diverse at the same time that effort made and money spent no longer have the same impact as in former years. Add to that the diminution of popularity of certain genres (for example, middle of theroad, top 40, and rock and roll in all of its manifestations) it is indisputable that radio promotion has diminished among the menu choices that an artist or record company can utilize. Even as top 40 radio changes its spots from a pop song aggregator to an urban and country source, even that genre, which has survived cultural and societal changes over the years, has itself changed its form. And top 40 radio will no doubt change again. Nationwide programming by Clear Channel and other station owners and, while welcome on some level, satellite radio genre-specific programming, have all contributed to the homogeneity of music today making it even more difficult for a unique artist to be heard via what remains the most effective marketing device known to the music business: radio airplay.

With this in mind, I move on to discuss the often unsavory means by which airplay is achieved in the music business.

AIRPLAY AND PAYOLA

In the world of radio promotion, some stations, known in the business as "parallel one" stations, have more influence than others on *Billboard* and other chart publications. (Although satellite radio channels do not currently have parallel one status, it is only a matter of time before SiriusXM, or even Music Choice, makes a profound impact on consumer awareness of new artists and new releases.) To have a record added to a playlist on, say, forty parallel one stations in the first week of a record's release will most likely assure it a spot on the hot 100. Therefore, record labels will usually see to it that those stations receive copies of the single, or, if available, copies of the album way in advance of the release date, usually at least four months. Radio stations know that receiving a record product on its release date, or even one to three weeks in advance, indicates a lower priority at the label. It suggests that less money will be committed, fewer marketing tools will be used, and there will be less follow-up from the record company divisions (field sales personnel, publicists, and others), fewer in-stores, less co-op advertising, fewer radio station personal appearances, etc.—all those things that will eventually confirm to the radio station's listeners the correctness and foresight of a particular radio station programmer or DJ for having chosen that particular record as "hit bound." The importance of a company manifesting its commitment to an artist and recording cannot be overemphasized.

A Brief History of Payola

A combination of FCC rules and federal statutes govern *payola*, which is defined as the unreported payment to employees of broadcast stations, program producers, or program suppliers of any money, service, or valuable consideration for the purpose of achieving airplay. In short, payola is a bribe. An FCC rule referencing the applicable statute and FCC policies on payola (47C.F.R. Section 73.4180) states simply that the Federal Communications Act requires persons who have paid, accepted, or agreed to pay or accept any consideration for the broadcast of any material to report that fact to the station before the material is broadcast (47USC Section 508). If the material which is broadcast is paid for, the act further requires the station to announce that fact on the air and to identify the sponsor (47USC Section 317). The 1988 FCC Public Notice referenced in 47C.F.R. Section 73.1480 explains the FCC's payola policy. Failure to adhere to these reporting requirements can subject the violator to a fine of up to $10,000 or imprisonment in a federal penitentiary of up to one year, or both.

On February 25, 1988, four persons were indicted in US District Court in Los Angeles, California, for payola violations. One of those indicted was charged with having made "undisclosed payments from 1980 to 1985 in the form of cash and cocaine" to station personnel in order to secure airplay for certain records. These four persons were later convicted.

What does this have to do with record promotion? Let's just say that in the absence of regulations like the ones cited above, there would be little chance for an artist to succeed on his or her own merits. Money talks just as loudly in the record industry as in politics. Just as an incumbent politician with millions of dollars in his coffers usually buries a newcomer, those in the record industry with easy access to the media can leave their less fortunate competitors in the proverbial dust. Remember, in the United States, and increasingly throughout the world, with the rare exception of a YouTube video clip which has gone viral, if you don't get played on the radio, you won't succeed. Period. Or at least succeed in a big way. Those who claim that touring has replaced radio-supported record sales are simply serving up a myth.

I like to believe that if a talented person stays in the game long enough, the person's creativity will win out despite such obstacles as better funded and/or more established competitors (for the airwaves), stations' preference for tried-and-true musical styles, and xenophobic arbiters of taste. Unfortunately, this idealistic view runs afoul of the incredible power of the broadcasting industry. Listener expectations that songs are always selected for airplay on the basis of their merit is historically naive. I will not restate the history of payola except to say that there have been times in our history during which illicit means to attain radio play (that is, bribes) ran rampant throughout the radio industry. These included cash payments to disk jockeys and radio programmers as well as other kinds of favors, such as expensive gifts (television sets, cars, etc.), sexual favors, and, of course, drugs.

For good reason, and throughout the 1990s and early 2000s, the federal government thought that it had done a fairly good job at terminating this practice. But the record industry could not quite give up the advantages gained during the heyday of payola. So the leopard merely changed its spots one day. The road between the record company and the radio station was irrevocably placed on permanent detour. Let me explain.

Chart Manipulation: The New Payola As EDM (electronic dance music) takes over hip-hop and rap as the most popular youth-driven genre (even Jay Z has signed several DJs to his label), payola has raised its head again—this time by controlling charts. If the important charts display your record among the top 100 (or better), you can relax . How to get there in the modern age? Read on.

Given the rise of the "playlist," curated by and for individuals signed up to streaming services, charts have become even more significant than merely written lists of the most performed/sold recordings. As this book goes to press, Beatport (an SFX subsidiary) is in the middle of the dispute as to whether charts can be manipulated. While that site is generally regarded as quite diligent in pulling from its playlists tracks that they suspect have been illegally charted, some artists/producers have claimed otherwise. Laidback Luke, having had one of his recordings removed from a Beatport playlist, was appalled. Having achieved the irreplaceable—and I think that I can say essential—goal of getting his record on the playlists of Spotify, Deezer, and Apple Music, Beatport decided that the activity attributable to the track was suspect. Arriving in the "streaming space" is the holy grail. To depart from it is to be moving in the wrong direction.

How does a track get added to a playlist on, say, Spotify? First, fans will add it to their personal playlists; then their friends will adopt it and add it to theirs (not only because it has gotten their attention and they like it, but also because in the world of social media, if you like, it, then it must be worthy of being liked by your peers (and online friends); before you know it, the song has gone viral and become unstoppable. Naturally, the payday is so great that adding a song to a major sites' playlist is susceptible of bribery, and once again, we're back to the tried and true, if not honest, days (years) of payola. Pay for play is a natural outgrowth of the scenario where one person, or a few persons, "curate" a play list. It has not yet been proven that payola exists in the curation of playlists, but when thousands of dollars, if not millions, and of course entire careers, are at stake, the record that gets the play, gets the influx of money for additional promotion. The money follows the money. Record companies do not throw money at records that are not making any noise; they throw it at records that are. Allegedly, adding a song to a watched playlist can cost upward of only a mere $2,000 to $10,000 for the privilege. This is a drop in the water when honest, straightforward, promotion can cost upward of $250,000. As in the past, new acts tend to fall behind the dividing line between legitimate and illegitimate ways to reach the public on anything that resembles a level playing field.

Worth noting, however, is that this kind of chart manipulation is not (or not yet) a crime. There may be other laws which might be asserted to protect consumers and creators such as the laws of unfair competition, anti-trust and the like. Manipulating charts and playlists of streaming services has nothing to do with broadcasting over FCC-licensed airwaves. The Payola Law (47US Code Section 508—the Federal Communications Act) simply does not apply.

The Independent Record Promoter

Record companies today rarely expend the lion's share of their promotion money on their promotion division staff's own efforts to promote radio play. For most of the history of the music business as we know it, one of the record companies' vaunted talents was to promote their products. They sold themselves on these strengths. Even today, they have sophisticated promotion departments. What is different?

Over a decade ago, in the midst of several federal investigations of the presence of payola in the record industry, the major record companies had a brilliant idea. Why should the suited executives subject themselves to these tawdry, tedious, and expensive investigations, all of which were centered around the foot soldiers of the industry? Why indeed when the risks were so great? For a CBS (which owned the CBS Radio and Television Network as well as several other stations) or an RCA (which owned the NBC Radio and Television Network, as well as several other stations), violations of federal payola regulations by their record divisions threatened the most lucrative assets the corporate giants owned, their broadcasting licenses. Simply put, broadcast licenses would not be renewed for felons.

What to do? Simple. Kill the messenger.

The record companies, as a group, fired most of their promotion department personnel. Now that the villains were no longer employed by the record companies, the broadcasters and record companies could breathe more easily. Only there was one problem. The record companies could not promote their records without promotion people. You might say that this was like cutting off your head to spite your body, but the record companies had a solution.

Enter the independent promoter. Who *was* the independent promoter? In many cases, the same person who had previously been employed by the record company. Now, instead of a W-2, the company filed a 1099 with the IRS. The independent promoter was an independent contractor and was not under the "supervision, guidance, or control" of the record company, let alone the parent company. The parent was safe. The record company was safe. Voilà! Saved from the Feds. If the "independent" promotion people violated the law, there was no clear line of authority and therefore no clear culpability on the part of the record companies that could implicate their parent companies and, among other things, jeopardize their broadcast licenses.

The internal cost of a promotion department decreased enormously (the companies retained a head of promotion and a skeletal staff), and there were lots of promotion dollars available to spread among the independent promoters. The promotion people thus hired, of course, did not let a good thing go unexploited. They began to charge more and more money to the record companies for their services. But the record companies were not so dumb. They insisted that the fees they paid be tied to the success of the promotion people: How about $4,000 dollars if radio station WXXX were to "go on" the record? Or $10,000 if radio station KZZZ were to add it to their playlist? Etc. This was getting expensive. But for whom?

Paying an Independent Promoter

The costs of external promotion were running far higher than the costs of the now-disbanded internal staffs. But the record companies had another brilliant idea. Why pay for these "extra" services to promote the artist? Why not let the artist pay for them? After all, the philosophy in the record industry had always been that the artist should pay for recording costs (out of royalties, so ultimately out of his or her pocket). Why shouldn't the outside services of people engaged to help promote the records be considered recording costs and additional advances?

Certainly a record company's investment is, as we have seen, considerable: the A&R department that finds the artist in the first place, the business affairs and legal departments that sign the artist, the enormous investment of the actual recording costs, the art department, the manufacturing and distribution facilities, the marketing department, the publicity department, and let's not forget the dozens of executives who run the company, or the rent that must be paid for the company's marble towers. Welcoming the reduction in overhead resulting from the downsizing of their promotion departments, the record companies were reluctant to suffer the increase of costs when a lucrative alternative was available to them: simply make it a contractual obligation for the artist to pay for independent promotion of his or her records. If the video clip, which was intrinsically promotional in nature, was now a cost to be borne out of royalties by the artist, why not the dollars spent on independent promotion, an absolutely essential expenditure? What more useful cost than one focused solely on the most proven way of establishing the artist's success: getting airplay for the record!

And so developed the practice of charging the artist with the cost of independent promotion. It is ironic that the artist and manager must fight with the record company in order to convince it to expend monies on independent promotion only to be obliged to pay for it themselves. Even the manager loses. If the money is charged against the artist's royalties, customarily the manager will not commission the earned royalties used to recoup the costs of independent promotion—thereby forfeiting the manager's commission on every recoupable independent promotion dollar spent. Some companies hand over the promotion money to the managers for disbursement. In such cases, assuming the managers are honest and do not skim anything off the top, they get to touch, but not spend, the money that, in part, reflects what would have been their own earned commissions if the promotion efforts had been successful. Ironic.

In recent years, the record companies have settled into a kind of standoff with the artists whereby they seek to be repaid (out of royalties) only one-half of the monies expended on independent promotion. This goes a long way—well, half way—toward ameliorating the damage to the artist's bank account. Two facts remain, however: one is that these are costs that the record companies traditionally bore themselves and now have found a way to charge back to the artist; the second is that the amount spent on independent promotion—and the timing of such expenditures—is totally within the control of the record company. Thus, if the artist's account is otherwise in the black (or if the cost of independent promotion can be recouped against other earnings such as mechanical royalty earnings), the record company can actually use the artist's own money, earned royalties otherwise payable at the end of an accounting period, for the purpose of further promoting the artist's records, avoiding all risk that would be associated with advancing its own funds for such a purpose. Hmmm.

Icons and Iconoclasts

Many books have been written about the excesses of independent promotion people and their actual or alleged associations with organized crime, drug dealers, and others (for example, *Hit Men; Off the Charts; Stiffed—The True Story of MCA, the Music Business, and the Mafia*). These are informative, occasionally amusing, and frequently disturbing. Feel free to read them. The point I want to emphasize is that whatever incarnation of payola exists today is a direct descendent of institutions originally established because of record companies' greed. I say "greed" because when the companies recognized the inherent willingness of a radio station programmer or DJ to compromise their ethical responsibilities, they simply reestablished the promotion system. But this time they did so in a manner that had the appearance of being more at arms' length than had previously been the case, when the promotion staff was employed by and under the supervision and control of the record companies themselves.

One day, in the 1980s, Warner Bros. Records' legendary chairman Mo Ostin unilaterally terminated the use of independent promotion people because of what he perceived to be abuses that were inherent in the system and that no one, however pure his or her motives, could control. It was an enormously courageous decision. Unfortunately, Mr. Ostin's solution was short-lived.

THE SAME OLD SONG (ONLY THE CODA IS NEW)

There developed a practice in the fairly recent era of independent promotion whereby the independent promoters themselves would cross the legal line drawn by federal and state laws of bribery, and in particular, the FCC regulation cited at the beginning of this chapter. The record companies, while having insulated themselves from their own employees' actions, were nevertheless anxious about having to pay such evidently tainted sums to independent contractors in return for such specific services as getting a record played on a particular radio station and being listed as among the top 25, top 15, top 10, top 5, or #1 songs on such station's play charts. For, as noted earlier, each of these successful "adds" would generate another few thousand dollars to the independent promoter.

One of the ways in which the record companies have further insulated themselves from the specter of association with unethical and illegal business practices rivals their most ingenious solutions of the past. They have figured out how to pay for independent promotion on the one hand but how not to pay for it on the other. I do not mean that they have found a way to charge someone (in this case the artist) with the cost. That we have already observed. No. Now, they do not even have to suffer the indignity of writing the check! How do they achieve this, the best of all possible worlds? The answer, as I alluded to earlier, is simple: they give the *manager* the money and the manager is expected to run the radio promotion campaign.

To nobody's surprise, the independent promotion people hired by the managers at the specific behest of the record company are usually the very people that the record company designates. But the manager, who has no one to whom he or she can shift the responsibility, is the one who will be the focus of governmental interest if the issue ever comes to the forefront again (as in 2006 it inevitably did). Here again there is a disparity between the experienced and the inexperienced. The independent manager who has little experience in such things, or who does not have a trusted network of (honest) promotion people who can present programmers and DJs with rationales for adding their records to playlists, is at a distinct disadvantage compared to the experienced manager who does.

And the record company's dilemma? How to obtain necessary promotional assistance with the least risk, both from a financial and from a liability standpoint. Promotion is essential if records are to gain the attention of those programmers who determine which records are to be played on their airwaves. Salespeople in all fields—from watches to books, from fashion lines to airplanes—are the front-line soldiers of their respective industries. How to ensure their effectiveness is a challenge that has to be faced constantly. Things are no different in the record industry. However, the potential rewards in the music industry are so enormous, and payola charges so visible, that promotion people in the record industry stand out from the crowd.

It is not an exaggeration to say that without promotion and promotion people, there would be few, if any, superstar recording artists. Many promotion people are stars in their own field and deserve the kudos they so infrequently receive. What makes music industry promotional people different from those in other fields with similar functions is that in the record industry the people engaging their services—directly or through the artist's manager—are so successful in detaching themselves from the process that sometimes all control is lost and anything goes.

Under these circumstances, the fact that the artist is expected to pay for all or a portion of promotional services is bizarre to say the least. The artist has no expertise in such matters, and probably does not even know one promotion person from another, and yet the artist's entire career can depend on the success of the promotion person's efforts.

THE BEGINNING OF THE END?

A bit of an earthquake hit the record industry in 2005. Then New York State Attorney General Eliot Spitzer, known for his crusades against various industries allegedly serving the public interest, had gone after what he believed to be widespread payola practices permeating the record industry. The result, in the summer of 2005, was a settlement with SonyBMG Music Entertainment in which Sony BMG acknowledged that they participated in bribing broadcasting stations to "spin" their music, thereby impacting the charts, other radio stations that were in the process of selecting records to play, and the perception of the public as to which records had merit, and which were becoming popular. Investigations continue, and indictments are sure to follow. Civil lawsuits have already begun.

According to Spitzer's press release, the inducements for airplay took several forms, including

- outright bribes to radio programmers, including expensive vacation packages, electronics (duh!), and other valuable items;
- contest giveaways for stations' listening audiences;
- payments to radio stations to cover operational expenses;
- retention of middlemen, known as independent promoters, as conduits for illegal payments to radio stations (remember them?);
- payments for "spin programs," airplay under the guise of advertising.

Reportedly, an unintentional result of Spitzer's investigation of broadcasters' criteria for adding new records to their playlists was that, for some time after the investigation began, the number of radio stations that in any given week added *no* new records to their playlists increased by 40%.

So, perhaps stations have stopped committing the above-listed sins for now. But what will happen down the line when an ambitious promotion executive gets a call from his CEO who says, "What do I have to do to get [name of act] on KXXX this week?" or he is told by his superior, "Johnny [name changed to protect the guilty] really wants you to do it, so cut the deal"? (Quotes are directly from the New York Attorney General's press release.) It's a pretty sure bet that the industry reform movement will have to take another ride on the roller coaster of life in the promotion lane.

• • •

Artists are ultimately responsible for achieving their own career goals. By the time they have found out that their undying faith that their record company, manager, lawyer, business manager, and agent know what they are doing is a chimera, it may be too late to achieve those goals, which, even if not specifically articulated, reside somewhere in their subconscious.

There are no simple solutions to this dilemma, but as with any problem one faces in life, there are several possible approaches. Although the following suggestions have all been covered, either explicitly or implicitly, in previous chapters, they bear repeating here:

- Stay in reality.
- Ask questions, then evaluate the answers with a degree of skepticism.
- Learn from your mistakes.
- Observe others. Learn from their mistakes and from their successes.
- Keep around you a variety of professionals with information and experience different from yours and absorb as much as possible.
- Make sure your team is functioning as a real team. All team members as well as key personnel at the record company must meet regularly (once a week before and during the high-activity release period of an album cycle). Set long-term and short-term goals, assign responsibilities with time tables, and establish mechanisms for communication when the parties cannot meet in person.

A BRIEF LOOK AT THE PROMOTIONAL PICTURE— FROM THE ARTIST'S POINT OF VIEW

At a standard, mainstream record label, promotion staff is broken down according to radio station/formats (top 40, easy listening, R&B, etc.). Each format has numerous releases each week, and the promotion people responsible for those formats make appointments with radio programmers to present the records they are pushing that week. A promotion person representing a major label may get a half-hour session, during which he or she will be able to play no more than five or six records out of the fifteen or twenty "singles" the company wants to promote. (People not from a major label will be lucky if the pitch session lasts ten minutes.) There is a good chance that yours will not be one of the five or six played. (Even if it is, it faces stiff competition. After all, the programmer's station may only add one or two new artist records a week—from all labels.)

So, you've gone through all of this effort—from putting your band together, working the clubs, finding your representatives, securing a deal, recording your record, and beginning your promotional tour—in short, climbing the rungs on the ladder that is the development stage of your career—only to find that your record does not even get played for the radio programmers. Maybe the promotion person really likes your band or your record. So what? He or she can do only so much. Maybe if you're lucky, the promotion person will hand over your record to the programmer and say, "Listen to this; if you can find a spot on the overnight, I'd appreciate it. I'm not going to play this for you because you don't have the time, but I'm sure when you get a chance, you'll love it." One thing the programmer may be thinking as the record is flipped into the circular file is why, if this is such a good record, was it not one of the five or six the promotion person chose to play for the station. That your record was an afterthought solves a problem for the radio programmer. It need not be considered at all.

Finally, it is not inappropriate to suggest that all team members recommend to each other self-help and/or management books that are sold by the carload at any major bookstore.[1] There is, after all, something to be learned from many of the writers of these books, and there is no reason why these lessons should be the private reserve of corporate America. I should also point out that many record companies are deeply invested in management training in the form of lectures, retreats, annual meetings, and even continuing education coursework. Since corporations and even our vaunted record companies care enough to provide education on management and self-fulfillment to their executives, why shouldn't the rest of us—lawyers, managers, business managers—take some courses also? After all, it is in our hands that the ultimate business responsibilities of the artist's career rests. (And it wouldn't hurt for the artist to pursue some of this knowledge as well.)

I speak as much for the professionals around the artist as for the artist because, after all, their common goal is success—artistic success, financial success, or some combination of these. For managers, lawyers, and others who have invested months and eventually years of their lives in the belief that a particular artist has what it takes to reach the level of success that will match the artist's promise, a mismanaged album release or a failed promotional effort has an effect on them only slightly less painful than the effect on the artist who has to start all over again.

I know of no law firm or accounting firm specializing in representing artists that has not had dozens of these experiences over the years. How much can one take before a decision has to be made to shift out of the "baby band" business representing talent and into real estate law representing institutions? Well, not to worry. Those professionals will always retain their love for music, their affinity for musicians and songwriters, and their willingness to negotiate the ups and downs of the music business.

---

1. Popular self-help books reduce to a small number (usually ten or under) the methods by which people can identify their goals and best achieve them—*Ten Ways to a Happier Life*, *Five Steps to Fame and Fortune*, *The Seven Habits of Highly Successful People*, and others—and the messages of these books are, at least in part, transferable to the needs and aspirations of the emerging musical artist. Some other possibly useful titles I recently observed at a local bookstore are *Don't Sweat the Small Stuff—It's All Small Stuff*, *The Dynamic Laws of Prosperity*, *Profiting from Experience*, *A Quick and Simple Guide to Taking Charge of Your Life*, *365 Daily Lessons in Self Mastery*, *Dare to Be Yourself*, and (I liked this title) *An Idiot's Guide to Managing Your Time*. And let's not forget the estimable *The Power of Positive Thinking*.

10 · TOURING CONCERNS
Trials and Tribulations

Recordings are really for people who live in Timbuktu.
—AARON COPLAND

This chapter is not meant for the faint of heart. The subject is touring: moving large numbers of people and huge amounts of equipment from place to place so that from one to ten singers and musicians can entertain even larger numbers of people. The fans do not have to find the artists; the artists will come to them . . . for a price. And that price is not just the price of the ticket; it is often the price of a career, a marriage, a life.

The secret of successful touring—club tours but especially what I call grand tours—is in the details. A competent tour manager will know whether all the equipment and transportation chosen for a tour fit together well and what it will take to make everything work. Although it should go without saying that one should choose a competent and experienced tour manager, many artists feel secure with certain people who have been associated with them since the days they were hauling their instruments around in a borrowed van, and they like to reward these people by advancing them to higher positions in their touring lives. While this is probably how most tour managers do get their starts, it still is important to be cautious when selecting people whose competence may mean the difference between success and failure of each performance and, ultimately, of the tour itself.

Before reviewing the nature and characteristics of the club tour and the grand tour, I offer these thoughts. While certain artists can perform anywhere (the Rolling Stones, the ultimate bar band, loves to play in small clubs on the way to 75,000-seat arenas), most have to balance the available options with an understanding of who they are, who their audience is (or should be), and how to reach their audience. It can give an artist a false sense of value to be part of a subscription series (for example, sponsored by performing arts centers, or PACs). The venue is sold out. The people are behaved, polite, and fairly responsive. Yet if the artist tried to sell a ticket across the street at a regular rock or pop venue, he or she might be surprised at the lack of interest. Subscription series also boast older audiences and little press. This scenario is particularly apt in the jazz field, but it applies in every genre. Other artists may follow the radio play of their records and mix and match money dates with promotional dates.

Artists take heed: making decisions regarding the right venues—at the right times— requires strategic planning. Artists, managers, and agents who chase the dollar in the short run may be overlooking initiatives that will build the artist's career over the long run.

The kinds of venues that have offered opportunities for young artists to be seen and heard, but just as importantly, to develop their identities and performing skills, are harder to come by than at any time in the last fifty-plus years. In a word, they are disappearing— and not just in the United States. Many reasons explain this phenomenon, including economics—those of the venue owners and those of the potential customers. Most countries, the United States included, have experienced a serious recession (or recessions) in recent years. Yet those recessions have been followed in many instances by incredible building booms throughout the country—gentrifying depressed neighborhoods which are often the locations of basement clubs appealing to the cutting edge newbys that enter the music industry every day. So they move—in New York City, for example, from midtown to the Village, to the Lower East Side, to Brooklyn's Greenpoint, Williamsburg, and lately, Bushwick. Take the trip (virtually on a map or actually on public transportation) and you will essentially have experienced a travelogue featuring the former (and the next) exponents of cutting edge music comprising our culture.

Many articles have appeared and punditry expressed which present the view that touring income is replacing the income of artists who, in a different, though recent, era, would earn the substantial part of their music business/career revenue from the sale of records and from mechanical royalties derived from the reproduction on their or others' records of musical compositions they wrote. A recent study by SeatSmart (www.seatsmart.com), the online ticket broker, suggested that while touring is still generating real money for artists, in this era of lower record sales, it is no wonder that record labels want a piece of it. Remember, record labels are now demanding, and obtaining, a share of touring income via their "360" exclusive agreements with their artists. Still, while tour revenues have gone up, they have not come close to replacing the lost income resulting from the sinking sales of CD albums. Indeed, ticket sales *numbers* over the past several years have gone down, and we all know that the cost of a ticket has gone way up. My reference in chapter 9 to touring income replacing record income is due to the fact that overall data supports this conclusion. However, it should be noted that this data is skewed due to it coming from large grossing acts (with a great percentage of touring income). Touring for all but the 1% is no panacea for the losses of revenue resulting from the diminution of actual physical CD sales taken together with the puny royalties payable by streaming services, all in the face of rampant piracy which still continues throughout the world. Reduced performance venues, the high price of gasoline (or at least the irregularity of such prices), insurance costs where the act bothers to protect its van and its instruments and sound systems—all further impact the economics of the other 99%. It is not a pretty picture. Those articles and blogs that say otherwise (and "touring is replacing record sales" has become the conventional wisdom among the noncognoscenti) are simply wrong. No, they don't know it all.

Thank goodness for the festivals whose prominence has risen many-fold in the last few years. Not only do they offer a lot of bang for the buck, but the artists who perform at the festivals are a far broader cross-section of the evolving musical scene than are tour dates featuring one act only with perhaps an opening act. What the Rolling Stones would do by offering opening act opportunities to an array of new artists over the course of a world tour, festivals are now doing in spades. There is no problem with attendance at (most) festivals, and often the least-known participant reaches an audience that it could never reach via half-baked marketing and promotion that too often characterizes the efforts of those who "do it themselves." (See chapter 16.)

THE CLUB TOUR

New artists are marketed in essentially two ways: via radio and via live performances. Other options do not have the same success rate. Whatever the Internet does to ease the distribution of their music, artists and their art must first come to the consumer's attention.

Distribution is everything. Social media sites and other indie-oriented sites can provide some exposure. But the major league, the mainstream? That is still usually only achieved via airplay and touring. We explored radio promotion in chapter 9. It is time to talk about live touring.

It will come as no surprise that in order to fashion a successful endeavor, there must be an enormous amount of coordination among the artist, the record company, and the artist's lawyers, managers, business managers, and booking agents. You may say that this is beginning to sound as if it is going to cost real money: You're right. A young rock-and-roll band will need subsidies to travel from club to club and city to city. And the travel map is not haphazardly drawn; it very carefully traces the response to the record on radio and among fans.

Of course, not only does the artist not make any money from this process, his or her unrecouped red position at the record company begins to rise astronomically.

Another characteristic of the club tour is that just as little kids do not always understand the value of a dollar, artists at this stage of development generally do not understand what they are supposed to be doing; thus, the record company, which usually pays the deficits incurred by such tours, places the artists in a totally dependent mode. Like children, they are given allowances (although they are called per diems), told where they can stay, what they can afford, and what to do. They awake to different rooms and different cities on an almost daily basis. A tour during the promotion of an album can last a year or more and take the artist to fifty or more cities, often more than once, and a half-dozen countries. Their lives are no more similar to yours and mine than are the lives of minor league baseball players traveling from game to game by bus.

This process can continue for years, and it is no wonder that by the time artists get to the grand-tour years, they are likely to be out of touch with what most people consider reality.

Out of the Clubs and Out of Business

Most professionals who live and breathe the world of live performing are of the opinion that club business is no longer a viable part of the global concert business, where many millions of dollars are at stake. Attendance is down across the country, and very few clubs can do anything resembling profitable business absent the implementation of other money-making methods such as merchandising, satellite radio broadcasts, Internet distribution of live shows (for example, via eMusicLive), beer deals—you name it. Despite the fact that club owners, often with the help of record company subsidies, still do all they can to keep open these venues, which have been such a vital means of disseminating the music and musical ideas that reflect an evolving culture, it has become extremely difficult for record companies and promoters to focus on, and invest in, developing acts on the club circuit.

THE GRAND TOUR

Sounds like a movie and sometimes it must feel like one. *Almost Famous, The Rose, Truth or Dare, Helter Skelter*—their depictions of the "road" are not exaggerated.

For artists who reach this privileged stage, the ultimate financial return for the years of effort by the artists and their representatives can be astronomical. Yet no matter how much is made, it can be squandered as a result of any number of excesses, errors, and extravagances of the artists and their handlers.

SAMPLE TOUR BUDGET

INCOME

Performances:
$100,000/show x 65 shows $6,500,000
Sound and lights (reimbursed by venue):
$17,500/show x 65 shows $1,137,500
Merchandising (guarantee) $1,000,000

Total **$8,637,500**

EXPENSES

Commissions:
Management @15% (excluding sound and lights reimbursement)*† $1,125,000

Agency @10% (of performance fees only) $650,000

Business management @ 5% (excluding sound and lights) $375,000

Hard production costs (including trucking, sound, lighting, equipment rental, equipment supplies, set construction & design, set fee, misc.) $700,000

Pre- and post-tour expenses (such as airfares, advance, equipment purchases, transportation, wardrobe, immigration [i.e., cost of services to obtain permits or visas for countries in which performers are not citizens]) $120,000

Ancillary production and tour costs (e.g., band members' payroll and fees; entourage [road managers, security, etc.]; stage crew, including guitar and drum techs; keyboard programmer; carpenter; grounds man) $350,000

Per diems (individual band members, entourage, and crew) $120,000

Hotels (band, entourage, crew, and drivers) $425,000

Transportation (airfares, auto and bus rental, limousines and taxis) $400,000

Tips and gratuities $11,500

Miscellaneous expenses (e.g., wardrobe, shipping, dues) $300,000

Insurance (nonappearance, liability, equipment, Workers' Compensation) $300,000

Legal $45,000

Publicity (independent/not paid for by record company) $20,000

Rehearsal costs (rehearsal studios in home city and on the road; local labor, hotels and apartment rental, telephone, food and drinks, equipment rental and supplies, transportation, payroll and fees, per diems at $4,250/month for 4 months) $17,000

Contingency $50,000

Total expenses $4,783,500

Net profit on tour ($770,800 per band member) $3,854,000

The Tour Budget

The accompanying table is a real-life example of a touring budget for a sixty-five-show tour—over a period of four months—for a moderately successful five-member band. Observe how many different categories of costs must be dealt with. Each category requires specific expertise, or experience, in order both to estimate potential costs and then to meet these costs on budget. For this tour, the net profit would be divided by the five members of the band: $3,854,000 divided by five equals $770,800 for each member.

The issue often facing artists and their representatives is not so much whether costs are reasonable or should be cut, but whether there has been sufficient time and expertise invested in preparing the budget to justify getting the tour under way in the first place.

Even a cursory glance at the budget numbers listed in the table reveals that it costs a lot of money to mount a major tour. When so much money is involved (and note that the profit margin is usually much smaller than in my example), the difference between success and failure can be the result of fine decisions in one area or another. A small mistake in estimating personnel costs, multiplied by many persons over a long tour, can be nothing short of disastrous. Both the projected income and the projected expenses must be analyzed carefully, and the projections for both must be flexible enough to allow for all kinds of contingencies over and beyond such things as weather and illness and other insurable events.

Now, what if you put on a tour that is supposed to attract one million people and no one comes? What if the current single of the artist goes from a bullet on the charts to an anchor? What if the next single is a bomb? What if the entire promotion staff of the record company leaves for another company? What if the promotion staff at the record company is forced to shift its attention from the touring group's record to a different one that is exploding well ahead of and beyond expectations? I have seen these things happen time and time again. But, although there is really no way to control events, what *can* be controlled is the financial discipline necessary to avoid disaster. Timing is very important in planning a tour. And it takes time to plan a tour to promote an artist's latest release. By the time the stage is built, or the venues are booked, the record may have tanked, or the economy may have gone south, or both. In 2002, no less a star touring group than the Rolling Stones postponed a potential hundred-million-dollar tour because they feared that their demographic was getting too old at the same time the economy was experiencing a downturn. Seductive as it may have been to the group and their advisors, all of whom stood to make a fortune, the decision protected them from what could have been a financial, as well as an image-destroying, debacle.

While it is customary for an artist and the artist's business manager to find a way to help out a promoter who has taken a bath at a show, this is not something that anyone wants to experience. A misjudged and poorly planned tour can easily result in one of these sad late-night negotiations where the artist has to help out the promoter by waiving fees, bearing unplanned expenses, and perhaps agreeing to terms for a future date that are less favorable than they should be.

Tour Riders

Performance riders are the multipage addenda to the (usually) one-page employment contract that establishes the basics of a booking: the date, the location, the price, the terms of payment, the number of shows, and whether the act is headlining or not. The rider is where the fun begins. Rather than review all of the customary provisions, suffice it to say that they cover everything from staging, sound, lighting, and electrical requirements to backstage food and drink (a generous serving of moo goo gai pan was my favorite—but for sixty-five dates?). Included among the more important provisions are restrictions against recording (audio and video); a commitment to provide comprehensive general liability insurance (in case something happens at your concert to someone attending it—that needn't be as dramatic as what happened to the Rolling Stones at the Altamont); and satisfactory accommodations (always with 24-hour room service).

What is important here is, again, not so much the content of the rider, but the thought that goes into drafting it. It matters who writes it, who reads it, and who sees it. There are hidden costs included within the rider that can bankrupt a tour if the person who draws up the budget is not aware of them. While the costs of advertising (for example) and the nature, variety, and extent of the backstage food are usually borne by the promoter, what happens when the promoter suffers significant losses and looks to the artist for help? After all, in the promoter's opinion, it is the artist who failed to draw the crowd—not the inefficiencies of the record company, not the local radio promotion people who awoke too late to the fact that the artist was coming to town, and not the inept (or nonexistent) advertising by the promoter. So, the more costs the promoter incurs because of the artist's whims, or the artist's manager's misjudgment or mismanagement, the bigger the financial hit the promoter may experience later—and the less likely it is that the promoter will be willing to accommodate the artist when he or she wants to play that venue again.

Even in the event of a successful concert, these superfluous costs can have a considerable impact on the artist's net income derived from the date. The profits of a concert are customarily shared by the artist and the promoter on some percentage basis, with the much larger share (upward of 80%) going to the artist. When the expenses incurred as a result of excesses sought in the rider are higher than they should be, the net to the artist is naturally lower than it could be. Remember, in traditional arrangements, the manager, business manager, and agent are all commissioning the gross, so they do not have the same stake as the artist does in controlling costs, which ultimately determine the net profit.

Most of the time, the artist has no clue as to the goings-on behind the scenes that cause expenditures to spiral upward, expenditures that, in a nanosecond, can exceed those imagined in the artist's wildest dreams mere months before. That is too bad, since the artist will end up paying for *all* of them.

Another reason why it is important that each artist's rider be carefully vetted and drafted by the artist's representatives who care about that particular artist's specific interests, deals with how he or she deals with his or her own celebrity. Without intending to slander any particular artist for being excessively paranoid, or egotistical, suffice it to say that some riders require the promoter to ensure that no eye contact is made between the artist and backstage personnel. "No autograph or photo requests" are quite prevalent, although one can appreciate how artists, thrust into environments of strangers, and seeking to establish a cocoon of comfort before facing a crowd of 2,500 to 100,000 fans, do not wish to be disturbed—especially while preparing for the show to start.

Foundations of Success: Team Planning

The preparation (or lack thereof) for a grand tour can have a profound effect on an artist's future. A poorly planned tour can not only destroy the fiscal health of an artist, it can also kill a career. In no other area is it more important that planning time be spent wisely by the artist's team of advisors, and nowhere is it more appropriate for all of these advisors to be in constant communication with each other. The purpose of establishing and maintaining fluid contact among advisors is not to make it impossible for any of them to claim innocence if something goes wrong—that will not help revive a bank account or a career. Rather it should be established so that the advisors will be able to truly test each other's judgment when critical decisions are being made. In a finely tuned organization, all the information gained as a result of following the guidelines in this chapter would be shared by all of the important decision-makers within that organization—including, of course, the artist.

Cash Flow

Cash receipts and cash outlays are not always in synch. Accordingly, it is crucial that the band's business manager establish a line of credit with a bank to ensure that cash will continue to flow despite unanticipated glitches. For example, the band's own agent may hold back funds that have been paid by promoters for dates already played. Similarly, some agents inexplicably take deposits for future shows well below the recommended 50%, meaning that if the date is not played because of a default by the promoter, the artist is left without any of the budgeted fee for the date. The impact of such actions on the finances of a tour can be devastating. Some agents "settle" accounts, after a date is played, once a month. This is bad practice. Remember, they already have their commission (usually 10%), and they should remit the money they collect without delay rather than sit on it. The band's business manager must keep on top of the agent to ensure that the band's money is in the band's hands as soon as possible. This issue should, of course, be dealt with in the written agency agreement, but even when it has been, the band's business manager must take steps to keep the cash flow going. Remember, the contract is in the filing cabinets of all parties.

Trucking and Busing

There are a number of issues that must be explored before projecting a budget for this extremely expensive category. First and foremost, or course, is the reputation and track record of the companies you will deal with. If you have knowledge of a reputable firm, fine. If not, will you need a broker (who will add to the cost)? Following is a comprehensive list of items that need to be evaluated in the planning stages by the artist's professional representatives—and occasionally by the artist as well. (For simplicity's sake, I have used the pronoun "you" to refer to the artist and the artist's team, collectively.)

Contingency Planning

- How committed must you be to reserve the vehicles—for example, once the deal is agreed, what is the cancellation policy? Seven days? Fourteen days?
- Is everyone absolutely clear about dates, and has some flexibility been provided, in case there is a need to change start and end dates as well as venues in between?
- Has anyone thought of negotiating a renewal option if the tour does particularly well and the artist is in a position to extend it?
- Has anyone thought of negotiating a termination option if the tour does not do particularly well and the artist is in a position to end it? What is the "kill" price and is it reasonable?
- If there is a mechanical failure, what kind of damages can ensue and what kind of costs will the trucking company be required to bear to provide alternative transportation? In the case of buses, who decides what this alternative transportation will be to ensure that the artists arrive at their destination in the same shape as they would have if there had been no mechanical failure? The same issue applies to gear in the trucks that obviously must be at the venue in time for sound check and, of course, the show itself.

Insurance and Liability

- What are the claims procedures?
- What kinds of insurance must be provided, how much does it cost, and how secure is it?
- Is there a way to make sure that the trucking company bears some liability in the event the drivers commit acts of negligence or incompetence due to poor training or substance abuse? Or worse?
- Who is responsible for mechanical failure and can it be insured against?
- How are third-party liability and property damage dealt with?
- Since the artist will have to reimburse the trucking company in the event the artist's guests trash the bus or cause damage, the artist (and, if a band, each member) and the entire entourage (wives and husbands included) had better be forewarned of the possible liability.
- If the vehicles are used for any illegal or unlawful purpose (such as a violation of a federal, state, or even municipal statute or law applicable to the operation of the vehicle or possession of drugs), the vehicles themselves can be subject to confiscation by the authorities. This would be a disaster! Who knows what the damages could be? At the least, the artist would be liable for the fair market value of the vehicles (as depreciated) or even the actual cost of replacing them with brand-new vehicles. The artist might also be liable for lost profits if the vehicles were scheduled to be leased to a customer following the expiration of the current contract. Even if the artist does not do anything illegal or unlawful in the bus, many of these contracts require the artist/group to agree not to permit the vehicle to be

used for such purposes. Thus an affirmative obligation is placed on the artist regarding the eventual risk of cost.

- Even if the artist is completely insured, if a loss occurs, the insurance rates on the next tour will be even higher. It is a good idea for the attorney, or business manager, to inform the artist about this issue.
- In the event of injuries or death of the artist's personnel or passengers resulting in claims in excess of the insurance, or in the event of damage to or loss of baggage, cargo, or personal property not caused by the artist, who is responsible for the costs incurred or, for that matter, the legal fees to defend the eventual lawsuits?

The Drivers

- Who is responsible for the drivers? Their accommodations? Their insurance? Their withholding taxes? Their benefits? Their Workers' Compensation fees? Their per diems?
- How do you know if the drivers have good driving records?
- How do you know if the drivers are familiar with the particular type of vehicles you are leasing or with their unique characteristics?

Day-to-Day Expenses

- Is there a basis for comparison to determine whether the projected costs (per day/week/month) are reasonable?
- Who pays for the diesel fuel? Oil?
- Who pays for ordinary repairs?

The Vehicles

- Has anyone examined the licenses, permits, and certifications of the trucking company and compared them to the vehicles that are being leased? This and similar nitpicky details can be delegated by the tour manager, but *someone* needs to be responsible for them.
- Did anyone see the vehicles before they were selected for rental?
- Have the selected vehicles been inspected by someone on or hired by the artists' team? It is a good idea to have someone who knows about these things inspect the vehicles before possession is taken because, like rental cars, they will have to be returned in the same condition they were in when first handed over to the artist. Photographs or video would not be a bad idea—put an issue of that day's newspaper in front of the photographs to establish the date on which they are taken.
- Is there a list of the vehicles' serial numbers so the touring group can be sure it is getting what it paid for?
- Has there been an understanding reached about security of the vehicles? For example, where will they be parked and under what kind of protection when they are not moving? The lessee (artist) will be responsible for sabotage, vandalism, floods, etc., and will customarily be insured against these eventualities. However, if the vehicles are damaged or stolen

after being left unlocked or unguarded, the insurance claim on behalf of the artist might be rejected by the insurance company asserting that negligence on the artist's part contributed to the loss.

- Is the artist responsible for the cost of moving the trucks or buses from their places of origin to the location where the equipment can be loaded (insofar as trucks are concerned) or to the location where the band and crew are to be picked up (insofar as the personnel are concerned)? Is the artist responsible for the cost of returning the trucks or buses to their places of origin?

- Are all concerned aware that the vehicles must not be altered in any way? (The owners really do not like their buses and trucks repainted with advertisements screaming out how many booties the band will shake.)

Security Deposit

- What is the security deposit and are the terms of its return clear?

- If the security deposit is to be returned "less damage," does this mean "less damage caused by the artist or the artist's entourage"?

Breach of Contract

- What kind of cure period is available to the artist and to the trucking company? Is a one- or two-day period practical when taking as long as two days to cure a particular breach can result in a cancellation of a date, the attendant loss of guarantees, and the possible incurrence of additional damages due to the promoter's losses?

- If there is a breach by the artist, can the trucking company (1) terminate the lease, (2) recover the vehicle, (3) accelerate damages—such as by demanding payment of the entire remaining portion of the lease fees, (4) charge interest, and/or (5) seek reimbursement for other costs and expenses, such as attorneys' fees?

Boilerplate Finally, has everyone paid sufficient attention to the so-called "boilerplate" provisions (the standard language found in most contracts)? We are dealing with vehicles worth hundreds of thousands of dollars, and simple things like notice provisions—including those regarding who receives copies of notices and those relating to the choice of applicable law and location of any lawsuits—can either protect the artist or put the artist at incredible risk. In the arts world, in general, it is customary to provide that the laws of the states of New York or California or Tennessee apply to the interpretation and construction of contracts. There are three main reasons for this:

1. These states have a long precedential history of cases affecting entertainment industry contracts.

2. Their courts are familiar with the entertainment industry and will be able to comprehend factual situations that arise as entertainment industry contracts are performed (or breached).

3. Both the courts and the laws of these three states are sympathetic to the artist's interests in such situations because the entertainment business is so important to their economic health.

Sound and Lights

It is not a stretch to say that the quality of sound and lighting at a concert is the most important production value on any tour. Achieving anything less than perfection can jeopardize the tour and a career. To assure artists that all of their art and work will not be lost in a haze, more time and energy must be invested in formulating agreements affecting sound and light facilities than in agreements involving any other elements of the tour.

Design The first contractual obligation should be with the artist's sound and lighting designers. Following that, the contract with the vendor of the sound and light equipment and operating personnel must be carefully drawn to provide that the equipment and services will be provided strictly in accordance with these designs. It is appropriate and wise to attach to the vendor's contract a paper copy of the sound designer's and lighting designer's drawings and specifications. Otherwise, there is no way to pinpoint what it is that is being contracted for.

Standard equipment and services are provided by a variety of companies. Specialty equipment and services are provided by a company such as Vari-Lite, Inc., owners of the patents to the remote-controlled "self-propelling" lights. If an artist's manager does not know whom to deal with, the artist's agent or lawyer or business manager will know.

Standard Versus Specialty Equipment The companies that provide sound and lighting equipment to artists on tour often offer two different levels of equipment and services: (1) standard equipment and services pursuant to designs provided by the artist's sound designer and lighting designer and (2) specialty equipment and services provided by companies that own their own technology. The deals are essentially the same, but because there are occasionally two sound and two lighting companies providing the product and the services, a little coordination is needed.

Personnel and Transportation Costs It is customary for the servicing companies to provide personnel familiar with the equipment. Their cost is built in to the price of the lease. When this is the case, the artist will be expected to bear not only the cost of the technicians, including their salaries, but also payroll taxes and Workers' Compensation. Most of these are not subject to negotiation; however, the following costs are usually negotiable:

- transportation of equipment and personnel from the home base of the lighting company
- transportation of equipment and personnel to and between all rehearsal locations and concert locations
- transportation of equipment and personnel back to the home base of the lighting company
- cost of accommodation for the personnel commencing on their arrival at the first rehearsal
- cost of per diems for each member of the technical staff

Insurance As with other elements of the tour, insurance (liability, damage to equipment, equipment failure, delay in replacing or repairing equipment, etc.) is an important issue and all of the concerns applicable to the failure of the trucking and bus companies to accomplish what is expected of them apply here as well. In particular, many tours experience, and actually plan for, a hiatus in the touring schedule. What must the artist pay during such a break? Sometimes the fee is reduced for the equipment; more often, the personnel are sent home and the equipment is moved to a secure location for the hiatus period. There may be scheduled downtime as well as unscheduled hiatuses, and the professionals negotiating these agreements must provide for these contingencies in the contract. Surprises are costly.

PRIVATE CHARTER

You're tired of buses. You're tired of weather and traffic delays, breakdowns, and the sheer time it takes to go from place to place. Speed is now in your vision of how you would like to conduct your tour. Time to rent an airplane and hop on.

Now that you have forsaken the bus for the airplane, and have factored in the additional costs (and savings), let's discuss the unique issues that arise from your newfound adventurousness. What is the main difference between a bus and a jet plane? No, it's not the wings. It's the availability! Whereas buses can be replaced and substituted for fairly easily, airplanes cannot. There are several important differences between these two modes of transportation:

1. Planes are inspected more regularly than buses, and if they do not pass inspection, they will be grounded. This happens far more frequently than you can imagine.

2. It is easy for a plane to fail inspection or to be grounded voluntarily because a part is needed; most airports do not keep a lot of spare parts around.

3. Air routes are much more closely monitored and controlled than ground routes.

4. Weather and traffic can wreak havoc on flight schedules; buses can more easily locate alternate routes.

5. Finally, if you think that bus drivers have to be rested periodically, imagine the rules affecting jet plane pilots!

One detail that is true of *both* buses and planes concerns location. Whether you are traveling by bus or by plane, you will have to find a way to get it from its home base to the city in which you are rehearsing and from which you will depart for your first date. And—you'd be surprised at how many people overlook this detail—you actually have to return the vehicle to its city of origin.

An attorney for one of our era's biggest touring acts told me that he actually has a solution to these problems—one that I think is more easily achievable than to open up a new air route in an otherwise overwhelmed traffic lane: he prays. Here are some other approaches.

The Bigger the Broker, the Better One of the tricks of the trade is to deal only with brokers who have access to other planes. While we in the music industry like to encourage young, small entrepreneurs in many areas of the business, here is one situation where the bigger the broker, the more likely it is that you will get what you need when you need it.

Force Majeure All air travel is subject to the vagaries of weather and air traffic conditions. That is why it is a good idea to try to insert in touring agreements involving moving from venue to venue a little extra language in the *force majeure* clause (the clause that essentially says that if a failure to perform is the result of an "act of God"—such as hurricane, earthquake, strike, or other disaster—neither party to the agreement will be held to be at fault). The extra language would include "failure of transportation" outside of the control of the artist. This would include a failure of the aircraft to pass inspection; it would also cover a delay due simply to too much traffic. August is usually one of the busiest months for air travel, and it is also one of the preferred months for large touring acts. Capacity problems at airports can wreak havoc on a tightly scheduled tour. There may be more takeoff and landing slots authorized by federal law than existed just a few years ago, but there also is a backlash by commercial travelers against private carriers. Airports have been forced to delay private planes because of pressure from commercial travelers. A big-time rock band will not engender a lot of sympathy when it is a question of their being on time for a gig versus a grandmother trying to arrive in time for her grandchild's birthday celebration. In 2015, 18% of all flights (that's a *million* flights) were delayed by at least fifteen minutes (one flight to Atlanta was delayed 97% of the time!), 2% (90,000) were canceled altogether, and three out of ten were diverted—the worst record in years. Some of the causes of flight delays are maintenance problems, fueling. extreme weather, airline glitches/scheduling (the top cause), congestion of air traffic, late arrival of connecting flights, and security issues. A well-oiled, tightly scheduled tour can be severely disrupted if the artist's jet has to idle for three hours on the runway. According to the air traffic division manager for the Eastern Division of the Federal Aviation Administration, "You don't have to be the sharpest knife in the drawer to know that I'm going to have aircrafts left over that I can't accommodate when ten flights are scheduled to leave and twelve are scheduled to arrive within four minutes on a typical day."

Variations on Leases   There are actually not a lot of variations or provisions open to negotiation when it comes to airplane leases. Probably the most important one is whether the plane comes with or without fuel. This may sound like a no-brainer, but believe me, when the cost of fuel is factored in to the lease price, what appeared to be a good deal, one within one's budget, can go south in no time. Aircraft are traditionally leased in "wet" or "dry" conditions. A "dry" lease may mean not only that the aircraft comes without fuel, but that it comes without crew or maintenance also. In that case, an aircraft management agreement must also be entered into with a vendor of such services in addition to the aircraft lease agreement. Oh, the legal fees!

Warranties Unique to Aircraft Leases   In the ordinary course of events, you might expect to receive at least these warranties from the leasing company: that the lessor owns the aircraft and has the right to enter into the lease and that the aircraft has been maintained in compliance with applicable federal regulations and is "airworthy." But many other, similarly reasonable, warranties that one might normally expect to receive are not always available from the companies that lease jet planes. In view of the fact that many tour schedules are poorly thought through and the pressures of time and availability provide for few, if any, alternatives, warranties such as "merchantability or fitness for a particular purpose" are often specifically excluded and disclaimed. There is simply nothing you can do about it if you want that plane *now*.

Similarly, leasing parties—the artists or their service corporations—often have to make certain warranties with respect to things they do not have knowledge of. For example, they may be required to affirm in the leasing contract that the artist's corporation is authorized to assume the enormous responsibility of undertaking a costly aircraft lease. This authorization may not in fact exist, and the certificates of incorporation of traditional industry corporations often do not permit such an undertaking, and a warranty made and breached can have dire consequences to the shareholders.

Paperwork Bet you didn't know that your touring company has to file a signed copy of the lease with the FAA, Aircraft Registry, Flight Standards Technical Division, P.O. 25724, Oklahoma City, OK 73124, within twenty-four hours after the execution of the lease. And, at least forty-eight hours before takeoff of the first flight under the lease, the lessee needs to notify the FAA Flight Standards District Office, General Aviation District Office, Air Carrier District Office, or the International Field Office nearest the airport where the first flight under the lease will originate informing them of (1) the location of the airport of departure, (2) the departure time, and (3) the registration number of the aircraft.

Pricing All charter leasing companies have rate cards for renting their planes. Often they offer "specials" on short notice when they have leased a plane to one destination and have no one paying the cost to return it or to fly it to another destination where it can be rented by another party. These might include a one-way rental from Houston to Miami, for $5,500 or from London to Paris for $11,000. The dates are specific and will not always mesh with the artist's tour plans and therefore short-notice opportunities do not serve a touring artist very well. Nevertheless, these options are widely available and should be considered in a pinch. Ownership or fractional ownership of aircraft is another alternative, but this characteristic of convenient travel is on the wane because newer planes are always available for lease at a fraction of the cost of maintaining all or a portion of a self-owned plane. Private charter is the preferred choice nowadays for many touring acts, and the leasing industry is becoming more adept at juggling charters so as to make the process less complicated. A variety of pricing plans are available to fit any particular needs such as purchasing block hours where you pay on completion of the trip (not coincidentally when the fee for the concert is also paid). Finally, charter companies offer one-way private jet flights. While these one-ways are based on availability, you would be surprised at how many planes are sitting just where you want them and available to go just where you are going. Yes, they have more stringent cancellation policies, but this is an option you might not have considered. Check out Blue Star Jets (www.bsj.com) for an array of available itineraries.

Are you beginning to get the idea that your life and those of your representatives (and bankers and insurance companies) may be a lot more complicated now that you have forsaken the bus for the airplane? Nevertheless, plane transportation works most of the time. As long as your cabin pressure transducer doesn't fail! And as long as the lessee's (the artist's) $100 million insurance policy is actually in force! And don't forget the "engine reserve" and "airport-related expenses"!

All of this is to emphasize that aircraft leases, like any other contract entered into on behalf of an artist in the music industry, must be considered carefully and by expert counselors. And the cost for the lease as well as for the maintenance services and the legal fees must be calculated into the total cost of the project in sufficient time for the artist to be fairly—and safely—represented. Sufficient time means time to drop the idea and find an alternative way to transport your equipment and personnel.

Pyrotechnics

Many performing artists seek to enhance their live shows with pyrotechnics, the name given to special-effects displays that use explosive materials. Silver fountains, concussion effects, airburst effects, flame effects, fireworks, gerbs, waterfall gerbs, flame additives, flash powders, saxons, bullet hit simulators, fireballs, comet effects, flashpaper comets, shock tube initiator, and crossette effects have entered the lexicon of the live tour.

My favorite pyrotechnic device is the remote fire pickle, which is just a variation on a television remote—and which doesn't really look like a pickle. Luna Tech, Inc., located in Alabama, is probably the top supplier of pyrotechnics for performing acts. Here are some of their instructions for use of the remote fire pickle:

> There are two buttons located on the pickle and both must be pressed simultaneously to fire. This provides an extra margin of safety, in the event the pickle is dropped or knocked out of the operator's hand. The pickle has a red LED to indicate the SAFE/ARM status of the Master . . . . It is recommended that no more than five feet of cable be used to ensure that the Master is within sight of the operator.

Sounds like fun. Anyway, here are some of the things groups need to consider when planning the pyrotechnics part of their shows.

Costs In addition to being hazardous, these effects are not inexpensive. A full-effects show at an arena venue can cost upward of $5,000 per show. In addition to the equipment and personnel supplied by the pyrotechnics company, some states require a locally licensed "shooter" to be present—one more body to travel, accommodate, feed, insure, and pay.

Safety Issues Some of the pyrotechnics-related equipment used in a performance can endanger the safety of all personnel and customers at the venue. A recent notice from the principal pyrotechnics supplier to all artist productions that use its pyrotechnics services warned that certain "IR-controlled video projectors can result in premature firing" of explosives (benignly referred to as "effects"). Testing effects ahead of time can help, but given current advances in electronics, and remote digital equipment, ranging from sound and lights to laser and pyrotechnics, it was only a matter of time before there was a major tragedy resulting from an erroneous signal initiated innocently or from some other mistake.

Sure enough, on February 20, 2003, the ultimate showstopper occurred. Fire, caused by carelessly placed pyrotechnics, killed some one hundred people during a Great White concert at the Station Club in Rhode Island. Among the legal consequences? Million-dollar fines, lawsuits galore, bankruptcy, even jail for one hundred to two hundred counts of involuntary manslaughter (maximum sentence ten years). It was the fourth deadliest nightclub fire in US history. People, not just limited liability corporations, paid.

Following this tragedy, the National Institute of Standards and Technology (NIST) (bet you've never heard of *them*), a division of the Commerce Department that, among other very obscure functions, sets the official clock in the United States, suggested a number of recommendations for venues involved in conduct that could lead to flammable results. In a report issued in June 2005, NIST recommended to all state and local governments national model building and fire codes for venues operating as new nightclubs or existing nightclubs holding at least one hundred people. Among NIST's recommendations are the installation of sprinkler systems, restrictions on the use of flammable materials, and improved means of egress and signs. It also recommended that sufficient fire inspectors and building plan inspectors be on staff to fulfill these responsibilities. The report also addressed pyrotechnics specifically:

> Recommendation 4 calls for the NFPA 1126 standard [referring to the National Fire Protection Association] on the use of pyrotechnics before an audience to be strengthened by addressing the need for automatic sprinkler systems; minimum occupancy/building size levels; the posting of pyrotechnic use plans and emergency procedures; and setting new minimum clearances between pyrotechnics and the items they potentially could ignite.

Whatever pyrotechnic effects you are planning to use, dealing with a reputable pyrotechnics company has obvious advantages. Among them is the likelihood that when pyrotechnics equipment is aged or stressed through use, the company providing the services will ensure that either new equipment compatible with the old is provided or that the old or damaged equipment is refurbished properly, expertly, and safely. Whether you are buying or renting a car, a jet plane, or a pyrotechnics stage display, it is always wise to ask about its age, in whose hands it has been, how many "miles" it has been driven, and where it has been used. Among the pieces of equipment that your production manager should be sure to examine are the cables that connect the active parts. Most of these pyrotechnic effects come with complicated diagrams of the firing connections. A typical diagram showing how to hook up a flame projector looks like it belongs in a World War II film about blowing up a bridge. This work is, in a word, scary—and as incredible as the effects are, fortunately the steps taken, and instructions provided, to ensure the safety of the personnel and the concertgoers are usually equal to the task.

For example, the PYROPAK Grid Rocket is a tube device attached to a steel cable stretched between two points designed to be fired to simulate a rocket-propelled projectile. The Grid Rocket burns approximately three seconds, which translates to approximately 120 feet (36.5 meters) of level "flight." This effect is so powerful, and the rocket covers so much ground, that special precautions must be taken to prevent the effect from burning the material around it. According to Luna Tech's instructions:

> A minimum vertical Safety Clearance of 20 feet (6 meters) is required between the Grid Rocket and any people or flame sensitive materials. This is, of course, subject to any applicable local regulations. As always, when using any pyrotechnic effect outdoors, be sure to calculate the possible effects of wind on your Safety Clearances. Always test-fire your system before the performance.

Most pyrotechnic effects are designed to work with certain equipment only. Start to extemporize and you're asking for trouble.

Other Preventable Tragedies

From the Rolling Stones debacle at the Altamont (two killed) in 1969 to The Who disaster in Cincinnati in 1979 (eleven died), crowd control and security have been taken more seriously. In the former, members of Hell's Angels, untutored in law enforcement, and the restraints of force, took matters of discipline in their own hands and two concertgoers died. In the latter, carefully laid plans to ensure the safe exit of concertgoers in the event of fire neglected to include protection against a surge of people rushing into the venue—Riverfront Coliseum—when the undesignated "festival seating" construct resulted in an uncontrolled mass of eight thousand people pushing their way into the venue seeking a better location to watch the band during a late sound check—because they thought that the concert had already begun. Unfortunately, lessons were not always learned from these tragedies. From mosh pits to soccer crowds, there remain many dangers to concert and sports watchers throughout the world (for example, the 2000 Pearl Jam concert in Roskilde, Denmark, during which nine died). The music goes on, but not always the lives of the attendees.

Local Licenses and Permits

Needless to say, numerous local licenses and permits will be required, and all competent tour managers/production managers know that. Here is another in the long line of reasons for hiring only experienced personnel—from personal manager to attorney to business manager (who, more than anyone else, will know all of the details of such regulations because the business manager is the one who writes the checks) to, of course, all touring staff members.

Where Did You Say My Fireworks Were?

UPS, FedEx, Airborne Express, RPS, and Viking all provide Internet facilities to track the shipment of goods, and you can find out literally within seconds exactly where your shipment is. This is particularly useful when your shipment contains hazardous materials, which, if in the wrong hands, could present more than a few problems.

ELEMENTS OF TOURING AGREEMENTS: COMMONALITIES AND IDIOSYNCRASIES

All agreements written to cover elements of tours are related to each other in many ways even though the subject of one is to move equipment, another to move and accommodate people, a third to provide the equipment that is transported, etc. Some elements are common to almost all of them: the need for an equipment manifest; language stating that all technicians work at the direction of the artist's production team; language that makes it clear that payments due to the lessors of the equipment are "lease payments," or "rents," not simply "payments," which might be interpreted to connote a sale; the right to terminate the agreement on short notice. Others, such as clauses related to equipment provided by specialty vendors and clauses related to liquidated damages, are not as common.

The Equipment Manifest

Neither the trucking company nor the airplane lessor will agree to transport the equipment unless and until certain information regarding the size, content, dimensions, and other details, of the equipment is provided. They will need materials and parts to secure the equipment during transportation, and they want as much information and notice as possible to ensure that they can transport the equipment safely and securely. Before they will transport anything, an *equipment manifest*, spelling all these things out, must be drawn up, approved by the business management, the personal manager, and the technical staff of the artist, and given to the company responsible for transporting the equipment. The sooner the equipment manifest is finalized, the better.

Termination Clauses

The artist must have the right to terminate all or many of the touring agreements on short notice in the event the tour is not succeeding or selling tickets. There is nothing worse for an artist financially, and emotionally, than to have to cancel a tour for lack of interest and at the same time have to pay the megacosts of the tour just as if the tour had proceeded on schedule.

Back to Basics: Counting Seats

Some promoters and venues play a special game. While they are more than happy to acknowledge the sale of tickets for the number of seats they have put up for sale, sometimes they also have "unmanifested" seats at the venues. There is no accounting for these seats, whether they are sold or not. After all, they do not really exist on paper, on websites, or in venue promotional literature. They only exist in front of the eyes of those who know their venues like they know their checkbooks. These unrecorded seats can number as many as two or three hundred. At $100 a seat, that reflects income of from $20,000 to $30,000—per night! At $250 (after all, these are often the prime seats—on stage, for example), we're talking about $50,000 to $75,000. Have you ever seen a permanent seating chart for a rock or pop venue? You think you have, but you haven't. Seating plans are as fluid as the weather in an outdoor stadium in New England. An artist's tour manager must be charged with the responsibility of counting seats—as mundane as it may seem. Lots of money is involved. Further, in owner-operated venues, suites that are rented by the owner-operators at a premium to season ticket holders or sponsors—even scalpers—are not included in the calculation of the artist's share of earnings. They are not considered "seats."

Specialty Vendors

Given the sensitivity of some of the equipment, some companies require a special kind of truck to transport it, for example, an "air-ride" trailer. And, believe it or not, some of these companies insist that their equipment ride "in the nose" of the trailer. This may seem a bit technical to you, and it certainly is to me, but I am mentioning it because these companies are putting incredible value into the hands of the artist and the artist's staff. Whether or not the artist's staff in fact has the right kind of experience to handle the specialty equipment, the leasing companies have nothing to do with the choice of the touring staff and their insistence on some kind of control over how the equipment is handled and transported should not surprise the artist's team.

Liquidated Damages

Liquidated damages (that is, an amount of money agreed in advance of a problem) in favor of the artist are more easily negotiated in sound and light agreements than in trucking and busing agreements. A smart equipment vendor will negotiate a fixed sum of money to be paid if for any reason the vendor is in material breach of the agreement. This is customarily established as daily fees for each day of a scheduled performance that is missed and a similar amount for each day for which the artist must find a substitute vendor.

Owners and Operators: Who Nets the Net?

The traditional model of the concert business is the net deal. The artist receives a guarantee against a percentage of the net—typically 85%. Any marquee headline attraction will try to get this deal. Another common model provides the artist with a percentage of gross—typically 60%. Both of these structures are known as the "four-wall" model because essentially the promoters rent the venue—the four walls—empty, and take care of the rest themselves. Of course, the rental cost includes the essential features of the venue such as ushers, some security, etc.

But the four-wall archetype has become archaic because so many venues—particularly amphitheaters and even some arenas—are now owner operated. In such buildings, the standard 60% or 85% models can be bettered. The risk is substantially lower to owner-operators because there is a whole litany of ancillary income streams available to them such as parking fees, concession profits, a piece of the income derived from merchandise sold by the artist, and the insidious facility maintenance fee. Much of the income generated by these "add-ons" supplements the ticket price—did you wonder why they have gone so high? (One oddity of this paradigm is that the parking fee is collected per ticket, not per vehicle. For 20,000 tickets, at $3.00 a ticket, that's $60,000. A recent hard-rock all-day festival added $13.50 to each $60 ticket. None of this went to the artist or the promoter. Talk about an add-on!)

As noted, the artist does not usually share in add-on income. Accordingly, there is an upward pressure on the owner-operators by artists and their promoters to increase the standard model percentages. Remember, the owner-operators are not paying rent. While they may be contributing their receipts to service their debt on their buildings, they are nevertheless, in essence, renting out their own homes. Note that with municipal facilities such as Madison Square Garden or the Staples Center most of the money generated by a performance is still accounted for within the 60/40 gross or 85/15 net calculation. It is when so much income is "outside" of the deal that booking agents on behalf of their artist rosters try to squeeze even more out of the gross, or net, reflected by the portion of receipts that they can claim a percentage of.

As of this writing, upward of 80% of the country's amphitheaters are owned and operated by a huge concert promotion organization called Clear Channel, which has absorbed most of the independent promoters in the country. The remaining 15% to 20% are controlled by House of Blues concerts.

Holograms: The Tour Never Ends

Holograms (virtual images of dead artists) are the new rage. Whether an artist can legally replicate Elvis Presley dancing on stage with a live artist is questionable. But estates of deceased artists are not reluctant to glean money from the touring font of the 21st century. When Elvis was performing, ticket prices seldom reached $10. The multi-millions earned nowadays on the road is a vein of gold just waiting to be mined. Thus, estates of deceased artists are working out terms with performing acts and their promoters to "participate" in the live shows and in the revenues derived from them. With the permission of the representatives of the deceased artist, one need not get to the issue of infringing name and likeness rights, the so-called civil rights of the deceased (which may actually not exist at all in the United States absent state laws to the contrary, such as those in Tennessee and Indiana—the Supreme Court has not ruled on the issue). Their permission is eminently exchangeable for cash.

Product or Service Sponsorship/Identification

One way to promote your brand is to become identified with a product that reaches millions of whom comprise (or you wish to comprise) your core audience. Product sponsorship has become quite routine in recent years, and there are numerous companies which specialize in developing sponsorship relationships for artists. While the whole area of sponsorship is a bit outside of the subject of this chapter, let me make this one observation as to what needs to be considered: your exposure, which heretofore had been limited to a known audience, will expand and reach a far a greater audience of people who will not have the same sympathies for you. For example, Markey Mark's relationship with Calvin Klein famously ended in embarrassment over a bigoted remark attributed to him. Some feel that his replacement was simply a change whose time had come, but we will never know if it was really his "morals clause" (see chapter 7, pages 116-117) that ended his relationship with the apparel manufacturer. Similarly, the front man of Blood Sweat & Tears, a Canadian, had been involved in a minor marijuana problem in Canada and the US State Department offered to turn the other cheek if the band would perform in Eastern Europe on a State

Department initiative. They did, and lost the entire right profile of their audience. So they decided to recapture it by playing Las Vegas. They did, and lost the entire left profile of their audience. Seller beware!

• • •

One final thought about the sharing of grand tour money. In the merchandising area, it used to be that the venue would either simply make room at no charge for the artist's merchandise to be sold, or would provide booths and sometimes staff, in return for a small percentage of the merchandise income—routinely 3% to 10%. Those days are over. Now the venues charge as much as 40% of the merchandise income in return for permitting the merchandise to be sold in their halls. This is the main reason why the price of T-shirts has risen from $10 to $30 and why the cost of other tour merchandise is similarly high.

11 · MERCHANDISING
Your Band, Your Brand

I was, however, approached by Chinese journalists, one of whom observed how interesting it was that I combined politics—which is practical—and music—which is fantasy. I replied that they had it the wrong way round!
—EDWARD HEATH (PRIME MINISTER OF
THE UNITED KINGDOM, 1970–74)

While the purpose of this book is to explore those things that "they will never tell you," it is sometimes necessary to put the previously unknown into a familiar context. So please bear with me while I provide a brief overview of merchandising.
One does not merchandise people or things; one merchandises intangible rights. In the case of the performing and recording artist, these consist of

- artists' individual name
- artists' trade names
- artists' likenesses, including photographs
- logos and artwork identified with artists

There used to be two principal ways in which artists exploited their merchandising rights: touring and retailing. Now there are three: web merchandising has come into its own in the past few years. Obviously, many of the issues discussed below will not have particular application to bands engaged in touring via small club performances or festivals, but some will.

There are a variety of companies that specialize in marketing merchandise to fans; some are actually owned by the record companies and, more frequently, some merchandising rights are actually granted to the record companies at the time the original record deal is entered into. This chapter contemplates a more traditional situation, one in which an artist is free to license merchandising rights to one or more independent companies. In the case of touring, the period of the license most often coincides with the length of the artist's forthcoming tour or album cycle. Retail deals are traditionally for slightly longer periods.

The following sections deal both with issues that are specific to tour merchandising and with issues specific to retail merchandising.

TOUR MERCHANDISING

Delivering Heads
Touring agreements differ depending on whether or not the act is a headliner. The main *characteristic* of these deals is that, while the merchandise company will provide a substantial advance to the artist—an advance that will help finance the production elements of the tour—the company will insist on the artist "delivering" a certain number of audience

members—affectionately called "heads"—and the failure to do that will have fairly dire consequences. It is a rare deal that does not include such a delivery commitment, so it is worth explaining how these provisions work.

Contract provisions identifying the kinds of heads that are to be delivered are often ambiguous. For example, does the artist have to be a headliner? This becomes important because when the contractual requirements to deliver heads have not been met, there arises an issue as to whether the artist, or an individual member of the artist's group, can fulfill those requirements at some future time by live performances *other* than as a headliner.

If the artist is not a headliner, the parties determine a formula in the contract by which the number of heads is "imputed." For example, the particular mix of headliner and supporting act or acts may suggest that one artist, the supporting act, is likely to draw only about one-third of the total audience. Thus, a per-head dollar figure will be negotiated and divided into 33.5%. If that dollar figure (which is the figure that the parties minimally expect the fans of the supporting act who are attending the concert will pay for merchandise) is, say, $4, then each person who actually shows up at the concert (this is a count that is attainable after all) will be deemed to be contributing about 8% toward the "imputed" total (33.33 divided by 4 equals 8.33). Thus of every 12.5 people that show up, 1 (or 8%) will be deemed to be attributable to the supporting act. The reason the merchandise companies do not simply divide the total attendees by 3 (which would represent one-third of the audience) is that it is presumed that the two-thirds of the audience that is there to see the headliner is far more likely to pay money—and pay more money—for merchandise than those who are present to see the supporting act.

Suppose, for example, a merchandiser is prepared to offer $1 million as an advance to a headliner, and intends to sell merchandise at its stands for the supporting act, which is expected to draw one-third of the audience. The headliner has "guaranteed" that over the course of the tour, the act will perform before 450,000 concertgoers, and in fact the number of attending concertgoers over the course of the tour does add up to 450,000. Yet of that number the 150,000 that are likely to be fans of the supporting act are only counted as 12,000 people (that is, 8%). Adding the 300,000 heads imputed to the headliner to the 12,000 heads imputed for the supporting act yields 312,000 heads, 138,000 short of the contractually promised 450,000.

No matter how cleverly one can try to calculate the value of a head, the fact is that in most situations, merchandisers would rather not impute *any* heads to an opening act. In fact, most merchandisers assume that no one is showing up at all at the gig, let alone someone to see the opening act. At the same time, they will tell you that even if some of the 19,000 people showing up at Madison Square Garden are there to see the opening act, and not the headliner, even they will probably buy the headliner's T-shirt, not that of the supporting act.

In the end, it is really an issue of how much money the artist can negotiate by way of an advance and how much has to be paid back if projections do not meet expectations. Anyway, this is the thinking.

If the "guaranteed" number of heads is not "delivered," the artist will owe the merchandiser either an amount of money that was advanced against the guarantee that has not been met, or (get this), the artist will owe the merchandiser an amount of heads at some future date on a tour that has not yet been scheduled!

There are numerous problems with this solution. One is that, for liability purposes, artists customarily establish separate service corporations to present each tour and the corporation is often dissolved, or at least put into mothballs, after the tour ends. (Dissolving a corporation is an act that can expose the shareholders to liability for the corporation's actions and promises and therefore is not an action that should be taken lightly.) Merchandisers are aware of this process, and, since the promise made by the defunct corporation to owe future heads is of no particular value, the merchandiser does not want to hear about the artist's touring corporation: it will insist on personal guarantees and usually will get them.

Personal guarantees are also problematic because once an individual member of a band guarantees something personally, that band member is in potential danger for a long period to come—even if the member leaves the band and joins another or goes solo. A well-known band from a British commonwealth country was on its third album and third tour. Unfortunately, the interest in this group suddenly waned and the tour failed. However, a lot of money had been paid to this group by way of an advance by a merchandising company. The money was naturally spent—mostly on preproduction expenses—building the stage, designing the lighting and sound, guarantees for trucking, buses, etc.—but the band did not perform to the required number of heads. The manager commissioned the advance, as did the business manager, for a total of 20% of the advance. Unfortunately, the entire advance was lost by the merchandiser, so each individual member of the band owed the merchandiser 100% of the money (not 80%) until the merchandiser was fully compensated.

Complicating this was the fact that only one member of the band had any funds set aside from previous earnings and that same member of the band was the only one who would have a career following the demise of the band itself. Thus, this one member was suddenly the one targeted either for the return of the money or for delivering the *un*-delivered heads at some future date. She (she was the lead singer) ultimately honored the obligation of her band, took a role in a Broadway show for four years, and paid back the merchandiser.

In negotiating a band member's agreement at the inception of a group artist's career, an understanding should be reached as to what will happen in the event of a loss such as that just described. Under customary partnership law, if one band member is liable for the acts of the group, the member can cross-claim against the other band members for damages. Provisions of the band member agreement may supersede or even controvert this result.

Whose Fault Is It Anyway? In the example related above, neither the manager nor the business manager returned their share of the merchandise advance—in part because they felt they had done the job they were hired for. They deserved to be paid out of the gross because, essentially, they would have worked for nothing unless and until some money found its way into the artist's coffers. Clearly, however, this was not a good result for the artist. Suppose the artist felt that the tour should not have been structured so ambitiously, that the people who planned it had not made a realistic assessment of whether the band could support such a tour financially. And to whom would the artist have looked for the proper guidance? The manager and the business manager, of course.

As with many such situations, various factors go into determining whether management has or has not been effective. It is difficult for nonmanagers to put themselves in the place of managers in given circumstances and to understand the pressures these people face. On the other hand, in most other businesses (including the "businesses" of government and war), people are expected to take responsibility for their actions. Shouldn't the same rules apply to those of us in the music industry who are responsible for doing a particular job to assist the artist to achieve a full potential—record company personnel, the business management office, the tour management office, the attorneys' office, the agent's office, etc.? There may be hundreds of people involved in planning a tour, but when an artist does not deliver the sufficient number of heads, guess who pays? It is not out of the question for an artist to ask his or her professional representatives how they define their jobs and what responsibilities they believe they are undertaking. What comes out when those discussions take place might surprise everyone. Before agreeing to a heads-delivery condition in a merchandising contract, there is every reason for the artist to require from his or her manager and business manager a promise to return their share of the merchandising advance. In fact, the management agreement, in anticipation of such circumstances, should provide specifically for such an eventuality.

Accruing Interest and Accrual Date   Once a merchandise deal is breached due to the failure of the act to fulfill its promise to deliver a minimum number of heads, financial consequences begin to multiply. (Of course, the minimum number of heads might not have purchased the projected amount of merchandise anyway, but the breach is in the failure to deliver the heads, not in the failure to sell the merchandise.)

Some deals require that the unrecouped balance at the point of the failure becomes subject to interest charges (at various, not always easily discernible, rates). If the rate is a variable one, and has increased at the time or times the interest becomes chargeable, the consequences can be enormous. If the interest accumulates for however long it takes for the artist to mount the next tour, the artist can be looking at a very large debt indeed. One thing that the artist can do in advance is to limit the "debt" to an increased number of heads that he or she must deliver; so that, at worst, the artist will not owe real cash to the merchandiser. This is a better result, if not a totally satisfactory one.

In addition, there is always the question of *when* this interest begins to be charged.

For example, some deals provide that it begins to be charged sixty days after the tour ends or is supposed to end. Some provide that the interest begins to accrue after the final accounting, which can occur quite soon after the end of the tour. As far as the merchandising company is concerned, it is out the money on the day the advance is paid, and the calculation of the number of heads the artist is required to deliver takes into account that the requisite number of heads (concertgoers) will be delivered only over a period of months after the money has been advanced. That is, a merchandising company will often increase the number of required heads proportionately to the time frame during which it expects to be recompensed for its investment. Thus, the argument goes, the failure of the band to deliver the number of heads over the anticipated period will cost the merchandiser more than simply the unrecouped balance, and, once the contract is breached, the merchandiser will want the interest to accrue from the date the advance was given, not from the alternative dates mentioned above. Of course, there are ways to modify this extreme position, but it is important that the artist and the artist's team understand what the merchandiser is likely to try to do. As with any unsatisfactory provision, negotiations may result in (1) doing away with it entirely; (2) specifying another date; (3) reducing the advance, and therefore the risk; or (4) some combination of the three.

It is also possible, on occasion, to negotiate an interest hiatus—a period during which no interest will accrue or during which a reduced rate of interest will accrue. The hiatus might be, for example, a period not to exceed six, nine, or twelve months between tours, the purpose being that the artist then can record a new album and carefully prepare the tour associated with the new album without worrying about paying interest on an "advance" that was turned into a "loan" due to circumstances that might have been the fault of any number of people. As with all entertainment industry deals, contract provisions will be more or less favorable, or harsh, in direct proportion to the amount of the advance. It is not always cause for celebration when the manager announces a $1 million deal. The flip side is buried within the contract language!

Unrecouped Balances   Obviously, if the artist promises to pay back the merchandiser in the event of a failure to deliver the agreed-upon number of heads, and then the tour is canceled for reasons beyond the artist's control (illness—maybe even an act of God), the artist should not have to pay back more than the unrecouped balance, at most. Merchandisers will object to this result because they want not just to receive their advance back, but to make a profit as well. Nevertheless, if the advance has been recouped because enough dollars per head were accumulated before the tour was canceled, even if the contractual number of heads was not technically delivered, the artist should be relieved of the promise.

Shared Risk   On occasion, the merchandise company will permit the operating company of the act (which, as you will recall, is usually a corporation with limited liability) to assume *some*, if not all, of the risk and thereby get the artist off the hook on a personal level for at least that portion of potential liability.

Saying "No"   As noted earlier in this book, sometimes negotiating strength lies solely in the power to say "no." Merchandising is an option, not a necessity. To be sure, there is income to be had, but there are tremendous risks involved as well. Gambling with the future financial security of an artist by foolishly making guarantees that might bankrupt the artist—or the artist's group or any of its individual members—is not a game that I think most artists would want to play. As with everything, there has to be a balance between risk and reward. It is true that merchandising money will often assist the artist in getting the tour off the ground by providing the seed money to organize the tour in the first place. But there are other sources of money that involve far less risk, and an artist in a secure financial position will have a stronger negotiating position down the road, when it *does* makes sense to enter into a merchandising deal. However, those other sources are not commissionable by the artist's manager and business manager and not always presented as an option.

When a Band Member Moves On   Special problems can arise when a member of a band that owes a debt to a previous merchandise advance wants to join a new band. As stated above, depending on the language of the original merchandising agreement, each band member may be responsible for that debt. For example, suppose the bass player of a now-defunct band is under an obligation to deliver the entire number of heads agreed upon by the previous band. If the bass player were, say, offered an opportunity to play with Garth Brooks during his upcoming world tour, he wouldn't be able to accept it because Garth Brooks would never take on a musician with such a debt. It is here that the issues of whether an act's responsibility to pay back the merchandising company only via income received as a headliner is of particular relevance. If in the original merchandise agreement, only headliners were liable for making up deficiencies in delivering "heads," or if the bass player had the option of paying back all or some of the unrecouped debt (plus interest) in money, rather than in heads on behalf of his or her band mates, the bass player would be free to take a job with another touring band.

The marketplace may also provide a solution for the band member who joins an existing band. The old merchandise company can make a deal with the new band's merchandiser, so that some of the merchandise of the old band member might be sold through the new band's outlets. Although, because of Mr. Brooks's status and power, this is unlikely, it is an option that has been exercised in some instances.

Head obligations, like others involving a situation where an advance is paid and the contractual commitment is not fulfilled (for example, in an exclusive songwriter's contract), the delivery of a minimum number of songs or the recording or release of a minimum number of cuts can theoretically extend for a lifetime. At some point, however, such obligations become impossible for the artist to meet. Most states' laws will permit a party to ultimately walk away from a never-ending duty to fulfill a contractual commitment that is either out of the party's control or is virtually, or actually, impossible to fulfill. The artist's representatives should understand the state laws in this area that apply to "head" provisions in the contract so that they can determine just what the artist's true burden will be in the event promises are made and not kept. This is an example in which the boilerplate provision known as "applicable law" can have enormous negative (or positive) impact on the artist, notwithstanding many lawyers' (and clients') inattention to this provision—which, on its face, has nothing specifically to do with the deal. Here is another reason why, as indicated in the previous chapter, New York, California, or Tennessee law is often chosen by artists as the applicable law by which the provisions of an entertainment business contract are interpreted. The courts in those states have often considered entertainment-industry issues involving commitments extending far into the future.

One practical way to stop the nightmare before it starts is to provide that in no event will the obligation to continue to provide heads last beyond the commencement of the recording of the album following the one that is the subject of the tour that failed to fulfill the merchandise contract's promises. Even if the artist ends up owing money to compensate the merchandiser, money is a finite thing, and a promise to pay money is always open to later compromise. For example, if a merchandise deal ended up unrecouped by, say, $100,000, the artist might pay the money back when he or she was able to pay, pay it off over the course of time, or work out a compromise when the artist's next tour was about to commence whereby a new deal with the original merchandise company would be negotiated, part of whose terms would be a reduction or forgiving of the old debt.

Territory

While in the United States, the United Kingdom, Australia, and Canada, it is customary to specify the number of heads that must be delivered, in the rest of the world, the preferred route, even for headliners, is to *impute* heads according to a predetermined formula (see above, page 180).

As with all agreements that go beyond one's own country's borders and that apply to a territory that is less than "the world," the contract must be clear as to what exactly the territory covered by the deal is. It is important to list each country and even each portion of certain countries (for example, French-speaking vs. German-speaking Switzerland) separately. "Europe" may or may not include the United Kingdom. The "European Community" will not include Switzerland unless specifically added. It is a good habit and a money-saving (and face-saving) step for the attorney or manager who is negotiating the contract to take the time and trouble to look at a map and list the countries making up the "territory" for which the artist is seeking to grant merchandising rights—or, for that matter, any rights.

Hall Charges

As noted in chapter 10, the venue itself customarily charges a significant percentage—up to 30% or 40%—of the gross sales in return for which it allows the artist the space within which to sell merchandise to the concertgoers. Outside of the United States, however, many venues have not yet caught up with the sophistication of the American halls, and considerable savings can be had there. For many venues, getting the act in the first place is the primary consideration—particularly in situations where the act can just as well ignore a particular city or country in its world tour. Sometimes the hall charges are less than what is anticipated (or predicted by the merchandiser); the artist's contract with the merchandiser can specify that when this occurs, the artist will share any such savings with the merchandiser.

Partial Advances

Some merchandise companies (particularly the more established ones, which have learned from bitter experience) will spread the advance (that is, the amount of which is "guaranteed") over the course of the tour, paying in installments so that they can protect themselves in the event that things go awry and the artist fails to deliver the requisite number of heads. Doing this makes the "advance" more of a "guarantee." The problem for the artist is, of course, that installment "advances" are not really advances at all. The "guaranteed" money, while still money, is of a different nature than advance money. First of all, the artist will be more tightly held to the head-delivery promises that have been made. In this scenario, the merchandise contract will break down the number of heads into segments of the tour—usually weeks or a number of shows, frequently eight. The head-delivery requirement will be proportioned to those segments. Thus, the number of guaranteed heads will be parsed into so many heads per week. If the weekly number is not met, the now-weekly advance will not have been recouped and the next "advance" payment will not be paid. Thus, if the number of heads guaranteed is 450,000 (as in the example above), 45,000 heads per week might be the number that has to be achieved before an "advance" is deemed recouped so that the next "advance" payment will be paid. As soon as delivery promises are not kept, the money flow will stop. Second, the amount available to the artist as seed money to set up and begin the tour before the initial flow of money from ticket sales is in hand will necessarily be significantly less than what would be available if the entire amount were advanced.

The ramifications of this dependence on installment advances can be enormous. One potential problem—the inability of the merchandise company to fulfill its promises to deliver the money when due—can be covered if the merchandiser's bank agrees to issue a letter of credit stipulating that if the merchandiser does not pay the promised sums when due, the bank will remit the promised sums on the merchandiser's behalf. Another, which involves the cash flow that is the currency of any well-planned tour, is not so easily solved. If a hunk of money is taken out of a tour precisely when the attendance levels of a particular leg of the tour drop, the effect on the remainder of the tour—a remainder that may include the biggest dates—can be catastrophic. After all, the costs of the entire tour—the trucks, buses, sound, lights, personnel, travel, etc.—are all prorated across the entire tour, not in equal segments per leg of the tour. These are very significant concerns to the business manager and personal manager, who are trying to plan the tour efficiently. In this case, the tail—the merchandise agreement—may indeed wag the dog. Among the consequences of having to halt a tour due to lack of funds are, of course, the claims that will arise from promoters and venues with respect to the canceled dates and the mess that the record company will be in for having incurred promotion expenses in cities in which the artist fails to appear.

Some Practical Considerations

Music lawyers are not used to multiple agreement transactions. The record deal, the publishing deal, and the producer agreement are made one at a time, have little to do with one another, and are addressed on a per-artist basis very irregularly and over a course of years. When an artist decides to embark on a major tour—in particular a world tour—there are dozens of major agreements to be entered into over a very short period of time. Some law firms, management firms, and business management firms are not staffed to cover all the bases in such circumstances.

I can attest to the fact that when a major artist decides to mount a major tour, the lawyer's world changes very quickly. But just because the merchandise agreement is only one of a dozen major agreements to be entered into does not mean that it deserves less attention to detail. This attention can take time and cost the client money, and the lawyer must weigh relative benefits of spending time and the client's money against the practicalities of just how much total time and money are available. Nevertheless, if the following issues are not specifically dealt with, the agreement that is eventually signed may bear no resemblance to what the parties desire or expect out of the relationship:

- Whose personnel will be used?
- What is the itinerary of the tour and how are revisions to be dealt with?
- Who transports the merchandise and at whose cost?
- Will the merchandise be offered for sale in display cases provided by the artist?
- Are the display cases provided by the merchandiser? And who transports the display cases and at whose cost?
- If there are not display cases, should they be built? At whose cost? Who will own them after the tour is over?
- What kinds of controls will ensure sufficient supplies for the expected demand?
- Is the insurance adequate to cover the possible loss of merchandise?
- Is the product liability insurance adequate?
- Who is responsible for protecting the venue and the tour city against pirated merchandise?

Advertising

Imagine an artist who has made a commitment to avoid commercial advertising and the stigmas that go with it. (Note that such resistance is much less widespread in the United States than it used to be—undermined, perhaps, when icon Bob Dylan opted to participate in a Victoria's Secret commercial.) The artist is backstage preparing to go onstage for a performance before 20,000 people to whom he or she will be representing the values of an "outsider"—a unique spokesperson for the "not ever to sell out" class—and that artist picks up a copy of the souvenir program for the tour and discovers pages of advertising by liquor and tobacco companies proclaiming the qualities of their products and identifying with the values of the great artist who is about to perform. The job of an attorney is not just to review the written word in a contract submitted by the merchandiser; he or she must also "imagine" the things that are not there. This is one example. The attorney should insist on a provision that prohibits the inclusion of advertising material on, near, or in association with the artist's merchandise (for example, on concert tickets) unless the artist or the artist's representatives have given their approval in writing, in advance.

Even if the artist does not care about the products he or she is associated with, or has approved the inclusion of advertising in connection with his or her merchandise, one must be careful to ensure that the money derived from the advertising is included among net receipts of the merchandiser (or the venue itself) and therefore shared with the artist. Tour merchandise royalty structures do not usually take into account this kind of income, and the issue should be dealt with directly and clearly during the initial negotiation.

Exclusivity

While the artist may be exclusive with the merchandiser, is the merchandiser exclusive with the artist? One would think it would be very disturbing—emotionally and financially—were the artist to find, among the merchandise being sold at the merchandise booth, merchandise of other acts that had performed at the venue over the past season or even merchandise featuring the logos of the venue itself (for example, Madison Square Garden or Radio City Music Hall). The sale of this merchandise will naturally reduce the net sales of the artist's merchandise and should be prohibited if possible. This is an example of why it is useful to work with an experienced merchandiser who knows what can and cannot be done at various venues; the issues will be on the table from the beginning—to be resolved, if possible, in plenty of time before the date is played.

RETAIL MERCHANDISING/WEB MERCHANDISING

Most tour merchandising agreements have a retail component as well. The Internet is having a revolutionary effect on retail sales, as opposed to tour-oriented sales. Although this is not yet having a significant effect on the royalty rate structure, eventually it *will* have an effect because there will no longer be any intermediary vendors to justify the kinds of commissions retained by merchandisers. In the meantime, in negotiating a retail agreement, care must be taken to address the difference between customary store distribution and Internet distribution. Certainly, the artist will want to reserve the right to sell uniquely designed merchandise on his or her website, in addition to merchandise manufactured and designed for touring or ordinary retail sale. For example, T-shirts, program books, and CDs are customarily offered at all concert venues; umbrellas, shot glasses, tour jackets, and other products with custom logos are offered at some concert venues and via the website. Expensive specialty items like sweaters and crystal are usually offered only via the website (1) because they are too costly or too fragile to carry as inventory on tours and (2) because they can be manufactured on demand. Today artists' online stores are their major source of merchandise income.

In traditional retail deals, the term of rights is longer than for those limited to touring. The latter are based approximately on the length of an album release period (about nine months to one year). With retail deals, three years is not unusual.

Even though the immediate concern of parties negotiating a tour-merchandising contract involves the tour aspects of the relationship, the retail portion should be very carefully negotiated to protect the artist's rights. It should not be treated as an afterthought.

Some other issues that arise with regard to retail sales include the following.

Cross-Collateralization

If an artist decides to place retail rights under the control of the tour merchandiser, two specific financial distinctions should be made: first, there should be separate royalty terms pertaining to the two areas because the services to be rendered are totally different; and second, there should be no right on the part of the tour merchandiser to apply success from one realm against failure from another. In other words, the income from one realm should be separated from the debt from the other. Whether or not this distinction is achievable may depend both on the artist's leverage and on the amount of money at risk. As noted previously, as more money is advanced or guaranteed, fewer rights can be reserved and deal terms benefiting the licensing party (the artist) will suffer.

Exclusivity

Does the artist wish to reserve the nonexclusive rights to issue certain licenses directly or through another agent, or must the artist give exclusive retail rights to the tour merchandiser? There may be opportunities brought to the artist's attention that involve areas in which the merchandiser is not actually involved or has no relationships; the contract can permit the artist to license those areas even if the deal with the tour merchandiser is otherwise substantially exclusive in nature. A problem may arise if the artist wishes to make available for retail sale through another vendor or agent some of the same merchandise that has been created by the tour merchandiser who has been eliminated from the retail side of things. This possibility must be dealt with as well. Artists' control of the trademark and ownership of all designs created on their behalf will give them appropriate leverage in this area.

Even when the retail rights extend beyond the term of the tour merchandise license, the artist may want to restrict the tour merchandiser from licensing the use of the tour logo, which has been designed for use with a specific tour. The first tour—and term of agreement with the tour merchandiser—may be long ended at the same time that the retail rights continue and a second or even third tour, each with its own logo, may have commenced. The artist may want to control these separately, particularly if the artist grants tour merchandising rights for tours two and three to a competitor of the first tour merchandiser.

Sample Approval

The need for the artist to have the right to approve samples of the merchandise is obvious; how to deal with the issue of the time it may take to provide those approvals is not. If the artist is responsible for approving designs and samples—as he or she should be—and the merchandiser must move so fast in manufacturing the products that the rights are not cleared properly, the merchandising company will jeopardize both itself and the artist. At the same time, if the merchandiser does *not* move quickly (and to the merchandiser, that is the name of the game), sales opportunities may be lost that will never arise again. As with a Broadway show or an airplane flight, once the curtain goes up, or the plane takes off, the empty seat—a commodity that had real value five minutes before—is worthless. Systems should be established early on to facilitate, insofar as possible, prompt submission of materials for approval and response by the artist or his or her designated representatives.

Trademarks

The laws and cases regarding trademark protection are complex. Trademarks are not like copyrights; once you acquire or create a copyright, it stays with you practically forever, no matter what you do (or do not do). In contrast, you can *lose*—through misuse or even nonuse—a trademark. Music business lawyers usually refer trademark legal work to others who live and breathe it daily and who read up on the latest changes regularly. Large law firms, including large entertainment law firms, have trademark specialists. There is a body of law in the area of trademark that establishes that a trademark owner must maintain almost absolute control of the reproduction of the owner's marks; failure to do this may result in losing the federal, and possibly state, protection that has been acquired through years of use and official trademark registrations.

This issue becomes concrete when an artist sublicenses his or her name, likeness, logos, trade names, and trademarks either directly or, through a merchandise "guru," to a variety of third parties. Mere approval by the trademark owner of these licensees is not enough to establish the kind of control that the law requires. The artist, either directly or through an agent, must have total control over the manner in which the trademark is reproduced, the quality of the reproduction, and the manner in which the trademark is used.

Once a licensee misuses an artist's trademark, if the artist does not take significant steps to cause the error to be corrected, the artist's trademark may be in real jeopardy. If the artist has been careless in monitoring the use of the trademark, or if he or she, or a licensee, uses it in a manner that, under trademark law, can divest the artist of his or her rights, it may not be possible to stop a third, unauthorized, party from using the trademark, and this party will raise the defense that the artist has abandoned the trademark. The culprit will claim that he or she can continue selling the product and will be exempt from infringement claims and all of the attendant liabilities that infringers can suffer. An example might be when an unrelated, and unauthorized, third party manufactures and distributes a coffee mug with a Rolling Stones "tongue" or a Prince "no name" symbol. As with other clauses in entertainment-related contracts, merely identifying the issue and requiring control over the use of one's trademarks is not enough. Someone must be put in charge of, and be held responsible for, ensuring that those steps that are necessary to protect the marks be taken, and taken consistently over the course of the term of the merchandising agreement.

In the area of trademark protection, one of the parties from whom the artist should be protected is, ironically, his or her own merchandiser. It is wise to put into the merchandise contract a provision that ensures that the trademarks, trade names, copyrights, and other intellectual property rights of the artist will *not* be disputed or attacked at any time by the merchandiser *and* that by being authorized to use and to license the use of these rights, the merchandiser is affirming that the rights are indeed vested in the artist and that the merchandiser is not acquiring any of those rights.

The merchandiser should also be familiar with the rules governing the requirement that manufacturers identify the source of the product (that is, who manufactured it and where), and there is still some vestigial belief that proper copyright notices and trademark notices must be affixed to products to protect the intellectual property rights in the logos, trade names, etc., although such formalities are, in fact, no longer necessary. As noted earlier, many artists have a problem with corporate names being used to identify the owner of a trademark or copyright. "Neil Young, Inc." is not something that an artist who has evidenced an antiestablishment bias in his career would like to see plastered over all of his program books or T-shirts. In this scenario, the merchandiser thinks (mistakenly) that

"Neil Young, Inc." or whatever the artist's name is, must appear somewhere on the T-shirt, and so it includes those words on the T-shirt, together with a copyright symbol © and the year of copyright. But the artist might well be—rightfully—annoyed because of his lifelong opposition to the "establishment." In fact, the merchandiser could simply have used the initials NY, or whatever his initials are, which would satisfy both Neil artist and the law—or used no copyright noticess at all as that formality is no longer necessary under the US Copyright Law or those of the signatories to its various international copyright conventions. The lawyer in charge of your merchandise licenses must be familiar with the laws of copyright to determine if the merchandise can be distributed without this designation, or, if the merchandise company or the artist's lawyer prefers, they can try to reach agreement as to what designation satisfies them from a legal point of view and their artist from a public relations point of view.

The Role of the Tour Merchandiser

One of the first issues to be dealt with is whether the tour merchandiser will act as a manufacturer and distributor or as an agent, licensing to third parties the manufacture and distribution of merchandise. The latter involves considerable risk to trademarks and quality control.

Net: Gross Less Sales Tax?

Interestingly, in deals in which royalties are calculated as a percentage of net receipts, "net" is often defined as gross less all applicable taxes. Let's see what this means. A product is sold for $10.00. Sales tax on this is an additional $0.8375 in New York City. Thus the consumer pays $10.84. If the royalty is to be paid on "gross less applicable taxes," $0.84 is deducted from the $10.00, leaving $9.16 as the net. Here is an example where imprecise language affects the artist's pocketbook. Obviously, the intention (probably of both parties) is that the royalty will be paid on $10.00, not $9.16, but when push comes to shove, it is surprising what disagreements may ensue (and then maybe be settled in return for some compromise elsewhere). Therefore, the definition of net receipts should be "gross *net* of sales tax," not "gross *less* sales tax."

Of course, depending on the nature of the merchandise and the location of the sale, there may be other taxes other than sales taxes, such as import duties, value-added taxes, etc.—that may be added to the suggested sale price of a particular product, and these should be dealt with specifically in each case. The same issue applies to shipping and handling charges, which can be significant in Internet sales. (Note that Internet sales are soon going to be subject to sales taxes also.)

Boilerplate: Don't Overlook the Obvious

Many of the boilerplate provisions found in tour merchandising agreements—such as insurance and territory issues—are also applicable in the retail area. Just because these are routine provisions does not mean that they do not have weight and should not be fought over vigorously. For example, in the insurance area, among the warranties an artist should require is that all of the goods and materials that are used in the merchandise are safe and fit for the purpose and use intended. One of the mechanisms utilized by artists who are subjecting themselves to potential liability by depending on the quality of products produced by third parties is to require that the third parties themselves be sufficiently insured against eventual claims by people claiming injury from the products. One way to guarantee that this is the case is to require that the third party (in this case the merchandiser) provide a certificate of insurance proving the existence of whatever amount of insurance the artist's representatives feel is sufficient to indemnify the artist in the event of adverse claims. In addition, the artist will usually want to be named as an "Additional Insured" on the merchandiser's own insurance policy. This is customarily provided when requested (if, of course, the company is in fact insured in the required amount). One thing to watch out for is the possibility that the insured amount may be used up by claims against the merchandiser from completely unrelated parties.

Therefore, the contractual clause requiring a certificate of insurance naming the artist and the artist's touring company as "Additional Insured" should also provide that the amount of insurance that is sought to be provided is isolated from claims from any other parties against the merchandiser.

• • •

Many other merchandising issues are applicable both to tour merchandising and retail merchandising. A primary consideration in both areas, of course, is to maintain what I refer to as "institutional memory." As time passes, and particularly when an artist has switched representation, the artist and the artist's team must be very careful to be sure that there are no previous agreements or provisions of agreements that have carried over into the present (or the future).

Often merchandising companies request that the artist sign irrevocable letters of direction to the artist's record company, music publishing company, even performing rights society, requiring them to pay to the merchandising company, in the event the merchandising deal does not play out as expected, earnings generated by the artist and otherwise payable directly to the artist. This is a disaster for a variety of reasons—not the least of which is that, although the amount of money cited in a letter of direction is by necessity a fixed number, the actual sum of money due the merchandiser at any given time is, more often than not, a matter open to considerable dispute. The "deficit" number is always changing and, in changing, becoming less and less; yet it is unlikely that the merchandiser will send follow-up letters to the artist's record company, publishing company, etc., changing the original number.

Among the other areas of general concern are confidentiality, compliance with local laws, sell-off and inventory, the disposition of artwork and photographs, audits, and life and disability insurance. In addition, remember that the merchandise licensing agreement is usually entered into by the artist's touring corporation, not by the artist. The artist's personal guarantee to provide rights to the merchandise company in the event that the touring corporation defaults flies in the face of the artist's claim that the touring corporation is a legitimate entity worthy of beneficial tax treatment. If the corporation is in actuality a gimmick, then the chances that a third party will be able to breach its limited liability protection is increased.

CONFIDENTIALITY

For some reason, people are very nosy about the relationship between artists and their merchandisers. Perhaps it is because the deals are so straightforward (advances, royalty rates, heads attending concerts, etc.) that it is easier to comprehend the value of these deals than to get into comparison shopping with information about record royalties where a royalty "point" can mean anything you want it to mean. There is no reason to educate other competitors for artist's rights or merchandiser's money as to what deals can be squeezed out of the merchandisers. After all, the artist and the merchandiser pay substantial fees to professionals to work their way through the complexities of these deals and both the information about them and the process that accomplishes consensus are, in a way, proprietary. Accordingly, there should be included in these agreements a clause, with teeth, protecting that confidentiality.

COMPLIANCE WITH LOCAL LAWS

Nothing pleases a small-minded prosecutor more than a little publicity that can be garnered from attacking a high-profile artist for "participation" in breaking a local law. The contract with merchandisers must address the fact that the tour, and retail licensing deals as well, will involve many different states with many different laws, rules, and regulations. The merchandiser must be responsible for compliance with these laws and regulations, and most merchandising agreements so provide. But the ultimate impact of any such provision will be found in the indemnity provision, which should be carefully considered when the initial contract is negotiated.

There are innumerable laws with which most of us in the music business have no contact whatsoever at any time in our professional careers, yet these laws can cross our paths in the merchandise area suddenly and with devastating result. For example, many types of products must bear posted warnings if the merchandiser and the artist are to be insulated from liability in every state. If merchandise products with small parts are designed so they might appeal to children, specific child safety warnings often must be posted. Sleepwear for children must usually be fire-retardant. Claims arising out of the failure to abide by these laws may result in a court award of damages in an amount so high that no amount of insurance typically maintained by the merchandiser will be enough to offset the possible liability to the artist. There may be criminal liability as well. The artist's representatives must use all due diligence to satisfy themselves that the merchandising company knows exactly what it is doing in the area of compliance with local and federal laws—yet another reason to use a company with a proven track record.

END-OF-TERM INVENTORY AND SELL-OFF

Any contract that involves inventory has to come to terms with what happens when the term of the agreement is over. In the area of tour and retail merchandising, the artist and the artist's representatives have to ensure that the merchandiser does not manufacture or authorize the manufacture of goods—at any time, let alone toward the end of the contract term—in excess of approximate market demand. It is customary to seek a written inventory (allowing an auditor of the artist's choice to actually physically assist in counting the inventory) both at the end of the license term and after the sell-off period (usually six months to a year after the term expires). Believe it or not, it has happened more than once that more inventory was on hand *after* the sell-off period than at the end of the official license term.

Once the rights to sell have officially ended, the artist should have the option of either purchasing the remaining inventory in stock at cost (plus maybe 10% handling) *or* demanding that the remaining inventory be destroyed. In the latter event, the artist should have the right to send in an auditor to observe the destruction, and the merchandiser should have the obligation to provide an "affidavit of destruction" to put the final nail in the coffin on that deal.

In the retail arena, a problem sometimes arises when inventory somewhere out there in the marketplace is returned to the merchandiser by sublicensees long after the events described above have taken place. Under these circumstances, the merchandiser will itself have inventory on hand after its rights have expired. The provision stating that the artist has the right to purchase (or destroy) remaining inventory doesn't help in this situation. This kind of anomaly can be avoided if the artist has been apprised of the identity of all the merchandiser's sublicensees and their addresses. Of course, if the artist maintains control over the choice of sublicensees as part of his or her trademark-monitoring responsibilities, the artist will likely know their identities anyway. Artists who are hands-on in this regard are more, rather than less, likely to be able to protect themselves if merchandisers glut the market with products. And those who are not hands-on? Well, you know the answer.

ARTWORK AND PHOTOGRAPHS

The artwork used for tour merchandise may duplicate the artwork on the record album (which the record company owns), or it may be created by a designer or photographer hired specifically for the tour merchandise. In either case, the artist's rights to exploit this artwork beyond the tour itself may be severely restricted. Even if separate permissions for retail licenses are acquired from the record company or the designer (or photographer), the artist's attorney must make it clear whose responsibility it will be to clear these rights, and at whose cost, as well as whether the rights clearance will include providing camera-ready artwork. The costs include the costs of obtaining the rights themselves, as well as the cost of attorneys' fees for clearing the rights and negotiating and processing the contract establishing the terms of the rights clearance.

Both the artist and the merchandiser must insist that all persons who create art or text for the merchandise (for example, in program books) sign, wherever possible, work-for-hire agreements establishing the artist or the artist's service corporation as the owner of the result created. In this regard, the representatives of the artist must be careful, in acquiring rights to artwork, designs, and photographs, to make sure that the artist's team has the right to crop, reshape, edit, or even adapt the artwork. Note, however, that in many countries of the world, even if there is a total buyout of rights, the "moral" rights of the artist or photographer may be violated by such actions, and there is no concept of a work for hire outside of the United States. Using a French photographer for an album cover, and then fiddling with it in a way that transforms it into something that the photographer feels damages his or her art, and therefore his or her reputation, may be problematic. The unacceptable change can be as simple as cropping a painting or photograph to fit a CD jewel box and then cropping it again to fit a DVD and then cropping it yet again to fit a cassette J card. I have actually had to deal with a situation in which artwork for a tour was purchased and for which agreements were signed, where the artwork had to be reinstated in its original form for use outside of the United States under the threat of litigation for violating the artist's moral rights. I am not suggesting that one never use foreign nationals to create or license artwork for a United States–based group, but I do want to alert those artists and their managers and other representatives whose artistic reach extends beyond our borders that they may be acquiring fewer rights than they think they are acquiring.

COUPLING

Just as the artist may be dismayed (at the least) to discover commercial advertising attached to the souvenir program for the tour (or, heaven forbid, the T-shirts), he or she may be very confused (at the least) to discover that some of the merchandising products feature not only the artist but another artist as well. This possibility is yet another reason to be careful to approve everything that is manufactured. Nevertheless, some things slip through the approval cracks and it is important for the contract itself to forbid the coupling of other artists' names and likeness or other logos, trademarks, etc., on the subject artist's merchandise—or even on advertisements for the merchandise.

LIFE AND DISABILITY INSURANCE

Companies that are investing substantial monies in pursuit of the purchasing capabilities of fans of a particular artist are naturally concerned lest the artist die or become disabled through illness, and seeking life and disability insurance against such contingencies is neither unusual nor unreasonable. There is, however, a practical problem: The artist usually has to undergo a physical examination—one that is conducted by a doctor other than the artist's own, and not necessarily one that is conducted by someone who is bound by any privacy or confidentiality concerns beyond those of the medical profession. Add to this an artist who is prone to taking drugs of any sort—or even one who smokes marijuana occasionally—and you are inviting a lifetime problem. (For example, suppose the examining doctor denies the artist insurance, and, years later, the artist has to complete an insurance form that asks the question, Have you ever been denied insurance?) And then there is the problem of a female artist, especially a "star" who is required to submit to an examination by a male doctor (or doctors) who has not been scrutinized by her own doctors. (I have had many situations in which my female clients—and not just the supermodels—have been made to feel very uncomfortable during physical examinations by doctors who come to their homes and either behave like star-struck fans or, worse, act in ways that are, to put it euphemistically, less than "professional.") The solution, of course, is to have one's own doctor do the examining, and this is something that is often permitted by the insurance company. The contract itself can prescribe this option.

PIRACY

Bootlegging, or copying an artist's logo, trademarks, and trade name, and selling merchandise without authorization, is as old as show business itself. Ordinarily, merchandisers will have mechanisms (and lawyers) in place to keep piracy to a minimum—especially during tours. The days of bootleg merchandisers setting up shop in the parking lots of rock-and-roll arenas are pretty much over, but the days of bootleggers are not. Different genres of music invite different styles of stealing, and it is important that the merchandiser be skilled at stopping these thieves in advance if possible. In recent years, courts have become educated in the ways of this unauthorized underworld and have been willing, in many instances, to grant temporary restraining orders, in advance, against the John Does, the as-yet-unidentified thieves. Enjoining behavior before the person has his or her day in court is generally anathema to all courts (and a remarkable remedy in a democracy when you think about it), but in bootlegging cases US courts have come to embrace this procedure as the only way to stop the piracy of artists' merchandise by people who would otherwise simply disappear in their vans never to be identified and never to be caught.

Of course, taking any formal legal action requires a coordinated effort, and there is considerable cost involved. Who pays for this? Who is responsible for initiating actions to prevent the sale of unauthorized merchandise? Are these costs cross-collateralized against the retail side? The language in the contract should answer all of these questions.

Bootlegging will occur wherever there is a vacuum. In the retail area, bootlegged merchandise runs rampant where the subject of the piracy doesn't see to it that the retail shelves are filled with legitimate merchandise. Doing so actually minimizes the risk that illegal products will appear. In the course of selecting a merchandiser, the artist should determine whether the merchandiser is effective in distributing product to the retail side. (If Internet sales are going to be part of the deal, is the merchandiser adept at ensuring that *its* website is placed up front on a search engine?) At the time the basic merchandise agreement is being considered, artists' representatives should raise the issue of the efficacy and the reputation of the merchandiser in pursuing bootleggers and in filling up distribution channels in response to demand for the artists' products.

AUDITS

I would like to mention briefly the issue of audits and general examinations of the books and records of merchandisers. I cannot think of another situation in which the ability to check books and records on a regular basis is more appropriate. Most dealings for merchandise on the road are in cash, the road personnel of merchandise companies are often picked up for temporary duty and are not known (or bonded), and merchandising income is derived from many sources and in many locations outside of the centers of the music business. These unique characteristics of the tour merchandise business leave open a lot of room for carelessness, let alone abuse and downright stealing. The tour accountant, who, it goes without saying, should have a familiarity with merchandising operations in general, needs access at all times to the books and records of the venue and the merchandiser so that these monies can be monitored on a daily basis. Remember, we are not just talking about the artist losing some money; we have also seen that there are considerable consequences to the artist in the event that guarantees are not met. Even when all of the provisions of an agreement have been honored, sloppy accounting can have the same effect as a material breach of the performance-guarantee provisions of the agreement.

12 · AUDITS
Truth or Consequences

Money doesn't talk. It swears.
—BOB DYLAN, "IT'S ALRIGHT, MA (I'M ONLY BLEEDING)"

After all the negotiating is over, the career has slowed down or stopped, and the records have run their course, when the action is all in the past, the shining knight finally appears—ready to bring sense out of chaos, truth out of lies, rationality out of illogic, money out of nowhere. Who is this hero? The accountant! This may seem an unlikely role for this often-disparaged professional whose salient personality traits are supposed to be passivity, cordiality, and conservatism. But the accountant may be the only person who has the understanding and experience to turn failure into success, to turn short-term earnings into long-term security. In football, success or failure starts with the quarterback. In the record business, success or failure at the beginning may well depend on how good the lawyer and manager are, but in the end, it surely rests with the accountant.

EXAMINING THE AUDIT

Useful and effective audits do not have to wait until the end of an artist's career to be conducted. In fact, as we saw in chapter 4, the longer one waits, the more likely a person who wishes to audit another will be shut out. Except as otherwise indicated in this chapter, when using the term *audit*, I am referring to audits of record companies by artists or producers. In brief, an *audit* is an examination by an expert of the financial books and records of a company that has agreed to make periodic payments—in particular, royalty payments—to another person: the artist or producer, or, as you will see later, the songwriter.

When most of us hear the word *audit* we think of the government breaking down the door, or a fancy accounting firm certifying the financial statements of a public company. But in this chapter, I am not referring to audits that actually "certify" whether statements are correct; indeed, this will never occur because in the end compromise is the name of the game in the music business, leaving precision in the dust. In my experience, record company or music publishing statements have never been certified as accurate. The only purpose of an audit—an examination of books and records—is to determine if there can be raised a convincing argument on behalf of the auditor's client that there are any significant underreportings or underpayments by the party that is supposed to write the check.

The parties in whose interest an audit is customarily performed are:

- The *artist* who audits the record company.
- The *producer* who audits the record company. This audit may have to piggyback on the artist's audit because the record company may limit the producer's access to the record company records rather than open them up to multiple audits of essentially the same data.

- The *publisher* who audits the record company either directly or through the efforts of its agent, most often the Harry Fox Agency, Inc.
- The *writer* who audits the publishing company.
- The *writer's own publishing company* that audits the writer's administrating publishers or subpublishers.

When the Artist Audits the Record Company

After the record has been produced and released, and the costs of and returns on its active life are in, the auditor enters the game to determine if the record company has accounted for and paid the artist what the artist was entitled to pursuant to his or her agreement with the record company. Record company audits will examine issues such as free goods, returns, mathematical calculations of statements (do *you* remember your multiplication tables?) and cut-outs. (*Cut-outs* are records taken out of inventory because of their totally poor sales history and, essentially, given away for a pittance and marked accordingly so that they cannot reappear as a "return" at the other end of the record company's distribution system.)

Interestingly, the accountant within the record company whose job it is to defend the company's interpretations of the contract and its practices does not ordinarily report to the chief financial officer of the company, but rather to an operations executive, or even to the head of legal or business affairs. Why is this? Because the audit is looked upon as just another deal to negotiate, to settle, to compromise. It is the end game of the process of identifying and signing the artist, selling the artist's recordings, and turning them into "catalogue." The audit is expected, it is anticipated, and in a way it is welcomed, because for the first time, the open questions—crucial questions as to accuracy in payment calculations—will be closed for all time. Closure, both for the record company and the artist, is a good thing. And when the record company has to make a settlement as a result of the audit procedure, it is not just a vindication or victory for the artist; through settlement, the record company closes a chapter in which it has often miscoded charges, miscalculated royalties, and distorted the intention of the parties as reflected in the written contract.

In fact, record companies often view audits as a group—they review the annual audit picture and balance the costs of defending the onslaught of the artist's (or publishing company's) auditors. If an artist is important and handled by an important auditor, there may be a generous settlement. If not, probably not. In effect, audits are a profit center.

Even when the record company pays up, it may be just so the artist and the artist's auditor will go away. Rarely, if ever, will the record company provide a statement that indicates with any specificity how much they erred or in what categories. Audit settlements do not ordinarily specify the rationale behind them. Even when the particulars of a settlement are quantified by category, companies are unlikely to change their practices in the future, or even admit to the errors of the past. Their goal is to get the auditor out of the building and close a chapter in the life of the artist and record company. A cash settlement is a small price indeed to pay for that.

When Is an Escalation an Opportunity?

Often recording contracts provide for escalating royalties once a record reaches a particular sales threshold. Sometimes, these royalty provisions provide for retroactive adjustment upward. Depending on the contract's definitions of "sales" and "net sales," the upward adjustment might well apply even though the sales threshold is not net of free goods.

In other words, for royalty *payment* purposes, record companies will calculate net sales, after free goods are excluded. But for royalty *calculation* purposes, they may have inadvertently defined the sales threshold in terms of *sales*, rather than net sales. On a greatest-hits recording on which the royalty rate is increased retroactively on older tracks as a result of the achievement of a certain amount of sales, this distinction can amount to hundreds of thousands of dollars gained—or lost. Furthermore, the contractual definitions of records and phonorecords may allow the record company to increase royalties only on vinyl or CD versions of record sales, but not on, say, downloads.

When a Publishing Company Audits the Record Company

A publishing company's audit of a record company most often is pursued by the Harry Fox Agency, Inc., which represents about 80% of all publishers in the United States, and, through its affiliated mechanical rights societies around the world, most publishers based outside of the United States as well. Two issues that are unique to audits initiated by publishing companies are (1) unmatched lists and (2) controlled compositions.

Unmatched Lists The term *unmatched lists* (also referred to as *suspense lists*) refers to data collected, more or less efficiently (often less), by the record company with respect to musical compositions on which mechanical royalties are payable but where the party entitled to the royalties is not identified. Even if the record company knows whom to pay, it may not pay because it has no executed license agreement from the publisher or from the publisher's agent (again, usually the Harry Fox Agency). The careless and haphazard way that unidentified compositions are listed and accounted for by record companies is legendary in the music industry, and if an auditor does not know where to look, the income will be lost for the audit period. Remember, once a period has been the subject of a resolved audit, that period is, absent outright fraud, closed for all time, and is no longer subject to question. Further, you may be sure there is nobody at the record company who is pointing the auditor in the right direction. If the auditor is not plugged in to the idiosyncratic ways in which record companies hide—or misplace—royalty-generating events and income, the audit's effectiveness will be lessened accordingly.

Controlled Compositions Controlled compositions are dealt with at some length in the next chapter. Suffice it to say at this point that controlled composition clauses are often "custom" negotiated for each artist, and a full and complete comprehension of the particular clause at issue is essential if an auditor is to be able to verify the accuracy of accounting statements from the record company. Some countries—in particular, Canada—have established certain floors on controlled-composition clauses that will have the effect of overriding some of the clauses now written into contracts. Sophisticated thinkers are at work here, and the auditor will have to muster all of his or her insights and experience just to keep up with them.

Auditing Copublishers and Subpublishers

Copublishing agreements are between two entities that agree to share ownership of the copyrights to a given body of compositions as well as the compensation due to the owners of the copyrights. The term *subpublisher* refers to a foreign publisher who represents the interests of a US publisher. In either case, the companies involved are often multinational corporations.

THE FLOW OF MONEY

We will see in chapter 13 how multinational companies or companies whose rights are themselves represented overseas by subpublishers have different views as to what "receipts" are and whether they should pay royalties on those receipts or the royalties should be paid "at source." The multinationals (and I am using this term intentionally, because these companies are not set up and have never been set up to be "global" in the sense that they create one concerted worldwide effort to exploit artists and their copyrights) move their money around so facilely that it is a wonder that even the home office knows where it is.

Sometimes, in fact, the home office doesn't. Until PolyGram Music Publishing was sold to Universal Music, it had its headquarters in Baarn, the Netherlands. Yet its home office was in London. When you made a deal with the US affiliate, it was impossible to figure out who would possess the books and records of US sales, or of the foreign sales. What's more, PolyGram counted its money in Dutch guilders!

Money is exchanged and moved back and forth faster than it is at the World Series of Poker—and with much more success. Like good poker players, these companies keep their information close to the vest—so close, in fact, that it becomes prohibitive to try to follow it without the aid of the CIA (which, hopefully, has other things on its agenda).

Moving money from country to country—paying, receiving credits for, and simply getting the benefit of international tax treaties (as to which, be assured, these multinationals are expert)—will befuddle even the most astute auditors. How much more baffling the money chase became with respect to PolyGram Music statements when this company was finally absorbed into another multinational—the Universal Music Group—in 1999. And that was before Universal (owned predominantly by Seagrams of Canada, but partly by Matsushita of Japan) was sold to Vivendi (of France) and before a consortium of investors in 2011–2012 purchased EMI Music Publishing and Universal Music group purchased EMI's record assets. See what I mean?

There is an inherent disadvantage in dealing with a multinational publishing company in that the Harry Fox Agency—previously owned and run by the American National Music Publishers Association, and since 2015 by SESAC, theoretically the songwriters' last chance for an honest count—does not always audit the affiliated record companies. For example, Harry Fox does not audit the major record companies on behalf of their publishers that license their sister record companies directly, bypassing the Fox agency entirely. The publishing companies will tell you that they conduct internal audits by their own in-house people, but these are easily tinkered with so that the combined company can produce a profit-and-loss picture that says what the company wants it to say. This is an obvious impediment to achieving an accurate "count," and more importantly, as will be seen later, it will reduce the chances that an efficient and conscientious audit will be able to correct registration errors, whose correction, ironically, would benefit both the original publisher and its administrating publisher.

This disparity among music publishers and the lack of vigor with which some pursue audit rights can be a serious handicap, and, while it should not discourage songwriters or their self-owned publishing companies from entering into administration or copublishing arrangements with a multinational, it would be appropriate to address this issue at the time the contract is negotiated rather than after earnings that might otherwise have been uncovered by a more zealous publisher have been lost forever.

ACCESS TO REGISTRATION INFORMATION

It is important for auditors to have access to copies of the foreign societies' accountings to their publisher members—whether these publishers obtain rights of representation directly, for example, in the case of music indigenous to their territory, or through a worldwide or regional administrator. No foreign society will allow a US (original) publisher to audit them directly; but each country's societies operate differently, and depending on the copyright owner's negotiating leverage, it is at least within the range of possibility to obtain access for the auditor to so much additional data that the success of the audit process will be geometrically more promising.

Occasionally, the impediment established by foreign societies can be overcome by the original publisher when *it* becomes a member of the foreign rights society itself or when it establishes in the foreign country an affiliate company that becomes a member of the foreign rights society. This avenue is not widely taken for a variety of good reasons—not the least of which is figuring out what to do with the foreign entity (if one is created) once it is established. For once the original publisher has created a new tax entity in a foreign country, it may find that there are tax consequences beyond the publisher's original expectations both in that country and in the United States. Even the possibility of dissolving the entity can have severe tax implications.

THE BLACK BOX OR "SOMETHING IS ABYSS HERE"

The infamous Black Box phenomenon is discussed in several chapters of this book. In the context of audits, let me make a few observations. The mechanical and performing rights societies of each country around the world, which are usually combined into one society per country, quite regularly realize that they cannot attribute the earnings of a particular song to a particular owner or publisher. What are they to do with this money? Customarily, they drop it into an account for later distribution. There are several kinds of income that end up in the abyss of Black Box accounts: unallocated income, unclassified income, and unidentified income. While they sound alike, they are not, and only your auditor knows for sure which is which.

In addition to the three above-mentioned categories, Black Box income will include monies which were set aside by a foreign rights society for expenses but that were not needed because the organization did not spend its full budget. There is also income representing monies reimbursed by rights societies by way of specific rebates of society commissions: for example, the *Restausschutung* payments by GEMA (Gesellschaft für musikalische Aufführungs- und mechanische Vervielfältigungsrechte) in Germany and similar payments by SDRM (Société pour l'Administration du Droit de Reproduction Mécanique), the mechanical rights society in France and STEMRA (Stichting Stemra), the mechanical and performing rights society in the Netherlands.

Some of this income represents surplus proceeds or collections (such as the *Verwertungsverfahren* proceeds in Germany), including those received by way of newly introduced types of distribution or newly introduced types of income in which monies are not separately allocated and attributed to specific musical compositions.

The sums that find their way into the Black Boxes of various countries can be enormous. For example, it is estimated that the Italian Black Box absorbs more than 30% of the gross income collected by SIAE (Società Italiana degli Autori ed Editori). Indeed, entire catalogues whose income has never been allocated correctly have been "lost" into one

Black Box or another. One would like to think that the inability to allocate income from musical compositions on such a scale is due to carelessness and lack of diligence. However, I would be remiss if I were not to mention that over the years, a lot of Black Box income has been found to have been accumulated because various parties, including the foreign publisher members themselves (some of which were merely subsidiaries of the original US publisher in which writers placed so much trust), intentionally misallocated funds or misregistered (for example, registered with misspelling of authors' names or the wrong author or copublisher shares) songs.

You may wonder how in the world an auditor could get access to the information needed to verify the accuracy of royalty statements from countries in which the Black Box exists. The answer varies from country to country, but if a knowledgeable auditor can get into the books of the company that is the official member of the relevant performing rights or mechanical rights society, the information is all there.

TELEVISION CAMPAIGNS

As stated in chapter 9, record companies often reduce the artist's royalty rate—by as much as 50%—during the period in which they mount a television campaign to promote a record. No record company executive dealing with an auditor will volunteer the basis for the reduced royalty arising out of such a provision. The entry on the royalty account will merely indicate the reduction, and there will be a notation that the reduction in the royalties was due to promotional expenditures. It may cite the contractual provision: for example, "Promotional expenditures pursuant to Paragraph 7.07(b)." While there is nothing the artist can do about this, it is important for the auditor to verify that the promotional expenses in question were not only incurred, but incurred in an amount justifying the royalty reduction. For example, was the expense in the nature of a one- or two-time television buy, or was it a real campaign as contemplated by the contract? Frequent consultation with the artist's attorney is appropriate in such situations.

INTEREST CHARGES

It is not unusual that when one party is adjudged to owe another party money damages for breach of contract (which would include the submission of inaccurate accountings), the party claiming the deficiency will seek (and occasionally receive) interest on the monies due that were either not paid at all or not paid on time. Both the federal government and state governments charge interest when taxes due have been underreported (and will often pay interest or credits when money is due to the reporter). This would seem to be an equitable way to compensate the damaged party with the intended salutary effect of discouraging similar acts in the future.

Record and publishing companies offer no such compensation—even in egregious situations. Nevertheless, it is customary to at least *make* the interest calculation. If the deficiency is due to a misunderstanding, or to a disagreement, or to a different interpretation of a contract clause—that is, mistakes in interpretation that do not represent a pattern of deception—the record company or publishing company can claim "innocence," which will usually frustrate a claim for interest. However, processing errors, a total lack of payments, or cataclysmic underreporting or underpayments—like tax evasion versus tax avoidance in the IRS's world—will more likely give resonance to the claim that interest is due. Merely asserting a claim for interest may be enough to ratchet up an eventual settlement.

The methodology of settlement between artists and record companies, or publishing companies and writers, is so entrenched that interest is rarely paid; indeed, it is often not even sought in view of the remote chance of recovering it. More likely, the auditing party will receive an "interest factor" in the context of an overall settlement. It will not be designated as such, but as long as the auditing party is satisfied with the total settlement figure, why should it matter how one categorizes the elements that make it up?

STATUTES OF LIMITATIONS

Most states have statutes that limit the number of years during which a person can assert a contract claim arising from a perceived breach. These statutes customarily establish the limits at six or seven years. However, record companies and publishing companies traditionally seek to modify these statutorily granted protections by reducing to one, two, or sometimes three—the number of years during which a person can assert such a claim. Their justification is that it is too difficult and costly to maintain records back as far as six years. The fact that such records must be kept longer under the rules and regulations of the Internal Revenue Service is conveniently ignored.

The goal obviously is to chip away at artists' and writers' opportunities to review their careers—and the attendant income—after as short a time as the company can get away with has passed. Even with today's intricate global banking network and vast communications facilities, it can take at least a year and often two or more years before income earned in various parts of the world is reported. To require that an audit be conducted within days or weeks following (or preceding!) the submission of accounting statements is to deny the artist or writer the fair opportunity underlying the logic of states' more generous statutes of limitations.

There are a couple of things that a negotiator can do to ameliorate this problem before the contract is entered into. In particular, in dealing with a multinational company, audit rights should be expanded to extend to subsidiaries and affiliates. (I have had deals fall through when such requests were refused. There is enough paranoia among artists to not add to it by a company's reasonable request to audit wholly-owned subsidiaries.) Similarly, one can seek a provision permitting, under certain circumstances, a year-to-year extension of the period during which the right to audit remains viable if the gross sales of product reach certain levels. For example, the time period during which the artist or writer (or producer) experiences a substantial financial success is not only the time that an audit may really matter; it is also the time period in which the record company might be most receptive to the argument that a fair evaluation of one's career cannot be made with blinders on. That is, it is reasonable to stipulate that when large blocks of income are to be reported, transferred, and examined, the artificial statute of limitations sought to be established by the record company should be extended.

While long-term (more than three years) audit provisions are never specifically granted, it is not unusual for a royalty-paying entity—particularly a music publishing administrator like a Universal Music Publishing Company—to agree to audits to be performed *during* the term, or to one comprehensive audit covering the entire term to be performed within one year following the end of the term. For a five-year contract, this audit would occur in the sixth year after commencement of the term. Sometimes, audits are conducted and no formal audit report is submitted. There are two reasons for this: first, the auditors may not have found anything significant or may want to wait to see how the company deals with a future accounting period; second, the auditors may have found an error in the client's favor and are reticent to bring this to the company's attention. Hence, this audit is *never* completed.

Mechanical Licenses and Mechanical Variances

A *mechanical license* is a license granted by the owner of a copyrighted musical composition giving another entity the right—for a fee—to record, manufacture, and distribute copies of the composition. Legally, however, the mechanical "license" document frequently used by music publishers is not a license agreement at all, which would be subject to the usual statute of limitations period of six or seven years, but a "variance," or modification, of a provision in the US Copyright Act. The statute of limitations for claiming copyright infringement is three years from the date of infringement. Failure to pay, or pay correctly, gives rise to a copyright infringement claim rather than a breach of contract claim. Chapter 15, page 235, discusses mechanical variances in more detail, but let me point out three issues that are relevant to the statute of limitations on audits.

One California Federal Court has ruled that the copyright law's three-year statute of limitations might only apply to the period during which claims are sought—so that an infringement that continues well beyond the end of the initial three-year period following publication (even twenty-five years later) can give rise to ongoing claims for profits derived from ongoing infringements during the most recent three years of the copyright term. If affirmed on appeal, this ruling will be a godsend to songwriters and publishers who have always thought that their right to sue for an ongoing infringement would have expired years earlier. The jury is still out, as they say, as to whether these late-date infringement claims would allow the plaintiff to claim some of the special remedies of the Copyright Act such as minimum statutory damages, injunctions, and other remedies, or whether they might be limited to claiming only the profits of the infringing party.

1. In a contract negotiation in which a writer or music publisher (which may be the artist's own company) is trying to extend the right to audit a record company's books until, say, one year following the expiration of the deal (as mentioned previously, for a five-year deal, this would extend to as long as six total years), is it possible to recapture infringement claims that would otherwise have expired?

2. Record companies traditionally try to encapsulate *all* rights to object to royalty accountings in a fixed and predictable schedule—usually of two years' duration—and to pursue such objectives in the courts. Under US copyright law, can the record company, by contract, reduce the three-year copyright infringement provision to two years?

3. Recording agreements now customarily *include* a "license" to mechanically reproduce the musical compositions on the record rather than have to comply with a separate variance document.

CONDUCTING AUDITS IN FOREIGN COUNTRIES

Naturally, it can be very expensive to conduct an audit of a record company in the United States. Yet both the cost and the logistics of conducting audits in more than one foreign country on behalf of a small publishing company or owner to the rights of a record catalogue can be even more daunting. I have two practical suggestions in this regard:

1. Audit one country at a time and proceed to other countries only if claims are detected in the first country or countries. When auditors begin to see common errors, they can move on into other countries.

2. If possible, combine resources and audit foreign companies in tandem with others similarly situated. For example, the Association of Independent Music Publishers (AIMP), based in New York, comprises hundreds of small companies. Banded together, these companies can— and do—pursue audits of companies that are common to their colleagues' subpublishing schemes.

While there are very experienced music business auditors available outside of the United States (particularly in the United Kingdom), if you want to have the privilege of personally knowing your representative or using one you have successfully worked with in the United States in the past, there is no reason you should not engage that person's services for audits outside of the United States. In addition, many US accounting firms have offices or correspondent firms outside the United States (again, particularly in the United Kingdom). Even if you ask your US representative only to oversee or review a foreign audit, or act as a consultant, you may be better served than if you let a foreign auditor, no matter how qualified, conduct the audit alone. Your US representative will know you better, know your catalogue and history better, and have a continuity with you that one-time auditors will not, by definition, have. I should also note that it is no more costly to have a US auditor go to Milan (the center of the Italian music business) than for a United Kingdom–based auditor to go to Milan. Airfares (we're not talking Jet Blue or Ryan Air for these guys) and lodging expenses are similar, and the only issue is whether professional fees are competitive, which in large part they seem to be.

A FEW PRACTICAL SUGGESTIONS

It is not necessary for "fear" and "audit" to be spoken in the same breath. And an audit need not be expensive. In fact, it need not be formal. Remember, an audit is merely a process by which accounting statements are verified.

Desk Audits

There is often sufficient information within the recipient's control such that regular monitoring of the statements will serve essentially the same purpose as a formal audit. If a recipient, attorney, or accountant has kept track of the recipient's writing and recording activities, a fairly satisfactory job can be done on a regular basis to determine the accuracy of statements and accountings.

Here the issue is how to verify whether song licensing and master licensing—usually done by separate parties—show up consistently in accounting statements by publishers and record companies respectively; allowing for some overlap in accounting-period data, they should match. Most artists can identify their discography and their music catalogue (and if they cannot, it is not such a bad idea to hire someone to organize and categorize this information so it can be used). In addition, most artists these days have the right to approve the licensing of their recordings in films, TV programs, and commercials, and on compilation or flashback-type records. Those artists who control their own publishing administration may also have the right to approve the licensing of their songs, so there is some awareness of these uses that can be documented and filed for future use in an audit.

In cases in which the recording right is automatic by virtue of Section 115 of the Copyright Act (Scope of Exclusive Rights in Nondramatic Musical Works: Compulsory License for Making and Distributing Phonorecords), publishers are notified formally and in writing. All of this data is readily available, and the information can be checked against accounting statements easily, without the delay or expense occasioned by a formal audit.

On receiving an accounting statement, it is advantageous and judicious to review it immediately. In doing so, the recipient should determine the following:

- Has the statement been received in a timely fashion?
- Does the statement cover all applicable copyrights (or masters)?
- Are the splits (for example, those between artist and producer, between artist and record company, and between the writers, cowriters, and publishers) correct?
- On the statements of the record company, do all the catalogue numbers match the actual releases?
- Do the reported releases match the master-use licenses entered into by the record company? For example, Rhino is charged with licensing, TV, films, and record compilations, master recordings owned and controlled by the Warner Music Group's record companies. Customarily, permission to issue these licenses is sought from the artist or the artist's representative, and these requests should be maintained in a separate file so that they can be compared with the actual accounting statements when they are issued, sometimes years later. A license for a *Greatest Rock Songs of the '80s* compilation record in New Zealand or some other foreign territory will not generate a royalty on an accounting statement for as long as three years after the sales occur.

Technicalities Do Matter

Do any notices have to be sent to preserve rights? Most contracts require that specific objections be made within a brief time after receipt of statements or any right to raise objections during an audit will have been waived. Believe me, when it comes to these "details," the record company most certainly knows its standard contract provisions relating to audits and follows them to the letter. For this is where the money is, and *their* bottom line, like the bottom line of any business, it is *the* bottom line.

Errors in Excess of 5% to 10%

Artists' and writers' lawyers and accountants like to insert into contracts a provision that if an audit determines that an error of 5% or 10% has occurred in favor of the auditing party, the party being audited must pay for the costs of the audit. What is the value of this? Actually, very little (other than the representative's bragging to a client that he or she got this into the contract). Why? Because, as indicated earlier, most audits result in settlements, and a settlement is just one way for an audited party to tell you to go away. (The settlement figure will always take into account the costs of the auditing party, and this is so even when this item has not been specifically addressed.) There is rarely, if ever, an admission of liability, so it is usually futile to seek to particularize the audit result.

The record company does not want to be precluded, in future audits, from asserting the same defenses it has chosen to raise in a current audit. Paradoxically, the more the deficiency, the more likely there will be a settlement and the less likely there will be a detailed breakdown of the areas being settled. Although the preliminary audit claim will particularize the areas in which the claims are being asserted, in the end, a lump sum payment will probably be offered and accepted.

It should be noted that in Europe and in Australia, settlements are less the norm, and these provisions are easier to obtain. It is therefore more viable in deals outside of the United States to seek a provision providing for compensation for audit costs where a deficiency amounting to 5% to 10% has occurred.

THE RIGHT TO AUDIT: A CONTRACT ISSUE

In New York State, there is no inherent right on the part of a royalty participant (or a party who has received a promise to be a royalty participant) to have access to the books and records of the promising party. Record companies that do not insert audit clauses into their artist contracts or permit them to be included in mechanical license agreements are impeding access to the very information on which *all remuneration* to the artist or publisher is necessarily based. Companies that refuse to insert such clauses after a request that they do so are acting in bad faith and should not be trusted.

In addition to ensuring that a reasonably and clearly worded audit clause is included in an agreement, it is a good idea to check with a professional auditor *before* any royalty-based agreement is signed. As we have seen, a traditional audit clause may not be sufficient to protect the royalty participant. For example, if the publishing agreement between a songwriter and the songwriter's publisher (or copublisher) is in the nature of a "receipts" deal whereby the administrating publisher pays the writer based on its receipts, how is the infamous Black Box income to be treated? The receipts contract may limit the writer's income to "money allocated to specific songs." Yet Black Box income is just a pot of money that is paid to publisher members of foreign rights societies. It is not necessarily money allocated by specific title. If it were, it would have to be shared with the writers or original publishers. For example, if an original publisher's catalogue represents 10% of the total income of a particular German subpublisher, and the German subpublisher is rewarded by GEMA with $1 million of "unallocated" income, rebates of rights society commissions, etc., then, theoretically, 10% of this should be attributable to that catalogue. The way to obtain this Black Box income is to provide specifically that the original publisher be paid in the same proportion as the original publisher's catalogue earnings are allocated to the society member (that is, the subpublisher) by the society. If the subpublishing deal provides that for every $1 collected by the subpublisher with respect to a specific song, 15% is to be retained by the subpublisher and 85% is to be paid to the original publisher, then, in the $1 million example above, 85% of $100,000 (which is 10% of the million dollars of Black Box income received by the subpublisher) must be paid to the original publisher.

Since upward of 30% of all publishing earnings in Italy (and 15% and more of such earnings in France and Germany) flow into the Black Box, a goodly portion of a writer's income may be unintentionally diverted right out of his or her bank account—all because of the use of the phrase "specific songs," which appears, on its face, to be straightforward but may in fact lead to the loss of substantial monies.

Obviously, once an agreement has been signed, it is too late to patch up the deficiencies in the audit clause.

• • •

What does a formal audit—as opposed to a desk audit—accomplish for the client? A survey has suggested that a 10% to 15% recovery over and above the accountings presented by the record companies is not unusual. Settlements are reached in 95% of all audits, and only 10% of the remaining 5% end up in court. Chances are that the audit settlement will end for all time any controversy that may have arisen about the issues raised by the audit—whether these be substantive (for example, nonreporting of income) or definitional (for example, disputes over the meaning of contractual words or phrases). A careful choice of an auditor and cooperation among the auditor, the attorney, the manager, and the artist are essential to achieve a fair result.

13 · MUSIC PUBLISHING
The Odyssey of the Song

When asked: "Why do you write?" Frederick Delius
answered, "Because I cannot swim."

No man but a blockhead ever wrote, except for money.
—SAMUEL JOHNSON

Let's talk about music publishing. It worked for Beethoven; how will it work for you?

This is the most intriguing, most complex, and surely the least understood area of the music business. Yet every budding recording artist (and his representatives) should have a high degree of awareness and sensitivity to this stepchild of the industry. For even the novice songwriter knows that long after the records are relegated to the oldies bin and the live performances are a distant memory, music publishing income will endure. This is the annuity, the social security, of the songwriter. How an artist's songs are owned, exploited, and, most of all, protected, can determine whether or not the artist's career will, in the end, be a financial success, or whether the artist will have to, God forbid, get a job.

Those who are interested in music publishing are not lonely. The company enjoyed by the songwriter includes the music publisher who, in exchange for services, participates in the income and the asset accumulation as each musical composition gains value. Users of musical compositions have a distinct interest in them: record companies, film and television companies, product owners who use compositions in commercials, etc. And let's not forget video game companies, website owners, and Apple's (and others') online music stores. Everyone wants (needs?) a good song.

In most respects, music publishers' and songwriters' attitudes toward, and interests in, musical compositions coincide. There are areas in which their interests diverge, and these are covered later in the chapter, but predominantly they have the same goals: protecting the controlled use of the song, maximizing the eventual income from the song, and ensuring that copyright protection, and attendant compensation rights, are as broad as possible throughout the world.

Music publishing is a creation of the music business. Yet music publishers are the most significant contributors to the maintenance of all copyright rights throughout the world and the most effective lobbyists for those rights. Collectively, in many ways, they are the engine that makes the entire music industry run.

WHAT IS A MUSIC PUBLISHER—AND WHAT DOES IT PUBLISH?

There is no simple, universal definition of what a music publisher is, and the term appears in the US Copyright Act only twice. Yes, there are references to copyright owners, authors, and "rightholders"; many references to "publication" (the distribution of copies or records of a work to the public by sale, rental, lease, or lending); and language about performing a work "publicly" (that is, at a place open to the public or at any place where a substantial number of persons outside of a normal circle of a family and its social acquaintances is gathered). But the lawmakers were not the ones who had to figure out how to commercialize the concept of publication. Others did. They created the "publisher." A publisher can be as simple as a name under which the author does business (dba, or "doing business as") or as complicated as a multinational such as Universal Music Publishing Group, which looks after the rights of more than 1 million musical compositions.

This chapter will explore the changing role of the music publisher in the 21st century, discuss some of the traditional concerns of publishers and songwriters alike, and identify some of the ways in which music publishers' interests and methods diverge from those of the writers. Before we proceed, however, let me define briefly some of the terms that I will be using in this chapter.

- An *administrating publisher* is the entity responsible for the myriad tasks associated with licensing and collecting income derived from the exploitation of musical compositions. There may be one or more administrating publishers, each responsible for a portion of the song.

- A *copublisher* refers to a publisher that actually owns a portion of the copyright to a song, the so-called "publisher's share." A copublisher can be an administrating publisher, but is not necessarily one. For example, an artist who writes may copublish his or her own songs, but it is usually the other copublisher—perhaps a major such as BMG Music Publishing Company—that provides the administrating (or song management) services.

- A *subpublisher* is the foreign equivalent of the American administrating publisher. Subpublishers are vital to domestic publishers because they belong to performing and mechanical rights societies around the world and can collect directly, and monitor accurately, the monies generated by the exploitation of musical compositions in their respective territories.

Traditionally, music publishers have had two major roles:

1. To administer, exploit, and nurture copyrights. The rights specifically granted to copyright owners of musical compositions under the US Copyright Act are the right to perform, to mechanically reproduce, to synchronize, and to print. Music publishers seek to ensure that federal and world copyright protection is sought and acquired, that users of their musical works throughout the world are properly licensed, and that users of the works pay the requisite fees—for mechanically recording the works on records, synchronizing them on film or video, performing them live or through broadcast, or reproducing them via visual notation. Music publishers also actively seek out potential users of their copyrights, for example, by convincing a musician to record a song or a film or television company to include the song in a film or video production.

2. To provide sufficient funds (a) to help a songwriter live while he or she is writing, (b) to cause songwriters to meet each other wherever they are in the world for the purpose of encouraging cowrites, and (c) to pay for the cost of demonstration recordings that are the means by which potential

users of the works get to hear them in the first instance. This chapter is primarily concerned with the first of these functions: administering, exploiting, and nurturing copyrights.

COPYRIGHT: A BUNDLE OF INTANGIBLES

What exactly is a copyright?

The concept of *copyright*, that is, the right to reproduce an original work, has undergone an extensive evolution since the first US copyright law was passed in 1790. For example, the 1909 copyright law protected musical compositions from being mechanically reproduced, without permission, by any "parts of instruments." At the time, the "instruments" (devices) in question were player piano rolls and eventually Edison cylinders—the first record players. It was not long before circular records were being produced (from 78s to 45s to 33s), then tapes (from eight-track to cassettes), then CDs, DVDs, etc. Eventually, we began to refer to the various devices by which musical compositions are reproduced as "sound carriers" because we could no longer specify what form the "parts of instruments" might take. Now, of course, we do not even work solely with *forms*. We work in cyberspace (MP3 and other digital download formats) with digital phonorecord deliveries (DPDs). Thus, over the last one hundred years, the rights of copyright holders under the copyright law have been found to apply to every one of the devices used to reproduce them, even though most of these "parts of instruments" had not been invented, or even imagined, in 1909. We are introduced periodically to new technologies, such as computer programs and Internet applications, which invite expansion of what are often referred to as the "bundle of rights" subsumed under copyright legislation.

Establishing Authorship

Under United States Copyright Law, the exclusive right to own, control, and protect one's creation from unauthorized reproduction is a right granted upon the *creation* of the work. Most people do not realize this. They think they have to "copyright" the song first. Well, rest easy. Upon creation, any original work of authorship "fixed in any tangible medium of expression" has federal copyright status and protection. (Note that copyright protection does not extend to any "idea, procedure, process, system, method of operation, concept, principle, or discovery" [Section 102 of the Copyright Act], nor does it extend to any work "authored" by the US government.) However, the subsequent registration of a claim to copyright in Washington, DC, gives the creator some wonderful additional benefits:

- The right to sue in federal courts for specific statutory damages and to seek injunctions for unauthorized copying.
- The right to collect compulsory license royalties according to the rules established in the Copyright Act of 1976 (misnamed, because the act didn't actually take effect until 1978). Section 115 of that act provides that "to be entitled to receive royalties under a compulsory license, the copyright owner must be identified in the registration or other public records of the Copyright Office. The Owner . . . is not entitled to recover *these* royalties for any phonorecords *previously* made and distributed."
- Concrete and credible *evidence*, via the Certificate of Copyright Registration issued by the US Copyright Office, proving that the work had indeed been created and was in existence at the time the claim to copyright was filed.

The copyright certificate rendered by the US Copyright Office obviously does not prove that the person claiming authorship or ownership actually wrote or owns the work, but it does prove that the *claim* to ownership in the song was in fact filed on a certain date. It is also *prima facie* proof of the facts stated thereon. This means that if the copyright registration form says that writer A wrote the song, and writer B says that he or she actually wrote the song, the burden of proof in any legal proceedings is on writer B to prove that he or she, not writer A, wrote the song. This can be a very valuable piece of paper indeed. This does not mean that for every composition a songwriter creates, he or she must register a separate claim to copyright in Washington. The Copyright Office will accept multiple registrations (for example, a CD or tape containing ten songs can be the subject of one registration). Finally, if for some reason—usually financial—a songwriter cannot formally register a work or works with the Copyright Office, the writer can still mail a registered package to him- or herself (or to an attorney) containing a copy of the work and leave it unopened. (In 2016, the cost to register claims to copyright in a musical composition was $85 via physical/paper registration, but the online cost is only $35, or sometimes $55, per registration.) In any copyright infringement action, it is necessary to prove not only that the defendant had access to another person's work, but that it was substantially similar as well. But if the defendant can prove that the work existed *before* the plaintiff's work was even written, the rest doesn't matter and the defendant is home free.

Digital Print Rights

This represents a new world for music publishers. Whereas for most of the 20th century, phonograph record owners became used to the addition to their financial vocabulary of new and different means of transmitting music for home use to consumers, music publishers have long been reduced to concerning themselves with the *four* rights mentioned above: performing rights, mechanical rights, synchronization rights, and print rights.

A millennium gift to the music publisher is, virtually, a fifth right: a new product that has been developed in the digital age—digital sheet music. This is an awesome addition to the arsenal of music publishers and one that has not yet been entirely recognized for what it is: a revolutionary method of distributing "sheet music" inexpensively, instantly, and with a great deal of variety and satisfaction—24/7 and forever "in print."

Digital print rights are the rights to digitize musical notation and graphs (such as guitar tablature) as well as textual information (such as lyrics) in a manner in which they may be used through all means of digital delivery, such as the Internet, on CDs, as part of DVDs, and via music scanners. As of this writing, one distributor of digital print rights, Musicnotes.com, includes digital data representing pitch and duration that can be accessed through midi (musical instrument digital interface) or by way of CDs themselves. Digital print rights are exploited the same way digital audio rights are exploited, except they can be translated into a readable visual text identical to musical notation. As with digital audio rights, they provide immediate access to content and do not require a trip to a music store, nor is any concrete medium, such as a CD, involved. Unlike audio rights owners, digital print rights owners have thus far conquered the problem of protecting their assets from unauthorized appropriation.

There are approximately eight thousand dealers of musical instruments and products in the United States. About four thousand of them carry printed copies of music; perhaps one hundred of these specialize in the print area, and it is estimated that those one hundred do not provide more than 1% of the world's printed music to their customers, despite the fact that some do order the music for later delivery. (Note that a similar situation exists in the record industry: Probably fewer than 1% of the sound recordings in existence are actually available from your local CD chain store, if you even have one of these days.)

Thus, the vast majority of music is not available to the public in traditional ways. In fact, the vast majority of music never sees the light of day in the music publishers' offices either. Talk about intangible rights! The title of the song "For Your Eyes Only" is apt: No matter how hard you try, you will not be able to find, in a store, a printed sheet music copy of it to perform or record yourself. Go ahead. Try! But you *can* find more than a dozen versions on the Internet in the form of digital "sheet" music—everything from piano to solo alto saxophone.

And yet, music publishers uninitiated in the ways of the digital world carelessly "bundle" digital print rights along with traditional print rights. Whether you label it a fifth right or merely a distinct part of the fourth right (the print right), the digital right should be regarded as a different asset from the traditional print right, neither replacing nor supplanting it. Ironically, digital print may save the sheet music business because the efficiencies of print companies over the past fifty years have so steadily declined that there is a danger that the lack of profitability of this area of the music publishing business may kill off what remains of this business—from manufacturers (print companies) to dealers.

As everyone knows, finding the particular edition of sheet music that one may seek is nearly impossible. Either the work is not in print, or it is not in stock. Or it may be part of an expensive music "folio" and not be available on its own. With digital versions, there are no warehouse, inventory, selection (read: "labor"), or shipping costs. A digital version is always in stock. And it is *instantly available*.

Time was that sheet music of a hit song would sell in the 1 million copy range. From "Bicycle Built for Two" around 1900 to "Over the Rainbow" in 1939, million-sellers were frequent. The heyday of sheet music sales ended around the time that phonograph records took the place of piano rolls and player pianos. Singing in the living room or in the ice cream parlor had lost its flavor, and vinyl records took over from real live people who followed sheet music to create sound on a piano. Sure, the song from *Titanic*, "My Heart Will Go On," sold a million copies in the late '90's, but this was an anomaly.

In the wake of the exploding digital market, traditional print companies have fallen on hard times. Their $25 folios, which one had to buy to acquire a preferred song like "Memory" or "Over the Rainbow," have been ambushed by the broad availability, world-wide, at any hour of the day, via the Internet or one's own home, of digital sheet music. On top of this, recording artists and record companies have begun to "monetize" the licensing of artist photos placed in music folios or on individual sheets of music. One record company authorized the use of a photo, but only after demanding and receiving, a fee for every two thousand copies of music sold—an astronomical royalty when all was said and done.

Therefore, it is incumbent on the music publisher to insert a provision in its contract with artists (and for artists to do the same with their record companies) to allow the publisher to use artist photos on sheet music. The print company of one major rock band had to beg (and pay) for permission to use a film logo on its special sheet music edition of a song which the music publisher licensed to the film company for a substantial synch fee. Unfortunately, the interests of their own print licensee had been ignored in the process and was reduced to having to use a postage-stamp-size version of the film logo ("as heard in . . . . film")—ultimately to the detriment of the music publisher and songwriters. Better communication with all of the elements on the side of the song owner/writer would have avoided this debacle.

Today those involved with the digital distribution of sheet music are finding that the desire to possess the actual musical notation of a sought-after piece of music has not only not disappeared, it has probably increased! Given the huge population of music makers in the world, the desire may have been there all along, but the potential consumers were stymied by their inability to obtain the product they wanted. Those days appear to be over.

Finally—a perfect application for the Internet!

• • •

Enough about the bundle of rights—except to wonder, What next? It was only a few years ago that we were talking about sound carriers embodying the intangible rights of a song; now we are trying to comprehend intangible delivery systems sending the intangible rights into your computers, television sets, MP3 players, cell phones, and, yes, even your watches—unless they are otherwise engaged doubling as digital cameras! Let's go back to the real world, where songs are the motivation behind some heinous behavior displayed by record companies toward copyright holders and to which publishers often respond with deplorable judgment.

FINANCIAL SECRETS AND REALITIES

The fact that the majority of musical compositions are controlled by music publishers that are themselves owned and controlled by the biggest users of music—record companies, film companies, television production companies, and (for example, for a while after the AOL acquisition of Time Warner) Internet companies—makes for some interesting negotiations, and not a few potential conflicts of interest. Three important areas in which songwriters' and publishers' interests are not always the same are controlled compositions, buy-outs, and audits.

Controlled Compositions

"Controlled composition." Perhaps the most feared words in the songwriter's galaxy. Under the Copyright Act of 1976, the copyright owner has the exclusive right to authorize the first recording of a work; after that original authorization, anyone else can record it pursuant to certain specific rules. The most relevant rule here is that the new user must pay to the author or publisher a minimum statutory rate—aka the compulsory rate. Since 1978, the rate has risen periodically. Since 2008, the Copyright Royalty Board left unchanged the per-song rate for physical product (the so-called mechanical royalty rate), and established an identical $0.091 (and .0175/minute-long song) rate for permanent downloads. Still, $0.091 seems low given the fact that for downloads, the record label nets about $0.69 from a $0.99 download after paying the $0.091 to the publisher, the online service gets about 23% of the selling price, and the songwriter and publisher 9%. But I suppose it depends on what hat you're wearing. The physical record industry does not see the rationale for keeping the $0.091 rate given their reduced profit margins. (But see chapter 4: "360 Deals," as the record companies try to make up for that loss of market) The songwriter/publisher community had asked for an increase to $0.15 from $0.091. Nevertheless, the prevailing industry view is that the current rates will continue indefinitely. The Copyright Royalty Board (CRB) also established a $0.24 rate for a master tone (for example, a ringtone on a cell phone). The rate for interactive streaming and *limited downloads* (downloads that expire after a period of time) have also been set for the time being. Their 2008 decision establishes the current rate for five years and was the first rate set since the onset of legal online music delivery services. It has recently been renewed for another five years, adding an array of new compulsory rates affecting lockers in the cloud and other more recently developed technologies that require copying musical compositions. It will be interesting to observe how the CRB will handle these rate issues in the future when the music industry has righted itself after years of sinking out of control. If Kelly Clarkson wishes to record your four-minute song, her record company must either obtain the copyright owner's permission for the first-ever recording of it or, if the song has already been the subject of an authorized recording, the record company can automatically record the song upon payment of the requisite fee. As discussed in chapter 4, on royalties, the record companies have found a way to contractually circumvent this rule so they don't pay the full fee. Recording agreements between artists and record companies invariably include a provision that results in you—the artist—promising to license to them, customarily at three-fourths of the statutory rate, all songs you write, all songs you cowrite, including the cowriter's portion, all songs your producer writes or cowrites, and in fact *all* songs you record—and this holds whether or not you "control" (have ownership of) these songs. Effectively that means that if you record a song that you neither wrote nor cowrote, and that your producer had nothing to do with, if the owner of that song (who is a complete stranger to you) does not agree to license it at three-fourths of the statutory rate, the excess over three-fourths of the statutory rate will be taken out of your artist royalties! *This* is the controlled composition rate.

The amounts involved can be staggering. Three-fourths of the $0.091 rate is $0.06825, and the difference, $0.02275, is retained by the record company. If you record ten songs on an album, the difference is $0.23 per album. Sell 1 million albums and you begin to get the idea of what you (and your publisher) are losing ($230,000 in this example). Over a ten-album career, if each album sells 1 million copies, the total is $2.3 million. If one sells more (Celine Dion had an album, *Falling into You*, which sold 10 million copies in the United States alone), as they say in the vernacular, forget about it. In addition, record companies inevitably try to limit to ten the number of titles on any given album on which they will pay even the reduced rate. Thus, even if your record contains twelve songs, the maximum mechanical royalty, continuing with the number used above, the company will pay $0.6825 rather than $0.819, which is what they would have to pay if they paid three-fourths of the mechanical rate on all twelve songs, or $1.09, which is what they would have to pay were there no "rate" given at all. Why do the record companies do this? Why not?

Of course, the major music publishers are controlled by giant media conglomerates, and while the music publishers are biased in favor of maximum exploitation of copyrights, their bosses are biased in favor of big bottom-line profits of the entertainment unit, which counts the music publisher as a poor cousin to the record or motion picture company affiliate. For if the record company had to pay to the music publisher (its own affiliate) the $2.3 million referred to above, one-half, or $1,150,000, would have to be paid to the writers of the songs.

A nightmare scenario occurs when the artist has agreed to a "rate," but his or her cowriters have not—and, on request, will not. The excess paid to the cowriters will be extracted from the artist's publishing and record royalties. See chapter 4, page 31–32.

Recently, a one-third writer of one song refused to grant a three-fourths rate which caused the entire remainder of the cowriters and their publishers to reverse themselves in light of the most favored nations clause in their original three-fourths rate authorization. The cost to the artist was enormous. If there were twelve songs on the album, and all were co-written with one writer only, then the total relief sought by the record company would be one-fourth of the mechanical rate for all twelve songs. That's $0.02275 per song × 12 or $0.273. This would be divided by one-half since the artist would have already agreed to the one-fourth rate reduction; the cowriters' rate reduction would total $0.1365. That's $13,650 for each 100,000 records sold. If the record is a hit and sells a million records, the total that the artist would have to bear out of mechanical statements and artist statements because of the intransigence of one writer would be $136,500. Even more damaging would be the fact that the artist's publisher's advance to him, as a writer, would often be tied to the amount of mechanical royalties that would be paid by the record company. If the publisher is receiving 12 × one-half of $0.091, it would expect to receive $0.546 for each record sold. This sum represents the artist/writer's share in a perfect world. If the record company is paying only three-fourths rate, then this would be reduced to $0.4095. However, if the cowriters do not license their songs at a three-fourths rate, then the differential ($0.1365 per the above calculation) would be taken out of the mechanical royalties otherwise payable to the artist/writer's publisher. Thus, the publisher would receive only $0.273 rather than $0.4095. The impact of this would be that the publisher would reduce the advance payable on delivery of this album by a percentage representing the reduction it was going to have to suffer as a result of the cowriters' unwillingness to grant the three-fourths rate. So, if the advance for the album is $500,000, one-half paid on signing the agreement and one-half paid on release of the album, the artist will have received $250,000 already; when the album is released, he or she will be expecting to receive the remaining $250,000. However, the artist will have failed to deliver a record generating $0.4095 for the publisher. Therefore, the publisher would reduce not just the remaining portion of the advance not yet paid, but the entire $500,000. The differential between what they thought they were going to receive ($0.4095) and what they will receive ($0.273) is 33⅓%. Therefore, they will reduce the $500,000 by 33⅓% to $333,333. Having already advanced $250,000 to the artist/writer on signing the publishing agreement, all they would owe him now would be $83,333 rather than the $250,000 that he was expecting.

Thus, the impact of one, often irrelevant writer (the one-third writer of one song) can have a devastating effect on the artist/writer both in terms of the reduced advance he or she will receive and the ultimate amount of mechanical royalties that he or she will net after the publisher takes its share out of what it receives from the record company.

All of this could have been avoided if the cowriters had merely entered into a standard cowriter agreement in the first place covering this contingency.

What can be done to correct this situation? Presumably, there would have to be legislation outlawing this practice in its present form, but the record companies insist that they would merely have to reduce artist royalties accordingly if this profit cow were to be reduced or eliminated. But at least in that case, the artists would be responsible for negotiating their own royalties and the writers and publishers would not be forced to choose between being straw men or victims. The way it works now, either the song side of the creative team is blamed for the reducing the artist's royalty, or it has to bear the brunt of the royalty reduction. (In most countries of the world, the mechanical rate payable to copyright holders is calculated as a percentage of the selling price of records. Therefore, whether the record contains ten songs or twenty songs, the mechanical royalty is the same for all. Medleys are actually financially feasible outside of the United States and Canada.) Antitrust litigation is a possible solution to this state of affairs. However, small, independent music publishers have generally elected not to sue their best customers—the record companies—for fear of destroying what little cordiality there remains in their relationship.

In the event that one of their songs is used on a record and it is not written by the artist or producer, and therefore "controlled," the record company might still threaten to remove it unless the publisher agrees to license it at the controlled composition "rate." These small independents would have no negotiating room in this situation were they in the process of suing the hand that was feeding them.

Buyouts

To reproduce a song as part of a motion picture, television show, or television or radio commercial, it is necessary to obtain a synchronization license from the copyright owner. The purpose of this license is to give the user the right to synchronize the song in a timed relationship to what is going on "around" the song—usually visual images. Upon the invention of the home videocassette player (Sony's Betamax and later the Matsushita version, the VHS videocassette recorder) in the 1970s, the music publishers (who controlled the majority of musical compositions that would comprise the soundtracks to films and other video presentations) considered the per-copy reproduction of the film in the same way as a per-copy reproduction of a phonograph record, but were unsure as to how much to charge for the per-copy use. There might, for example, be as much as two hours of music in a videocassette. There were long uses, short uses, and background orchestral score uses. There could be as many as fifty or more "cues" containing music, all of which would have to be reckoned with. Some films were heavy on the music. Some were not. A videocassette was indeed a copy, like a record, and presumably the songs used on a videocassette for sale to the consumer would be subject to per-copy mechanical reproduction fees, but many music publishers assumed that the formula used to calculate the per-copy fee for a record would not work given these disparate lengths. Nevertheless, some publishers wanted to charge fees on this basis, and others established a fictional "fund" for song royalties of about 5% of the wholesale-selling price of the cassette, whereby the fund was to be split among the song owners as their interest appeared.

This concept of dividing a specific percentage of the videocassette among the various song owners would be modeled on the European approach, which is based on time. However, before the family of copyright holders, as a group, could figure out how to charge for the use of songs in such devices that would now be finding their way into homes via videocassettes, and later videodiscs and DVDs, Paramount Pictures (which coincidentally owned one of the premier music publishing companies in the world, Famous Music) came up with the concept of the buyout: If the copyright owner allowed its song to be included in the film—in return for which it would be paid many thousands of dollars as a synchronization fee plus additional performance royalties generated upon the presentation of the film in motion picture theaters outside of the United States and on television in the United States—it would have to agree to forgo a per-copy royalty upon the sale of the device.

MECHANICAL ROYALTY RATES OUTSIDE OF THE UNITED STATES

Foreign record companies, as a rule, pay just as high, and very often higher, royalties to the music publishers and do not seek to reduce artists' royalties to keep their costs down. Outside of the United States and about a dozen other countries where the mechanical rate is set by statute or collective bargaining, an association of mechanical rights societies (Bureau International des Sociétés Gérants les Droits d'Enregistrement et de Reproduction Mécanique, or BIEM) and record industry lobbying organizations, such as the British Phonograph Industry (BPI) in the United Kingdom and the International Federation of the Phonographic Industry (IFPI), periodically negotiates mechanical royalty rates to apply in their territories. While these rates vary somewhat from country to country, they are currently in the range of between 8.5% and 9% of the published price to dealers (PPD) of a record, excluding value-added tax (VAT), which is, essentially, a built-in sales tax.

The PPD represents the cost of a record to a record retailer. In the United Kingdom, the rate is currently 8.5% of PPD. With a 10 pound sterling PPD for most top-line CDs, this amounts to 85 pence or just over $1.25 per CD. The US equivalent for ten songs—even absent the special "rate"—is $0.91, far below the UK rate. This mechanical royalty is shared collectively among all of the writers and publishers—usually based on percentages of total music contained on the CD, calculated by time.

TOP GUN—A TOP BUYOUT FOR PARAMOUNT

Top Gun: Paramount Pictures' once-maligned investment in a feature film starring a relatively unknown Tom Cruise—a film that had been reworked, reshot, rewritten, and refinanced so many times that its future was not only uncertain, it was most likely nonexistent!

Paramount's music licensing supervisors had put together a marvelous score featuring some of the hottest recording artists of the day and presaging the phenomenal musical soundtracks to come over the next two decades that would result in the sale of tens of millions of albums. But they did not want to pay a per-copy mechanical royalty rate upon the sale of videocassettes—if indeed anyone would ever be interested in buying copies of this risky film. (This is an example of the brilliant anticipation of the future that the motion picture industry is known for. Here's another. Decades before television was invented, there were provisions in film contracts with screenwriters that prohibited the screenwriters from authorizing a version of the film to be shot and broadcast on "television." It's true!)

Paramount offered a one-time, $2,500 payment to each music publisher who controlled a song in the soundtrack without regard to the ultimate number of videocassettes, videodiscs, etc., that might be sold. The music publishers broke ranks, and most of them agreed to the deal, thinking that at $0.05 a copy—the audio-only copyright rate at the time the film was made—a 50,000-unit sale would not amount to all that much in the long run and $2,500 in hand was better in the short run than a gamble that the film (especially this film) would break all previous sales levels, including Jane Fonda's workout video. Had you seen the trailer for the film, you would have jumped on the same bandwagon. Oh, you're wondering how many copies the *Top Gun* videocassette/disc combination sold? 1.2 million copies.

Music publishers and writers in the United States customarily grant to their affiliates or subpublishers outside of the United States the exclusive rights *in their respective territories* to exercise most rights under copyright. Included among these are mechanical reproduction rights. But each subpublisher, as well as the US publisher, is also usually authorized to issue *worldwide* synchronization licenses only on a *nonexclusive* basis, for music embodied in motion picture soundtracks. In this way, the film company, wherever it is, can rest easy in the knowledge that it can distribute its film worldwide, without regard to where the film has been shot, without having to seek licenses in each other territory of the world in which the film might be presented.

However, when it came to determining whether a worldwide synchronization license for a *film* also covered the videocassette or videodisc embodying the film, problems arose. Was the reproduction of music on a videocassette a mechanical reproduction or just an extension of the synchronization right? If the right to *mechanically* reproduce musical compositions was *exclusively* granted to the various publishing affiliates or subpublishers around the world *for their territories only*, the value of the synchronization license would be defeated for uses outside of the traditional film medium. What's more, in many countries the manufacture and sale of individual videocassettes and discs would generate a per-copy obligation to pay royalties to the copyright holders, much like a mechanical royalty on the sale of records.

With respect to films made in the United States, since the worldwide synchronization license was entered into in the United States, the powerful film companies decided that the provisions of the synchronization contract—with its worldwide effect—prevailed, superseding foreign countries' laws and society rules. Basically, the companies were saying to the publishers who had granted exclusive mechanical reproduction rights around the world to their affiliates or subpublishers: "Work out your contractual breaches with your subpublishers. We don't care to hear about your view that you have already given away the rights we are demanding. We insist on a worldwide buyout of *all videogram reproduction rights* even if you have previously given away the rights to grant us these and you no longer own them. Either work it out, or we will not include your song in our film." ("Videogram" covers all physical audio and video devices, including videocassettes, videodiscs, and DVDs.)

The buyout concept prevailed and continues to this day. Do you think that Sony/ATV Music Publishing Company (Columbia/Sony Pictures), Warner/Chappell Music (Warner Bros. and New Line Cinema) or Universal Music Publishing Company (Universal Pictures) will fight this take-it-or-leave-it approach? No way. Sorry, writers. (BMG, which had no affiliated motion picture company, can no longer come to the rescue and litigate the issue; BMG has merged with Sony.)

Audits

While I have dealt with the audit process in some detail in chapter 12, it is appropriate to expand on the discussion here because some aspects of the music publishing business require a more in-depth review of this subject.

As noted earlier, when a songwriter licenses the right to mechanically reproduce his or her song on a record, a mechanical royalty is payable pursuant to a license agreement with the record company. This license agreement ordinarily contains an audit right, allowing the songwriter to examine the books and records of the record company to the extent reasonably necessary to verify that he or she is being paid properly.

Songwriters who utilize the services of the Harry Fox Agency, Inc., or other mechanical rights licensing agencies, have the benefit of their agents' auditing the record companies on their behalf. Indeed, the Harry Fox Agency audits the major record companies regularly not only on behalf of those independent songwriters and publishers who are their principals, but also on behalf of some of the major publishers who are owned by the major record companies. While this appears to avoid any potential conflict of interest between the major music publishers and their affiliated record companies, it also is a mechanism through which the major music publishers can pass off their responsibilities to a third party. However, when it comes to their sister record companies, the major music publishers choose to license them directly, thereby—not coincidentally—bypassing the Harry Fox audit juggernaut.

Independent songwriters who control their own publishing rights and license record companies directly also have the opportunity to audit the record companies, threaten lawsuits, and participate in settlement discussions. This may be an advantage for them because, if they utilize the massive audit capabilities of the Harry Fox Agency—where an enormous number of songs are the subject of an annual or other periodic audit of a record company—while the audit costs are certainly reduced pro rata, the opportunity for the record companies to make broad settlements increases at the same time that the probability of obtaining a satisfactory settlement for individual works, or groups of works, decreases. And, while the major music publishers have an incentive, as do all copyright holders, to maximize their receipts and profits, it is unlikely that they will go to the wall against their own record company affiliates.

Foreign Audits As might be expected, the major music publishers' record company affiliates in other countries are not used to being audited or being the initiator of an audit. For example, since Warner/Chappell (US) does not audit the Warner Records Group in the United States, Warner/Chappell (France) is not likely to audit Warner, Atlantic, or East/West Records in France. On the contrary, it will leave this responsibility to the mechanical rights society in France, the Société pour l'Administration du Droit de Reproduction Mécanique (SDRM), and let the settlements be made in the customary manner in that territory. This is not the right scenario for inquiring aggressively to ensure that (1) the songs that should have been registered at the foreign mechanical (and performing) rights societies were indeed registered, (2) the money that should have been collected has in fact been collected, and (3) the division of this money is in accordance with the songwriter's agreement with the publisher. Nevertheless, SDRM is independent of the US parent publishing companies and at least some audit is conducted.

THE ADMINISTRATING FUNCTION

The previous section discussed audits—the process by which financial records are verified. But it is important to note that unless the administrative responsibilities toward a song are properly discharged, there may be no financial records to verify! The importance of the administrating role of the music publisher cannot be overstated. And, without the proper information from the songwriter, the administrator's performance capabilities are extremely limited.

What happens when a writer's or recording artist's music publishing rights are controlled by a music publisher that is so overloaded with administrative responsibilities that it fails to do some of the things it needs to do to fulfill its administrative responsibilities? Simple. Everyone loses. The writer loses his or her share of the income that has not been collected. The publisher, of course, also loses its share of the income, but if it has given cash advances to the writer and has the right to keep the writer's share of income until those cash advances are paid back, its losses are doubled. So it is in both the writer's and the publisher's self-interest to accomplish the first two administrative tasks effectively: registration and collection. For at least in these two areas, their interests coincide exactly. A song properly registered results in a dollar collected, which in one way or another works to the benefit of both the songwriter and the publisher.

FAMILY TIES (TOO CLOSE TO SUE)

A hot recording artist was signed to a major record company, and, of course, the major record company's publishing affiliate was the first to hear about it. So the music publishing affiliate offered to enter into a long-term copublishing agreement with the artist (read: "they would control the administration rights in the compositions forever"). They offered the artist lots of money, calling it an advance. (This advance would later be recouped against the artist's song earnings, and therefore, except for the short-term risk on the part of the music publisher of losing the investment, the artist would have paid his or her own advance!) Well, when the recording was done, lo and behold the CD contained twenty songs, not ten, and so had to be released as a double CD, though the recording agreement provided for only a ten times three-fourths statutory rate rather than twenty times three-fourths.

What's more, there were outside songs on the album, and the publishers of those songs were unwilling to reduce their royalty to less than three-fourths the statutory rate, which is exactly what happens when the ten times formula is applied to twenty songs! So who ate the difference? The artist. What did the artist's publishing company do? It punted.

Although the publishing company had a financial interest in fighting this deal, it had no stomach for it, especially because the record company affiliate's CEO was, ultimately, the boss of the publishing company president. So a double CD that contained twenty songs was licensed to the record company for three-fourths of the statutory rate for a CD containing ten songs.

There are arguments on both sides here. The fact that the double CD cost twice as much to manufacture, and the retail selling price was less than twice that of a single-album CD was certainly an argument in the record company's favor. Then again, the packaging cost was not twice that of a single CD. Yes, the union pension and welfare percentage that is applied against the retail selling price of the CD was now increased, since the double CD would be sold at a higher price than a single CD, but the cost of promoting the double CD would, of course, be the same as it would have been for a single CD. In the end, the record company prevailed.

Could an independent publisher have gotten a better result? Probably not, since if the record company had to pay more for the mechanical royalties than it had contracted for, it would simply take the excess out of the artist's royalties. But at least an independent publisher would raise hell over it and maybe get something in return.

In early 2002, Warner/Chappell's foreign affiliates were directed to report not to the head of Warner/Chappell in Los Angeles, but to the record company heads in their own territories. The result is more potential conflict of interest insofar as musical composition rights are concerned.

I used the word *fails* above, rather than "neglects," because too often the errors of administrators are due solely to the fact that they are so big and have so many copyrights to administer that they are bound to slip up sometimes. And sometimes an administrative "failure" is actually caused by the songwriter and the songwriter's representatives, not the publisher at all. Here's an example that illuminates this point.

One of my clients, the principal songwriter of a popular rock band, assigned responsibility for administering his worldwide publishing rights to a major music publisher, which at the time was administering several hundred thousand copyrights. The administrating publisher paid the songwriter lots of money in return for a percentage of whatever it collected over a period of years as a result of the worldwide exploitation of the songwriter's musical compositions. What the songwriter failed to do was to advise the administrating publisher adequately as to what he was writing and what he was recording. It was as if once the deal was in place, such details would magically find their way into the administrating publisher's computer.

Subsequently, the band had a hugely successful worldwide hit that sold more than a million singles and millions of albums. Everyone was happy. Except one thing went wrong. The B side of the single was an instrumental that, although it did not appear on the album, received a lot of radio play because it was the theme of a major world sporting event—the Olympics. The publishing administrator had never heard of the song. In the course of a full-scale examination of the status of the songwriter's songs around the world, lo and behold, this song's title appeared. All concerned were surprised to find that no one had communicated the necessary information to the administrating publisher and therefore the song had never been licensed, registered in Washington, or registered with any performing or mechanical rights society anywhere in the world. The lesson? Songwriters must treat their copyrights as any other precious offspring. Like children, they must be nurtured, cared for, and paid attention to. And just as no one but the parents can be expected to be responsible for developing a child to his or her full potential, no one other than the person who created a song should be responsible for developing a copyright to its full potential.

WHEN YOUR PUBLISHER FORGETS YOU

What happens when songwriters and their heirs find that their music publishers have totally forgotten them, and their songs? In many cases, the music publishers have no clue as to what the songs in their catalogue even sound like. Often the only evidence that a song exists is the title on an ASCAP, BMI, or SESAC schedule or a Copyright Office printout. There are three reasons for this:

1. Recordings, and more likely lead sheets or sheet music, have long gone missing. Whether a song was "published" or "unpublished" under the 1909 law, registrations of copyright could be made, and would be accompanied by so-called "deposit" copies of the music—most often in musical notation on paper format. These deposit copies presumably still exist, but probably in a pile of music that has not been disturbed in fifty or more years. Thus, how could a music publisher exploit a musical composition whose very essence (the music and words) is a mystery to them.

2. Music publishers have undergone significant changes of ownership over the past fifty years—such that current owners, who focused on the "top 25" earners when they valued the catalogues prior to purchase, either have

no idea what else is in the catalogue or have no interest in these songs as they are not particularly reflective of the stream of income generated by the catalogue's biggest earners.

3. You may have guessed by now the third reason. Yes, the venture capitalists and investment bankers who are often behind the purchases of music catalogues have no idea whatsoever as to the inherent vitality of a musical composition. The composition is represented to them merely by a numerical column of earnings or a title in a Copyright Office search report. Why would they—no, how *could* they possibly be even aware of musical compositions outside of the financial heart of the catalogue? They do not even need to be aware; after all, the key to the acquisition is the growth of the numbers, not the activity (or lack of it) of any particular song. The opportunities granted to authors and their heirs by Section 304(c) of the Copyright Act (see chapter 20) serve to overcome some of these problems by removing the publishers from the position of "caregiver" over these copyrights, but unfortunately, in many cases, the songwriters or their heirs are unaware of their termination rights. Furthermore, music publishers who were charged with the responsibility of keeping the copyrights alive and available are the only ones with the files and records that can uncover the identity of a song years after it first made its way into their catalogues.

FOREIGN TAXES

Although the issue of foreign taxes is too complex to be covered in depth in this book, one observation should be made in the context of audits.

Many countries tax money paid by their music companies to writers or artists, whether or not located outside of their countries. For example, some countries' tax laws dictate that only $0.90 will be transferred. The other $0.10 is paid by the subpublisher to the particular country's tax authorities, and the original publisher in the United States will never see it. This 10% takeout represents a not-insignificant loss of income. Suppose the publisher is a "doing business as" of a songwriter and is in a 30% tax bracket. If the entire dollar were transferred as income, the taxes paid would be $0.30, leaving the publisher with $0.70 for every dollar collected. But if only $0.90 is transferred and taxed at the 30% rate (for a $0.27 tax bite), the publisher is left with only $0.63—$0.07 less—for every dollar collected in Japan.

Such a situation exists in Japan, Australia, and Mexico, as well as many other countries.

The United States has special tax treaties with some countries (for example, the United Kingdom, France, Germany, and, most recently, Japan), which provide that instead of a tax being withheld by the foreign government, it will be reinstated and paid to the American publisher *once a special tax form is filed*, in a timely manner, with the inland revenue of the foreign country (equivalent to the IRS). (This works something like a value-added tax that a US traveler can be reimbursed for at the airport upon leaving the country that affixed the tax to the purchase in the first place.) Under these treaties, the publisher pays taxes in the United States on the entire amount of the monies collected, but it collects 100%, not a lower percentage, net of the tax, of the royalties due. They usually require that the American publisher be in good standing with the American tax authorities, having filed a federal and state tax return for the prior year.

This process can be handled very smoothly, or it can be a nightmare. And if the appropriate forms are not filed correctly, or are filed late, the withheld money can drift around such that it may take months and even years to capture it—if indeed it is ever captured. Delays will hold up paying the after-tax portion of the monies, the $0.90 cents in my example, as well. Paying—or receiving—companies can go bankrupt by the time the United States and foreign tax authorities process these documents. It is essential that your accountant or business manager and your lawyer coordinate these filings to avoid the loss of the tax benefit they afford—or worse. Have you ever thought of asking who among your representatives is responsible for filing your RF3EU form in France? I'm sure not. You might want to start thinking about it now.

AT-SOURCE VERSUS RECEIPTS DEALS

When a publisher says it will pay a writer and the writer's solely owned company a given percentage of the earnings of the songs worldwide, can the writer take that statement at face value? Of course not. In a typical copublishing situation—where the US copublisher administers the songs worldwide and supposedly retains only 25% of the earnings, the following issues arise:

- What happens when the copublisher makes an arrangement with an overseas subpublisher whereby the subpublisher gives the copublisher substantial advances in return for a percentage of the earnings?
- Does the copublisher own its own companies overseas or have such a close affiliation with them that they might as well be part of the same company?
- Does the copublisher pay on the basis of at-source earnings or receipts earnings?

By way of illustration, let's say a writer's songs are copublished in the United States by a respectable administrating publisher. (Hereafter I will refer to the writer as the "original publisher.") For every dollar earned in the United States, the original publisher receives $0.50 as a writer and $0.25 as one of the copublishers. To collect monies earned in France, the copublisher retained by the original publisher must obtain the services of a French subpublisher or administrator. That subpublisher keeps, let's say, 25% as its share. (After all, it has paid substantial advances to the American publisher and has provided substantial services registering the songs, promoting them, liaising with the local record company, exploiting them for television and commercial uses, etc.) That means that for every dollar earned in France, the US copublisher (the administrating publisher) will receive only $0.75. If the copublisher's deal with the original publisher is a receipts deal, the copublisher will take 25% of the $0.75 and pay the balance—$0.5625—to the original publisher.

Now, if the administrating copublisher is, say, Universal Music or Peermusic (to use two of many possible examples), and does the same thing, there is something wrong with the picture. Sure, the subpublishers have the same job to do, but the parent company in the United States is now receiving either directly or indirectly much more than the 25% the original publisher thought had been bargained for. When an administrating copublisher ignores the introduction into the mix of a subpublisher that *it* owns or controls, and pays the original publisher as if the administrating copublisher had collected the money directly, it is known as an *at-source distribution*. For every $1.00 earned in France, the administrating copublisher will retain $0.25 (either through its subsidiary—or close affiliate—in France or through some combination of sharing with that subsidiary or affiliate), and it will pay the original publisher $0.75. This is an at-source deal. And it is a lot better result than the $0.5625 the original publisher would have received under a receipts deal.

You may say that this is a fine result for the original publisher, which is obtaining the services not only of the United States administrating publisher, but of its foreign affiliates as well, for the same price. Or you may also say that this is not fair to the US administrating copublisher because, in financial terms, it will essentially have become a domestic copublisher only, and all of the earnings outside of the United States will either go to foreign affiliates or have to be shared with them; its ability to recoup its advances will be hindered and the efforts to "break" the song or the record that embodies it in the home country of the writer, which is where the rest of the world is looking before it pays attention to the song or the record, will not be rewarded—so why try?

Not surprisingly, the various interests have tried to come up with some kind of compromise that serves the needs of the original publisher on the one hand and the administrating copublisher on the other. There has been a tendency in recent years to establish a receipts deal at the beginning of a relationship and to convert it into an at-source deal later. Whatever is the result of your negotiations as an original publisher, you must keep in mind that there is a significant difference between the receipts deal and the at-source deal.

THE BLACK BOX REVISITED

As stated previously, money collected in many countries outside of the United States that is not attributable to any particular song or writer finds its way into what is known as the Black Box. You will recall that monies budgeted for expenses that are not used get dropped into the Black Box, as do monies reimbursed to member publishers as rebates of collection society commissions and, in some countries, additional monies with respect to newly introduced types of earnings that are not separately allocated and attributed to specific musical compositions. However, there are two major categories of Black Box monies that an administering publisher's subpublisher can directly affect through its administration services:

1. Monies that that have accumulated as a result of the failure to communicate—on the part of the original publisher or administrating publisher—the necessary information on song titles and writers

2. Monies that have accumulated as a result of inaccurate registration or misallocation of funds

One way for the original publisher, or administering copublisher, to ensure that access to Black Box income is attained is for an attorney or accountant to examine, on a regular basis, both the registration lists of foreign collection societies and the actual accountings that are issued by those societies to each foreign subpublisher or to each foreign affiliate of a United States–based multinational publisher. Unfortunately, this is more easily said than done, as those who have tried to unravel the tangled web of foreign accountings have discovered. But with the increased globalization of the music business, it is inevitable that a more open sharing of such information will be achieved in the future. The world's societies are even now talking among themselves to deal with such global issues as how and to whom to allocate performance and mechanical income emanating to copyright owners via the digital download and streaming of sound recordings, and, by extension, the musical compositions embodied on such sound recordings. The same will apply, no doubt, to digital downloads of sheet music as well. They are also in the process of establishing central databases that, for the first time, may allow accurate identification of song titles and their writers and publishing interests on a global basis, thereby reducing the possibility of error in allocating income. Regrettably, the European Commission has determined that such deals among societies constitute antitrust behavior. Government regulators do not like it when competitors talk to each other. (Of course, once global tracking of songs is instituted, an error made at the initial registration will only be exacerbated as it is replicated throughout the world's data systems. That is all the more reason to have someone looking "over the shoulder" of the publishing administrator of the writer, the artist-writer, or his or her own music publishing company to check and double-check that the registration process is being handled with absolute precision.)

COPYRIGHT REVERSIONS

Music publishers are in the business of acquiring copyrights. Or at least that is what one would think. They make substantial investments over incredibly long periods of time in writers of every stripe: songwriters, theatrical show writers, songwriter–recording artists, and others, and they lose a lot of money in the process. When their investment has been successful, one would think they would want to finally own what they have risked capital on and in many cases nurtured so significantly that the songs might never have been written in the first place—or been successful—but for their creative input and financial support. Yet many music publishers today agree to allow the songs they acquire pursuant to various forms of songwriter-publisher agreements to revert in their entirety to the writers five, ten, or fifteen years later. Why? Perhaps it is due to increased or more sophisticated competition from other publishers—especially those who do not identify with the conservative values of the old-time publishers who are used to owning, not renting, copyrights. Some believe that the major reason for this phenomenon is that the multinationals would rather make hay while the sun shines and let someone else harvest the crop in future. That is, they are willing to trade long-term prospects (future income generated from control of copyrights) for short-term bottom-line profits (the market share resulting from the work of a few hot writers whose first wave of income is usually the largest).

There is another reason the music publishers may be less avaricious than in earlier days. As we have seen (page 138), under the Copyright Act of 1976, for any works created in 1978 or later, even if a writer transfers to another entity the copyright on those works, the rights can be recaptured by the writer at any time during a period of five years beginning at the end of thirty-five years after the date of execution of the grant. If the authors are going to get their copyrights back anyway, why shouldn't publishers entice writers to place the works with their companies by offering an even earlier reversion? (Note that the work-for-hire exceptions to this right to reversion do not, in general, apply to musical compositions written in traditional ways by traditional songwriters, which are *not* works for hire.)

Reversions come in many varieties: reversion of copyright after X number of years; reversion of administrative control, but not copyright; reversion of copyrights in songs not covered or otherwise exploited during X number of years; reversion of one or more portions of the above. Most of these variations depend on whether or not the writer's account with the publisher has been recouped. Once the account is recouped, reversion may occur five to ten years later. If it is not, then reversion will not occur until years after recoupment, if at all, until the thirty-five-year recapture provision takes effect.

Sometimes a publisher will allow reversion when the writer's account remains unrecouped, provided the writer pays back to the publisher 110% or 115% of the unrecouped balance. This option may be very appealing to a writer. For example, if the writer's copyrights have attained an asset value of from five to ten times earnings, taking control of the copyrights in return for a small fee represents a sound investment. And besides, I have rarely met a writer who does not think that he or she can more diligently exploit copyrights than the publisher can (though I have not often met a writer who *can*). These options are all intricately worked through in the course of negotiations. Let us not forget, after all, that no publisher really wants to lose the asset (the copyright) if it can be avoided.

14 · WHEN RODGERS MEETS HAMMERSTEIN
Determining Songwriter Credits

When asked, "Which comes first, the words or the music?"
Ira Gershwin responded, "The Contract!"

The songwriter who works alone is rare. Irving Berlin did it. So did Cole Porter, Jerry Herman, and Frank Loesser. Diane Warren, Bob Dylan, Leonard Cohen, and Paul Simon do. George Gershwin did not; neither did Jerome Kern or Leonard Bernstein, nor do most of the pop songwriters of our day. In fact, sharing authorship is increasingly the norm nowadays as the structure of songs has changed from pure "music and lyrics" to "track, lyrics, melody, and rap." Different people bring different talents to the mix; so does the studio owner, who may create tracks to songs he or she never imagined would be written over them.

COWRITING AGREEMENTS

Normally, the arrangement among cowriting songwriters is that of equal partners. A lyricist and a composer write a song together, each counseling the other. They go to a third person who owns a studio and who introduces an arrangement and perhaps a word or two and a riff or two to the song. It has become increasingly fashionable for all three writers to agree to share the authorship, and the copyright, three ways. (They also contribute in equal parts for the cost of the demo—the hired musicians, singer, etc.—but not the studio, since that is one of the contributions of the third "songwriter.") Once they agree to do this, they often sign a scrap of paper, register the song in Washington in their three names, and forget about it.

But what governs the *rights* of the three cowriters? Not surprisingly, copyright law.

And what are these rights? Very simple. All the cowriters are entitled to equal control over their shared copyright. The copyright in a musical work is like owning a piece of land as a "tenant in common"—the legal jargon for a situation in which, for example, three people each own only one-third of the land, and yet each of them can nevertheless walk over the entire property without restriction. No one owns a particular, definable, one-third.

This sounds very fair and balanced. But what this also means is that each cowriter has the right to

- issue the highly prized (and protected) first mechanical license—whether to an artist chosen by all three cowriters or to whomever he or she pleases;
- authorize changes in lyrics, title, etc., without the permission of the other cowriters;
- authorize the use of the song, at whatever price he or she wants, in a commercial or film. Even if one cowriter has rejected, say, a use by Coca-Cola or feels the song should be isolated from commercial identification for a time, or should command a higher fee, another cowriter can circumvent that person's wishes without even telling him or her.

This kind of free-for-all can be avoided by having the cowriters sign a joint songwriter's agreement that deals with all of these contingencies. In other words, the cowriters will modify the general rules of the copyright law that essentially treat all cowriters as tenants in common, sharing identical nonexclusive rights. Upon signing a proper songwriter's agreement, all cowriters will understand precisely what is expected of them and what they may and may not do. For example, it will provide that money received by one writer that is attributable to the song in general will be shared properly by all cowriters and that the money attributable to other cowriters will be held "in trust" by the first cowriter, thereby placing a fiduciary burden on him or her to do the right thing. Many major music publishers do not bother with a songwriter's agreement and maintain an unwritten policy of dealing with each songwriter *as if* they had signed such an agreement, blocking, for example, first-use licenses or synch licenses absent the approval of all writers. But they don't *have* to honor this policy.

Don't think that a verbal understanding among songwriters—or people who believe themselves to be contributing songwriters—is enforceable. The fact is that in most states, a contractual agreement must be in writing to be enforced. Furthermore, under the US Copyright Act, a "transfer" of copyright must be in writing as well. Finally, you should be aware of the fact that a court will not automatically take your word for it that you are or were intended to be deemed a "coauthor" or "co-owner" of a song.

Recently, a number of court cases have established that when a song is originally written, in order for a person to claim coauthorship, with all of its attendant privileges, there must have been an intention to do just that—that is, an intention to share in the earnings of the song, an intention to be referred to as a cowriter, and an intention to share artistic control—in short, to be a co-copyright owner.

How is an "intention" most effectively expressed? In writing.

When a song has already been written, the intentionality must be even more pronounced. The writer of the musical *RENT* was sued by his "dramaturge," a person who apparently made considerable, lasting, and perhaps even fundamental additions and changes to the musical play—and to its songs, but *after* the fact—that is, after the work was first written and thus after the copyright was vested in the original author. The trial court in the ensuing case held that unless the dramaturge could show—in writing—an absolute intention by the original writer to share authorship, and therefore copyright ownership, with her, her case would be dismissed. She couldn't, and it was.

During the appeals process, the parties settled, so we will never know how this case would have eventually evolved, but the implication is that without a piece of paper that documents the intention of the parties, the participants in creating a song will not be certain as to their rights and will be susceptible to claims and cross-claims once the song succeeds—which is, of course, the only time that it matters anyway.

The Multiple Writer Mess
Since urban music and pop music joined artistic forces and Max Martin (boy bands) and Dr. Luke (Katy Perry, Ke$ha) became the kings of contemporary record sales, a phenomenon unknown in earlier years became the norm in the mainstream, pop, urban genres: performing rights societies were beginning to see multiple writers claiming authorship shares. And I don't mean two or three (music, lyric, and sometimes "beat"), but five, seven, even eight or nine. One hit song recently boasted a writer whose interest was 0.78%—less than 1% of the writer's share. Cowriter agreements such as those described above are no longer regularly entered into. The music publishers have no interest in going to the

considerable expense of negotiating terms, nor do the writers whose lawyers are charging them upward of $600/hour (and neither do the lawyers who are commissioning their client's income—after all, no income is directly related to the time and effort necessitated by negotiating a cowriter agreement). So the parties are left to signing a "splits" letter which merely sets forth the respective percentages claimed by the writers and their respective music publishing companies. If, as is so often the case, all of the cowriters cannot agree on the splits, then mechanical royalties will not be payable by the record label. Several hundreds of millions of dollars of such monies were held "in suspense" by United States record labels until recently, so you can see the extent of the financial damage such circumstances cause the copublishers and the cowriters.

But collaboration with successful writers or writers who, doubling as producers, can create their own recordings, is too valuable a course of conduct to refrain from doing so because the number of writers becomes cumbersome. A cowriter (often the artist) who has contributed 5% (or who has been allowed to claim this share even if he or she didn't) is happy to hook onto the star of a legitimate, emerging, or proven, writer and the proven writer deals with him or her as part of the dues he pays for getting the cowriter gig in the first place.

COWRITERS WHO ARE BAND MEMBERS

What if two or more cowriters are band members? Now we have a much more complicated situation, where nothing is standard. Often bands have a principal writer or two, and the remainder of the band contribute very little in the way of authorship or assistance during the recording process.

How do bands compensate the cowriters? And how much should the principal writer or two give up in order to keep peace among the band members? After all, it is not particularly healthy in a community of four or five band members for one to receive significantly more than the rest of the members. Jealousies are exacerbated and financial inequality makes for even more problems—not just among the band members, but also among their spouses as well, who always seem to get involved on behalf of their husbands or wives. Now *that's* trouble! Decisions as to how the band should structure the song ownership and authorship are made at the beginning of the band's relationship, when not all of the data about the band, its future, the dynamic of the band members, etc., are in; yet, most often, all of them must live with the decision for better or for worse—and for all time. How have different bands dealt with this issue? In a word, differently.

How to Split the Splits

One band—predominantly an instrumental group—decided that although two of the six members wrote all of the songs, the remaining four should share equally in the publisher's share, to the extent they were able to retain it (and they were able to retain all of it in this case). Therefore, while a song's authorship might list two names, the publisher's share would be split six ways. The justification? The band members, and specifically the two writers, felt that the other four contributed, if only in the studio, to the sound and arrangement of the songs sufficiently to deserve credit for having established the song's identity for all time. I am not saying that they were thought to have "created" or "authored" the song. In fact, they were explicitly excluded from the writer's credits and the writer's share of royalties. But it would be acknowledged that although the two principal writers had created the "essence" of the song, on one level it was the result of the combined efforts of all six.

Another band followed the above pattern, but added the following twist. Since so much work had been done arranging the songs in the studio during the recording process, the band as a whole was considered to have contributed authorship to some extent. Therefore, a song by this group would have perhaps three writers: the two principal writers, who might share 80% of the writer's share, and a third (fictional) writer who would be entitled to the remaining 20%. This latter portion would be shared by all six writers, whose "name" would be a contraction of the band's name. Thus, the share of one of the two main writers would be 43.33% (one-half of 80% plus one-sixth of 20%), while the share of one of the writers who was not a main writer would be 3.33% (one-sixth of 20%). The songs would be registered with the performing rights societies with this authorship breakdown, and all income would be divided accordingly by the band's publishing company and its licensees.

Here are four more possibilities:

1. A band has one main writer who shares his or her retained publishing interest equally with another member of the band who is instrumental in taking care of just about everything and who has been with the band since the beginning (unlike all of the other members). But the *writer's share* is his own and is not shared with anyone.

2. A band has one main writer who shares her or his copyright and (possibly) the entire writer's share with one other band member on one or two songs per album to acknowledge the other band member's musical contribution to arranging all of the songs on the album and for being with her or him in the studio 100% of the time, as opposed to other band members who recorded their tracks and went to the beach.

3. Each band member receives his or her appropriate writer's share, but the publisher's share is dealt with as follows: Any band member who does not write a particular song (or any song for that matter) receives 10% of the net publisher's or copublisher's share (that is, 5% of the whole song's earnings) as long as he or she is a member of the band through to the end of a given accounting period. If he or she writes or cowrites a song, the band member receives his or her pro rata share of the publisher's or copublisher's share left after the various 10-percenters are paid. Thus, if two members cowrite a song equally, they share 50/50 in the writer's share of each dollar earned. And, if there are, say, two other members of the band who did not write that song, they each get 10% of the publisher's or copublisher's share, leaving 80% of the publisher's or copublisher's share to split equally between the two main writers.

4. The band members all agree in advance that the authorship and the publishing share will be split equally among them. Even if one writer only sets up the loop that "inspires" the rest of the song and the other writer goes home and finishes the song, or one band member writes all the lyrics and the rest contribute the music, everyone is treated the same.

Are there other variations? Sure. A multitude of them. The important thing is that the issues be discussed openly—preferably with the band's manager, business manager, and lawyer—and a consensus arrived at. For, as in any partnership (and what is a band if not a partnership?), consensus is the way to go. If the situation ever arises in which a majority outvotes the minority, trouble is not far behind.

Problems can set in when the splits become weird. A client of mine authored one-third of a song and therefore the writer's share was split one-third, one-third, and one-third. The publisher's share was dealt with differently, however: first of all, she split *her* publisher's share with a company whose job it was to obtain a recording of the song (and who succeeded in doing so), so her publisher's share went from one-third to one-sixth. But then, for some reason, she agreed to split her remaining publisher's share even further—but not equally—with another of the cowriters. Somehow or another, she ended up with a one-third writer's share, but 11.89% of the publisher's share. That was more or less what she wanted to accomplish, and she stood by her deal with her cowriter. Subsequently, however, she faced an unanticipated problem.

The performing rights societies in the United States will most likely honor an instruction to pay to a copublisher an odd sum like 11.89%. Cowriters should be aware of the fact that the performing rights societies around the world conceive of writer's and publisher's shares of songs in terms of twelfths as opposed to percentages (for example, 25, 25, 50, etc.). Dividing twelfths into two (as would two writers sharing their interest 50/50) or three (33⅓, 33⅓, 33⅓) or four (25-25-25-25) parts is easy, but what do you do with eight songwriters, one of whom contributes 5%? That's .04167 of ¹⁄₁₂th! Even if the societies overseas will agree to such parsing, and many of them will not, the errors likely to occur are practically guaranteed.

In this case, the author wrote one-third of the song. The writers as a group were entitled to six-twelfths of the song, so each one, including my client, was entitled to two-twelfths of the writer's share of song earnings.

So far so good. The problem arose with the publisher's share. How could the performing rights societies outside of the United States handle a copublisher whose interest was 11.89% of six-twelfths? Question: How many twelfths does 11.89% of 100% of the publisher's share equal? Something between one-twelfth and two-twelfths. See what I mean? In fact, this writer had created a nightmare for the performing rights societies around the world. Even if she managed to correctly and successfully register her claim with every performing rights society in the world and convince them to pay her publisher's share correctly, who knows what the other cowriters or their publishers might have done? The publisher's share of six-twelfths (100% of the publisher's share) was broken down so that one copublisher retained 11.89% and the remaining copublishers shared 88.11%.

Oh, to add confusion to an already complex issue, the mechanical rights societies around the world do *not* work in terms of twelfths, but in terms of percentages, just as the US, mechanical rights societies do. Believe me, the societies around the world will not have the patience to register and pay royalties according to the whims of coauthors in the United States—not least, perhaps, because the United States is currently one of the few territories in which songs are routinely cowritten.

15 · BEING YOUR OWN MUSIC PUBLISHING COMPANY
Pros and Cons

And therfore, at the kinges court, my brother
Ech man for him-self, ther is non other
—GEOFFREY CHAUCER

Songwriters who have succeeded in retaining their copyrights have established for them-selves an annuity that in innumerable examples has allowed them options they would never have had were they to have placed their copyrights in the hands of traditional music publishers. Songwriters who are not also recording artists really need the help of music publishers to obtain cuts on their songs. Songwriter–recording artists, on the other hand, obtain their own cuts. Some songwriters relinquish their copyrights because they need the money that large publishing companies will often pay them to acquire ownership or co-ownership, and administration rights, to their songs. Even those who can afford to do so may not want to forgo the benefits that come from an association with a fully staffed music publisher. Circumstances will necessarily be different for each songwriter, and it is a worthwhile exercise for all songwriters to sit down with their representatives and analyze whether, to what extent, and when it would serve their immediate and long-term goals to self-publish or whether it would be better to align themselves with a large music publishing company.

SELF-PUBLISHING

If you're a songwriter who wants to self-publish, you must take the steps outlined below. If you don't have the time or inclination to take them yourself, you should ask for help from an attorney experienced in copyright law or one of a multitude of small publishing administration companies. The Association of Independent Music Publishers (AIMP; www.aimp.org) is a great resource. Most managers and business managers don't have the interest or experience to discharge the tasks required in the administration of copyrights, although some do.

Registration

The first step is to obtain PA (Performing Arts) forms from the United States Copyright Office in Washington, DC, or online. In 2016, the cost to register "paper" claims to copyright is $85, but the online cost is only $35 or $55 per registration. The Copyright Office will accept claims for multiple songs if the forms are accompanied by a tape or CD containing all the songs. This will save a lot of money. Although some copyright lawyers will argue that there is some question as to whether a compulsory license fee can be maintained on a per-song basis if a group of songs has been combined on one registration (it is possible, if unlikely, that only one mechanical license fee would be collectible for songs registered as a group), the cost advantages of multiple registrations outweigh the risks.

GETTING IN TOUCH WITH THE COPYRIGHT OFFICE

The Copyright Office (accessible via the Library of Congress site, www.loc.gov, or directly via www.copyright.gov, is a division of the Library of Congress. Some feel that the Copyright Office should be a part of the Department of Commerce, as are the Patent and Trademark divisions. Those who disagree argue that deposits (copies of books, songs, records, and other creative materials) made in the course of registering copyrights are a principal reason the copyright law exists; it provides the Library with a copy of just about everything that is created in this country and much of everything that is created in the rest of the world. The address of the Copyright Office is Library of Congress, Copyright Office, 101 Independence Avenue, SE Washington, DC 20559-6000. Courier delivery should be addressed to CCAS, 2nd Street and D Street, Washington, DC The telephone number for questions is (202) 707-3000. Call between the hours of 8:30 a.m. and 5:00 p.m. Eastern Time.

The Mechanical Variance

Once registered, if your work is recorded for release, you will have to issue a license to the record company. As stated previously (see chapter 12, page 205), the preferred form of this document is not drafted as a license at all. It is designed as a variance of the copyright law. The reason for this is if a license is breached, the entity granting the license can take only a breach of contract action against someone who fails to honor its terms. In contrast, breaching a mechanical variance opens the door to a suit on the basis of federal copyright infringement, offering far greater remedies.

The language of the variances provides relief from some requirements of the Copyright Act applicable to those who record songs pursuant to the provisions of the compulsory license clause, Section 115, of the Copyright Act. These requirements include

- rules concerning the timing of the request
- extremely detailed formal requirements of the notice of intention to use the musical composition
- the calculation of royalties on the basis of every record made and distributed, rather than made and sold
- various accounting and payment requirements, such as those requiring accounting and payments on or before the twentieth day of each month (under oath, no less!), and additional accounting requirements promulgated by the Register of Copyrights, such as the obligation to produce annual detailed cumulative statements of account, certified by a CPA.

And that's just a sample. The actual language of the Act formalizes these already burdensome requirements to an almost farcical degree. It is no wonder that the "variance" has been a welcome relief to record companies. What the variance accomplishes is to put these formalities on hold: They do not go into effect unless the user does not honor the "varied"provisions set forth in the variance. In particular, if the record company does not pay, accurately and on time (usually every three months), royalties due, the company will have itself waived its benefits and will be an infringer—not a contract breacher.

In contrast, although a traditional license agreement provides for the same royalties to be paid at the same times and intervals, the record company's failure to pay royalties accurately and/or on time will generate damages only in the amount of the royalties the songwriter should have been paid plus perhaps interest and a few costs. But this is *nothing* compared to the remedies available against infringers under the Copyright Act, which include such things as the right to sue in a federal court, secure injunctions, claim statutory damages ranging up to $150,000, and recover costs and attorneys' fees. Now that is *something*. None of these remedies would be available to a prevailing party suing a record company for failure to pay royalties under a traditional license agreement.

Registration with Performing Rights Societies

Once you have determined that your song may be performed (most importantly, if it is going to be played on the radio), the musical composition should be registered with the performing rights society with which you are affiliated. In the United States, there are three such organizations: the American Society of Composers, Authors, and Publishers (ASCAP), which is a membership organization comprising writers and publishers only; Broadcast Music, Inc. (BMI), which is a corporation owned by broadcasters (although it is very sympathetic to the concerns of writers and publishers and actually has more writer and publisher affiliates than ASCAP has members); and the Society of European Stage Authors & Composers, Inc. (SESAC), which is a privately held corporation. Once you secure a record release of a song you write, or expect a performance to be broadcast on radio or television, or secure a synchronization use in a motion picture, one of these societies will be happy to allow you to join—as an affiliate in the case of BMI or SESAC or as a member in the case of ASCAP.

Foreign Collection Agreements

You must also ensure that if your recording is made available for sale in countries outside of the United States (with the exception of Canada), someone is appointed as your representative to register the song with the performing and mechanical rights societies in those countries.

Customarily, Canadian rights are handled by issuing licenses from the United States directly to Canadian record companies. Nevertheless, although the performing rights will be collected sooner or later through your US performing rights society, there are several advantages to appointing a Canadian publisher to assist in administering copyrights in that country:

- Performing rights income will be paid at least a year earlier than would otherwise be the case.
- There will be someone "on the spot" to keep an eye on the uses of your songs.
- The Canadian publisher can hire a local auditor to verify your song's activity. You may even be able to get an advance against earnings.
- The Canadian publisher may be able to obtain cover recordings of your songs.

Outside of Canada, a local publisher is all but essential. Without one, the odds of losing income due to inaccurate identification of performance and mechanical uses increase to a level which is simply unacceptable if you care at all about the income your songs generate.

As noted previously, a foreign publisher that represents the interests of a US publisher (or songwriter–self-publisher) is known as a *subpublisher*. Subpublishers may be selected on a per-country basis or on the basis of a larger regional division of the world. The value of per-country deals is that you can select each representative personally, and each advance paid by a representative selected on that basis stands alone—that is, it is not subject to recoupment against earnings from other countries for the simple reason that neither the various subpublishers nor the deals themselves are related to each other. On the other hand, processing one or two dozen agreements for purposes of representing one song or a small catalogue can be very time-consuming and expensive. In some circumstances, it may be appropriate to make separate agreements with subpublishers that are capable of exploiting a song or catalogue, and are motivated to do so because the song may be a big earner, or because in this way they can prove their competence and perhaps convince you to let them handle your entire catalogue. But more often than not, it makes financial sense to make an "ex-US and Canada" deal with one publishing company whose various affiliates or subsidiaries will provide the same services and actually coordinate with each other to help promote the song or catalogue, or the artist's recording embodying the copyrights that are the subject of the subpublishing agreement. ("Ex–North America" won't do because it inadvertently adds Mexico to the reserved countries instead of licensing rights to that country to your foreign representative.) Nevertheless, high-earning catalogues often warrant country-by-country deals.

The Black Box, One More Time

Since Black Box monies can amount to many millions of dollars annually, anything that a United States–based writer or publisher can do to gain access to some of this money is likely to be well worth the effort.

One often-used means to gain access is to establish companies in the countries themselves rather than enter into traditional subpublishing agreements. Sony did it. BMG did it. For example, once a US publisher has established a company in Germany, that company can become a member of Gesellschaft für musikalische Aufführungs- und mechanische Vervielfältigungsrechte (GEMA) and have access not only to information but to a proportionate share of the Black Box income as well. The fact that many companies established for this purpose are shell companies, whose sole reason for being is to obtain information and increase income, does nothing to negate their legitimacy. Of course, some US publishers have set up such companies for more questionable purposes, such as hiding the money thousands of miles away from the offices of capable auditors whose principals cannot afford to send them around the world to verify accountings.

The Subpublisher as Liaison

I would like to make an observation about an anomaly in most subpublishing agreements. There must be tens of thousands of traditional subpublishing agreements in effect throughout the world today. All of them provide for the administration of the copyrights that are the subject of the agreements. All of them provide for the collection of earnings and the periodic payment to the copyright owner or original publisher of the compositions. Rarely, however, do they actually state the underlying hopes, wishes, and expectations of the original copyright owner or publisher, which, simply stated, are that the subpublisher will make a reasonable effort to exploit the copyrights covered by the subpublishing agreement within the subpublisher's territory.

If the songwriter is an artist, there is all the more reason to include such language. While it is anathema for a publisher to state in so many words what it will do to exploit the song, the writer, or the artist, it is not unreasonable for the artist-songwriter to request (1) that the subpublisher be the artist-songwriter's liaison with his or her record company's affiliates in the territory of the subpublisher, and (2) that the subpublisher act as the artist's "eyes and ears" in the territory in order to keep the artist and the artist's representatives informed of what is happening (or not happening) in the territory with regard to the artist's recording. It is also not unreasonable to want the subpublisher to go beyond the basic collection function, for example, to participate in selecting the single the subpublisher might think would best appeal to the consumers in the territory, and to communicate this to the local record company. In essence, it is completely appropriate to ask your subpublisher to maximize not only the commercial exploitation and promotion of the musical compositions, but promotion of the artist-songwriter as well. Below is a sample provision that serves this function. No doubt some subpublishers will not accept the language as it appears here, but written provisions are negotiable, and something is better than nothing.

> Owner hereby appoints Subpublisher its nonexclusive representative for the Licensed Territory for the purpose of promoting Owner's publishing interests and the recording and performing artist [name of artist] (hereafter referred to as the Artist). To this end, Subpublisher shall use its best efforts to maximize the commercial exploitation and promotion of the Compositions in the Licensed Territory, and the sale in the Licensed Territory of phonograph records embodying Compositions. In connection with the foregoing, Subpublisher shall:
>
> 1. Generally liaise with personnel of record companies based in the Licensed Territory to maximize the exploitation and earnings of the Compositions.
>
> 2. Use its best efforts to liaise with the professional representatives of Artist including, without limitation, Artist's manager, business manager, and attorney, to maximize the commercial exploitation and promotion of the Compositions in the Licensed Territory the sale in the Licensed Territory of phonograph records embodying Artist's performances of Compositions and the commercial success of Artist's personal performance tours in the Licensed Territory.
>
> 3. If Owner shall notify Subpublisher of any corrections or changes in any Compositions including, without limitation, the author(s), title, lyrics, copyright, etc., Subpublisher shall notify the applicable performing rights, mechanical rights and other collection societies in the Licensed Territory thereof and use its best efforts to ensure that such corrections or changes are made by such societies in an accurate and timely manner.

Print Rights in the Digital Age

In chapter 13, I discussed the subject of print rights in the digital age. For a self-publisher, as for any publisher, print rights have more value than they did ten years ago. More and more small publishing companies are recognizing that they can license digital downloads of their sheet music—including guitar tabs and lyrics—to the few companies that are specializing in this new world of music exploitation. The sheet music "button" can be placed on the artist's website, and the consumer can benefit from instantly being able to access visual notations of his or her favorite music.

Of course, no publisher should count out traditional print rights, which can also be licensed individually on a per-song basis or collectively by catalogue. There are a number of outstanding print companies in the United States. If you can't find one, try to find a store that sells print music and look at the names and addresses of the companies that provide this product to get an idea as to which one fits your particular needs. Your attorney will also be able to guide you in this area.

WHY BOTHER DOING IT YOURSELF?

There are basically two options songwriters have for exploiting the rights to their compositions: (1) self-publishing, which usually involves asking their agents or attorneys to provide those services, or even hiring someone to do so; and (2) entering into an administration agreement with an established publisher. Clearly the least costly way to go—provided the artist-songwriter feels sufficiently organized to accomplish efficient administration of his or her songs, or trusts his or her attorney or staff person to do the job—is the self-publishing route. The costs of *hiring* an attorney for this purpose will be substantially less than the percentage of income traditionally charged by an established publisher. There are, however, disadvantages: There will be no cash advances to operate with; there will be no introductions to cowriters; there will be no effort to introduce your songs to motion picture music supervisors, and the like. In addition, the large publishing companies are connected to just about everything that is going on in the music business—particularly now that those companies have been absorbed into huge global entertainment conglomerates—and the companies that are most efficient in exploiting global synergies are more likely to be able to create opportunities for you that you would never be able to create yourself.

The option you choose will ultimately depend on the kind of catalogue involved. For a self-generating band that is recording its own material and that does not reasonably anticipate that third parties would be interested in recording their songs, self-publishing is a real option. A "stand-alone" songwriter may not be as comfortable following this route. That said, it should be noted that Diane Warren found a way to self-publish successfully at the same time she was lining up her Academy and GRAMMY Awards on the mantel.

You *can*, however, have it both ways. As an artist-writer, you can self-publish copyrights within the United States (and often Canada as well) and subpublish with a major multinational, giving the multinational worldwide synchronization responsibilities. In this way, you get the services of the multinational where you most need them, and, as you are part of their "family," they will often assist you in obtaining cowrites with their other writers, in marketing your songs, and in helping your US (or Canadian) record company to market your records.

ACQUIRING COPYRIGHTS

In past decades, songwriters gave to their publishers 100% of their publishing share, including the copyright and worldwide administration rights. The deal was, essentially, for all time—or at least as long as the various world copyright laws would permit (all rights end at some point). When the original publisher would license subpublishing rights overseas, even for a limited period of years, it would at the same time agree that if the subpublisher were to obtain a cover recording of a particular composition by a local artist, the subpublisher could retain control over that song for the entire remaining term of copyright in that country.

Those days are gone forever. Currently, the term during which owners grant foreign rights to covered compositions is usually two to three years.

Publishers today do not customarily acquire 100% of the copyrights in the songs they administer; more often they acquire 50% of the copyrights, although they continue to control (administer) 100% of them.

It may surprise you to learn that when a songwriter assigns his or her copyright to a publisher, the publisher usually pays nothing for that right. For in the music publishing business, as in the recording business, the companies do not actually purchase the assets they acquire. Yes, the record companies advance the cost of recording, etc. But uniquely in the record business, as we have seen, the artist winds up paying back the cost of recording out of what would otherwise be due in royalties. In the music publishing business, the writer may receive advances against royalties for the assignment of his or her copyrights (or 50% of the copyrights) and the worldwide administration rights. But once those advances are recouped out of the writer's share, the portion of the copyrights that the publisher "acquired" normally belongs to the publisher for the entire term of copyright, which in most countries of the world today means for a term extending seventy years after the death of the last of the cowriters. In other words, the publisher owns an asset for which it has paid only advances. Of course, there is always the risk that exploitation of the copyright will yield nothing, in which case the publisher will not get the advance back (no earnings, no reimbursement), but with a little bit of luck, the advances will be returned to the publisher out of the writer's share of writer royalties and, if applicable, the writer's 50% interest in the publisher's share.

REVERSION OF COPYRIGHTS

Being your own publisher sometimes requires a fairly sophisticated knowledge of the technical requirements that the copyright law establishes to protect innocent third parties from being taken advantage of. The law provides that if a copyright is originally registered in one party's name (for example, the established publishing company) and the copyright is later assigned to another party (for example, another publishing company or, in the case I am about to discuss, to the original writer), if the change in assignment is not registered in the Copyright Office in Washington, a third party (for example, yet another publishing company), who in good faith checks the Copyright Office records to make sure the party selling the copyright that it desires to purchase actually has the rights, will have no idea that the reassignment has occurred. Thus, the third party will think that it has acquired something from a publisher that in fact no longer owns the rights. In the world of million-song catalogues, these situations occur more frequently than you might imagine. For all intents and purposes, a *reversion*—which, quite simply, is an assignment back to the writer, should be registered as should any other assignment. There is no official concept of reversion in the copyright law. But the rules and legal decisions affecting assignment have consistently been applied to the situation in which copyrights revert from an established publisher to a songwriter in the manner described earlier. Not only is there the danger of a third party acquiring copyrights that have reverted, or might at some future date revert, to the songwriter, there is the added complication that if technical requirements are not followed carefully, other potential sources of income (such as performing rights) will assume that the original publisher remains in charge of the copyrights. Let's see how this potentially dangerous situation can be avoided.

As discussed in chapter 13 (page 227), permitting reversion in deals in which the writer has some leverage results in a shortening of the period during which the publisher retains rights to the writer's copyrights. As is becoming the custom, control and/or ownership will revert to the writer after a number of years: five, seven, ten, twelve, whatever. The circumstances under which the period can be shortened are customarily tied to the success of the music. If the songs and the records embodying them are failures, the publisher can keep them. If the advances are never recouped, the publisher can keep them. If, however, the songs and the records are successful, even with the often invaluable assistance of the publisher, the publisher will lose them. The publisher will wake up one day after a good run with a catalogue and it will have lost the catalogue permanently. Strange, but true.

Once it appears that the songs may revert to the songwriter, he or she should refocus from being a royalty recipient to being a self-publisher, who will need to take all the steps—and more—that would have been necessary had the songwriter decided to self-publish in the first place. Beyond the basic steps such as registering claims with a performing rights society, there are some additional technical requirements that can become a virtual nightmare. Most particularly, for example, the reversion of the rights that had been held for a time by the publishing company should be registered with the Copyright Office in the same manner as if they had been assigned. But what happens if there is no document signed by the publishing company that effects the reversion? I have already pointed out the dangers in failing to register an assignment. If there is no actual document representing the assignment, what can the writer send to Washington? There are three possibilities:

1. Should the writer register the entire original publishing agreement that contains the reversion clause?

2. Should the writer have added to the original publishing agreement for later use an affidavit saying that the conditions set forth in the clause have been met and that therefore the copyrights have reverted to him or her?

3. Should the writer have required the music publishing company to execute (sign) for later use an assignment of copyright for filing in Washington should the conditions of reversion occur?

The third procedure may be the most efficient. The assignment can be held in escrow by one of the parties' attorneys together with a precise set of instructions as to when the attorneys can release the document to the songwriter for filing in the US Copyright Office. In this way, when the songwriter's relationship with the music publisher is long over, and the copyrights have reverted, the songwriter does not have to go back to the music publisher, hat in hand, and ask that the formal assignment document be signed—something to be avoided if at all possible. If you are going to be a self-publisher and you are depending on rights reverting to you from your established publisher after a period of years, you must be very careful to follow the formalities of the copyright law. If you fail to follow them, a third party may be able—in all innocence—to walk off with your copyrights. If that happens, your only recourse may be to sue your original publishing company, which, by then, may have disappeared from the face of the earth. Unfortunately, unless the conditions of reversion are unconditional, it is not likely that you will be able to follow the "most efficient" procedure; instead, you will have to fend for yourself by following either option 1 or option 2.

THE VALUE OF THE COPYRIGHT

How can the value of copyrights be measured? Let us say that a recording artist writes ten songs per album and records five albums over five years—one each year—all of which sell 500,000 copies (gold in the United States). Although, as we have seen, there is a difference between "sold" records and "royalty-bearing net sales." Let us assume that each one of these records is a royalty-bearing record. Let us also assume that each song's length is under five minutes in duration so that we do not have to deal with the "long" copyright rate. Finally, let us assume that the artist's agreement with his or her record company requires that each song be licensed for three-fourths of the statutory rate with a maximum per album cost of ten times three-fourths of the statutory rate. The mechanical royalty income per record sold will be:

Current rate ($0.091 per song) × 10 × 75% = $0.6825

For each album selling 500,000 copies, the record company will have paid $341,250 in mechanical royalties. For the five albums—with a sales figure of 2.5 million units—the total is $1,706,250.

The writer and publisher share this $1,706,250 on a 50/50 basis; both get $853,125. In a typical situation, 50% of the publisher's share (or 25% of the total), amounting to $426,563, is paid to the writer's own publishing company and the remaining 50% of the publisher's share (25% of the total), also $426,563, is retained by the administrating publisher. So, absent any advances that the administrating publisher may be able to recoup from the writer's or the writer's publishing company's shares, this works out to $853,125 for the writer, $426,563 for the writer's publishing company, and $426,563 for the administrating publisher.

Returning to the sales of just one of the five albums, we have a writer's share of $170,025, an original publisher's share of $85,313, and an administrating publisher's share of $85,313. A rule of thumb in catalogue acquisition is that a buyer will pay anywhere from five to ten times the net publisher's share of earnings of a group of musical compositions. If the writer wishes to sell his or her 50% publisher's share, on the basis of a five times earnings calculation, that means that he or she can sell it for $426,563 (that is, 5 × $85,313). On the basis of ten times earnings, the amount is $853,125. On the basis of fifteen times earnings, the amount is $1,279,695. So, for an investment (therefore merely a recoupable advance) that business managers deem to be nothing more than a short-term loan (which, in this example, will certainly have been paid back), the copublisher has acquired from the songwriter an asset that is worth anywhere from $426,563 (5 × 85,313) to $1,279,695 (15 × 85,313)—after one album!

The administrating publishing company has it even better because it, and not the writer's company, actually controls the administration rights. Companies purchasing other companies' copyrights will pay a premium to the company that can assign to them the control of the copyrights (along with right to collect the writer's and copublisher's share) rather than just a passive interest in earnings. Different copyrights generate different kinds of income, and buyers who think that these copyrights may have a better financial life in their hands than in the original copublisher's hands may choose to pay more—as much as fifteen times earnings.

Note that to keep it simple, I have intentionally excluded from these calculations other forms of copyright-generated income, such as performance income, which can be *substantial*; income from licensing synchronization rights, which can also be substantial—particularly if the songs are used in films or in commercials; income from print licensing; income from cover recordings; etc. The net publisher's share of all of these other forms of income would similarly be multiplied by from five to fifteen times earnings. And don't forget, if a buyer becomes the administrating publisher, the buyer will have the right to use (read: "invest") the writer's share and the writer's own publishing company's copublisher share until it has to account for and pay these shares to the writer and copublisher.

Of course, the writer's own publishing company's 50% copublisher share is also worth approximately the same as the administrating copublisher's share, with two important caveats. First, the writer may be contractually obligated not to sell that share to anyone except to the administrating copublisher. Second, to a potential buyer, the writer's own publishing company's share would be of considerably less value than the administrating publisher's 50% copublisher share. That is because the former does not come unencumbered; it is still administered by the administrating copublisher, and the buyer would have to have faith that the administrating copublisher could be trusted to do a good job and to account regularly and honestly—a leap of faith that a buyer would not necessarily want to make.

THE IMPACT OF ADMINISTRATING COSTS ON TRUE EARNINGS

When a publisher acquires administrative control over the copyrights it represents, it is free to enter into foreign agreements for representation (which it will have to do in order to responsibly collect mechanical and performance royalties earned in foreign countries) in return for which it may be able to obtain advances. However, it will not have to share these with the writer whose songs are being parlayed into these foreign deals. Conversely, a self-published writer will have lost an opportunity to fund his or her career, and will have to remain dependent on the goodwill of others, including the outside publishing company, for support.

Furthermore, when an administrating publisher enters into such agreements, it will establish a fixed percentage for its own subpublishers to retain—a percentage that customarily exceeds 15% and can be as much as 25%. (As noted on page 225, these subpublishers are often affiliates or divisions of the administrating publisher.) Conversely, a songwriter who retains control of administration of his or her own copyrights is likely not to have to give away as much as a large administrating publisher would give away in return for the services it requires of the foreign publishers. For example, an important writer–self-publisher who has not entered into an agreement with an administrating publisher, but who nonetheless needs collection agents (subpublishers) in different countries, can give these subpublishers the right (and obligation) to collect income attributable to the compositions in return for anywhere from 90% to 95% to 100% of what they collect. Letting them retain 10% is tacit recognition that subpublishers have a job to do that takes time, staff, expertise, and experience; where the songwriter is also the recording artist, letting subpublishers retain 5% gives them a small "taste" of the earnings that have been generated not by their efforts, but by those of the artist and the artist's record company; zero gives them nothing but the right to use the money they collect for a short time and the "prestige" of saying they represent the important writer's catalogue.

THE COST OF GIVING AWAY A "PIECE" OF THE PUBLISHING

We saw in chapter 2, page 14, what giving away a "couple of points" can do by way of crushing an artist's income possibilities. Similarly, giving to others one's songs, administration rights, or copyrights can have serious deleterious effects on the writer's career. Nowhere is this more true than with the songwriter who is also a recording artist. It is worth mentioning here—once again—that a recording artist's record royalties for a given body of songs may be minimal. Remember, the artist has to pay—out of what would otherwise be received as record royalties—recording costs, video production costs, tour support, equipment loans, at least one-half of the costs of independent promotion, and, nowadays, a growing list of costs that used to be paid by the record companies. The possibility that *all* recording royalties will be totally absorbed by recoupment of these costs is unfortunately quite real, particularly when one considers that the recording costs, etc., for the follow-up album will undoubtedly be debited to the artist's account before any royalty from the prior album becomes payable. Thus, in many cases, the song income is likely to be the largest percentage of a songwriter–performing artist's earnings.

Most people have one career. I do. But a person who is not only a songwriter but an artist and a performer as well, has three careers and such a person should not mortgage one for another if he or she can help it. At a minimum, the recording artist–writer–performer should be fully aware of the consequences. As we have seen, there are ways to give, while keeping.

• • •

In conclusion, there are a host of reasons why one would want to retain one's copyrights and, in particular, administrating control over them. Irving Berlin was perhaps the first writer who saw the value in doing so. Even though he lost almost all of his savings in the 1929 stock market crash, his continuous earnings from the copyrights he retained kept him and his family solvent and permitted him the peace of mind to continue to be a productive songwriter. While self-publishing is not brain surgery, it is extremely complex, and if you are seriously considering taking on the challenge, you should most definitely make sure that your attorney is equipped to meet the challenges. Self-publishing is not for everyone, but for some, it can be a lifesaver.

16 · INTERNET ENTREPRENEURSHIP
Doing It Yourself

So, the lunatics have taken over the asylum?
—ATTRIBUTED TO RICHARD A. ROWLAND, PRESIDENT OF METRO PICTURES

Clearly, the Internet is transforming the manner in which music is promoted and sold. How now can it be used to assist fledgling recording artists to come to the attention of a public eager for the creative wares bursting forth all over the world—a public that is willing to part with money, thereby making the effort worthwhile financially?

Enter the high-octane world of Internet commerce. Never have the relationships among art, technology, and money been so complex. For several years now, those composers and performers who desire to communicate with eventual fans have had a variety of means open to them via the Internet: their own websites; use of ringtones, apps, and other mobile methods of communication; links to others' sites; clever use of Facebook and Twitter; Instagram or Snapchat; the new, new, new MySpace; fulfillment sites through which one's CDs, sheet music, and merchandise may be sold in hard-copy form; sites that highlight and even review new music; webzines; and the ubiquitous sites through which one's music may be uploaded, downloaded, streamed, and otherwise transmitted to and among computers and computer-compatible devices. So you can see, it's not easy to sell music online. Sure, sound quality is poor, but who cares? Many Internet entrepreneurs fall back to the "old-fashioned" technique of simple emails in order to divert consumers' attention to their product. And believe it or not, such methods are actually quite effective.

One truth has evolved from the recent period during which the myth of "opportunity for all" gained a certain credibility: traditional resources must still be assembled and utilized. And here is the $64 million question: Do you want to make a living, or do you want to try to compete with the majors?

You will note that my point of view in this chapter jumps back and forth between advocating the do-it-yourself approach and warning that many artists would be foolish to try to become entrepreneurs. Perhaps this is endemic to the field of law, where attorneys must be able to see all sides. But I think that it has just as much to do with the inherent complexities of the Internet and of e-commerce. In any case, there is much to think about before embarking on this kind of pursuit, and I will explore some of the issues you will have to consider before doing so.

COMPETING WITH THE BIG BOYS

At whatever level you decide to compete, you will need money, facilities for writing, rehearsing, and recording; good songs; tour equipment; clothes; a techie (or two or three); maybe a van; cowriters; producers; engineers; videos; etc. In short, you'll need to get for yourself everything customarily provided by a record company.

And, if this is not daunting enough, don't forget that you still need to obtain the services of the same types of professionals any working artist (whether individual, group, or band) traditionally requires: personal managers, accountants, and lawyers of various disciplines—music business lawyers, trademark lawyers, possibly immigration lawyers, and, where minors are involved, lawyers knowledgeable in the area of minority contracts. You may even need to consult corporate and tax lawyers. These professionals will be necessary to help you budget your recording; to organize your expenditures, receipts, check stubs, etc., for the purpose of preparing and eventually defending tax returns; to form affiliations for you with applicable unions, if appropriate; to negotiate your partnership and internal band agreements; to negotiate agreements with cowriters, with studios providing services for promises of future payment, with investors providing money for promises of future payment, with trademark services (including clearance of band names for the E-commerce, the unions, and the various states and countries of the world in which a conflicting name may already exist), with photographers regarding ownership and use of photographs for promotion, advertising, merchandise, and artwork on CDs and digital downloads, and with unions.

You will need to develop databases and print and distribute flyers, mailings, posters, and other merchandise. You will need assistance in mixing, mastering, and manufacturing or otherwise distributing your musical output. You will have to deal with encryption technology and requirements both for your own protection and that of your Internet distributors. You will have to seek reviews and mention in the press. You will have to identify, negotiate with, and service foreign companies with whom you hope to ally yourself for the exploitation of your products outside the United States. You will have to either deal with the venues yourself or find people who will do this for you—both agents and managers. You might even have to release your record via free download, foregoing all financial return from this segment of your career, but hopefully expanding your fan base, hoping that there will be more—and better—records in your future for release more traditionally—whether via major traditional labels or indie labels—all the while playing and thousand gigs and selling some merchandise, and eventually making a living doing what you do best.

You think all this sounds a lot like a record company? You're right. Sure, the Internet is a wonderful new outlet for the discovery and dissemination of new music, but it is a whole lot easier to be on the receiving end than on the selling and distributing end. It always has been.

ARTIST, SONGWRITER, PERFORMER—AND E-COMMERCE EXPERT?

Artist, songwriter, performer. Enough professions to keep three people busy. Yet many of our music industry creators are all three. But if you are going to exploit your music via the Internet, you will have to add a new profession: e-commerce expert. And much of what you will have to know is mysteriously similar to what you used to depend on your record company and publishing company to handle for you.

However you cut it, you used to have one item on your plate: your music. Now you have two: your music and your website. Both have to be marketed and promoted, and the expertise and services required to succeed in one are actually quite different from what is required to succeed in the other. Search engines (some of which charge per hit), newsgroups, other bands' sites, banner ads, reciprocal links, common interest sites, affiliated sites—all are Internet destinations that you will want to feature your product.

And, if you want your website to distribute your music as well, you should be aware that outside of the United States, the sale and exploitation of product can range from expensive to prohibitive. Licensing the manufacture and sale of hard goods overseas is complex enough: royalties, accountings, tax systems, the sometimes idiosyncratic procedures of foreign rights societies, the infrastructures of other countries governing how music is delivered to consumers—all these have been in place for decades, and old systems do not dissolve overnight. Selling music products overseas via the Internet can be even more complex.

Insofar as digital downloads are concerned, while the politicians have been struggling with this issue for some time, no taxes are yet chargeable in the United States. However, it will likely come to pass one day that taxes or some kind of tariff will have to be charged as the Internet begins to interfere substantially with bricks-and-mortar stores—or even catalogue sales. The European Union has been struggling with the tax issue for a while, and, although it is not yet resolved, one must remain alert to the fact that there are government institutions around the world that are intruding on the free and unrestricted distribution of music via the Internet. It is only a question of how intrusive they will choose to be, how alike or different the intrusion will be from country to country, and how complex and costly compliance will be.

But there is hope. A number of options have become available to artists seeking a presence on the Internet. Once you have acquired your domain name, companies such as cafepress.com can design your website to your specifications, and there are "powers" who can arrange for your modes to be designed, manufactured, and sold, taking care of all financial aspects of the transaction. For an example of how this has been constructed by a small independent artist with a specific target audience in mind, check out www.righteousbabe.com, Ani DiFranco's website.

MAKING A LIVING

What's wrong with just making a living? There is a level of success in the music business that may not be up to the multiplatinum level demanded by the multinationals or the venture capitalists in the mainstream music world, but that for many is nonetheless worth pursuing. In fact, while you may not sell enough records to make a dent in the *Billboard* Hot 100, you can still make an awful lot of money if you do it right—in fact, a whole lot more money than most artists will ever see as a result of contracts with major labels.

A client of mine refers to artists with such modest goals as the middle class of the music business. Think of Ani DiFranco; think of Prince, after he discarded his career-long dependence on a major record company (and before he welcomed it back into his life). To the argument that you have enough to do as an artist, my client answers that you will no longer have to spend time wondering (or trying to fix) what others are doing on your behalf. That saving alone buys you a lot of time.

What we are really talking about is a good, old-fashioned mail-order strategy with a contemporary twist: the use of the Internet as a means of advertising, funneling traffic, and utilizing digital technology to transmit music via downloads and other means.

You may be thinking, "But I can't reach the people this way!" Do you mean the people you want to reach or millions of people? If you mean millions of people, then you are right: you can't reach the platinum people. But if you mean the people you *need* to reach, then you *can* do it. There are ways to target the very audience that will find your artistry appealing—people who appreciate what you do and what you have to say.

Remember, as an entrepreneur you have total artistic control and you need not make any compromises to fit the agenda of a record label. You *are* the record label.

Now you may be thinking, "How can I compete with one hundred years of collective experience represented by many of the major labels?" The answer, of course, is, "How many times does a major label screw up?" Whenever a company is in the volume business, there is the likelihood—in fact, the guarantee—that it will mess up along the way in discharging its responsibilities. A label with fifty or one hundred acts—hoping one or two will succeed—is in the volume business. You are not.

When you are an artist, as a perusal of chapter 4 of this book will attest, you are at the bottom of the food chain. You are the last to be paid. Some artists compare their royalties to the last little morsels of a cookie. If you do not have the stomach or the patience for the major label paradigm, then don't complain. Do it yourself.

STEALING AND PROTECTING AGAINST IT

The illegal download phenomenon has received almost as much attention and publicity as an elected official's extramarital affairs. Those who will never set foot in the music business are nonetheless aware of the fact that Internet companies have been making music available for "sharing"—or, as copyright interests put it, "stealing." One of those consequences has been the heightening of sensitivity of the world's populations regarding the validity of copyright in the works that are being "shared." When you make your music available on the Internet, the boundless opportunities to reach consumers is matched only by the boundless opportunities for those consumers to appropriate your product without compensation. This is the lesson—good and bad—that the Napster, Grokster, and RIAA litigations has taught us.

Thus, we come to the only protection copyright owners can depend on: encryption. Encoding is the sine qua non ("without which nothing") of digital distribution. Imprecise, inefficient, careless encoding—or even the total absence of encoding that, believe it or not, is still fashionable among many artists (but not their record companies)—will provide uncountable numbers of web surfers with the opportunity to copy—effortlessly—a product that was created only after the infusion of an incredible investment of time and money on the part of the creator.

I cannot say enough about the necessity of encryption. Such sites as those run by Microsoft, Spotify, iTunes, and e-music, as well as the major record company sites that have finally made their presence known, are fairly well encrypted, although the imagination of the hacker has not had much opportunity to be fully tested. This is another reason artists must trust the institutional sites, rather than the fly-by-night sites, with their music—no matter how appealing they might find their philosophies or demographics.

DOS AND DON'TS OF INTERNET ENTREPRENEURSHIP

Don't be surprised if your search for success through an effort to do it yourself results in exactly the opposite: an inability to fund that effort, a lot of disappointed fans, and even an accumulating debt resulting from the expenditure of money necessitated first by seeking customers and second by trying to satisfy them. The ultimate irony of pursuing Internet entrepreneurship in the manner described in this chapter is that, as a musician, you live in the world of the idea. The abstract. The dream. Doing it yourself on the Internet is another world entirely. Columbia and RCA Records have almost two hundred years of experience between them. (Now they are joined as one company under the Sony umbrella.) Can you really expect the well-meaning efforts of one individual to duplicate this experience?

Perhaps I have (almost?) dissuaded you from accepting the daunting challenge of becoming an Internet entrepreneur. That was not my intention, and to prove it, I offer a few pointers in case you want to take the chance of offering your creations to the vagaries of cyberspace. Here is my top 11 list of dos and don'ts (actually nine dos and two don'ts):

1. Don't make any exclusive arrangements with anyone. The Internet is still too fluid a system to give up the flexibility of trying alternative means to achieve your goals.

2. Do try to find a distribution method or methods that can aggregate your music in such a way as to focus it sufficiently in a specific genre, for example, so as to target a specific demographic that you must reach in order to have success.

3. Do make certain that the sites with which you establish links and/or affiliations are trustworthy, both as to the manner in which they make and fulfill promises and as to the manner in which they protect your music.

4. Do try to use the facilities through which you distribute your music so as to develop databases of persons, Internet addresses, or other sites that inquire about your music so that you can use this extremely valuable information when offering other products and when touring.

5. Do focus yourself first before trying to target what audience you are going to try to reach. Know who you are, what you stand for, what you are trying to communicate, and who you are trying to reach (their age, their location, and their tastes).

6. Do view other bands' and artists' websites, including those that are not in the same genre as your music. You will be able to quickly distinguish between those websites that are effective and those websites that are not.

7. Do be careful when you design your website. If it does not effectively articulate your image and does not have the technical means to achieve the sales and interest in your music that is your goal, it will fail. And so will you.

8. Don't expect a lot of sales (for a new artist, anything more than ten CDs a year would exceed the average, believe it or not), but use your site as an information-gathering resource. Through links to, and with, other, similarly styled musical acts, you can begin to collect data that you can use to target and reach new audiences when you are touring. Eventually, you should attract the attention of radio programmers—perhaps find a friend at a station who would program a track or two. This data, at its most basic, will also help you develop a mailing list for gigs and flyers for your tours and for sales of records. MySpace.com—which is more user friendly and better structured than MyMP3, and Facebook.com which surpasses all other social network sites and has easily integrated music files in its algorithms—provides the wherewithal to make your artistry available to the audience you want to reach.

9. Do constantly update your website. Nothing turns off a fan more than a rusting and dust-gathering image.

10. Do be flexible in how you utilize the Internet. There are a variety of means by which you can do this in addition to the traditional goals of promotion

and distribution. (The *Blair Witch* phenomenon is a case in point: The film was introduced via the Internet, but then distributed and promoted via traditional means.) You can learn from the example of an inspired record company, which will try to find a way to coordinate with artists to utilize the Internet in new and creative ways that not only can reach hard-to-contact consumers but can achieve a certain level of "cool" as well.

11. I saved the least likely and most unexpected "Do" for last: Do learn double-entry bookkeeping. One hundred years ago Max Weber, and before him the Dutch, understood that absent a proper sounding in double-entry bookkeeping, no one really knows where they are financially and, according to Jacob Soll, where they are morally as well. He said that double-entry bookkeeping is the very source of accountability, that capitalism itself could not exist without it. In those days, *everyone* who owned land or were merchants knew double-entry bookkeeping. While it's an ethical idea at its foundation, it is the very essence of fiscal management. Anyone in business that does not understand it runs the risk of failing without warning. For purposes of this section, I will just define it briefly, but will leave it to the reader to bone up on its elements because I cannot suggest a more pertinent body of knowledge necessary to "do it yourself" than understanding the financial underpinnings of how to operate a business. It really is quite simple. *double-entry book-keeping* is a system of maintaining financial records whereby every entry to an account (for example, a purchase) is balanced by another entry to the account (a charge). Each entry has a corresponding opposite entry. Each side of an accounting ledger (credits and debits) balances out the other. There is a reason it has formed the foundation of all business since the 13th century.

A special mention of Snapchat, Facebook, Instagram, and Twitter: Social media have become indispensible in spreading the word about their devotees. In addition to their obvious personal appeal, artists who wish to expand their audience have been utilizing these media to full advantage.

MANUFACTURING AND DISTRIBUTION

Using the Internet effectively—as a way to reach potential listeners via your website and by marketing your art, as an information-gathering tool, or as a way to organize the manufacturing and distribution of your CDs—requires time! Time away from writing; time away from rehearsing; time away from thinking about who you are and what the purpose of your art is; time away from performing. Consider the time it will take merely to set up your home studio at the level necessary to produce high-quality recordings. Thus, at all levels of the recording process, time is a commodity that must be husbanded carefully.

And it requires money! Money for designing the website and keeping it current; money for encoders (software to convert your newly recorded CD so that it can be disseminated via the Internet without risk of having it stolen); money to raise the level of such encryption to CD level, which is not as easy as you think; money for manufacturing and packaging CDs; money for mailings; money for production of the music; money for instrumental rental; money for registering copyrights in both the songs and sound recordings; money for registering trademarks and service marks; money for tape; money for market research; money for club distributions; money for shipping the CDs; money for lawyers, accountants, and managers to negotiate with studios and investors; money for cowriters, professional engineers, and producers; money for negotiating contracts with foreign distributors and representatives; money to manufacture merchandise and then ship it; money for being featured at the top of search engines' lists; money for designing banner ads. And don't forget the cost of *getting* the money for all of the above.

KICKSTARTING YOUR CAREER

But behold, Kickstarter to the rescue: Kickstarter is a website service that helps a fledgling artist to establish a fund-raising mechanism to produce and eventually promote, market, and distribute the artist's record(s). Potential contributors make pledges which eventually turn into donations. The donations may be as little as $1, and depending on the amount of the donations, the artist can give the donor everything from a free download, to a bonus download, to tickets to an upcoming show, to whatever the artist feels is a fair exchange for helping him or her out in the first place (that is, giving the artist a kick-start). To date, already tens of millions of dollars have been raised utilizing this site. According to Kickstarter's "Stats" page, more than half of all music projects on this site are successful in meeting their financial goals. The service is not limited to music projects, but also includes creative projects in general. Other sites that have developed in the wake of Kickstarter such as PledgeMusic and Indiegogo are supporting this model whereby artists function—at least at the beginning of their careers—without the aid of major labels. Along with a larger piece of the (admittedly small) pie, this business model ensures that, for a time at least, the participating artists do not relinquish creative control. The model is in its early stages and results on average in relatively small sums being raised—surely not enough to replicate what a major label can do with its far more vast resources. (The exception is Amanda Palmer who raised more than a million dollars and then offended her donors by neglecting to pay side musicians who she invited to join her on her tours.) But some artists are making inexpensive albums as a loss leader for their touring, and then are able to raise even greater sums via Kickstarter, and others to finance concerts in costly venues.

As I noted in chapter 2, while crowdfunding is more practical than borrowing in that it does not lead to an accumulation of debt, there may be securities issues that need to be addressed if the nature of the return to "investors" is more than a gift. Once the return is tied to levels of success, it might be said to have morphed into an investment with respect to which other laws come into play.

Word to the wise, however: don't try to be all things to all people. Using funds raised by means such as the above will help a fledgling career to get under way. But once you try to become a "record label," you will merely be repeating what too often represents misdirected time and money to achieve something that is, frankly, beyond even the most business-oriented creative people.

An instructive story. In 1919, Charles Chaplin, Mary Pickford, Douglas Fairbanks, William S. Hart, and D. W. Griffith—all frustrated in their efforts to control their own business and artistic lives—established their own motion picture company, United Artists Studios. Apt name. It was not long before they learned that they could not do what they did for a living and run a picture company at the same time. Although Mary Pickford did not leave the studio until 1951, it had been clear for a long time that United Artists would eventually morph into a First National/Republic/Paramount/Columbia/Warner/ MGM–type motion picture company—and that was that. Actually, today, United Artists and MGM are one and operate under the same management. So it goes.

PODCASTING

What is a *podcast*? Essentially, podcasts are audio or video programs that are recorded, much as a radio or television program is recorded, then "broadcast"—transmitted—over the Internet. These programs are created by a wide variety of entities, including national magazines, radio stations, politicians, religious groups, and bands and artists, and made available to subscribers whenever they want to play them, via any digital audio player or computer. Podcasting differs from streaming in that a streamed broadcast is live, whereas podcast programs have already been archived by the provider of the service, and the user can store them for future access, much as TiVo stores broadcasts for future playback. Once the program has been downloaded, it can be played and replayed, as well as sent to like-minded friends. Check out www.PodcastAlley.com, which is a directory of podcasts available on the Web. The software you'll need to download podcasts—or transfer them to your smartphone, tablet, or other MP3 player or transmit them to one of your friends—options can be reviewed via www.podcast-software-review.toptenreviews.com.

The legal issues pertaining to the use of copyrighted elements, such as music, on podcasts are complex. The creators of the podcasts face one set of licensing issues; the users, another. Some podcasters are avoiding the payment of substantial licensing fees by using music whose authors have waived their right to royalties. If you, the user, however, choose to give your friends access to a program that contains copyrighted music, you are inviting the same legal problems faced by peer-to-peer sharers of music, about which we all know more than we want to know.

First among the responsibilities for podcast distributors is the mechanical royalty. The Harry Fox Agency has been approached by innumerable podcast producers who want to take responsibility for the mechanical royalties due each time a podcast is downloaded/ streamed. The problem is that the producer has no idea how many people will access any particular podcast. The result is that the producer risks bankruptcy if the public finds any particular podcast of his irresistible. If ten thousand podcasts are streamed, and the podcast contains only one copyrighted musical composition, then $0.091 will be due for each stream, for a total of $910. This is something a producer can build into his budget. Then again, anything can go viral. What if one million podcasts are streamed? In that event, the producer will be stuck with a bill for $91,000, most likely far more than the podcast cost to produce—and this sum represents the cost of only one song. So the producers try to make a deal with the copyright owners to cap their liability in the "unfortunate" circumstance of a hit podcast. The net result is that thousands of podcasts are not made available at all because the producers are afraid of the consequences of success. When a classical show is offered to be broadcast over a classical music radio station, and podcasts are a suggested supplement to the live broadcast, the radio station will demand that the producer indemnify the radio station for any liability arising out of claims from copyright owners. No producer in his right mind would do this given the ramifications of success as noted above. So the opportunities presented by the live broadcast are dead on arrival.

INSTANTANEOUS DISSEMINATION OF LIVE PERFORMANCES

There are plenty of new opportunities for live performers to expand their audiences via simultaneous webcasting and making CDs of concerts instantaneously available (with photos!). All of this costs money, but if managed carefully, it can generate money as well. Internet service providers such as AOL will often finance such ventures. The opportunities are enormous, and it will not be long before live performances that you attended will be available on your cell phones—before you have left the venue! It will, of course, be easier for independent artists to disseminate their performances in this way than it will be for artists signed to record labels.

CREATING A WEBSITE

Domain Names

If you launch a business on your own, you will need a website. You can create your own site, or you can enlist the aid of any one of a number of services that exist for that purpose. Obviously, your want the *name* of your site to be one that people looking for your music on the Internet will be most likely to type in on the search line and/or the name that the various search engines will display at the top of their hit lists.

Pursuant to the rules of the Internet's *domain name system*, each website is identified both by a long IP (Internet protocol) address and also by a more-or-less easy to remember domain name, which consists of several parts. (Note: The initials URL [universal resource locator) are not synonymous with "domain name"; the latter does not include http://.]

The *top-level domain* (TLD) is one of a short list of generic names—for example, .org, .com, .info, .biz, .net, .pro, etc.—*or* a territory extension—for example, .au (Australia), .us (United States), .eu (European Union). TLD assignments are regulated by the Internet Corporation for Assigned Names and Numbers (ICANN) and the government of the country in which the site originates. The creators of websites do not have free choice when it comes to choosing top-level domain extensions. For example, .pro is restricted to credentialed professionals. The fact that your company does business in a particular country does not automatically entitle you to use the territory extension of that country; the rules governing which entities qualify vary from country to country.

Within a given top-level domain extension, users are free to select any unallocated domain name on a first-come, first-served basis. You can obtain a domain name from one of several companies; register.com and networksolutions.com are two of the largest. These companies will guide you through the name-choosing and registration process; sell you the name for a period of time, renewable from year to year or from multiyear period to multiyear period; and offer support services once your website has been set up.

If the domain name you want is already in use, you can sign up for a service whereby you essentially sit quietly behind the registrar waiting for the name you want to become available again. This can happen if the original owner fails to renew registration, and when it does, your application is ready to slip through the back door, so to speak, making you the new owner.

Cybersquatters

Cybersquatting refers to a practice whereby people deliberately register domain names connected with known celebrities, companies, or groups—for example, an up-and-coming band—with the purpose of reselling them at inflated prices. In late 1999, the

Anti-cybersquatting Consumer Protection Act became law, giving trademark and service mark owners legal remedies against those who have registered a domain name with a "bad faith" intention to profit from use of the mark. For example, someone may register a name that is similar to the name used by a well-known musical group with the intention of diverting consumers from the legitimate website. The courts will almost always rule against a cybersquatter who has at any time attempted to sell the name. However, all court cases are costly and time consuming, and an alternative to bringing a lawsuit against a cybersquatter is to appeal on the grounds that ICANN's Uniform Domain Name Dispute Resolution Policy rules—which must be followed by any party registering a .com, .net, or .org name—have been violated. Here again, the concept of "bad faith" use is crucial. For example, ICANN will determine whether the company claiming ownership of your band's domain name has a legitimate business purpose justifying their use of the name (such as a fan club), or, alternatively, whether its sole or most significant reason for claiming rights in the name is to hold you up. Another example of a bad-faith use of a domain name is when the name is confusingly similar to a trademark or service mark that your band may have registered for commercial use, such as for sale of tour-related merchandise.

The bottom line here is that you should actively establish your trademark rights wherever they exist, building up what amounts to an entitlement to the name, however used. Trademark status is not like copyright; it is not automatically granted on creation, and your legal right to use your registered trademark(s) as a domain name is established through usage of your trademark in the various areas (recording, performing, merchandising) you pursue. For more information on trademarks, see chapter 11, pages 188–90.

WHICH PEOPLE SHOULD DO IT THEMSELVES?

There are four kinds of artists who, I think, have the best chance to become successful do-it-yourselfers in the world of e-commerce: urban and reggae artists, classical artists, jazz artists, and currently and formerly successful pop and rock artists. The ways in which urban and reggae artists and classical artists can benefit from the Internet are covered in chapters 18 and 19, respectively. Following is a brief discussion of how formerly successful artists might go about doing it themselves.

As to currently, or quite recently, successful artists, creating one's own label is definitely becoming quite popular. Joss Stone (Stoned Records), Jack Johnson (Brushfire Records) and the pioneers Ani de Franco (Righteous Babe Records) and Aimee Mann (Super Ego Records) have all gone this route successfully—at least for the artists who established them for their own recordings. The Delgados' Chemikal Underground, Jack White's Third Man Records, and other indie bands' efforts to create a home for their community of like-minded artists have also succeeded. The successes (among a bunch of attempts that have failed utterly—for example, Mariah Carey's Crave label and George Michael's Aegean label. I guess that it's not as easy as it seems.)

And, of course, there is Nettwerk Records which had the brilliant idea of reversing the policy of seventy-five years earlier by becoming the record company of the artists it was managing. They gave up on the majors a long time ago and now have a much better handle on their artists' records than they could have had via a "major." Similarly, Emily White's and Brendan Benson's Readymade Records perfectly aligns the needs of artists for their records—first, to see the light, and, second, to be "managed" and supported by attentive, commission-based employees (they call them "participants") in publishing, distribution, digital marketing, synchronization licensing, and promotion and public relations. This time, "sounds like" a record company, *is* one.

An artist who has had a great deal of success almost invariably still has hundreds of thousands, if not millions, of fans who recall their feelings years earlier when they were first introduced to the artist's music. Record companies that tried to specialize in such artists have, for the most part, failed. Assuming that an artist from the 1970s or 1980s (or earlier) has something left to say, that artist can record a CD fairly inexpensively and make it available via the Internet—either as a hard-copy CD or via download or streaming technology—for $10 or so if not for free and sell a few hundred thousand copies.[1] Not bad for a minor investment. Like Tori Amos and Foreigner there are a large number of formerly successful artists whose appeal is broad, but apparently not broad enough to warrant the majors granting them an exclusive recording relationship. The appeal of Internet distribution will resonate with these artists especially, and there is no reason why such artists cannot "do it themselves."

There is a fifth kind of artist who can do it him- or herself. This is the artist who already has a grassroots following and is original and creative enough to continue growing musically and relevantly. For example, Aimee Mann, late of 'Til Tuesday, or Ani Di Franco, or especially Amanda Palmer who discarded her record label in favor of a totally populist approach to her fans. When her record label called a 25,000 unit sale of her album a failure, she collected well over a million dollars through Kickstarter—from—yes, 25,000 fans. These artists' appeal to their fan base is not concocted or manufactured using new technological methods. They are not fake, and uniquely, they effectively replace traditional methods of distribution and marketing. The Grateful Dead may have been the best exemplar of this type of artist. A word of warning though: an obscure act such as Hollywood Undead "did it" themselves, but did not really succeed in any real terms until it obtained major label distribution. A&M/Octane, James Diener's label, funded with Wall Street money, does it backward: it acts like an indie until a certain success level is attained, at which point the awesome power of the Universal Music Group takes over. Maroon 5 was a notable beneficiary of this approach.

A WORD OF WARNING—AND ENCOURAGEMENT

As profits and market share of the majors diminish, the owners and distributors of "content" (read: the traditional record companies) are finding ever new ways to diminish, or at least keep under (their) control, the percentage of income they wish to share with the creators. So I suggest that you and your representatives review royalty provisions ever more carefully to ensure that they cover new and untested forms of exploitation. It used to be that hard sales, performances—and maybe licenses—were the entire universe of exploitation. Today, although that universe is expanding rapidly, the record companies are clinging to old models of royalty computation. For example, most traditional record companies maintain that the digital download of a recorded song should bear the same royalty as if the sale were made over the counter at a record store.

As we saw in chapter 4, a $16.98 "record" royalty base in the United States is customarily subject to a 10% or 15% breakage deduction, a 25% new technology deduction, a 25% packaging deduction, another 10% to 15% to make up for so-called "free goods," and perhaps even an additional 10% to 15% reduction just for the hell of it. A download is viewed in precisely the same way. Instead of sharing in the traditional 50/50 split of income from what are essentially licenses (via Napster—formerly Pressplay—or Musicnet, iTunes, etc. for example), record companies have figured out how to glom as much as 92+% of receipts from downloads. Streaming presents even more challenges to the recording artist. Many lawyers and business managers rue the day they receive "statements" from the principal streaming sites.

The record companies argue that their investment risks are the same whether the music is on a CD or downloaded. The costs for production, promotion, radio promotion, advertising, touring, video exploitation, etc., are justification enough to the record companies to exact precisely the same royalty reductions as they do for actual hard-copy sales. While there is some justification for this rationale, there are equally strong arguments for a more equitable sharing of the income.

This brings us back to doing it yourself. If you can find a way to reach your audience—even a substantially diminished audience compared to what a traditional record company can reach—you can profit enormously. Precisely because you do not have to reach mega-levels of buyers, you can present your art in an economically feasible way without having to learn all of the tricks of the trade discussed in earlier chapters of this book.

Finally, here is another top 10 list with which Kathleen Marsh, CEO of Musicnotes .com, recently closed her lecture on music entrepreneurism at the Neilson School of Management at the University of Wisconsin:

- Recognize opportunity and act on it.
- Be careful who you partner with in both business and finance.
- Don't underestimate the power of inertia.
- Don't underestimate the resistance from those who are threatened by your business.
- Make allies in your industry.
- Use experts, including legal and business experts.
- Decision-making is not always logical . . . it is emotional. Get people excited about your idea or product.
- Be brave. Getting started is scary.
- Never give up. Tenacity is your greatest weapon.
- Pray for luck.

---

1. It is not out of the question to create a workable studio with 36-track recording capabilities for a cost of under $40,000. Further, the usually outlandish costs of mixing and mastering can be achieved via the Internet. A record recorded in Los Angeles can be sent via FTP (file transfer protocol) to New York or London for mixing, and sent back again via FTP, all in a day's time. Customs delays, air courier charges, shipping time, and lost time are all absent in this fast-moving—and cheap—electronic world. There are, of course, huge security issues, but by the time you have learned the tricks of this particular trade, hopefully you will have learned methods of encryption that will protect your music.

17 · LOST, MISPLACED, NEGLECTED, AND ABANDONED
Royalty Opportunities You Were Never Told About

What is a cynic? A man who knows the
price of everything, and the value of nothing.
—OSCAR WILDE

In a previous edition of this book, the topics included here were incorporated into the chapter on royalties. In part, I did this because at the time I wrote the book, some of the royalty opportunities now available either did not exist or the means of collecting them were nonexistent or in their early stages of development. Things have changed.

AN INTRODUCTION TO NEIGHBORING RIGHTS

First, an explanation of the somewhat mysterious island of intellectual property protection known as *neighboring rights* is in order. These rights apply only to performers, record companies, and record producers. Its universe encompasses only the sound recording—not the underlying musical composition. Frank Sinatra's heirs receive nothing from the multitude of "New York, New York" performances presented at Yankee Stadium—many of which are televised; Bing Crosby's heirs receive nothing from the incessant play of "White Christmas" during the Christmas season. Nor do Ringo Starr and Paul McCartney receive anything from the innumerable performances in the United States of The Beatles' recordings broadcast on radio or television. Nor do Coldplay, Garth Brooks, or Josh Groban. Nor do their record companies or producers. Nor do the musicians or singers who performed on their recordings. Why not? Because the United States has never recognized neighboring rights—rights not actually conferred by existing copyright law but, rather, rights that are "neighbors" of traditional rights conferred by copyright laws. Most other industrialized nations do recognize such rights. But because the United States does not recognize their citizens' neighboring rights, they refuse to recognize ours. Some neighbors!

The following is a brief introduction to neighboring rights—which generate a type of music income that is practically unknown to Americans, one which the US House and Senate have systematically refused to acknowledge, effectively preventing our artists, record companies, producers, musicians, singers, and writers from sharing in that income. In fact, almost all European countries, as well as many Eastern European countries, South American countries, and China and Japan have their own versions of neighboring rights laws. For example, in Russia and in some other countries, the performance that is the subject of the neighboring law may include a dramatic production, and need not be recorded on a "record"; if a live dramatic production is broadcast, a neighboring right has been exercised. Japanese record companies, alone in the world, are permitted to rent sound recordings to consumers as long as they pay performers as if the CDs were in fact sold.

The fee structures and payment processes established by the organizations set up to license neighboring rights are not dissimilar to those established by the performing rights and mechanical rights societies around the world. Customarily, fees are negotiated separately from negotiations between performing rights societies and broadcasters. Of course, all of these organizations are champing at the bit now that the term "broadcasting" has taken on new meaning due to audio transmissions via the Internet. Some dot-coms are attempting to dismiss the expansion of neighboring rights to the Internet because there is no actual "wire transmission." Or is there? Stay tuned.

At present, neighboring rights money comes predominantly from radio and television broadcasters that play music for profit. While these broadcasters are used to paying fees to music publishers and songwriters for performances of their music, in many countries—including the United States—they have no obligation to pay record producers or artists a similar fee. These rights have been debated for years in the United States, but resistance to the passage of broader neighboring rights laws has been generally effective in the United States. Broadcasters are resistant to the expansion of their payment responsibilities beyond intellectual property holders, and performing rights societies are also resistant to this expansion because they fear that the fees applied to neighboring rights licenses would come out of a fixed-fee pool, thereby reducing monies traditionally paid to them. (However, the Digital Performance Right in Sound Recordings Act [DPRSRA] of 1995 broke some new ground by permitting the owners of digital rights in sound recordings to license these rights for fees—particularly via satellite radio transmission. Since this new right is actually incorporated into the US Copyright Law, technically, it is a "copyright" right, not a "neighboring right.")

Internationally, there is a growing trend toward expanding neighboring rights protection. Canada has recently instituted a neighboring rights law that, for the first time, allows Canadian recording artists (such as Celine Dion, The Weeknd, Drake, and Avril Lavigne) to share in the broadcast success of their CDs, just as the writers and publishers of the songs do.

The lesson to be learned here is that where recording artists or record producers are citizens of countries that recognize neighboring rights, there is a substantial likelihood that they will earn these rights not only in their own country, but in all other countries of the world that recognize neighboring rights. A citizen of the United Kingdom who produces an American artist will have an opportunity to increase his or her income significantly if someone registers the records he or she produces with all of the organizations in the European Union. There are, as one would expect, international collecting federations whose strength is the identification of works around the world via sophisticated data-processing techniques. They can assist artists and record producers in asserting their claims to neighboring rights money that would otherwise simply drift away to someone else via the Black Box or disappear entirely.

Unfortunately, the neighboring rights traditionally vesting in United States citizens who produce artists or who perform as recording artists cannot substitute the status of a foreign citizen for theirs. Therefore, an American producer who has a foreign manager is unable to access neighboring rights simply by assigning them to the foreign citizen. Simply put, the societies will not permit these transfers of rights. This rule will apply even if the manager, for example, acquires the services of the producer as an employee for hire, a concept which in itself is "foreign" to the societies outside of the United States.

BROADCAST MECHANICALS

Ironically, the very technology that has made it possible for radio stations to automate the broadcast process (gone are the days when DJs actually spun discs; music is stored on file servers and selections are accessed via computer) has also made it possible for various rights societies to collect broadcast mechanical fees. *Broadcast mechanicals* are royalties payable to copyright holders when their music is played on broadcast radio. The act of reproducing the sound recording on a broadcast tape for automated play gives rise to a mechanical reproduction "event," and many countries in the world—including Canada (see below), many European countries, and some Asian countries—are right there pursuing song and sound recording reproduction rights. Not so the United States. Sorry. In fact, the United States Copyright Act creates a specific exclusion: On the theory that it is not possible to broadcast a song without first copying it from the medium in which it originated (that is, the CD distributed by the record company) onto a broadcast tape, or CD, the copyright law provides a safe haven for broadcasters by permitting them to make such copies as are necessary to fulfill their principal goals—the broadcast of the sounds on the tape.

Nevertheless, as noted, there is a font of money available, outside of the United States, to publishers and record companies from broadcast mechanicals, and unless this pool of money is specifically designated as a source of income in music publishing administration agreements—for example, subpublishing agreements—it will reside in the ozone with so much other royalty income that the copyright owner so often fails to claim. No one else will tell you about broadcast mechanicals. I have. Go find them!

NEIGHBORING RIGHTS IN OUR OWN BACKYARD: CANADA

Canada—the largest trading partner of the United States, with a land mass larger than the "lower 48"—is merely one of many countries that have figured out how to fine-tune the dissemination of authors' and artists' rights (that is, royalties) to a degree that United States legislators and lobbyists cannot begin to fathom, and reviewing the Canadian model is an excellent introduction to how neighboring rights (and certain other rights) *can* work. What does our northern neighbor know that we don't know? I'll tell you.

Two Canadian societies are responsible for collecting neighboring rights royalties on behalf of their members: the Society of Composers, Authors, and Music Publishers of Canada (SOCAN), which also serves to collect performance royalties in much the same way ASCAP and BMI do in the United States; and the Neighboring Rights Collective of Canada (NRCC), a nongovernmental organization that administers the rights of performers and makers of sound recordings. (I am using the word "makers" rather than "producers" for reasons that will be evident later.)

As mentioned above, Canada has secured a tariff (some call it a tax) on music broadcast over Canadian radio stations: The rate for all formats but talk radio is 0.8% of the station's gross, and is distributed on the basis of airplay data (now easily collected thanks to automation). This money, which is a form of broadcast mechanical, is collected by the Société du Droit de Reproduction des Auteurs, Compositeurs et Éditores au Canada (SODRAC) and by the Canadian Musical Reproduction Rights Agency—Canada's Harry Fox (CMRRA). Together they are a joint venture named CSI—not the TV show. (The imaginative Canadians have dared to demand other rights affecting income-generating sources of the 21st century: direct licensing of digital downloads, tethered downloads (downloads that disappear after so many listenings or so much time), and interactive streaming. CMRRA, and its fearless former leader David Basskin, cleverly utilized the leverage that comes with those rights to increase the amount, the accuracy, and the timing of payment of mechanical royalties that these new technologies generate. Similarly, the Canadian Recording Industry Association (CRIA), rather than spending its time and its capital suing its best customers (unlike the Recording Industry Association of America [RIAA]; see chapter 23, page 339), has made inroads in effecting a change in the mechanical license rate from specific per-song rates, as in the United States, to a percentage of the selling price of records. This revolutionary change (revolutionary for a North American country at least) would eliminate the controlled-composition clauses. Music publishers in Canada, as in the United States, are strenuously resisting such a change by, among other things, insisting on a minimum fee per song, which of course negates the purpose of a percentage rate. But, as stated above, things are changing, and Canada is certainly one of the prime movers behind the changes.

LOST, MISPLACED, NEGLECTED, OR ABANDONED: WHICH CATEGORY ARE YOUR ROYALTIES IN?

Every year millions of dollars of royalty monies that might be paid to musicians and song-writers are never collected, or misplaced and ultimately abandoned, due to the failure of our country—more specifically, our industry's legal and financial community—to keep current with (1) international copyright developments that provide certain entitlements to intellectual property holders and (2) relevant advances in technology. Even lawyers who regularly practice entertainment law find it difficult to keep current with the "initials of the day": GVL, AHRA, WIPO, GONG, GATT, and TEA, to name just a few. However, the economic health of the music industry is strongly impacted by the laws and treaties and interests represented by these letters. Here I will mention two of the most important, GVL and AHRA.

Gesellschaft zur Verwertung von Leistungsschutzrechten mbH

One neighboring rights organization, Gesellschaft zur Verwertung von Leistungsschutzrechten mbH (GVL), due to the strength of the deutschmark during the 1990s, has become one of the more financially successful versions of income-generating organizations that go beyond the traditional mechanical, performance, synchronization, and print classifications. This German collective captures compensation for neighboring rights in Germany and beyond. GVL is not the only organization in the world that has succeeded in enforcing claims of record producers (that is, independent producers as opposed to record companies under whose auspices records are "produced"), but it has generated large sums of money for those producers who are citizens of European Union countries. Record producers' claims are based on the argument that producers' contributions to the creation of the ultimate master recordings are as worthy of ongoing fees commensurate with the success of the recordings as are artists' contributions, and hence producers are just as entitled to neighboring rights income as the artists themselves.

The Audio Home Recording Act

In 1990, Congress passed the Audio Home Recording Act (AHRA) in direct response to the concern of music rights owners that home copying of recordings was having an enormous impact on the sale of records through traditional means. (This source of royalty income is not a "pure" neighboring right, since it does not relate to performances of sound recordings, but neither is it a pure copyright right.)

The AHRA requires the manufacturers of devices whose primary purpose is to make digital music recordings for private use (for example, audiocassettes and Minidisc and DAT recorder/players) to pay a statutory royalty on each device and piece of media sold, with the receipts to be distributed to those whose income would be directly diminished by unauthorized copying: songwriters, record companies, and musicians' unions. It also requires manufacturers to implement *either* the Serial Copy Management System (SCMS), which prevents all but first-generation copies, or a system that has the "same functional characteristics" as the SCMS.

The royalty, about 2% of manufacturers' revenue, is collected and divided into two funds—the Sound Recordings Fund and the Musical Works Fund—as follows:

Sound Recordings Fund: 66 ⅔%

Nonfeatured musicians and vocalists (via AFTRA and AF of M): 4% (of 66 ⅔%)

Featured recording artists: 40% of balance

Copyright holders: 60% of balance

Musical Works Fund: 33 ⅓%

Songwriters: 50%

Music publishers: 50%

But the AHRA is less than meets the eye. First, it does not cover copying via computer hard drives and CD-Rs (CD-recordable devices), the method of choice for 99% of today's music copiers. Microsoft and its allies in the computer industry can be thanked for this successful lobbying disaster to rights owners. Second, there are numerous possibilities for technically circumventing systems designed to prevent any but first-generation copying. In other words, Congress in its wisdom (or lack of it) actually passed a law that ties itself to a particular technology rather than to the use sought to be protected against. As with neighboring rights, the fallout reaches beyond our borders. Why would countries whose laws *do* cover AHRA-excluded copying methods pay royalty income to US interests when the United States does not provide reciprocal rights to their copyright holders? They won't.

The Musical Works Fund is administered jointly by ASCAP, BMI, and the Harry Fox Agency. The Sound Recordings Fund is administered by the Alliance of Artists and Record Companies. The Alliance of Artists and Recording Companies (AARC) is in fact the only US collective representing featured artists and recording companies regarding domestic and foreign home taping royalties.

With respect to the collection of home-taping (and rental) royalties from certain other territories in the world that have laws similar to the AHRA and that authorize AARC to act for them, the list of countries is small, but growing. (Home-taping royalties overseas are sometimes referred to as *private copying remunerations*.) Over time, AARC hopes to be in a position to collect any and all home-taping and/or rental royalties owed to featured artists and independent labels on US sound recordings. Currently, such royalties generated in Spain, the Netherlands, and Japan are represented exclusively by AARC. Remember, many countries do *not* have similar laws (for example, England and Ireland), but with a lot of foresight, AARC is busy negotiating with foreign collectives such that when and if such laws are passed, AARC will be the collecting agent for them in the United States. AARC's executive director, Linda R. Bocchi, quite naturally recommends that individual artists sign up with AARC not only for the royalties they currently collect, but for those that will eventually come into their control in the future once they enter into appropriate agreements with respect to countries that have laws similar to the AHRA.

The AARC maintains a list of artists whose money is "on hold" because they are not registered with AARC. Notwithstanding herculean efforts to locate these artists, in a huge number of instances, they cannot. To the extent the monies reflect home taping and rental royalties originating outside of the United States, AARC is permitted to hold these monies for a period of three years while they try to locate the artist who is entitled to them; however, to the extent such royalties originate within the United States, if the artist is not registered, the money otherwise allocated to the unregistered artist will go into the AHRA "pot" and the artist's entitlements, in such cases, may be lost. I invite you to check the list of artists for whom AARC is holding royalties, which it generously provides on its website. You will be surprised when you see how many artists (or their heirs) have not bothered to collect royalties due them.

Note that while AARC collects AHRA royalties, these are not the same as digital performing rights—true neighboring rights, which are collected by Sound Exchange. In other words, you will require at least two collectives to capture all of the money to which you may be entitled—and probably more. Keep reading.

Sound Exchange

In 2008, Sound Exchange became the official negotiator on behalf of copyright owners and performers with Internet radio services. While their role was limited in time, Sound Exchange probably will continue to serve the needs of their participants in negotiating webcasting rates without ruffling the feathers of these radio services as had a previous decision by the Copyright Royalty Board in 2007. Sound Exchange collects and distributes royalties generated by the use of sound recordings, on the World Wide Web, via satellite services, and via cable services *only*. The beneficiaries are both featured artists identified on the recording and nonfeatured artists. Spoken-word artists are covered as well. These are the only digital performances for which DPRSRA has created a special category of rights that are "neighboring" to traditional copyrights. The royalty arises solely from the public performance of a sound recording via *digital* audio transmissions (performances on analog radio or television are not covered by this act) and has nothing to do with the underlying copyright in the musical composition. The royalty rate is statutorily determined; performers are paid their shares directly, and not through recording artist agreements

There are, of course, exceptions to when digital performance royalties are generated—for example, a digital audio transmission that is part of an "interactive" service does not generate such royalties. (*Interactive* refers to services that allow a subscriber to a digital radio or television service to select *one* song rather than a genre-channel list, and/or manipulate the transmission by fast-forwarding, rewinding, or downloading.) In fact, the exceptions are so numerous and complex as to be absolutely mind boggling. All the more reason to have an expert collection agency deal with these rights.

The royalties collected by Sound Exchange are split as follows:

1. 45% to the featured artist
2. 5% to artists performing auxiliary functions—paid to AFTRA and AF of M
3. 50% to the sound recording record company (which may not be the actual label)

Sound Exchange not only collects applicable royalties generated in the United States, but collects those generated outside of the United States as well, to the extent the foreign laws permit it and they can negotiate to collect them. Note that the fees collected outside of the United States are subject to the same limitations as the fees collected in the United States: performing royalties for which the United States Copyright Law provides reciprocal relief for foreigners—in other words, digital performing rights only. And they don't collect from Canada!

Sound Exchange, as of this writing, does not have an "unpaid" or "unregistered" list of artists like the list available at AARC's website and at Royalties Reunited's site (see below). This convenience will come soon. Sound Exchange pays quarterly and is working on a "play service" that members (at no charge) can use to check real-time information as to their (hopefully) accumulating royalties.

SHOW ME THE MONEY

Unfortunately, with some exceptions, a recording artist or songwriter based in the United States, even with top attorneys and business management, will experience enormous difficulty trying to identify—let alone collect—all of the varied royalties that are just sitting out there waiting to be collected. This is not just because there are a bewildering array of performance rights collection societies throughout the world, but because, as I have stated previously, the various countries that offer neighboring rights will do so only for their own citizens or for citizens of those countries that offer reciprocal rights. And, as also stated previously, the sole piece of legislation in the United States that provides for what can be considered a neighboring right is the DPRSA of 1995. Notwithstanding the fact that a broader rights system works quite well in almost every other country of the world, the broadcast industry in the United States has so far successfully blocked neighboring rights legislation by raising the specter of the virtual apocalypse that would ensue were they required to pay anything more than they already do for rights to perform music. The electronics industry (in particular the computer industry) has also had a good run in blocking tariffs on recordable cassette tapes and CDs that, in other countries, serve to compensate, in some small part, for the losses resulting from illegal or excessive home taping and computer copying.

Still, boundaries are falling. The rule of reciprocity referred to above requires that the artist claiming neighboring rights be a citizen of one of the countries on the schedule of qualifying countries. However, it also allows a citizen of a nonqualifying country to bypass the residency restriction if the recording is *produced* in a qualifying country. Unfortunately, Canada, like the United States, is not on the reciprocal list, so stopping over in Toronto or Montreal to record your album will not help you here.

TWO NEIGHBORING RIGHTS–FRIENDLY COUNTRIES: THE UK AND THE NETHERLANDS

You may be wondering why, if historically the issue of neighboring rights has been all but dead in the water in the United States, I am making such a fuss about them to readers of this book, most of whom are US citizens? Because some of the countries that *do* have broad neighboring rights policies—and their resident societies—will pay neighboring rights royalties to US citizens under certain circumstances. For example, if the producer of a sound recording is a citizen of one of those countries (I will call them NRF—neighboring rights–friendly—countries), he or she is eligible to receive these royalties; if the producer or artist is an American, but records in an NRF country, he or she may be entitled to those royalties.

Throughout the world, NRF countries are holding millions of dollars of royalties. It is not as if these royalties have been abandoned by them. Indeed, once a defined period of time has passed (different for each society), these monies will find their way out of the societies' coffers and into those of non–United States companies' and artists' pockets—or into the Black Box. To say that it takes a specialized service to capture all, or a majority, of these royalties is an understatement. The following section describes some routes that can be taken to recover royalties that would otherwise be lost forever.

The Rental Directive

The United Kingdom and the remaining members of the European Union offer reciprocal protection in "qualifying countries" (not, of course, including the United States) for the purposes of paying remuneration to performers. This is a result of a European Commission "directive" to encourage the collection of royalties under a newly created "rental and lending" right for recorded performances. A performer is entitled to claim equitable remuneration if the sound recording in which his or her performance is embodied was included in a cable program service, broadcast, or played in public in the United Kingdom after December 1, 1996 (the "exploitation"), and either (1) the country in which the recording was made appeared in the schedule at the time of the exploitation or (2) at the date the recording was made, the performer was a national, citizen, or resident of a country appearing in the schedule at the time of the exploitation.

NEIGHBORING RIGHTS COLLECTION AGENCIES

As neighboring rights are expanded in the United States, whether technically copyright-driven or otherwise, a number of companies have created worldwide-connected collection services to wade through the various conditions that need to be met in order to justify a claim. For example, now that Sound Exchange collects satellite-generated performance royalties for record companies and artists (and producers), the lack of reciprocity whereby other countries would honor our citizens similar rights in their countries has been largely erased. The same result occurred with AARC, which collects blank-tape and related income for its members. Some countries require that an artist be a citizen of that country in order to collect neighboring rights from that country. The lead singer of Foreigner, Mick Jones, is a beneficiary of this rule, being a citizen of the UK. Recordings that were produced in, say, England, such as the CARS' "Heartbeat City" are also eligible.,

Every artist should enter into some kind of agreement with one of these agencies as there may well be money just waiting for collection. Some of the agencies that have entered this field will even pay advances to eligible artists. And, of course, the artists need not have a foreign connection when it comes to royalties payable by Sound Exchange and AARC.

Here are some of these collection services:

Fintage House (www.fintagehouse.com) This is one of two important agencies originating in the Netherlands—it is a spin-off of a large banking organization. Fintage has tons of experience in extracting money from countries around the world that are traditionally very difficult to deal with.

Kobalt Music Group (www.kobaltmusic.com) This Netherlands-based company with a huge US presence is an independent music publisher, which offers global administrative and creative services to writers, publishers, and other publishing rights holders.

Sony Music Entertainment (UK) This is a division of Sony Music and is obviously very well connected throughout the world. When the English company does not know the idiosyncratic rules of a particular country relating to neighboring rights, they have experts in place in most countries of the world to help them. This is a tremendous asset for them and for their licensors/artists.

PremierMuzik (www.premiermuzik.com) This is a Canadian company based in Quebec but with reach well beyond our own "neighbor." This is a boutique with all of the benefits of a small company. They will get to know you, your attorney, your accountant, and you will consider them part of your personal team to maximize your income from all neighboring rights sources.

Royalties Reunited/PPL (www.ppluk.com) Royalties Reunited collects airplay royalties, including royalties resulting predominantly from analog radio and television transmissions. These are the true neighboring rights. The entity that actually collects these royalties is Phonographic Performance Limited (PPL). Royalties Reunited claims to have royalties just waiting to be claimed by more than five thousand performers totaling several million pounds. Those qualifying for the royalties are the individual performers on the recordings, including session performers, not the "band" entity per se.

The Association of United Recording Artists AURA based in the UK, represents featured artists, and the Performing Artists' Media Rights Association (PAMRA, www.pamra.org) collects for both featured and nonfeatured musicians and singers. At either of these sites, you can enter your name (or if you are an artist's representative, your client's name) in the applicable field, and if money on your behalf—derived from radio and television transmissions, bars, clubs, gyms, and wherever else recorded music is played—is being held on you or your client's behalf, that information will be provided. Try it.

Through subagreements, all of these companies collect performance royalties not only for performances of sound recordings in their home countries, but also for those generated in practically all other countries of the world and particularly in at least fifteen of the most lucrative countries, including the United States (thereby running into competition with Sound Exchange). Others include Austria, Belgium, Denmark, Finland, France, Germany, Holland, Ireland, Italy, Japan, Norway, Spain, Sweden, Switzerland, and Brazil. As noted, Sony is one of the neighboring rights collection agents that have their own divisions throughout the world. Other companies such as peermusic and the other majors are getting into the game as well.

As to all of these companies, once you sign up with them, you do not need to fill out the burdensome, and burdensome number, of applications for collection rights. Nor will you miss out signing on with some obscure companies/collection services that you, and even your attorney and accountant, have never heard of. The agents I have identified, and others, are members of the major music societies around the world and collect directly from them, thereby reducing the amount of time it takes for a person entitled to such royalties to receive them. They have changed the traditional standard for issuing accounting statements which was stuck forever on a semiannual or quarterly basis. Some will account on a monthly basis, and their websites offer private and confidential account information reports on a

24/7 basis. Of course, they themselves are accounted to most often semiannually, or perhaps quarterly, so the great majority of your income will not be received by them, and reportable to you, monthly, but rather every three or six months.

I should point out something that might help you in deciding whether to appoint a worldwide agent or to pick and choose among other neighboring rights societies before granting to the worldwide agent whatever remains. For example, the UK, France, Canada, and many other countries have neighboring rights societies all their own. And the United States has Sound Exchange and AARC. Why not sign directly with them and then appoint an agent to handle the outliers? Because it is thinking small. To deny a collection agency that you have appointed the ability to collect neighboring rights in the big territories by signing directly with their respective societies and to give the collection agency merely the rest of the world is not always wise. First, even with respect to the countries' own societies, your agent can keep a better eye on their processes than you can; that's what they do. Second, dividing up the world detracts from their power to help you when things get dodgy. Third, by giving the agent only the smaller territories, it is more likely to lose money than make a profit (even if they do not provide advances) as the amount of work to register your recordings in every applicable country of the world is enormous. The best thing that you can do yourself is to give your appointed agent at least a chance to make a profit. If they cannot share in the worldwide rights, the economic model on which they structure their companies and their staffs fails and it would not be surprising if their attention to your particular catalogue turns out to be less than energetic. I should add that the time it would take to act out this bifurcation of the world hardly will ever be worth it. If you are a recording artist or a small record label, don't you have better things to do with your time than becoming the world's most clever licensor of neighboring rights?

PERFORMING AND OTHER OBSCURE RIGHTS IN SOUND RECORDINGS

In most of the world outside of the United States, rights to perform sound recordings are considered neighboring rights. Thus, the inclusion of this section here. Until very recently, lost, misplaced, neglected, and abandoned would be an accurate description of them. But they are slowly being discovered through a combination of legislation and jurisprudence.

Analog Performing Rights in Sound Recordings: Still Waiting

For decades, recording artists and their record companies have sought to create a performance right for analog performances by an amendment to the Copyright Law. They have been characterized by major PR events in Congress where the recording stars of the time (Frank Sinatra anyone?) would lunch and chat with Congressmen only to see their long-sought law discarded as unpassable.

Currently, the US Copyright Law, unlike those equivalent laws of most other countries in the world, does not recognize a federal performance right for analog radio. The proponents of a law granting recording artists performance income from analog performances point out that only China, North Korea, and Iran fail to have legislation in effect that causes analog radio stations to pay artists. Unless the performances are of a digital nature (for example, via webcasting, cable, satellite or stream), even a Taylor Swift record, produced in 2015, would not garner performance royalties no matter how much it was played on AM or FM stations throughout the country. Foreign performing rights societies will not, of course, pay performance royalties for performances of American-originated recordings performed on their radio stations because American performing rights societies are barred from collecting performing rights monies in the US for *their* artists' recordings. If things change, then the foreign societies will be bound to reciprocate and pay American recording artists on this use. Since American recording artists are still the most important source of contemporary music in the world, (along with a few Brits, an occasional Australian, and a masked French duo, a lot more money is lost to Americans than would be earned by foreign artists. It has always seemed to be a no-brainer to pass legislation permitting this. It would even help the US balance of payments. But things have not changed for the better. During years of failure, the proposed legislation was referred to as the Performance Rights Act. Maybe they should change the name, as the publishers did in pursuing their legislative agenda, now called the Songwriters Equity Act. Still, the resistance of the National Association of Broadcasters and many others is unremitting, so I do not expect an amendment to change the copyright law anytime soon. In the meantime, performing sound recordings on analog radio do not generate any money whatsoever for sound recording owners via federal copyright law.

The Discovery of Performing Rights in Pre-1972 Sound Recordings

Flo & Eddie of The Turtles brought a lawsuit in 2013 that might turn upside down the law as we have known it for over a hundred years—that is, that until the US copyright law was changed to grant federal copyright to sound recordings (that is, anything recorded commencing January 1, 1972) was passed, no such rights existed for any recordings issued prior to that date. The Flo & Eddie claim was that their recordings, released in the 1950s (!) were nevertheless protected by common law copyright regardless of when they were recorded. They acknowledged that the Copyright Act gave them nothing in terms of protection, but in the absence of federal law, they believed that the rights of people to their own property was sacrosanct. If these rights were not preempted by the federal government, then they still exist. They claimed that it was wrong for courts to deny them their property rights in sound recordings granted by the various laws of the fifty states that impacted private property (the venerable "common law"). The proponents of this claim acknowledge that similar protection may not exist in every state, but they believe that it surely does in New York and in California (where the lawsuit was brought). In their view, therefore, SiriusXM, the defendant, would be liable not for federal copyright infringement *per se* but for a kind of infringement characterized by the conversion of assets, unfair competition, theft, and the kitchen sink for performing their sound recordings on satellite radio, webcasts, and cable networks without permission.

The plaintiffs claimed that their sound recordings, created prior to the date on which the US Copyright Law was changed to grant federal copyright to sound recordings (that is, January 1, 1972) were nevertheless protected by common law copyright regardless of when they were recorded. The proponents of this claim acknowledge that similar protection may not exist in every state, but they believe that it surely does in New York and in California (where the lawsuit was brought). If they are right, then SiriusXM, the defendant, would be liable not for copyright infringement *per se* but for conversion of assets, unfair competition, theft, and the kitchen sink for performing their works on their satellite radio transmissions. To the shock of the Copyright Bar, a California court agreed with them. Similar lawsuits have been brought against Pandora and eventually against terrestrial radio. CBS Radio, iHeartMedia and Cumulus, the country's largest radio station conglomerators have all been sued. Others who have not yet been sued will inevitably be called before their state courts by similar claimants.

Ironically, Flo & Eddy have found common bond with Sony Music Entertainment, Universal Music Group, and Warner Records Group, all of which have sued SiriusXM as well, and which have apparently achieved several hundreds of millions of dollars in settlements. Whether they will succeed when the last appeal is decided, especially in view of the fact that the federal law is likely to change soon with respect to analog performances, is not predictable. It is not even clear whether the next iteration of the Performance Rights Act will protect analog performances of pre-1972 recordings. But if they do prevail, what a boon to the record labels and their artists (who are destined to receive the lamb's share of the newfound monies). Then the only issue will be how much, if any, of their recoveries (which will likely be blanket sums, not attributable to any particular artist's recordings) will be shared with the artists and their producers. The second most important court in the land, the Second Circuit Court of Appeals, based in New York, will hear an appeal on this issue about the time this book is published. Which way will they come out on the question of whether there exists a public performance right outside of federal law in New York, California, or other states? One of the dilemmas that the court will have to consider is what to do with a sound recording if they agree that it requires permission to be played on the radio in New York or California, but may freely be performed on the radio in any of the other forty-eight states. Will that reality alone constitute interference with interstate commerce so as to negate the claim that there exists such protection in New York and California? We will see.

Laws, priorities, rules, regulations, technology, and perceptions change so fast that to indicate one state of facts existing at the time this book is composed is most likely to not resemble the same state of facts existing at the time of publication—or for that matter for several years thereafter. The Flo & Eddie claim described above is one example. Another involves streaming. Streaming services are becoming so widespread in the second decade of the 21st century that standards and customs are still being worked out in the marketplace. As of 2015, most streaming services paid about 10% of their total revenue for the reproduction and distribution of musical compositions. Apple, in its wisdom, and in part to put itself on the map—being a bit of a latecomer in the field—pays one-third more. These disparities are bound to reach an acceptable level over time. The parties need not conspire illegally with each other for rates to coalesce to an essentially identical number. The market will lock in a standard. A download cost of $0.99 was established only by Apple several years ago, but when other companies entered the field, at first every competitive service also chose $0.99 to consumers. Then competition pricing began to appear with $1.29 becoming the expected price for a new release or a hit sound recording for download purposes. These things are not forced on the public; they establish themselves.

The parallel between this "discovery" of rights that had never before been acknowledged parallels what I discussed earlier in this book regarding whether the three-year statute of limitations on federal copyright infringement renews itself on a continuous basis and that the statutory provision does not refer only to the initial three years of the claimed infringement. Two enormously surprising decisions that, if affirmed on appeal, will mark the most profound changes in the law of copyright in decades.

18 · URBAN MUSIC
The Beat Goes On

The Music Business is a cruel and shallow money trench.
A long plastic hallway where thieves and pimps run free
and good men die like dogs. There's also a negative side.
—ATTRIBUTED TO HUNTER S. THOMPSON

Beating on a beat box—making a snare and a kick drum—that people can rap to. What else do you want? What else do you need? On street corners—starting as DJs—promoting others' music and then making their own. Rhythm is the beginning and rhythm is the end. Provided it's *new*. And has never been heard before! Can you believe that DMX went platinum (1 million sold) *bootleg* before it hit the music stores. Why? Because it was so different from everything that came before. This is the currency of hip-hop! Make them hungry. Establish the buzz. The fans are no slouches. They know what they want; they know what they hear; and they know what they see!

ROOTS

First, a little history. In 1984, Harry Belafonte produced a small film, *Beat Street*, which featured urban ghetto kids break dancing, painting graffiti on walls, rapping, and generally developing a musical style that was light-years from what had gone before. Fast cuts by the camera, head spins, windmills, even some pop lockin'. What was this music? Surely, its origins and references (rhythm and blues) were well established and even mainstream by the time this seminal film was released. And maybe that was the reason for the explosion into a new dimension. But hip-hop really started much earlier.

A wonderful website www.B-Boys.com traces the evolution of hip-hop from Kool Herc, in 1973, so-called father of hip-hop. Born in Jamaica in 1955, he introduced to New York the raw rhythms and structures that we know today as hip-hop and laid the foundation for the Break-Boys. After Kool Herc came Grandmaster Flash and the Furious Five in 1979; Kurtis Blow, Afrika Bambaata, George Clinton (and his funky contribution), Ice-T, and Michael Jackson's legendary moonwalk during the early 1980s; Salt-N-Pepa and Run-D.M.C., N.W.A.'s gangsta' rap, and Tribe Called Quest, followed by Dr. Dre, Tupac Shakur, Notorious B.I.G., Missy Elliot, and Lauryn Hill in the 1990s. An array of adventurous and talented groundbreaking artists, including Eminem, 50 Cent, and Kanye West, bring us to the 21st century, and the explosion of hip-hop and rap's influence, which extends beyond the world of music. Hip-hop is a genre of music, to be sure, but it also represents a culture that defines urban life as much as urban life defines it.

THE MILIEU

At first glance, the world of hip-hop seems to be very different and to operate by different rules than the pop music world. Seemingly, one would need a cultural historian, a psychiatrist, and a translator to make sense of it. But the essential characteristics of the music business—minus a few idiosyncrasies—are no less applicable to the world of hip-hop than to other kinds of music. The same concerns facing the pop artist and songwriter—the same copyright laws, the same laws of contract, the same federal and state income taxes, and the same international treaties—are faced by hip-hop artists, although often these artists do not realize that the models applicable to the pop music business apply just as much to hip-hop. (Reportedly, Cheryl James of Salt-N-Pepa was surprised at the consequences of contracts that she and her partner signed. "We never even thought of a lawyer," she stated when testifying against her record company.)

That said, it must also be acknowledged that the musical vocabulary of hip-hop—and R&B and rap—is different from that of traditional pop songwriting. Whereas the rest of the popular music world divides songs into music and lyrics, and customarily collaborators will be credited as having written "words and music," in the hip-hop world, songs are divided into three parts: the track, the melody, and the words. And true to the traditions of Tin Pan Alley in the 1950s, everyone involved in producing a hip-hop song tries to get his or her name into the authorship list—whether they are true contributors or not. This is not only because there is a lot of money in music publishing and writers automatically own part of the copyrights of their creations. Being one of the writers has something to do with pride of authorship as well; the entire team of people who participate in creating a musical work in the hip-hop area see themselves as cocontributors and being named as an author is merely a manifestation of this phenomenon. Even the musician who creates an incidental keyboard part over the background track will claim to be an author. In truth, in the world of hip-hop, in contrast to the rest of the musical scene, the keyboard contribution alone can make or break a song; it can be the single defining contribution that justifies the creator's rise to the level of author. Thus, with a hip-hop song, it is likely that from five to ten names will find their way into the authorship list, often including writers whose works were recorded and released years earlier but whose music has been sampled.

This is a world of emergency lawyers, late-night calls, tinkering and manipulating with sounds that can date a song as being old-fashioned or mark it as the latest thing simply on the basis of a "sample." Hip-hop represents the nanosecond when a member of a disadvantaged community explodes into mainstream society. And, as with any immigration or emigration from one economic or social community to another, this migration carries with it all of the attendant dangers that such moves engender.

The music of hip-hop, because of its very reason for being, is on the cutting edge of the culture. It is a fast-moving art form that changes almost daily. If a record is not catching on in the clubs or at the radio stations within two weeks, many record companies will simply kill the record and release something new, no matter what the financial consequences.

The artists bringing you this music change almost as rapidly. From Tupac Shakur and the Notorious B.I.G. (both of whom were killed—possibly by their compatriots), to Lil' Kim and Busta Rhymes, who, mere weeks after their stars had begun to climb, were referred to by insiders as the "rap elders" as Nelly's debut album passed theirs by in an extremely brief period. The speed by which these transfers of status occur is mind boggling.

Beyond their charismatic live appearances—on- as well as offstage—hip-hop musicians are very well schooled in the rhythms, riffs, and songs of the '50s and '60s. The phenomenon is mostly black, but, as we saw with Elvis, The Beatles, and the Rolling Stones, music that originates in the black community does not stay there for long. At this writing, Eminem, of course, is still the breakthrough white artist who has emerged to express the hip-hop ethos.

URBAN MUSIC: THE PRODUCER'S COSMOS

The current trend toward producer-driven music makes the producers of this music as important as, or even more important than, the artist. This oddity creates a lot of different priorities, methods of payment, and abuses.

On the positive side, the team effort of the production company, writers, producer, sidemen, and artist constitutes a real creative effort. The contribution of the production company is much more visible here than in the pop world. The logistics alone of creating tracks and adding melody, raps, ad-libs, and instrumentation—often seeking the input of musicians, producers, or rappers with a reputation—is mind-boggling.

On the negative side, particularly in the touring area, there has emerged quite a lot of violence and a not-so-new phenomenon in the live performing world—the unscrupulous promoter. With a few exceptions (noted below), hip-hop touring has been a bust, with the unfortunate result that new young hip-hop artists do not have access to the traditional avenues to long-term success.

The urban music market is so huge that the record companies have begun to invest massive amounts of money to claim their fair share of the charts in this area. The producers, alone or through surrogates, create tracks by the dozen, called "beats." They often incorporate samples. The artist essentially shops for a beat that he or she likes and adds his or her own rap to it. This is an electronic world and very little music is produced acoustically. The artist is the only real, live, contributor to the sound.

DIFFERENT STROKES FOR HIP-HOP FOLKS

"Guerilla" Marketing

From the beginning, hip-hop and rap have used unconventional ways to reach their target markets. For example, record companies or producers often hire groups of kids—known as "street teams," to sticker as much of the city as they can afford to. They will paper the side of a van and drive around; they will go into the clubs at night and hand out flyers; they will "snipe" any blank space available on the side of a construction site. You have all seen them. The artist's representative builds this kind of promotion into the recording and distribution agreements. Who should be in charge of the process of establishing street teams? The artist, producer, or manager—certainly not the record company. Why not? It is not that the record company is not capable of doing so, although mainstream record companies are not likely to be as effective as someone who is part of the community. It is, rather, the resistance of eventual record buyers to the image of corporate America doing the promotion. In addition, some of the things street teams are asked to do are illegal, but the underage kids who are paid a few dollars to snipe the city are not as likely to be arrested. And these kids are the ones who congregate in the areas where the promotions will be most useful.

Among the production companies known for their use of guerilla marketing teams to establish artists' popularity and credibility perhaps the most celebrated was Notorious B.I.G.'s Undeas, which gave New York City's Junior M.A.F.I.A. (Masters at Finding Attitudes) almost instant notoriety.

Bootlegs

Bootlegs. The anathema of the music (and film) business. But wait. Can bootlegs help build a artist's career (and the attendant profits of the artist's record company)? Sure. Some record keepers note that hip-hop sales are higher in white America than in black America. But what they fail to note is the fact that in black America—particularly in the communities of New York, Los Angeles, and Florida—there is a preponderance of bootlegs over ordinary commercial copies of records. The Midwest has no bootlegs, so the only way to acquire this music is to buy it. So the SoundScan numbers that show that the majority of buyers of rap music in Wisconsin are white are misleading. The truth is that blacks in Wisconsin are as, or more, likely to possess hip-hop records than the white population. They just acquire them differently. Rapper "Cheech" reports, "They say White America is picking up our rap? It's not true. *Everyone's* picking up our rap."

White Label

What is a "white label" recording? Just another means of promotion. Preferably, the recording is a lousy copy, with no artwork, but it's fresh, and it's hot! A producer of white label recordings is happy to sell a few hundred copies and go home. Maybe he'll give them to the club or radio DJs, who then bootleg them if they're half good. White label recordings (actually mixtapes) contain more than one track. They are akin to compilation records, but the songs tend to blend into each other. Something new is actually being created and duplicated in a wholesale way without anyone's authority or any documentation establishing ownership. Illegal? Sure. But so what. In fact, even the artists' record companies have been known to turn a blind eye toward white label recordings and actually encourage them because they reach a market that the record companies could only dream to reach.

The Rap

If anything distinguishes hip-hop, it is the rap, the sometimes mesmerizing poetic, lyrical monologue we have all heard. There are many varieties of rap. For example, in freestyle rap, the artist raps spontaneously, without prepared lyrics. Freestyle rap, which is common on the streets, is also an exciting characteristic of the MC battles between and among rappers. People always want to know if a rapper can freestyle. Not all rappers can. Freestyle lyrics are not listened to and absorbed in the same way that the traditional hip-hop lyric is. The message of the traditional hip-hop lyric is more important than the beat, and the rapper who communicates best is the rapper who will succeed in the commercial world.

In the world of hip-hop, the power of an artist's rap—the words and the rhymes—determine whether the artist succeeds or fails. Artists in the R&B genre do not have the rap to fall back on, and their music, more than hip-hop music, tends to achieve immediacy and relevance via image and style. Of course, looks and style are also an essential element of hip-hop, but a compelling rap can transcend a less-than-powerful image.

Ironically, the more successful the rapper, the more likely he or she is to slip into the mainstream and move away from themes born and nurtured in the inner cities, concentrating instead on a quest for money and success. Such a shift in focus, no less than overexposure, can damage a rapper's image. Rappers who become celebrities risk being branded as sellouts.

Production Costs

One of the major practical differences between hip-hop music and other forms is the cost of recording. Budgets for one hip-hop track can exceed $100,000; the cost of an album-length CD can run over $1 million. Included among these costs are the costs associated with sampling. In fact, sampling costs are where recording budgets often go off the track. It is difficult to estimate what those costs will ultimately turn out to be, and the contract is usually signed after the samples are already in place, when it is too late to make a change in the track. Since the records are producer driven, the producers or production companies can retain as much as one-half of the gross royalties paid by the record company plus a flat fee per track of as much as $100,000.

Royalty Points

Royalty points in hip-hop contracts are also higher than those in hard-fought, highly publicized rock and roll deals. Further, the control over the points and the artist is often in the hands of the producer. The record company neither speaks the language of the artist, nor is it particularly trusted by the artist. Indeed, the artist often does not even meet record company personnel: the producer or manager or independent label assumes total negotiating responsibility and forms the only connection between the hip-hop artist or group and the record company. This one-step-removed line of communication, in which the artist or group is not a part, makes the connection between the artist and the record company, already tenuous at best in the pop field, even further detached. It completes the alienation that naturally results when people do not physically relate to one other. Ironically, this alienation parallels the detachment that motivated the artist in the first place to express him- or herself through the hip-hop genre.

Sound and Lyrics

Hip-hop producers, like rock producers, often establish a distinctive "sound." Since the beginning of rock and roll (or at least since Phil Spector and his "wall of sound"), individual producers have had their own sound. To capture and to replicate this is the key to continuity and continued success. If Jermaine Dupri's sound guarantees sales and attention, why not stay with it?

Much of the hip-hop lyrical focus is shocking. Many who hear hip-hop lyrics for the first time come away with the impression that the *only* purpose of the words is to shock, and that therefore the music is not art. For those who think that a piece of music (or a painting, or any other creative work) with shock value is somehow not art, I submit a story about the internationally renowned Russian composer Igor Stravinsky (1882–1971). Stravinsky was asked what he thought of a work by the American composer John Cage (1912–92), which contained six minutes of silence. (Cage's work was at the time considered avant-garde). Stravinsky said that he looked forward to Cage's next work, which he hoped would be even longer!

RAP AS PROTEST

Rap as protest—protest against violence, unemployment, lack of opportunity—is alive and well even as it incorporates other styles featuring more melodic lines. It is also often "anti-"—antiwoman, antiestablishment, antitradition, and sometimes anti-Semitic. The advocacy represented by the rapper's points of view is repeated over and over again in different ways and finds an ear not only in the black population, but in the white, suburban, well-to-do population as well. The ultimate consequences of this commingling of cultures cannot be all that bad. The protesters of the '60s, while never fully realizing their dreams, made their point and the consciousness of our entire society has changed as a result. What societal changes are in store for us in view of the protests of the new century are obviously speculative, but changes there will be, and some of them will certainly be the result of the consciousness raising effected by the widespread communication of the hip-hop generation's messages to the world at large. One rapper, when asked why there was so much violence at hip-hop shows, referred to the fact that the things that make the youths in the audience angry at their situation in society are the very things that are pounded at them by the rappers. Since hip-hop constitutes an expression of what the audience itself is living, and since the subject matter is not saccharine material like that of the pop (read: bubble gum) world, the audience is naturally engaged and, sometimes, aroused to the point at which violence regrettably can and often does erupt.

THE IMPORTANCE OF THE MIX: MIXTAPES

The mix can make a huge difference in hip-hop. Mixers are not always paid royalties, but a simple remix of a commercial release, for radio purposes only, can transform a work. Enormous amounts of money are at stake here. Do you like a particular pop song? Change one chord and you have a hip-hop song and a killing. The music "bed" is different. Then a rapper "raps" on it, thereby transforming it into a cutting-edge track. With the addition of some musical elements, such as strings, you have hip-hop. (Sometimes I think of the joke about ravioli as a metaphor for hip-hop. Two square noodles and a piece of cheese constitute no more than just that; twist three corners and you have two square noodles and a piece of cheese with three ends twisted. But twist the fourth corner, and voilà—ravioli!) Drake, and many other urban artists in recent years, have discovered the value of the mixtape. The appeal to the public is that these compilations of music are created by individuals who are not connected to the record company. Sometimes the mixers/DJs are not even known to the artists. Yet they constitute a valuable tool in addition to those described in chapter 9. But this time they are tools not of the label but of the team identified with the artist—even if the mixers are not officially associated with the artist. There are undoubtedly copyright infringement issues raised by these activities, but most artists suffer the impingement into their area of artistic control on the theory that cutting edge, new, and different outweigh the technical arguments offered by their labels or lawyers. Many artists support a variety of mixtapes being introduced into the marketplace even before the artist's official album is released. The tease alone serves an important promotional purpose.

CAREER CEILINGS

With a few notable exceptions, a successful career is as difficult to achieve in the hip-hop world as in other mainstream genres. The audience for *all* pop genres is very fickle. Its fondness for a particular artist or "look" or "sound" can die as rapidly as it was born. And, as noted above, tour success has in the past eluded most rap/hip-hop artists. Again, there are exceptions, and the phenomenal touring success of hip-hoppers starting with 1999's Hard Knock Life Tour and the Up in Smoke Tour of 2000 promises venues and outlets not only for known acts, but for up-and-comers as well. It is, after all, show business, and the more that the proponents of the genre get the chance to communicate their art to others, the more it will be fine-tuned to fit the needs of the population and the more it will reflect the population's own needs, wishes, desires, and fears—a nice return to the point in the circle from which it began.

HIP-HOP AND POP CULTURE

Hip-hop musicians are idols and role models not just to black kids, but to white suburban rich kids as well. Identifying with hip-hop raps is the ultimate rebellion for white kids.

Some hip-hop romanticizes killing, drugs, misogyny, and bravado, in many cases using language of jarring crudeness. Yet hip-hop, as an expression of rebellion and the conflict between generations, is no different from a lot of popular music from the 1950s or 1960s or just about any other decade before or since. The manner of expression has changed, and the force from which the expression gains its energy certainly has different origins, but the melding of music, yearning, anger, and politics reflecting cultures, trends, and styles spins a common web. Certainly the birthplace of hip-hop and rap was the ghettos and projects of urban centers in America. But the characteristic rawness of this genre is not unique to the inner cities.

Almost twenty years ago, the (white) country singer David Allan Coe recorded two underground albums of songs that are considered to be among the most racist, misogynist, homophobic, and obscene songs ever recorded. Ironically, at the beginning of the new century, the white rapper, Kid Rock, invited Coe to open his acts for him. Coe's music has taken on a new life through the Internet and through the welcome that the new "interpreters of the culture" have given it.

Currently, in the truest tradition of the music business, hip-hop artists *and* their audiences are beginning to embrace all sexes and all cultures. Women artists, for example, have quite publicly and vocally urged a diminution and even a cessation of misogynist features of hip-hop. It is no coincidence that Destiny's Child, a female group, was *VIBE's* Artist of the Year in 2000 or that Beverly D'Angelo has risen in profile to present the women's response to the "booty shaking" that is rampant in male hip-hop. By 2005, *VIBE* was honoring Mariah Carey for her "Emancipation of Mimi."

BUSINESS MANAGEMENT AND THE MANAGEMENT OF BUSINESS

Rappers and hip-hop artists in general are no different from other artists in that they hardly ever listen to their business managers. This behavior creates an environment where it is simply a matter of time before taxes and debts will overwhelm the artist. There is little that a business manager can do to help the artist avoid judgment day; the bankruptcy laws are around, but they have been seriously diluted. Further, declaring bankruptcy is not a panacea.

If an artist can convince the bankruptcy court to allow him or her to walk away from most debts, the consequences will be felt for many years to come—certainly for the remainder of the artist's "youth." And hip-hop artists who play in the financial world must wake up to the fact that the game has rules and that there may be tragic consequences if they don't take steps to guard against the day when their music-generated earnings begin to dry up.

Rappers, even more perhaps than their counterparts in other genres, must pay attention to their financial security. Often they do not have family resources to fall back on. Lacking a college degree, they may not be able to make a good living outside of their chosen profession. Their music is less likely than mainstream music to be picked up for Broadway shows, for film and television soundtracks, or for commercials, etc., as more mainstream music is. Finally, the incredible speed with which their genre evolves breeds obsolescence.

One money-earning solution for many rappers, MCs, and hip-hop artists who have signed exclusive agreements to provide services either to a record company or to a particular project is to do side projects without the knowledge of their record company (or the business manager or the lawyer for that matter). The financial equivalent of sneaking a smoke or hiding from Mom may or may not catch up with them, but there are a lot of more traditional, and safer, ways to accumulate capital and maximize earnings.

Whether you are a Wall Street wunderkind, a young classical pianist, or a band of underage rockers—or rappers—you need advice from trustworthy representatives: lawyer, business manager, personal manager, whomever. It is these (mostly state-licensed) professionals who are qualified to provide guidance and to protect you from grasping fans, producers, record companies, and, yes, even family members. Hip-hop artists and rappers are no different, yet it takes a special professional to understand these young people and care about what they have to say. Fortunately, there are a growing number of lawyers and business managers who practice in this field and who believe that to represent hip-hop artists is no less a privilege than to represent any young creative person.

THE CHANGING IMAGE

Across the spectrum of hip-hop artists, managers, and producers, a number of individuals have achieved considerable financial success, an ascendancy that automatically makes them once removed from the world of the streets. Others have deliberately turned away from the violent, antisocial, "thug" image cultivated by some of the genre's most visible icons. Before Destiny's Child broke up, they were actively involved in raising awareness and funds for the National Alliance of Breast Cancer Organizations and the National Breast Cancer Coalition, and I understand that their members retain their commitment to this cause. Common, a Chicago-based hip-hop musician, has set up a foundation, the Common Ground Foundation, which raises money to be spent on such things as instruments, travel, computers, and post–high school tuition for low-income youths. Talib Kweli rejects the hustler/thug image out of hand. He uses the medium—which he calls "alternative music"— to entertain, yes, but he also uses it to "bring information and to promote literacy and multicultural education in Brooklyn." This changing image is not, unfortunately, universal. According to rapper-turned-activist Chuck D, "Hip-hop is caught up in a time where one's worth and status are contingent upon money rather than a genuine love for the music. The degradation of women and the ubiquitous use of the N-word are not what . . . Afrika Bambaata, Kool Herc, Grandmaster Flash, and all the pioneers started way back."

CONTRACTUAL ISSUES

Hip-hop artists, and their representatives, must be cognizant of specific contract issues that exist only in the hip-hop field. For example, while most rock groups are self-contained and are largely, if not totally, responsible for writing the songs they perform and record, in the hip-hop world, it is equally customary for most, if not all, of the songs to be written and controlled by others, in whole or in part. In the urban world, therefore, one needs what is known as "outside protection"—that is, protection from the contributors of the songs so that they will (1) license the first use of the songs in the first place, and (2) license them at a rate and according to the provisions of the artist's controlled compositions clause in the artist's agreement with his or her production company or record company. Failure to agree on splits (see chapter 14) in time for royalty accounting periods—or ever—will merely result in the record company's holding all royalties. If you don't think that this is significant, at one point, the US record companies were holding over $300 million in royalties due music publishers and their writers because either they were not advised with finality as to what the agreed splits were, or because they had no recent address to which royalty statements and payments were to be sent.

Guest Artists

Remember that when a record company brings in a guest artist who has to write his or her own verse, the principal artist's record company cannot give the guest artist–writer a part of the copyright—only the original authors or their publishers (if they are signed to publishers) can. However, since the principal artist's record company has a stake in the result, the guest artist can make this a condition of his or her agreement to participate. One might think that when an artist (or record company) calls in a guest artist, this issue will have been dealt with. Often, however, it has not. Such issues are often worked out over time, but the legal fees (for all of the parties) can be enormous. It has become customary in recent years for everyone involved in the production of a song to share in the authorship credit (if not the actual authorship) in some proportion depending on the power of the respective parties. When an artist is "featured" on another artist's record, even when one is significantly more important than the other, it has also become customary that the two artists and their record labels merely "swap" services with each other, often without a royalty being paid to the artist providing the services. The mutuality of spirit is welcome in a world which is often characterized by adversity.

Remixes

Another situation often arises now that remixes have become big-ticket items that record companies have found can increase record sales. The producer of the remix receives a fee, but not always a royalty. The theory is that the producer has entered the situation too late in the game to claim a "producer" share in the income of the record. This is wrong, but it is the custom. Again, this issue should be dealt with in advance if the remix producer is going to have a chance for success in seeking a royalty participation. The producer who waits will run into enormous resistance and expense—and, most likely, will fail.

Interludes: Their Impact on Mechanical Royalties

Most hip-hop albums are full of what are known as *interludes* or *ad-libs* (usually described as musical elements one or two minutes in length or less), and record companies simply will not pay for them. If a record contains five to ten of these interludes, the costs of obtaining the rights from third parties will reduce the artist's royalties considerably, and may even absorb all or a major part of them. Even if the producer, and not the artist, is responsible for the interludes, the artist—however excellent he or she feels the choices may be—will ultimately pay for them. Or, if the party contracting with the record company is a production company rather than the artist, the production company will also be hit with the cost of incorporating these interludes in the recording. Whether it is the production company or the artist who pays, there are only two ways to avoid this debacle: (1) raise the mechanical cap, or (2) cut way back on the number of interludes. Otherwise, what appears to be merely a mechanical royalty issue will end by actually reducing the artist's (or production company's) royalties payable on the sale of records containing those interludes. If you don't resolve this issue at the contract-negotiation stage, your royalty flow will be littered with land mines that may blow up in your face.

THE RAP COALITION: SELF-HELP EXEMPLIFIED

Go to the website www.wendyday.com and surf the various websites recommended on the site . This accumulation of sites (crossed with Ms. Day's original, www.rapcoalition. org , provides something that rockers and blues artists of the past were never offered: the information necessary to control their own fate! The not-for-profit organization, Rap Coalition (www.rapcoalition.org) provides help to fledgling artists (and those not-so-fledgling artists who did not do it right the first time) in the form of management guidance and legal services. Here is an extraordinary example of how the Internet is helping not only to disseminate useful information, but also to break the walls of secrecy that have for so long and so effectively kept doors from opening for young artists. And, although Dr. Dre and Eminem have publicly questioned the value and impact of the Internet, they, too, are benefiting from Internet exposure.

It should be noted that these sites, as well as others that exist to help artists maximize their chances of success, have a bit (okay—more than a bit) of a bias against record companies which can skew the credibility of the advice. However, as I have pointed out more than once, record companies serve a genuine and often underappreciated purpose in developing the careers and selling the records of artists and so, as with any resource, one must weigh the information carefully in order to make an informed decision.

For example, one of the sites, which does some calculations on the bottom-line "mathematics" of the record business, concludes that even an artist whose records may have sold hundreds of thousands of copies is working for about $12 per hour. Even if this is not an accurate figure, it is undeniable that, given the long hours performing musicians put in, the average per-hour return is quite low. However, it is my hope that artists and their managers and other representatives will be able to use this information to enhance their negotiating capabilities rather than to give up entirely on an industry that, like it or not, has enormous global strengths and value.

In any event, owning one's own record company or Internet distribution service is not going to be everyone's cup of tea. The wheel has been invented before, and probably better than most of us can reinvent it today. Each artist is different, and each artist has a distinct milieu and environment, so no one formula for whether to leave the traditional system or embrace it will work for everyone. Nevertheless, the information and advice provided by the Rap Coalition is well worth considering. This organization has established a division—Visionary Management—whose sole purpose is to act as a school for managers. In chapter 5, Personal Management, I noted that managers, unlike other professionals such as accountants and lawyers, are not trained by means of any consistent, approved, and universally respected school or method. The Rap Coalition and its progeny may prove to be an exception. Let's hope so. As they say on their website, "We believe it's time for hip-hop artists to take control of their own art form!" This is a truly out-of-the-ordinary organization whose sole purpose is to help hip-hop artists to control their own fate.

HIP-HOP RULES

Never, at least since Ira Gershwin, have words in song meant so much. Rap, after all, is talk. Ja Rule, a well-known rapper, says, "What else can you rap about [than] sex, violence, and materialism." Apparently a lot. Lyrics have taken on a much more vital level of meaning. Ira would be envious.

But hip-hop is not really the sea change from rock and roll that it appears at first glance. Rebellion, women, the good life, the hard-knock life—these are still the staples of the music. Only the environment is new. And the expression.

Given all of the congressional criticism of hip-hop, and the willingness of the major record companies to cave in to this criticism by censoring the music or placing warning notices on labels, it is actually quite remarkable that so much of what is expressed actually gets disseminated—whether through broadcast, podcast, traditional record channels, or downloads, which remain largely unlicensed and uncontrolled. While there remains a tendency for the majors to go with the sure thing, change is possible and indeed change occurs on a continuum that would perhaps shock our founding fathers. Mos Def, commenting on the corporate music industry's practice of promoting the same overexposed, clichéd product, said, "If all you make available is acorns, people will eat the f*&$*n' acorns." Yet whenever the art of hip-hop—which after all is a reflection of our culture—is able to offer alternatives to the corporate-sponsored musical pabulum that dominates the charts, everyone wins.

Electronic Dance Music

Electronic dance music (EDM) is the latest "style" to break through what, during the early part of the 21st century, had become a rather stifling and rigid creative marketplace, with urban music (mostly hip-hop) holding on to its role as having replaced rock and roll in the consciousness of the youth of the world. Technically, EDM is not actually a genre, but a name given to a generic group of several music genres (and subgenres) such as house, techno, and many others. It is concocted in a studio, but presented via DJs live in venues like any other music, although it is most effective when presented at festivals and in clubs.

EDM evolved by focusing on the live DJ presentation. Add dance and you have a phenomenon. The physicality of the EDM audience (who actually form an essential element of the genre) is breathtaking. It is inexpensive to present, inexpensive to tour, and inexpensive to enter for enterprising DJs. The instrumentation of EDM emphasizes drums (kick and snare) and bass, mixed into recordings by the genre's producers (such as David Guetta, Swedish House Mafia, Skrillex, and others). EDM itself began to break down into subgenres, such as dubstep. Dubstep, which dates to the late 1990s, although given its name around 2003, features dark, instrumental dub remixes of recorded tracks (especially garage tracks) that would otherwise not have seen the light of day. As with many experimental musical structures, dubstep eventually became less dark, and more commercial, over time and furthered the ascendency of producers over artists. The producers are the "authors." Are we to expect Bob Dylan to incorporate the wobble bass in his next iteration?

Ironically, it was just as this new form of engagement with the youngish audience began to take hold in the late 1990s (Google Daft Punk to observe its beginnings) that physical record sales (vs. digital downloads and rentals via subscription) began to slip dramatically. The more that EDM succeeds in replacing rock and roll and other genres, the greater its impact on the record industry which will be, of course, still depends largely on the sale of physical units.

One of the more unusual acronyms arising out of the EDM genre is BPM. This stands for "beats per minute" and refers simply to the number of beats in a recording that appear in the course of a minute. It is almost a photograph of the tempo of a song, and it has two effects on the genre: first, it actually describes the energy emitting from a track in terms that people can read rather than feel—thereby providing them with a metric by which to choose recordings that appeal to their desire for fast tempos; second, it is one more means by which data can be communicated to a third party—for example to a music supervisor looking for a track to promote to a third party seeking to synchronize a recording with its film, TV episode, or commercial. The greater the BPM, the more one could say it represents something that can grab a current audience's attention. When a synchronization department submits a track for consideration, it must provide a lot of data such as title, authors, Performing Rights Organizations (PROs) of the authors, publisher, timing, etc. BPM is yet another piece of data that has relevance. Not only does it describe the energy of a song in terms that can be understood without listening to it, it also helps to identify it when streamed. The unique BPM of a recorded track, then, can be used almost as a fingerprint.

19 · CLASSICAL MUSIC
Dead or Alive?

Classical music is the kind we keep thinking will turn into a tune.
—KIM HUBBARD

The difference between a violin and a viola is that a viola burns longer.
—VICTOR BORGE

What is classical music? Of course music composed during the so-called classical period, from the mid-17th to the early 18th century, especially the classical symphony and concerto, qualifies. But are there any characteristics that apply solely to classical music, but not to the so-called "popular" genres, including country, pop, rock, and rap? One possibility is structure—formal structure that goes beyond melody and beat, incorporating complex orchestration, exposition of theme, development, and recapitulation. Perhaps the best way to define it is explain what it is not. It is not mainstream; it is not something that spontaneously touches a large percentage of all listening populations. It is for specialty, though eminently varied, tastes; it appeals to knowledgeable buyers and listeners who want to have a profound experience of the kind that they do not find in what we call popular music; it is remarkably resilient and takes on different meaning in the hands of different interpreters (which, of course, also fits jazz; so be it).

Whatever it is—and I submit that we know it when we hear it—it is in trouble.

A LITTLE HISTORY

The classical record business was wildly profitable from 1980 onward for many years. Profitability on sales pushed the 30% level. On $100 million in sales at one company, the pretax profit was $27 million. Yet by the 1990s, under management that chose to apply popular music standards to classical music divisions, things went south fast. The few record companies that continued to invest in new classical artists and young composers had precious few outlets to bring these artists and composers' works to the attention of potential record buyers. *The Ed Sullivan Show*, which made household names of Ezio Pinza, Renata Tebaldi, Robert Merrill, Risa Stevens, Anna Moffo, and Mario Lanza during the '50s and '60s, was long gone, and nothing had replaced it. The most recent opportunity for a classical opera singer to "hit it out of the park" came in the 2014 Super Bowl when Renée Fleming did just that—reaching more people in under three minutes than Ed Sullivan did in his entire career. Watch it here: https://www.youtube.com/watch?v=7xuQxuE8SYk. Then, in the second decade of the 21st century, what happened? TV competitions such as *American Idol* and especially *America's Got Talent* began to feature opera singers; while the contestants have obviously not achieved any high degree of success, at least they have the opportunity to showcase their talents, and to introduce opera to the viewers who otherwise would be completely ignorant of the appeal of the genre.

For decades, while even as record labels supported the genre, most senior executives knew (and cared) nothing about classical music, its heritage, or its extraordinary worldwide market potential. They were of the mind that this genre could not possibly earn enough by way of sales to recoup their companies' investment. They saw their company's involvement largely as a charitable contribution to culture. But then, the numbers crunchers put a stop to what they perceived to be the excesses of prior generations. The major labels then made a fundamental and disastrous decision to look at themselves not as libraries (catalogues) or nurturers of great artists, but as large-scale bookstores. Once they began to demand that Beethoven sell the way James Patterson novels or *The DaVinci Code* sell, and that their recordings be judged on the number of units sold, they found that they could never meet their goals. So the companies gave up. BMG Classics, successor to RCA Red Seal, one of the diamonds of the lot, had essentially dismantled itself by the late '90s. EMI Classics was spun off from EMI when it was acquired by Universal. It was an albatross that they somehow convinced Warner Records to acquire.

By 2010, the operations of Universal Classics and Sony Classical were significantly curtailed, although the latter has been reborn with much smaller expectations, even as it revived the venerable name "Columbia Masterworks." Today Masterworks labels can be found on "crossover" records that try to simulate the emotive power of classical music, but rarely do.

DEMISE OR REJUVENATION?

Much has been written about the demise of the classical music industry. Companies are shutting down; artists are being dropped in huge numbers from every classical record label, and sales that were so promising upon the introduction of the CD have plummeted. Even though the proposed AOL/Time-Warner/EMI, and BMG/EMI mergers never took place, the fears of the classical music community were nevertheless realized in 2001 when Warner closed down two of its three classical record labels, Erato and Teldec, and EMI essentially shut down its US classical division, Angel Records. In the course of acquiring EMI Records in 2012, Universal agreed to "discard" some elements of the EMI assets, starting with EMI Classics. (At least they consider them "assets.") While some new labels that record and release classical records have appeared in recent years, these records are not offered to the public in significant quantities. One unforgettable SoundScan snapshot of a particular label's sales history revealed that only 13 copies out of the label's entire year 2000 offering (25 or so releases) were sold in the United States in the first seven months of that year. (They shipped 400 worldwide just to fill the distribution pipeline, but no one was buying. No one.)

We have also seen the end of the exclusive recording agreements for each and every one of the world's greatest orchestras, including one of the last holdouts, the renowned Berlin Philharmonic.

Music ensembles (from trios to quartets, quintets, and chamber and symphony orchestras) are going to have to make their own recordings if they want to preserve their legacies and enjoy the recorded fruits of their labors. They can no longer rely on the record companies to provide these archives. Even the New York Philharmonic is selling archival records that they have long kept in the vaults (for example, the Bernstein and the Mahler collections), as are the great London orchestras. Indeed, the London Symphony Orchestra has sought to fill the void by initiating its own recordings—and guess what? Its first, *Les Troyens*, won several 2002 GRAMMY Awards, including Best Classical Album and Best Opera Recording.

Artists of worldwide stature have gone begging, not just for an exclusive record company relationship—but even for a single record! Even if they or their patrons find the money to pay for the cost of the orchestra, the recording venue, the engineer, the conductor, and the producer, they still have to find a record company that has the budget to pay for the artwork and the manufacture and release of the record. In most cases, finding such a company is impossible, so they must reluctantly decline the kind offer of backing.

At the same time that the majors have all but abandoned the classical music genre as a viable commercial proposition, the number of staff members who specialized in classical music, particularly those who were the bearers of the "institutional memories," has declined drastically. Some have died; others have retired, not to be replaced; still others have been laid off. What this does to a record company's intangible assets is incalculable. The abandonment of classical music programs by the major record labels comes, ironically, at a time when more creative marketing—via reissues or compilations and use of the Internet—(think streaming) can generate substantial income while at the same time incurring no additional production expenses and resulting in records bearing minuscule royalty obligations, compared to the standards of today. Yet those who know the catalogues best have, one by one, left the companies whose legacies they are best able to exploit.

The closing of major retail outlets, such as Tower Records and Virgin, is putting additional nails in the classical music coffin. Now Tower Records is essentially out of business, as is HMV, both major purveyors of classical CDs in the last quarter-century.

Yet there is some good news. Record labels such as Sony Masterworks, noted above, is substantially fueled by soundtrack recordings such as *Titanic* and *Star Wars*, the phenomenal success of which so enriched the label's budget that it could invest in the development of Tan Dun (who, in addition to his impressive symphonic and choral works, made a mark in his soundtrack for the film *Crouching Tiger, Hidden Dragon*) and the extremely successful Joshua Bell's *West Side Story*—with a home video, no less. And Peter Gelb, the former head of Sony Classical, invested a considerable amount in commissioning new works by composers such as Tan Dun and John Corigliano. Similarly, individual instrumentalists and music publishing companies are initiating commissions across the board that are feeding programs of symphony orchestras and individual instramentalists' recitals. With present-day recording and notating capabilities, there is almost an underground industry developing which is generating ever-newer works for performance. Hilary Hahn, the violinist, felt that too many commissions were being granted for large orchestral works or operas, but not for shorter works such as encores. She commissioned twenty-seven composers to write encores, then performed them worldwide, recorded them for Deutsche Grammophon rather than drag out one more classical encore (Bach, anyone?) that had been recorded and performed endlessly by herself and every other concert violinist for time immemorial. She then caused the new works to be eventually published digitally and physically. (How else can violinists of all levels access these works so that they themselves can perform them or learn them in the course of their development?) "In 27 Pieces: The Hilary Hahn Encores" are a framework for others similarly inclined. No wonder the innovative ones rise to the top of public awareness. And now, her twenty-seven composers have that opportunity, too.

A Gift from the American Federation of Musicians

Most of the cost of recording new classical works is the orchestral cost. After about 1960, American record companies found it economically more feasible to record outside of the United States, whenever possible, without using members of the American Federation of

Musicians (AF of M), the musicians' union. Orchestras in the United States suffered as European orchestras—particularly, after 1990, eastern European orchestras—flourished.

The AF of M has made great strides in recent years to accommodate orchestras that wish to return to the world of recording. It now offers to many North American orchestras special rates for live recordings, the right to own them, and an opportunity to participate in a revenue-sharing plan on the sale of both physical media and digital downloads. It also offers special terms to permit US record companies to release on soundtrack recordings the soundtracks of motion pictures, the music of which has been recorded by American orchestras; an agreement according to which if the budget is under $99,000, the session fees will be considerably less than they would be if the budget were higher; and a deal according to which if the record company agrees to limit pressings to 10,000 copies, the session fees will be even lower. This relief from the most costly portion of a recording budget not only permits record companies, and artists who raise their own funding, to actually record works that they could only dream of before, but also encourages them to use American musicians rather than foreign orchestras.

Another promising development for world-class orchestras is the new Universal Music Group (UMG) initiative to work in partnership with orchestras to produce live (read: cheaper) downloadable concerts over the Internet. In June of 2005, there were 1.5 million downloads of free Beethoven symphonies offered by BBC Radio 3. In March, 2006, the New York Philharmonic concert of Mozart's last three symphonies was similarly, and successfully, offered for downloads. The participants were shocked at the size of the audience for classical music. Where have they been all these years? The days of sending artists to eastern Europe solely for cost benefits may soon be behind us.

The Star Factor

Another reason why classical record sales have plummeted in recent years may be that there are so few overpowering musical personalities such as Vladimir Horowitz, Leonard Bernstein, and Maria Callas. There are very few classical artists whose records consumers "must have." Yet there *is* an audience out there. Look what happened with The Three Tenors' records. Pavarotti, Carreras, Domingo, Yo-Yo Ma, now the violinist Mark O'Connor, the Chinese pianist Lang Lang, and the superb sopranos Renée Fleming and Anna Netrebko—there is still a great deal of big-time talent out there. But try to name a couple of instrumentalists today who have a similar hold on the public's imagination—or a conductor who is making magic with his orchestra. Perhaps violinists Joshua Bell, Sarah Chang, Hilary Hahn, or Anne-Sophie Mutter, pianists Yuja Wang or Evgeny Kissin, or Simon Rattle, long-term conductor of the pre-eminent Berlin Philharmonic. But names of "stars" do not come easily to mind these days. How did this happen? The demise of popular TV outlets and the ever-increasing competition from other media are some of the reasons. Some say that current performers tend not to be as idiosyncratic as the old guard. For example, musicians today are much more respectful of the printed text, and the original-instruments movement has made everyone more conservative and historically conscious—a sort of musical "politically correct" stance, according to Steven Blier, co–music director of the New York Festival of Song. This movement showcases musical instruments (or replicas) and techniques of earlier eras. The music is stylistically as well as technically similar to the music played in the era—often the Baroque period—in which the musical work was originally introduced.

But there are other things at work here: Publicists and press agents who create opportunities for some and cut off opportunities for others; being in the "in" group in this extremely tight-knit and competitive world. Unfortunately, the latter example is a recurring theme among musicians and conductors, and they do not really know any way out. Christoph Eschenbach is a magical musician but has not the profile of Muti or Abbado or Bernstein. Why not?

The Relevancy Factor

One often-asked question is why there is a need for any of the world's great (let alone near-great or mediocre) artists to record one more time the world's classics, all of which have been recorded *ad nauseum*. Who would want to pay today's $16.98 price (which inevitably must be charged) for an unknown pianist interpreting Chopin's *Nocturnes* when you can get Arthur Rubinstein's renowned recordings for far less. The latest *Tristan und Isolde* two-CD set released by EMI in 2005, which is the last studio-made operatic recording made by that company, retails for more than $50.00. While it is receiving rave reviews, it remains a bit pricey for most people. (As we shall see, some unknown pianists' recordings—of almost the entire classical repertoire—are now widely available on budget labels for $6.99.)

Why bother, then, to examine the secrets of an industry that has become all but irrelevant? Simple. It *needn't be* irrelevant. Consider the following:

- In 2005, sales of classical CDs were down 7% from 2004—21% since 2000. Since then things have gotten only worse, although streaming income and access to neighboring rights income have begun to take hold.

- Millions of classical music enthusiasts from all over the world visit the shrines of music annually to pay homage to its interpreters: from Carnegie Hall to Lincoln Center; from Tanglewood and Chicago's Ravinia Festival to concerts in Central Park; from the Connecticut Early Music Festivals, in southeastern Connecticut, to Wolftrap, in Virginia.

- According to *New York Times* music critic Allan Kozinn, "Concert halls are sprouting like mushrooms." New symphony halls have opened in Sonoma, Miami, Nashville, and Costa Mesa, California, and Toronto has recently opened a new opera house.

- According to the American Symphony Orchestra League, 1,800 orchestras in the United States give about 36,000 concerts a year, 30% percent more than in 1994.

- Not only are the numbers of concertgoers growing, they are getting younger: witness the attendees at the Los Angeles Philharmonic's Minimalist Jukebox festival and New York's Bang on a Can Festival.

- Bon Jovi's keyboard player is actually conservatory-trained, at Juilliard. Believe it or not, this is not unusual. Two of The Cars (Greg Hawkes and Elliot Easton) attended Boston's Berklee School of Music, which, while primarily a jazz and pop conservatory, offers respected programs in the classical field as well in conjunction with the Boston Conservatory of Music.

- A surprisingly large percentage of digital print distribution (some estimates are as high as 50%) consists of classical music.

- More than 40 million Americans study a classical instrument each year. There are 3½ million keyboards sold each year in the United States.

- The American Symphony Orchestra League (ASOL) has announced that its subscription audiences for classical music are getting younger—and larger.

- In 2005, public attendance in the United States for orchestra concerts was over 34 million, up 35% from 1990.

- Classical music sales have almost regained their historical 3% to 3.5% market share of total record sales inclusive of digital downloads of classical albums, which increased by 94% in 2005.

- In December 2004, 47% of the television-viewing audience in Germany (14 million listeners) tuned in during prime time to hear the great Russian soprano opera singer Anna Netrebko.

- According to the American Symphony Orchestra League, the number of classical music concerts is actually increasing—mostly via community or school concerts, park concerts, and even concerts featuring orchestral renditions of music with appeal to a young demographic: music from *Star Wars*, music from *The Lord of the Rings*, and even music inspired by the video game *Final Fantasy*. (The video game garnered seven sold-out concerts in the United States and Japan in 2005. The only advertising consisted of email blasts to the 2.5 million fans of the game.)

THE METROPOLITAN OPERA

The great achievements of Peter Gelb, now the general manager of the Metropolitan Opera in New York, deserve special mention. Obviously, the Met cannot tour like a pop or rock group—or even a musical—can. Mr. Gelb, fresh from his successes at Sony Classical where he joined audio and video performances to great acclaim, established a few years ago the *Live in HD* transmissions of live Saturday matinee performances at the Met, which are being delivered into movie theaters throughout the world. While other arts institutions, particularly classical ones, have begun to copy this model, the MET's success is noteworthy.

One reality of the opera world is that the cost of presenting an opera is mind boggling. Not only can it cost millions of dollars to mount a new production, but even to raise the curtain on an evening's performance can burden an opera company with an astronomical cost approaching $1 million—each night! Opera companies in countries outside of the United States enjoy subsidies from their governments that are truly amazing. For example, France subsidies the Paris Opera's $263 million annual budget with $133 million each year. In contrast, the United States provides funding of about $490,000 toward the Met Opera's annual budget of $327 million!

With a budget of that size, it is fortuitous that the Met is enjoying new sources of revenue never imagined only a few years ago. In 2015, the HD broadcasts were delivered into 1,900 theaters in 64 countries around the globe. There are usually twelve cameras in the house, not the customary few which were the mark of other *Live at the Met* broadcasts delivered only in the US via PBS. In 2010, *Carmen* was seen by 330,000 people. All paid about $25 for the experience, which included produced intermission features such as scenes backstage as the huge sets were being pulled down and set up for the next act. While the audience members per season at the Met Opera House itself amounted to 700,000 (approximately 92% capacity) in 2010, 3 million additional viewers attended the live broadcasts, which have reached 11 million tickets sold since the program launched in 2006. This represents a 375% audience increase with no added seats. Gelb estimates that 20% of the live HD audience had never seen an opera before. Each time they do now, the experience amplifies their interest to see more.

The HD live opera presentations begin at 10:00 a.m. on the West Coast, 1:00 p.m. on the East Coast, 6:00 p.m. in England, 7:00 p.m. in Europe, etc. Breakfast and a fulfilling morning in California; dinner and opera in France. And the Met Opera everywhere. What's not to like? I know people in LA who "go to the opera" with a friend in New York City, one in Madrid, and one in Stockholm. And they text or use social media during the intermissions to share their experiences. The world is definitely getting smaller.

Another benefit of this extraordinary program is the creation of intellectual property content and the opportunity to showcase new singers who eventually, and much faster presumably, will become household names. As to the content, the performances can be replicated on DVD's or even shown on television in areas such as Asia and Australia where live attendance is not really practical.

AN ESSENTIAL FOR SUCCESS: SPIRITUALITY

There is a long-perceived need in human beings for a connection to things spiritual. In most societies, this connection is achieved, in part, through music. We are in an age in which spirituality and an effort to come to grips with the nonmaterial aspects of our civilization are important aspects of our daily life, and entire populations are searching for ways to manifest this vision and to experience this way of looking at the world. They are finding it in literature, religion, film, the outdoors, and, of course, in music. However, for some reason (and this time I cannot easily tell you "what they'll never tell you"), the "nourishment" people are searching for, at least in the world of music, is not so easily found. Whether they do not know where to look for it, or do not find it in records or live performances, or simply do not have the ability to decompress from the pressures of 21st-century society is not clear.

This failure is not the fault of Brahms.

In the concert area, most live performances are merely a reiteration of what has been done previously. The creative spark that recasts a work for a new generation is too often missing. You often come out of a concert wondering why you have gone.

When the 150 or so leaders of the members of the United Nations gathered in New York for the UN's fiftieth anniversary in October 1995, the New York Philharmonic "entertained" them with Beethoven's Ninth (Choral) Symphony. It was a concert remembered only for Mayor Guiliani's asking Yassir Arafat to leave the concert because of his aggressive past history in the Middle East. Everyone was checking their watches; the concert was not televised. Happily, it ended and everyone forgot it. Why? Because it had no meaning other than one more iteration of a familiar work. Sponsoring a big-deal event? How about the Ninth? In 2005, some 175 heads of state were back in New York City for the sixtieth anniversary of the United Nations. No one even bothered to present a gala concert. Then there is the Boston Symphony Orchestra's final concert each summer—year after year after year—at its summer home Tanglewood. How many times can they present the Ninth without the effect of minimizing its specialness? Sure, it is still as brilliant a work as ever, and the performance gives Tanglewood the opportunity to showcase its renowned youth chorus, but enough already. How about the Berlioz or Verdi *Requiem* next time?

Classical concerts featuring great works such as the Beethovan Ninth do not have to be uninspiring. Rarely was this great symphony's resplendent spirituality ever evinced more effectively than when Leonard Bernstein conducted it in 1989 at the recently dismantled wall in Berlin. Televised, newsworthy, an absolutely memorable event—not just for the million or so Germans who were there, but also for those additional millions around the world who did, and will for all time, experience it on video and on CD.

We do not have to go back to the 19th century to find music that in its ineffable way can touch the soul. Nonesuch Records' mid-1990s release of Henryk Górecki's 1963 Symphony No. 3 (in its third recording—not even its premier release) sold more than a million copies. This is a Polish symphony about a very sad and troubling subject—World War II—with a soprano performance in the Polish language and a symphony orchestra and conductor not among the most famous or sought-after in the marketplace. Yet it had an extraordinary appeal. A memorable performance by the great soprano Dawn Upshaw didn't hurt. Was it a fluke? Certainly, records do not sell themselves. In the Górecki case, the hook was the use of a portion of the score in the famous crash scene from the motion picture *Fearless*. Word of mouth boosted US sales; once people were connected to this symphony's wordless message, sales took off worldwide.

The first Three Tenors' album—recorded at the Baths of Caracalla in Italy on the occasion of the World Cup Soccer finals—sold 3 million units in the United States. And let's not forget Andrea Bocelli, who, after a 1997 PBS special, grabbed the imagination of US consumers just as he had won over the hearts and souls of Europeans over the prior two years. Let's also not forget that companies fought each other in almost embarrassing ways to grab the follow-up records of The Three Tenors, but the second didn't do as well as the first, nor did the third do as well as the second. There is also the lesson of *Chant*, the bizarre recording of Spanish monks that sold several million copies, beginning in Europe in the early 1990s and spreading to the United States. The lucky record company (EMI—again) began spending its windfall profits on other artists and other projects, as though the success that was experienced with the *Chant* recording was going to replicate itself over and over again. This "brilliant" reasoning almost bankrupted EMI's US classical division, Angel Records.

Some blame conservatory education, or the lack of it, on the blandness of instrumentalists' performances. I suppose it has always been our nature to idealize past styles and artists and to find fault with the new. There are so many competitors for so few places that young musicians are unreasonably forced into trying to win auditions by replicating an acceptable, renowned rendition of a work. Individuality and innovation are not, for them, a goal, but a distraction and a sure way to lose the audition. The absence of vitality is not theoretical; you can feel it when you hear it.

A fluke is only a fish. No way is it a harbinger of the future. Fortunately, the nonfluke examples of classical recordings that have made it big—almost always helped along by artists like The Three Tenors, Kiri Te Kanawa, and Renée Fleming who have found ways to distinguish themselves from the ordinary—are numerous. No, the classical music industry has not drowned. It is still swimming, if in fairly deep water.

NEW LIFE FOR AN OLD GENRE

It is important for anyone reading this chapter to understand that much of what has been written before in this book about royalties, music publishing, audits, management, investments, etc., is applicable to classical music, and to classical musicians and composers, as well. Indeed, a clear understanding of those issues previously discussed may be essential to the survival of the classical music industry. All of the elements of the classical music industry—from the artists to the record companies, from the lawyers and the managers to the agents—must find a way to comprehend how the successful and financially sound portion of the popular music business works so that they can find a way to apply this knowledge to their own world.

Here is a telling example from my experience. I represented a classical music ensemble that performed mostly public domain material—you know, Bach, Telemann, Vivaldi. Yet all of their arrangements of public domain works were copyrightable. This particular group understood this on some level and registered their arrangements in the Copyright Office and with their performing rights society. But what they did not know (until I told them) is that the performance of their recordings outside of the United States and Canada generated significant performing rights income (collected automatically by the performing rights societies around the world) for which publishing companies would be willing to pay substantial advances, while at the same time administering their copyrights around the world and making sure that they were properly registered with foreign performing rights societies. As discussed in chapter 15, proper registration of a work is absolutely essential in order to collect both performance and mechanical income. In this case, the music publisher administrator also ensured that the mechanical royalties generated by the sale of this particular group's recordings overseas were properly credited, paid, and collected. Not only was the money accurately collected, but it was collected years earlier and at considerably less cost than it could have been had the group tried to take on this collection and administration function itself.

Arrangements like this are made every day in the popular music business, but those in the classical world have either no idea or very little understanding of the cash-generating options staring them in the face. A lot of money is involved. Maybe that is what scares them, since money is something that classical musicians and their representatives rarely expect to see from the exploitation of their careers outside of live performing. I have never encountered so many low self-images in any group of like-minded people in my life. Maybe it is because the piano teacher's ruler was wielded too often; maybe it is because, like all artists, they are dreamers, not strategizers; maybe it is because there are so many of them competing for the same work that the circumstances of their lives reduce their confidence and keep their spirits low. Whatever the reason, it is time to get over this resistance and to start using the tools and resources available to them.

THE CD ARRIVES: BOTH A BLESSING AND A CURSE

In the early 1980s, classical record companies finally got what they wanted and needed: a new technology. Not only did CD recordings sound fabulous, but they also were virtually indestructible, at least compared with the LP. The companies were able to mine their catalogues, reconfigure all of the recordings they had long ago forgotten they owned, and resell them all over again. How incredibly lucky they were!

But as with many good things, this one came with a curse. Once the (perceived as) limited classical music market absorbed all of these new releases, the consumers stopped buying! They had been given everything they could ever want. And they did not want anything else. What spiked at a 20% share of the total record market dropped to under 2.5%.

The Rise of the Budget Label

The budget labels have done fantastic things for a slew of new artists—most of whom are quite accomplished musicians. The revolution in the pricing and structures of classical recordings in recent years has had a tremendous impact on the availability and the reach of new recordings.

In order to induce sales, record companies have always priced long-released recordings or "lesser" artists' recordings lower than top-line recordings, but they considered those records low-end products. Then a brilliant German entrepreneur, Klaus Heymann, decided to glamorize so-called "budget records" by offering recording opportunities to heretofore unknown artists—from violinists to pianists, flutists to singers. His record company, NAXOS, is based in Hong Kong, and Mr. Heymann's extraordinary sensibility toward classical music and the effect it traditionally has on populations all over the world has combined with a sound sense of marketing and distribution in a way that changed the classical music business forever.

NAXOS, whose CDs retail for about $7, does not customarily pay royalties to the artists, but the artists get to record what they want, their records fill the record store bins (such as they are) and digital catalogues with all the new recordings the stores could possibly desire, and everyone wins. It is A&R without the A—almost totally repertoire based. The choice of music is a more salient marketing point than the name of the artist. If, at the same time, the artist can build on the record catalogue to enhance his or her celebrity, performing career, and finances, all the more power to the artist. (NAXOS, notoriously, neither signs major artists nor does a great deal to promote the artists it does sign.)

But, like the CD phenomenon, the budget juggernaut came with a curse. As it turns out, the budget-record scenario has also lowered the perceived value of classical records and has inadvertently damaged, perhaps forever, the willingness of consumers to pay a sufficiently high price to allow record companies and artists to produce truly memorable, even legendary, recordings. A standard cost for an orchestral recording of a world-class orchestra, such as the Philadelphia Orchestra or the Chicago Symphony, ranges from $150,000 to close to a quarter of a million dollars. Sad to say, symphonies of this caliber rarely record anything anymore.

This consequence of setting prices so low that the public perceives that the records are not worth very much may turn out to be the ultimate legacy of the budget label. In the popular music field, try to buy a Rolling Stones or a Pink Floyd record for less than full retail. Sure, there are sales, but the going price for these records, some of which are more than forty years old is still for sale at a suggested retail price of $18.98—three times *more* than they cost when they were originally released! But select a Eugene Ormandy, Philadelphia Orchestra recording, and you'll pay a whole lot less.

THE INTERNET: IS IT THE ANSWER?

Supply and Demand

It did not help record companies (or artists) when a late 1990s change in the tax law made it impossible to deduct the cost of retaining huge inventory stocks. The record companies can no longer keep the large back orders of inventory they used to maintain, and, accordingly, they do not. The customer who wants to back-order a work heard on the radio can forget about receiving it any time soon. But, as with so many clouds, there is a silver lining to this one as well: in this case, the internet.

There are fewer applications of the Internet more important than the ability to make available huge choices of music 24/7. The technology needed to provide for real-time downloading has already been invented, and baby steps toward distributing new and old music have already been taken—most notably by UMG, which has established Deutsche Grammaphon and Decca concerts: live, downloadable musical events. Many of the new classical music artists that are utilizing the Internet are paralleling what pop artists are doing—making available their music via downloads *and* hard copy delivery. MP3 files are just as applicable to classical music as to popular music, and the energy level and innovations of the classical music Internet enthusiasts are no less sophisticated than those one can see in the popular field. Further, one of the things that makes classical music exploitation on the Internet more feasible than exploitation of popular music is that, in many instances, the music performed is out of copyright. The time and cost of clearing rights is totally absent, making the process a whole lot more efficient. Of course the quality of the sound of MP3s is another story entirely. (See chapter 4, page 63)

Reaching the Surfers

Theoretically, the Internet is a place where independent artists and labels can have the same direct access to consumers as the big companies. Nevertheless, the lesser- known names all face an uphill battle to prove their bona fides. Known trademarks are still more valuable than unknown trademarks; an authorized Van Cliburn recording of the Tchaikovsky *First Piano Concerto* will usually have more resonance than one by an unknown performer.

Classical Music Websites

The almost absurd number of competent instrumentalists and singers who play and sing classical music in the world today makes it incumbent on all of them to find new and effective ways to reach an audience. The Internet affords this opportunity for the classical artist almost more than it does for the popular artist. Why? Because there are hardly any other outlets for the classical artist. Numerous music sites have sprung up featuring young artists, and it is only a matter of time before these artists figure out how to use Internet opportunities to create a kind of branding that will begin to exploit their names and talents.

There are also a large number of classical sheet music sites on the Web. Downloading this music is usually accomplished via PDF files—in other words, files that are like photographs. The downloading and printing of PDF files is fairly cumbersome and time-consuming, and not at all interactive, but the music is visible and readable nevertheless. Other sites, whose main target is the popular music buyer, have far more sophisticated options and some are interactive in that they will play back via your computer's sound card all or portions of a work and will change keys, repeat measures, etc. A client of mine, Musicnotes.com, is the industry leader.

The generic sites that are currently affording classical artists visibility are mostly sites whose financial models have not done well over the years, and it would be a shame for these sites to disappear just when they have begun to become "branded" (translate: "trusted"). You know what you get and you get what you ask for. We have to cross our fingers and hope that these few compatible sites remain available to surfers.

Promotion Via the Internet

One new option available to record companies in the digital world is Internet radio. By utilizing Internet radio sites to do what they have done since time immemorial, record companies can now extend their reach globally in an effort to promote artists. Cable television stations feature 24-hour classical music programs originating at Sirius XM and Music Choice, so they do not have to establish their own programming—or, worse, not program classical music at all. Coincidentally, this new opportunity can be used to introduce a broader population to new music, new artists, and new composers much more efficiently than ever before. Instant access (for a price) to these new works will make these artists and composers ever more valued in the marketplace, benefiting both the record company and the artists and generating an enhanced demand for the artists' performances. And soon, via webcasts, these live performances—which many feel present the ultimate musical experience—will be available via the Internet.

The Internet permits a multiplicity of performances on demand. It will not be long before every concert hall is wired for instant download or streaming. There are already dozens of performances currently available on a number of websites. These are not "cooked" performances, presented through the filter of an editorial process; that's why they are called "virtual." The Vienna Philharmonic customarily presents a concert on Saturday nights, yet its concert hall can seat only 2,400 people. How wonderful if those concerts could be experienced virtually live in one's home—with video. The popular music industry has www.allmusic.com, which makes available live performances, by mostly unsigned bands, in one of the wide variety of music clubs throughout the United States and around the world. Why not a similar approach to classical venues?

Many of the prayers and promises of the last dozen years to reignite interest in classical music have been answered, since various web services have been introduced to take advantage of the easy transmission of MP3 files. Apple introduced the iPod, which is now obsolete given the range of the iPhone and the iPad. But iTunes keeps growing, and the massive catalogues that used to be represented only on physical discs are now available for streaming and even by download. The world's music has been treated to the largest audience it ever had. In 2011, Spotify began operations in the United States. The large record companies, down to three upon Universal's absorption of EMI's wondrous cache of great recordings (particularly vocal recordings), have cooperated enormously with digital music services now that they have actually seen in dollars the results of the expansion of monetization in the digital space. While audiophiles may object to the sound quality which is something less than they enjoyed with LPs and CDs, the incredible choices made available by these music services more than balances their artistic concerns. Furthermore, as the *New York Times* pointed out, the metadata (search information such as artist, conductor, soloist) is much more complex, and poorly served by the industry, than that of pop recordings. One can only assume that now that the foundation and the receptivity of the content owners and users have begun to be established, and both sound quality technology and metadata are coming of age, revenue collections will improve as well.

THE ROLE OF RECORD COMPANIES

Whatever one's ideas about promoting artists, it is undeniable that unless the artists are brought to the attention of consumers, there is little likelihood of success. With (most) television opportunities a thing of the past, and motion picture biographies of instrumentalists and singers unlikely, the best way to do this for classical artists is through recording.

Besides, even if the artist is able to generate a semblance of a live performing career without records, the impermanence of a live concert itself dictates that only through recording can these works and these new artists be made to last. The record becomes a means of promotion rather than a product for sale.

Having a record deal has another crucial function—one that is understood by classical managers. Being with a major label is simply irreplaceable as a calling card. Classical managers will take an artist associated with a major label more seriously. Purchasers of talent will take the artist more seriously. Being signed to a major label really *can* contribute a lot to one's status and prestige and economic viability. If a major record label says, "This artist is important," then he or she *is* important. It becomes a self-fulfilling prophecy.

How should classical artists entice record companies to record them?

Although there is nothing wrong with the concept, it is really not necessary to record CDs entitled *Mozart for Cats* or *Songs Your Russian Grandfather Sang While Hoeing the Steppes*. The marketplace is more flexible than that.

The disparity between the appeal of the known and the appeal of the unknown, which is endemic in all fields of entertainment, will require artists to find creative ways to generate interest in their work. A few years ago, the conductor Gilbert Levine, named a Knight Commander of the Papal Order of St. Gregory for his work in using music to further interfaith relations (the last musician so honored was Wolfgang himself), recently presented Haydn's *The Creation* with the Philharmonia Orchestra of London in several of the great cathedrals of the world, including Baltimore's Basilica and the Vatican's St. Peter's (for the eightieth birthday of Pope John Paul II). This inspired presentation of a work with a somewhat tired past gave the work a new vitality, which did not go unnoticed by the media. Many of the concerts were televised (by, among others, PBS in the United States). Again, the Internet would seem to be a perfect venue for these magnificent concerts, whether presented live or via recordings.

Suppose a pianist discovers a previously unknown work by a great composer. Or suppose a pianist identifies a work that has been underperformed because its cadenza is poorly conceived and the pianist writes a new cadenza, lifting the work to the level that it aspired to but fell just short of. Or pianists—or composers—who have been largely forgotten or abandoned by the mainstream, but deserve to be revisited or visited for the first time through a technology that can do them justice, find work.

Once a recording exists, its value is limited only by the imagination of the artist, the artist's representatives, and the artist's record company.

The High Price of Low Pricing

When retailers made the transition from the LP to the CD in the early 1980s, they were concerned with the response of customers to a new price structure. Compact discs were expensive to produce, and were not, in fact, manufactured by all of the record labels when the format was introduced because they did not have the facilities to do so. The extra cost to the retailers was considerable, and CDs were not in great supply. During the first roll-out, competition and demand were very high, so retailers decided to use the CD as a loss leader to get rid of LPs, expecting that they would eventually be able to raise prices to a more appropriate margin of profit. They have never recovered from that decision. Even when the cost of making CDs dropped considerably, the record companies continued to charge the same price to dealers and the retailers felt they could not reverse their earlier actions and raise prices, leaving them with the same small profit margin.

The only way retailers could figure out how to make up the difference was by literally selling the store. As competition became fierce in the classical music industry, as the retailers had to discount even more drastically, and as budget records began to fill up space in record stores, the record stores actually began to construct a complex system of selling advertising within their stores themselves. This system became extremely sophisticated. Every inch of a store was available for sale. Some methods are obvious, such as window dressing and listening stations; some are surprising, such as stickering headphones at listening stations and pasting advertisements on light boxes. The record company had to pay for all of this. With most stores no longer extant, and with the decline in profitability of the brick-and-mortar record business, this creative scheme has become all but extinct. Bad as it was to "sell the store," at least there were stores to sell. Not so anymore, unless you consider Walmart a valid substitute. The Internet at least offers some consolation to those who want to "thumb through" a variety of choices, and YouTube clips are also useful for potential purchasers of classical music records, but that site too often serves as the listening experience itself and streaming opportunities continue to threaten the very existence of physical unit sales.

Budget labels for classical music did not have the money to buy in-store advertising. They had to rely on rock-bottom prices, made possible because their production costs are low and there are no royalties due to the artists. Just as today's kids fiddling around with MP3 files and other Internet transmissions over their computer "sound systems" seem to be satisfied with degraded sound quality, classical music buyers have shown that they are quite happy buying a Beethoven symphony performed by the Bulgarian Opera Orchestra for $4.98 rather than one performed by the Berlin Philharmonic Orchestra conducted by Herbert Von Karajan for $10.98, or the latest version by the London Symphony Orchestra conducted by [insert "name" conductor] for $18.98. One sad side effect of this practice is that the consumer, while presumably enjoying the recording, will not have had the magical opportunity to experience the ultimate greatness that made the artists, or the conductors and their orchestras, almost as legendary as the masterpieces, with their unique visions, that they recorded. Without this experience, it is not at all certain that the consumers who purchase budget-price records will ever be totally captured by the possibilities of classical music.

Promotion Methods for Classical Records

Record promotion in the classical business can be considerably more potent than in the popular music business if handled carefully. And it *must* be handled carefully, as there is so little money to spend on promotion. How much can a classical record company expend on promotion when it expects its new release to sell 10,000 units? A rule of thumb is around $3 a record, or, in this example, $30,000. How the allotment is spent is interesting. Artists, and their inexperienced managers, will have a million ideas about how to draw the consumer to its product: quarter-page ads in the *New York Times*, for example, radio spots, some of those highly visible "in-store" displays. But $30,000 doesn't go all that far. Only experienced artists' managers, or record company product managers, are likely to know how to get the most bang from the buck. And believe me, they need that knowledge. Remember, if the records don't sell, the artist can move on to another label, try to make a go of it via Internet distribution, or make a living performing. The record company will be left to collect "returns."

While the proliferation of independent record companies in the classical field mirrors, in part, the development of independent popular record companies, the smaller labels cannot compete with the big companies. The small label, even more than the big label, must rely on smart promotion. A small label that does not have the *Titanic* soundtrack millions to dip into may have only one shot to "break" an artist. So savvy record companies and wise managers commit their limited resources to press and publicity. You will more quickly buy a record recommended by a reviewer or a radio station than by the record company telling you why you should own it. However, if its one-shot promo campaign does not succeed, that may be the end of promotion for that particular record and perhaps also for that particular artist. A major label does not face these constraints. (Some of the major classical record labels have begun to establish focus groups in order to determine whether a record has a chance of catching on. Stokowski would not be amused.)

While the promotion effort is being mounted by the record label, the distributors are simultaneously supposed to be picking up the baton and continuing the push toward the retail account. This used to be called selling. But nowadays, it is more common for the distribution companies to respond to the accounts rather than vice versa in order to sell them on a particular project. They take orders and collect money. There is no "sell"—hard or soft—in the classical record business.

No wonder the artists are depressed.

Interestingly, retailers, whose stake is in the artist's ultimate celebrity, notoriety, and record-selling prowess, have never, to my knowledge, actually made their own commitment to develop artists and careers. While this is not particularly surprising, it seems shortsighted, since promotion at the retail level would seem a perfect way to create demand for a product.

Balancing Supply, Demand, and Optimism

One thing the record company must avoid: responding too quickly to a surge in interest. As noted in an earlier chapter, records are shipped on a 100% return guarantee; this means that if records do not sell at retail, or if middle-level distributors (such as rack jobbers) do not receive orders from retailers to match what they have purchased from the ultraenthusiastic sales staff of the record label, those records that the rack jobbers and the retailers were unable to sell can, and will, be returned to the record label for credit. On the other hand, the record company will have only a brief window within which to respond to a surge of interest. This is a very delicate balancing act when dealing with classical records, which, on average sell 1,500 copies, but which in extraordinary circumstances can sell 1 million copies.

In a perfect world (the popular music business?), a record released in one month can have a slow buildup over many months until it is selling a few thousand copies a week, then five thousand, etc. until it begins to chart and build sales based on its radio play. Soundscan counts, the buildup due to touring—all of these things construct a steady growth of demand, and the supply of records is increased to meet it. When there is no such trend, the record companies have a problem. And trends like this are rarely observable in the classical music world. Without records in the racks, no matter what the demand, there will be no sales. How many records of a particular title are required to fill all of the slots in the distribution chain? About 60,000. (In the popular music world, this number is much larger—probably as many as 200,000.) The cost of manufacturing this much product is enormous, and I think it is evident that it is simply not feasible for a company—particularly a small company—to fill this supply line, except in very rare instances. It's no wonder YouTube and iTunes have taken charge of getting recorded music to customers.

THE COMPOSER-ARTIST: SPECIAL CONSIDERATIONS

Unlike the situation with most popular music recording artists, those music recording artists who have a classical bent (for example, Michael Bolton, Elvis Costello, and Billy Joel) and those who are more traditionally schooled in the classical arts often have aspirations to compose more extensive works than short lyric or art songs. These composer-artists often find themselves in a conflict with their record companies, which want them not only to record exclusively for them, but to record the works they write exclusively for them—preferably radio-ready-length songs.

This kind of restriction can cause quite a dilemma for the composer-artist—especially for an instrumentalist. For example, a violinist is likely to compose works for the violin. Unlike works written for the popular music audience—which are created spontaneously by the artist—classical works are often commissioned by organizations that not only seek to present the world premiere of the work that they have commissioned, but also to have the composer present the work at that event. And of course, the commissioning party may wish to record the work as part of its archive or even as a commercial recording to enhance the funding of its not-for-profit institution.

Many times these works are no more than ten or twelve minutes in length, and yet when the commissioning institution is restricted from including the work among those in a recording of the evening's performance, the commissioning institution is harmed. Indeed, the threat of such a restriction may even keep the institution from commissioning the work in the first place. Given that the work would never have been written but for the hard-fought-for funds and artistic imagination of the creative personnel in the organization, this seems hardly equitable for the institution, the composer, or the community at large, which would presumably benefit from the availability and celebrity of the work for decades to come.

Another argument in favor of some flexibility toward this kind of composer-artist is that the work that person composes may have nothing to do with the nature of the works to be scheduled or likely to be programmed for recording by the artist for the record company. Even if the artist's record company desires to promote the artist via the 19th-century-repertoire format, what harm would it do the company to allow the composer-author-artist to record a 20th-century work on an album of 20th- and 21st- century material? It would seem sensible not to impede the artist from pursuing a composing career, even if that entails allowing the artist to step out of his or her exclusivity obligations—as long as this does not unreasonably interfere with the artist's recording responsibilities to the record company.

It should also be noted that many classical composer-artists write for instruments other than their own primary instrument, for ensembles (full orchestra or chamber-size ensembles), or even for duos, trios, quartets, and quintets. Frequently these composer-artists could not perform such works even if they wanted to, yet they may be asked to appear at the premiere as a guest, or they may have a role in these works, for example, as featured instrumentalist. And they may want to participate in the recording of them—perhaps as one of several instrumentalists or even as conductor.

While just about all recording artist agreements require the exclusive services of the artist for a period of years or a number of albums, the situation described here is relevant only to classical artists. It is rarely the case in the popular field that an exclusive recording artist for one label writes such a significant work that his or her services are requested, or even appropriate, for a competitive label. The only time that an exclusive artist's musical services (either as singer or instrumentalist) are typically sought by another artist's label is when the exclusive artist is requested to appear as a sideman on the other label, and the right to do so is subject to yet even more verbiage in the traditional recording artist agreement, covering such things as how the artist's name can be used on the packaging and in advertising and promotion (usually in a size and placement no different from that of other musicians appearing on the recording), whether the artist's photograph can be used (usually not), and whether the track on which the artist is appearing can be released as a single. This is not, in general, the case in the world of motion picture soundtrack composers-artists and in classical music.

Whoever is responsible for negotiating the artist's recording agreement must understand the choices the artist may desire to have in his or her musical career and must seek relief from the rigid exclusivity rules customarily imposed on artists by their record companies. Many negotiators view any contract as if it were a document writ in stone and are reluctant to negotiate its terms; they are paralyzed by the appearance of finality that these fifty- to one-hundred-page behemoths suggest. That is a major mistake. Most provisions in most documents are negotiable, and if artists' representatives do not attempt to craft their artist's contracts specifically to the individual needs and desires of their artists, almost certainly provisions will be included that will negatively affect the artists' careers.

CLASSICAL COMPOSERS AND THEIR PUBLISHERS: SOME PITFALLS AND SOME OPTIONS

Most competent, and many up and coming classical music composers who have been recognized by the industry, have the benefit of classical music publishers which assist them in innumerable ways in their craft. They do not just provide all of the traditional roles of a music publisher, worldwide, including the administration of copyrights and the rights comprising copyright such as mechanical, performing, print, and synchronization rights. They also provide editorial advice, or obtain commissions from third parties, introduce their writers to opportunities for master classes and "composer in residence" opportunities. As with most companies, some are stronger in some areas than in others.

Synchronizations

Synchronizations, in particular, however, suffer from the classical music publishers' unique specialization. They are far less "connected" to the film, television, and advertising community than pop music publishers. They are rarely as aggressive, or effective, as their colleagues in the pop music field in obtaining uses of music tied to video images. Indeed, they are in many ways alienated from the mainstream because their composers, their personnel, and those who perform or record their music are as well. One of the difficulties they face is obvious: historic classical music is in the public domain and easily and cheaply available to film, TV, and advertising companies. There is no cost for the composition and the availability of sound recordings of this kind of classical music is so vast that the supply dictates a low price for licensing. Things are different for contemporary "classical" works: first, there are few styles that lend themselves to synchronizations; they are either too avant garde, or they are simply too jarring to a public used to melodic alternatives; second, sound recordings rarely exist of contemporary works, and the cost of recording is astronomical, especially if done in the United States; third, companies seeking music to synchronize with their films, TV shows or commercials like to acquire finished product and have little or no interest in actually paying to produce recordings of works whose end-product might disappoint them in any event for being inaccessible to the public at large; finally, where recordings do exist, they are usually archival recordings of live performances—often by seventy-to-one-hundred-piece orchestras—but for which no union fees have been paid. To bring these recordings to the public, the cost would be prohibitive.

Accordingly, if possible, classical music composers should consider carefully if they want to place their works exclusively with a classical music publisher as opposed to reserving those works for which, for example, a pop music publisher might use its extensive synchronization department and connections to exploit. Similarly, pop music publishers can request composers to write specifically for a project—such as a television commercial. This would never happen in the classical publishing world. These options are not available to classical music composers simply because access of the composers to the pop publisher is closed off due to their contractual relationship with their publisher in which they park their works permanently and exclusively with a classical music publisher. I have had some success in bifurcating rights between classical and pop music publishers whereby they function as partners in a cause. Egos are set aside and the pull of those who constantly need new content for their audiovisual works is met by two naturally opposing cultural forces now working together toward a common goal—synchronizations—which are fast becoming the most income-producing segment of the music publishing business.

Subventions

Subventions—an unfamiliar word and concept—are unique to the classical music world. When a classical music publisher either obtains, or is offered, a commission for one of its writers, there is a considerable cost to create readable and playable orchestral parts of the commissioned work in order for it to be able to be performed. The cost of such parts varies depending on the nature of the orchestration and the length of the work. Someone has to pay for these costs. The way music publishers and commissioning parties handle this reality is by adding a *"subvention" fee* to the cost of the commission. This fee can amount to many thousands of dollars and is *in addition to* the commission fee itself. The publishers and the composer's manager will usually commission the base fee payable for creating the work in the first place. However, many publishers (but fewer managers) forgo this fee, recognizing the reality that it is via these commissions that the composer often lives from day to day. Often these additional fees are not disclosed or, if they are, they are built into the commission agreement just when the composer needs the commission fee to pay his or her rent and has no opportunity or flexibility to question the language of the document he or she is expected to sign. Furthermore, there is often no rationale provided to the composer as to how the subvention fees have been determined. A $20,000 commission might be accompanied by an $8,000 subvention, which goes to the publisher to cover the cost of creating the "parts." If the work is designed for a string quartet, or for a hundred-piece orchestra, the costs obviously will differ; but the composer is usually not privy to the breakdown and the third-party editors who often are independent contractors and not part of the staff of the publishing company—and therefore inaccessible to the composer.

The question then becomes: for what is the publisher receiving 50% of the copyright as well as 50% of all earnings of the composition if one of the principal services it is supposed to provide is actually provided by a third party (the editor), and if the cost of providing them is covered by another third party (the commissioner)? Yes, of course, the publisher is often responsible for finding the commission, and the publisher provides a myriad of services to supply performing entities with parts, once created, for subsequent performances (as to which they share in the rental fees, of course). And they are registering the composer's works in the US Copyright Office and at the composer's performing rights society, and they are soliciting interest from the performing community in attempts to cause them to perform the composer's works, but traditionally, their advances to writers are minimal whereas the significant costs of creating parts for instruments are covered by third parties. Some composers "do it themselves." They hire a couple of professionals who can (1) administer the rights directly on the publisher's behalf, (2) provide a website or email address to process rentals and collect rental fees, and (3) solicit commissions or work for film, etc. directly or via agents who are specialists in the field. The administration of copyrights is not difficult, as important as it is to do so accurately and completely; for everything else, the independent, nonaligned composer, has multiple options at his disposal that would not exist were he or she to be signed exclusively to a music publisher. This option to "do it yourself" is not appropriate for everyone, but is an alternative that deserves to be considered carefully before the composer relinquishes 50% of the copyright and worldwide control over his or her works for at least thirty-five years (in the United States—see Termination of Grants or Copyrights chapter 20) and essentially forever outside of the United States.

Compositions with Audio or Audiovisual Features

Many contemporary compositions utilize electronic backgrounds or audio and/or video features that are costly to produce. Composers and their representatives (lawyers or agents) must make clear to both parties who is expected to pay for these recordings: usually no one thinks about it until it appears as an issue, and then the composer is usually charged with 100% of the cost. The illogic of this is evident in that the composition is unperformable without the audio component, yet the publisher thinks of it as separate and apart from the composition. Does this mean that the composer should negotiate with the commissioning party for a separate subvention? After all, there are costs of production involved in preparing an audio component for performance. You decide.

Quick Checklist to Refer to in Negotiating Classical Publishing and Commission Agreements

Here is a list for a classical composer or his or her representative to check off when entering into a publishing agreement—these are issues peculiar to classical music publishing agreements; the array of concerns of all composers discussed in chapter 13 obviously applies as well?

❑ Can the cost of samplers be reimbursed to the composer

❑ Most of these agreements provide for automatic extension for the same number of years applicable to the initial term—which can be as little as three years and as many as five. These opportunities to terminate should be dealt with very carefully. Even if the composer has every intention of extending the term of the agreement, provided a few matters of concern are fixed, the composer's leverage to obtain those changes is reduced to zero if he or she does not exercise the right to terminate the agreement prior to the last applicable date before the automatic extension takes effect. The termination notice can be quite friendly and acknowledge the composer's desire to stay with the company provided a few of the composer's concerns are dealt with, but when the company receives the notice, it will undoubtedly comprehend the reason for it coming at a time following which the composer will have lost all negotiating power had he or she failed to exercise it. A friendly phone call from the composer prior to sending the notice would be wise as well.

- ❏ Third-party commission agreements should be reviewed on each occasion by the composer's representative; times change, leverage changes, and things that might have been okay in prior years might no longer be okay in later years. The publisher might be processing these agreements automatically without focusing on things that the composer might deem important after years of foregoing objection to them.

- ❏ As noted earlier, subventions should be discussed, and labeled as such in commission agreements.

Here is a another check list—this time for a classical composer entering into commission agreements:

- ❏ Commissioning entities usually want the exclusive right to premier the work and sometimes to record the work for the first time as well (which is an exclusive right of the copyright owner until the owner has actually licensed that right to a third party). Both might be perfectly agreeable to the composer, but there should be outside dates set, beyond which the exclusivity as to each promise expires. Usually, there is such a date for the premier performance; less often do the parties realize that if they do not insert an outside date for the recording, the work will be tied up indefinitely, unavailable for recording.

- ❏ The composer will usually obtain a contractual commitment to provide economy air and first class hotel accommodations for the premier; certain composers might wish that his or her manager or family member accompany him or her to the premier. This is not something that all composers want, or need, all or even some of the time, but if it is important to a composer, it is better to raise it at the inception of a negotiation and not later when the answer will more likely be "no." The composer's publisher and staff members who are dealing with the commissioning agent should be attuned to the particular composer's requirements.

- ❏ Wherever archival copies of the first performance are created, even if for the orchestra's own library, a copy should be provided to the composer and another one to the composer's publisher.

- ❏ Each commission agreement should provide that the premier performance (and subsequent ones, of course, as well) be in a hall subject to a performing rights society license for the PRO of which the composer is a member (ASCAP) or affiliate (BMI or SESAC). (Non–United States composers' performing rights societies license their works, by default, through ASCAP, unless otherwise instructed specifically by the composer.)

- ❏ Finally, it is incumbent upon the composers' publishers to ensure that their performing rights societies are advised of the live performance of a composer's work—especially the premiere performance. Performance fees may be small, but they add up. The publisher will probably know the idiosyncrasies of each performing rights society's rules and regulations insofar as they relate to crediting performances of a classical composition. ASCAP likes to receive an actual copy of the program booklet (or if necessary, just the program) because it needs to be able to (1) verify that the performance took place and (2) comprehend where the work for which performance royalties are sought falls within the repertoire of the particular program itself. For this process to be effective, of course, the work must first be properly registered with the composer's (and publisher's) society. Those who do not have outside music publishers but "do it themselves" should be very careful to follow the PRO's rules in order to generate funds that are, in a word, waiting for them to collect. Commission agreements should include a clause requiring the commissioner to provide a program booklet to the composer or the composer's publisher. If the composer is a performing artist as well, his or her agency should request the program as well so there are two chances for the composer to notify his or her performing rights society of the fact that a performance took place.

One last comment on this subject: where a composer can establish that a work has been performed at a variety of venues, but the performing rights society does not pay much in terms of royalties (for what can be a variety of reasons), good communication with the society and its affiliated foundation will often result in an "award" on an annual basis of several thousand dollars which is paid to the composer in recognition of the composer's serious effort in making a mark in the classical music performance field—if not one that yet has generated any significant performance royalties in the ordinary course. As for ensuring that the composer's works are actually registered (1) in the US Copyright Office and (2) with his or her performing rights society, the composer or his or her representative should regularly (once every year perhaps) double-check with the society and the Copyright Office records (both available free online) to ensure that the composer's works are being administrered properly. The administration of copyrights may seem to be not a big deal, but it is. Significant potential revenues are awaiting payment to composers, but these payments will not be made unless their works have been properly registered with their PRO. Copyright registrations are essential for a variety of other reasons, all of which significant.

CLASSICAL MANAGEMENT

At one time, classical management was really mostly about booking. With the voluminous increase in talented and accomplished singers and the numerous alternatives available today to disseminate information about young artists, classical management companies today must do much more than arrange bookings. They must use public relations (worldwide), publicity (radio, TV, magazines, newspapers), records, videos, creative types of demos, and a large number of other tools—in particular the Internet—to assist an artist in building a career. They do, however, still act as booking agencies, which is why they must be licensed by their states as employment agents. (By the way, just as in the popular music business, not only are many managers who seek and obtain employment for their artists not properly licensed, but if you were to ask them if they were licensed, they would not even know what you were talking about.) For this two-pronged service, a classical manager customarily charges a 20% gross commission rather than the 10% that a traditional booking agent charges. This standard is not followed in the area of the classical music business specializing in vocalists, where multiple performances are the norm, and the gross income is naturally higher than for a single recital or performance with orchestra. In these situations, the management commission is usually 10%.

The Big Agencies

The world of classical management is hard to penetrate; most people do not know how, or to what extent, managers are successful—or unsuccessful for that matter. As with personal managers in the popular music field, one of the great strengths of classical managers is their relationships with the buyers of talent, but as with managers in the popular music field, this is also one of their great weaknesses. Yes, you want them to have access to the opera companies and orchestral managers as well as to the record companies. Yet you do not want to think about whose interest they may have at heart when you learn that they are spending winter and summer holidays with the very same people. You begin to wonder whether there might be a conflict of interest present here—albeit not an official, actionable one.

Classical managers represent conductors of great orchestras; presumably, then, they have unlimited access to those conductors, to whom they can offer their instrumentalists. Do they? Of course they do. Will they? Should they? You figure it out.

One of the problems that I alluded to earlier (see chapter 5, page 75) is that often an artist does not know whether a big agency is using its clout for him or her, or for other artists. Certainly large agencies are involved in more "action" than smaller ones. They deal with more people more often because of their volume of clients and the multiple attendant deals. But there is an intriguing flip side. The large agencies are so big that some of them actually break themselves down into divisions, even within disciplines. Ostensibly, these divisions are set up to create "boutique" units within the larger institution, but many feel that as a matter of practicality, this approach does not work. In many cases, each division continues to grow until it is so large itself that any benefits that were sought are lost, if not totally forgotten. Even if the divisions remain relatively small, they rarely communicate among themselves—often distrusting one another—making it impossible to generate the very synergy that attracted the artist to the big agency in the first place. In fact, such synergy turns out to be a myth; there is no more spirit of cooperation within the agency than there is between Warner Records and Warner/Chappell Music—notwithstanding their fervent claims to the contrary.

Not only do these divisions distrust each other, but, where the disciplines are different, they do not understand each other. Having no taste for embarrassing themselves by admitting their own limitations of knowledge and experience, they decide not to talk to each other. Part of this results from natural competition, part from poor management at the top. Some of it is just plain neurotic. But the consequences for the individual artist are unfortunate. The artist is unable to see how he or she fits into the agency's operations, and is unaware and uninformed as to the available opportunities—which indeed, for reasons that will never be disclosed, may never have been presented to the artist at all, but declined out of hand by the agency.

Is Smaller Better?

In the classical music world, as in the popular music world, many new small management boutiques have begun to spring up. In both instances, it is extremely difficult for any young artist to find a professional that will put the resources of the management office behind the artist for free. That is, if there is no income, there is no commission. Under these circumstances, a small management company, even more than a large management company—notwithstanding its ambition and the fact that its heart is in the right place—will not be able to pay its bills. But unlike the popular music business, where artists can self-book at the important start-up venues, if there is no classical manager to book dates, there will be no dates on which the artist can build a career and reputation. (This is where a recording contract can make a valuable contribution. Once a classical artist has been signed by a record company, competent management will be more open to the possibility of working with the artist. At the same time, of course, record companies know who the effective managers are and can recommend them.)

The music world has changed a great deal in the last forty years. The big management agencies, like any institutions that try to do too much for too many, are perceived by many as being waterlogged. Of course, they probably always have been, yet several of them are still here whereas most of the artists who complained are long gone. Still, many feel that these institutions have lost their ability to take care of the needs of artists—in particular new artists—many of whom are being drawn to small boutique agencies headed in large part by refugees from the big agencies. Smaller agencies often gain their credibility by beginning as small service agencies in the public relations/press/publicity area. They are assigned work by the larger agencies, and may eventually inherit the larger company's artists when the artists see what life might be like with someone who is paying attention. And maybe the boutique manager even loves the music the artist is creating. The large agencies, in fact, have a reputation of not even understanding the music, the heritage, the difference between good and bad, on-pitch or flat. What they do understand is power and influence, and they usually have the instincts to spot a remarkable talent in the bud.

Will the boutique agencies get too big one day? Probably. But in the meantime, there is an acknowledgment by many artists that smaller is better and it is their own talent and hard work rather than the contacts and power of their manager that will determine the success or failure of their careers.

Assessing Classical Management

At their best, classical managers, like personal managers in the pop world, open doors and facilitate and develop relationships. They create possibilities for the artist—recording, performing, and others. They take charge of the business of music, thereby allowing the artists to do what they do best. But—and I have seen this time and time again with artists from every genre of music, and classical musicians are no exception—too many artists abdicate responsibilities they should shoulder themselves. Yet classical artists, like all artists, are ultimately responsible for the decisions affecting their careers. If an artist chooses the wrong representatives, they should be replaced. An artist who does not question the advice he or she is given is responsible for any negative consequences.

The reason this is of particular relevance to the classical music business—and why I am emphasizing it here—is that the classical music industry is so small that a dent in a classical music career is communicated with the speed of light to all of the people who can harm an artist. A poor performance or a poor review gets telegraphed throughout this relatively small business, which is fraught with jealousies and envy. Generosity and sympathy for artists who have had an off day are not sentiments that one finds in the classical music industry. ("Yes, the orchestra is good, when Mr. X is not conducting." "Did you notice that she won't even attempt to sing the high C in the aria at the end of Act 1 of *La Bohème*?") Performing in a poorly directed or conducted program—or even simply being miscast—can ruin a classical singer's career. The "high society" of Monday Night Opera-goers is only a cracked note away from throwing rotten tomatoes and eggs at the culprit. The same holds true for instrumentalists—some of whom do not know when to stop performing certain repertoire and do much to destroy their reputations in a fraction of the time that it took to build them. Decisions have more immediate impact than in the popular music business and alternatives are far fewer in the event an error or stupid mistake is made. No wonder classical artists tend to leave all of their decision-making to the managers. They do not really want to know. If they did, however, maybe they would have fewer complaints because they would understand the lengths to which their representatives have to go to set the table for them.

So, it is not easy being a manager either.

PRESENTING THE SINGER

Many of you are familiar with the Grateful Dead and Phish, the touring acts that actually encourage(d) their fans to tape-record their performances. Well, in the classical music field, this kind of taping is so prevalent today that many concert halls around the world have simply given up trying to stop it, and people arrive not just with hidden DAT recorders in their vests, substituting a microphone for a lapel flower, but with actual camcorders that they place on their shoulders as the concert begins and do not put down until the battery starts to beep. Some say that on any given night at the Metropolitan Opera House in New York, at least five first-class DAT tapings are going on.

Now DAT taping of concerts is against copyright law (and most likely a violation of the terms of the performer's and the ticket buyer's contract with the venue as well), but it does provide a neat answer to a pervasive problem in the classical music world. Given the large number of competent singers and instrumentalists in the world today, how does one present an artist to a record company, manager, or buyer of talent? One obvious answer is tape the artist's recitals and concerts. Once you have a DAT tape of the artist's recital or other performance, you can then burn a CD containing a selection of these performances and off you go with a convincing package. While this action is obviously not one that an attorney can endorse, it is certainly an attractive alternative to sitting and waiting for the phone to ring.

As in the popular music business, another route would be to make a demo recording of the artist—you know, an aria with piano background or something similar. But this kind of product simply cannot compare with a DAT recording of your artist singing with the renowned Metropolitan Opera Orchestra!

There is another possibility, however, which is entirely legal: recording with a great world-class orchestra for little more than the cost of a good demo. How is this achievable? Well, given today's extraordinary technology, one can record an orchestral program without the singer. Then the tapes can be brought to a high-end sound studio, where technicians can actually reconstruct the sound texture of the original recording environment. Add the singer's voice, and voilà! A fantastic recording that would never be available to an up-and-coming artist.

Then there is Music Minus One (www.musicminusone.com), a company that sells recordings of a selection performed by orchestra, jazz group, or chamber ensemble, minus the solo part—either instrument or voice—which the user, with their permission, then adds. This alternative does not run afoul of copyright or other laws, and the background orchestral tapes can be used over and over again by more and more artists, as long as Mozart's, Verdi's, Puccini's, and Rossini's tunes have resonance. As their website announces: "Your Orchestra Awaits."

MUSIC EDUCATION

What can or should be done to "hook" today's youth on classical music? Educators will talk in terms of the educational matrix: the system. Make music part of the curriculum, they say. Others say this is not enough, that love for music is more effectively nurtured if it is introduced in a way more central to the students' "lives and feelings." Presumably, that means private instruction.

In my opinion, a three-pronged approach is best—emphasis on music in the home, private instruction, and expanded programs of music education in schools. The reality is, however, that as more and more parents defer to the schools for all kinds of learning and introduction to new things, emphasizing music in the schools is probably the most practical way to inculcate a love of music—especially classical music—in young people. But once schools accept that this is *their* obligation, we need to consider what the overall goal should be. Knowledge? Inspiration? A level of performance ability so that the child can function in an ensemble such as a high school band or orchestra? Or a dance band or trio? Or, simply, pleasure?

Whatever the goal, a preoccupation with making sure that all students have a common level of achievement in the arts is no more practical or wise than insisting that all students develop scientific skills. It is not always appropriate for all children to be strongly pointed toward one field or another. Nevertheless, it is the careful and effective introduction of the subject that is key to students' future passive *or* active appreciation of what the arts can bring to their lives.

Music education, like needed medication or nourishment, must be served up on a regular basis. The best music programs begin in kindergarten and develop in an age-appropriate manner with the students being invited to experience new and broader challenges as they grow older. By fourth grade, instruments are traditionally introduced and the beginnings of dramatic musical performances (for example, musical theater productions such as *Annie* or *Pippin*) are presented. The most financially sound schools can follow this pattern to the letter; most schools cannot.

There is an assumption that well-to-do suburban and ex-urban communities offer what is not available in the inner cities. Except in very few situations, this is not true. Seldom do these school systems have the money or the trained personnel to provide the resources necessary to achieve a high level of teaching. But there are other resources.

In New York City, for example, where I live, the Department of Cultural Affairs has a program that helps schools present live performances in schools. As many adult music lovers will attest, their motivation to pursue music as a avocation or a career was first fueled by hearing a particular live musical performance—whether in school or at a concert hall or watching one of the *Live at Lincoln Center* performances on PBS.

We have heard a lot in recent years about the incredible work of faith-based institutions in lending support to local, state, and federal governmental efforts to help people in need. Among their services, in some instances, is the introduction to young people, at the grassroots level, to the richness that music can bring to their lives. As one example, in 1995 the United Jewish Appeal Federation of New York established the Music for Youth Foundation to support and advance music education programs in the New York City metropolitan area. It has since expanded, through a partnership with the National Foundation for Advancement of the Arts, and now provides annual cash scholarships and educational opportunities for young people—both individuals and groups—nationwide.

Included within the New York State Council on the Arts mission statement is the following: "The Council believes in the rights of all New Yorkers to access and experience the power of the arts and culture." Among other things, this philosophy is what drives the Council's grant-making decisions. One of their grant recipients, the New York Festival of Song, which is dedicated to the reinvention of the art song recital, has a significant educational outreach program. It is worth repeating their philosophy:

> Exposure to music as a creative endeavor is an integral part of a student's education, requiring specific thinking skills, an active imagination, a fresh look at history, and an appreciation of cultural differences. We have the greatest impact when we go beyond simple music appreciation, and actively engage students in applying their new understanding to the creation of their own music and poetry.

Nevertheless, the road of a talented classical instrumentalist remains a hard one. Blair Tindell, oboist and author, estimates that in 2005, over 5,000 graduates with degrees in music were pursuing only 250 orchestral vacancies.

Why is the classical music audience so old?

I wrote earlier about the comfort that concertgoers experience listening to music. They do not need to know what is happening on their smartphone every few minutes. Their concentration span is more than a few seconds. I find it interesting that the "gray" audience was young not so long ago. What drew them to classical music is not the same thing that was appealing to them when they were young. Their needs and desires change over time. Unfortunately, the growth rate of audiences is slowing and the young are less likely to replace them than at any time in history. The arts institutions (from the LA Philharmonic to the New York Philharmonic, from small orchestras to smaller chamber music and vocal organizations) are beginning to open up avenues of communication between their performers and the young people who would not have ordinarily attended a concert. They are accomplishing this in many instances via social media. Texting and tweeting back and forth before and during a concert have become as routine as summer picnic concepts on the lawns of Tanglewood, Ravinia, and Wolftrap. Some instrumentalists are distracted by the appearance of cell phone illumination across the audience spectrum, but some arts institutions are sticking with the effort, hoping to appeal more to the culture-savvy population. However they try, one thing is a proven fact: get someone into a concert that is transcendent, and you will have a classical music lover for life. Whether they'll spill for the cost of the ticket (and the parking and the dinner and the gas) is another story entirely.

• • •

Is there still room in our lives for classical music? My answer is a resounding "yes!" For the same reason that Kenneth Branaugh's *Henry IV* and Ralph Fiennes's (or Mel Gibson's) *Hamlet* resonate with 21st-century audiences, new recordings of Bach, Beethoven, and Brahms can be exciting and commercially successful. Just as we have Laurence Olivier and John Gielgud—all the great Shakespearian actors in the last fifty to seventy-five years on film in one format or another—we also have multiple versions of all the classical masterpieces. Obviously, there is a perceived need to replicate these performances again and again. Why? Because each generation needs to make these masterpieces work for them—and for us.

And in a fundamental way they do. This is why they are called masterpieces.

An instrumentalist, a vocalist, or a conductor identifying him- or herself with prestigious, if obscure, music, or mounting a performance that will have publicity value (as one Hungarian pianist did by playing all of Beethoven's thirty-two piano sonatas in chronological order over the course of two daylong concerts) is one way to develop a career. Some of these projects are sponsored, and some receive terrific press and publicity. The artist's reputation—and career—builds over time. Everyone in the small and insular world of classical music reads the same things—the same reviews, the same articles, the same news stories. The more they read about a particular artist, especially when the news is positive, the better will be the artist's chance to establish a long-lasting reputation.

Which brings me to another rationale for record companies to record classical artists regularly. I am not talking about artists whose appeal is tentative and fleeting, as is true of so many artists in the world of popular music. An artist who stays in the classical ring and is willing to pay his or her dues for ten, twelve, or fifteen years, and records regularly, will accumulate fifteen to twenty records over that span of time. (Sarah Chang, the great violinist, started recording at the age of nine. At twenty, she had already recorded two dozen CDs!)

This scenario has numerous benefits for both artist and record company. Not only will the records show the maturation of the artist during the period of recording, but they will also constitute a sort of minicatalogue. The record company can highlight the artist by showcasing the artist at record stores via personal appearances. And the record company will have innumerable options with which it can market an artist, and not just a record. For once, volume counts.

20 • TERMINATION OF GRANTS OF COPYRIGHTS
For Every End, a Beginning

Life never presents us with anything which may not be looked upon as a fresh starting point, no less than as a termination.
—ANDRÉ GIDE

BASIC TERM OF PROTECTION

Before going into the incredibly complicated issue of termination of grants of copyright in the United States, a brief review of the history of the basic term of copyright protection is in order. Most of this chapter only deals with works whose copyright terms began before January 1, 1978. Any works created on or after that date are governed by the 1978 Copyright Act and the term of copyright for those works lasts for the duration of the author's life plus seventy years.

Between 1790 and 1909, US copyright law provided for a maximum term of protection of forty-two years (a twenty-eight-year initial term plus a fourteen-year renewal term). The 1909 Copyright Act stipulated an initial copyright term of twenty-eight years, renewable for a second twenty-eight years, for a maximum of fifty-six years. The current Copyright Act, which took effect on January 1, 1978, extended the maximum term for an additional period of nineteen years for a total term of protection of seventy-five years. On October 28, 1998, the maximum term was extended for an additional period of twenty years pursuant to what is known as the Sonny Bono Term Extension Act, for a total term of protection of ninety-five years.

That is where the law stands today. Both the nineteen- and twenty-year extensions were to apply only if the works were protected at the times the extensions were enacted. The renewal term for a work originally published in 1977 (and thus *not* under the 1978 Act), would be ninety-five years (original terms of twenty-eight years plus twenty-eught-year renewal plus nineteen-year extension plus twenty-year extension). Thus protection for a work published in 1977 will expire in 2072.

In anticipation of the passage of the 1978 act, Congress extended the maximum term of protection under the 1909 act several times, for a total term of seventy-five years, and so a work whose copyright term began in, say, 1921, did not enter the public domain fifty-six years later, on December 31, 1977, but rather in 1996. By the time the 1998 twenty-year extension was enacted, the work copyrighted in 1921 had already entered the public domain, and so the twenty-year extension did not apply to it. The same calculations apply to *all* works published on or before December 31, 1922. However, any work published or registered on or later than January 1, 1923, was still protected in 1998 and thus the twenty-year extension *did* apply. The protection for the first of these copyrights will expire on January 1, 2018 and for every work whose copyright protection began after

January 1, 1923, various expiration dates, counted from 95 years following the original copyright date will apply.

To summarize: Any copyrights published or registered before January 1, 1923, are in the public domain now. Period. (For an example, see box, page 307.) Any copyrights published (with proper notice, which was a requirement under the 1909 law) or registered *after* December 31, 1922 (and renewed in timely fashion) are currently protected by copyright.

"K-K-K-KATY"

"K-K-K-Katy" was originally registered on February 1, 1918. Under the 1909 Act, the original term of protection was due to end in 1946 (twenty-eight years after 1918). The copyright for "K-K-K-Katy" was properly renewed in 1946, which added twenty-eight years to the term of protection, giving the song a total term of fifty-six years, a period which ended in 1974. However, the various extension bills (the first was in 1962) extended the renewal term of "K-K-K-Katy" until December 31, 1976. The 1978 Copyright Act provided that any work still in copyright between December 1, 1976, and December 31, 1977 (which this song was), would be protected for a maximum of seventy-five years. "K-K-K-Katy" therefore entered the public domain in 1993—seventy-five years after 1918—and was therefore ineligible for the twenty-year extension enacted in 1998.

Note that any new arrangement of this work made after 1993 is entitled to its own copyright—and copyright term—although only with respect to the new material embodied in the arrangement.

TERMINATION OF GRANTS

In the United States, alone among nations, an author or the author's heirs can reacquire their copyrights—that is, terminate their grants—by the mere exercise of a notice to that effect. This can be done regardless of neglect of, inadequate attention to, or even incompetence in the administration of the copyrights—or even the total opposite, outstanding care and attention! Thus, a total failure to account and pay royalties has usually not been sufficient to warrant the cancellation of the assignment and the return to the assignors of their rights. The following sections discuss several aspects of US copyright law that are relevant to the issue of termination of grants. The list is not exhaustive, but should be sufficient for an understanding of all but the most convoluted examples. Note that these points apply in all cases:

1. If no grant has ever been made, there is nothing to terminate.
2. If a work has entered the public domain by virtue of the fact that a renewal has not occurred on time, there is nothing to terminate.

DURATION OF COPYRIGHT: SUBSISTING COPYRIGHTS

Section 304 of the 1978 Copyright Act is entitled Duration of Copyright: Subsisting Copyrights. Section 304(c), Termination of Transfers and Licenses Covering Extended Renewal Term, and it covers the conditions under which an author or the author's heirs can terminate certain grants or transfers of copyright (or rights under copyright) that the author may have made during his or her lifetime. (Section 203, Termination of Transfers and Licenses Granted by the author, applies to grants made after December 31, 1977, and does not affect any works which acquired copyright protection prior to January 1, 1978.)

The "author" can be the lyricist or the composer, and the termination rights apply only to that portion of the copyright that the author owns. (If there are two authors, each usually owns one-half.) It does not matter for purposes of the termination right whether the grants or transfers were exclusive or nonexclusive.

The reasoning behind the enactment of this right was that once the 1978 Copyright Act had established an additional nineteen-year extension of protection, authors who had, under the previous law, thought to have given away up to fifty-six years of rights—usually to the authors' publishers—were faced with a seventy-five-year loss of rights, with the grantees reaping any windfall profits that might accrue during the additional nineteen years. The same logic applies to the 1998 extension of twenty years.

WHO CAN TERMINATE

Any grant—whether by the original author or the author's heirs—is terminable by the author (if still alive) or the currently surviving heirs of the author (or his deceased heirs). That's it. If the author is deceased, the rights can be exercised by the author's successors as follows:

- 100% to surviving spouse when there are no children
- 100% to the children when there is no surviving spouse
- 50% to the surviving spouse and 50% to the children, the latter to be divided equally

The surviving children of the author, and the surviving children of any deceased child, are each dealt with as an entity. This is what is referred to in legal jargon as sharing *per stirpes*.

Example: A deceased author is survived by a wife and three children. Each of the children is entitled to one-third of the 50% children's share of the termination rights. One of the three children dies, leaving two children, who will share equally in their parents' one-third (of 50%) termination rights. (*Note:* The inheritance of rights does not extend beyond the level of grandchildren of the original author.)

THE CONTROL OF TERMINATION DECISIONS

Where an author leaves a number of heirs, how is a majority achieved among them? The Copyright Act stipulates that the author's spouse has a 50% interest in the author's share of the copyright. In cases in which there are children, the spouse still maintains a 50% interest, and the children divide the remaining 50% equally. Thus the termination decision can be made by the spouse and one child, because no matter what the split, the spouse plus one child's share will be more than 50%.

THE RIGHTS GRANTED

The ownership of the copyright asset which has been recaptured has enormous value (up to fifteen times earnings), much of which is gained from the rights referred to below. Note that these rights apply only to the United States:

- the right to administer 100% of the copyright and the rights under copyright (including the performance right, the mechanical right, the synchronization right, the display right, and the print right)
- the right and opportunity to negotiate with a new publisher or renegotiate with an existing publisher the following: royalty splits, audit provisions, advances, and exploitation requirements by a new publisher

should the acquiring party wish to place the copyrights in the hands of a US music publisher

- the right and opportunity to isolate rights under copyright (for example, print rights, foreign rights, synch rights) and license them to one or more parties at a time, rather than assign the copyrights themselves to one publisher. These rights can be licensed exclusively or nonexclusively and for limited periods of time (five years, ten years, etc.) rather than for the entire length of the term of copyright.

- the right and opportunity to use the power acquired by having recovered total control over the copyrights to change the terms of existing agreements, and therefore to stay with a long-term publisher and maintain old relationships—only now on more favorable terms. For example, the acquiring party might offer to return some of the US rights to the original publisher in return for an improved position with that publisher vis à vis rights *outside* of the United States.

THE WINDOWS FOR TERMINATION

This is where things get complicated. There are two time periods (windows) that concern us. First, according to Section 304(c), the termination *may* "be effected at any time during a period of five years beginning at the end of fifty-six years from the date copyright was originally secured, or beginning on January 1, 1978, whichever is later." But to "be effected" does not preclude sending a notice before the fifty-six-year period expires. The second time period addresses this: These notices may be served not more than ten years prior to the date on which the notice is to become effective, as long as they are served *not later than two years prior to the last possible effective date.* The reason that one must give at least two years' prior notice of termination is that the law accommodates the original grantee (usually a music publisher) by giving it an opportunity to prepare for the impending loss of its copyright.

> *Example:* A copyright was secured on January 1, 1964, and the renewal copyright was registered as required. The maximum copyright term pursuant to the 1909 Copyright Act will end on December 31, 2019 (that is, fifty-six years later). The earliest possible effective date of termination is January 1, 2020. The earliest possible date on which to *send* the termination notice was January 1, 2010 (that is, ten years prior to the earliest possible effective date of termination. In order not to lose the chance to recapture the copyright *entirely*, that is for the entirety of the remaining years of protection, the terminating party would have to send the appropriate notice no later than two years before the end of the five-year window which began on the expiration of the original fifty-six-year term (December 31, 2019). On January 2, 2023, it will be too late.

Your *own* actions determine the effective date of termination. In the example above, you could choose to terminate at the *earliest* possible time, in which case the effective date on which you could recapture the copyright would be January 1, 2020. Alternatively, you could choose to terminate at the *latest* possible time (January 1, 2023) in which case you could not recapture the copyright until 2025.

One important detail to remember is that the dates on which termination notices can be served and the effective dates of termination are not calendar year ends (that is, December 31st of a given year). Normally, copyrights are registered on odd days during the calendar year.

> *Example:* "A Pretzel, A Beer, and A Burp" was registered by the copyright owner—the publisher—on October 6, 1952. The copyright was renewed in 1980 pursuant to the original grant, which gave the publisher the right to renew the copyright. The fifty-six-year term provided for under

the 1909 act ended on December 31, 2008. (The term ended on the last day of the fifty-sixth year). However, the "effective date" five-year window began on October 6, 2008, and ended on October 5, 2013. Notice to terminate could have been served with respect to the thirty-nine-year extension period (that is, nineteen years plus twenty years) as early as October 6, 1998, ten years before the expiration of the fifty-sixth year after registration. The *latest* date by which a termination notice could have been given was October 5, 2011, which was two years before October 6, 2013, the end of the five-year window. If the author or his or her heirs terminated as of the earliest possible effective date, they have recaptured the entire additional thirty-nine years of copyright protection after 2008, and they would have been the owner of the copyright until 2047, when it will enter the public domain—finally. However, if they waited to terminate until the latest possible time—October 5, 2011, for an October 6, 2013, effective date—they would have lost five of the thirty-nine years of protection. Nevertheless, they still would recapture the copyright on October 6, 2013, and will be the owner of the copyright until 2047 when, as noted above, it will enter the public domain.

WHEN AUTOMATIC RENEWAL APPLIES

In 1992, Congress passed a law that provided that any works first copyrighted between January 1, 1964, and December 31, 1977, need not be renewed formally; the renewal (for, by then, a renewal term of forty-seven years) would be automatic. (This benefit would not have applied to "Pretzel" because its renewal date preceded the new law.) Since 1998, when the twenty-year extension was passed, the renewal term of sixty-seven years (that is, twenty-eight years plus thirty-nine years) would be automatic. By 2006, this issue became moot because any copyright first published with notice or registered under the 1909 law before January 1,1978, advanced into its sixty-seven-year renewal term (twenty-eight plus nineteen plus twenty) renewal term prior to January 1, 2006. For example, the initial term of a copyright registered on January 31, 1977 would have expired on December 31, 2005. Its renewal term would have commenced on that date. Any copyright coming into existence after December 31, 1977 would be governed by the new law whose term now extends to the life of the author plus seventy years.

THE SONNY BONO TERM EXTENSION ACT

What happens if you forgot or chose not to terminate the nineteen-year extension to an original fifty-six-year copyright term? Do you lose the chance to terminate the new twenty-year extension as well? Not necessarily.

For example, suppose that a copyright was in its renewal term on October 28, 1998, the date the twenty-year extension law took effect, but that the person or persons with a termination right had not exercised it by that date with respect to the nineteen-year extension, and it was too late to exercise it. In that case, the termination right could still be exercised with respect to the additional twenty years. (for example, a work copyrighted on or before October 28, 1939). The termination process exercised with respect to that extension is the same with respect to the seventy-fifth year as it is with respect to the fifty-sixth year. The time windows within which the right could be exercised, as described above, would still apply.

KEEPING RECORDS

All copyright owners whose works were created prior to January 1, 1978, should, for each work, make a schedule that notes all relevant dates and extension periods, as follows:

Date of copyright	1st extension?	20-year extension	Earliest termination date	Latest termination date	Name/ address of entity to whom termination notice is to be sent

Remember, all copyrights originally secured between January 1, 1923, and December 31, 1977, are now in their renewal period, at the end of which the copyrights will enter the public domain. Except in the special case described in the Sonny Bono Term Extension Act above, it is not useful to identify which portion of the renewal period the copyright is in (that is, the first twenty-eight-year renewal period, the nineteen-year extension, or the twenty-year extension). It simply doesn't matter. Copyrights registered after December 31, 1922, and properly renewed, are still in their renewal period. Copyrights coming into effect (that is, works created) after December 31, 1977, have no renewal period. Their copyright terms are simply the life of the author plus seventy years.

THE TECHNICAL REQUIREMENTS FOR TERMINATION

To terminate copyrights under Section 304(c) of the Copyright Act of 1978, notice must be given to (served on) the copyright owner to whom the rights were transferred, and these notices must be recorded in the Copyright Office pursuant to regulations published by that office.

Section 304 (c)(4) lists the specific notice requirements for a termination to be effective. One important issue *not* addressed by the copyright statute is how to find out where the notices of termination must be sent. Many music publishers no longer exist in their original form. Is a notice to Harms, Inc., sufficient to terminate the copyright now owned by Warner/Chappell? And vice versa? To what address should the notices be sent? What is the effect of notices that are returned by the post office? Is the terminating party required to secure a Copyright Office search report in order to find out the "official" owner of record of each individual copyright?

A full Copyright Office search can cost several thousand dollars. The Copyright Office bases its charges on hourly rates, so any cost estimate you or your representatives are given will be just that—an estimate. Many old-timers were members of the Songwriter's Guild, which continues to maintain a fairly accurate up-to-date list of copyrights created by their members, and the Guild's list is often enough to identify the current owner. Regrettably, without patching together information via databases such as those of ASCAP or BMI, perhaps the Harry Fox Agency, and maybe even foreign societies' records (less likely), there is simply no place other than the Copyright Office to which one can turn to search efficiently for the needed information.

Agreements Not to Terminate May Be Invalid Of course, you can make an agreement not to exercise the termination right, but if the party you make that agreement with is not the current renewal rights holder, the grant will be invalid. Therefore, any money you received for the invalid grant would have to be returned . . . if you still have it. You can also serve the applicable termination notices and then make a contingent transfer effective after the termination actually occurs.

• • •

Suffice it to say that most scholars feel that the termination right is simply not waivable—for any amount of money. In fact, Section 304 (c) provides that termination of a grant is still effective even if an agreement to the contrary is entered into, including an agreement to make a will or to make any further grant.

Another issue that has reared its head only in the past few years due to the proliferation of samples involves the question of what happens when a sample makes its way into a new copyright. What happens to the underlying, original song used in the new work? The transfer relating to the original work can surely be terminated, but what about the new work? Can the termination pull the rug out from under the new work and render it useless? Is the new work a derivative work such as a movie with a soundtrack where Congress specifically denied termination rights to songs not to mess with the other contributors?

As should be abundantly clear from the preceding text, the subject of termination rights is enormously complicated, and many issues will be resolved only through litigation or legislation in the future. It is beyond the scope of this chapter to deal with these issues, so I will refer the reader to his or her own attorney for guidance in effectuating the authors' or heirs' intentions in this regard.

The Gap This one is a doozy. The problem some people describe as "the straddling work" transfer arises when a contract entered into during the pre-1978 period refers to songs or recordings not yet created, and indeed not created until after 1977. Are the copyrights in these works terminable under the provisions of Section 203 or 304 (c). One permits termination after thirty-five years and the other after fifty-six years. The preconditions of termination differ under each section and the parties permitted to terminate differ as well. The Copyright Office and Congress have not yet resolved this dilemma which has inserted such uncertainty in commerce that deals have fallen through because potential buyers have no clue who the termination class is comprised of. The Copyright Office is endeavoring to determine if the date of the grant of rights in a non work-for-hire occurs on the date of the contract signing or upon the creation of the work. Say that in 1978, a songwriter signed an exclusive term contract for existing songs and songs not yet written. When does the thirty-five years run for each song? From the date of the contract even though some songs did not even exist at that time? When did the "transfer" occur? Here's another one: what if their contract was signed in 1977 before the new law, with the thirty-five-year termination right, took effect? Some of the songs would be ruled by the 1909 law and others by the 1976 law (which took effect in 1978). Or would all songs be ruled by the 1909 law because the contract was signed before the new law took effect?

Stay tuned as this is merely one of dozens of issues still to be resolved and probably litigated in the future, especially after 2013—or, hopefully, legislation will resolve the ambiguities in the law. As should be abundantly clear from the preceding text, the subject of termination is enormously complicated.

No, when I speak of the Gap, I don't mean the clothing store. In copyright circles, there is only one gap: the mysterious status of copyrights that fall within the proverbial cracks. Let's say you signed an exclusive songwriting or an exclusive recording contract in 1975—before the Copyright Act of 1976 took effect in January 1978. The first set of songs you delivered or the first album you delivered (let's say in 1977) was clearly covered by the 1909 Copyright Act. Under that law, there existed no termination rights affecting these songs, or recordings. (The 1976 act granted a limited right of termination to these transfers [Section 304], but only after fifty-six years had passed, in order to give the author a chance to recapture his works before the nineteen-year extension took effect [now thirty-nine years]).

If you signed an exclusive songwriting or an exclusive recording contract in 1979, and delivered your first set of songs or first album in 1980, clearly the termination provision (Section 203) of the new copyright law would apply to the transfers made in 1979.

But what if you signed the first long-term agreement in 1975 affecting five years' of your songs or sound recordings, and you didn't deliver your second set of songs, or album, until 1979. Are those copyrights terminable under Section 304? Section 203? No one knows. Therein lies the gap.

Some attorneys, faced with this dilemma, take the safe road and advise clients that unless there was a separate grant of rights occurring after 1977, only the fifty-six-year termination right applies (Section 304) under the current law. Period. Of course, a copyright cannot preexist the creation of a work. And the language of termination under the fifty-six-year provision speaks in terms of "renewal copyrights" which do not exist under the law containing the thirty-five-year provision. So the preponderance of the academic thinking is that a work created after January 1,1977 can be terminated after thirty-five years, not fifty-six years, and that the termination class is defined under the thirty-five-year provision. Nevertheless, this is something that will not be clear until Congress fixes the problem it created.

The Copyright Office cannot resolve the dilemma on its own; it will require legislation which, if passed, will raise its own set of problems if it is not carefully drafted. For example, will it matter if the songs delivered prior to 1978 were published or not published (an important consideration under the 1909 act)? if the songs delivered afterward did not arrive in the publisher's (or record company's) hands until years later? if there was any correspondence between the author (writer or recording artist) and the publisher/record label after 1977 that might constitute an actual "transfer?" This set of facts would make the issue moot as the transfer will clearly have taken place under the new law, even though the exclusive songwriting or recording agreement was entered into before 1978. What if the songwriter delivered a "splits sheet" after 1977 for the songs being delivered? Could this constitute a transfer after 1977? What if the song or the recording was created before 1978, although delivered afterward? What if the song or the recording was created after 1978, which is more likely the case?

Copyrights vest under the current law upon creation. If it can be established that the songs or recordings were created before 1978, the songwriter or recording artist would take the position that the copyrights to them were not actually registered as such until after 1977; whereas songs or recordings written after 1977 would instantaneously be covered by copyright upon creation, thereby identifying them for all time as being affected only by the new law—yet the transfer of rights would have occurred before 1978.

One final scenario to explode an already almost impossible problem to solve: What if there are multiple authors and they cannot agree on which provision covers termination (because the termination class is comprised of distinctly different people)? Who is going to resolve this self-made dilemma?

A further complication would occur if there are multiple authors whose contractual relationships with publishers or record companies differ. One may have signed an agreement in 1977, although he or she may have delivered the songs in 1979; another may not have signed an agreement in 1977 at all, but owned her own publishing or recording rights; creation and "fixing" the songs or recordings after 1977, and assigning them to her own publishing company pursuant to an agreement entered into prior to 1977 would create yet new problems. If the author sells the company one day, can she terminate her own transfer to what had been her own company? And joint authorship raises its own set of rights which can trump the issues just discussed.

Some dilemma.

Without prognosticating too much, I think that the weight of the arguments dealing with the gap issue is in favor of having the termination provision affecting post-1977 works to apply. Even though the transfer document may have been entered into pre-1978, in most cases, the copyrights were created post-1977 and therefore were subject to section 203, which allows termination after thirty-five years following the transfer. Section 304, which required fifty-six years to pass before termination, has sufficient language (for example, renewal language that only applies to works created under the 1909 law) that reinforces the argument that the old law could not possibly apply to these post-1977 works. I think, therefore, that the issue will be resolved—possibly through legislation—in favor of the argument that Section 203 applies to these works. The date of termination would be thirty-five years after the actual date of creation. It would probably be that date that would effectively constitute the moment the transfer of rights occurred. I use the word "probably" because dates of creation are not always discernible, but absent clearer language in the statute, there really is no other date which could constitute the moment of transfer. The fact that identifying the date of creation is difficult is not dissimilar to the difficulty of identifying the date of an oral transfer of a nonexclusive license, which clearly is subject to termination. So the framers of the legislation did not seem to be troubled by the difficulty in assessing a precise date as opposed to something simple, like the date a contract is signed, where the date is usually embedded right on the first page.

It is only logical to interpret the statute to mean that the transfer of rights to the publisher or record company could not possibly occur until the works were actually created, not before. How could one be an author, in whom the statute establishes the right to terminate a grant, until he actually has authored something? Jane Ginsburg, esteemed Columbia Law professor, and the daughter of Supreme Court Justice Ruth Bader Ginsburg, supports this position by pointing out the seemingly uncontrovertible logic that no copyright could preexist the creation of a work. Furthermore, she points out that the thirty-five-year time clock begins to run after the transfer has been "executed," and she argues quite convincingly that execution can only occur once the work is created. Executed, in her interpretation, does not mean "signed." Therefore, the statute in her mind is absolutely clear. There is no gap!

This issue has vast financial consequences, so I would expect that it will not be long before it is finally resolved one way or the other. The consequences of each of the two choices are so different that you can expect lots of lobbying and arguing before this occurs.

21 • COMPLIANCE WITH COPYRIGHT LAWS
Hints for the Corporate Counsel

Corporations cannot commit treason, nor be outlawed,
nor be excommunicated, for they have no souls.
But they can be sued for copyright infringement.
—ME, AFTER EDWARD COKE

Most corporations, their management, and their corporate counsels have never needed to comprehend or to process music rights. Certainly some companies, both large and small, have crossed paths with performing rights societies when they have utilized music on their telephone "hold" buttons, or when they have used music in a fairly sophisticated manner at store openings, at retirement or holiday parties, or in break rooms via television broadcasts, etc. But few of these companies had any idea what they would be getting into when they took their trademarks and products into cyberspace.

Some of what I am about to discuss is mentioned in other chapters. However, for those who may selectively choose chapters to read and, in particular, for those who counsel corporations (whether as in-house counsel or as outside counsel) and may not be as interested in some of the other portions of this book, a brief review of the legal underpinnings of music copyright is in order, highlighting what facts must be reckoned with and what myths need to be debunked.

INTANGIBLE RIGHTS AND THE INTERNET

Music rights do not exist in tangible form. You can't touch them; you can't put them on a table; you can't pour anything into them. Music rights are an idea—a concept. Most of the humanmade items that the world has valued since time immemorial are the tangible assets created by the hard work of people: everything from buildings to automobiles, from farm products to steak, from electronics to furniture.

A copyright is an accumulation of intangible rights. The bundle of rights that makes up a copyright consists of an indeterminate number of rights—long-established ones (for example, print rights, recording rights, performing rights, display rights, and synchronization rights [the recording of sound together with visual images]), and the "new" rights that seemingly emerge with each passing decade. Of course, many of the manifestations of intangible rights are real: sheet music, scores, CDs, etc. But the rights that allowed these manifestations to be created are nevertheless intangible. Got it?

It is the second decade of the 21st century, and we are faced with an entirely new mother lode of rights: There are digital download rights, webcast rights, podcast rights, and streaming rights. As discussed in chapter 23, page 352, maybe there is even an "Internet right" that will be discovered to exist within the protective coating that copyright provides for the expression of ideas!

This period of expansion and accompanying uncertainty is not the first time rights owners and users of music have had to face anomalies such as these. When the video-cassette was first introduced in the late 1970s and early 1980s, it was unclear whether the reproduction of a song on the videocassette was a mechanical reproduction (for which copyright law provides copyright owners with certain privileges and users certain responsibilities) or a synchronization (for which copyright law provides mostly responsi-bilities). The question has really never been answered—except by virtue of the fact that the entertainment industry (film and music divisions, in particular) has decided to consider these reproductions to be synchronizations so that the original license fee for the use of a song in a movie, for example, covers all subsequent reproductions on videocassettes, discs, and DVDs (together called *videograms*).

The federal copyright law (Title 17, United States Code), does not entirely distinguish among many of these rights, nor does it make much of an effort to catalogue them. It prefers the bundle to be flexible—evolving. The problem this presents to those who own music and those who use music is that they are forced to squeeze newly discovered rights into old definitions. Thus, to some a webcast is a performance and a mechanical reproduction as well. Is a download a mechanical reproduction (and, to some extent, a performance as well)? Is streaming . . . well, maybe a performance *and* a mechanical reproduction—maybe even a synchronization? When confronted with such questions, rights owners have universally concluded that the answer is always "yes." That the rights owners are not exactly sure why they answer in the affirmative does not weaken their resolve.

So, we have law achieved by consensus. Is the same type of law-without-legislation taking place now in the world of the Internet? It seems so. Digital downloads, webcasts, and streaming uncover rights that the copyright owners *decide* exist. Perhaps this is payback time for what the rights users did to the rights owners in the videogram area. Of course, until these issues are litigated, legislated, or arbitrated, the question as to what rights exist and who owns or controls them will not be resolved definitively.

LICENSING FROM MUSIC PUBLISHERS AND SOUND RECORDING OWNERS

Nothing in the law establishes a legal definition of "music publisher." This is totally a creation of the music industry, and it has served the industry well over the years. Authors' rights are dealt with in the writers' contracts with their publishers. Of course, since this relationship is not legislated, room for bargaining exists, so each writer's relationship with his or her publisher is unique.

The administration of songs can be quite complex, and large publishing companies have developed over the years to take the administration responsibilities out of the hands of the smaller publishers and writers. Therefore, it is most often these music publishers with whom rights users have to deal in order to obtain permission for the use of musical compositions. Insofar as performing rights are concerned, music publishers have bundled their rights and placed the responsibility to license such rights into the hands of monopolies, the two largest of which are ASCAP and BMI. These two entities, together with SESAC, control the performing rights to almost all of the musical compositions in the world. They represent just about all of US authors' songs, and they share the representation of the remainder of the world's music. For all practical purposes, these organizations are obliged to give licenses to anyone who requests them. The rates, however, are different for each organization, since their negotiating strengths differ, in part because of the difference in number and quality of their music catalogues.

Since the performing rights societies in the United States are not permitted to control their rights exclusively, they differ significantly from their affiliates in other countries in that those who seek performing rights can go directly to the source in the United States because the original copyright owners retain the right to license performing rights directly. Notwithstanding the hybrid nature of the American societies (that is, while they act as monopolies, the rights they have acquired from the music publishers are nonexclusive), they are still considered by the US government necessary, although dangerous, aggregators of the performing rights in essentially 100% of the world's music. In particular, ASCAP and BMI are controlled quite closely by the Justice Department and operate under consent decrees that are regularly reviewed. SESAC is not—yet.

Under certain circumstances, performing rights must be obtained for sound recordings as well. Specifically, certain rights must be obtained for sound recordings created since 1995 (the year in which the Digital Performance Right in Sound Recordings Act [DPRSRA] was passed), and copying of sound recordings created after 1972 is also subject to a plethora of protections that must be dealt with. Sound Exchange, a spin-off of the Recording Industry Association of America (RIAA), has begun to assume the responsibility for the licensing of the performing rights in sound recordings that ASCAP, BMI, and SESAC have assumed with respect to musical compositions.

Clearance of the mechanical reproduction and synchronization rights to most, but not all, songs (but not with respect to rights to synchronize musical compositions or to reproduce sound recordings) can be obtained through the Harry Fox Agency, Inc., or through its principals, the music publishers, most of whom are members of the National Music Publishers' Association (NMPA). As with the US performing rights societies, the Harry Fox Agency, in the United States, acts on behalf of the mechanical rights societies around the world that control equivalent rights. Contrary to the Harry Fox Agency's general refusal to issue synchronization licenses on behalf of its members, it has facilitated arrangements to assist its members in tracking and licensing such synchronizations as occur on YouTube, VEVO, and similar web outlets.

With the exception of certain qualifying users of music who can obtain a statutory license automatically from the government to webcast or otherwise provide noninteractive digital audio services, the clearance of the rights to mechanically reproduce sound recordings must be obtained from the sound recording copyright owner. This is usually one of the four major entertainment conglomerates (Universal, Sony BMG, Warner Music Group, and, recently disappeared, EMI), innumerable labels distributed by them, and yet even more independent (indie) record labels that are nearly impossible to quantify or, in many cases, to identify and locate.

One result of the many mergers that have recently taken place (for example, MCA with PolyGram and A&M, forming Universal; Geffen and Interscope with Universal; Virgin and Chrysalis with EMI, Sony with BMG, and, in 2012, EMI Records with Universal Music Group for sound recordings and EMI Music Publishing with Sony/ATV and its partners for music publishing rights) has been huge staff cutbacks, so that companies that have doubled and tripled their catalogues need to get by on the administration side with the same size staff that they started with prior to the mergers. (A similar diminution of the combined staffs of Warner Music Publishing Company and Chappell Music Corporation occurred when Warner bought Chappell, forming Warner/Chappell Music Publishing

Company.) Clearance procedures that were always a nightmare in the past are now even more difficult to negotiate, particularly within a time frame that is commercially practical. Note that when Sony Records merged with BMG Records, their music publishing divisions remained separate. BMG has since sold off its interest in Sony BMG and its publishing companies as well, only to be reborn as BMG Rights Management where it has been actively acquiring independent music publishing catalogues, thereby joining once again the top three of music publishing companies.

COPYRIGHT PROVISIONS APPLICABLE TO THE INTERNET

The Digital Millennium Copyright Act

The Digital Millennium Copyright Act (DMCA), which was signed into law in 1998, was designed to address issues relevant to the age of digital transmissions:

- *Title I* prohibits unauthorized access to a copyrighted work by circumventing technological protection measures (for example, encryption software), as well as civil remedies and criminal penalties for violation.

- *Title II* exempts from liability certain online service providers. This provision includes an exemption (the "safe harbor") for Internet service providers who make a temporary copy of a piece of music for the purpose of delivering the music to online users.

- *Title III* exempts Internet service providers from copyright infringement merely because they have turned on a computer to make repairs.

- *Title IV* extends to digital transmissions the "ephemeral" recording exemption of the Digital Performance Right in Sound Recordings Act of 1995, which applied to analog broadcasts.

Title IV also adds a paragraph to Section 112 of the Copyright Act containing a laundry list of limitations and exceptions to the necessity of seeking permission from copyright owners, which are analogous to those in Section 114 of the Copyright Act exempting certain transmissions and retransmissions of music from claims of copyright infringement by copyright owners. In the one case, however, the law helps users of music and then limits the help, and in the other case, the law helps copyright owners and then limits their remedies. Anyone who has to deal with this area should certainly seek out expert counsel. Just to give you an example of how incomprehensible the law can be, here is one sentence from a Congressional "explanation" of Section 114:

> Among those limitations is an exemption for non-subscription broadcast transmissions, which are defined as those made by terrestrial broadcast stations licensed as such by the FCC. 17 USC. 114(d)(1)(A)(iii) and (j)(2). The ephemeral recording exemption presently privileges certain activities of a transmitting organization when it is entitled to transmit a performance or display under a license or transfer of copyright ownership or under the limitations on exclusive rights in sound recordings specified by section 114(a) . . . .

Who says lawyers don't earn their fees?

In 2000, David Nimmer, a highly respected copyright law expert, wrote an article in the *UCLA Entertainment Law Review*, preparatory to including it in his (and his father's) invaluable treatise *Nimmer on Copyright*. It was entitled, "Ignoring the Public, Part I: On the Absurd Complexity of the Digital Audio Transmission Right."

Enough said?

Actually, not. In the world of copyright exploitation, one's truly innocent behavior can have dire consequences. This law can actually have the effect of freezing the development of the Internet. Innocence is no defense, so be careful.

The Government to the Rescue: Statutory Licenses

As noted above, the statutory license available to users of certain sound recordings for certain subscription services is fraught with exceptions and limitations. Actually, there are two statutory licenses established by the DPRSRA. One deals with performances of sound recordings that meet certain programming and other requirements, and the other deals with certain ephemeral (or incidental) reproductions of sound recordings, usually an interim step taken to store the music in the hard drives of computers known as "servers" prior to an authorized use such as a webcast. (The term *webcast* is generally used to refer to audio streaming on the Internet, or nondownloadable "Internet radio.") Under the ephemeral recordings exemption, for example, a radio station can record a set of songs and broadcast from the new recording rather than from the original CDs, which would otherwise have to be changed rapidly during the course of a broadcast.

The law is enormously complex and filled with exceptions and limitations. To stream sound recordings that are subject to copyright protection requires a statutory license. Securing one is not easy. (Note that one-artist-only webcasts and channels that perform the recordings of one artist continuously are not permitted to obtain a statutory license.)

Determining whether a statutory license is available for a particular use is no piece of cake. Yet, without a statutory license, a website utilizing music will have enormous, and probably overwhelming, difficulties in attempting to comply with the law. Seeking specific permission from sound recording owners is expensive, time-consuming, and, ultimately, prohibitive in every way. (A recent attempt to clear Internet rights with Universal Music Group was met with the following [paraphrased] response: "We don't do that. How about an 'up to' thirty-second license? We can do that!" What kind of "Internet radio station" can exist without the recordings of the largest company in the world?)

The fine print in the law that governs whether or not a statutory license is obtainable is very fine indeed. And provisions change frequently as the law's impact becomes more understood and modifications are sought and obtained. Consider yourself warned.

Blanket Performance and Synchronization License Agreements

The underlying principle behind all of the current standard agreements from each of the "blanket licensing" organizations (ASCAP, BMI, SESAC, the Harry Fox Agency, Inc., and the RIAA) is to charge fees based on revenue—with a minimum fee per year. The revenue-based model itself is susceptible of variations. For example, as with the all-industry-negotiated rates in the traditional broadcast media, ASCAP and BMI could one day seek to charge webcasters a percentage based solely on revenues less some agreed-upon percentage of operating expenses, or they could charge a percentage based solely on revenue derived from digital sales, but not hard goods sold via an Internet interface. But the websites that engage in webcasting are balking at this method. They argue that much of what is available on their websites does not include music, and only a percentage of those portions that do include music are devoted to streaming, that is, the real-time performance of the music. Variations on the theme abound, and it will not be clear for years how the societies will deal with this issue. Blanket license agreements for a variety of music uses can be viewed or downloaded from these websites:

- Performing rights—www.ascap.com, www.bmi.com, and www.sesac.com.
- Mechanical and synchronization rights—www.nmpa.org.

The agreements are still evolving, but even an *attempt* to comply, and regular communication with these organizations, will be useful in defending a claim from either the organizations or their members in case of a problem. SESAC has a particularly user-friendly site whereby one can download the license agreement relevant to a user's particular needs.

Some people have recommended that the societies create a "hobbyist" license for $25 to $50 a year. Unfortunately, as the DMCA now reads, a hobbyist would not qualify for the DMCA exemption because a hobbyist would not be able to meet the sound-recording criteria of the law. Said hobbyist would have to seek and obtain permission from an array of writers, publishers, record companies, and performing and mechanical rights societies every time he or she wanted to make an ephemeral copy by which legal, authorized rights could be exercised. This seems too bad, as the hobbyist license approach would afford a marvelous opportunity to "sign up" millions of young Internet users while educating them in the niceties of copyright compliance at the same time.

TERM OF COPYRIGHT

The copyright in a song written in the United States in the 1990s now extends for the author's life plus seventy years. (See chapter 23, page 356, for a discussion of anticopyright interests' unsuccessful attempts to reduce the term of copyright to the author's life plus fifty years.) A copyright secured by a company as an employer who has contracted for a work for hire extends for ninety-five years. Works for which copyright was secured under the 1909 Copyright Act (the one preceding the current act) also enjoy a copyright term extending ninety-five years, provided certain formalities—no longer necessary—were followed when they were supposed to be pre-1993.

Throughout the rest of the world, the copyright term is essentially the same as exists in the United States, although most other countries do not have the work-for-hire option: everyone who creates is an author. In addition, the copyright terms in countries outside of the United States were not subject to the renewal formalities provided under the 1909 Act and therefore the determination of whether a US work is in or out of copyright outside of the United States is much easier to calculate.

SAMPLING, BORROWING, AND STEALING

As chapter 23 discusses in some detail, "borrowing" copyrighted material is not permitted. Using any copyrighted work without permission, for just about any purpose—especially one with a commercial aspect—constitutes an intentional act of copyright infringement: Although the copyright law permits some uses as noninfringing under its fair-use provisions, most "borrowing"—including sampling—does not meet fair-use criteria. The idea that using a *de minimus* portion of a song is entitled to a fair-use defense is just plain wrong. (This defense is not to be confused with the defense of *de minimus non curat lex*, which is a general defense, not specific to the intellectual property field, available to all when a claim is of such little consequence as not to be worth the court's time.) The fiction perpetuated by those who are unfamiliar with copyright law that borrowing up to eight measures—or four measures—of music is permitted by law should be abandoned once and for all. Courts have actually held that copyright pertains to a single note on a sound recording when that note is distinguishable and original.

As part of its Friends of Active Copyright Education (FACE) initiative aiming at copyright education, the Copyright Society of the United States has established a website for teenagers that cites several examples of when a fair-use defense can be asserted and when it cannot. These are useful not only for teenagers but for corporate counsels as well, and the information can be found at www.copyrightkids.org.

RIGHTS MANAGEMENT

There are a myriad of state and federal laws, case interpretations, and customs affecting the use (commercial or otherwise) of photographs, models, film clips, etc. Corporations that face these issues must establish a management plan that invites the easy and broad sharing of information. Ironically, much of this can be exchanged through the mechanism of the Internet itself; many companies (including law firms) have established intracompany websites through which information and decision making can be opened up to the widest possible audience within the companies.

The task of managing intellectual property and complying with copyright and associated laws consists not just of identifying the problem; it includes controlling how the intellectual property rights are used and how they can be cleared in a reasonable fashion under the particular circumstances of a given use. That is why it is necessary to establish guidelines for identifying whether a proposed use will require special counseling in the event it actually takes place. In particular, companies whose legal counsel are dispersed and decentralized throughout the world should establish an intellectual property network so that lawyers and managers who are involved can keep each other informed, possibly by selecting a central rights-management person as well as one person in each division designated as the contact person for corporate compliance.

Another valuable means by which a company can manage its risks is to issue educational pamphlets on copyright, rights of privacy, and other intellectual property issues. Some of these will be "timeless" so that they can become a permanent part of the company's office manual. Other pamphlets, newsletters, etc. can be issued as the circumstances, such as changes in the law and the changing needs of the company, warrant. This is a particularly useful procedure because as new managers are hired, the total level of intellectual property education of a company's managers is necessarily diluted. The rights-management attorney can be charged with this responsibility.

In order to accomplish the information-exchange goals alluded to above, attorneys throughout the spectrum of the company's deal making should be informed of the availability of the rights-management attorney and the function of that office. In this way, language that appears in any contract that has intellectual property aspects can be scrutinized by an expert.

DANGEROUS LANGUAGE ALERT

A contract dealing with webcast distribution (including podcast distribution) may include the following language, tucked in well toward the end of the document, in the middle of other standard boilerplate language (where they hope no one will notice it—let alone understand it):

- Customer holds all rights *throughout the world* [italics added] material to its obligations under this agreement and to the licenses granted hereunder [including the rights of] . . . , transmission, distribution, performance, display and broadcast of the event and materials . . . and all copying . . . , necessary to effectuate these activities.

- Webcaster's exercise of any . . . , rights granted . . . , herein, will not violate or infringe any right of privacy, personality or publicity, any Intellectual Property Right, or any other right of any party.
- Customer has the worldwide right to license to Webcaster the right . . . , to publicly distribute, transmit, and perform the event . . . , via streaming video protocols . . . and to use, reproduce, and display . . . , the materials contained in the event . . . , and to maintain the archive of the event . . . , for on-demand access and distribution, transmission, and performance.

Pretty inclusive language. Pretty dangerous language. Does the person negotiating the overall agreement have enough familiarity with the DMCA and the DPRSRA to sign off on language such as this? Does that person understand technically what the company is actually seeking to accomplish or to present to the public to be able to counsel the company on this language?

Would it not be a lot more efficient and risk free to seek the counsel of someone who lives and breathes this area of the law every day? It is unwise for a corporation to parcel out its contract-negotiating responsibilities among a variety of lawyers who are not acting as mutual resources for each other. It is far better to consult outside counsel who specialize in Internet and copyright law, to create the position of rights management person, as suggested above, or to expand the job description of one inside counsel to assume this responsibility.

The infringement issues raised above do not present insoluble problems. On the contrary, they merely require a different kind of attention and decision-making. Copyright infringement consequences can be significant, but if a company is diligently trying to do the right thing, the damages anyone will be able to recover can be significantly reduced. For example, the statutory damages for *copyright infringement* (which, by definition is intentional, even if "innocent") are dramatically lower than those for *willful copyright infringement* (which, while also intentional, is subject to much higher damage penalties).

Of course, the issues explored here are exacerbated when a company has many divisions and—even more so—when those divisions exist in different states and countries. The need for corporations to establish rights use and clearance guidelines is as compelling as it is to have general corporate policy and other legal guidelines that have become routine over the past decades. There is no other responsible way to manage the risks of infringement of copyright or other intellectual property rights. Among these risks in the copyright area are the attendant costs, including not only the legal fees of the company (the defendant), but also, potentially, the legal fees of the prevailing party (the plaintiff) for which the US copyright law includes specific provision, to be assessed at the discretion of the court.

MUSIC CLEARANCE: THE MUSIC INDUSTRY'S REVENGE

People who want quick solutions have no idea how complicated it is to clear music rights. First of all, there are multiple rights involved. Even in a live-performance webcast of any sort, one must deal with the mechanical and performance rights emanating from the webcast; in-store uses of footage from the webcast (for example, a CD or a videogram, that is, cassette or DVD); and perhaps a TV special, perhaps more than one (one for the United States and one for Europe, one for South America, and one for Asia). And don't forget pay per view. Oh yes. One more thing to add to the "don't forget" list: the moral rights of authors and their heirs outside of the United States. This is a wild card courtesy of foreign intellectual property laws that will allow the heirs of *their* John Philip Sousas (whose music in this country is in the public domain) to stop cold any use of their ancestor's music that they believe is inimical to the ancestor's moral heritage. The concern is particularly relevant in the area of commercial advertising. Thus a Mercedes Benz commercial using a French song long out of copyright protection might offend the heirs of the writer of the song, while a Citroën commercial using the same song might not.

For a company whose principal function has nothing to do with music, it is virtually impossible to understand how difficult it is to clear the necessary rights for something as seemingly straightforward as a webcast—or even the simple use of a song on a website. What's more, the rights have to be cleared both for the song and the master. And if the song is a particularly current "edgy" one, the likelihood is that there are multiple writers and copublishers on the music publishing side who will have to be dealt with. For a five-song presentation, there are upward of fifty to two hundred rights that have to be cleared. For example, if, for one song, three writers and unaffiliated publishing companies are involved together with one master rights owner, seven rights would have to be cleared for one work, but if all three writers and their publishing companies were in partnership with third-party music publishers (like Sony/ATV or Warner/Chappell), then there would actually be six publishing companies to deal with—for a new total of ten rights. Multiply this by five songs and you get fifty different rights to clear. And that's just the song. To clear the master recording can be even more daunting, especially if samples are incorporated into the recording. Obtaining these rights can be so expensive as to be practically prohibitive for the average marketing budget—or they can be managed efficiently and cost effectively.

INTERNATIONAL ISSUES: ONE-STOP SHOPPING

One-stop shopping is impossible in the current global environment. Even the collection societies have not figured out what to do.

Slow responses are the norm. *No* response is, unfortunately, not rare. Yet decisions must customarily be made on very short notice. And even where the responses are quick and satisfying, the process of drafting and negotiating the formal licenses is enormously burdensome. Every music company would prefer to use its own form, none of which really fits the imaginative uses that the licensee comes up with (at least *someone* is being creative!). The staffs of the music companies are simply too small to deal with the avalanche of paperwork generated by the multiple uses and clearances involved, neither the music companies nor their prospective licensees have a clue as to what to charge, and both legal fees and clearance company fees multiply to unconscionable levels. Further complicating the issue is the fact that most, if not all, of the rights owners will undoubtedly insist on most-favored-nation treatment—which can put a real crimp not only in one's budget, but in determining whether it is even worth proceeding with the project. The concept of "most favored nation" (MFN) originated in the world of international trade: an agreement between nations would stipulate that the receiving nation had to be granted terms at least as good as any other nation with respect to the same deal. Here's an example from the world of music: A client of mine cleared fifty-three of fifty-five songs in a documentary film for $5,000 each, but one publisher demanded $30,000. The difference, dictated by the MFN clauses in the agreements, amounted to more than the cost of the film—$25,000 × 53 = $1,325,000! Needless to say, the film remains in the can, never to see the light of day.

Some adventurous lawyers think they have found a way around the strictures of the most-favored-nations agreement. They suggest optioning another song and never using it, obtaining rights they never need and will never use and therefore never pay for, and paying extra for rights they will never use. Needless to say, those who make their living licensing rights are tuned in to these tricks and they won't often be fooled.

There is some question whether MFN provisions constitute antitrust behavior and are therefore illegal. But do you want to take on the fight for everyone else and make new law? I don't think so.

For a more detailed discussion of the trials and tribulations of the copyright industry's attempts to make things easier and cheaper rather than harder and more expensive, see chapter 23, pages 353-356.

SO YOUR CORPORATION HAS ALSO DECIDED TO BECOME ADVENTUROUS?

Times have changed. Corporate counsels are dealing with matters formerly left to rock and roll attorneys and their offspring (hip hop lawyers?). Corporations are using music as never before. Gone are the days that IBM looked only to its advertising agencies to clear rights to music used in their commercials. All major and minor corporations in the world today are utilizing music on their websites, on phone lines, and in their offices, lobbies, and meeting rooms. Holiday parties feature "Do You Hear What I Hear?" and "Little Drummer Boy" not to mention "I Saw Mommy Kissing Santa Claus" and "Silver Bells." Websites include music clips to bring down the age of their visitors and potential customers and to characterize them as more hip than their competitors. All are copyrighted and require permission to be used.

Many fairly mainstream companies have begun to introduce, via their websites and links with other websites, creative and contemporary marketing ideas into their general approach to sell their products and image to the public. Whether they are offering downloads, streams, or podcasts, music rights are implicated to one degree or another. Downloads require mechanical licenses, streams require synchronization licenses and probably performance licenses, and who knows what is required to offer podcasts legally. I say the latter because these on-demand programs clearly require mechanical licenses, yet one won't know what is owed until the podcast offering has ended. There may have been a thousand recipients who have accessed the podcast or 1 million. No one can control this, and budgets don't accommodate uncertainty. Sound recording owners similarly don't know how to allow the use of their masters pursuant to any rational basis for compensation. So, all I can say about a company which wishes to offer podcasts with music is "Be careful" and try to make a flat-fee deal with both rights owners, or you are opening up your company to unknown risk. See chapter 16, page 252 for more detailed discussion on podcasts.

22 · CATALOGUE VALUATION
How to Improve Your Odds at Winning Big

Price is what you pay. Value is what you get.
—WARREN BUFFETT

Music publishing is widely regarded as both an excellent profit-making venture and a good long-term investment. Hardly a day goes by without my having (or hearing) a conversation that ends by someone asking, "Do you know of any catalogues that are for sale?" This view derives partly from fact and partly from myth.

In the early 1980s, Boston Ventures purchased Chappell Music from PolyGram Music for about $100 million. They sold it to Time Warner a mere four years later for $275 million. Of course, this incredible increment in value occurred *before* the historic rise in publishing income derived from legal digital downloads and other technological advances that have coursed through the music business in the years after the millennium. It is too early to evaluate how "historic" this rise will be given that copyright rates for streams are in flux, and there are as yet insubstantial returns on the mechanical side from full downloads. The estimated cumulative mechanical revenue from the more than 1 billion iTunes downloads that have accrued from inception through the date of publication of this book amounts to about $500 million. While this may seem like a lot, it is roughly equivalent to about 100 million *album* sales—what just fifteen or twenty top artists would, until a few years ago, cumulatively sell on a regular basis annually.

Not the least of the reasons for the increased value in copyrights is the fact that artists have begun to withdraw their resistance to licensing their works for commercials—something that was anathema to them for decades—at least in the United States. It didn't hurt to change the overall attitude for such icons as Lou Reed (Honda motorcycles), Sting (Jaguar), Bob Dylan (Victoria's Secret), and Ric Ocasek and The Cars (Circuit City) to support such practices. Ringtones (most often note sequences that emit chords and melodies alerting a cell phone holder that a call is coming in), which did not even exist a few years ago, are now a multibillion dollar business worldwide. (For 2007, the market has been estimated at 2 to 3 billion dollars, less than 2% of the US music business, and down 50 percent from just a few years earlier due to record labels offering actual "master" ring tones, the ability to create one's own ringtones, and the availability via digital music stores when coupled with the sale of downloads). Yet video ringtones are now available in advanced economies, so the growth and expansion of the use of music continues. Whatever their future, ringtones are just one of a myriad of heretofore unknown exploitation opportunities in which the Internet is serving the music publishing community in ways the music publishers and writers never imagined (and still do not comprehend in many cases).

Many factors go into the valuation of a music catalogue. Many that seem to be self-explanatory are not. Where they are not, I have added some clarification or example. All of them serve one goal only: *the ability to project future cash flow*. If one can value a catalogue at a specific point in time, one can evaluate the catalogue's potential earnings at various points in the future. But it is not enough to determine what is driving the revenue. One must also be able to figure out how to increase future revenue. This is about money, not music; interest rates and inflation, not market share; projections, not dreams.

FACTORS IN VALUING CATALOGUES: AN OVERVIEW

Earning Trends

Is the income going up or down? (Five years' history is the norm for such evaluations, but depending on the nature and the extent of the peaks and valleys, five years' history may not be enough.). Did a spike in income result from the death of an artist? A tour? A film? How enduring, then, might the income be? (Note that, depending on the catalogue, synchronization income may spike, but the likelihood of repetitive spikes is usually quite small—particularly with respect to the same song—and particularly if the synchronization is for an advertising use. United Airlines has utilized "Rhapsody in Blue" for years. On the one hand, if United stops using this song, upward of $1 million per year will be lost. At the same time, it is unlikely that any other company would want to associate that song with another product for some time to come.

What is driving the revenue? Cover recordings, which may continue ad infinitum, or original recordings, whose earnings life will naturally be limited? Singles, tracks from albums, entire albums? Do the earnings come from "best of" records? The source of the money is very important, as some sources dry up more quickly than others.

In stock market parlance the term *anomaly* refers to situations in which the price of a stock seems not to reflect its real value. An example in the music world would be "Tie a Yellow Ribbon," which always sells well when US troops are in combat overseas, but it would be a mistake to overvalue the catalogue containing that song on the basis of those sales.

Who's Buying What? The better the information you, as a potential purchaser, have as to who is going after what, and how much potential buyers might be willing to pay—especially when others are interested in bidding for the catalogue that you are thinking of acquiring—the more power you will have.

Getting the Most for Your Money: Identifying the Unidentified Astonishingly, many music publishers own songs that they simply cannot identify by melody or by written notation. They exist only as titles. While these may represent only the more minor earners (perhaps generating money only via obscure radio performances) and therefore not be of particular relevance to determining a purchase price, they should not be overlooked.

Trends in Taste: What's Hot and What's Not Here is where the advice of an expert who has a grasp of the current value of different genres such as rock, rap, classical, adult contemporary, reggae, R&B, Latin, EDM, etc., can be useful. There are now as many radio formats as there are genres. If the music in the catalogue is predominantly reggae, does this explain a growth in the catalogue's income during the first part of the 21st century with such top-selling reggae artists (throwing in a little rap on the side) as Sean Paul and Kevin Lyttle? Is country music on the upswing or the downswing? Boy bands and disco have already seen their finest hours, and the timing of their fall from grace might well have been predicted by a savvy trend watcher.

Evaluating the Artists When purchasing a catalogue that predominantly comprises songs by a particular artist, it is useful to be able to predict the ongoing viability of that artist—both in the recording and in the performing realm. As we have seen, an increasing number of older artists who seemed to have fallen off the radar screen have had remarkable comebacks. Even Cream, which had not performed together for almost forty years, toured again in the early 2000s. Why? Surely their members—Eric Clapton, Ginger Baker, and Jack Bruce—enjoyed some artistic and personal pleasure, but with ticket prices being what they are these days, it is likely that the most important motivation was money. Some purchasers of catalogues are Wall Street (or even Boston) venture capitalists; a purchaser grounded in the music of an era may well be able to approach an artist or artists and encourage him or her (or them) to revisit their past—not coincidentally reviving the music copyrights identified with that artist.

It is, of course, not possible to make precise, accurate projections of *any* artist's long-term viability. But purchasers should evaluate the possibilities as thoroughly as possible, preferably with an expert in the field—for example, a booking agent or a promoter, both of whom know long before anyone else what the real story is.

SATELLITE RADIO, INTERNET RADIO, MOBILE PHONE STREAMING, AND HD RADIO

In recent years, satellite radio has increased its subscriber list by as much as 200% per year. In 2005, revenue increased by almost 300% over 2006, and media watchers predicted over 40 million subscribers by 2020. Satellite radio has given listeners an unprecedented choice of both genres and individual tracks, but the returns are not yet in on the extent to which this medium will affect the sale of records—either in physical form or via digital download—or how much it will represent in terms of performance royalties. Nevertheless, new possibilities continue to present themselves. It is only a matter of time before listeners will be able to push a button when they hear a song they like, instantaneously copying it into their iTunes libraries. Another developing trend involves new devices being introduced by SiriusXM satellite radio that will allow users to "record" (the language used by SiriusXM is "retain") permanent copies of musical works transmitted by satellites. Notably, these copies cannot then be burned onto CDs. Both NMPA (the National Music Publishers Association) and RIAA (the Recording Industry Association of America) are monitoring all trends closely. Some feel that, as a result of these initiatives (with more to come), satellite radio might be a negative, and not a positive, entry into the music distribution wars—at least for record companies and artists.

But do not despair. Other platforms are exploding, all of which are generating new and undreamed-of income for song and master owners.

Digital Downloads, Digitally Distributed Video Games, Streams, Apps As we know, digital downloads may have seen their best days. After a period during which digital download sales far exceeded expectations, they are on a descending track just as streaming passes them by. At one time, record "clubs" thought that they could salvage their role in providing consumers direct access to music via the download route. They never developed a model that worked, and the downward trend continues across the board without their involvement. Although the total number of song tracks downloaded is still considerably less than the equivalent number of CD tracks that were sold historically, several billion DPDs have been purchased, putting a crimp into at least some of the illegal peer-to-peer music sharing that still occurs in high numbers. Digitally distributed video games are experiencing a huge growth of over 200% since 2010 alone . . . and all of these use music, much of which has to be licensed. But it is clear that streaming has become the medium of choice for music consumers. Subscriptions for unlimited streams, via such platforms as Spotify and Internet radio such as Pandora are generating new sources of mechanical and/or performance income never before possible, and accordingly, the value of song catalogues is increasing daily in ways that most often cannot even be predicted or calculated. The jury is in insofar as justifying faith in the future of music, but out insofar as making it possible to predict the monetization of these new sources of exploitation. The introduction of smartphone apps has made it all the easier to capture music from an unlimited array of sources on a moment's notice. In 2012, Spotify alone was the seventh highest rated app in AppData's 2012 list of top apps in the world, and it was also the highest rated music app. Not bad for a company that had operated in the world's biggest market, the USA, for less than two years.

Digital Jukeboxes　The "digital jukebox," like satellite radio, is a relatively new medium. Digital jukeboxes offer hundreds, and even thousands, of tunes direct from central servers to your table at your favorite diner. Different companies have different technologies for delivering these recorded works, but once again, the wider choice simply expands the reach of all music in ways never dreamed of before. Still, they do not present a real challenge to personal and industry-created playlists.

Sources of Income

Cover Possibilities　Obviously, some songs are more coverable than others. We have yet to find out if rap songs will have the second (or third) life that has historically followed Gershwin, Porter, and even Holland–Dozier–Holland songs (for example, the Supremes' hit "Can't Hurry Love" found a new audience after the release of a cover by Phil Collins that became hugely successful). Cover possibilities vary depending on the nature of music (and radio) at the time the valuation is taking place. During the boy-band era, these artists recorded mostly new songs, even though the genre was predominantly middle-of-the-road and presumably 'NSYNC and the Backstreet Boys could have recorded "standards"; however, the beginning of the 21st century has seen such phenomena as Peter Cincotti, Michael Buble, and so many others (not to mention Bob Dylan, Barry Manilow, and Rod Stewart!) rediscovering (and more importantly reminding us of) some of the greatest "chestnuts" of the last century—for example, "Sway," "Stardust," and, yes, "Moments to Remember." Sometimes, an unrecorded song will have excellent cover potential, but only an expert in the particular genre or genres represented by the catalogue is qualified to assess whether the unrecorded songs in a catalogue are in shape enough to be able to be evaluated for purpose of cover recordings. No accountant, lawyer, or financial investor will have a clue. If a catalogue consists of various genres of music, then hire various experts. A worthwhile investment.

Print Rights　Print rights have not meant very much in relation to other forms of income for more than seventy-five years. But with the advent of digital sheet music, and the intricate cross-promotions made possible by the Internet, the good days are back. If you believe that the music in a catalogue is likely to be of interest to specific classes of purchasers (students, churchgoers, fans of an artist, attendees at weddings, other celebrations, or funerals, etc.), by all means ask the expert you have selected to evaluate that catalogue to consider these possibilities.

Song-Specific Exploitations It has often surprised me—perhaps "shocked" would be a better word—that many music publishing companies have evidently given little or no thought to the potential of using specific songs in ways that will generate revenue. One use that springs to mind is commercials. Hiring a consultant from a marketing company or an advertising agency could easily come up with ideas to exploit titles of lyrical portions of songs for this purpose. A potential purchaser could engage such a person for a brief amount of time to give an opinion as to the viability of such an option.

Another possible song-specific exploitation is use of a song that has particular resonance in terms of a widely celebrated holiday. For example, a dynamic, though small, publishing company owns a song called "Oh My Mama." When was the last time it was used for Mother's Day in any creative way? Certainly 1-800-Flowers would know what to do with it on the biggest day of the year for flower sales. But what about digital sheet music or downloads offered on the Internet? Radio play? Products identified with the title or lyric? Greeting cards? If this song—or songs like it—is in a catalogue, the fact that its earnings may be moribund should not necessarily discourage a purchaser from assessing its potential value.

When stock prices go down, new management often switches gears, thinks out of the box, and tries innovations that cause the stock prices to rise. The same is true with a music catalogue that has been gathering dust for fifty years. The numbers don't tell it all.

Added Value You, as a buyer, may determine that a given catalogue may be of more value to you than it might be to other potential buyers. For example, when a client of mine decided to sell half of the Buddy Holly catalogue, several players were interested, but the one who should have bought it, and did, was the new company which Paul McCartney had just formed. This was his first catalogue, and soon Linda Ronstadt had recorded two of the catalogue's biggest hits, and had hits with them; the film *The Buddy Holly Story* was released; and the musical *Buddy* was on the boards. MPL Music Publishing (McCartney, Paul and Linda) was on its way. It is fair to say that few, if any, other publishers could have lit a match under this catalogue as MPL did. Whether it was the work of one or many people is not relevant; both the purchaser and the seller (Buddy's producer who was also one of his cowriters, Norman Petty) benefited. Now that's synergy.

EVALUATING DATA

Before discussing the pitfalls in evaluating data, let's first agree on what data we are going to evaluate. Most buyers will require at least the following as part of their due diligence. Copies of all relevant royalty statements received from any source within the prior five years, including but not limited to the following:

1. Music publishers through the world broken down per territory
2. Copyright administrators
3. Mechanical rights licensing organizations and agents
4. Performance rights societies/organizations

5. Copublishing administrators
6. Subpublishers
7. Any statements from any source directly licensed by the owner
8. Copies of all of the relevant agreements and copyright registrations, notices of use, renewal certificates where relevant, all applicable assignments including US Copyright office recordings of such assignments, mortgages, etc., and pertaining to any of the entities detailed above, including a schedule for each agreement detailing:

a. Titles subject to such agreement
b. The author(s) of each title and each author's authorship share in percentage terms
c. The publisher(s) of each title, and each publisher's percentage share
d. The date of creation for each title
e. The date of copyright registration for each title
f. The date of assignment for each title

Finally, if possible, the potential buyer will want to audit/review the books and records of the seller to make sure all songwriters and others due royalties pursuant to the agreements mentioned above we're in fact paid their due.

On their own, of course, the buyer will want to do copyright searches on its own, as well as credit and UCC and state record searches to make sure no liens exist on the copyrights or assets generally of the corporation.

When all is said and done, the seller may wish to not depend solely on a nondisclosure agreement with potential buyers as they might not even want the potential buyers to know certain confidential facts about the company in the event the sale does not eventually occur. Nowadays this will entail filing the data in the cloud and providing potential buyers with various codes and keys to access ever-widening amounts of information.

Now, let's discuss how the data is evaluated.

Third-Party Data

What happens when the income on the seller's records do not match the data from SoundScan or other third-party data sources, the "across the counter" data that keeps track of record sales in most traditional record stores. At least a question can be raised and an answer evaluated. But unless the data is questioned, a significant deviation from accuracy might slip through. Of course, neither SoundScan nor the other data sources are precise. SoundScan is merely an extrapolation that provides the appearance of scientific accuracy and *may or may not* be statistically accurate. But it is not a one-for-one count. Financial records, therefore, should be read only in part in light of third-party data sources. Other data are necessary to obtain a full picture.

Net Publisher's Share

Often, publishers are paid on one-third of a song when they actually own one-quarter (or vice versa). These are 5% to 10% errors (in this case 8%), but they add up, and on an important earner, they can mean a big difference, especially when multiplied by 15, or whatever the multiple is that the parties are using to arrive at the net publisher's share (NPS) for an eventual sale of one's ownership interest.

Quality of Documentation

By "quality of documentation," I mean the quality of record keeping insofar as contracts with writers—or the absence of such contracts—are concerned. Obviously, some catalogue files will be in better shape than others. The absence of precise information on the chain of ownership of the titles in a catalogue can devalue a catalogue just as it would in a real estate transaction. The reality is that some catalogues are simply in a mess. This puts the seller at some risk because the asking price will be subject to attack—and reduction; it puts the purchaser at risk because he or she may be buying a pig in a poke. A costly Copyright Office search may be the most effective way to trace a song's title, but the absence of songwriter agreements can put in jeopardy a company's right to the composition in the first place. A long history of paying royalties to authors is always a good sign, but there are risks, and purchasers will have to depend on attorneys to evaluate just how serious these risks are.

Contracts with Writers

Sometimes the person who takes over administration of a catalogue is so respected and so comfortable in dealing with writers that he or she is able to forestall adversarial responses to the sale on the part of the catalogue's writers. Another person might not be as good at easing writers' before-sale concerns. Yet not dealing with such concerns can affect the price a purchaser is prepared to pay for a catalogue. When I represent an artist-owned and artist-created catalogue, I invariably find myself in the annoying role of insisting that where there are cowriters, they all (and all of their music publishing administrators) enter into a cowriter agreement establishing exactly who owns what and who controls what. This can become very important when one writer—usually the artist—does not want to permit certain uses of his cowritten songs. Absent such a document, cowriters are equally authorized to do essentially whatever they wish to do with the song—provided they ensure that all cowriters receive their fair share. But this may not be good enough for an artist-cowriter, and his or her cowriter agreements may well place restrictions on the others. Purchasers who are acquiring the "others'" interest will want to know whether there are such restrictions on the titles being purchased. Similarly, the absence of such an agreement might cause one to question the accuracy of the splits among the cowriters. More risk!

Sufficiency of Accountings to Writers

The purchaser's accountant—who, hopefully, is expert in valuing and evaluating music catalogues—will be able to advise the purchaser as to whether the writers of the catalogue's compositions (or their heirs or assignees) have been properly paid on time or not. While in most states, there is a six-year statute of limitations on claims for royalties, some states provide for the statutory term to be extended when fraud is present, and purchasers should make sure to have a pretty good picture of where things stand in this area in order to avoid surprises later on. As noted earlier, some writers and their heirs avoid controversy with the original owner for reasons of fear or otherwise, but have no such hesitation once the catalogue ends up in the hands of a good-faith purchaser—particularly one with deep pockets.

Number and Diversity of Songs

The number of songs in a catalogue is significant in the sense that administrative costs can be a significant deterrent to profitability. Purchasers tend to look at the top twenty-five or one hundred earners and calculate the worth of the company on this basis. Even a company with 25,000 titles has twenty-five top sellers. But consider the cost of registering the assignments in the Copyright Office and upgrading an old-fashioned accounting and record-keeping system to present-day standards. Certainly many hidden gems may be in the 24,975 less-significant titles, but the cost of uncovering them is as much of a burden to a buyer as is the cost of extracting gold from an abandoned gold mine. A buyer has to be able both to identify the overall value of the catalogue as a whole and to evaluate the cost of managing it.

Another factor to take into account is diversity. On the face of it, diversity would seem to be an advantage, but it can work the other way, too. A catalogue may be so diverse that its owners are unable to take advantage of any of the parts of which it is composed. If country music is making a comeback, for example, and the catalogue is 2% country music, the trend will have little positive effect.

Administration Issues

The numbers are only as good as the administrative talent and detail behind them. Those handling the due diligence should be able to evaluate how likely it is that the income data from various sources, including various regions of the world, is (1) accurate and (2) likely to be well administered. If the foreign collecting agents are reputable, and not companies connected with the seller, the chances are the numbers are accurate. Some publishers either join foreign societies or check periodically on the registration facts at the various societies, and those records are valuable sources of confirmation as to the accuracy of the numbers.

As for the *quality* of the administering function, there are two concerns:

1. Once again, the reputation of the foreign collecting agents or the potential connection to the seller (which will make their numbers suspect) is important.

2. Whenever the administration of a catalogue is in the hands of a third party, the contractual terms of the administration agreements should be very carefully examined. Are the earnings calculated at source? Have the foreign subpublishers been audited? If foreign subpublishers have retention rights, how long do they last? (It used to be that a cover record obtained in certain European countries, however insignificant in terms of sales, would entitle the subpublisher to represent the song for the entire remaining term of copyright; nowadays, retention rights usually extend two years if the cover record has strong sales or is high on the charts.)

Quality of Registrations

There is not usually sufficient time for a potential purchaser to double-check the accuracy of the registrations with the various societies that handle copyrights, including US societies, leaving purchasers pretty much in the dark as to whether the numbers they are depending on reflect reality. Errors, however, tend to benefit the purchaser because the numbers on which the purchaser will base the multiple will be lower, not higher. Catalogue owners (sellers) who pay attention to such things will have society printouts of registrations, and these can be compared with catalogue master lists. These are particularly useful because no society is likely to allow a potential purchaser to obtain information on catalogues he or she does not own or control.

Limitations on Recovery of Royalties

Agreements between the seller and its licensees will often contain a contractual statute of limitations that will limit the ability of a purchaser to audit their books and records. Those doing the due diligence will have to schedule these so that a conclusion can be reached as to what limitations the purchaser will have to accept.

Timeliness of Data

Naturally, the more recent the data, the more valid it is. The purchaser should be wary of companies that cannot provide a clear picture of recent activity—through such verifiable means as statements issued from record companies or collection agents, or from other users or administrators of the music (such as subpublishers). Confirming letters from such companies or societies will help the purchaser to get a picture of more than a years' worth of current activity. They can also confirm what earnings have yet to be paid to the catalogue owner—known as *pipeline earnings*.

Translations and Adaptations

Many songs that originate overseas are successful in the United States only because of their translations and/or adaptations. The publisher's share is not often affected by the presence of translators or adaptors, but sometimes it is. More often, in the modern era, songs are cowritten, and co-owned, by multiple writers, so that the valuation of a more current song may require checking a bit more thoroughly into songwriter contracts (if indeed there are any) than cases in which a song has been written by a single songwriter whose exclusivity is established by a clear written contract.

For songs that originate in the United States and are translated and/or adapted for use overseas, royalty splits with respect to the affected songs are often controlled by foreign societies, and not by contract. To the extent that songs have originated in or are particularly successful in foreign languages, in foreign countries, it is useful to ask the seller what they actually control, and what, by virtue of society regulations, they may have been forced to relinquish to, say, a foreign adaptor and the adaptor's publisher.

Advances

Unrecouped advances benefit the purchasers as long as they can keep song earnings coming in until those advances are recouped. They act, on a dollar-for-dollar basis, to reduce the risk of the purchaser. Sometimes, however, writers receive loans or advances from their publishers. The efficacy of a company's bookkeeping records that should disclose these loans or advances can avoid a lot of confusion and unhappiness down the road. Otherwise, a buyer might pay royalties to writers whose accounts are in fact unrecouped. This again is an area in which the purchaser will traditionally look to his or her accountant for guidance.

Contractual Carryovers with Third Parties

Whether carryovers with third parties are positive or negative, they will have an impact on revenues. Ordinarily there will be both: unrecouped advances from third-party publishers or administrators, and unrecouped advances to writers and copublishers. These carryovers should be on the books of the company and can be verified by checking the agreements giving rise to them. These will have an impact (again positive or negative) on the true value of the catalogue and should be looked at very carefully.

WHO OWNS THE CATALOGUE?

When a company that is all about legitimate business and legitimate profit owns a catalogue, potential purchasers are likely to be dealing with honestly obtained and presented facts and figures traditionally used to evaluate any business. But when the catalogue owner is the writer or the heir of the writer, or someone who has a reputation for sharp dealings with his or her writers, there are often big-time problems, especially with regard to a purchaser's ability to perform due diligence. And, of course, for a variety of reasons, the records simply may not be available.

I recall performing due diligence on a catalogue the owner of which was an alleged mobster, whose name was regularly inserted as "author" on copyright registration certificates and on "amendments" to copyright certificates following a loan to the real author, which was granted in return for an "acknowledgment" that a mistake had been made in the original copyright registration application. The alleged mobster decided to sell, and negotiations for the sale of the catalogue began. Two companies were interested. One pulled out, on the correct assumption that the risk was enormous that the owner had so carelessly, and/or criminally, acquired the rights that the documentation available to the lawyers performing the due diligence was practically worthless. The other company, which eventually did purchase the catalogue, faced the same problems, but it was headed by an executive who had a way with writers and who knew that the first step was to find the legitimate authors and their heirs, then announce that for the first time, their royalties would be properly accounted for and paid and their songs exploited. This turned out to be enough to forestall almost all of the threatened lawsuits; the catalogue became stable and made the new owners (and the songwriters) a lot of money. (Coda: Two of the writers did choose to sue the new owner, claiming that they were really the writers of a song, but that they had been afraid for twenty-five years to present a claim to the dishonest owner because they feared they would be killed, and on this basis, they sought to extend the statute of limitations on their claim, which had expired almost twenty years earlier. The court rejected their argument, and threw out the case. Too bad.)

TERMINATION ISSUES

Termination issues are discussed in detail in chapter 20, pages 308–316. Suffice it to say here that copyrights to which either Section 304(c) or 203 applies are ticking bombs. When *any* notice of termination becomes effective, all newly licensed (although not all formerly licensed) revenue stops. Period. While one may never be able to get a precise fix on whether the author of a particular composition or group of compositions—or the author's heirs—is even aware of, let alone willing to exercise, his or her rights under Sections 304(c) or 203, the mere *possibility* that the rights could be exercised should give a purchaser pause (and impact the price he or she is willing to pay for the catalogue).

Of course, the composition of some catalogues is such that it is highly unlikely that the heirs of an author will elect to disrupt a flow of income and to simultaneously be willing, or financially able, to take on the cost of hiring advisors to help them prepare notices of termination, and then, once they acquire the copyrights, help them administer them. I don't know the percentages of copyrights whose termination windows pass without a peep from the authors or their heirs, but I would guess it is very high. Nevertheless, would-be purchasers must take this factor into account and assume that it is more likely that the termination rights for the more important songs (at least those with the highest earnings) will be very much on the radar of their authors or the heirs of their authors.

THE "TRUNK"

Robert Kimball, the theater historian, archivist of the Ira Gershwin estate, and the country's leading expert on the American song, has written many of the exhaustive studies of Cole Porter, Irving Berlin, the Gershwins, and other American songwriters. Mr. Kimball was asked by Warner Bros. Music (the predecessor to Warner/Chappell Music) to investigate a box of miscellaneous musical material in a warehouse in Secaucus, New Jersey. He found the proverbial "trunk" of George and Ira Gershwin, as well as works of Cole Porter, Jerome Kern, and Richard Rodgers. This contained a mother lode of musical compositions, musical shows, and fragments of both. When I first started practicing law, my firm was providing legal services to Frank Loesser, composer, lyricist, and book writer of *Guys and Dolls*, *The Most Happy Fella*, *How to Succeed in Business Without Really Trying*, and many more. It was then that I learned of the trunk. Frank had one. Paul Simon has one. And the discovery that the Gershwins also had a trunk was so miraculous that it deserved a front-page *New York Times* story and a feature story in *Time* magazine.

WHO'S SORRY NOW? THE BLACKBIRD

In valuing a copyright catalogue, the potential purchaser must evaluate whether a composition, once terminated, still has some life left as an income provider to the catalogue. The courts have held that a mechanical license, issued by a music publisher prior to termination, remains valid and the income derived from that license remains the music publisher's, to share with the author or the author's heirs in accordance with the author's original grant. (This principle was established in the "Who's Sorry Now" case decided in 1985 by the Supreme Court.) That mechanical license, issued to a record company, remains the legal document affecting who receives the mechanical royalty from a digital download of the subject song. (Note that a digital download of a *new* recording requires a separate mechanical license.)

What happens once an author, or the heir of a musical composition's author, terminates a grant—for example, a US license to use the composition on a recording? Can the original music publisher continue to license the use of the song as embodied on the recording for, say, a motion picture soundtrack?

In 1998, the Second Circuit New York Court of Appeals said "no" in a case which involved "Bye Bye Blackbird." While it was pointed out that a terminating author's (or his heir's) rights are not unlimited because there exists in the Copyright Act an exception to the usual rule that all rights return to the author (or his heirs) upon termination. This is the so-called "derivative works exception," which permits a grantee or licensee (for example, an original publisher) who creates or authorizes the creation of a derivative work (that is, a work that combines an original copyrighted composition with independently created modifications—such as a recording, or even a ballet based on a song) to continue to utilize it. (The section of the Copyright Act that covers this is Section 304[c][6][A].) In this case, both the original publisher and the successor publisher, which received its rights from the heirs of the author, wished to exercise the right to license a Joe Cocker recording (a derivative work) in the soundtrack and soundtrack album of the motion picture *Sleepless in Seattle*. In the end, the successor publisher was allowed to control the use of the derivative work in the film. The original publisher was prohibited from issuing posttermination licenses of pretermination derivative works. The original publisher's claim was thrown out.

Why are we interested in these two cases? Because any purchaser of a catalogue who includes, in the course of his or her valuation of the catalogue, income receipts from a song that has been, or may well be, terminated needs to know what assets he or she will be able to exploit (in this example, not the derivative work).

Anyone purchasing a music catalogue must seek to understand the catalogue sufficiently to know, or have reason to know, whether one or more of its songwriters might actually have a trunk. Some writers will; some won't. But it might surprise you to learn that most of the rock-and-roll writers I know *do* have a trunk. Hundreds of songs, in the style, and from the creative mind, of a popular songwriter—most of which are usually recorded at least in demo form—can certainly add value to a catalogue. If the writer was exclusively signed to the music publishing company for the period of time during which it acquired the disclosed songs of that writer, then most likely the publisher also owns the copyrights to the trunk songs. One challenge is simply (or not so simply) to identify who these writers might be and another is to actually talk with them prior to the date the sale takes place. However, even the mere identification of the existence of such a trunk might justify purchasing a catalogue at a slightly higher price than otherwise would be the case.

23 · COPYRIGHT ISSUES
A Sampler

To see itself through music must have an idea or magic. The best has both. Music with neither dies young, though sometimes rich.
—NED ROREM

This chapter will explore the dialogue—many would say battle—between procopyright and anticopyright forces, a dialogue that has moved beyond the hallowed halls of universities and spread across the editorial and front pages of our newspapers and magazines. But first, let's spend a little time examining important principles of copyright law that affect songwriters, musicians, recording artists, record producers, and record companies in the digital age. There is no better place to begin than by exploring where you end up if your so-called "creative" actions wind up constituting copyright infringement. There is no less appealing place to end up than in the dock, having been hit with the full force of copyright law.

CHANGING COPYRIGHT'S IMAGE

Despite the fact that most people would agree that creators of original works should have the right to earn income through the sale of those works, or through fees paid for the use of those works, copyright interests have received a bad rap over the last few decades. For example:

- In 1967, United Artists tried to stop a Community Antenna Television Company (CATV), fortnightly, from delivering television signals over a mountain to people who could not otherwise receive the station's programs.
- In 1983 and 1984, Universal City Studios tried to stop sales of Betamax tapes.
- In 1999, the American Society of Composers, Authors, and Publishers (ASCAP) was perceived as trying to stop Girl Scout camps from performing copyrighted music around their campfires.
- In 2000, A&M was the lead plaintiff in the recording industry's successful effort to stop Napster in its tracks, a move that many, especially teenagers, perceived as an undeserved victory by the establishment over our basic rights to listen to music via the Internet.
- In 2003, the Recording Industry Association of America (RIAA) began its series of litigations against individuals, including college students, for illegal downloads. By 2007, these suits numbered more than 20,000. Only 4,000 of them have been settled. Defendants of thousands more have defaulted—with consequences one can't even imagine.
- In 2006, a group of Canadian musicians, including the Barenaked Ladies and Avril Lavigne, formed the Canadian Music Creators Coalition to keep the Canadian Recording Industry Association from adopting, in Canada, the practice initiated by RIAA of suing those who share digital music for noncommercial purposes. The headline? "Recording

---

its members' rights to license ringtones; it was pilloried by headlines such as "ASCAP Wants to be Paid When Your Phone Rings." The proponents of this attack forgot that AT&T was paid every time the phone rang with songwriters' intellectual property forming the sound.

- In 2012, ASCAP and BMI suffered more indignation when the Pacific Coast Farmers Market Association (whose executives thrived on salaries generated by their markets' fees) complained bitterly that the PROs wanted to charge fees to those markets which presented live performances. The cost of a BMI license, by the way, for one of these markets, was $165 per *year*. One gets the impression that whatever the cost, the concept of private copyright creators and owners receiving money for the exploitation of their works was anathema to these users. Their philosophy is really not all that different from the points of view of others, described later in this chapter and in chapter 24, who simply cannot accept the fact that a culture's intellectual property is not, and should not be, free. Of course, in this situation, the markets had no objection to paying the local electric company for electricity for lights, sound, public address, and power for the food and other vendors (from onion ring stands to game booths and booths selling clothes, generators, roofing services, etc.) that many of the farm markets provided to their attendees. So everyone could make money from their professions, but not the songwriters. Described this way, the songwriters and their PROs don't seem so selfish after all, do they?

- In 2013, Jennifer Nelson, an independent filmmaker, sued Warner/Chappell Music Publishing Company to establish once and for all that the venerable song, "Happy Birthday," was actually in the public domain. She, along with every other filmmaker who wanted to use the song in a film, customarily had been charged a license fee for synchronizing the song in their films. This displeased her sufficiently that she did what thousands of other users of the song wanted to do for years, but either did not have the resources to do so, or did not wish to pursue a litigation that for the most part would only serve to relieve countless *other* parties of the obligation to pay license fees for the use of the song. For decades, the saga of "Happy Birthday" has seen law review articles, Copyright Society analyses, even lawsuits. But in 2015, new evidence of the song's public domain status may have brought Warner/Chappell's copyright defense to its knees. The Second Circuit Court of Appeals postponed decision until it could examine the new evidence that the song was published, with the authorization of the copyright owner, *without* a proper copyright notice—at a time when copyright notices were obligatory to avoid having a work enter the public domain. If true, those few remaining years of copyright protection claimed by Warner/Chappell will end and Warner/Chappell might even have to repay those from whom it sought and obtained license fees for years past. The only claim that Warner/Chappell made with respect to the song was that the lyrics—not the music—were protected intellectual property. The music itself was not the issue. This case has now been decided in favor of the public domain point of view. Decisions of the Federal Court of Appeals can be subject to rehearings, reviews, and, of course, appeals to the US Supreme Court. The income to Warner/Chappell derived from this legendary work was sufficiently large to justify that they pull out all stops until they ran out of options. Warner/Chappell will now have to return much that it has received from the exploitation of this seminal work. "Happy Birthday" is now clearly a public domain song.

Copyright Kids is aimed at junior high school–aged children and older. It teaches copyright basics and registration procedures. It provides sample permission letters for school kids to request authorization to reprint, say, lyrics, in a yearbook, or to use recorded music in a video yearbook. Schools welcome this education aid, and some teachers use the tools offered by these sites to assist their students, individually or as a group, to create a work and to register it.

What can copyright interests do to improve their image? One answer is to educate young people so that along with learning about music, and how to create enduring music, they also learn how important it is that the music be protected. The Copyright Society of the United States of America (www.CSUSA.org) has set up, as part of its FACE (Friends of Active Copyright Education) program, a section of its Website called Copyright Kids (www.law.duke.edu/copyright). The basic message is that the copyright laws of the United States and of other countries are necessary and, basically, fair: they protect creators' (including the kids') works; they protect the music and literature that the kids love; and they encourage creation.

Even YouTube has gotten into the act. This Google-owned company does not appear to have been dissuaded in its efforts to teach the parameters of copyright protection, fair use, and copyright compliance/infringement by its parent's total annihilation of the PIPA and SOPA bills. Now this juggernaut of online video has established Copyright School. It's really just a video, but whatever works, I guess.

The Music Publishers Association is developing a unique educational curriculum called the COPY-FREE ZONE targeted specifically at school music programs. It fosters a commitment to copyright recognition and compliance and guides schools and their students away from inadvertent copyright infringement as well. Hundreds of secondary schools throughout the country are participating. Sounds like something that should be applied to corporations that infringe music wholesale (see page 323).

SOPA (Stop Online Piracy Act) and PIPA (Protect Intellectual Property Act) were two acronyms given to what were originally perceived to be rather innocuous, though necessary, bills in Congress to control and stop online piracy. Mozilla and Google, early supporters, killed the bill with a public relations onslaught that totally ambushed the copyright interests. They felt that protections against foreign websites might result in limitations on their own businesses. Freedom of speech is once again invoked on behalf of the interests who would not exist but for the protections afforded intellectual property. The more things change, the more they stay the same.

COPYRIGHT INFRINGEMENT

A word about infringing others' songs. Don't. A copyright owner wronged ranks right up there with the proverbial scorned woman as among the most fearsome adversaries that one might have to face. And do not think that even a small incursion into someone else's private property will not be noticed. It will. The copyright owner is likely to find you out even if your song is a hit only in Timbuktu. And he or she will use every tool in the book—national laws, international treaties, courts up to and including the Supreme Court—to make you pay.

Under the Copyright Act, anyone who violates any of the exclusive rights of the copyright owner or author is an infringer of the copyright or right of the author, as the case may be. Period. The remedies (if you are interested, and you should be) available to a successful copyright owner, or author, are impressive: injunction; minimum damages (in cases in which the author or copyright owner cannot prove the actual financial extent of the damage) of from $750 to $150,000; in many cases, costs and attorneys' fees; impoundment and "disposition" of the "infringing articles"; and, in some cases, seizure, forfeiture, and imprisonment. Not a pretty picture.

There are two basic types of infringement: plagiarism (that is, copying another's creation and representing it as one's own) and more traditional violations of copyright, such as recording another's song without permission (whether or not with the intention to call it one's own creation); performing another's song on the radio or in a club without the broadcast station or club having obtained permission; or printing, selling, or merely sharing copies of another's song without permission. (The Internet has provided new and imaginative ways to accomplish this kind of infringement.) True, many infringements are unintentional, but that does not matter. Nor does it matter if the infringements are unconscious. All that matters is that the two works being compared are *strikingly similar* and that the defendant had *access* to the work of the plaintiff. And let me state right here that the broadly held belief that copying a maximum of eight notes does not constitute infringement is a myth. Nowhere is there any statute or case law that supports this contention.

As noted earlier in chapter 17, one California federal court has ruled that the copyright law's three-year statute of limitations bar to copyright infringement claims might only apply to the actual period during which claims are sought (that is, the three years preceding the lawsuit) so that an infringement that began decades earlier continues well beyond the end of what was always considered the end of the three years after publication. The only thing that is limited is ability of the copyright claimant to sue for infringements preceding the three years prior to bringing their lawsuit. If this ruling is upheld, the defendant in an infringement action will be susceptible of being liable for profits during the three years prior to the commencement of the lawsuit in addition, of course, to having to face all of the usual remedies afforded by the Copyright Act such as alternative statutory damages, an injunction, and all of the other remedies provided for by the Copyright Act.

Access and Substantial Similarity

Access to others' recordings and musical compositions is the key to copyright infringement lawsuits involving plagiarism. And, believe me, the intellectual property community—from Disney to Mattel, from music lawyers to Atlantic Records—understands this full well.

As you can imagine, millions of CDs—mostly demos—are mailed or messengered into music companies' offices every year. Most sophisticated companies—record and music publishing companies, law firms, and management firms—take steps to ensure that they cannot successfully be sued for copyright infringement when a product is released that may (or may not) bear some resemblance to the unsolicited material. These companies routinely choose to not open—and, in fact, immediately return to the sender—the material they receive which has the appearance of including an unsolicited tape or CD, or which comes from a person or company with whom they are not familiar. Recent court cases have bolstered these companies' confidence in that they have held that unsolicited materials received by these companies do not constitute such "constructive corporate receipt" as to render them liable if it turns out that something they are subsequently involved with "sounds like" the product that was sent to them without their solicitation. (We shall have to wait to see whether unsolicited MP3 files sent via email to these same companies will be regarded in the same way by the courts.)

It is, of course, quite within the range of possibility that a musical work substantially similar to or even identical to another work can be the result of independent creation. A finding of "access" is a damaging, although not necessarily fatal, blow to the defendant in a situation like this just as a finding of lack of access may not deal a fatal blow to the plaintiff. "Substantial similarity" in and of itself might give rise to an inference that there was access to the plaintiff's work. But, in the lingo of the federal district courts, the courts now require "significant, affirmative, and probative evidence" of access, and, as noted above, it no longer appears that the mere sending of a demo to the defendant's record company will meet this criterion.

Yet, whenever one gets into a courtroom—and ends up staying a while—anything is possible. The Isley Brothers' claim against Michael Bolton and his song "Love Is a

Wonderful Thing" regarding the claimed infringement of their song of the same title survived the district court and appellate court and was, in effect, upheld by the US Supreme Court when it declined to consider the case on appeal—even though there was no proof whatsoever that Mr. Bolton ever heard the plaintiff's song and even though the songs of the two litigants were really not so similar after all.

Five million dollars in judgments and lots of legal fees later and you can begin to appreciate the paranoia that is rampant among music business companies when it comes to opening that envelope that looks so enticing. Okay, it is not so enticing to those of us who receive loads of them, but sometimes the package gets through (perhaps a temporary secretary is opening the mail, or there is a particularly inviting cover).

An earlier Michael Bolton case involving "How Am I Supposed to Live Without You?" had a more favorable result for Bolton. Even though the plaintiff had recorded a demo of his musical work featuring the very artist that Atlantic Records used to make the song a worldwide hit, Laura Branigan, the court held that the lack of substantial similarity in itself was enough to negate the plaintiff's claim. But the proof of access in that case must have taken the breath away from Mr. Bolton's litigator.

Then there was the claim against Ric Ocasek of The Cars in which the plaintiff had sent his "substantially similar" song in demo form to the very A&R person who acted on behalf of The Cars for its record company, Elektra Records, a full year before The Cars' version was released and became a hit. Curious timing, one would think. But this particular plaintiff's argument had a problem—one that was fatal to his case. The Cars and their principal writer were able to prove that their song was actually written *and* recorded two years *before* the plaintiff's song was sent to The Cars' record company! Luckily they had saved the tape and it was computer dated! The plaintiffs slunk away from this one.

How Can Similarity Be Blurred and Still Be Substantial?

I will not go into the details of the lawsuit regarding the claim that Pharrell Williams and Robin Thicke's "Blurred Lines" infringed the Marvin Gaye song "Got to Give it Up." This lawsuit received exhausting international attention. But I do want to discuss the consequence of the jury verdict which has yet to be affirmed or reversed on appeal.

Because of the basis on which the jury made their decision—which revolved around the "feel" of the recordings of the two works as opposed to the substantial similarity of the notations—the graph that defines the songs—musicians are now beginning to think that they can claim infringement for reasons that never existed before. And contrarily, composers and producers who always felt it was artistically valid and even exemplary to "quote" or "refer" to prior art in their original works are now beginning to worry that they risk copyright infringement lawsuits if they continue to follow this practice.

In this case, similarities of orchestration that have nothing to do with compositional elements of the copyright (which after all are the essence of the copyright) led the jury to consider the two songs to be too close to have existed without one copying the other. That one was inspired by the other was acknowledged at the beginning of the case. Both Thicke and Williams were fans of Marvin Gaye's music and "sound" and sought not so much to replicate it, but rather to "reference" it in their original work "Blurred Lines." In fact, Thick and Williams initiated the lawsuit in the first place to seek a declaration by a relevant court that their work did not infringe the Gaye song. (This technique—of a potential defendant initiating a lawsuit as a plaintiff—is a fairly recent gimmick of lawyers from California and Texas—(and presumably other states as well now—in order to gain some one-upmanship on an unsuspecting party—and at the same time, not coincidentally, establishing the venue of a lawsuit more favorable to the initiating party than the one where it would have had to litigate had it waited to be sued by the party who was actually damaged.)

So, now a jury has been allowed to consider the "total concept and feel" of a recording as having equivalent (if not more) weight as that of experts' analysis in determining whether the actual notes, their relationship, place in time, etc. of the two works make them substantially (or strikingly) similar. The "Blurred Lines" case suggests that external "vibes" have a role to play even though those elements usually come via the *recording* and not the *literary expression* found in the notes themselves.

Compare the wisdom (or lack of it) of the Blurred Lines judge compared with Shakespeare. Yes, Shakespeare. When attending his play *Richard III* a few years ago, I heard something that bowled me over. Whatever the bard's background was in music or music education, and I do not believe it was significant, or even present, at all in his life, he so totally comprehended the essence of music that it is a wonder that five hundred years later well-educated judges, most of whom one would think had some musical training, could get it so wrong. Shakespeare's words: *How sour sweet music is when time is broke and no proportion kept.* He understood the essential *relationship* between notes on a staff (the graph that gives structure to the musical code forming a song), and time, which together differentiates one piece of music from another. When a court allows a jury to consider the "feel" of a piece of music, it is denying the very essence of musical expression that constitutes a song: the relationship of notes within a time signature on the staff.

Infringement Via Another Form of Intellectual Property: The Droit Morale

The tendancy toward creative, though ill-advised, theories are challenging other long-established concepts of infringement. The European Union has come up with a blockbuster: trademark infringement by iPhone.

I am one of many attorneys who have had clients perform at Carnegie Hall in New York. When they sought to title their CD: "Live at Carnegie Hall"—with photo of course—they were dismayed at the voracious response of the trustees of that renowned institution: they were told that they would be infringing not just the trademark "Carnegie Hall," but also the façade of the building which they claim is protected by copyright. Fast-forward to 2015: the European Parliament is debating whether to adopt an exemption to copyright called the Panorama Exception. Essentially, this new rule/law would protect the "moral right" or the "*droit morale*" of the architects of public buildings from unauthorized reproduction. This "right" has no expiration. It lasts forever. Thus, a photo of your best friend standing in front of the Eiffel Tower would infringe the rights of the heirs of Gustave Eiffel who died almost a hundred years earlier in 1923. To be violative of this law, the use of the photograph need not be anything more than one more addition to the tourist's photo diary of a trip to Paris. The concern over the Panorama Exception, of course, is that this law, if passed, will presage similar laws that might also affect the reproduction of music—whether public domain or not. The United States is one of the few countries in the world that does not recognize the *droit morale*; but the concern now is that the concept will be expanded well beyond how it has been interpreted and applied for hundreds of years. The result would impede the free flow of information. Beware those who might want to turn John Philip Sousa's marches into a rap opera. Oh wait: isn't there a hit Broadway hip-hop musical based on the life of Alexander Hamilton?

Fair Use

Be very skeptical concerning what you hear about "fair use"—use of copyrighted material that is not considered infringement. The rules covering fair use are contained in Section 107 of the Copyright Act of 1976, which states:

> The fair use of a copyright work . . . , for purposes such as criticism, comment, news reporting, teaching scholarship, or research, is not an infringement of copyright. In determining whether the use made of a work in any particular case is a fair use the factors to be considered shall include:
>
> (1) the purpose and character of the use, including whether such use is of a commercial nature or is for nonprofit educational purposes;
>
> (2) the nature of the copyrighted work;
>
> (3) the amount and substantiality of the portion used in relation to the copyrighted work as a whole; and
>
> (4) the effect of the use upon the potential market for or value of the copyrighted work.

The fair use provisions in the Copyright Act merely create a framework for identifying when and under what conditions copying will be allowed. It does not excuse infringements that fall outside of the guidelines. On the contrary, federal courts are beginning to resent the four-step "test" because they feel it has unreasonably, if unintentionally, boxed them in when reviewing a set of circumstances that does not fall neatly within the four conditions. They are tending now to use the four conditions as guidelines (which indeed they were intended to be in the first place), but not as the "final word" on when an alleged infringement is or is not fair use.

In considering your rights under the statutory provision regarding fair use, you should note several things: First, as you can imagine, the phrase "shall include" invites a great deal of interpretation in each particular case. Second, even the most highly respected copyright law experts cannot tell you in any particular case what a court might conclude in applying the provisions of Section 107 to that case. Third, as a rule of thumb, if you are thinking of using a copyrighted work for what you think is a good cause and according to what you think should be permitted under this section, if there is any commercial gain whatsoever to you or to the people to whom you are thinking of offering your services, the odds are that the use will be prohibited and all of the hefty infringement remedies of the Copyright Act will come bearing down. And, as I noted previously, there is nothing that says it is okay to "borrow" a limited number of notes or bars from a musical composition.

Similarly, recent cases have suggested that unless your creation "transforms" the one you are "borrowing" from, it will not constitute fair use. What is *transformation*? Legal pundits call it a Humpty Dumpty word. It means what a judge says it means. Basically, it means changing the original, borrowed, work into a new mode of being. This kind of change is not likely in a song context unless the new work is a parody—that is, a lampoon or a spoof.

Do note, however, that whatever fair use is, its scope is narrowest with respect to unpublished works. While you can get away with infringing a work generally available to the public, as long as you fit within the guidelines mentioned above, or some version of them, fooling around with a work that is not intended (yet) for public dissemination is just asking for trouble.

For those of you who are interested in taking existing works and parodying them, yet another word of caution is advised. Parody, briefly, simply mimics an original, and to the extent that its intention and execution are clear, parody can survive a claim of infringement.

Satire, however, is a different story. Satire is parody that lampoons society itself. Satire can stand on its own two feet and is considered to be as original as a nonsatirical creation. Courts have tended to categorize satire as "direct" or "indirect." Directly, satirical parody is not fair use; indirectly, satirical parody is. These distinctions may aid a court in reaching the conclusion it believes is just given the particular circumstances of each case—but it surely confuses the rest of us. While judges have recently resisted having a knee-jerk reaction to a property owner's will, this is an area fraught with uncertainty, and an attorney's guidance might be called for. (Note that even an attorney might not want to speculate on what a court would say about a particular work of parody or satire.)

Finally, if you are thinking of copying someone else's work and are prepared to argue a defense of fair use, do not think that setting up a corporation will protect you. Under the Copyright Act, the officers of a corporation that commits the infringement cannot hide behind the corporate protection of limited liability. The officers of the corporation are as culpable as the corporation itself.

SAMPLING

Sampling is the practice of capturing sounds from a previously recorded and released recording and incorporating them into a new recording. Sampling is subject to the same infringement criteria as any kind of borrowing. When technological advances put sampling within the reach of even novice record producers, many thought that this kind of copying was of no particular significance—that using a loop from an old song was even a compliment to the original songwriter or songwriter–recording artist. Then one day, a federal district court judge in New York was asked to look into a situation of "sampling" from the point of view of the person whose song was "borrowed." Was it fair use? In the first sampling case, which was decided in 1991, Judge Kevin Duffy, a highly regarded federal judge whose understanding and perceptions of the copyright law are legendary, needed only five words to answer that question for all time: "Looks like stealing to me." And that was that. Sampling is not fair use. It is theft.

But what if the use is *de minimus* (of no particular significance)? What if the public would not recognize the appropriation? Is a three-second use *de minimus*? Don't bet on it. (A favorite excuse used by law school students who empty out their roommates' beer supply is *de minimum non curat lex*: the law does not concern itself with trifles. But use this justification for sampling another person's creation and you do so at great risk.)

Is recognition of the appropriation essential to constitute actionable infringement? What if the material sampled cannot be scored? What if it is simply a combination of sounds that an artist had produced? The Atlantic Records recording agreement, in the grant-of-rights paragraph, says, "Company has the exclusive and unlimited right to own, control and exploit Artist's services as a recording artist and to all the results and proceeds of such services." Is reggae spoken rather than sung? Is the voice rhythmic? To what extent can you sample the rhythm without fear of a lawsuit?

Can a doorbell ring from a film be sampled with impunity? What about a police siren from a television program?

Sampling is not limited to audio. An example of both at once is the sampling of a portion of a motion picture: Not only are the motion picture company's rights being compromised, but those of the actors as well. Sampling a moment, or a phrase, from *Casablanca* would pit the sampler against not only Warner Bros. Pictures, but against the estates of Humphrey

Bogart and Ingrid Bergman as well. Let alone Sydney Greenstreet, Claude Rains, or Peter Lorre. If you think the George Clintons, the Average White Bands, and other musicians whose music is frequently sampled are insistent on pursuing their rights under the copyright law, wait until you meet the heirs of Paul Henreid and Conrad Veidt!

Fair Use Turned on Its Head

Once again the Ninth Circuit, known for its "imaginative" rulings (and disdained by many for them) has come up with a theory that defies past views of a copyright owner's right to stop others from infringing their works. In 2015, in a case involving a twenty-nine second video clip of a toddler dancing to the 1984 Prince hit "Let's Go Crazy" (that came to be known as "Dancing Baby"), the copyright owner was reprimanded for not considering the possibility that the use of its song fulfilled the statutory and judicial requirements of fair use. Instead of looking at fair use as simply an affirmative defense of what would be technically considered an infringement, the court supported arguments by Google, Twitter, and Tumblr that the copyright owner should itself have the burden of establishing that at a minimum, it "considered" that the claimed infringing action might have been a fair use before issuing takedown notices to the ISPs presenting the clip. This view of a copyright owner's responsibility to the public is appearing in other areas in recent years, not the least of which is in the area of music licensing discussed in chapter 21, page 318.

Not to Worry; They'll Never Find Out

A client of mine once performed a song live (with an appropriate ASCAP license) at a rehearsal for a television special when something went awry and news photographers and television cameramen who were present for PR reasons, recorded the problematic moment. The live show was about an hour in length; the problematic moment was over in thirty seconds. The producers reshot the scene. The copyright owner of the song that was performed, an Italian music publisher, had declined a request for a television synchronization license. So the performance of the song was replaced with another for the upcoming television special and all was well in copyright land. But the copyright owner found out about the live performance and, wrongly, presumed that the song was being used on the television program. She threatened to bring a willfull copyright infringement lawsuit, hired Wall Street litigators, and was riding a very high horse of self-righteousness when I contacted her, explained that the song was performed only live, with an ASCAP license, and was not to be included in the television program. She backed off with an apology. I then asked, "By the way, how did you know the song was performed? The set was closed and you were in Europe." She answered with a response that I shall forever remember and repeat to any of my clients who use anothers' property without permission and who assert that "they will never find out." She said that she was in Austria, on holiday, with her two children. They had just come back from skiing. She was making fondue in the kitchen while she sat her sons in front of the television to watch CNN so that their English would improve. Suddenly she overheard her song on the TV. She ran into the living room and saw the film of the moment that I described earlier when something went awry at the live show—the clip lasted no more than four seconds. And whose music was playing behind the video at that one moment in the one-hour show that was never actually televised? Hers! The press which had attended the live show had filmed the scene and filed a clip with their news services. What were the odds on that happening? You never know—except that we do know: They'll Always Find Out.

Infringement Insurance

I do not know of a successful artist who has not faced a claim of copyright infringement. From George Harrison to Paul Simon, it is just one more risk of being in the music business—and a costly one at that. But writers can obtain insurance against infringement. That's right. There is a certain logic to this in view of the fact that unintentional and unconscious acts are as actionable as intentional and conscious ones. (So-called "willful" acts—usually infringements after warnings are communicated to the eventual defendant—will, however, usually incur higher damages. But willful acts are not usually the result of plagiarism but of the other kind of infringements noted at the beginning of this chapter—recording or performing another's song without permission.) This insurance, which is known as errors and omissions (E&O) insurance covers "honest" mistakes. It is fairly expensive, but definitely worth considering.

Sometimes the administrating publisher will agree to share in the cost or add the writer to its own E&O policy (another reason to engage a publisher). Most of the standard E&O policies are issued by insurance companies in the ordinary course of business to protect against an occasional lapse in the due diligence process in producing television programs or motion pictures, and do not really fit the need here. I advise my clients as a matter of course to obtain plagiarism insurance, which has come in handy more often than you can imagine. Instead of simply signing off on a standard form of E&O policy, however, the artist-songwriter's lawyer and business manager should read the document, consider the wording carefully, and, if necessary, rewrite it where appropriate to fit the need it is supposed to serve.

Specifically, the "covered acts" are not defined specifically enough to meet the needs of the songwriter or artist-songwriter, so the traditional E&O language is obsolete when it comes to the kind of coverage songwriters need. Exposure to liability is couched in terms of "products" instead of songs, and some policies actually *exclude* intellectual property such as copyrights. In that case, all the money spent on premiums has been spent on insuring against the wrong kind of injuries. Coverage should extend not just to recorded songs, but to all creations that are musical compositions, or parts of musical compositions, which the creator can prove existed as of a certain date and time. This can be accomplished via computer-dated demo recordings or copyright registrations or even by mailing tapes to oneself by registered mail, return receipt requested, with the title(s) of the work(s) on the front of the envelope. Rather than mount a full-bodied assault on the contract language, which will be strenuously resisted by the insurance agent and company, it may be sufficient to modify a standard E&O policy binder by simply expanding the definition of covered products.

THE IMPACT OF THE INTERNET ON RECORDING AND PUBLISHING AGREEMENTS

Now that we have dealt with the awesome power afforded copyright owners under US copyright law, let's consider contemporary copyright issues that have been thrust into the collective consciousness of the music fraternity since the advent of digitization and the Internet. There are battles going on between those who are for the strongest possible copyright protections, no matter what the medium, and various anticopyright troops. Who wins these battles will impact not only the creative and business elements of the music business, but, in economic and cultural terms, our very civilization.

Technical solutions to distributing music via the Internet have been found. iTunes, Tidal, GooglePlay, Rhapsody, Microsoft, and Slacker for example, as well as numerous other portals offering authorized recorded music, are currently in operation, as are Spotify and Pandora, which serve different purposes but are steadily having a negative effect on download services. Now it is in the hands of the music rights owners to find a way to put them to effective e-commerce use. One of the reasons the "old" Napster and its progeny, Grokster and Morpheus, were so popular is that there is obviously a great demand for one-source and one-stop shopping. Apple, Microsoft, Google, and now Sony and others have now figured out how to supply that demand in a cost-effective and efficient way.

There are numerous implications of the total absence of a standard with respect to how and to what extent the digital download is dealt with in recording and music publishing agreements: We have discussed royalty escalations and net sales in chapter 4. In addition, there is considerable indecision with respect to this most important consideration: the location of the download. Depending on where the act of use takes place, different rules and laws may apply and different parties will claim an interest in licensing (or refusing to license) the use and collecting the money generated by the use.

Digital downloads occur *somewhere*. We are not always sure where, but the location of the content provider seems to be the location of choice. Of course, private agreement may not survive legislation in the many parts of the world that are beginning to discover that they are themselves "players" in the international entertainment complex. (For example, if the United States or other countries eventually tax downloads, why not place one's server in Guyana, where the tax may be less or nonexistent?) The European Union is already recommending a sales tax on all online purchases. The United States is resisting it.

Some lawyers have thrown up their hands in the course of negotiating recording and publishing agreements precisely due to the fact that there are no standards—let alone global standards—established for determining where a digital transfer to a user occurs. Ordinarily, when negotiators either compromise on a point, or decide it is not worth arguing, they understand the implications of what they are doing. In this case, however, no one can even imagine the consequences of failing to get it right, and no one even knows what getting it right means.

Where indecision abounds, rather than try to solve the issue with the record company's lawyers, the artist's lawyer or manager, in understandable frustration, will often view all things that are not negotiable, or not immediately capable of solution, in terms of money. Increase the advance and we'll drop the subject, they will say. But in the end, the artist will indeed pay for the lack of precision in the negotiation and for the lack of clarity in achieving an understanding as to where a digital download occurs. Writers and publishers will also suffer as a result of this lack of precision.

There are innumerable issues inspired by the fast-paced technological changes occurring in the digital world: 1s and 0s have never been so complicated. Here are a few of those that must be considered in attempting to wedge new ideas into traditional structures:

- Are digital phonorecord deliveries (DPDs) to be treated the same as direct mail, with its attendant lower royalty rate? Are Internet transfers to be dealt with differently if they constitute digital downloads or simple Internet e-commerce sales via Amazon or www.CDUniverse.com? Is one in the nature of direct mail and the other not? Even if the prices are the same as retail prices in record stores, should there be an increase in the royalty rate since there is no packaging as such?

- A digital download is different from a hard copy because transfer via the Internet does not involve the manufacturing and distribution process, as the sale of a hard copy does. Does a record company satisfy its release commitment obligation by offering DPDs?
- Where royalties are reduced until such time as a change of policy occurs at the record label, is the royalty rate change to be retroactive? Is the new rate to apply to United States sales only or worldwide?
- Are coupling restrictions a thing of the past? If iTunes offers three DPDs for the price of two, does this constitute coupling?
- If two tracks of an artist's album are offered via digital download, what happens to the A-side protection of the producer when the A track may well be coupled with a track that he or she has not produced? The record company that has promised the protection will not be able to control coupling.
- Is every digital download a DPD?

HOW THE INTERNET HAS PROVIDED CONTEXT FOR SONGWRITERS' AND PUBLISHERS' SEARCH FOR EQUITABLE TREATMENT

David Israelite, the chairman of the National Music Publishers Association (NMPA), the songwriters' and music publishers' trade organization, has pointed out, in the clearest terms, those aspects of copyright law and how it is administered by the government, which place songwriters and publishers in a distinct disadvantage vis-à-vis record companies—their alleged partners in aggregating sound to be carried to the public. He points out two incredible facts: the first is that a 1909 law, passed during William Howard Taft's presidency, continues to force onto songwriters and publishers a "statutory compulsory rate" that they have no choice but to accept. This is the mechanical rate that we have discussed many times earlier in this book. The rate was originally set at $0.02 for each recording of a song; it eventually (seven decades later) was raised to $0.0275 and ultimately to today's level of $0.091. Recordings of songs in excess of five minutes command $0.0175 per minute or fraction thereof. But, given the value of the dollar in 1909, this increase has not kept up with inflation. Furthermore, and this is David's principal point, songwriters and publishers have no opportunity to negotiate in a free market, as willing sellers, rates that willing buyers are able, and would be willing, to pay. The net effect is that record companies and download and streaming services are essentially subsidized by the songwriters/publishers.

The second fact that David reminds us of is that the consent decrees that allow ASCAP and BMI to exist as monopolies (necessary monopolies, of course—what radio station wants to negotiate with a million song owners) were established during Franklin D. Roosevelt's presidency. The US Justice Department constructed the situation whereby rates that ASCAP and BMI are allowed to charge those who perform music (principally analog radio stations) are not set in an open market, but by one of two federal judges (one for each PRO) who themselves have no required knowledge of music, the music industry, its past, or its future. The PROs are restrained from the ability to negotiate freely with users of their music. They feel that the process established to set the rates is artificial and arbitrary, yet they can do nothing about it.

The result of these two vestigial means of controlling songwriters and publishers is the following:

1. Outside of the United States and Canada, mechanical rights royalties are paid based on a percentage of the publisher price to dealers of sound recordings embodying the songs. In the United States (and Canada), mechanical rights royalties are force-fed to songwriters/publishers by the fixed statutory rate, the concept of which was established more than a hundred years ago. Thus, for a $0.99 download on iTunes, about $0.22 is retained by Apple. Of the $0.77 remaining, $0.091 is paid to the music publisher/songwriter. Of the $0.676 remaining, all of it goes to the record company to share with the recording artist and producer (on terms mostly favoring the record company). Thus, the music publisher and songwriter share $0.091. The record company and artist share $0.676. That is, 88% of the price of a download that is paid by iTunes *after* it takes its share, goes to the record company/artist . . . 12% goes to the publisher/song-wrwriter. That is, the record company/artist receives *seven times* what the publisher/songwriter receives.

2. With respect to the performing rights organizations' share of streaming revenues, the federal judges have determined that they are entitled to 1.85% of the streaming services' revenue. The PROs feel that the rate is ridiculously low given what the record companies likely receive. No one knows for sure what the record companies receive because their deals with Spotify and other streaming services are secret—but we do know that (a) their share is dramatically higher than 1.85%, (b) the record companies receive millions of dollars in advances which they do not necessarily earn back and therefore can keep for themselves, (c) some record companies charge a management/administration fee over and above the rate which establishes their base share of revenues, and (d) some powerful music publishers have sought and received equity shares in the streaming services which they need not share with their artists.

One further note about how the consent decrees hamstring the PROs: if a radio station or a streaming service wishes to use the millions of compositions controlled by the PROs, they do not have to obtain a license to do so; all they need to do is to *request* a license, reject the rate that is sought to be charged, and freely use the music for years while they fight the PROS on the amount of the cost; in essence, the publishers and songwriters are subsidizing the radio stations and digital service providers. And when all settles down, and a retroactive rate is established, even if the streaming services still exist or are still solvent, it is the publishers and songwriters who receive a miniscule percentage of what the licensees pay to the record companies due to other restrictive aspects of the consent decrees. A double whammy.

In 2010 and 2011, the major music publishers sought to withdraw their digital rights from ASCAP and BMI so that they could license them directly. Soon, however, the PROs rate court judges blocked them from doing so, But in the interim, these companies they negotiated directly with the streaming services. What did they achieve in an open market? They obtained rates substantially higher than what the judges determined the PROs were entitled to charge for these rights. While they did not entirely close the gap between what the sound-recording owners were being paid, which was about eight times what the rate courts allowed ASCAP and BMI to charge, they improved the rate substantially. The free market was doing its thing, but both rate courts summarily denied the publishers the results of their negotiations by prohibiting them from withdrawing only their digital rights from the PROs. They said that once their long-term licenses issued via the PROs had expired, they were free to leave *entirely*. But that would have produced havoc among the hundreds of thousands of companies—radio, TV, live venues, etc.—that depend on licensing their music directly from the PROs. They would have had to negotiate separately with the music publishers, and the music publishers would have had to negotiate separately with the hundreds of thousands of users of their music. Furthermore, Pandora, the Internet radio station, which complained that it was being asked to pay a greater percentage of its revenues than terrestrial radio stations, purchased a small station in South Dakota, KXMZ, thereby justifying a lower terrestrial radio rate for its Internet radio station. David Israelite called out Pandora. "Make no mistake," he said, "Pandora has now proven that it is the enemy of creative people everywhere." The company has since agreed to not take advantage of the loophole it had qualified for, and in fact voluntarily doubled its rates payable to publishers. A start!

It is also worth noting that the one place where neither the government imposed a mechanical statutory rate nor the federal courts interceded to block the PROs to negotiate a free-market rate, the ratio between record companies' share of licensing revenue and publishing companies' share of licensing revenue was 1 to 1. That is, in the area of synchronization licensing, it has become customary, in the marketplace, that the licensee—the user of a sound recording and the musical composition embodied in it—splits the synchronization fee equally between the sound recording owner and the music publisher.

The NMPA and other entities are diligently seeking to protect the rights of songwriters and publishers from being marginalized financially by laws established between eighty and more than one hundred years ago. The Justice Department has announced that it is examining the rules that govern the performing rights organizations with a view toward relaxing some of the restrictions that have caused their members/affiliates to object at being treated so differently from record companies and their artists for reasons solely due to the fact that one set of rights owners are hamstrung by ancient laws and the other set is not subject to anything close to such regulations. Susan Butler, the publisher of Music Confidential, notes that the music business is one of the most regulated industries in the country; in my opinion, there is no class of people for whom the regulations are designed to protect—given that one wonders if the industry and its consumers cannot fare perfectly well without them.

THE INTERNET IS GLOBAL: SO WHAT? I'LL TELL YOU WHAT

One of the problems in clearing music rights, of course, is that the Internet is global, and it is very difficult to effectively limit the exploitation of music to individual territories. For example, ASCAP's rate structure, while one that does not require time-consuming negotiations, is limited to the territory of the United States. So anyone who wants to webcast or use a song as part of a conventional website beyond US borders is going to be back into the negotiation mode, like it or not.

The music publishing and record industries have always been designed along territorial constructs. Rights licensing has necessarily found its solutions in territorial determination. Subpublishers and record company affiliates are institutionalized throughout the world, and the processes of international licensing have, traditionally, followed a certain model, a model that is *not* global.

The Internet Right Model

In view of the difficulties being experienced by companies that wish to clear music rights for their websites and for other exploitations, and that are at the same time expected to comply with a myriad of laws, several concerned industry lawyers and executives have recommended that there be established an *Internet right*—essentially combining (or neutralizing) the various rights that are being exercised when a piece of music is dancing around in cyberspace.

This right would combine the transmission, distribution, and performance rights; it would supersede the synchronization right, the mechanical reproduction right, and the performance right solely for Internet use. There is naturally a lot of resistance to this idea because, among other things, the various entities that might own the separate rights would have to determine who owns, controls, and administers the combined right. In addition, the wording of the original rights grants by the writers to the publishers is not likely to have addressed the issue of the Internet right. There are two possibilities with regard to an Internet right. One is that courts would have to "discover" it among the "bundle" of rights within copyright. If such a new right were "discovered," publishers and record companies would require new assignments from writers, artists, or their heirs—a virtual nightmare. The other is that the Internet right would have to be established solely by legislative means; that is, it would be a statutory right. This most likely would take the form of a compulsory license—something that is disliked intensely by virtually all copyright owners, who feel they are in a better position to put a value on a specific use and charge appropriately for it in each specific circumstance, rather than be told that all uses and all content are essentially equal and should either be licensed for the same fee or licensed according to a limited selection of predetermined fees.

Currently, ease of distribution and access to music via the Internet are virtually impossible to achieve. For example, let us say you want to webcast a live event and to preserve the event for other forms of exploitation in the future. At a minimum, you will have to clear the following ten rights (for each song and for each master—that's already twenty, and it's just a beginning) *before* the webcast takes place:

- webcast itself—both performance and mechanical rights
- pay per view simultaneous with the webcast
- pay per view after the webcast
- television special derived from the webcast
- edited television specials of indeterminate number for different countries (for example, Europe, North America, Asia, South America)
- CD release of the soundtrack of the webcast
- videocassette/videodisc/DVD of the webcast
- videocassette/videodisc/DVD of the various television specials
- in-store displays via looped minutes of the webcast—worldwide
- actual television commercials using footage from the webcast

The above list is not comprehensive, but includes the most important uses. Did I forget to repeat that most songs today are written by more than one person and that each person has his or her own publishing company? And that each of these publishing companies commonly shares responsibilities and income with another? And that even the master rights are often controlled by more than one party? So, the twenty clearances—ten per song, ten per master—can easily multiply to forty or more transactions *per song*. Ten songs? Four hundred transactions!

WHAT IS TO BE DONE?

The performing and mechanical rights societies of the world met in November 2000 in Santiago, Chile, under the auspices of the Confédération Internationale des Sociétés d'Auteurs et Compositeurs (CISAC), determined to find a partial solution to the music performance portion of the problem—to figure out how to offer world licenses via reciprocal agreements among themselves. While the temporary solution they agreed upon would still require users to enter into licenses for their territory, multiple negotiated licenses would have seen their last light, at least in the non–sound recording arena. Of course, many, if not most, eventual users wish to use the songs *with* the masters. Nevertheless, some progress toward establishing a global licensing structure had been made. This is how it was supposed to work.

- The prospective licensee contacts the content provider (usually that is the music publisher).

- The content provider is represented by a society in the country in which the content provider is located.

- The society licenses the rights worldwide, but on a nonexclusive basis only and on a nondiscriminatory basis as well (to avoid territory shopping).

- Prompt distribution of the license fee is arranged.

- Any taxes that are payable are charged in the country of use (that is, the download), if that country in fact taxes the transaction.

This procedure produces not only ease of licensing and a sort of one-stop buying, it also provides legal certainty for the licensee. That appeals not only to the licensee, but to the licensee's attorneys as well, who are being asked, if only by implication, to "certify" that the licensee won't be sued for copyright infringement.

Following the CISAC World Congress in Santiago, a number of the world's most important societies—including Broadcast Music, Inc. (BMI); Vereniging Het Bureau voor Muziek-Auteursrecht (BUMA, the Netherlands); Performing Rights Society (PRS, United Kingdom); Sociedad Général de Autores y Editores (SGAE, Spain); Società Italiana degli Autori ed Editori (SIAE, Italy); and Gesellschaft für musikalische Aufführungs- und mechanische Vervielfältigungsrechte (GEMA, Germany)—established a "fast track" licensing procedure designed to optimize business cooperation and ease of licensing. At this conference, a majority of the world's active international repertoire representatives entered into agreements that authorize each other to grant licenses for online music use on a worldwide basis. This was a remarkable achievement, although long overdue.

The official statement issued by the parties signing these bilateral internet licensing agreements states:

> The parties recognise that one transmission of music over the Internet may result in performances in multiple countries. It is clear that online music users do not want to enter into license agreements with each performing right organisation in the various countries where their musical works may be performed online. We realise that the extensive use of copyrighted music is not limited to territorial boundaries in the online world. We hope that others will agree that this is a necessary step to assure the legal performance of music online, and that many other societies will enter into such agreements.

The agreements cover webcasting, streaming, and online music on demand, as well as music included in video (TV, motion pictures, etc.) transmitted online. They provide for a mechanism to assure proper distribution of license fees to authors, composers, and music publishers on a worldwide basis. The agreements were effective as of the issuance of the document, but as you will see, they met an unfortunate, and early, demise.

A year after the Santiago Agreement, this time in Barcelona, the principal *mechanical rights* society members of BIEM (Bureau International des Sociétés Gérant les Droits d'Enregistrement et de Reproduction Mécanique, a group of forty-five mechanical rights collection societies from forty-three countries, and CISAC's sister organization, picked up the ball passed to them by the *performing rights* group CISAC. They, too, agreed to a mechanism by which their member societies would offer a license for multiple countries, and to deal internally with the matter of identifying where exactly the mechanical reproductions took place.

Amazingly, the European Commission and BIEM found that the agreements reached by both CISAC members and BIEM constituted a monopoly in restraint of trade and was therefore in breach of European Union competition rules. As of January 1, 2005, the Santiago Agreement was declared null and void, and the agreements signed in 2000 expired on December 31, 2004. Similarly, the Barcelona Agreement, being analogous to the Santiago Agreement, became invalid as of January 1, 2005. It is truly remarkable that rather than welcome a fantastic solution to what has been a commercial disaster for those who wish to use music via the Internet, the European Commission essentially forbade the members of both confederations to implement the agreements they had reached.

The decision of the European Commission to void both the Santiago and Barcelona Agreements has had a chilling effect on efforts by various international confederations, including IFPI (the International Federation of the Phonographic Industry, which is the world recording industry trade arm), to establish an integrated music industry standard for Internet licensing and other digital services.

Still Trying: Database Integration

In April 2002, the Executive Bureau of CISAC persuaded ASCAP and SACD (Société des Auteurs et Compositeurs Dramatique, a French rights society) to transfer to CISAC two database subsystems—the Musical Works Information Database (WID) and the International Documentation on Audiovisual Works (IDA). They also managed to establish some general guidelines for fixing an applicable price scale for system access. These institutions, along with BIEM, are discussing the establishment of an integrated music industry *identification* standard through which information about songs and recordings will be collected, tagged, and stored in a database—whether WID, IDA, or some new system—that can be integrated with existing management systems.

Once competent and accurate song and recording identification is established on a global scale, it will be relatively easy to facilitate the licensing of rights wherever they may be requested and to whatever extent their use may be sought. Whether their efforts will come to fruition or be countermanded by actions on the part of the European Union remains to be seen.

Similarly, CIS (Common Information System), a series of tools that establish a global digital copyright administration standard, has been developed under the auspices of CISAC. According to the CISAC information releases, it will streamline the exchange of information among member societies and is the foremost international development effort being pursued in the field of online collective administration of intellectual property rights.

In the spring of 2006, a group consisting of major record labels, technology companies, and publisher groups formed the Digital Data Exchange (DDEX) to create standards for communicating information necessary to license and sell digital information globally.

The Internet is forcing copyright and technology interests throughout the world to address and reconcile—quickly—issues involving music clearance, rights licensing, and the transfer of digital music, videos, artwork, photographs, and other information accurately and speedily. As a result of the cooperative efforts noted above, the interoperability of the world's licensing organizations has already been greatly enhanced, and the best is certainly yet to come.

THE FAIRNESS IN MUSIC LICENSING ACT

For as long as people and companies have had to pay for the right to publicly perform music for profit, there have been attempts by the users to chip away at both the amount of the cost and the obligation to pay. The latest attempt resulted in the passage by Congress of an amendment to Section 110(5) of the Copyright Act. This provision, the Fairness in Music Licensing Act (FMLA) of 1998, exempts an enormous number of users of music, including restaurant owners, from the obligation of having to obtain licenses to perform (play) music. The name of the act belies its intentions. Writers and publishers see nothing fair in this new law, nor do our trading partners around the world, most of whom are signatories to international treaties that provide for the payment of license fees for the very uses exempted by the US act.

The ostensible purpose of this act was to protect mom-and-pop stores from having to dig deep into their pockets to pay for the use of music in their restaurants. Of course, the copyright interests' position is that people pay for electricity, heat, interior decorators, and decoration, all of which create ambience for restaurant owners, and that music provides a similar bottom-line value. Indeed, if it has no value, why fight so hard to use it? It became apparent to everyone that the self-righteousness expressed by the proponents of "fairness in music licensing" was a smokescreen for the simple desire to save money, and some of the exemptions the original drafters of the legislation wanted to include did not find their way into the act as passed.

Passage of the FMLA has already had serious financial consequences for writers, publishers, record companies, and artists in the United States. Over 50% of the income from the world's music performance and mechanical fees is generated by US creations. A phenomenal amount of income that would have otherwise flowed into the United States has been, and will continue to be, lost because countries whose income-producing laws are diametrically opposed to the US "fairness" statute will not apply those laws to US authors' works.

THE COPYRIGHT TERM EXTENSION ACT: A LESSON IN LEVERAGE

As part of a quid pro quo in the world of congressional compromise and intrigue, many procopyright interests (particularly those representing music catalogues that were fast racing toward expiration of copyright protection—such as the big-time Broadway writers and their heirs, the Gershwins, Rodgers and Hammerstein, Cole Porter, Irving Berlin, and Leonard Bernstein—as well as the Walt Disney Company, which was concerned that early Mickey Mouse drawings would become part of the public domain) looked the other way when the FMLA was passed so that the Copyright Term Extension Act of 1998 (widely known as the Sonny Bono Copyright Term Extension Act or CTEA) would also make it through Congress. The Sonny Bono extension was duly passed, extending the term of copyright protection from fifty years after the death of the last artist or author of a work to seventy years. Most observers of this trade-off thought that FMLA would eventually be voided but that the copyright extension would stand.

It didn't happen. In fact, anticopyright interests are aggregating their bullets and hoarding them for the next receptive Congress, hoping to restore some of the initiatives that did not find their way into FMLA as enacted.

MP3: HOW TWO LETTERS AND A NUMERAL TERRORIZED AN ENTIRE INDUSTRY

As most people living in our society know by now, a number of companies have figured out how to compress musical sounds (that is, entire recordings) and to transmit them over a relatively narrow bandwidth to consumers who acquire them via the Internet, transpose them back into sound, and go their merry way enjoying the music they have downloaded. The ease by which this methodology works has caught the attention of millions of people across the globe. You have read enough, in this book and elsewhere, to understand the enormous threat that such processes present to the recording industry, which, one must not forget, includes the artists and songwriters whose art is virtually exclusively expressed in the audio tracks themselves.

MP3.com, Inc. is a publicly held company that operates a commercial Internet site at www.mp3.com. MP3 is a free technology protocol, developed by the Moving Picture Expert Group (MPEG), that enables a user to convert large .wav files contained on ordinary music CDs into files that are ten to twelve times smaller than the originals. Since MP3 files consume considerably less computer storage space than .wav files, they can be transferred much faster and have accordingly become the preferred modality for moving audio files through the Internet and among computers (the latter being the catalyst for Napster-type exchanges among users).

MP3 has not been greedy. Unlike Sony and its Betamax, or Apple and its Macintosh, MP3 has generously allowed its conversion software to be made available for free in order for consumers to create MP3 files, with Microsoft, RealNetworks, and others providing the conduit for such availability.

NAPSTER AND POST-NAPSTER

What was Napster? This was the well-publicized software created by a then nineteen-year-old which permits multiple (read: upward of 250 million) Internet users to access each other's collections of MP3 files for free. Most of these MP3 files were never licensed, and accordingly the users had been shown the way to wholesale infringement. No one was paid: neither the record companies, nor the artists, nor the union pension and welfare and health funds, nor the record producers, nor the mixers, nor the songwriters, nor the music publishers.

In the fall of 2001, the big guns of the recording industry, having at least temporarily stopped Napster, were trained on the USA's MusicCity Networks' Morpheus and Grokster Ltd., a West Indies–based firm. Both base their music sites on Kazaa, a program developed by the Amsterdam company FastTrack, which does not rely on computers operating through a central clearinghouse, as Napster does. They are file-sharing networks that allow users to search the network of users for those with the most powerful computers, or those with fast modems such as DSL or cable modems. The large worldwide network of other computers, for the time they are being captured, become a search hub, or "supernode," that other users can utilize in order to search the rest of the network—and do multiple transfers, one at a time, from other users. In effect, Morpheus users are "borrowing" the power of others' computers to complete their own private tasks. Sounds like something extraworldly (and maybe it is).

Unlike Napster, Grokster and Morpheus had absolutely no means to suspend users and therefore they cannot possibly be expected to control those users. At issue, then, was whether peer-to-peer file-sharing services could, if they did not control their networks but merely facilitated their creation, be held liable. In 2005, the Supreme Court once again ruled in favor of copyright interests. In a unanimous decision, the Court stated, "We hold that one who distributes a device with the object of promoting its use to infringe copyright is liable for the resulting acts of infringement by third parties." The opinion for a unanimous Court, delivered by Justice David Souter, found that Grokster was clearly taking "affirmative steps . . . to foster infringement," by third parties participating in peer-to-peer sharing. And what happened to that nineteen-year-old Sean Parker who was portrayed so effectively by Justin Timberlake in *The Social Network*, the film about the development of Facebook? Parker owned a bunch of shares in Facebook which he purchased with his (some would say ill-gotten) gains from the company he created, Napster. When Facebook went public in 2012, those shares were worth $2.5 billion. Enough said.

• • •

THE MORE THINGS CHANGE, THE MORE THEY REMAIN THE SAME (OR DO THEY?)

Changes in the music world are happening fast and furiously. Methods of distributing music are challenging the government's ability to figure out how to monetize them. For example, there are webcasts, podcasts, limited downloads, variations of performance-based communications via the Internet and those with mechanical reproduction characteristics which foreign societies can handle more efficiently than our American system where performance and mechanical organizations are separate. The Webcaster Settlement Bill of 2008 is aimed at resolving rate disputes among webcasters (such as satellite radio) and rights owners, but the challenges of figuring out what rights are being exploited and how to monetize them is just beginning. What only a few years ago we considered a finite number of exploitation possibilities is now exploding in the area of streaming alone. Social networks —particularly Facebook—are further complicating the analysis of what rights owners can claim and how they can either prove the use of their music or how to charge for it.

Podcast producers don't mind paying mechanical royalties for the music which is embodied on the program, yet they have no control over how many people access (perform/download) the programs. A company with a $100,000 budget for a podcast will be very surprised if a million people access it, thereby resulting in mechanical royalty obligations which would bankrupt the producing company.

YouTube presents yet another array of problems. Neither YouTube nor rights owners have any control over what is posted on its site. Only when an owner comes forward to identify its song will YouTube either take down the posting or, with the copyright owner's permission, attach advertising to the post and share income with the rights owner. Notwithstanding YouTube's claimed good faith effort to avoid infringing works on its site, Viacom sued them claiming that they should have known more than they claim they did. This is yet one more lawsuit by a rights owner which, while legitimate on its face, can only delay the day of reckoning when extraordinary new means of authorized, licensed distribution are the order of the day. Ben Sisario, in a recent *New York Times* article pointed out another quirk in the modern-day music business which is making rights owners and users crazy: the constant reshaping, resizing, and reprising of the very same product. For example he points out that a recent Dave Matthews record has a CD version, a deluxe version, a super-deluxe boxed set and even an accompanying live disc. (He notes that the Beastie Boys "hid" a new single among random copies of a deluxe edition reissue of its 1992 album "Check Your Head." Once these variable products hit the Internet, who is to know which versions are being distributed? One artist, Ben Folds, has even considered re-recording a song, or at least modifying it, for a fee, so that the person ordering the recording can hear his or her own name or the name of a spouse or other loved one actually sung by the artist on his hit recording. Whatever floats your boat, I guess.

A larger social policy issue here involves the conflict between making commercial products available to all at reasonable prices and at the same time respecting the creative and financial investment of those individuals who bring the property to fruition in the first place. For example, it costs just pennies to manufacture numerous brand-name drugs sold by major pharmaceutical companies, but the R&D investment required to both create the first of the pills and put them through development and testing, as well as go though the Food and Drug Administration approval processes in each country, can cost hundreds of millions of dollars. How do you suppose the pharmaceutical industry would respond to the idea that peer-to-peer sharing is a citizen's right? Currently, the copyright interests, in association with or at least in the same ballpark as, the technology industry, are trying to develop a business model for the MP3 delivery via a Napster-style software that will permit peer-to-peer sharing but at the same time protect the artists and copyright owners.

What of the future? New and powerful partnerships are developing that will force copyright issues onto the public stage for courts, legislatures, and, ultimately, the people themselves to resolve. There is an ebb and flow of political sensibilities toward, on one side, copyright protection, and, on the other, the right of the public to have free and easy access to public domain material.

All of this brings us to where we are today: a disgruntled public used to getting music for free (whose culture is it anyway? they ask), a rigid legal doctrine blocking peer-to-peer sharing, and a barrage of news coverage—all imagining a world without copyright, but positioning themselves, and expressing one level of hysteria or another, on totally opposite sides of the issue.

Copyright: Can we live without it? Can we live with it? Read on.

24 · COPYRIGHT
Can't Live With It—Can't Live Without It

And art made tongue-tied by authority, . . .
—WILLIAM SHAKESPEARE, *SONNET LXVI*

Rarely have governments conceived of a more obscure body of law. Even more rarely has something so ephemeral, and intangible, affected so many. What a surprise, then, when, at the dawning of the 21st century, technological developments catapulted copyright into the public consciousness. Many believe that a world without copyright would be a world without art, literature, and music—a virtually cultureless society. Others believe the opposite. Most governments acknowledge that a world without copyright would devastate most of the advanced economies on earth. Why, then, have so many in the world disdained copyright? Why is there so bitter a dispute among equally intelligent people about whether it is a good or bad thing that a person can be identified as the *owner* of a melody, a lyric, an image, a word? Has copyright gone too far in protecting "artists"? Have the multinational conglomerates abused their "copy" rights by controlling their markets to such an extent as to actually impede the flow of ideas whose very manifestation into fixed forms like books, records, and films was the goal of copyright in the first place?

Many feel that nothing can be said that hasn't been said before and that it is illogical to give exclusive copyright protection to something like *West Side Story* or *RENT* when their debts to *Romeo and Juliet* and *La Bohème* are so obvious. Many celebrate the fact that digital technology has opened to shared expression what they perceive to be prison gates, which have long been closed to the average citizen. Others believe that the gates in question are more aptly compared to floodgates, the opening of which will let loose into the public's control hard-earned assets that would never have *been* assets were it not for copyright law.

The Internet has laid bare some inherent flaws in copyright law. Whereas copyright law (and lawyers) used to be concerned about performance and copying violations, now an anonymous infringer can *distribute* copies around the world in a matter of seconds. Indeed, merely calling up a file on one's computer constitutes a copying of the underlying work.

Is this the end of copyright? No. But it certainly is the end of copyright as we know it. The battle between copyright as a property right, and society's right to have unfettered access to its own musical heritage, is something worth contemplating as an opportunity rather than as a problem. Call it a wake-up call in this era of changing business models and perceptions. The whole world is struggling with this conflict, so let us examine it and see if we can identify its causes and perhaps offer some solutions that will help to strike a balance between the two conflicting viewpoints.

BATTLES OR BATTLE-AXES

First, let us consider to whom the benefit of the work of an author passes. Surely not only to the creator. The consumer and society tend to benefit as well. But, as we will see, there is an evolving view among the populace that copyright law no longer succeeds in serving the interests of *both* authors and consumers. In fact, it is arguable that the perfectly lawful acts of copyright owners may actually diminish the inherent value of their own copyrights. Is it possible that the copyright law itself, which has served society so well, now threatens the very rationale behind it?

There is a war going on, and you may be surprised when the combatants are identified. Here are some of the important issues involved:

- first and foremost, of course, CD burning and illegal song swapping, and the ever-increasing sophistication of the software that facilities the co-opting of music for personal use
- the need for database protection (see chapter 23, page 355)
- piracy
- cut-rate retail prices
- deregulation and consolidation of radio and television ownership
- the continuing consolidation of the major players in the entertainment industry
- the paucity of "new music" in major media, which goes hand in hand with the record companies' dependence on the "super artist"
- a growing trend among hardware manufacturers to give away "content" to sell their gadgets
- the growth of satellite radio, with its attendant opportunities and challenges
- the incredible cost of A&R and motion picture and television production
- the location and relocation of servers to offshore countries where no copyright laws apply
- the continued chipping away, by the US Congress, at copyright (for example, the ill-named Fairness in Music Licensing law)
- the claim, by Internet users, that they have First Amendment protection
- nonexistent or insufficient harmonization of rights clearance procedures worldwide
- insistence on most-favored-nation provisions, forcing prices to rise to the highest quoted license fee, but limiting the price paid for the most valuable songs to the price paid to the least valuable
- the need to establish acceptable and reasonable rates for permanent download, limited download; on-demand streaming; subscription services, etc.
- mechanical rate issues: per copy or percentage? more or fewer compulsory licenses, for an array of uses?
- expansion of the tariff on digital audio tapes to analog tapes and blank CDs and DVDs

- resolution of the conflict between support of intellectual property rights vs. the fear of dampening developing technology
- the continued shrinking of music education initiatives
- the ignorance of professionals, at every level, of the source of copyright in the United States, its progenitors, and the importance of copyright protection for our society and our economy
- enormous disparities among nations and their courts with regard to identifying responsible parties among distributors of music and other intellectual property via the Internet
- artists' frustration with record companies whose greedy actions speak louder than their soothing, fraternal words
- incompetent—or shady—accounting practices
- the change in work-for-hire provisions that matured in 2013

COPYLEFT (AKA COPYWRONG), BUT NOT COPYRIGHT

Many of the issues just listed are part of the driving force behind the copyleft, or copywrong, movement.

Lawrence Lessig, one of the most outspoken of the critics of monopolistic behavior among copyright owners (and self-appointed 2016 candidate for President of the United States), refers to the "remix" culture in the world of music, a culture in which the creativity of artists is built on the creativity of others. Appropriating others' material is, according to Lessig, an essential ingredient of our culture, justifying borrowing (and more extensive adapting) that is so pervasive in the music field. Had *Romeo and Juliet* been in copyright when Leonard Bernstein and Stephen Sondheim wrote *West Side Story*, there would have been no such musical masterpiece. Lessig reminds us of *The Grey Album*, produced by the DJ Danger Mouse, which is a remix of The Beatles' *White Album* using vocal tracks from Jay-Z's *Black Album*; *The Grey Album* was a musical breakthrough in 2004 and remains an Internet download favorite, notwithstanding its questionable copyright status. Some call it the "ultimate remix." But in our world, Mr. Mouse (actually, Brian Burton) was lucky that EMI and Sony/ATV decided not to pursue their considerable legal remedies. He would have lost.

Mr. Lessig, who was the (losing) primary counsel on behalf of Eldred in *Eric Eldred et al. v. John D. Ashcroft*, the Supreme Court case that affirmed the constitutionality of the Sonny Bono Copyright Term Extension Act, sees our very culture as a "remix." He sees oppressive copyright laws (in particular the aforementioned extension of the term of copyright to life plus seventy years) and the practice of embedding codes in musical offerings that prevent copying as clearly running counter to the intent of the framers of the Constitution, who offered protection to authors and inventors in order to "promote the progress of science and useful arts, by securing for limited times to authors and inventors the exclusive right to their respective writings and discoveries . . . ." How can extending the term of protection for George Gershwin (who is dead) and Mickey Mouse (who is dead in an entirely different sense) promote the progress of the arts?

He and other copyleft proponents contend that laws in general are continually being adjusted to take into account new technologies. Why not copyright law? What has happened, they say, is that instead of the law being a facilitator, it has become a major impediment to doing business. And if anything riles a legislator in Washington, it is that! Yes, copyright is supposed to reward the creators and to encourage innovation and creation. But no one foresaw that the copyright owners (most often the music publishers and record companies, not actually the creators) would use their monopoly rights to *discourage* innovation and creation—yet this is, in fact, what they are doing.

Creative Commons

Quite a lot has been written about Lessig's positions and his establishment of Creative Commons (www.creativecommons.org), a nonprofit organization that has conceived of what might be called a "middle ground" between full copyright protection and the absence of all copyright protection. Creative Commons encourages the relinquishment of an array of copyright protections via a license agreement (which they provide) that permits variable conditions on use of copyrighted materials. For example, depending on the circumstances, the license may limit a user to "noncommercial" use, while retaining the commercial rights for the author. It may permit changes in the licensed work, or not. It may require credit to the author, or not.

Here is what a sample license from Creative Commons might look like:

> You are free to copy distribute, display, and perform the work, to make derivative works, and to make commercial use of the work under the following conditions. You must attribute work in the manner specified by the author or licensor. For any reuse or distribution, you must make clear to others the license terms of this work. Any of these conditions can be waived if you get permission from the copyright holder. Your fair use and other rights are in no way affected by the above.

Some refer to this process as a sort of lawyer-assisted suicide. Why? Because under the Copyright Act of the United States, and under the copyright laws of other countries, while a mere license that relinquishes certain rights under copyright does not, in and of itself, place the work in the public domain, once a right is relinquished to the public for no compensation, and pursuant to no control whatsoever, the consequences to the author can be considerable—and unpredictable. For example, an author who allows a derivative work to be made may have lost the right to make a derivative work him- or herself, or via another licensee, for all time. If I write a song (recall "Rhinestone Cowboy"), and someone wants to make a play out of it, a Creative Commons license may well authorize this. The resultant musical (or nonmusical) play (which is quite well protected by worldwide copyright) and the subsequent film and television series and attendant books, videos, etc. (which are also well protected), and all of the earnings derived from them, will be completely beyond the author's right to participate—whether in creative decision making about how the song is used or in any of the earnings derived from the exploitation of the play or film.

Why would any artists, then, want to give up the ownership or control of their intellectual property and relinquish the possibilities of earnings derived from it? Creative Commons explains:

> Many people have long since concluded that all-out copyright doesn't help them gain the exposure and widespread distribution they want. Many entrepreneurs and artists have come to prefer relying on innovative business models rather than full-fledged copyright to secure a return on their creative investment. Still others get fulfillment from contributing to and participating in an intellectual commons. For whatever reasons, it is clear that many citizens of the Internet want to share their work—and the power to reuse, modify, and distribute their work—with others on generous terms.

Many of the different forms of license agreement offered by Creative Commons require only that the originator of the intellectual property be given "credit" for being the originator. But after that, it's a free world. Its detractors point out that intellectual property license agreements are wordy for a reason. The absence of carefully drafted language can result in ambiguity and a whole lot of disappointment and even outrage in the licensor when he or she finds out how imprecise the Creative Commons license is. For example, the Creative Commons license provision dealing with credit is silent insofar as how the credit is to be provided, in what size, where and how often it is to be given, how it is to be given in proportion to the other credits, etc., yet these are the meat of traditional industry agreements dealing with the issue. Credit provisions are often the most hotly contested parts of an agreement imparting intellectual property. You can't imagine what someone can do with a clause as bereft of protective language as the credit provisions in the Creative Commons license.

Creative Commons has established itself in dozens of countries, including most European countries and some South American countries—encouraging the anticopyright movement there. Creative Commons has been embraced by many musicians who are looking for ways to get their music to the public with no restrictions. Jeff Tweedy, of Wilco fame, is a huge supporter, even as he rakes in the royalties from his Nonesuch (that is, Warner Bros. Music Group) releases, all of which are quite well protected. Yet having made his music free for a time via the Internet, he attracted a sufficient enough following that his touring alone drew the attention of the majors. Sometimes free is good. He actually created stronger copyright exploitation by initially offering his music free.

Creative Commons has interrupted, in part, the attempts by copyright owners to control the Internet, and has opened up a brand new paradigm for the distribution of intellectual property to the public at a price they can afford—zero. At its inception, in 1709, copyright protection was merely a license to publishers as an exercise of the royal prerogative to prevent unlawful copying of printed material. But over three hundred years of international lawmaking, the rigid controls enjoyed by proprietary asset holders have grown ever stronger. At its best, Creative Commons provides a means to dilute those controls, ending the virtual hegemony now enjoyed by copyright holders. At worst, it opens up many cans of worms (and litigations). One thing seems certain: if copyright reform catches on worldwide, the result will be nothing short of a revolutionary reshaping of our very social structure.

At the end of the day, I think that the Creative Commons concept may survive in some form; perhaps a sampling license can be attached to a digital recording as a data file. Yet "shorthand" license agreements like the one quoted above are fraught with hazards—that is, unaddressed issues—and open the door to unlimited litigation down the road. For example, telling an anonymous user via the Internet that he or she can make a derivative work but cannot use a work "commercially" is clearly ambiguous, opening the door to countless lawsuits brought by parties with differing interpretations of that language. Lawyers who advise clients to sign such agreements are themselves open to claims of negligence. Why should it be otherwise for Creative Commons?

Worse still, the carefree use of contract language encouraged by Creative Commons encourage people who think they "know better" to write their own "creative commons" contracts, which will merely produce yet more frustrated licensors, as well as dissatisfied licensees. There are good reasons for the sometimes extreme length of contracts between licensors and licensees: they must address and answer the myriad questions that may arise once the contract is signed. Shortening a five- or fifty-page license agreement to five sentences is an invitation to disaster—for both parties.

Killing the Goose That Laid the Golden Egg

This may all sound perfectly reasonable on some limited level: why not let people decide how much protection they want and how much they are willing to relinquish? But what many people do not know is that the seemingly rational and reasonable arguments promulgated by Lessig and "solved" by the Creative Commons licensing scheme have resulted in the proliferation of movements in many territories of the world—in particular in undeveloped countries—to extend the intent and limits of the free culture movement. Lessig himself has supported this expansion of global resistance to copyright hegemony that Creative Commons has fueled.

The World Social Forum (WSF) is an annual meeting held by the "alternative globalization" movement to "resist neo-liberal globalization" and challenge its capitalist-model rival, the World Economic Forum, which meets—usually in Davos, Switzerland—at exactly the same time. WSF originated with the *encuentro*, an activist Latin American movement. Its annual meetings were originally held in cities such as Caracas, Nairobi, and Belém, Brazil, but lately the meetings have featured polycentric/decentralized venues around the world at the same time, including some in the United States. Their participants have occasionally been violent, such as when they destroyed the genetically modified crops of Monsanto in 2001. These enthusiasts objected to the global agribusiness of Monsanto which they thought was unethical for harming rural farmers. It is not a reach to carry forth this philosophy into demonizing copyright laws as smothering the downtrodden masses they claim to represent by denying them unfettered use of the world's creative output. Talk about a counterculture! (Depending on your point of view, WSF is dangerously far to the left on the political spectrum, progressive, or simply out of touch.) (There have been fifteen meetings through 2015. The 2016 Forum will be held in Montreal.) In Porto Alegre, Brazil, at the Fifth World Social forum, in 2005, free culture advocates encouraged the idea that the establishment and maintenance of property rights in music, films, and computer software are just one more (and overwhelming) example of the rich countries' dominance over the poor countries. Limiting access to these materials—which to a large extent form the underbelly of these countries' *own* culture—by copyright laws and conventions is regarded by WSF as tantamount to occupation by a foreign power.

The World Social Forum is still not much more than its annual meeting. And, although it hasn't yet come close to being a movement, many feel that its tenets are aimed at property ownership of all kinds, not just intellectual property. The attendance in Porto Alegre of more than 100,000 participants suggests that we have not heard the last of what I consider to be a particularly venal form of anticopyright enthusiasm.

Using phrases like "proprietary culture" in an address to the WSF, Lessig (yes, him again) demonizes copyright by distinguishing "culture" from the control that copyright places over creations that are, of course, the fundamental elements of our culture. He points to what he calls an "error" in the 1909 United States Copyright Act that used the word "copy" rather than "publish" as the right that law was primarily intended to protect. "Copying" was at the time simply the act of reprinting a work. It required intentionality; guilt was easily established and punished and just as easily avoided. But with the development of digital transmissions via the Internet, copying has become not just routine, but ubiquitous. There is no way that a document can be called up onto a computer screen without it being a copy. In addition, the opt-in copyright system, where federal registration was required to claim copyright ownership, had already changed to an opt-out system: copyright is automatic unless waived. Under such circumstances, it seemed likely to many observers that seemingly innocent activities like visiting a website and even just reading a copyright-protected document was, by implication, copyright infringement. Everything created after 1978 was automatically "copyrighted," and every click on the mouse resulted in a "copy." Things that used to be "free"—like playing a song on the piano via sheet music—became liable to a charge of infringement if the sheet music was obtained via an illegal site on the Internet. Reading a book became an infringement if the book happened to be an e-book. Giving your sheet music or a Coldplay recording to a friend is fine; forwarding it to a friend via the Internet is not. Selling used music at a flea market has always been a convenient way to disseminate music to lovers of certain genres; selling it on the Internet is an invitation to a federal lawsuit. Why then should we be surprised that the eruption of so-called copyright violations (beginning, of course, with peer-to-peer sharing) has provoked everything from discord to near riot (at the 2005 World Social Forum) by those who claim that "their" culture has been stolen.

Is Copyright a Violation of the First Amendment?

This is not something that you really need to know, but in keeping with the theme of this book, here is something you might never have thought of. There are those who believe that copyright, being a protection of expression, actually infringes on the First Amendment rights of the public. When a painting is stolen, the thief walks away with a canvas, but the canvas itself means nothing. It is the depiction of the painting's subject—the expression of the artist depicted on the canvas—that has value. A copy of a musical score constitutes notation in a certain order by means of a graph that describes the movement of the notes depicted and the rhythm to be given to the notes. Does protection of this "order" represent an impingement on free speech—free expression? Thankfully, both the copyright law and the courts have decided this question in favor of the creators. They do not agree that the government, by granting copyright protection, is interfering with individual's rights of free speech. On the contrary, the copyright law specifically separates the "idea" from the expression. The idea is as free as the wind; only the expression by which the author expresses his or her idea is protected by copyright—constitutionally as well as by statute—a hard test to overcome.

THE CLEARANCE NIGHTMARE

Although it is not entirely clear *what* destabilized the relationship among copyright owners and users, a relationship that had been on a relatively even keel for many, many decades, the culprit may have been the nightmare of copyright clearance. Those who object to the way copyright law works today see abuse wherever they look, and they see the benefits of technology being twisted in order to support protections that are no longer valid. No one, they say, should write a law that requires three different licenses for one use. But that is exactly what we have. An interactive Internet file involves mechanical, synchronization, and performance rights. (A karaoke producer has to clear those three rights, but also has to clear print [display] rights to the lyrics.) Some entertainment lawyers recommend that music industry players work on developing a composite license. But to date, there really is no such thing available. An EMI Music Publishing spokesman pointed out, before his company's demise, that the "law couldn't be clearer." All of these separate rights *can* be cleared—whatever the costs in terms of labor, time, and fees. That is the problem. And that is the solution as well. Once Congress hears the cries of the bedeviled users of music, they will see that the law indeed could not be clearer. And they will change it. The fear is that they will change it in ways that will satisfy no one. And no one in the music industry is happy when Congress forces itself into their world—especially when their world is so complex, so filled with custom and tradition, and so beholden to the industry's own peculiar sense of balance among authors, publishers, and recording companies.

Lawrence Lessig, in his book *Free Culture*, gives the following example. A filmmaker was producing a documentary based on Wagner's *Ring Cycle*, a four-opera marathon. As Valhalla was crumbling in the final act of the final opera in the cycle, *Götterdämmerung*, the camera operator drifted backstage and caught the Met Opera workers watching *The Simpsons*. Everyone, including the creator of *The Simpsons*, Matt Groening, thought this was delightful, but Fox Television, which owns the audiovisual rights to *The Simpsons* wanted so much money for the three- or four-second background use that the filmmakers were forced to delete it from the film, which itself was costly, and to replace it with three or four seconds from another TV show, the inclusion of which would make a similar point. Chalk up one for inauthenticity.

The reality is that even some of the wholly legitimate and legally sanctioned actions of copyright owners are enough to make one wonder if reason has totally taken a vacation. The stories are legion, and the following examples merely scratch the surface.

- Recently a public company was planning a promotion with DJs appearing at several hundred of its stores. I reminded the company's representative that it would require performance licenses from the three American performing rights societies: ASCAP, BMI, and SESAC. "Well," he sputtered, "We want to do the right thing, but we now learn that in addition to your legal fees, we have to pay SESAC, the smallest performing rights society, three to four times what ASCAP, the largest, is charging."

- Also recently, I was asked to clear five songs and five masters for use in a television show that initially appeared on PBS (the songs and masters were covered by a special provision in the copyright law for those specific broadcasts). Subsequent negotiations for nonpublic television rights, a DVD, foreign broadcast rights, etc., involved more than thirty different companies and departments and the paperwork took six months to complete.

- You want to use a photograph or likeness of Elvis Presley in a book? Forget about it. Whereas the right of publicity was always assumed to have died with the subject, many states are now passing laws to keep their citizens alive. I call the Tennessee law reviving Mr. Presley's publicity rights from the afterlife the "Help the Balance of Payments of Tennessee—Keep Elvis Alive" law.

- You want to use the likeness of Marilyn Monroe by Andy Warhol on the cover of a book, *The Culture of the 20th Century*? The Warhol estate doesn't care, but the Monroe estate does. You can't do it.

Documentaries

Documentary filmmakers, in particular, are up against what they consider to be the excessive demands of copyright owners: They *must* quote existing transcriptions (whether print, video, or audio) in order to tell their story. The budgets for documentary films are notoriously small, and the films are usually completed before the directors know exactly what footage they will use to tell their story. They fear the costs when they can find the owners; the risks when they cannot; the eagle eye of their insurers, who demand proof of

100% clearance; the need to self-censor rather than take their art where their muse carries them; the fact that the fair-use provisions of the copyright law offer no concrete guidance and present problems for even the most experienced attorneys.

When documentary filmmakers shoot a scene in a room in which a television set or radio is playing, they must be conscious (and cautious) enough to turn off the TV or radio lest they end up having to negotiate with the copyright owner for the right to use the material—and these rights don't come cheap! Documentary filmmakers refer to this recurrent nightmare as "the clearance culture trap." It is no wonder. A recent panel of experts selected by the Copyright Society of the United States entitled their discussion "Is Copyright Killing the Documentary Film?" They firmly believe that documentary film-making is threatened by the licensing demands of copyright owners of film and television footage, music, photographs, and other source materials. Unfortunately, as noted above, their fears are well documented (pun intended).

Here is another example. Many of the songs written by Irving Berlin were written with Fred Astaire in mind—and, in fact, were introduced on film by Fred Astaire. Documentary filmmakers treating some aspect of Irving Berlin's life and work customarily seek permission from the Astaire estate (his widow) to incorporate a film clip from an Astaire film into an Irving Berlin retrospective, even though they do not have to. But Robin Smith Astaire regularly blocks these uses, to the obvious detriment of the veracity and power of the films themselves. Although she has no right to block them (the original film companies own the clips for all purposes), the documentary film companies are paralyzed because they apparently fear retribution or lawsuits or something, if not with regard to the particular project for which the use was requested, then with regard to some future project. Errors and omissions insurance (E&O) policies may not be obtainable if the documentary filmmakers cannot demonstrate that they are insulated from claims from the Astaire estate. (It is some-how not very comforting to know that Mrs. Astaire did *not* object to the use of an Astaire clip to promote the Dirt Devil Dynamite Vacuum Cleaner.) Now you know why Gene Kelly (whose estate regularly and generously approves uses of his filmed performances) is better known to the youth of America than Fred Astaire. Charles Wright, an A&E televi-sion network vice president, has pointed out that even those who do not own intellectual property are wielding power over those who want to use it.

The (Independent) Empire Strikes Back

The *New York Times* recently reported that the Independent Film Channel, on advice from its counsel, Michael C. Donaldson, a former president of the International Documentary Association, has decided to avoid (evade?) the huge cost of clearing film clips by pro-mulgating a copyright law–based fair-use position. They feel that film clip–dependent documentaries in particular need to find an alternative to the paralyzing fees charged by copyright owners—usually other motion picture companies. The future will tell whether this creatively aggressive application of the fair-use doctrine will hold up in court.

Searching for the Owner

What happens when a company desires to use a copyrighted work, is willing to pay any price for a license, and cannot locate the copyright owner? An honest company will be discouraged from using it and presumably the consumer is worse off as a result. Works whose progeny or current ownership is unknown or uncertain are often referred to as "orphan works." While the owners or administrators of music and film works are fairly well documented and public, the same is not true of works of art, illustrations, cartoons, etc. This issue has drawn the attention of the Copyright Office and Congress, but their proposed solutions are suspect, as you will see below (page 374).

Sampling

Contrary to the belief of some, most sampling is not simply an easy way out for producers and other authors who are too lazy or untalented to create the sounds themselves. Their real intent is to capture a mood, a memory, a feeling of a specific time or experience, and to blend that into their own creation. DJs have "sampled" for years. But what they are permitted to do in a club—live—is prohibited on a permanent recording, even if the recording is available only via the Internet via downloading or streaming. Most composers, and the courts, find sampling anathema to the concept of private property; others find the process similar to making a salad—the ingredients that make up a contemporary recording naturally include elements that went before. What else is culture than the accumulation of a civilization's art over time? Sampling is now part of most every genre of music—from hip-hop to rock to pop. Even electronic classical works are utilizing samples from our everyday culture just as a hip-hop composition might.

Consequences of the Clearance Nightmare

Another challenge for entertainment lawyers are laws written during the predigital–pre-Internet age (or their application) that are not relevant in today's music world, where legitimate creators of music want to reach citizens around the world and convey to them the fruits of their creations.

Among the most important of entertainment attorneys' functions is to provide their clients with a "rights road map" showing them how to comply with copyright laws, identify the risks they must avoid or manage, and somehow find them a way within the law to publish their book, write their musical, or record their song.

Too often, we are unable to achieve these goals for our clients. Our frustration is mirrored in the frustration and anger of those who wish to use copyrights in a responsible manner. The possibilities offered by the Internet have merely added exponentially to the mood among copyright users when they keep running into stone walls in an effort to seek permission, and—yes—pay a reasonable fee for the rights they seek. Their frustration is finding support among academics and, more importantly, powerful lobbies that single-handedly are reversing the thinking of the author-friendly Congresses of the past 230 years.

COPYRIGHT AND PERSONAL PROPERTY

In the past, building on the art of others was the hallmark of genius. Now it is an invitation to a lawsuit. Is this simply borrowing, or is it outright copying? Sampling without the permission of the owner of the music sampled is illegal. Fine. But the effort (not to mention the cost) involved in clearing rights ranges from impossibly difficult to nearly impossible. This discourages the creative use of our culture's output and, at the same time, encourages widespread violation of copyright owners' rights. Both results are unproductive and destructive.

Is intellectual property "owned" in the same way that a house or a car is owned? The Recording Industry Association of America (RIAA) and the National Music Publishers

Association (NMPA) say it is a property right. *Period!* What I create is mine. *Period!* This view permeates the copyright owners' world. What, then, is our culture? An accumulation of other people's property? Whose culture is it then? Certainly not "ours." How can it be "ours" when we have to ask permission to use it? And how can a culture survive and expand when innovation is stifled by the threat of lawsuits?

In his book *The Dark Heart of Italy*, Tobias Jones, in attempting to identify a core essence of Italy and Italians, compares the culture of Italy to a chemical reaction: "*Nothing is created and nothing is destroyed but everything is transformed.*" Tell that to a copyright owner whose music has been "transformed."

If copyright were mere property, it would be subject to state and federal laws that enforce property rights. A primary difference between copyright as property, and ordinary property in the form of goods and services, is that the cost of producing a copyright does not reflect either the cost of its reproduction or the cost of its distribution. Another is that intellectual property is more vulnerable to theft (which we call piracy) than, say, manufactured products like clothes, cars, and toasters. Finally, stealing a song file via peer-to-peer sharing does not take the property from an eventual buyer, as does stealing a CD from a store. The property still exists—a copy of it has merely been relocated.

The value of intellectual property is not just the intangible MP3 file reflecting it. The idea that a user of intellectual property may pay less than the value of providing the property via distribution means such as radio, television, motion picture theater presentations—even the Internet—is anathema to creative people and their supporters, publishers, record companies, film companies, etc. And why not? People are willing to pay for water that they *could* get for free? Why not copyrighted works?

Work for Hire: Co-Opting the Author

Generally in this book, I have referred to the author as the person who actually creates the song—whether the lyrics or the music (or even the "beat"). There is s bizarre exception to this concept which used to be judge-made and ultimately appeared in the "new" copyright act of 1976 (taking effect on January 1, 1978). This is the "work for hire" doctrine. Briefly, this concept deals with situations where companies actually engage a creator to author something just for them—and just for a particular purpose. For example, a screenplay for a film, or a marching band arrangement of a musical composition. This is a very old concept dating back to 1903, and which has been codified in the 1976 law. To be a work for hire, the author needs to agree in writing that the work is indeed a work for hire, that the work was "specially ordered" by the employer, and that the work is of a nature that would fall within nine specific categories of commissionable works cited in the Copyright Act. If the work does not do so, it will be deemed to have fallen into the company's hands solely by virtue of an assignment. The difference is enormous. An transfer of an "authored" work can be terminated (see chapter 20) after thirty-five years. But a work for hire will stay with the company for ninety-five years! Recording artists who, since 1978, have signed agreements acknowledging that their records have been created as works for hire are now disputing whether there is any legitimacy to such representations given the fact that the nine categories do not explicitly set forth sound recordings. The record labels are relying on the wording of the statute which includes "contributions to collective works." Are recorded tracks collective work? We'll find out soon as the first tests of this dispute will be made after 2013.

MISUSE OF COPYRIGHT

The doctrine of misuse of copyright was first developed in patent law, another law derived from the US Constitution (Article I, Section II). "Misuse of patent" is a defense raised to counter a claim of patent infringements. It is cited when companies that own patents abuse their monopoly in order to overwhelm a defendant (the alleged patent infringer) with the power they derive from the federally granted patent. This is usually framed as an antitrust issue rather than "unfairness" per se.

There exists no fully fleshed-out doctrine of misuse of copyright, but it is bubbling under many litigations brought by copyright owners. Many observers feel that it is only a matter of time before the courts or Congress, in an effort to protect citizens from the abuse of the monopoly that is inherent in copyright ownership, extend the doctrine to music publishers. After all, music publishers, not being authors, are not even the targeted beneficiaries of the copyright law or, for that matter, the constitutional provision underlying it. Why allow them to use their power in this way?

Let me explain.

Let us take as a given the fact that holders of copyright monopolies have the means to abuse their powers. Now, *who* is damaged by their actions? Certainly consumers. But authors as well. Because authors do not, usually, control their own copyrights but have relinquished control to huge multinational companies such as EMI and Warner/Chappell, which together control almost 1.5 million copyrights. Even when the multinationals do not actually own the copyrights, but merely administer them, they still control them. The same applies, on a much smaller, but nevertheless important, scale for hundreds of smaller music publishing companies that completely control decisions as to whether, and for how much money, songs are licensed.

When a music publisher denies a license for whatever reason (for example, the publisher is nervous about technological advances), or asks for so much money that its demand destroys a carefully negotiated most-favored-nation rate among many other copyright owners, is it merely exercising its near-holy property rights, or is it conducting itself in a way that violates the express intentions of the Constitution and the copyright law? And if the latter, what can be done about it? Can its copyright be invalidated? Should it? These are questions that will be raised and pursued in the future. The trend is anticopyright, and I agree with David Israelite, the CEO of the National Music Publishers Association (NMPA), that if the music publishers that control most of the copyrights in the world today do not address these issues themselves, and soon, they will run into a wall of US Representatives and Senators whose constituencies are, collectively, a lot more powerful than publishers who want to maintain the status quo.

SOME SUGGESTED SOLUTIONS

How can the industry solve these problems themselves before the anticopyright forces prevail? Following are a few suggestions.

Expanding the Function of Societies or Agencies

In many countries outside of the United States, the performing and mechanical rights societies, working together, have managed to create either a blanket license for users of music or a composite license in situations, such as those described earlier, where many different rights under copyright are implicated: a kind of one-stop shopping. The United States has neither. There are moves afoot among private organizations and the government to rectify the situation among frustrated users of music. The Harry Fox Agency, the three performing rights societies, NMPA, digital rights companies, the Songwriters Guild of America (SGA), the Recording Artists' Coalition, the National Academy of Recording Arts and Sciences (NARAS, the GRAMMY organization), the Nashville Songwriter's Association, and RIAA are all trying to figure out how to do this—either by industry consensus or by lobbying strongly for appropriate legislation. Reforming the licensing of intellectual property is high on Congress's agenda, and it *will* make changes in what it considers to be an outdated system of clearing rights. The compulsory license provision of Section 115 of the copyright law is no longer viable; it will be changed. The only question is when, how much, and to what extent will the copyright owners (and controllers) themselves have a say in the change. Mr. Israelite has it right when he says that the greatest fear of the copyright owners is that a bill that they can live with will be bound together with a bill they *cannot* live with.

The "21st Century Music Licensing Reform Act"

Just when the private institutions representing copyright interests are beginning to recognize the problem and are trying to fix it, the US Copyright Office has preempted them by proposing a significant change in the copyright law. While in many ways the proposed revision reflects the thinking of a large number of foreign countries in dealing with the complexities of Internet licensing, it is revolutionary for the United States. It is not useful to explain in any detail the nature of the draft legislation presented by Marybeth Peters, the register of copyright, in 2005, as any eventual bill will undergo significant changes before it is passed. But something will eventually pass. Following are some initiatives that have already taken effect, or are likely to take effect in the future.

Section 115

Section 115 of copyright law, the compulsory license provision, which has for almost a hundred years established a right to record a cover version of a musical composition already licensed at least once, for a fee (the statutory rate), and which set the maximum rate for such a right, will be eliminated.

Multiple-Use Licenses

The performing rights societies in the United States will have the authority to grant multiple-use licenses, which will include licenses for mechanical and synchronization reproduction.

The Harry Fox Agency's Role

The Harry Fox Agency, which, as stated earlier, is not a society, but a corporation owned and governed for most of its existence by America's largest music publishers, and sold in 2015 to SESAC, the United States' third performing rights society. Now SESAC will be able to bundle licensing for interactive digital services that require both performance and mechanical licenses. Theoretically, it will also allow the Harry Fox Agency to more accurately track uses by digital services because it will have both mechanical and performance sets of data.

The Formation of New Societies

There already exists a proliferation of societies or agencies representing rights owners. The European Union has blocked efforts by the large performing and mechanical rights societies to work together to solve the problems created by their very numbers. As more rights are discovered, or created, the proliferation will continue, putting the eventual user back into the soup insofar as knowing where to go to clear rights and being able to estimate costs. A positive development occurred in 2006 when the British corporate regulator, the Office of Fair Trading, proposed the merger of three collecting societies representing performers: the Association of United Recording Artists (AURA) and the Performing Artists' Media Rights Association Limited (PAMRA) will be merged into Phonographic Performance Ltd. (PPL), the goal being "distribution of equitable remuneration due to performers from the broadcast and public performance of sound recordings on which they have performed." It's a start.

The Creative Commons License

As noted earlier, Creative Commons has offered a solution to the "clearance culture trap": its own license (see above, page 363), which invites the public to use what otherwise would have been protected intellectual property as if it were not protected at all.

Documentaries

Special rules will apply to documentary specials. As stated earlier in the chapter, impossibly high clearance fees are making it difficult if not impossible to complete documentary films. In some cases, filmmakers have actually falsified footage rather than discard years' worth of work.

A group of documentary filmmakers have gotten together to encourage the passage of federal legislation that will protect documentary filmmakers from these problems. (One of them refers to the proposed legislation as the "Michael Moore Protection Act.") The makers of documentaries are what the name suggests: they document—create a permanent record of—aspects of the social-political-cultural milieu around them. Filmmakers believe that in-context use of images that advance their cultural function should be permitted without cost, or at a set rate. At this writing, their most visible action has been to develop a "statement of best practices" (drafted by the Association of Independent Video and Filmmakers, the Independent Feature Project, the International Documentary Association, the National Alliance for Media Arts and Culture, and Women in Film and Video), which honest filmmakers would adhere to. This would establish signatories as companies that have agreed not to abuse their authorization to utilize intellectual property. While this would not have the force of law, it would afford some insulation from the likelihood of lawsuits, even if what the company was doing technically violated one right or another. The uses that would be freed up include name and likeness rights—which, alone, can destroy a documentary if not granted.

The filmmakers who sign the statement of best practices would be deemed good-faith users of intellectual property, and copyright owners—film and television companies; music companies; and actors, artists, and musicians' unions; among others—would "recognize" them by not trying to stop them from using materials for which others would have to seek authorization. Documentary filmmakers want to protect and preserve our culture. This mechanism would seem to be a good way to go about permitting them to do so. Whether

E&O companies will insure productions on the fairly flimsy basis that the filmmakers have signed a statement of best practices and belong to the estimable club of good-faith makers of documentaries remains to be seen.

Section 118

Section 118 of the copyright law authorizes, among other things, the performance of music by a noncommercial educational broadcast station (for example, public television) of "published nondramatic musical works" pursuant to voluntarily negotiated terms that are reviewed and renegotiated every five years. The problem is that the authorization is in effect for only a week. After that, the film, or video, designed for broadcast will require clearance from all of the music rights holders for all uses: continued public television runs, free television, cable and satellite transmissions, Internet transmission, videocassettes and DVDs, and all other manifestations of technology now or hereafter created. Broadcasting on PBS is a privilege, but the broadcasts reach relatively few people, and Section 118 is no substitute for a broad rights license—which puts us back to square one when it comes to the clearance issues described in this chapter. Expanding its coverage, or creating a central clearing house such as exists in England for music used on television, would, if nothing else, go a long way toward removing the obstacle that exists for producers whose modest use of music should not be so costly as to be prohibitive.

Orphan Songs

At a time when registrations were necessary to renew copyrights, and thereby maintain them as proprietary assets, an incredible number of copyrights, some say as much as 95% of all copyrights secured in the United States were abandoned and thus entered the public domain. Most registration requirements were withdrawn in 1978, and even renewal registrations were made automatic in 1993; subsequently, all of those works that under prior law would have entered the public domain remain in copyright. All of them! Part of the clearance nightmare for potential users of these copyrights is locating their owners. As this is often an impossible task, the alternatives are to abandon any intention to use the works or to pirate them, hoping to avoid discovery. This is obviously an unenviable situation for a film or record company that merely wishes to reproduce a musical composition in ways other than would be permitted by Section 115, the compulsory license (itself at risk of being discarded in the near future). These works have come to be known as *orphan works*. Their owners cannot be found. The paper trail by which civilization traces back a title to its owner has disappeared.

Most of the master recordings currently identified as orphan works were produced prior to legislation investing sound recordings for the first time with federal copyright protection on February 15, 1972. It is estimated that ownership of up to 25% of these recordings cannot be traced. But ever since registration requirements lapsed according to the Copyright Act of 1976 (which became effective on January 1, 1978), the number of musical compositions suffering this fate has become astronomical. Many music interests have been working with the Copyright Office and the House Judiciary Subcommittee involved with intellectual property issues. Their efforts resulted in the January 2005 "Report on Orphan Networks," which proposes legislation to relieve a company of liability if it can show that it tried in good faith to identify the owner of a work. Marybeth Peters, the register of copyrights, is working closely with rights owners such as the Association of

American Publishers, as well as many music business organizations, to prevent Congress from pursuing the ever-present panacea loved by content users and abhorred by content owners: a compulsory license automatically relieving a user of any liability provided a minimum fee is paid for the use. The salutary effects of Congress passing a reasonable law based on the Copyright Office report go beyond those connected with predictable and ordinary commercial uses of these works; the entire industry of rediscovering, restoring, and redistributing (if only for archival purposes via museums such as the Smithsonian) these reminders of our cultural heritage will benefit from such a law.

Registration Requirements: Bring Them On (Again)

Registration of claims to copyright used to be the sine qua non of maintaining ownership lest the copyright fall into the public domain. This requirement was done away in 1978 with the advent of the Copyright Act of 1976. Remember, federal copyright protection now vests on creation. Registration is still useful to establish a record of the existence of a work on a particular date, and it is still required for such things as enforcing statutory damages, compulsory licenses, litigating in the federal courts, etc. But for all intents and purposes, registration for the purpose of *establishing or maintaining copyright ownership* no longer exists in America. Any change in that status would violate the Bern Convention absent an amendment to the contrary. And the other countries that have adhered to the Bern Convention never had, and would likely never permit, such a requirement for ownership as registration. Nevertheless, Creative Commons has suggested a registration regime in order to maintain copyright ownership after a number of years. In Lawrence Lessig's opinion, "copyrights that are doing nothing except blocking access and the spread of knowledge" are harming culture *and* commerce—both of which are supposed to be *enhanced* by copyright. His concept works best in the situation of orphan works, but he also recommends establishing a copyright owners' list for public dissemination, with the burden of keeping it up to date the copyright owner's responsibility. Once such a list no longer reflected the correct address or contact information for the owner of a work, a potential user of presumably copyrighted material, stymied by being unable to clear the rights being sought, would be able to use the material without fear of legal action.

Lessig is not alone in encouraging establishment of a central registry. Many musicians and copyright owners, in fact, feel that registration requirements, like state car title registration requirements, both authenticate ownership and make a statement that the copyright owner intends to continue to claim an interest in his or her copyrights. According to Lessig, a registration requirement, fifty years after the commencement of a copyright term, would result in 98% of copyrights entering the public domain—copyrights which are lying moribund, copyrights that even the owners are unaware of. How can anyone argue against an easy system for locating a copyright owner? How can anyone justify "life plus seventy" copyright protection when the commercial life of so many works has long ago expired?

Many organizations representing rights owners point to the cost of creating a registry. Other countries subsidize or even fully pay for the cost of registries—whether for music, or visual arts, or other areas within the protection of copyright laws. They also point out that shifting the burden of diligence (for example, registering claims to copyright with a central registry) from users to copyright owners flies in the face of the most fundamental guarantee afforded creators by the Copyright Act: the exclusive right to authorize *or withhold* reproduction, display, or performance rights, as well as the exclusive right to create derivative works. Stay tuned.

25 · SOLVING PIRACY IN THE 21ST CENTURY
How to Avoid a Greek Tragedy

Originally presented at the Institute for Cultural and Media Management—
University of Hamburg, Germany

Back before the Internet, we had a name for people who bought a single copy of our books and lent them to all their friends without charging: we called them "librarians."
—CHARLES STROSS

What do you want to be a sailor for? There are greater storms in the music business than you will ever find at sea. Piracy, broadsides, blood on the decks. You will find them all in the music business.
—PARAPHRASING DAVID LLOYD GEORGE

The music industry is in a mess. Some would say this is a problem of its own making and that it continues to make things worse, what with its lawsuits against college kids (the Recording Industry Association of America [RIAA] has reported on its website that it has instituted more than 35,000 such lawsuits), its bludgeoning (their word, not mine) of companies, Girl Scout camps, and performing venues for performance fees, and generally with all of the negative press it has received. I don't think it would be inaccurate to say that the music industry (and by implication, intellectual property generally) faces the most intensive attacks from anticopyright interests our society has ever known—attacks that find themselves on the front pages of our newspapers and among the lead stories on our electronic media, SOPA and PIPA (see page 341). Whether as intellectual property lawyers or entrepreneurs, we can either continue to move blindly forward justly enforcing our rights, or stop and reflect on what we are trying to accomplish, the reasons we are not succeeding, and the ways in which we can fix the problem.

There are actually a multitude of problems facing the music industry today. I will address two of these: first, illegal downloading by consumers; and second, the self-destructive behavior by copyright owners themselves arising out of the way they have chosen to exercise their monopoly. Even though I am a practicing attorney in the intellectual property field, it is my belief that we are going nowhere by following the advice of contemporary legal sages. So I thought a better solution to this problem might be achieved with a little help from the ancient Greeks.

But first, let me explain the peculiar view that we in the copyright bar have of that otherwise dry concept called "copyright." One of the legendary music lawyers in our field, my mentor, Harold Orenstein, would regularly compare copyrights to children.

"Nurture them," he would say. "Feed them. Protect them." I had no clue as to what he was talking about.

Over the years, I learned. A copyright that lies fallow is like a child starved. Paul Simon once offered millions of dollars to purchase an entire publishing company where he once worked as a low-level employee before his success with Art Garfunkel. During his brief employment, the company had acquired six of his copyrights (the only significant ones being "Fifty-Ninth Street Bridge Song [Feelin' Groovy]" and "Red Rubber Ball," a hit with the 1960s group The Cyrkle).

After Simon's success, he tried to buy the music publishing company for the sole reason of getting back his six songs at any cost. He was distressed that his six copyrights were not being exploited, nurtured. I began to understand what Orenstein meant.

Yet, while likening copyrights to children is a fine sentiment, warranting such noble efforts as that of Mr. Simon in the early 1970s, it appears that songwriters and their "children" today are in jeopardy much more than were they merely experiencing a lack of attention. Indeed, they are watching helplessly as their "children" are being killed off first by peer-to-peer "sharing" and second, most surprisingly and disappointingly by the copyright proprietors themselves, most often music publishing companies in whom the songwriters entrusted their copyrights. But more about that later.

What does this have to do with Greek tragedy? A lot, I think.

Remember Medea? She was the sorceress who was betrayed by Jason (of Argonaut fame) and who decided to pay him back by killing their children. Medea decided to "wring their father's heart" just as he had wrung hers.

I couldn't help but consider Medea as a perfect metaphor for the music industry.

"Go home," Medea says to her boys, "I cannot bear to see you anymore. I don't want to hand you over to someone else to be slaughtered by a less loving hand. I who gave you life will kill you."

And then, "For this short day, I will forget they are my children—and will mourn them later. The evil done to me has won the day. I understand too well the dreadful act I'm going to commit, but my judgment cannot check my anger, and that incites the greatest evils human beings do."

I know this is not the usual reference material of entertainment lawyers, but just as James Joyce, in *Ulysses,* saw a continuous parallel between ancient myth and modern life, I believe a similar parallel can be drawn between ancient Greek mythology and modern music copyright law.

ILLEGAL DOWNLOADING

As I describe earlier in this book, Napster was the well-publicized software created by a then nineteen-year-old, which permitted multiple Internet users to access each others' collections of MP3 files for free. MP3, of course, is the free technology protocol that enables a user to convert a large file contained on ordinary music CDs into files that are compressed to ten to twelve times smaller than the originals. Since they consume considerably less computer storage space than the form in which they were originally configured, they can be transferred faster and have become the preferred modality for moving audio files through the internet and among computers and digital download players. Napster was the mechanism for the deluge of illegal downloads that we have all read about and which has been nothing short of catastrophic for the music industry.

I think we all will agree that, for years, the music industry allowed illegal downloading to become totally out of control. We gave birth to mass infringements by neglect, by standing on the sidelines while technology advanced well beyond its ability to keep up with legal protections, and by seeking to remedy the situation by a bumbling array of solutions that really are mind boggling, given the perceived sophistication of the industry. The industry did not understand then, and still does not understand, that much of the record buying public today has been brought up *using* music, but not owning it, and that that's okay with the youth of the world today. The industry has not yet grasped this reality.

The examples of how the industry tried to remedy this situation are too numerous to mention, so I will limit myself to only a few:

First, the music industry tried to keep prices high even though it was becoming more and more obvious that consumers did not want to pay for the entire album when they were captured by the emotional pull of one particular song. Then it blocked, and later encouraged, the creation of compilation albums in order to increase sales volume. But all this did was remove even more album buyers from the food chain. Harold Vogel, the renowned economic analyst who is quite familiar with the music industry, reminds us that the population shift made a difference in demand. Baby boomers who were the primary buyers in the 1960s and '70s were no longer enthusiastic about standing in the rain and snow to be the first to buy an album and to push it into the top 10 overnight. Technologically, the industry fought invention and did everything they could to block it from the marketplace. More time and money was spent on encryption techniques than on education and adapting to the new paradigms. And then these lawsuits!

As I just noted, much of the record-buying public today has been brought up using music, but not owning it. My generation bragged about our record collections; we displayed them openly in our homes and in our entertainment centers. But today's consumer keeps his and her 10,000 songs on a little box and is quite content with that, or they just call up the song on their smartphones when they want to hear it. Needless to say, the industry has not yet grasped this new reality. They see it as a stopgap. But surely it is a replacement for the music business as we know it.

In all of its inadequate responses, the one consistent characteristic is that the entertainment industry has not, until now, acknowledged that the fault may lie within as well as without. It took an outsider, Steve Jobs, to figure that out.

Just as Medea was driven by the passion of a betrayed suitor, so the music industry seems to be driven more by passion than by reason. And in so doing, it has become the victim. The spurned woman.

So it just rolls right along, suing college kids, teenagers, and unsuspecting grandmothers—35,000 lawsuits before the RIAA suspended its campaign. Notwithstanding claims to the contrary, this remedy did not achieve what it was seeking. CD sales in the US continue to fall. The emphasis on suing pirates has been reduced to feeble attempts to penalize lyric and guitar tab sites and their unsuspecting visitors—mostly young musicians. Meanwhile, we are approaching 3 billion downloads from the Apple iTunes store. The company that has most benefited from legitimizing downloads is Apple, the same company that urged consumers to "rip and burn" music using their computers. Their share of every $0.99 download is around $0.23. Do the math. Talk about putting the fox into the hen house! The argument that the fight against piracy is intended to allow record companies to invest in new bands and develop more flexible legal Internet sites seems very weak when one considers that Apple has made billions from its preeminent position in the download business, but that artists and music publishers down the food chain have years to go before they will see any meaningful recovery from the reduction in CD sales.

None of us will personally recall that when the phonograph record was first produced, music publishers insisted on a head start of several weeks before the release of their songs on records so that they could sell sheet music—the predominant income-earner in the early part of the 20th century. The current century's version of this is the DRM-marked CDs which at their best require careful and sophisticated readings of the DRM warnings and at their worst result in the debacle resulting from (then-named) SonyBMG's use of rootkit cloaking technology. Even when the software was not secretly introduced into consumers' computers, the notice of the software's inclusion on the CDs resulted in the bizarre situation in which SonyBMG sold product which had so many disclaimers that even though the product did not work, SonyBMG took no responsibility. In other words, they sold a product that they knew did not work in a large percentage of cases and yet they refused to take the product back. What were they thinking? This copy protection intrusion into consumers' personal computers not only did not serve its security function—to impede piracy—but it actually threatened the integrity of hundreds of thousands, if not millions, of computers worldwide. At the close of 2005, SonyBMG settled many lawsuits brought against it for compromising the digital security and privacy of consumers who played the XCP-laced CDs on their home computers. The company also had to recall all of their copy-protected titles and make available uninstall software and security patches for infected computers. Just consider how Sony BMG's legal fund for fighting the multitude of lawsuits resulting from its invasive XCP software could have been spent more efficiently toward that too often forgotten goal—to increase sales, not just to reduce piracy.

We know that there is considerable tension between the life of a file sharer on the one hand and the music industry on the other. This is true whether the file sharer is a teenager or a college student or simply a music lover who is tired of being taken advantage of by the creative and commercial paradigms that have defined the music industry for the past fifty or so years—since the advent of the long-playing record.

Music is like air. It is going to be with us, however, and to whatever extent, the music industry seeks to put it in a protective box. It is a fundamental essence of humanity; only the expression is different. And, of course, it is the expression that the copyright laws seek to protect.

Professor David Lange of Duke Law School, in a talk given to the Copyright Society of the USA at its annual meeting a few years ago, asserted that "these kids are not pirates; they just love their music; they're just being kids." (Tell that to the copyright owners of the works that "these kids" are passing along to the million other kids comprising their "friends and family." By virtue of the technology offered by Kazaa via Grokster and other peer-to-peer software methodologies, one song on one unsuspecting person's computer can find its way in seconds across the globe and into unlimited numbers of computers of what we naively refer to as file sharers.) Given the awed reaction of the professionals who attended the meeting, those whose very beings scream EXCLUSIVE RIGHTS, it is a wonder Professor Lange was permitted to leave the conference in one piece.

But we can learn something from what Professor Lange suggested. Kids perceive that morality is on their side. Why? Partly out of youthful naivete, partly out of ignorance, and partly because of the well-documented perception that songwriters and artists have never been paid a fair share of the money they generate. They perceive the music industry as more likely to be avaricious, manipulative, and oppressive than fair and sympathetic.

This perception by a large segment of its customer base has resulted in a feeling that, like Jason, it is the music industry which has betrayed them. Yet the music industry feels betrayed as well. After all, did not the music industry invest heart, soul, artistic talent, and oodles of money to produce and distribute the very art that the consumers now feel entitled to take for free?

Ironically, it is the recording artists themselves who have recurrently publicized the fact that they are not getting what they consider to be a fair share of the income generated by their music. So why should the file sharers deny themselves the opportunity to "take from the rich?" (Regrettably, and very un–Robin Hood-like, these file sharers have forgotten the part about giving to the poor who are often the very songwriters and recording artists whose music they pilfer.)

As was inevitable in international commerce, copyright owners and those who depend on copyright sanctity looked to the courts to enforce what they considered to be their divinely given rights. In America, a long line of lawsuits culminated in the federal appeals court decision in the defining case A & M Records et al. v. Napster, Inc. (114 F. Supp 2nd 896 [ND Cal 2000], affirmed in part, reversed in part 239 F3rd 1004 [CA 9 2001] Decided February 2001) in which the court held that the Napster model, which I referred to earlier, necessarily harms the copyright holders. These file sharers were dealt an even harder blow in the recently decided Grokster case (Metro-Goldwyn-Mayer Studios Inc., et al. v. Grokster, Ltd: Case #04-480, Decided June 27, 2005). At issue was whether peer-to-peer file-sharing services could escape liability if their networks were used for illegal purposes, even though they did not control their networks, as did the Napster model, but merely facilitated their creation. The US Supreme Court had struck another victory for copyright interests. In a unanimous decision, Justice Souter wrote, "We hold that one who distributes a device with the object of promoting its use to infringe copyright is liable for the resulting acts of infringement by third parties." Once again, the legal system enforced its view that what some call borrowing was really no different than stealing,

So finally we saw that reason, according at least to those who value the federal courts' decisions, thwarted the passion of the file sharers. Maybe we have learned something since Medea rode off on her winged chariot at the end of her story. But has reason trumped passion? Is our story ended as well? I don't think so. Unlike a Beethoven symphony, the last movement is not the resolution the copyright industry sought. Indeed, the last movement has yet to be written.

What, then, have we achieved?

Right or wrong, moral or immoral, supported by the court system or not, there is still something wrong about putting your most passionate, avid customers in the dock. I have always felt that suing college students is a losing proposition—not because it is the wrong thing to do, but because it is self-defeating.

Suing four college students who are transferring a million files each is not effective if they are replaced by four million college students transferring one file apiece. And believe me, none of "these kids" are transferring only one file apiece. In my opinion, these lawsuits are like parents saying no to their teenage children. We all know what the response is likely to be. Add a layer of moral justification because their heroes are also getting taken advantage of, and you have an almost insurmountable scenario.

Now, of course, there is a certain logic to what the copyright interests are trying to do, just as there is a certain logic to what Medea did.

According to the RIAA, the lawsuits themselves constitute a form of education of the public, and the RIAA is actually quite encouraged by the willingness of their numerous defendants' acknowledgments of mea culpa. Unfortunately, as I noted earlier, the numbers of the converted are miniscule when compared to the actual damage being done on a worldwide basis. Furthermore, there is some considerable question as to whether the suits have any enduring value. There are also significant variations in analysis of the impact of illegal downloading on the one hand, and the effects of legal downloading options on the other. For example, according to the Harry Fox Agency, Inc., analysts significantly underestimated the appeal of subscription alternatives. They found that even legal downloading decreases the sale of physical CDs, while not particularly affecting piracy. The lawsuits by the RIAA have similarly had an impact far less than that which they had hoped for. The Fox Agency found that only 15% of illegal downloaders would have paid $0.99 anyway, so neutralizing and converting the illegal downloaders will not necessarily have the impact of creating legal customers.

Indeed, every time a well-founded action is commenced, the public is reminded of some of those lawsuits whose rationale and result were, in a word, absurd.

Take, for example the forty-one-year-old disabled single mother living in Oregon who countersued the RIAA for fraud, invasion of privacy, abuse of process, electronic trespass, violation of the Computer Fraud and Abuse Act, negligent misrepresentation, and the Oregon RICO Act alleging racketeering by the music industry. Her personal home computer had been secretly entered by the record companies' agents, MediaSentry. The fact that she had been up at 4:24 a.m. downloading "gangster rap" music failed to make the newspaper release.

In another case, the RIAA sued the mother of a thirteen-year-old when her daughter shared music over a file-sharing network. The suit was dismissed on a technicality. In order for the RIAA to sue the child, the court had to appoint a guardian to represent her. The mother was able to step out of the case, but not before having incurred substantial legal fees. The RIAA's position was that the mother was indirectly liable because she had purchased the computer, even though she had no clue as to how to use it. They failed—this time.

Many feel that the majority of those sued are innocent of copyright infringement, but the threats of legal costs, criminal prosecution, ruination of their credit, publication of their names, and eventually losing the case has resulted in thousands of settlements.

And so, we must ask again, "Is the desire for free music dictated by passion or by reason?" I would suggest that the weight of the evidence would appear to run toward the former and not the latter. But appearances are deceiving, for cannot passionate action actually be reasonable action?

What Medea has done is intelligible in the sense that what she did is what you do when you are ruled by passion. No, she is not behaving wisely, because she is driven by passion and anger—just as the illegal downloaders are driven by passion and anger. Interestingly, greed, something the music industry often points to as the underlying motivation for illegal downloads, is not really a factor at all. So, you see, Medea is beginning to seem a lot more sane.

So, what happens when reason is trumped by passion? Most philosophers—students of human conduct after all—believe that in such event, the most horrible consequences ensue. If to be driven by passion is to have passion rule reason, then is what the music industry has been doing to enforce its rights irrational? Is this kind of behavior actually *beyond* reason and not merely the manifestation of it? Is the end worth the means? Does the mission dictate the process?

Here is where a particularly strained use of reason intervenes to counter the passion argument. The freeloader feels that he has not been given what he wants, when he wants it, by the powers that be. If he is not offered what he wants, when he wants it, whether or not at a fair price, is he operating outside of the natural order by downloading music by unauthorized means? Is he a thief? Is his behavior the same as if he were to steal a CD from a record store (which, of course, he never would think of doing)? Herein lies the dilemma.

The loss to the industry via piracy is valued in terms of tens of billions of dollars. Efforts to stop it, by seizing domain names, legislating three-strike laws (for example, in France), enforcing laws generally, education of the public, suing college students, have all failed. The only rational solution has been to offer the same rights (and more) for a price. Streaming, subscription services, legitimate download services have all served to diminish the effect of piracy and, at the same time, led people to legitimate sites where the companies who financed the creators, and creators will be paid. Unfortunately, piracy in the copyright arena, as in the trademark arena, and others, will never go away, but its impact has been counterbalanced by the legitimate sources made available by rights owners!

So, we now know that if a freeloader is offered the chance to buy music at a fair price, as I predicted in my book, given that chance, he or she would do so.

Surprisingly, this new "model" has gone a long way toward solving the piracy problem absent the assistance of the courts or Congress. The good news, then, is that legitimate sources of music have become royalty generators for both record companies and artists.

Of course, we cannot talk about offering music legitimately at a fair price without pointing out Apple's extraordinary success in catapulting this model along. Apple's iPod fundamentally changed the way people listen to music. Who are these people? They are young; they are entering the commercial marketplace and, unlike us grownups, they are not used to owning music and they are not used to paying $18.00 or €25 for an album when they only wish to *possess* (I didn't say *own*) the right to listen to their favorite song. We cannot deny that billions of legitimate downloads (of mostly individual tracks) have indeed happened. While this may be a drop in the bucket of what sales used to be during the music industry's heyday in the 60s through the 80s, it is a significant turnaround from what were universally depressing statistics about record sales over the past five years. To show you just how successful the iPod has been for Apple, it now represents one-third of Apple's total revenue and 75 percent of the market for digital download players. Apple offers more than three hundred accessories. It is an industry unto itself, and this upstart company, known for its design marvels and rabid fans, while breaching a mere 5 percent of the computer market, has done it again.

WHEN AN APPLE BOOMERANGS

But all is not quite as it appears. Consider 100 million downloads of singles; divide by 10 and you have the equivalent of 10 million albums—something Whitney Houston, or Michael Jackson could have sold in a nanosecond during the now departed "golden age" just a decade or so ago. And now Japan has threatened to tax downloads. Just what the industry needed! And this, after 1 million songs were sold in just four days in Japan after the launch in August 2005 of the iPod in that major music business market.

Observe what we have seen.

We have seen that college kids and millions of others prefer to act according to their own whims and will pay attention to the laws of copyright only when sued. After all of the bad press the music industry has been receiving, there is a widely held perception that, given a chance, many in power in legislatures throughout the world will turn against the music industry. Indeed, observe the near disaster caused by the French legislature recently. In the US, the copyright interests are extremely worried that if they cannot negotiate a mechanical and performing "uni-license" with Internet subscription companies, the US Congress will do it for them—at considerably lower rates than they feel entitled to. Those negotiating against them, represented largely by the audio and video rights trade association DiMA (the Digital Media Association: www.digmedia.org) seem confident that if they do not get what they want via negotiation, they will by congressional mandate. This sense of entitlement by those who depend on their survival by the use of the content of others is new. Contrary to copyright interests' reluctance to look to Congress during this period of an anticopyright mood among citizens, DiMA is quite comfortable urging Congress to amend the Copyright Act. Similar sentiments will inevitably be pursued around the world. These interests' goals are not just to help facilitate technological development, but to make things easier for users of the Internet as well. Indeed, many of the changes they seek have the ring of reason behind them. For example, in the United States, tech companies are seeking to amend the Copyright Act by, among other things, replacing what they refer to as the "dysfunctional" Section 115 compulsory mechanical license with a comprehensive statutory blanket license.

Furthermore, there are not a few pundits who believe that the record and music publishing segments of the music industry will be taken over by the computer giants whose hunger for "cleared content" is insatiable. Elements of the music industry have even turned against each other. You may recall in the United States, the work for hire controversy (during which the RIAA sneaked an amendment into the Copyright Act in the dead of night to defeat the interests of "their" recording artists) wasn't exactly pretty. And the recording industry is relentlessly chipping away at music publishers' rights and control in all fields, not just the digital world. And why not? The major music publishers are all owned by the major record companies. We have seen newspaper headlines and talk shows that have eviscerated the music industry. We have seen avarice and ignorance succeed over wisdom and reason.

Yet I cannot help but believe—notwithstanding the instructive reread of the Medea myth—that the natural human state is one of reason, virtue, fairness, and justice. The music industry, and its counsel, have an opportunity to oppose the rule of passion and to apply reason to find ways to satisfy both their own vested interests in protecting the copyright structure on which our entire intellectual property industry is based, as well as the expressed needs of those who consider the music industry's creations as their own property. Some of this will be achieved through education, some through example, and some, inevitably, through lawsuits.

So, is the music industry living a Greek tragedy? Sounds like one to me.

WHEN CULTURE TRUMPS COMMERCE

Let us now consider the social, legal, and economic consequences of having multinationals own what citizens of the world perceive to be theirs.

Vogel calls music the most fundamental and widespread basic human need and emotion-inducing type of product in the world. As I noted earlier, only the expression differs from population segment to population segment, from country to country, from continent to continent. Naturally, people want to have what they believe is theirs. In a word, their own "culture."

For a discussion of how the changes in copyright law, technology, and enforcements have (in some peoples' opinions) changed our culture from one that is broadly open (if not exactly free) to one that is a closed, (ie. "proprietary," or "by permission") as Lawrence Lessig refers to it, see chapter 24, page 365-366.

How Copyright Owners Have Sacrificed Reason for Passion and Co-opted the (il)Logic of the Illegal Downloaders

I am not certain that a balance between copyright interests and consumers can be achieved without a better understanding by copyright owners of their customers—the consumers (yes, the very ones the RIAA was suing). As long as they do not understand them, the copyright community is vulnerable not only to the wholesale theft of its assets, but to the rejection by the public as well.

In the famous allegory of the cave, Plato showed us that darkness is tantamount to ignorance. In order to survive—or at least to survive with a semblance of the model in which we currently live and work—we have to teach "those kids" to penetrate the darkness. And we have to teach ourselves that unless we understand human nature, we will not have a clue as to how to fix this mess we're in.

Some of you will say that good conscience cannot be taught. In the myth of Gyges, the protagonist finds a ring that allows him to make himself invisible. What did he do when he could get away with murder and not be caught? He killed the king, raped the queen, and took over the kingdom. No punishment? No problem. Some will say that this is what we are seeing among the peer-to-peer sharers. But there's a reason they are called peers. They are of a similar mind that has neither been taught correctly nor effectively, and they act as if they can do whatever they want because they won't be caught. Like Gyges, they only think of what they *can* do—not what they *should* be doing or not doing. Yet, as we have observed in the record piracy area overseas, making available what people want, when they want it, at a reasonable price, is the best policing we can achieve in the marketplace. Wise business decisions will neutralize those who would take advantage of the vacuum and provide alternatives to hungry consumers. Apple's iPod has proven this point quite well indeed.

Which brings us to the second part of this chapter: the self-destructive behavior of copyright owners themselves.

COPYRIGHT OWNERS: POWER (NOT) TO THE PEOPLE

In addition to the digital evolution, something else tipped the balance between copyright owners and consumers which had stabilized the relationships among copyright owners and users for many, many decades.

It may have been copyright clearance that did it.

Those who hold firm to the outdated concepts of contemporary copyright law see abuse wherever they look and they see the benefits of technology being twisted into support for protections that are no longer valid. The last thing they want to face is one more technological breakthrough that threatens the status quo of their traditional licensing models. For example, no one, you would think, would support a law that would require three, four or more different licenses to be secured merely for one use. But that is exactly what has happened. An interactive Internet file will implicate the mechanical, synchronization and performance rights; a karaoke producer will do the same—but add print rights to the other three. (Some entertainment lawyers recommend that a composite license be composed—a so-called uni-license. But to date, there really is no such thing available.) An EMI Music Publishing spokesman points out that this is simply the way it is—that the "law couldn't be clearer." That is the problem. And that is the solution as well. Once Congress hears the cries of the bedeviled users of music, they will see that the law indeed could not be clearer. And they will change it. The fear among the copyright community is that they will change it in ways that will satisfy no one.

I will not reiterate the evolving concept of intellectual property law dealing with "misuse of copyright," which I discuss in chapter 24. But the wholly legitimate, and legally sanctioned, actions of copyright owners are enough to make one wonder if reason has totally taken a vacation. The stories are legion:

- Recently, a public company, was planning a promotion with DJs around several hundred of their stores. It was reminded that they would require performance licenses from the three American performing rights societies: ASCAP, BMI, and SESAC. Their new VP in charge of promotion complained that at other companies he had never cleared performance rights. "It's just music," he sputtered. "We want to do the right thing, but we now learn that in addition to your legal fees, we have to pay SESAC, the smallest performing rights society, three to four times what ASCAP, the largest, is charging."

- When I was asked to clear five songs and five masters for use in a television show that initially appeared on PBS (and were covered by a special provision in the copyright law for those specific broadcasts), negotiations for nonpublic television rights, a DVD, foreign broadcast rights, etc. were required among more than thirty different companies and departments and the paperwork took six months to complete.

- Use a photograph or likeness of Elvis Presley or Marilyn Monroe in a book? Forget about it. Whereas the right of publicity was always assumed to have died with the subject, many states are now passing laws to keep their citizens alive. I call the Tennessee law reviving Mr. Presley's publicity rights from the afterlife the "Help the Balance of Payments of Tennessee—Keep Elvis Alive" law.

- A prestigious art-book company wishes to digitize an Andy Warhol photograph of Marilyn Monroe on the cover of its book: *The Culture of the 20th Century*. The Warhol estate doesn't care; but the Monroe estate does.

- Documentary filmmaking is a particularly rich source of complaints about claimed excesses of copyright owners. By definition, documentary filmmakers have to quote existing transcriptions (whether print, video or audio) in order to tell their story. Documentary films' budgets are notoriously small, and the films are usually completed before the directors know what they are going to use to tell their story. They fear the costs when they can find the owners, the risks when they cannot, the eagle eye of their insurers who demand proof of 100% clearance, the need to self-censor rather than take their art where their muse carries them, and the imprecision of the fair use doctrine (which no attorney can assure a client he actually comprehends). When they shoot their factual moment in the frame of their documentary camera, they must be conscious (and cautious) enough to turn off the television or radio while filming lest they end up having to negotiate with Disney, or Fox, for a few immaterial, nonintegral, background seconds of *The Simpsons*; or they have to pay attention to the possibility of innocently reproducing the background sound of a cell phone ringing out the theme from *Rocky*. (Try it! It is not cheap.) Documentary filmmakers refer to this recurrent nightmare as "the clearance culture trap." It is no wonder.

- What happens when a company desires to use a copyrighted work, is willing to pay any price for a license, and cannot locate the copyright owner? An honest company will be discouraged from using it and presumably the consumer is worse off as a result. Works whose progeny or current ownership is unknown or uncertain are often referred to as "orphan works." While the owners or administrators of music and film works are fairly well documented and public, the same is not true of works of art, illustrations, cartoons, etc. This issue has drawn the attention of the Copyright Office and Congress, but their proposed solutions are suspect. One resolution of the problem has the potential user posting an "intent to use" on a public registry. The failure of the copyright owner to identify himself or itself will free the user from any liability unless and until the copyright owner shows up—at which point, his or her claim will be limited to a fixed fee for uses prospective from the date he or she appears. This amounts to the opposite of the exercise of the copyright owners' vaunted exclusive rights.

- Sampling. The practice of capturing sounds from a previously recorded and released recording and incorporating them into a new recording. Contrary to the belief of some, most sampling is not simply an easy way out for producers and other authors who are too lazy or untalented to create the sounds themselves. Their real intent is to capture a mood, a memory, a feeling of a specific time or experience, and to blend that into their own creation. DJs have "sampled" for years. But what they have been able to do in a club live is prohibited when duplicating their feat on a permanent recording—even if the recording is available only via the Internet through a download or streaming facility. Most composers, and the courts, find sampling anathema to the concept of private property; others find the process similar to making a salad—the ingredients that make up a contemporary recording naturally include elements that went before. What else is culture than the accumulation of a civilization's art over time? Sampling is now part of most every genre of music—from hip-hop to rock to pop. Even electronic classical works are utilizing samples from our everyday culture just as a hip hop composition might.

While another source of business for us entertainment lawyers, the laws written during the predigital/Internet age (or their application) often invite frustration and anger—not to forget the expense—of legitimate, creative users of music who want to reach citizens around the world and convey to them the fruits of their creations. No wonder some companies would rather hide than call us—or simply give up their creative urges and become engineers.

Among the most important functions of entertainment attorneys is to provide their clients with a "rights road map" to navigate: show them how to comply with copyright laws, identify the risks they must avoid or manage, and somehow find them a way within the law to publish their book, write their musical, or record their song.

Too often, we are unable to achieve these goals for our clients. Our frustration is mirrored in the frustration and anger of those who wish to use copyrights in a responsible manner. The possibilities offered by the Internet have merely added exponentially to the mood among copyright users when they keep running into stone walls in an effort to seek permission, and—yes—pay a reasonable fee for the rights they seek. Their frustration is finding support among academics and, more importantly, powerful lobbies that single-handedly are reversing the thinking of the author-friendly legislatures of the past 230 years. Are they justified?

It used to be that building on the art of others was the hallmark of genius. Now it is an invitation to a lawsuit. Sampling on contemporary sound recordings is illegal without the permission of the owner of the music sampled. Fine. But the cost and liability of clearing rights which ranges from impossibly difficult to nearly impossible is encouraging both a lack of creative use of our culture's output and a widespread violation of copyright owners' rights. Neither result is welcome; either result is unproductive and destructive.

Certainly intellectual property is a property right. The RIAA and the NMPA (the National Music Publishers Association) say it is a property right *period*! What I create is mine. *Period*! This view permeates the copyright owners' world. What then, is our culture? An accumulation of other peoples' property? Whose culture is it, then? Certainly not "ours." How can it be "ours" when we have to ask permission to use it? And how can a culture survive and expand when innovation is stifled by the threat of lawsuits?

The licensing archetype needs to be reformed. Everyone acknowledges this. In the United States, if the industry does not do it, Congress will do it for them. And no one is ever happy when legislatures interject themselves into their world—especially when their world is so complex, so filled with custom and tradition, and so beholden to the industry's own peculiar sense of balance among authors, publishers, and recording companies.

No, copyright is not mere property. It if were, it would follow the rules of property and government regulation that enforces property rights. A primary difference between copyright as property and ordinary property in the form of goods and services is that the cost of producing a copyright does not reflect either the cost of its reproduction or its distribution. Another one is that intellectual property is more vulnerable to theft (which we call piracy) than ordinary run-of-the-mill goods. For a user of intellectual property to pay less than the value of providing the property via distribution means such as radio, television, motion picture theater presentations, even the Internet, is anathema to creative people and their supporters, the publishers, record companies, film companies, etc. And why not? People are willing to pay for water that they can get for free? Why not copyrighted works?

WHAT WOULD THE GREEKS DO?

Back to the Greeks.

You may remember, in Sophocles's drama, *Antigone*, Polynices, Antigone's brother, has been killed; King Creon has ordered no one shall touch or bury him. Antigone is very upset by this command. "Don't touch the send button!" say the modern-day Creons. "Infringement suits await you!"

Anyway, Antigone disobeys the command and goes ahead and buries Polynices, and Creon comes out of the wings and says, "What—are you nuts? Why did you do this? Don't you know I'm the king and didn't you hear my order?" The point he wants to make is that his law is supreme. He is the king and his rule trumps everything. Or does it? Antigone's response, "Yes, that's true," she says. "But your law doesn't trump human nature. There is something bigger and older than your law. After all, it was always the right thing to do for a sister to bury her dead brother." There is something in all of us that tells us the course of action that is right for us.

Antigone is no dummy. She doesn't want to be jailed or killed by this bozo king, but she responds to her nature. Just as Medea laments the fact that passion has taken over reason, Antigone has answered the command to do what is instinctual in us. The laws of nature will force us to do right.

But what, then, is right?

Do you believe greed and stealing are less right than respect and discipline—following the rules?

Germany has a fair share of philosophers who have dealt with this question—from Immanuel Kant to Arthur Schopenhauer. What is moral to Kant requires actions whose imperative is "categorical." He dealt with universal truths and maxims. His sense of morality affects all the people, all the time, at all places. The moral worth of participating in what we call illegal downloading is something he would enjoy discoursing on. Schopenhauer, of course, differed in that he felt it was futile to attempt to base morality on reason. Kant postulated that freedom of action is an absolute prerequisite of morality. But what he meant by "free" required that people act on the basis of reason alone, independent of sensuous impulses. Schopenhauer, for his part, felt that the will obeys no law of reason and no law whatsoever. His reality is entirely irrational. This is not to say there is no morality in Schopenhauer's world. On the contrary, moral behavior is okay as long as we agree that it is derived only from the knowledge of what he calls "unity." In nonmoral action, the intellect merely facilitates the impulses of the will. Ironically, moral behavior turns us against these impulses. I wonder what he would have said about the dilemma facing the music industry today.

There is one memorable statement of Schopenhauer that indicates that he might be not so far from understanding at least the musical impulses of our 21st century culture. Perhaps anticipating the ever-changing musical landscape that we have been experiencing since Elvis Presley replaced Mitch Miller, he said, "I have long held the opinion that the amount of noise that anyone can bear undisturbed stands in inverse proportion to his mental capacity and therefore be regarded as pretty fair measure of it."

There is a battle going on now among the copyright and anticopyright interests. Some compare it to the book and film *The Perfect Storm*—except we don't have the confluence of three events creating the problem; we have dozens! In the United States, whether it is the effort to repeal the Fairness in Music Licensing Act, reestablishing in California the seven-year rule for recording contracts, establishing one in New York State, judicial modification of the line of decisions affirming state sovereignty smmunity where public universities can use music and other copyrights without care because of the immunity they have been granted by the eleventh Amendment, or now the French consumer body UFC-Que Choisir which is suing record companies and retailers over the production of copy-protected CDs because, in their mind, encryption penalizes customers by not permitting them to copy master recordings freely! How unattractive was it when the US Congress ran away from SIPA and PIPA, frightened of reprisals for the exercise of reason? This naturally is further complicated by the EU hegemony and yet another layer of bureaucracy. And last, but not least, the clearance nightmare, about which I have already written.

Whatever it is, wherever you find it, there is a war going on—and it is becoming stronger as I write.

In the digital rights area, as well as in the music clearance area, the battle is between those who use passion to define their strategies (while hiding behind the cover of reason)—the copyright owners—and those who use reason to justify their behavior (while hiding behind the cover of passion)—the consumers. Those who wish an easier and more economical access to the music of their cultures are battling with those who want to deny them such access except on their terms, their parameters, their paradigms, their conditions, their specifications, their financial demands. I am a lawyer. How does that qualify me to preach about the right and the wrong of music piracy? The Greeks help us out here as well, if I may extend the parallel between ancient myth and modern life.

In *The Republic*, Plato defined law as reason unaffected by desire. Not long afterward, Aristotle defined law as reason without passion, and wrote that reason applied to the law must benefit all, not just the few. Has the music industry got it backward?

CONCLUSION

When all is said and done, and the extremes on both sides are neutralized by the judicial process, legislative intervention, wiser choices by the copyright community, and the passage of time, the survival of copyright, as we know it, and as we believe it should exist, will depend on two things. First, does the citizenry understand the purpose of copyright? And second, if they do, are those who enjoy the benefits of copyright willing to recognize a balance between their interests and those of the rest of the population?

Whether or not this balance is achieved depends in part on education and in part on the behavior of copyright owners. Once the public processes the information that they have been presented with for the first time—that is, once the public deals with the fact that copyright is no longer invisible to them—hopefully, they will recognize that copyright is as much, if not more, in their interest than in the interest of the copyright proprietors.

The Grokster decision has most certainly reduced the need for copyright interests, at least in the United States, to sue the individual users in the peer-to-peer environment. (The new standard for secondary copyright liability, the Grokster standard, is whether the manufacturers created their software with the "intent" of inducing consumers to infringe copyrights rather than whether the software itself was capable of noninfringing uses—the test in the Sony Betamax case of 1984.)

Taken together with the preliminary success of legal download options and the fact that the music industry is slowly awakening to the needs—and societal rights—of consumers and not just of themselves, I am cautiously optimistic that this is not a time when we can bemoan the end of copyright, resulting from the pernicious exercise of remedies afforded by the world's diverse assortment of copyright laws, but rather a time to seek theirs transformation into the beneficial mechanism that it needs to be to serve the interests of all peoples and all industries.

Hopefully, the public will recognize that copyright is as much, if not more, in their interest, than if there were no copyright at all—a proposition that is not as unlikely as it sounds.

Back to Medea—and I quote:

> Things have worked out badly in every way, sings the chorus.
> Who can deny the fact? Nonetheless,
> You should not assume that's how things will stay.

I just hope that the chorus is singing in tune and getting it right.

INDEX

band members and, 183,
185–86
confidentiality and, 193–94
coupling and, 196
cross-collateralization
and, 190
delivering heads and, 181–86
end-of-term inventory,
194–95
exclusivity of, 189, 190
hall charges for, 180, 187
institutional memory
and, 193
insurance and, 192–93, 196
local laws and, 194
overview of, 181
photographs, 195
piracy and, 196–97
retail/web, 189–93
sample approval of, 190
saying "no" to, 185
territories for, 186
tour, 180, 181–89
trademarks and, 191–92
Merrick, David, 1
Merrill, Robert, 281
Message, Brian, 16
Metropolitan Opera, 286–87,
304, 367
MGM, 252
Michael, George, 254
Microsoft, 248, 261, 348,
349, 357
Midler, Bette, 62
Miller, Mitch, 125, 388
Misuse of copyright, 371
Mixers, 147–48, 274
Mixtapes, 274
MMF (Music Managers Forum),
3, 4
Moby, 78
Mod Def, 279
Moffo, Anna, 281
Momentum Worldwide, 50
Money management. See
Financial planning
Monroe, Marilyn, 367, 385
Monsanto, 365
Moral clauses, 116–17, 179
Morpheus, 349, 357
Most favored nations (MFN)
clauses, 60, 325–26
Mott the Hoople, 69
Moving Out, 72
Mozart, Wolfgang, 284, 293
Mozilla, 341

MPEG (Moving Picture Expert
Group), 357
MPL Music Publishing, 331
MP3, 357
Mraz, Jason, 143
MTV, 33, 34, 148
Musical Works Fund, 261
Music Choice, 152, 294
Music education, 305–6
Music for Youth
Foundation, 305
Music Minus One, 304–5
Musicnet, 256
Musicnotes, 293
Music publishers
administrating, 211, 221–
23, 242, 243, 318–19
audits of record companies
by, 200
conflicts of interest and, 222
copublishers, 200, 211,
225–26
copyright reversions and,
227–28
definition of, 210–11, 318
net publisher's share, 332–33
roles of, 211–12, 221–23
songs forgotten by, 223–24
subpublishers, 200, 211,
237–38
See also Self-publishing
Music Publishers
Association, 341
Mutter, Anne-Sophie, 284
Mutual funds, 102, 104
"My Heart Will Go On," 214
MySpace, 245, 249

N

Napster, 248, 256, 339, 349,
357, 359, 377, 380
NARAS (National Academy
of Recording Arts and
Sciences), 42, 372
NASAA (North American
Securities Administrators
Association), 12
Nashville Songwriter's
Association, 372
NAXOS, 292
Neighboring rights
in Canada, 258,
259–60, 265
collection agencies, 264–66
definition of, 139, 257
in Germany, 260

introduction to, 257–58
in the Netherlands, 263–64
producers and, 138–40
in the UK, 263–64, 265
Nelly, 270
Nelson, Jennifer, 340
Nelson, Ricky, 70
Netherlands, neighboring rights
in, 263–64
Netrebko, Anna, 284, 286
Nettwerk, 16, 17, 254
"New York, New York," 257
New York Philharmonic, 282,
284, 287, 306
Nickelback, 57
Nimmer, David, 320
NIST (National Institute
of Standards and
Technology), 175
NMPA (National Music
Publishers Association),
319, 329, 350, 352, 370,
372, 387
Nonesuch Records, 288, 364
Notorious B.I.G., 269, 270, 272
NPS (net publisher's share),
332–33
NRCC (Neighboring Rights
Collective of Canada), 259
'NSYNC, 26, 330
N.W.A., 269

O

Ocasek, Ric, 327, 343
O'Connor, Mark, 284
Ogilvy, David, 141
Opera, 281, 286–87
Orenstein, Harold, 377
Ormandy, Eugene, 292
Orphan works, 369, 374–75,
386
Ostin, Mo, 156
Overcalls, 14
"Over the Rainbow," 214

P

Pacific Coast Farmers Market
Association, 340
Packaging deductions, 30–31
Page, Patti, 80
Paid time off, 114
Palmer, Amanda, 251, 255
PAMRA (Performing
Artists' Media Rights
Association), 265, 373

cash flow and, 167
club, 162–63
equipment manifest for, 177
grand, 163–80
holograms and, 179
income from, 162, 166,
178–79, 180
insurance for, 166, 168–69,
171–72
licenses and permits for,
176–77
merchandising and, 180,
181–89
personal manager's role in,
70
planning, 167
product sponsorship and,
179–80
pyrotechnics and, 174–77
riders, 166–67
royalties and, 34
safety and, 175–76
sound and lights for, 171–72
successful, 161
support for, 34, 146–47
ticket prices for, 178–79
transportation for, 167–70,
171, 172–74, 178
trends in, 161–62
venues for, 161–62
Tower Records, 142, 283
Trademarks, 191–92, 254, 344
Translations, 335
Transportation, 167–70, 171,
172–74, 178
Travolta, John, 78
Tribe Called Quest, 269
Tristan und Isolde, 285
Tumblr, 347
The Turtles, 267
Tweedy, Jeff, 364
Twitter, 64, 143, 245, 250, 347

U

UFC-Que Choisir, 388
UK, neighboring rights in,
263–64
Undeas, 272
UNI, 122
Union requirements, 136
United Airlines, 328
United Artists Studios, 252, 339
United Jewish Appeal Federation
of New York, 305
Universal City Studios, 339

Universal Classics, 282
Universal Music, 26, 35, 45, 48,
49, 59, 78, 201, 204, 211,
220, 225, 255, 267, 282,
284, 293, 294, 319, 321
Unmatched lists, 200
Upshaw, Dawn, 288
Upstart, 16
USNRC (United States Normal
Retail Channels), 49,
123–24
U2, 34, 57, 69, 74

V

Vacations, 119–20
Value-added tax, 219

Vector Management, 76
Verdi, Giuseppe, 51
Vevo, 48, 142, 319
VH-1, 33, 148
Viacom, 358
Victoria's Secret, 188, 327
Video games, 330
Video promotion, 33–34, 148
Vienna Philharmonic, 294
Virgin, 76, 283, 319
Visas, 118
Vivendi, 201
Vogel, Harold, 378, 383
Von Karajan, Herbert, 294

W

Wagner, Richard, 367
Walmart, 47
Walt Disney Company, 356
Wang, Yuja, 284
Warhol, Andy, 367, 385
Warner Bros. Records, 49, 60,
156, 337
Warner/Chappell, 220, 221,
222, 319, 325, 340, 371
Warner Music Group, 25, 49,
51, 207, 221, 267, 282,
319
Warren, Diane, 229, 239
WEA (Warner/Electric/
Atlantic), 25
Webcaster Settlement Bill of
2008, 358
Webcasts, 321, 323–24
Weber, Max, 250
Websites
creating, 253–54

domain names for, 253–54
updating, 250
The Weeknd, 258
Welch, Jack, 113
West, Kanye, 144, 269
West Side Story, 283, 360, 362
White, Emily, 255
White, Jack, 254
"White Christmas," 257
White label recordings, 272
The Who, 176
Whole life insurance, 106
WID (Musical Works
Information Database),
355
Wikileaks, 58
Wilde, Oscar, 257
William Morris Endeavor
Agency, 17
Williams, Pharrell, 343
Work for hire, 138, 370
World Social Forum (WSF), 365
Wright, Charles, 368

Y

Yahoo, 48
Young, Neil, 63
YouTube, 34, 48, 61–62, 142,
148, 151, 319, 341, 358

Z

Zomba Music, 59

All rights reserved.

Published in the United States by Watson-Guptill Publications, an imprint of the Crown Publishing Group, a division of Penguin Random House LLC, New York.

www.crownpublishing.com

www.watsonguptill.com

WATSON-GUPTILL and the WG and Horse designs are registered trademarks of Penguin Random House LLC

Previous editions were published by Billboard Books, New York in 2002, 2006

Library of Congress
Cataloging-in-Publication Data

Names: Thall, Peter M.

Title: What they'll never tell you about the music busines : the complete guide for musicians, songwriters, producers, managers, industry executives, attorneys and accountants / Peter M. Thall.

Description: Third edition. | Berkeley : Ten Speed Press, [2016] | Includes bibliographical references and index.

Identifiers: LCCN 2016015721 (print) | LCCN 2016018133 (ebook)

Subjects: LCSH: Music trade—Law and legislation—United States. | Music—Economic aspects—United States. | Copyright—Music—United States. | Band musicians—Legal status, laws, etc.—United States. | Popular music—Writing and publishing.

Classification: LCC ML3790 .T43 2016 (print) | LCC ML3790 (ebook) | DDC 780.23/73—dc23

LC record available at https://lccn.loc.gov/2016015721

Trade Paperback ISBN: 978-1-60774-974-5
eBook ISBN: 978-1-60774-975-2

Printed in the United States of America

Design by Emily Blevins

10 9 8 7 6 5 4 3 2 1

Third Edition